MASTERING

ECONOMIC AND SOCIAL HISTORY

D1390711

MACMILLAN MASTER SERIES

Accounting
Arabic
Astronomy
Australian History
Background to Business
Banking
Basic Management
Biology
British Politics
Business Communication
Business Law
Business Microcomputing
C Programming
Catering Science
Catering Theory
Chemistry
COBOL Programming
Commerce
Computer Programming
Computers
Economic and Social History
Economics
Electrical Engineering
Electronics
English as a Foreign Language
English Grammar
English Language
English Literature
Financial Accounting
French 1
French 2
German 1
German 2

Hairdressing
Human Biology
Italian 1
Italian 2
Japanese
Keyboarding
Marketing
Mathematics
Modern British History
Modern European History
Modern World History
Nutrition
Office Practice
Pascal Programming
Philosophy
Physics
Practical Writing
Principles of Accounts
Psychology
Restaurant Service
Science
Secretarial Procedures
Social Welfare
Sociology
Spanish 1
Spanish 2
Spreadsheets
Statistics
Statistics with your Microcomputer
Study Skills
Typewriting Skills
Word Processing

MASTERING
ECONOMIC AND SOCIAL
HISTORY

DAVID TAYLOR

MACMILLAN

First published 1988 by
THE MACMILLAN PRESS LTD
Houndmills, Basingstoke, Hampshire RG21 2XS
and London
Companies and representatives
throughout the world

ISBN 0–333–36804–5

A catalogue record for this book is available from the
British Library.

Printed in Hong Kong

10   9   8   7   6   5
00   99 98 97 96 95 94 93 92

CONTENTS

Preface   xviii

Acknowledgements   xx

1 Population
- 1.1   Introduction   1
- 1.2   Population trends 1750–1820   4
- 1.3   Population trends 1820–1901   10
- 1.4   How useful are the nineteenth-century Census returns to the historian?   12
- 1.5   Population trends 1901–81   13
- 1.6   Conclusion   16

2 The Agrarian Revolution 1750–1850
- 2.1   Introduction: What was the open field system?   21
- 2.2   What were the disadvantages of the open field system?   23
- 2.3   What was the agrarian revolution?   23
- 2.4   Why did changes take place in British agriculture between 1750 and 1850?   24
- 2.5   The enclosure movement   24
- 2.6   Technical improvements and the agricultural pioneers of the eighteenth century   31
- 2.7   What contribution did the 'propagandists' make to the agrarian changes?   36
- 2.8   Conclusion   37

3 The Industrial Revolution
- 3.1   Introduction   43
- 3.2   Terminology   44
- 3.3   Alternative views of the 'Industrial Revolution'   44
- 3.4   Why was Britain the first country to become an industrialised society?   46
- 3.5   The controversy between the 'optimists' and the 'pessimists'   47
- 3.6   Conclusion   48

CONTENTS

4 The textile industry 1700–1850

4.1	Introduction	50
4.2	What processes were involved in the manufacture of textiles in 1700?	50
4.3	What was the state of the textile industry in 1700?	52
4.4	The domestic system	53
4.5	Why did the cotton industry develop more rapidly than the woollen industry from the late eighteenth century onwards?	55
4.6	Inventions of spinning and weaving machines	56
4.7	Why was factory weaving slow to establish itself?	62
4.8	Why did the cotton industry become concentrated in south-east Lancashire and central Scotland?	62
4.9	What changes took place in the woollen industry?	63
4.10	How important was the role of the cotton industry in the context of industrialisation?	64
4.11	Conclusion	64

5 The Luddites

5.1	Introduction	71
5.2	What were the origins of the term 'Luddite'?	71
5.3	The Luddite counties and main events of the movement	72
5.4	What caused Luddism?	73
5.5	How far did Luddism have political aims?	74
5.6	How and why did Luddism fade away?	75
5.7	Conclusion	75

6 The coal industry 1700–1850

6.1	Introduction	80
6.2	How was coal mined in 1700?	80
6.3	Why did the demand for coal increase after 1750?	81
6.4	The growth of British coalfields	82
6.5	What were the dangers of deep shaft mining and how did the mining industry attempt to overcome them?	83
6.6	How far did techniques of cutting coal improve?	87

6.7 Conclusion: How important was the contribution of the coal industry to the process of industrialisation? 88

7 The iron industry 1700–1850
7.1 Introduction 91
7.2 What were the main processes involved in the manufacture of iron in the early eighteenth century? 91
7.3 Why was the iron industry unable to increase its output in the early eighteenth century? 92
7.4 What contribution did the 'Darby Dynasty' make to the development of the iron industry in the eighteenth century? 94
7.5 What is the importance of Henry Cort in the mass production of iron? 96
7.6 What impact did the technical advances in iron-manufacturing have on the industrialisation of Britain? 98
7.7 Why was steel produced in small quantities in the eighteenth and early nineteenth century? 100
7.8 Conclusion 101

8 The pottery industry 1700–1900
8.1 Introduction 105
8.2 How and why did North Staffordshire become the main centre of the British pottery industry? 105
8.3 Josiah Wedgwood (1730–95) 107
8.4 What was life like for a pottery worker in the nineteenth century? 109
8.5 Conclusion 110

9 The development of power
9.1 Introduction 114
9.2 Traditional forms of power 114
9.3 What role did Thomas Savery play in the development of steam-power? 115
9.4 What role did Thomas Newcomen play in the development of steam-power? 115
9.5 James Watt (1736–1819) 116
9.6 How important was Watt's partnership with Matthew Boulton? 117
9.7 Conclusion: What impact did the steam-engine have on the British economy? 119

CONTENTS

10 Road transport

10.1   Introduction   124

10.2   What were roads like in pre-industrial
       Britain?   124

10.3   Why were Britain's roads in such poor
       condition?   125

10.4   Why was an improvement in the quality of
       the roads essential after 1750?   125

10.5   Government attempts to improve the roads in
       the eighteenth century   126

10.6   What was the role of the turnpike trusts and
       how successful were they in improving
       Britain's roads?   126

10.7   What was the contribution of 'The Great
       Road Engineers' to road improvement?   128

10.8   What were the benefits of road improvements
       during this period?   130

10.9   Why did the coaching era come to an end?   131

10.10 Conclusion: How far did road improvements
       1750–1830 contribute to the industrialisation
       of Britain?   131

11 Canals

11.1   Introduction   140

11.2   What forms of water transport were available
       before the mid-eighteenth century?   140

11.3   Why were canals needed?   141

11.4   How did the canal network develop in Britain
       between 1760 and 1830?   141

11.5   What difficulties faced engineers in
       constructing canals?   144

11.6   How were canal companies started and
       financed?   146

11.7   What beneficial results did canals have for the
       British economy?   148

11.8   When and why did canals decline?   148

11.9   Conclusion   149

12 Railways

12.1   Introduction   155

12.2   How and where did railways originate?   155

12.3   Who were the inventors of the early
       locomotives?   156

12.4   The tockton to Darlington railway 1825   157

12.5   The Liverpool to Manchester railway 1830   158

12.6	How quickly did the railway network grow?	161
12.7	What problems were encountered by the promoters when establishing a railway company?	161
12.8	What problems were encountered in the construction of railway lines?	163
12.9	How far did the navvies deserve their notorious reputation?	165
12.10	Why did amalgamations take place?	165
12.11	What was the role of the government in the growth of the railway network?	166
12.12	What were the social effects of railway growth?	168
12.13	What were the economic effects of the railways?	171
12.14	Conclusion	172

13 The development of shipping 1800–1939

13.1	Introduction	179
13.2	From wood to steel	179
13.3	The development of the steamship in the nineteenth century	181
13.4	Why were sailing ships able to compete with steamships for so long?	184
13.5	What developments took place in marine engineering?	186
13.6	What part did Parliament play in the development of shipping?	187
13.7	What effects did the steamship have on the British economy?	187
13.8	The age of the passenger liner	189
13.9	Conclusion	189

14 Factory reform

14.1	Introduction: The factory system	194
14.2	Who were the 'first generation' of factory workers?	195
14.3	What difficulties faced the first generation of factory-owners? How did they enforce a code of discipline?	196
14.4	What early attempts were made at factory legislation and why were they unsuccessful?	200
14.5	The struggle to reform the factories	201
14.6	Why and how was the Mines Act (1842) passed?	206

CONTENTS

14.7	The climbing boys	208
14.8	Conclusion	209

15 Social and economic conditions in Britain 1793–1822

15.1	Introduction: Background	219
15.2	What were the economic and social effects of the French wars (1793–1815)?	219
15.3	What caused the distress and discontent among the labouring classes immediately after the French Wars in the period 1815–22?	222
15.4	In what ways was the Parliamentary system outdated?	223
15.5	Who were the Radicals and why were they prominent in the period 1815–22?	225
15.6	What action did the labouring classes take to protest against their distressed condition?	226
15.7	What measures did the government take to deal with the disturbances?	229
15.8	Why did the government adopt a repressive attitude?	230
15.9	Was Britain close to revolution in this period?	231
15.10	Conclusion	231

16 The Poor Law 1750–1948

16.1	Introduction	238
16.2	How was the Poor Law administered before 1834?	239
16.3	What were allowance systems? Why were they introduced and what effects did they have on the poor?	240
16.4	Why was a Royal Commission of Inquiry into the poor laws appointed in 1832?	241
16.5	What were the terms of the Poor Law Amendment Act 1834?	243
16.6	How did the Central Poor Law Commission put the Act into operation?	244
16.7	How did the New Poor Law work in practice?	245
16.8	How far was the Poor Law Amendment Act accepted?	246
16.9	How successful was the New Poor Law?	247

16.10   What other changes were made in Poor Law
        administration after 1834?   247
16.11   Conclusion   248

17   Law and order   1700–1900
17.1   Introduction   253
17.2   Who kept law and order during the
        eighteenth century? How effective were
        they?   253
17.3   What improvements in law-enforcement took
        place during the eighteenth century?   255
17.4   What factors highlighted the need for a
        regular police force?   256
17.5   In view of the growing lawlessness why was a
        regular police force not established until
        1829?   256
17.6   What contribution did Robert Peel make to
        the reform of law and order?   257
17.7   How were police forces extended over the
        country as a whole?   259
17.8   How effective were the police?   260
17.9   What were prison conditions like in the
        eighteenth century and early nineteenth
        century?   261
17.10   What was transportation?   262
17.11   What steps did John Howard and Elizabeth
        Fry take in an attempt to reform prison
        conditions? How successful were they?   262
17.12   What were prisons like in the mid-
        nineteenth century?   265
17.13   Other legislation and measures   267
17.14   Conclusion   268

18   Education 1750–1944
18.1   Introduction   277
18.2   How were working-class children educated in
        the early nineteenth century? (elementary
        education)   278
18.3   What means of education were available for
        the middle and upper classes in the early
        nineteenth century? (secondary education)   281
18.4   What developments took place in elementary
        education between 1833 and 1862?   282

CONTENTS

18.5   What improvements took place in Public Schools and Grammar Schools in the mid-nineteenth century? (Secondary Education)   285

18.6   Why was the Elementary Education Act of 1870 passed and what were its terms?   286

18.7   What did the 1870 Education Act achieve?   288

18.8   Why was the 1902 Education Act passed? What were its terms and how far was it successful?   290

18.9   How was the Act received and what was its importance?   292

18.10   What developments took place in education between 1902 and 1944?   294

18.11   Conclusion   296

19   Public health in Britain 1750–1900

19.1   Introduction   301

19.2   What were the main environmental problems of the growing towns in the first half of the nineteenth century?   301

19.3   What was the health of the people like in the cities?   305

19.4   Why was so little done to improve living conditions in the first part of the nineteenth century?   308

19.5   Why and how did the 'sanitary reform movement' originate in the mid-nineteenth century?   310

19.6   How did the 1848 Public Health Act come to be passed and how effective was it?   312

19.7   Why did the government play a more direct role in public health legislation after 1865?   314

19.8   What legislation was passed between 1866 and 1900 to improve public health?   315

19.9   Medical advances   317

19.10   Conclusion   324

20   Trade and trading policy since 1750

20.1   Introduction   332

20.2   What were the main features of Britain's trading policy in the eighteenth century?   333

20.3   How did the free-trade movement originate?   341

20.4   What policies were adopted by William Pitt and William Huskisson to help transform Britain into a free-trade nation?   343

20.5   The achievements of Sir Robert Peel (1788–1850) – Tory Prime Minister from 1841 to 1846   345

20.6   What contribution did William Gladstone (1809–98) make to the achievement of free-trade?   351

20.7   Free trade challenged   352

20.8   What events led to protection returning?   355

20.9   Britain's trading policy since 1945   355

20.10   Conclusion   358

21 Working-class movements

21.1   Introduction   368

21.2   The origins of the trade union movement 1789–1850   368

21.3   New model unions 1850–80   374

21.4   Growth of the new unions 1880–1900   378

21.5   What legal set-backs did trade unions suffer in the period 1880–1910?   381

21.6   Industrial disputes 1910–14   384

21.7   Chartism   386

21.8   The growth of the Labour Party   398

21.9   Self-help movements: friendly societies and co-operatives   405

21.10   Conclusion   409

22 Industrial developments 1850–1914

22.1   Introduction   415

22.2   What was the importance of the Great Exhibition?   416

22.3   Why did Britain enjoy prosperity between 1850 and 1873?   419

22.4   Outline developments in the staple (basic) industries between 1850 and 1914, referring to coal, textiles, and iron and steel   423

22.5   What 'new' industries were developed in this period?   428

22.6   Why was Britain's industrial supremacy challenged in the last quarter of the nineteenth century?   430

CONTENTS

22.7	How far is it true to say that Britain suffered a 'depression' in this period?	433
22.8	Conclusion	435

23 Agriculture in Britain 1815–1914
23.1	Introduction	437
23.2	The landowners and farmers	438
23.3	The agricultural labourers	443
23.4	The 'Golden Age of Agriculture' 1850–73	448
23.5	Agricultural depression 1873–1914	453
23.6	Conclusion	460

24 The emancipation of women
24.1	Introduction	464
24.2	What was the position of women in 1850?	464
24.3	What improvements in their status did women achieve during the nineteenth century?	465
24.4	How and why did the suffrage movement originate?	469
24.5	Which groups made up the 'women's suffrage movement'?	471
24.6	What were the arguments used against the women's suffrage movement?	474
24.7	What were the main events of the suffrage movement between 1905 and 1914?	477
24.8	Did militant tactics further the cause of the suffragists?	479
24.9	How far is it true to say that the work of women during the First World War (1914–18) brought them the vote?	479
24.10	Conclusion	481

25 The social reforms of the Liberal Government 1906–14
25.1	Introduction	491
25.2	Who held the main Cabinet posts between 1908 and 1914?	493
25.3	What did the Liberals do to help children?	493
25.4	The elderly	494
25.5	What did the Liberal Government do to help workers who were exploited?	495
25.6	What legislation was passed concerning coal-mines?	497

25.7   What did the Liberal Government do to assist workers who were injured at work or absent from work due to sickness?   497

25.8   How did the Liberals deal with the unemployed?   499

25.9   How successful were the Liberals and how were the social reforms received at the time?   500

25.10 Conclusion   503

26 The First World War (1914–18) and its effects

26.1   Introduction   512

26.2   What measures were initiated by the government to deal with a total war situation between 1914 and 1918?   513

26.3   The economic and social effects of the war   514

26.4   Attempts at reconstruction 1918–22   517

26.5   Conclusion   520

27 The trade unions 1914–39

27.1   Introduction   521

27.2   The position of trade unions after the First World War   521

27.3   What caused the General Strike of 1926?   523

27.4   The nine days of the General Strike 4–12 May 1926   529

27.5   How and why did the strike come to an end on 12 May 1926?   531

27.6   What were the effects of the General Strike on the trade-union movement?   533

27.7   Conclusion: changed attitudes 1926–39   534

28 Industry between the wars 1919–39

28.1   Introduction   541

28.2   The basic industries 1919–39   541

28.3   The new industries   545

28.4   What developments took place in British agriculture between 1914 and 1930?   549

28.5   Conclusion   551

29 The Wall Street Crash and the depression of the thirties

29.1   Introduction: the international background   554

29.2   The Wall Street Crash – The collapse of the American Stock Exchange   555

CONTENTS

29.3 The economic and political crisis in
Britain – 1931 557

29.4 What immediate steps were taken by the
national government to deal with the crisis? 560

29.5 Which areas of Britain were hit most badly by
the depression and why? 562

29.6 What long-term measures did the national
government adopt to alleviate the effects of
the depression? 563

29.7 What were the social effects of long-term
unemployment? 569

29.8 How progressive were government policies
and were they successful in bringing a
recovery? 571

29.9 What alternative theories to combat the
depression were suggested at the time? 572

29.10 Conclusion 573

**30 The Home Front during the Second World War
1939–45**

30.1 Introduction 577

30.2 The blitz and evacuation 1939–41 577

30.3 How was the labour force mobilised? 579

30.4 What measures were taken to overcome the
shortage of food during the war and how
successful were they? 583

30.5 How were other shortages overcome? 584

30.6 How did the government finance the
war-effort? 585

30.7 In what ways did the war benefit British
society? 587

30.8 How was civilian morale maintained during
the war? 588

30.9 What plans were laid for reconstruction? 589

30.10 How much damage had the war caused? 591

30.11 Conclusion 592

31 The Labour Government 1945–51

31.1 Introduction 598

31.2 What immediate financial problems faced the
Labour administration? 598

31.3 Why did the Labour Government nationalise
key industries? 600

31.4	The Welfare State: National Insurance	605
31.5	The National Health Service	607
31.6	How successful was the Labour Government in other areas of social reform?	611
31.7	Financial and economic policy 1945–51	615
31.8	Conclusion – what was the achievement of the Labour Government?	620

32 Communications and transport since 1840

32.1	Introduction	626
32.2	How important was Rowland Hill (1785–1879) in the development of the postal service?	627
32.3	Why was the invention of the electric telegraph important?	629
32.4	How did the telephone come into being?	630
32.5	What have been the major developments in broadcasting?	631
32.6	The cinema	634
32.7	The press	635
32.8	Developments in transport 1900–1950	638
32.9	Conclusion	642

33 Britain 1951–86

33.1	Introduction: The Festival of Britain	647
33.2	The British economy since 1951	648
33.3	Trade unions 1951–86	655
33.4	Education since 1951	662
33.5	Industrial developments 1951–86	669
33.6	Energy since 1951	678
33.7	Transport developments	682
33.8	What social problems face modern Britain?	687
33.9	Conclusion: the future	691

Bibliography	696
Index	711

PREFACE

(a) *Mastering Economic and Social History* is geared towards preparing students for the General Certificate of Secondary Education.
This examination demands a much more analytical approach and
does much to make History a relevant subject which develops a
number of skills needed throughout life. No longer will it be sufficient
for a candidate to learn a body of historical knowledge in a
'parrot-like' fashion to regurgitate in the examination. It will now be
necessary to develop *skills* of analysis, selection, judgement and
source-evaluation. The factual background : ow forms a framework
which the candidate has to apply and use rather than memorise for its
own sake. I hope that this book will help the student to develop these
historical skills.

(b) The approach adopted in this book follows the successful format
of the *Macmillan Master Series* and has the following features
designed to help the GCSE student:

● Structured chapters which focus on the key issues.
● Sections which discuss matters of historical controversy and
  invite the student to make a judgement.
● Questions at the end of each chapter.

(c) The questions at the end of each chapter have been framed with
the GCSE directly in mind. The majority of them have been devised
by the author, but some have been taken from the syllabuses of the
new Examining Groups. It is worth noting that the *The National
Criteria for GCSE History* state that all History courses will test the
following assessment objectives:
'The candidate will be expected:

1. To recall, evaluate and select knowledge relevant to the context
   and to deploy it in a clear and coherent form.
2. To make use of and understand the concepts of cause and
   consequence, continuity and change, similarity and difference.
3. To show an ability to look at events and issues from the
   perspective of people in the past (empathy).
4. To show the skills necessary to study a wide variety of historical
   evidence which should include both primary and secondary

written sources, statistical and visual material, artefacts, text books and orally transmitted information by:

- comprehending and extracting information from it,
- interpreting and evaluating it – distinguishing between fact, opinion and judgement; pointing to deficiencies in the material such as gaps and inconsistencies; detecting bias,
- by comparing various types of historical evidence and reaching conclusions based on this comparison.'

(Quoted from *The National Criteria for GCSE History*, p. 1).
In all cases I have stated the assessment objective at which the question is broadly targetted.

(d) I owe a great deal to many people who have helped me to complete this book. In particular, I would like to thank Peter Oates of Macmillan who gave me every possible assistance and encouragement. My wife, Pat, gave me constant support and spent many hours typing the manuscript. This book is dedicated to her and my two understanding daughters, Zoe and Rachel.

(e) Finally, to the reader I apologise for any imperfections or errors in the book.

DAVID TAYLOR

ACKNOWLEDGEMENTS

The author and publishers wish to acknowledge, with thanks, the following illustrative sources:

BBC Hulton Picture Library (pp.77; 121; 234; 175; 191; 134; 270; 272; 273; 297; 326; 329; 330 top; 330 bottom; 411; 484; 540; 552; 593)
British Waterways Board (p. 146)
Controller of Her Majesty's Stationery Office (p. 679)
Durham Public Record Office (pp. 139–9)
Mary Evans Picture Library (p. 112)
Ford Collection, University of Southamton (p. 216)
Glasgow Bulletin (p. 539)
Hampshire Chronicle (p. 265)
Helmsham Local History Collection (p. 197)
Imperial War Museum (p. 595)
Ironbridge Museum Trust (pp. 103, 104)
London Express News and Features Service (pp. 594; 622; 623; 624)
Manchester Public Libraries (pp. 69; 236; 237)
Mansell Collection (pp. 18; 66; 67; 177; 211; 213; 214; 233; 271; 359; 360; 362; 364; 365; 461; 485; 486; 487; 488; 506; 508; 509; 510; 538)
Metropolitan Police (p. 275)
Nottingham County Council Local History Collection (p. 78)
The Open University (p. 152)
Science Museum (p. 121)

The publishers have made every effort to trace the copyright-holders, but if any have been inadvertently overlooked they will be pleased to make the necessary arrangement at the first opportunity.

POPULATION

1.1 INTRODUCTION

(a) The number of people living in a country (that is, the population) is an important factor in moulding its economic, social and political structure (see diagram below).

The importance of studying population trends

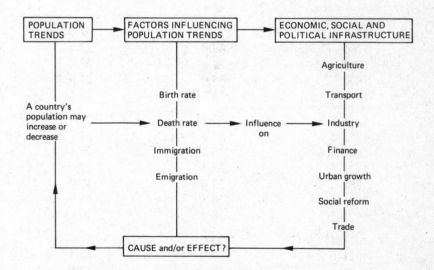

(b) A number of important terms needed to be grasped:

● *Birth rate* – the number born per 1000 of the poulation in a given year

- *Death rate* – the number of deaths per 1000 of the population
- *Immigration* – the number of people who enter a country to live and work
- *Emigration* – the number of people who leave a country to make their living abroad
- *Migration* – the number of people who move from one region to another region within the same country
- *Infant mortality rate* – the number of children who die in the first year of their life per 1000 births
- *Life expectancy* – the age to which people may expect to live calculated by studying the death rate and infant mortality rates
- *Demography* – the study of population

(c) Statistics

(i) *Population growth 1791–1971* (see opposite)

(ii) *Birth rate–death rate* (per 1000 of the population)

Year	Birth rate	Death rate
1740	33.0	32.0
1760	34.0	27.0
1780	34.8	28.2
1800	35.0	24.0
1820	33.9	20.1
1841–5	35.2	21.4
1851–5	34.8	22.7
1861–5	35.8	22.6
1871–5	35.7	22.0
1881–5	33.8	19.4
1891–5	30.5	18.7
1901–5	28.2	16.1
1911–15	23.6	14.3
1921–5	19.9	12.1
1931–5	15.0	12.0
1941–5	15.9	12.8
1951–5	15.3	11.7
1961–5	18.1	11.8
1970–5	13.4	11.7

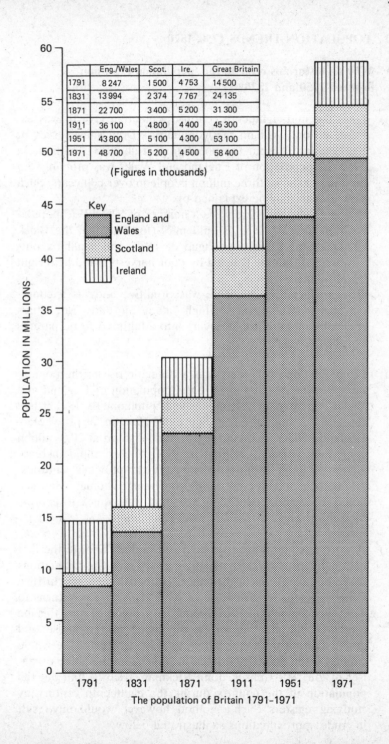

	Eng./Wales	Scot.	Ire.	Great Britain
1791	8 247	1 500	4 753	14 500
1831	13 994	2 374	7 767	24 135
1871	22 700	3 400	5 200	31 300
1911	36 100	4 800	4 400	45 300
1951	43 800	5 100	4 300	53 100
1971	48 700	5 200	4 500	58 400

(Figures in thousands)

Key

England and Wales

Scotland

Ireland

POPULATION IN MILLIONS

The population of Britain 1791–1971

1.2 POPULATION TRENDS 1750–1820

(a) Why do historians refer to the 'population explosion' between 1750 and 1820?

(i) Until the mid-eighteenth century population growth was extremely slow. William the Conqueror's Domesday Survey of England in 1086 put the population at about 3.5 million. In 1750 the population of England and Wales was probably 6.5 million – a rise of three million people in over 600 years. Such slow growth may be explained by:

● The fact that there were a number of 'checks' to population increase such as epidemics (for example, the Black Death of 1348, the Plague of 1665, and smallpox outbreaks), famine (caused by poor harvests), and heavy gin drinking.

● The fact that medicine was primitive and, as a consequence, there was a high infant mortality rate (thus children were not surviving into adulthood to be parents themselves).

(ii) From 1750 onwards there was a dramatic rise in the population. Between 1750 and 1801 the population of England and Wales increased by 2.4 million to 8.9 million. By 1821 it had reached 12 million. The figure for Britain as a whole – England, Wales, Scotland and Ireland – stood at 20.9 million compared with 15.7 million in 1801. Such a rapid increase amounted to an 'explosion' compared with previous centuries. A number of contemporaries, including Thomas Malthus, noted the demographical changes and were quick to express their misgivings.

(iii) A word of caution needs to be noted in that, prior to the first national census in 1801, the figures are only approximations based on tax returns or the analysis of parish registers. In 1696 Gregory King, for example, used the Hearth Tax returns to work out the number of rooms in a house. From this he estimated the number of people living in the house and gradually built up a cumulative total of people for the whole country – the figure he arrived at was 5.2 million. The organiser of the 1801 Census, John Rickman, tried to find out the population of the country during the eighteenth century by studying registers. Such a method, however, would only result in crude approximations as illustrated below:

PROBLEMS OF USING PARISH REGISTERS
TO ESTIMATE THE POPULATION OF A COUNTRY

Date back to 1538 when Thomas Cromwell ordered the Church of England clergy to record baptisms, marriages and burials in a register

Not all clergymen obeyed the order. Many registers have not survived: thus there are often 'gaps'

Some clergymen were rather slapdash in their record-keeping. Often baptisms, marriages, and burials appeared intermingled on the same page. Not until the 19th century did registers have a standardised format.

PARISH REGISTERS

During the 18th century the growth of the Methodist Church meant that many people would not figure in Church of England records. Thus parish registers do not include all the population

There were 15,000 parishes in England and Wales. Counting all baptisms and burials would be virtually impossible without a great deal of organisation

Thus only the census from 1801 onwards supplies the historian with relatively accurate figures.

(b) What factors might explain the rapid increase in population from 1750–1820?

(i)   Historians are still debating the answer to this question and opinions are likely to change as and when new evidence comes to light. It would appear that the population increased because of an increase in the birth rate combined with a fall in the death rate (immigration was very limited during this period and can be dismissed as a causal factor).

(ii) The following reasons have been forwarded for the birth rate increasing:

- The practice of 'living-in' began to disappear on large farms and labourers had to find their own cottage. This probably encouraged earlier marriages and thus more children (see chapter 23).
- The apprenticeship system was beginning to decline. An apprentice had had to stay single for a period of seven

years whilst he learned his trade. Once the system was discontinued, earlier marriages resulted and more children were brought into the world.

● Between 1795 and 1834 the Speenhamland (Allowance) system (see chapter 16) was widely adopted. It has been argued that this system encouraged larger families as the allowance of money received from the parish increased with each child. Thomas Malthus was very much of this opinion.

● It has been suggested that larger families became popular as young children were employed in the factories, and therefore were a source of income (there were no effective Factory Acts until 1833) (see chapter 14).

● The standard of living, including diet, began to improve at this time and this possibly helped mothers to survive childbirth.

These explanations are controversial and, in some cases, can seriously be brought into question. For example, the Speenhamland System was never adopted in the north of Britain, and, therefore, could not be a factor in increasing the birth rate in this area.

(iii) The following reasons are traditionally used to explain the apparent fall in the death rate:

● An improvement in the standard of living brought about by the enclosure movement which allowed arable and livestock farming to complement each other. Fodder crops, grown as part of the Norfolk Four Course rotation system, enabled animals to be kept alive during the winter months so that more fresh meat was available.

● Improved turnpike roads and canals enabled food to be widely distributed and, in particular, delivered to the growing urban areas.

● An increase in the availability of cheap cotton cloth (which could be washed more easily), soap and coal made life more comfortable for many people.

● Improved medical standards. More hospitals were opened, smallpox vaccinations were introduced (Jenner, 1798) and the training of midwives was improved. Thus, it is argued, less people died at an early age and survived to become parents.

Once again these explanations are contentious. For example, it is valid to question whether living standards did improve for all sections of society. The agricultural labourer suffered extremely harsh conditions between 1793 and 1820 when high bread prices and low wages dominated. Furthermore, it took many years before smallpox vaccination became widespread, and hospitals were filthy institutions. (Not until the 1870s was the importance of cleanliness realised.)

(iv) *Population growth and industrial change*

Another issue is whether or not the population explosion of this period 'caused' industrial take-off by stimulating demand.

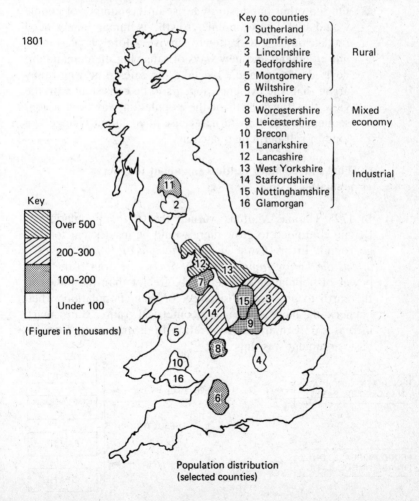

Population distribution
(selected counties)

It may have been that industrial growth resulted from the increase in population. Again no conclusive answer can be given but it is possible to make these points:

- The rise in the birth rate was greater in the industrial counties of the north (Lancashire and West Yorkshire) which suggests that families were becoming larger in these areas – at least there was employment available in factories.
- An increase in population occurred in Ireland (and is increasing in Third World countries today) but it did not stimulate an Industrial Revolution – so why should this happen in Britain?
- On the other hand, surely a rise in the number of people would stimulate economic growth, as human beings need food, clothes and shelter to survive. More people means more demand and new ways of satisfying the demand are devised. Deane and Cole take the safest line when they argue that 'the evidence appears to be consistent with the view that the growth of the population was both a consequence and, in its turn, a cause of economic change' – a kind of self-perpetuating circle.

(c) What did Thomas Malthus say about the increase in population?

(i) In 1798 Thomas Malthus warned that if the population of Britain continued to grow there would be insufficient food to go round. In his *Essay on the Principle of Population as it affects the Future Improvement of Society* he argued that 'the power of population is indefinitely greater than the power in the earth to produce subsistence for men. Population, when unchecked, increases in a geometrical ratio. Subsistence increases only in arithmetical ratio'. In diagrammatic form his basic argument was thus:

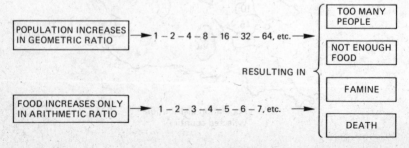

(ii) Malthus believed that the only way that this situation could be prevented was by 'natural checks' on the population occurring by accident, such as war, famine and epidemics. Malthus went on to launch an attack on the Poor Laws stating that the allowance system encouraged large families. His solution was 'the gradual and very gradual abolition of the poor-laws...[as]...their first obvious tendency is to increase population without the food for its support'.

Malthus was a disciple of Adam Smith and therefore favoured the *laissez-faire* idea, of the poor being made 'to help themselves'. He wrote at length about Savings Banks and stated that a poor man 'should be taught that his own exertions, his own industry and foresight, are his only just ground of dependence'.

(iii) *How far was Malthus correct in his theory?*

Malthus's argument cannot be totally disregarded, but his pessimism was not justified by events in the nineteenth century:

- The 'agrarian revolution' and the 'Golden Age' of agriculture (1850–75) enabled farmers to produce enough food to feed the growing population up to the mid-nineteenth century.
- From the 1870s onwards Britain adopted a policy of free trade, and cheap American grain was imported in large amounts.

Thus, Malthus did not foresee the rapid economic growth of nineteenth-century Britain.

(d) Distribution of the population

In the mid-eighteenth century the majority of the population was located in the south, south-east and East Anglia. Large areas of northern Britain were only sparsely populated. Apart from London which had a population of 500 000, towns were generally small; Norwich and Bristol, the next biggest towns, had populations somewhere between 30 000 and 40 000. 80 per cent of the population lived in rural areas earning their living off the land and supplementing their income by partaking in the domestic system.

By 1820 there were distinct signs that this pattern was beginning to change. With the perfection of the steam engine, the factory system became established on the coalfields of the northern English counties, South Wales and Central Scotland. This encouraged the growth of towns, together with the migration of workers over relatively short distances from rural districts. The population in the industrial areas grew more rapidly than the agricultural south, and became the most densely populated part of the country. (Note – there does not appear to have been any migration over large distances.)

1.3 POPULATION TRENDS 1820–1901

(a) What happened to the population in this period?

The population continued to grow. By 1851 the population of England and Wales had risen to 17.9 million and the United Kingdom to 27.3 million. In 1901 these figures stood at 32.5 million and 41.5 million respectively. In addition, the industrial towns grew quickly over the period as a whole (see chapter 19). By 1851 the population was equally split between urban areas and rural areas, indicative of the fact that Britain was becoming a nation of town-dwellers. In 1901 more people lived in towns than the countryside probably in the ratio of three to one. This re-alignment had important effects for the social framework of the country (see chapters 19 and 20).

(b) Why did the population continue to grow?

(i) *An overall decline in the death rate*

This more than anything else explains the rise in the population:

- Initially the death rate increased between 1820 and 1870 mainly because of the filthy conditions which prevailed in the industrial towns (see chapter 19).
- After 1870 the death rate began to fall steadily. This can be explained by the improvements in public health regulations which were heralded in by the *1875 Public Health Act* and the *1875 Artisan's Dwelling Act*. By this time the state had realised that it had to play a more dominant role in improving environmental conditions. At the same time rapid progress was being made in medical standards. Anaesthetics, antiseptics, vaccinations, bacteriology and the training of nurses had all begun to make their mark. By 1901 life expectancy had risen to 49 for a male and 52 for a

female. In addition, the infant mortality rate dropped from 162 in 1850 to 154 in 1900.

(ii) *Fluctuations in the birth rate*

Between 1820 and 1870 the birth rate increased gradually, but thereafter began to fall (from 33.8 in 1881 it dropped to 28.2 in 1901). The reasons generally forwarded for this are:

● The introduction of birth control. In 1877 Annie Besant and Charles Bradlaugh were responsible for publishing an American booklet on contraception. Victorian society was initially outraged and Sir Hardinge Giffard, the Solicitor-General, called the pamphlet 'a dirty filthy book'. Besant and Bradlaugh were arrested, tried, and found guilty of indecency. After the initial storm, however, birth control was gradually accepted and middle-class parents, in particular, deliberately limited the number of children they had.

● In the early part of the century a large family was an advantage as the children were a source of income. This was no longer the case after 1870. The *Elementary Education Acts of 1870, 1876 and 1880* made it compulsory for children to attend school, and the *Factory Acts* had banned child labour. A large family was now something of a liability and recipe for poverty.

(iii) *Emigration*

Taking the period as a whole, more people left the United Kingdom than entered, and consequently there was a net loss to the population (estimated at 1 200 000 between 1881 and 1911).

Why did emigration increase?

● In the 1820s William Huskisson lifted the restrictions which prevented skilled workmen leaving Britain.

● Periods of trade depression and unemployment such as the 1840s and 1880s encouraged people to try their luck in a new country.

● The Irish Potato Famine of the late 1840s caused many people to leave Ireland. Some went to Glasgow and Liverpool, others crossed the Atlantic to America.

● As the nineteenth century progressed, improved communications made emigration less hazardous in terms of travelling. The favourite destinations for emigrants were USA, Canada, Australia and New Zealand.

(iv) In the final analysis the population increased because the falling birth rate and increase in emigration were compensated for by a much steeper decline in the death rate.

1.4 HOW USEFUL ARE THE NINETEENTH-CENTURY CENSUS RETURNS TO THE HISTORIAN?

(a) General points

(i) The first official census took place in 1801 and has been held every ten years since, with the exception of 1941. Enumerators were employed to go round an area (a village or part of a town) to collect information which was then written up and collated. Statistics were then compiled for immediate use, for example, occupational structure.

(ii) A hundred years' rule operates on census returns. At the moment, census returns can be consulted up to 1881.

(iii) The early census returns (1801, 1811, 1821, 1831) do not provide very much information apart from basic statistics; they do not contain details, for example, on occupations and birthplaces. From 1851, in particular, they provide a wealth of evidence which allows us to reconstruct nineteenth-century life on both a national and local basis. Analysing census returns on a local level allows an historian to see how far a small area of the country fits in with the national trend.

(b) Census returns

Census returns have to be used carefully, but without doubt they are an extremely valuable source. The diagram below attempts to illustrate this:

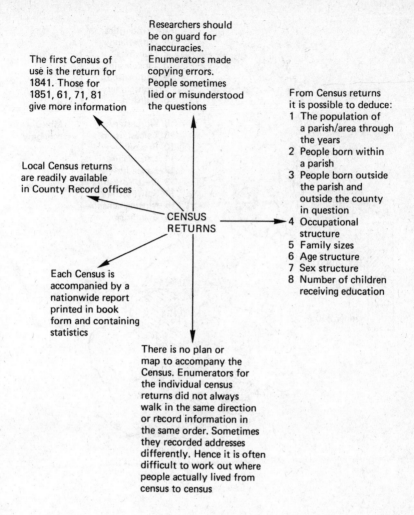

The first Census of use is the return for 1841. Those for 1851, 61, 71, 81 give more information

Researchers should be on guard for inaccuracies. Enumerators made copying errors. People sometimes lied or misunderstood the questions

From Census returns it is possible to deduce:
1 The population of a parish/area through the years
2 People born within a parish
3 People born outside the parish and outside the county in question
4 Occupational structure
5 Family sizes
6 Age structure
7 Sex structure
8 Number of children receiving education

Local Census returns are readily available in County Record offices

CENSUS RETURNS

Each Census is accompanied by a nationwide report printed in book form and containing statistics

There is no plan or map to accompany the Census. Enumerators for the individual census returns did not always walk in the same direction or record information in the same order. Sometimes they recorded addresses differently. Hence it is often difficult to work out where people actually lived from census to census

1.5 POPULATION TRENDS 1901–81

(a) What happened to the population during this period?

The population continued the pattern of growth. From 41.5 million in 1901 the population of the United Kingdom increased to 55.6 million in 1981. During this period life-expectancy has risen to 69 for males and 76 for females, hereby causing an increase in the percentage of elderly citizens within the population. In 1911, 6.8 per cent of the population were of retirement age, and this has risen to 17.5 in 1981.

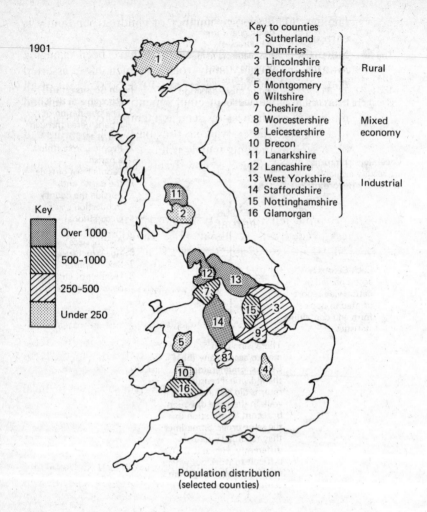

1901

Key to counties
1 Sutherland
2 Dumfries
3 Lincolnshire
4 Bedfordshire   Rural
5 Montgomery
6 Wiltshire
7 Cheshire
8 Worcestershire   Mixed
9 Leicestershire   economy
10 Brecon
11 Lanarkshire
12 Lancashire
13 West Yorkshire   Industrial
14 Staffordshire
15 Nottinghamshire
16 Glamorgan

Key

Over 1000

500–1000

250–500

Under 250

Population distribution
(selected counties)

(b) What were the underlying trends behind these figures?

(i) *The birth rate* has fallen steadily from 23.6 in 1911 to 13.4 in
1975, which can be explained by a number of factors:

● The First World War was responsible for the deaths of
750 000 males in the age group 18–45. After the war it was
hard for a young girl to find a spouse.

● The depression of the 1930s made working-class parents
re-examine their attitude towards family size. Unemployment and lack of finance caused them to have smaller

families. (The average number of children per family is currently put at 2.4.)

● Since the 1950s and 1960s attitudes have been changing towards traditional family roles. Women have asserted their right to pursue a career. In 1976, 50 per cent of all married women were in employment. Bearing a limited number of children is now seen as a temporary interruption to a woman's career, whereas previously child-bearing had been seen as the only female role.

● Birth control advice is now freely available via Family Planning Clinics.

(ii) *The death rate* fell from 14.3 in 1911 to 12.0 in 1931. Since 1951 it has levelled out at about 11.7. In addition the infant mortality rate has declined from 154 in 1900 to 16 in 1976. These statistics can be explained as follows:

● High standards of medical care now permit people to live longer.

● Higher living standards. Diet, housing and material comforts have gradually improved.

● The development of the Welfare State from 1906 onwards has also made a contribution – pensions, unemployment benefits, family allowances, school meals, free medical treatment are all provided by the State.

(iii) *Emigration and immigration*

● Overall, since 1945, emigration has exceeded immigration. Between 1945 and 1955 1.5 million people left Britain to settle in other countries. Many of these were 'skilled' workers and the term 'brain drain' came into use. Since the mid-1970s emigration has slowed down with the world recession. Countries like Australia, New Zealand and Canada have 'put the shutters' up as they have experienced their own economic problems.

● Since 1945 Britain has received a sizeable number of New Commonwealth immigrants from the West Indies, India, Pakistan and Bangladesh. In 1981 there were 2.2 million such immigrants in Britain, about four per cent of the population. European immigrants have also been received from Germany, Italy, Poland and Hungary (after the 1956 Hungarian Rising). In addition, since 1973 membership of the European Economic Community (EEC) has allowed the free flow of labour between the member states (in 1982 54 000 people entered Britain from other EEC states).

(iv) *Geographical distribution of population*

There have been a number of migratory trends during the period as a whole:

- In the 1930s there was a movement of the population from the north to the south and south-east of England (see chapters 28 and 29). This trend has continued into the 1980s.
- In 1939 40 per cent of the population lived in the six main conurbations of Greater London, South-East Lancashire, Merseyside, the West Midlands, West Yorkshire and Tyneside.
- Since 1945 there has been a movement out of the large conurbations into new towns such as Harlow, Stevenage and Skelmersdale. This is called 'secondary urbanisation'.
- There has also been the development of 'retirement migration' with elderly people moving to seaside resorts after retiring. The south coast towns, for example, Bournemouth and Brighton, have received most of these people.

Population (1000s)

	1951	1982
London	8348	6765
Birmingham	1113	1017
Glasgow	1090	761
Liverpool	789	510
Manchester	703	458
Belfast	444	325

1.6 CONCLUSION

Thus we return to the point at which we started. 'Population' is not an easy subject to understand – even demographers are unable to agree on a number of basic questions such as 'Why did the population boom take off in the late eighteenth century?' What is abundantly clear, however, is that the increase in population in Britain was accompanied by an increase in industrial output, trade, greater social provision and a basic framework within which people could live and work.

QUESTIONS

1. Objectives 1, 2 and 4

(a) What were the possible causes of the increase in population in the late eighteenth century?
(b) What were the results of the population increase?
(c) Why is the population a controversial issue among historians?

(Total = 30 marks)

2. Objectives 1 and 2

(a) Describe the way the population increased between 1820 and 1901.
(b) What factors influenced population growth during this period?
(c) How far were these factors (i) similar to, (ii) different from, those operating in the late eighteenth century?

(Total = 30 marks)

3. Objective 4

(a) What sources are available for investigating population trends between 1760 and the present day?
(b) Which sources, in your judgement, would be:
   (i) most useful
   (ii) least useful?
   Give reasons for your answer.

(Total = 30 marks)

4. Objective 3

How would the following people have viewed the increase in population in the early nineteenth century?
● a supporter of Thomas Malthus
● an overseer of the poor
● a landowner

(Total = 25 marks)

5. Objective 4

Study the sources below and then answer the questions:

Source A   cartoon drawn by George Cruikshank (courtesy of Mansell Collection) Taking the Census

Source B   The inhabitants of Jewry Street, Winchester, in 1881

The Inhabitants of Jewry Street, Winchester in 1881
Souce of Evidence: The Census Returns of 1881

A. Birthplaces

People born in Winchester	= 75
People born elsewhere in Hampshire	= 74
People born in other counties	= 51
	200

The Census is a count of the population. It is taken every 10 years

B. A Jewry Street Family in 1881

No	Name	Relation to Head of Family	Marital Status	Age	Occupation	Birthplace
29	James Thresher	Head	Married	38	Clergyman	Hamble
JEWRY	Sara Thresher	Wife	Married	36	–	Leicester
Street	Eliza Thresher	Daughter	Unmarried	13	Scholar	Andover
	Mary Thresher	Daughter	Unmarried	12	Scholar	Andover
	Lucy Thresher	Daughter	Unmarried	11	Scholar	Andover
	Edith Thresher	Daughter	Unmarried	9	Scholar	Winchester
	Frances Thresher	Daughter	Unmarried	8	Scholar	Winchester
	Edward Thresher	Son	Unmarried	4	Scholar	Winchester
	William Thresher	Son	Unmarried	3	–	Winchester
	Philip Thresher	Son	Unmarried	2	–	Winchester
	Constance Thresher	Daughter	Unmarried	11 months	–	Winchester
	Connie Fish	Servant	Unmarried	29	Nurse	Whitchurch
	Alice Biffin	Servant	Unmarried	42	Cook	Southampton
	Eunice Windebank	Servant	Unmarried	27	Cook	Kilmeston
	Annie Binard	Servant	Unmarried	25	Parlour Maid	Oxford
	Catherine Strutley	Servant	Unmarried	24	House Maid	Winchester
	Sarah Weeks	Servant	Unmarried	18	Kitchen Maid	Shirley

(a)   What views does Cruikshank have about the census count?

(b)   What evidence does Source B provide about the life-style of a nineteenth-century clergyman and his family?

(c)   'People in the nineteenth century tended not to travel'. How far do you agree? Explain your answer.

(d)   Are these sources reliable? Explain your answer.

6. Objectives 2 and 4

Study the graph below and answer the questions which follow:

Birth and death rates 1700–1840

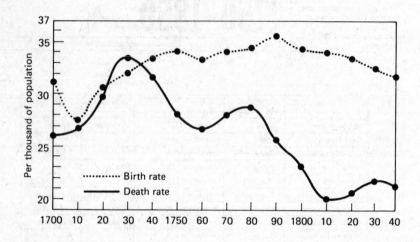

(a) In 1770, what were the total number of (i) births per thousand, and (ii) deaths per thousand?

(b) Use the graph to explain what was happening to the size of population in the periods (i) 1720–30, and (ii) 1780–90.

(c) What factors not shown on the graph might have made the population size increase and decrease between 1700 and 1840?

(d) The graph shows a dramatic change in the death rate between 1780 and 1810. What do you think were the most important reasons for this change? Explain your answer.

(e) What might have caused the death rate to change after 1810?

(Total = 25 marks)

(Northern Examination Association)

THE AGRARIAN REVOLUTION 1750–1850

2.1 INTRODUCTION: WHAT WAS THE OPEN FIELD SYSTEM?

(a) At the start of the eighteenth century about half of the arable farming areas of England were still under the open field system. This method was widely used in the Midlands, East Anglia and central southern England. In other parts of the country like the Lake District, North Wales, Kent, Devon and Cornwall, the open field system had never existed or had disappeared during Tudor times when the land was enclosed for livestock farming.

(b) There were variations in the number of open fields in each village but, by 1700, it is thought that the majority of villages had three. In addition, there was common land, waste land, and woodland, which were used for grazing livestock and gathering food and fuel. Each of the open fields was divided into strips measuring approximately 1 acre (0.4 ha) in area. Separating the strips were grass pathways or 'baulks'. A farmer's strips of land would be scattered between the three open fields; this meant that the good and bad soil was distributed amongst all the farmers.

(c) Within a typical open field village there existed a social structure:

- The Lord of the Manor or Squire was the main landowner in the village. Sometimes he did not actually live in the village, but he rented the land out as an absentee landlord.
- The freeholders were men who owned the land they farmed.
- The tenants rented their land either by copyhold (that is, a document dating back to medieval times showing proof of their right to rent land), or they were tenants at will, renting their land at the discretion of the squire.

- The cottagers were men who owned or rented a small piece of land but they were really dependent on the common land for a living.
- The squatters had no land in the open fields. They had a squalid hut on the common and they used the commons and waste to support their livestock.

(d) Open field farming depended on the farmers working together. Each year two of the three open fields were cultivated, the other one being left fallow (empty) on a three-year rotation (see diagram following).

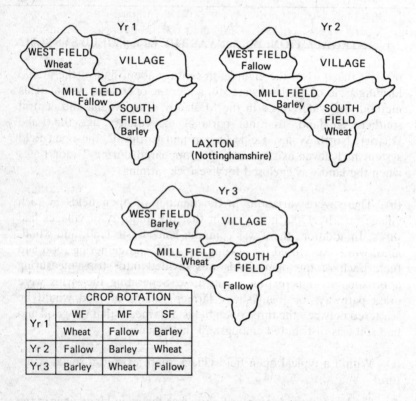

LAXTON
(Nottinghamshire)

CROP ROTATION			
	WF	MF	SF
Yr 1	Wheat	Fallow	Barley
Yr 2	Fallow	Barley	Wheat
Yr 3	Barley	Wheat	Fallow

All the farmers were required to grow the same crop in any given year. Sowing, harvesting and ploughing were done by everyone at the same time. Such communal organisation was necessary for the system to work efficiently. Machinery such as ploughs were also shared between the villagers.

2.2 WHAT WERE THE DISADVANTAGES OF THE OPEN FIELD SYSTEM?

(a) This system had a number of drawbacks:

- The employment of baulks and fallow meant that land was wasted.
- Machinery had to be moved between strips and this wasted time. This could involve moving equipment from one side of the village to the other.
- Individual initiative was thwarted with all the farmers having to grow the same crops by agreement, the decision being made at a meeting. This left no room for experimentation with new crops.
- There was no control of breeding on the unenclosed common land. Livestock was scrawny and thin, breeding was 'unscientific'.
- Root crops were not generally grown which meant there was little winter fodder for the animals. Livestock was killed off at Christmas and salted.
- Efficient farmers often had to suffer the encroachment of weeds if the adjacent strips were tended by careless farmers.
- It was difficult to drain the strips efficiently.

(b) The open field system was mainly a subsistence type of farming, each farmer growing sufficient for his family's needs, with little produce left to sell for cash. There were, however, exceptions to this general theory. For example, Daniel Defoe described large numbers of livestock being driven to market in London and sometimes farmers exchanged strips so that they could have a larger and more compact piece of land to till. Overall, however, such enterprise was on a small scale and the system in general was not suited to producing large quantities of food.

2.3 WHAT WAS THE AGRARIAN REVOLUTION?

(a) The term 'agrarian revolution' is generally used to describe changes that took place in agriculture between 1750 and 1850. The changes fell into two parts which were interconnected:

(i) The *enclosure* of the open fields.
(ii) The adoption of *new farming techniques, machines and methods*.

(b) The term should be used with caution as the changes were gradual rather than 'explosive' and the amount of change varied from region to region.

2.4 WHY DID CHANGES TAKE PLACE IN BRITISH AGRICULTURE BETWEEN 1750 AND 1850?

(a) An important factor was the rapid increase in population during this period leading to a much greater *demand* for agricultural products.

(b) The growth of the population also brought the expansion of large industrial towns which had to be supplied with food. British agriculture recognised this need and was prepared to change to meet the demand. With the home market expanding there were enough men in farming ambitious enough to innovate and change.

(c) This 'commercial attitude' was encouraged by a growing number of farming societies and even industrialists invested money in agriculture, sensing that they had a good chance of obtaining a profitable return.

(d) In the second half of the eighteenth century agricultural prices were generally high. During the French Wars (1793–1815) a series of bad harvests at the same time as a drop in foreign corn imports brought an upsurge in prices. Such economic conditions were an impetus for farmers to borrow money from the country banks and to invest in new methods of husbandry.

(e) During this period transport was radically improved. First the turnpike roads, then canals, and finally the railways, permitted farmers to transport their products to towns. In some cases farmers financed road improvements and canal-building.

Thus, agrarian change came about as a response to a network of causes working together.

2.5 THE ENCLOSURE MOVEMENT

(a) What were enclosures?

(i) Enclosure meant joining the strips of the open fields to make larger compact units of land. These units were then fenced or hedged off from the next person's land. Thus a farmer had his land together in one farm rather than in scattered strips. He now had a greater amount of independence. Enclosing land was not new; it dated back to at least the late Medieval period.

(ii) The area of England affected by the enclosure movement of this period was mainly the counties of the Midlands, East Anglia and central southern England.

(b) How was land enclosed?

(i) Before about 1740 most villages were enclosed by *agreement*. This was when the main owners of the land made a private arrangement to join their strips together. This may have involved buying some strips off the small farmers to eradicate any possible opposition. Where all the land in a village was owned by one or two men, enclosure by agreement was relatively straightforward. Unfortunately it is impossible to tell how much land was enclosed in this way as the documentation was rather informal.

(ii) Where a number of smaller landowners provided determined opposition to enclosure by agreement, an **Act of Parliament** had to be obtained. This became the accepted procedure after 1750. This had a number of factors in its favour:

- Each enclosure had legal documentation and certification.
- It provided the machinery for opposition to be heard.
- It permitted the *whole* of the village to be enclosed at the same time (that is, commons, waste, meadows and open fields). Up to 1750 many villages had been enclosed a little at a time.

(iii) Overall, Chambers and Mingay estimate that in excess of 2 400 000 hectares were enclosed by 4000 Acts of Parliament between 1750 and 1850.

(c) Why was Parliamentary Enclosure so widespread in the periods 1760 to 1780 and 1793 to 1815?

(i) Between 1760 and 1780 some 900 Enclosure Acts were passed. *Why was this?* Historians generally agree that high cereal prices motivated farmers to enclose land in order to produce a greater tonnage, thereby earning big profits (enclosure brought more land under the plough). In addition, where land was enclosed landlords could charge tenants higher rents.

(ii) The years of the French Wars (1793–1815) saw almost 2000 Enclosure Acts being passed. Once again this can be explained by high cereal prices – a record 126s.6d. (£6.33) in 1812 – which were the result of a series of poor harvests and the difficulty of importing foreign corn at a time when Europe was immersed in a major war. This led to widespread enclosure with even marginal waste land being enclosed. With enclosures the farmers could grow more food to feed the domestic population and make large profits.

(d) How was an Act of Enclosure obtained?

The process of obtaining an Act of Enclosure was a time-consuming activity:

- The starting point was when the owners of between three-quarters and four-fifths of the land in the parish decided that they wished to enclose. They then produced a petition giving notice of their intention to the rest of the village.
- From 1774 onwards this petition had to be fixed to the church door for three consecutive Sundays in late August/early September. Some landowners took the trouble to publish the petition in the local newspaper.
- Following this, a Bill of Enclosure for the village was drafted and it was read twice in the House of Commons.
- A Parliamentary committee then studied the Bill, considered any objections and wrote in any amendments or revisions to the wording of the Bill.
- The Bill was then given a third reading in the House of Commons and then passed on to the House of Lords.
- Finally, the Bill was given the Royal Assent and became an **Act of Parliament**.

Most Bills went through the procedure without too much hindrance.

(e) What were the General Enclosure Acts?

These Acts were an attempt to simplify the administration of enclosures.

In 1801 the *First General Enclosure Act* was passed. This laid down a model procedure for the enclosure of common lands in particular. The aim was to provide a guide to those who had the job of drafting Enclosure Bills. In 1836, a *Second General Enclosure Act* was passed.

This was concerned with the open fields and it gave local farmers the right to appoint commissioners (see section 2.5(f)) and to enclose land without direct reference to Parliament. In 1845 a *Third* (and final) *Enclosure Act* was brought on to the Statute Book. This established a group of 'specialist' commissioners who would travel round to the different villages to supervise the enclosing of land. They then reported back to Parliament and one General Act of Enclosure was passed for all the villages inspected during the course of the year.

(f) **What was the role of the Parliamentary Enclosure Commissioners and how well did they do their work?**

(i) Each individual Act of Enclosure stated that a number of commissioners (between 3 and 12, depending on the amount of land involved) should be appointed to carry out the enclosure.

(ii) After this surveyors and clerks were appointed by the commissioners. The surveyors had to draw up a plan of the village with its open fields and strips. The owners of the strips were recorded on the map. At a series of meetings called by the commissioners, landowners had to make a claim as to how much land they should be awarded under the enclosure. The commissioners then had to decide on the validity of each claim and come to a decision as to who was actually entitled to receive land in the award.

(iii) When, finally, the land had been allocated, the surveyors drew up a new map of the village displaying the new enclosures, boundaries between each parcel of land and the location of new paths and roads. With the new enclosure map went the award, a list of all the landowners allocated land in the enclosed village.

(iv) Commissioners, in general, have been accused of malpractice and of favouring the large landowners and aristocracy when allocating land. J. L. and B. Hammond, social historians of the early twentieth century, were particularly harsh in their judgement of the commissioners, stating that they usually ignored the claims of small farmers and cottagers in the award. More recent research has shown this to be an unfair judgement. Historians now tend more to the opinion that in most cases commissioners did their complex task admirably well, and they fastidiously considered the claims of the small man.

(g) How much did it cost to enclose a village by Act of Parliament?

The cost of enclosure varied from parish to parish. The amount depended on the size of the parish and whether it was the whole parish being enclosed or merely the commons and waste land. Every farmer who received an allocation of land in the award was obliged to pay his share of the cost. A contemporary estimate of the cost of enclosure by the Board of Agriculture was put at £1.40 per acre (£3.45 per hectare). More recent research carried out by J. M. Martin confirms the variations in cost between parishes. He concludes that in Warwickshire costs varied from £2.50 per acre (£6.20 per hectare) to £5.00 per acre (£12.35 per hectare). Such costs would have put quite a heavy burden on some of the smaller landowners who did not possess large amounts of capital.

(h) What were the economic effects of enclosure?

- The open fields gradually disappeared.
- Enclosures increased the amount of land under cultivation and this led to greater amounts of food being produced.
- Enclosures facilitated the adoption of the new methods of farming which were coming into use. (However, it should not be assumed that enclosure *automatically* led to the farmers using new techniques. In some areas the soil was too thin or the farmers were 'conservative' in outlook.)
- Enclosure enabled livestock to complement arable farming. More fodder crops were grown, livestock could be kept longer in the winter months and, in turn, they produced larger amounts of manure. Crop rotations could be used which did not necessitate leaving any land fallow.
- With enclosed fields, selective, scientific breeding could take place and animals, as a result, were fatter and more healthy.

(i) What were the social results of enclosure?

This a hotly debated issue.

  (i) The large landowners undoubtedly benefited from enclosure, particuarly if they were forward-looking. With their land parcelled off they were able to experiment and produce larger yields. During the war years they made excellent profits. Sometimes as the owner of a large enclosed farm the landowner's status was increased in the county. Chambers and Mingay argue that buying enclosed land during this period was a better investment than putting money into industrial developments.

(ii) *Did enclosure cause the demise of the small farmer?*

The Hammonds argued that the small landowners and tenants could not afford the expense of enclosure and were, therefore, forced to sell up and migrate to the industrial towns. More recent opinion challenges this viewpoint. It is possible that some men who owned very small amounts sold out, but it has been shown that the number of men farming between 40 and 50 acres (16 and 20 ha) actually increased during the period 1760–1815 when enclosure was in full swing. These farmers met the cost of enclosure possibly by selling a small amount of land or borrowing from one of the country banks. Some small owners sold their land to raise capital and then rented a farm. Although rents were high there was still an incentive to stay in business in this period because of the high prices and the demand for food from the increasing population. There is evidence, however, which suggests that small farmers began to decline in number after 1815, when prices went down but rents stayed at their wartime levels and the poor rates increased at an alarming pace. Thus, to blame enclosure for the disappearance of the small farmer after 1815 is rather unfair.

(iii) *What was the fate of the cottagers and squatters?*

The traditional argument claims that these two groups suffered terrible hardship and poverty as a result of enclosure, as they lost the right to use the common lands which were allocated to farmers in the enclosure award and probably ploughed up. Even a supporter of enclosure, Arthur Young, commented, 'by nineteen enclosure bills in twenty [the poor] are injured'. There may have been some truth in this in some parishes but, again, differentiation is necessary. If a cottager was able to show that he lived in a cottage with common rights attached to it he was allocated some land in the enclosure award. In some enclosures, the commissioners took the plight of the cottagers and squatters into account and gave them a small amount of land (about one hectare) even if they could not produce a legal claim. The degree of suffering may have varied from village to village.

(j)   How far was it true that enclosures led to 'rural depopulation'?

It has been claimed that enclosure caused widespread movement of landless labourers from the countryside to the growing industrial towns. However, there is evidence to contradict this:

● Enclosures initially required **more** labour, not less. It is likely that the 'landless' labourers would have been employed to build fences, dig ditches, construct roads and new farmhouses.

● Enclosures brought more land under cultivation which needed labour to work it. In arable areas, particularly, men were needed to plough, sow, hoe and harvest the crops. In addition, the increased output would have stimulated a number of 'associated' industries, for example, brewing and milling.

● More stockmen, dairymen and shepherds were needed.

It must be considered doubtful that enclosures caused rural depopulation. Statistics suggest that it was not until the late nineteenth century that any widespread exodus from the countryside took place.

(k)   There *was* poverty and suffering in the countryside in the period 1790 to 1830. If enclosure on its own did not cause this hardship what did?

 (i)   In the south and the east of England, the decline of domestic industries was one factor in bringing about increased poverty. Previously villagers had supplemented their income by, for example, weaving or hat-making.

 (ii)   The poor harvests and high prices in the 1790s, although bringing profit to the farmers, brought suffering to the labourers.

(iii)   Labourers in the areas where enclosures had taken place in the sixteenth century may well have suffered as they could not find employment in erecting fences, etc.

(iv)   It is also worth noting that poverty was rife in both open and enclosed villages. Rural poverty was a phenomenon well before enclosures.

2.6 TECHNICAL IMPROVEMENTS AND THE AGRICULTURAL PIONEERS OF THE EIGHTEENTH CENTURY

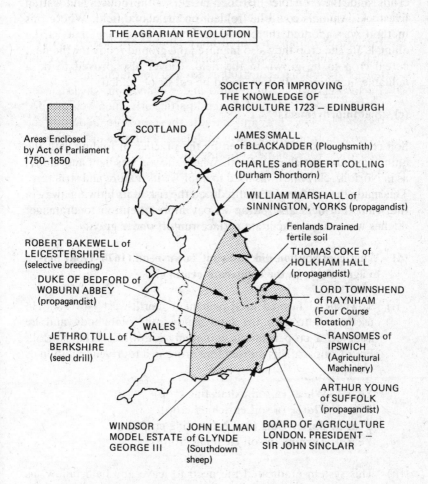

THE AGRARIAN REVOLUTION

Areas Enclosed by Act of Parliament 1750–1850

SCOTLAND

SOCIETY FOR IMPROVING THE KNOWLEDGE OF AGRICULTURE 1723 – EDINBURGH

JAMES SMALL of BLACKADDER (Ploughsmith)

CHARLES and ROBERT COLLING (Durham Shorthorn)

WILLIAM MARSHALL of SINNINGTON, YORKS (propagandist)

Fenlands Drained fertile soil

ROBERT BAKEWELL of LEICESTERSHIRE (selective breeding)

THOMAS COKE of HOLKHAM HALL (propagandist)

DUKE OF BEDFORD of WOBURN ABBEY (propagandist)

LORD TOWNSHEND of RAYNHAM (Four Course Rotation)

WALES

JETHRO TULL of BERKSHIRE (seed drill)

RANSOMES of IPSWICH (Agricultural Machinery)

ARTHUR YOUNG of SUFFOLK (propagandist)

WINDSOR MODEL ESTATE GEORGE III

JOHN ELLMAN of GLYNDE (Southdown sheep)

BOARD OF AGRICULTURE LONDON. PRESIDENT – SIR JOHN SINCLAIR

(a) The second ingredient of the 'Agrarian Revolution' was the introduction of new techniques and methods which were generally more marked in those areas where communications were relatively good and the soil was suitable (for example, Norfolk).

(b) Developments in the growing of 'new crops'

During the eighteenth century more farmers began to grow a greater variety of crops. Root crops such as parsnips, swedes and mangolds were popularised. Leaf crops and grasses, such as lucerne, sanfoin and clover were also grown to good effect. This trend reflected the growing demand for fresh meat. These 'new' crops were all fodder crops and they enabled British farmers to produce and fatten livestock. Animals could be 'folded' on the actual field. Where this method was adopted there was the added advantage that as the animals ate the crop they also manured the ground ready for the next cereal crop to be grown in the field. Clover also proved to be a valuable 'new' crop. It, too, could be cut or be folded.

(c) Soil improvements

Soil could be naturally improved by the practice of folding with the animal manure enriching the soil. Where the soil was light and sandy, as in Norfolk, clay marl was used to improve its texture and structure. This made the soil heavier and reduced the risk of its blowing away in the wind. Farmers also began to pay more attention to drainage; ditches were dug to facilitate surface run-off under gravity.

(d) What contribution did Viscount Townshend (1674–1738) make to agriculture in the eighteenth century?

(i) Townshend farmed at Raynham in north-west Norfolk. He used marl to give the light sandy soil some body and he adopted a crop rotation commonly known as 'The Norfolk Four Course'. This utilised four crops in a four-year rotation as follows:

Year 1. **Wheat** (a soil exhausting crop)
Year 2. **Clover** (a soil enriching crop)
Year 3. **Barley/Oats** (soil exhausting crops)
Year 4. **Turnips** (a soil cleaning crop)

(ii) This system eradicated the need to leave any field fallow, as had been the case in the open field system, and enabled Townshend to make full use of all his land each year. With such

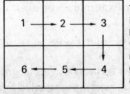

The field was divided into sections with wicker hurdles. Sheep grazed on first section before being moved on. This meant that grazing was systematic and not wasteful

The Practice of Folding

a system arable and animal farming complemented each other. Townshend favoured 'folding' the clover in order to fatten his sheep. The conditions at Raynham were suited to this particular rotation and Townshend gained a reputation for 'good practice'.

(iii) Townshend, however, did not 'invent' crop rotations and he was not responsible for introducing turnips to this country. He is often given the nickname 'Turnip' but this crop had been brought to England from Holland during the seventeenth century by Richard Weston. Townshend can be regarded as a pioneer in that he had the foresight to appreciate the advantages of the 'new' methods but his importance should not be exaggerated.

(e) **What developments took place in the breeding of livestock during the eighteenth century? What was the contribution of Robert Bakewell (1725–95)?**

(i) Greater attention was paid to the breeding of animals in the eighteenth century, particularly with farmers growing a larger variety of fodder crops. Although scientific breeding had been known before this period, in general, common lands were mainly populated by disease-ridden animals whose mating was uncontrolled. 'Old' breeds of sheep tended to be thin and to produce light-weight fleeces. Farmers began to experiment with improving livestock breeds, particularly where enclosure had taken place.

(ii) *Robert Bakewell* of Dishley Grange, Loughborough, is traditionally given the credit for pioneering new breeding methods. He produced the **New Leicester** sheep by using selective or 'in-and-in' breeding where parent and off-spring were mated. This particular breed was quick to fatten but the meat contained a deal of fat; the fleece also tended to be coarse. Bakewell paid careful attention to detail on his 440 acre (178 hectare) farm, making sure that stables and barns were spotlessly clean. He kept meticulous records and notes on his stock. Bakewell also produced the Longhorn cattle and a distinctive breed of black carthorses. His work was by no means perfect but he gained a reputation for thoroughness during his time. Farmers were keen to visit Dishley to study Bakewell's methods and also to hire rams from him in order to improve their own flocks.

(iii) Bakewell was just one of a number of men experimenting at the time. John Ellman of Glynde used in-and-in breeding to produce an improved version of the Southdown sheep. This breed was noted for its fine quality mutton and it could be folded on turnips. At Ketton, Charles and Robert Colling developed the Durham Shorthorn cattle which gave lean meat and large quantities of milk. George Culley of Northumbria was also successfully breeding Shorthorn cattle at the same time as the Colling brothers.

(iv) Bakewell's importance is that he made a platform for others to build on during the ensuing years. The amount of progress made in breeding in terms of average weight of livestock is shown below:

Smithfield Market

1710			1795	
	Beeves:	370 lb		800 lb
	Calves	50 lb		150 lb
	Sheep	28 lb		80 lb
	Lambs	18 lb		50 lb

(f) What was Jethro Tull's (1674–1741) contribution to agricultural change in the eighteenth century?

(i) Tull was a native of Basildon in Berkshire. In 1709 he took over Mount Prosperous Farm, Shalbourne, having previously farmed at Howberry, near Wallingford. It appears that Tull invented a seed-drill whilst at Howberry. He was unhappy with the normal 'broadcasting' method and his machine was intended to sow seeds in straight rows at at the same depth. However, he was not the first man to devise a seed-drill; this had originally been achieved by John Worlidge in 1669. It is not certain if Tull developed Worlidge's machine or made his drill independently. In 1711 Tull's poor health forced him to make a tour of Italy and France. He took the opportunity to observe farming methods in these countries and he was suitably impressed by the husbandry in the vineyards of southern France. Tull noticed that the vines were hoed rather than being manured. He adopted this idea on his farm when he returned to England, employing a horse-hoe in conjunction with his seed-drill.

(ii) Tull gained a reputation for being an 'eccentric' and it is possible that his lack of faith in the value of manure was the origin of such an opinion. However, Tull's ideas about drilling seeds and regular hoeing **were** sound, but they did not spread very rapidly. It was not until the early years of the nineteenth century that the seed-drill was generally accepted – by which time it had been improved by James Cooke, Henry Baldwin and Samuel Wells.

(iii) Thus, Tull's importance was that he provided an idea which later inventors were able to develop. The fact that his seed-drill did not gain immediate acceptance was due to prejudice, 'conservatism' and the fact that it had a number of 'teething problems' which he, himself, could not put right. Tull published a number of books and pamphlets describing his approach to farming, the most famous being 'The Horse Hoeing Husbandry' (or 'An Essay on the Principles of Tillage and Vegetation') in 1733.

(g) What other new machinery came into use in this period?

(i) In 1730 the 'Rotherham' plough was introduced. It was mainly used in the north of England and had an iron share and coulter. The source of this plough is something of a mystery. It was probably based upon a Dutch idea but the credit for its invention is often ascribed to Joseph Foljambe of Rotherham. As this plough was smaller it needed fewer oxen to pull it. It was later modified by James Small of Blackadder in Berwickshire. He experimented with the shape of the mouldboard until he produced a very efficient plough which was widely used in Scotland and generally accepted by English farmers.

(ii) In 1785 Robert Ransome founded a factory in Ipswich to make agricultural machinery. He made, amongst other things, cast iron plough shares. Andrew Meikle produced the first practical threshing machine in 1784 and Patrick Bell invented a cumbersome reaping machine in 1826. The use of such machinery was generally slow to spread.

2.7 WHAT CONTRIBUTION DID THE 'PROPAGANDISTS' MAKE TO THE AGRARIAN CHANGES?

The propagandists were a group of individuals – landed gentlemen and journalists – who were enthusiastic about the 'new' agricultural techniques. They either practised the new husbandry or wrote articles about its merits, thus helping to publicise the new methods.

(a) Thomas Coke of Holkham (1754–1842)

Coke was known for the progressive way he farmed his estate at Holkham Hall in Norfolk. When he began farming in 1776 the estate was run down and dilapidated. Coke transformed the estate spending a reputed £100 000 on the repairing of farm buildings. Being an advocate of the new methods he enclosed his land, applied marl, rotated his crops, and practised selective breeding. As a condition of obtaining a long lease, prospective tenants were asked to use the new methods. Every year, between 1778 and 1821, Coke held an annual meeting on his estate to demonstrate the best methods in farming at the time. He also took the opportunity to discuss farming with those who attended. The idea of an 'agricultural show' was also adopted by the Duke of Bedford on his estate at Woburn. It is believed that Coke increased the annual rental of his estate from £2200 to £20 000.

(b) Arthur Young (1741–1820)

Between 1763 and 1766 Young farmed at Bradfield, Suffolk, and Sandford Hall, Essex. He was not very successful and decided to devote his time to writing about agriculture, travelling widely throughout England, Ireland and the continent. Through Young's writing the historian can build up a picture of agricultural practice at the time. Young was a staunch supporter of the new husbandry and the enclosures. Among his publications were 'A Six Weeks Tour through the Southern Counties' (1768), 'The Farmer's Calendar' (1771) and, between 1784 and 1804, he was the editor of the magazine, 'The Annals of Agriculture'. Young wrote with enthusiasm about farming practice in Norfolk, which he observed as more progressive than many other areas. In 1793 Young was appointed Secretary to the newly-formed Board of Agriculture. Its purpose was to encourage farmers to adopt good practices so that increased amounts of food could be produced during the war against France. Young also helped to undertake a systematic survey of the agriculture of the country. Young surveyed six counties and displayed amazing energy. Young did help to publicise the new methods, but ironically, the gradual adoption of the changes is often highlighted in the comments he makes. For example, in 1791 he criticised the 'sloth . . . ignorance . . . and . . . backwardness' of the farming near St Neots.

(c) William Marshall (1754–1818)

Born at Sinnington, North Yorkshire, Marshall equalled Young in the production of farming literature. His main book work was *A General Survey of the Rural Economy of England*. The first volume, dealing with Norfolk, was published in 1787. It was Marshall, in fact, who suggested that the Board of Agriculture should be set up. Although invited to take part in the Board's work, Marshall preferred to publish his own surveys. It is claimed that Marshall's work is more objective than Young's and, as such, more reliable.

(d) King George III

The King was a keen farmer, knew Arthur Young, and contributed articles to the *Annals of Agriculture*. He practised the new methods on the Royal Estate at Windsor and in doing so gave them the Royal seal of approval. Many other farmers were pleased to follow the example of the monarch.

2.8 CONCLUSION

It is worth considering just how 'revolutionary' was the Agrarian Revolution. The word 'revolution' implies rapid, violent change. We have seen that new crops, rotations, selective breeding and new machines were, on the whole, gradually adopted. G. E. Fussell states that most farmers remained 'steadfast in their adherence' to traditional methods. Furthermore, many of the methods which claimed to be new to the eighteenth century in fact dated back to earlier periods. What probably may be judged as 'violent' was the widespread parliamentary enclosure of land, particularly during the French Wars of 1793–1815. This increased the amount of land in cultivation and enabled the progressive farmers to invest in the new techniques to maximum advantage.

QUESTIONS

1. **Objectives 1 and 2**

(a) What were the defects of the open field system?   (4 marks)

(b) Why was land enclosed in the late eighteenth century?

(6 marks)

(c) What were the social and economic effects of these enclosures?

(10 marks)

2. **Objective 4**

Study the following sources and then answer the questions which follow:

Source A *opposite*: The village of Helpston (before and after Enclosure). Taken from *The Northamptonshire Landscape* by John Steane (Hodder & Stoughton, 1974).

Source B

Ordered that the following Notice be exhibited on the several Church doors within the several Parishes and Places to be inclosed on Sunday next:

Maxey with Deepingate Northborough Glinton with Peakirk Etton and Helpstone Inclosure –

We the commissioners for the said Inclosure do hereby give Notice to the occupiers of the Lands to be divided and inclosed that they are not to sow any part thereof with Wheat this present Season Given under our hands this 23rd day of October 1811.

Source C

Ordered that the following advertisement be likewise published in the Lincoln Rutland and Stamford Mercury:

Maxey with Deepingate Northborough Glinton with Peakirk Etton and Helpstone Inclosure –

The commissioners for the said Inclosure will be ready to receive the requests in writing (sealed up) of the several proprietors as to the situation of the several allotments to be respectively made to

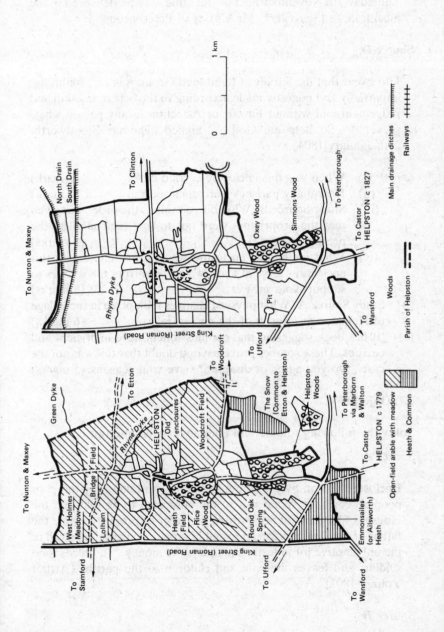

them at their meeting at the New Inn, Market Deeping on Thursday 7th November next or the same may be delivered in the meantime to their Clerk, Mr Morley of Peterborough.

Source D

I do swear that the Survey of Lands and Grounds is . . . faithfully, impartially and honestly made according to the best of my skill and judgement and without Favour or Affection to any person whatsoever . . . So help me God . . . Signed. Thomas Bloodworth. 27th January 1804.

(a)   (i)   When was this enclosure carried out?   (1 mark)
    (ii)   How many parishes were enclosed?   (1 mark)
   (iii)   Study Source B. Why, do you think, the order was given that the proprietors were not to sow their land in 'the present season'?   (2 marks)
   (iv)   What method of enclosure was used to implement this enclosure? Give at least two reasons from the sources to support your answer.   (5 marks)

(b)   Study Source A. What physical changes took place in the village of Helpston as a result of the enclosure?   (6 marks)

(c)   'It has been suggested that commissioners were inefficient and corrupt. These sources prove beyond doubt that this was not the case'. Do you agree or disagree? Give your reasons. (5 marks)

3.   **Objective 4**

Study the following sources and then answer the questions:

Source A

Enclosures go on by the commissioners, who take away the poor people's cows . . . What is it to the poor man to be told that the Houses of Parliament are extremely tender of property, while the father of the family is forced to sell his cow . . . Being deprived of the only motive for industry squanders the money . . . enlists for a soldier, and leaves the wife and children to the parish. (Arthur Young, 1801)

Source B

'Many of the poorer villagers suffered as a result of losing access to . . . fuel'. (R. Parker, 1965)

Source C

'A more ruinous effect . . . will be the almost total depopulation of their villages . . . driving them . . . into the manufacturing towns'. (House of Commons Committee, 1797)

Source D

'There is no evidence at all that enclosure led to depopulation of the countryside'. (R. Parker, 1967)

(a) How many of the sources appear to view enclosure favourably? Give your reasons. (3 marks)
(b) How might a poor villager lose his cow and access to fuel with enclosure? (2 marks)
(c) What arguments do you think could be put forward to support the view given in Source D? (4 marks)
(d) The sources above give the impression that many people suffered as a result of enclosure. Why, then, was enclosure so widespread in the late eighteenth century? (7 marks)
(e) 'Source C and Source D contradict each other, but Source C must be correct as it is primary evidence'. Do you agree or disagree? Give reasons. (4 marks)

4. **Objective 1**

Choose **two** of the following individuals associated with agrarian change:

Robert Bakewell
Jethro Tull
Viscount Townshend
Thomas Coke

(a) For each of the persons you have chosen briefly describe their work. (8 marks)
(b) What motivated them to take an interest in farming? (4 marks)
(c) Assess their overall importance in the 'agrarian revolution'. (8 marks)

5. **Objective 3**

The year is 1795. You are a leading farmer in an open field village in Norfolk. A group of landowners, yourself included, have decided to petition for enclosure. You have been selected to explain this decision to a meeting of the inhabitants of the village to be held at the local public house. What are you going to say?   (20 marks)

THE INDUSTRIAL REVOLUTION

3.1 INTRODUCTION

Beginning sometime in the late eighteenth century a number of changes took place which transformed Britain into an industrial and urbanised society. The changes involved were:

- Industry became the foundation of the nation's economy rather than agriculture.
- The bulk of the population became urban dwellers as towns developed on the coalfields of Britain.
- Most industrial activity took place in purpose-built factories, rather than people's houses.
- Steam became the main source of power to drive machinery, rather than muscle, animal and water power.
- There was a rapid growth of industrial output leading to the development of a large export trade.
- The industrial changes brought widespread social repercussions on the way people lived, worked and played.

It has become usual for historians to describe these changes as the 'Industrial Revolution'. This is a convenient term, but also one which has engendered widespread debate. It is also a term which appears to suggest that the changes were for the better, that is, progress. However, a number of historians have challenged this opinion, seeing the industrialisation process in negative terms, believing that the changes were for the worse (see section 3.5).

3.2 TERMINOLOGY

(a) What is the origin of the term 'Industrial Revolution'?

In 1837 Blanqui, a French economist, referred to the fact that Britain
had undergone an 'industrial revolution'. The term also appeared in
The Condition of the Working Class in England by Frederich Engels,
which was published in 1844. It is really from 1884, however, that the
term came into general use. This was after the publication of an
article based on notes taken from lectures given by Arnold Toynbee.
All three men felt that Britain had undergone such an industrial
upheaval in the late eighteenth century that the term 'revolution' was
an accurate and convenient description.

(b) Why should the term 'industrial revolution' be used with caution?

It is important to bear in mind that, like all labels of convenience, the
term has a number of shortcomings. Critics have pointed out:

- The word 'revolution' is misleading. It tends to suggest that the
  industrial changes were violent, dramatic and came about overnight. The changes, in fact, took place over a number of decades.
  Industrial towns like Leeds did not magically 'spring up', and
  many of the inventions (such as the power loom) took time to
  catch on. Thus, the word 'evolution' which implies gradual
  change would probably be more appropriate.
- It is also argued that the term 'industrial revolution' suggests an
  event which has a definite starting and finishing point. Some
  writers have actually stated that the industrial changes took place
  between 1760 and 1830. This assertion has caused widespread
  controversy amongst many historians, who point out that it is
  impossible to pinpoint exact dates as the industrial changes
  referred to were part of a *continuing process*.

3.3 ALTERNATIVE VIEWS OF THE 'INDUSTRIAL REVOLUTION'

(a) As with agriculture, there is a school of thought which argues
that 'dramatic' industrial changes had been going on a long time
before the late eighteenth century. Professor Nef, for example, cites
the increase in output of the coal industry which he dates back to the

mid sixteenth century. Historians of the Medieval period go further back and express the opinion that rapid industrialisation began in the fourteenth century with the expansion of the woollen industry. It is possible to see some substance in these claims, but the difference is that they did not have such far-reaching effects as the industrial developments of the late eighteenth century.

(b)   One of the most influential studies of recent years has been that of W. W. Rostow who, in 1956, published *The Stages of Industrial Growth*. This is an attempt to examine a nation's industrial growth based on a model of developmental stages. Rostow suggests that a country undergoes five stages of industrial growth. These are:

TRADITIONAL SOCIETY

↓

PRECONDITIONS FOR TAKE-OFF

↓

INDUSTRIAL TAKE-OFF

↓

THE DRIVE TO INDUSTRIAL MATURITY

↓

THE AGE OF HIGH MASS CONSUMPTION

The first stage of the traditional society consists of a pre-industrial economy based on agriculture. With the next stage some changes occur in the economy which take the form of increased coal and food production. Stage three is the most important, when the economy takes off into a period of *sustained* economic growth. This will then be consolidated when the stages of maturity and high mass consumption are reached.

Rostow has now come in for a deal of criticism. With Britain, he pinpoints 1783–1802 as the period when take-off took place. It appears that Rostow has fallen into the trap of citing exact dates for developments which cannot really be tied down so finely. Critics are also quick to point out that many features required for an industrial economy such as efficient communications (railways) did not occur until long after 1802. Furthermore, Rostow's theory ignores the social and political implications which accompany a period of intense industrial change. Finally, the question 'What lies beyond the stage of high mass consumption?' might well be posed.

(c)   There is, however, much to commend in Rostow's work. He attempts to see industrialisation in terms of 'development'. Industrial activity has been going on for centuries and it does make some sort of sense to plot industrial changes on a line of development through time.

3.4 WHY WAS BRITAIN THE FIRST COUNTRY TO BECOME AN INDUSTRIALISED SOCIETY?

An attempt to answer this question involves a case study of the many causal factors required to stimulate the transformation from an agrarian to an industrial society. These causal factors, or pre-requisites, were all present in Britain at the same time, and this is really the key to the question. In the late eighteenth century Britain had all the following pre-requisites necessary for industrialisation:

(a) Britain had large deposits of the necessary raw materials, particularly coal and iron ore.

(b) Britain's population was growing rapidly. This was important as it increased the demand for industrial products, provided a labour force for the factories and ensured that there was a ready-made market for the sale of goods.

(c) Britain's overseas empire was also growing during this period. This was advantageous as it was a source of valuable raw materials and also a market to sell products.

(d) Transport developments (roads and, especially, canals) were stimulated by the growing industrial activity and aided the movement of goods.

(e) With the growth of banking facilities money was available to finance industrial projects. There were a number of men who were willing to invest sums of money in industry. These *entrepreneurs* came from a wide spectrum of society, including the landed gentry. Many entrepreneurs were non-conformist in religion – for example, the Darby family of Coalbrookdale were Quakers. The most popular theory to explain this trend is that dissenters from the Anglican church were not allowed to hold positions of public office and thus they sought recognition in the field of industry. Vast amounts of money were not always needed to finance some of the earlier industrial projects, but later huge amounts were required to build the railway network. The early entrepreneurs were careful to put profits back into their business. During the period of the French Wars (1793–1815) the issue of paper money and credit notes by the country banks helped industrialists to solve the problems posed by the need to have current capital available to pay wages, etc.

(f) There was also a great deal of interest in applying science and technology to industry. A number of inventions were forthcoming often, it seemed, just as they were needed. More important was the fact that the inventions were made commercially viable by the support of the entrepreneurs. Asa Briggs quotes the partnership of James Watt (inventor) and Matthew Boulton (entrepreneur) as the 'classical partnership' of the period.

(g) The political atmosphere in Britain was receptive to innovation during this period. The government was relatively stable, there were no major wars fought on British soil, and the prevailing economic philosophy in vogue was that of *laissez-faire*. Inventors and commercial ventures were encouraged by such conditions. Adam Smith's book *The Wealth of Nations*, was published in 1776 and it deeply influenced the economic thinking of the period. In contrast, economic progress in France was hampered by the chaos of the Revolution and the ensuing wars.

(h) The fact that Britain could satisfy all of these pre-conditions simultaneously explains why she was the first country to industrialise. In the words of S. G. Checkland, 'Inventive activity is related to [the] general conditions of society'.

3.5 THE CONTROVERSY BETWEEN THE 'OPTIMISTS' AND THE 'PESSIMISTS'

A vigorous debate based on the issue of industrialisation and the standard of living has been going on for a number of years now. The debate began in the late nineteenth century, was carried on by the Hammonds in the early part of the present century and, in the last 20 years, has taken on a renewed impetus.

(a) What is the 'optimistic' point of view?

Those historians who take an optimistic view of industrialisation believe it brought an increase in the standard of living of the working population. The crux of their argument is based on a study of real wages. Furthermore, they argue, industrialisation brought wider job opportunities. This argument has been championed by T. S. Ashton, Professor Clapham and, currently, by R. G. Hartwell.

(b) What is the 'pessimistic' viewpoint?

The pessimistic viewpoint is that the early period of industrialisation brought a lowering of the standard of living, urban squalor, pollution and a general debasing of the quality of life. This is the view put forward by Eric Hobsbawm and E. P. Thompson, both of whom believe that industrialisation has resulted in the exploitation of the labour force.

(c) In the final analysis it will probably be a person's general political leanings which dictate the view they take of industrial society. The optimistic side is a reflection of capitalism, whereas the pessimists put forward a Marxist standpoint.

3.6 CONCLUSION

The whole question of the Industrial Revolution is a source of constant controversy amongst historians. When did it begin? When did it end? What caused it? What were its results? How accurate is the phraseology? – these are all questions which will provoke discussion for many years to come. In conclusion, Phyllis Deane makes an excellent point when she states that the arguments are ones brought about by 'differences in methods of historical analysis and interpretation rather than disputes about what happened'.

QUESTIONS

1. Objectives 1 and 2

(a) Why were conditions 'right' for industrialisation in late-eighteenth-century Britain?   (12 marks)

(b) Which of these conditions, if any, would you consider to be the most important? Why?   (8 marks)

2. Objectives 1 and 2

How do historians differ in their interpretation of the Industrial Revolution? In your answer make reference to:

(a)   When it started.
(b)   The effects it had on the standard of living.

(Total = 20 marks)

CHAPTER 4

THE TEXTILE INDUSTRY
1700–1850

4.1 INTRODUCTION

In the early eighteenth century the textile industry consisted of four materials – wool, cotton, silk and linen. The industry was organised on the domestic system using hand-powered machinery; wool was by far the most important fabric. By 1850 the textile industry had been totally transformed into one which was based on the factory system with steam-powered machinery. Output was vastly increased as a result. By now cotton was the dominant sector of the textile industry. How and why these changes occurred will be the main theme of this chapter, along with an assessment of the role of the cotton industry in the industrialisation of Britain.

4.2 WHAT PROCESSES WERE INVOLVED IN THE MANUFACTURE OF TEXTILES IN 1700?

(a) Preparing the raw material

There were slight differences as to the processes through which various raw materials were put, but by and large the following stages applied to all textiles:

- *Cleaning* – raw cotton and wood had to be washed.
- *Carding and combing* – two methods of disentangling and straightening out the fibres. This was achieved by using combs with metal teeth.

(b) Spinning and weaving

These were the two main stages of manufacture. Spinning was when a thread or yarn was obtained from the fibres by a pulling, twisting action. This was carried out on a spinning-wheel. Next the yarn was woven on a hand loom (threads were arranged vertically from the top of the loom (this was called the **warp**) and then the weaver passed a horizontal thread (the **weft**) through the vertical threads by means of a shuttle). Each time a weft thread was passed through the warp it would be pushed tight by a batten.

(c) Finishing processes

The cloth now had to be put through a variety of finishing stages:

- *Fulling* – woollen cloth was immersed in water and fuller's earth and then beaten with hammers (or walked on) in order to tighten the threads. Water-powered fulling mills were used in many areas.
- *Dyeing* – woollen cloth was soaked in large vats of dye to give colour to it.
- *Knapping and shearing* – woollen cloth was trimmed or sheared to get rid of the loose fibres.
- *Printing* – cotton cloth had colour or a design applied by a plate print.

After all this the cloth was ready for marketing.

(d) Other terminology

It is important to distinguish between 'woollen' cloth and 'worsted' cloth. Woollen cloth was heavy and was manufactured from short-fibred wools and underwent fulling. Worsteds were lighter, not fulled and were made from long wools. This cloth took its name from a small village near Norwich where it was originally made. Furthermore, in the early eighteenth century British cotton cloth was a mixture of cotton thread and linen thread and was called 'fustian'; at this time British weavers were unable to manufacture a pure cotton material.

4.3 WHAT WAS THE STATE OF THE TEXTILE INDUSTRY IN 1700?

In 1700 **the manufacture of woollen cloth** was found in many different parts of the country but three areas can be distinguished as the principal centres. These were West Yorkshire (Wakefield, Leeds, Huddersfield and Halifax), East Anglia (Norfolk, Suffolk and Essex) and the West Country (Gloucestershire, Somerset, Devon and Wiltshire). Raw wool was readily available and weaving skills, introduced by Flemish immigrants in the Middle Ages, had been passed down from generation to generation. The importance of the woollen industry was illustrated by the fact that in 1760 the export trade was worth £5.5 million. Wool's importance is also shown by the fact that Parliament was willing to pass legislation to protect it from the competition of Indian cotton. An Act of 1701 banned the imports of Indian cotton cloth and in 1721 it became illegal to wear imported cotton fabrics. The idea behind the Act was to increase wool production.

The cotton industry based in South-East Lancashire, was only of minor importance in the British economy. British people who were able to afford cotton fabrics bought the fine muslins and calicoes which were imported from India. Home-produced fustian cotton was coarse and much inferior. It was difficult to obtain raw cotton at this time and output was, therefore, limited. In 1760 cotton exports earned just £200 000.

The manufacture of silk was introduced to this country by the Huguenot immigrants who arrived from France in the seventeenth century. The most important areas were Norwich, Coventry and Spitalfields in London. Silk, however, was only made in small quantities, as it was difficult to obtain raw silk; it was imported from Italy.

Linen was produced in England but the most important centre was Northern Ireland, centred on Londonderry and Belfast. It was used to make sheets and shirts.

4.4 THE DOMESTIC SYSTEM

(a) What was the domestic system and how did it function?

(i) In the early eighteenth century all the branches of the textile industry were organised under the 'domestic system'. The main feature of the domestic system was that cloth was manufactured in cottages with all the family taking part. The children would clean and comb the raw material, women would spin the yarn and the weaving was done by men. Fulling was usually done in a fulling mill and dyeing and shearing would be undertaken in small workshops. In some areas it was usual for the manufacture of the cloth to be intermixed with farming. However, the phrase 'domestic system' can be misleading in that it suggests that a common system was used throughout Britain; in fact, domestic organisation varied greatly from area to area and took a number of different forms.

(ii) The operation of the domestic system is best illustrated by the West Country where the woollen trade was dominated by a few powerful master clothiers. They had enough capital to employ large numbers of domestic workers; the biggest clothiers had a work force of over 2000 people. In some cases these master clothiers owned all the looms which they rented out to the

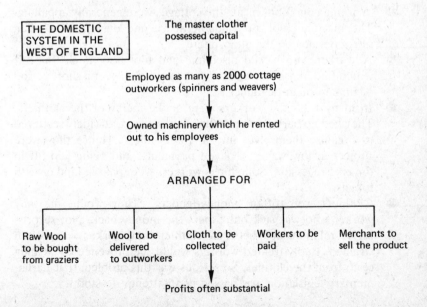

THE DOMESTIC SYSTEM IN THE WEST OF ENGLAND

The master clother possessed capital

Employed as many as 2000 cottage outworkers (spinners and weavers)

Owned machinery which he rented out to his employees

ARRANGED FOR

| Raw Wool to be bought from graziers | Wool to be delivered to outworkers | Cloth to be collected | Workers to be paid | Merchants to sell the product |

Profits often substantial

workers. They controlled all the stages of manufacture from the distribution of raw material to the collection of the finished product, and the payment of wages. They finally arranged for independent merchants to sell the cloth. It is sometimes assumed that the domestic system was 'backward', but this cannot be said of the woollen industry in the West of England where Pauline Gregg points out that '[even] before the Industrial Revolution, a highly organised form of capitalism existed'.

(b) What were the advantages of the domestic system?

● The spinners were able to organise their time in the manner they wished. Hours did not have to be regular, and there was no one in direct supervision imposing a code of discipline. This must have been one of the main attractions of the system for the workers.

● In some areas it allowed families to have a second income with farming being the main occupation and the rural location allowed fresh air.

(c) What were the disadvantages of the domestic system for the worker?

The drawbacks of the system outweighed the advantages:

● Working conditions inside the cottages were generally appalling. The machine took up valuable space and dust from woollen fibres permeated the atmosphere.

● A worker who lacked discipline and took too much time off would find himself having to work long hours over a short period of time to meet deadlines.

● In many ways the workers were at the mercy of the clothiers. They had no bargaining powers as they were too widely scattered to organise themselves into a 'trade union'. Hence they were subject to low wages, delayed payments, and being laid off in times of recession. Sometimes workers were paid in kind or with tokens.

● Clothiers were often 'money-lenders'. They would pay any worker who was sick but expect the money back. Not surprisingly, relationships between clothier and worker were often strained. Badly treated workers would seek revenge by stealing cloth from the clothier. So serious was this problem that Parliamentary legislation was passed in an attempt to stop it.

- The domestic system used child labour extensively. Children were expected to work at the same pace as the spinner and weaver otherwise a bottleneck occurred.
- The system was only geared to producing limited amounts of cloth. It could not have coped with any large increase in demand.

On balance, therefore, the presentation of the domestic system as a 'happy, pleasant experience' is not really accurate. It was hard, laborious and badly paid.

4.5 WHY DID THE COTTON INDUSTRY DEVELOP MORE RAPIDLY THAN THE WOOLLEN INDUSTRY FROM THE LATE EIGHTEENTH CENTURY ONWARDS?

From the mid eighteenth century conditions in Britain began to change rapidly. The population increased and there was a much bigger demand for textiles. Inventors were inspired to devise new machines capable of speeding up production. As the new machines were adopted the factory system gradually replaced domestic organisation. It was not wool, however, which responded first to the challenge but cotton. There were a number of reasons for this:

(a) Factors which restricted the woollen industry

- The Woollen Industry was riddled with outmoded laws, restrictions and regulations which originated during the time of the Medieval Guilds. It was, as a result, conservative and rigid in outlook. Many master clothiers, having established their businesses were suspicious of new methods and slow to assess the changing times.
- The mood of the market also militated against the woollen trade. People wanted a more versatile fabric; wool tended to be heavy and difficult to wash.
- The first textile machines were not particularly suited to the processing of woollen yarn which tended to snap easily. Not until the machines were modified in later years could they adequately work woollen yarn.
- The supplies of raw wool could not be rapidly increased. The rearing of more sheep was not practical at the time, and it was not until the nineteenth century that raw wool could be imported from Australia and New Zealand.

(b)   Factors which stimulated the cotton industry

Taken together these factors provided a powerful impetus:

● The Acts of 1701 and 1721 (see section 4.3) had the reverse effect to the one anticipated by Parliament. With imported cotton banned, the home cotton industry took the opportunity to increase its output to satisfy the demand.

● The demands of the textile market were for a cheap light fabric which could be easily washed. Such a material was cotton; in addition it lent itself to patterned designs via the printing process.

● As the eighteenth century progressed, supplies of raw cotton were readily obtainable from America and the West Indies.

● As the cotton trade was relatively young it was not held back by a traditional outlook.

● Finally, cotton fibres, in the right atmosphere, were ideal for the new machines.

(c)   Despite this, the first changes took place in the silk industry. As early as 1702 Thomas Cotchett had attempted, unsuccessfully, to produce silk in a factory on the River Derwent in Derbyshire. The Italians had developed a workable silk-throwing (spinning) machine for producing silk yarn. They kept their success a secret until John Lombe visited Italy and pirated technical data as to how the machine worked. He returned to England and, with his brother Thomas constructed the first successful silk mill near Derby (again, using the River Derwent for water-power to drive the machinery). Silk factories were subsequently built in Cheshire and Lancashire, but as an industry it never had the potential to mass produce because of the expense of raw silk, and only the richer classes could afford the finished cloth. The importance of the Lombe brothers, therefore, is that they set an example for future entrepreneurs to follow.

4.6   INVENTIONS OF SPINNING AND WEAVING MACHINES

The invention of new machinery did not just 'happen' but was a response to the needs of industry at the time. Also, each invention tended to have a 'knock-on' effect which demanded improvements in related processes.

(a) John Kay's 'flying shuttle' 1733

(i) *Kay (1704–64)* came from Walmersley near Bury in Lancashire, but he gained experience of the woollen industry when working as a weaver for his father in Colchester (Essex). He was well aware that a hand loom would only permit cloth to be woven which was the width of the weaver's arm. This was because the shuttle carrying the weft had to be threaded through by hand. It needed two weavers to produce broadcloth.

(ii) *Kay's flying shuttle* enabled the shuttle to be passed automatically across the loom, thereby speeding up the weaving

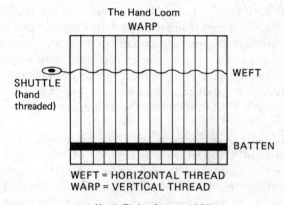

The Hand Loom

WARP

WEFT

SHUTTLE
(hand
threaded)

BATTEN

WEFT = HORIZONTAL THREAD
WARP = VERTICAL THREAD

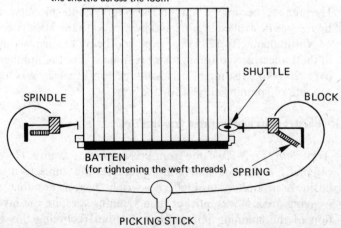

Kay's Flying Shuttle 1733

The spring, activated by the picking stick propelled
the shuttle across the loom

SPINDLE

SHUTTLE

BLOCK

BATTEN
(for tightening the weft threads)   SPRING

PICKING STICK

process and enabling broad-cloth to be woven by a single operator.

(iii) It took until the 1750s for the Flying Shuttle to be generally adopted. Hand-weavers saw the machine as a threat to their livelihoods and in 1753 attacked Kay's house in Bury. Kay went into exile in France and never gained financially from his invention.

(b) James Hargreaves's spinning jenny 1764

(i) *Hargreaves (1720–78)* was born at Oswaldtwistle near Blackburn (Lancashire) and started life as a weaver and carpenter. Hand-spinning had always been a slow process with only a single thread being produced at a time on the traditional spinning wheel; keeping the weavers fully supplied was, therefore, a problem. It took five spinners to provide a continuous supply of yarn to keep one weaver occupied. With the flying shuttle speeding up weaving further, spinners were under even more pressure to produce adequate amounts of yarn. To rectify the situation a quicker method of spinning was required.

(ii) In 1764 Hargreaves invented the *spinning jenny* (it was not patented until 1770) which was capable of producing eight threads simultaneously. The machine was worked by hand and, like the flying shuttle, could be used inside a cottage. Later modifications to the jenny meant that up to one hundred threads could be produced at the same time.

(iii) Hargreaves became a target for angry hand-spinners. His house was destroyed in 1768 and he moved to the hosiery town of Nottingham. By 1785 the jenny was being extensively used in the Lancashire cotton industry (estimates put the number at over 20 000). Its main disadvantage was that it was only capable of spinning thread for the weft.

(c) Richard Arkwright's water frame 1769

(i) *Arkwright (1732–92)* came from Preston in Lancashire. He was originally a barber and wig-maker, setting himself up in business in Bolton in 1760. Arkwright was aware that the weaving process was quicker than spinning, despite the invention of the spinning jenny. He set about rectifying this gap supported by the financial backing of John Smalley of Preston. In 1769 the first *water frame* was constructed out of wood, with a horse providing the motive power.

(ii) Arkwright went to Nottingham and established a small spinning mill and in 1771 he established a partnership with two hosiers, Samuel Need of Nottingham and Jedediah Strutt of Derby. Fully aware that water-power could be applied to the spinning machine, Arkwright and Strutt built a factory at Cromford on the River Derwent in Derbyshire. At first they produced cotton yarn which was used by the hosiers of the East Midlands. The main advantage of the machine was that it was capable of spinning a yarn strong enough for the warp, albeit coarse in quality. English manufacturers could therefore make a pure cotton fabric for the first time. Then in 1774 an Act of Parliament removed excise duty on cloth made entirely from pure cotton. From this time the water frame started to be adopted on a wide scale by the cotton industry; this resulted in newer, bigger ranges of products for the home and international markets.

(iii) Arkwright expanded his activities rapidly. His partnership with Need and Strutt ended in 1782, but he formed a new enterprise with David Dale, and was involved in the building of the New Lanark Mills in 1784. In addition, Arkwright built a second factory at Cromford plus mills at Bakewell, Wirksworth, Chorley and Manchester. Arkwright also invented a carding machine in 1785 and in 1790 he applied steam-power to the water frame (called the 'throttle'). Arkwright did suffer some setbacks, for example, his mill at Chorley was burnt to the ground by hand-spinners, but at his death he had made a fortune of some £500 000. Arkwright was the supreme entrepreneur – conscientious, ambitious and with a keen sense of opportunism. The water frame marked the beginning of the move from domestic organisation to the factory, and for this reason Arkwright is regarded as 'the father of the factory system'.

(d) Samuel Crompton's 'mule' 1779

(i) *Crompton (1753–1827)* was brought up in a family which made its living from farming and domestic cloth-making. He worked under the supervision of his mother and at his home, 'Hall-in-the-Wood', near Bolton, and he had soon mastered the skills of spinning and weaving. Crompton felt that the spinning jenny could be improved, and he determined to invent a machine which could produce fine, strong thread.

(ii) By 1779 he had succeeded in producing the *mule*, a spinning machine which combined the best features of the jenny and water frame. The result was a machine which was capable of spinning a thread of excellent quality which, in time, enabled the British cotton industry to match the finest Indian muslins and calicoes.

(iii) Crompton, however, was lamentably devoid of business sense. He did not apply for a patent nor did he try to obtain any financial backing to establish a chain of spinning mills like Arkwright. Other manufacturers were free to adopt his invention without any royalty payments. He eventually received a small grant from Parliament which was scant reward for his brilliance. The first mules were made of wood but by 1783 a metal version had been produced. Gradually, the mule began to outstrip the water frame as the main spinning machine in factories. In 1790 William Kelly produced a mule which had 300 spindles and was water-powered. This machine was further improved in 1825 when Richard Roberts (1789–1864), a Manchester engineer, invented *the self acting mule* which was capable of producing 2000 threads simultaneously. By this time steam-power had been applied to the mule and mills no longer had to be located in rural areas near fast-flowing streams. They now started to be located in towns near coalfields.

(e) Edmund Cartwright's power loom 1785

(i) *Cartwright (1743–1823)*, a clergyman, had no knowledge of textile machinery, but he realised that spinning was now far quicker than weaving and a power-operated loom was required to balance out the two processes.

(ii) A visit to Matlock in 1784 provided the motivation for Cartwright. He saw, at first hand, Arkwright's mills in operation, and was certain that weaving could be mechanised. By 1785 he had built a prototype power loom out of wood which was powered by an ox. It had many faults but provided a basis for other men to improve upon. Cartwright obtained a patent and established a small weaving factory at Doncaster in 1787. In 1789 he installed a steam-engine to drive the looms, and he also patented a wool-combing machine. Cartwright was, however, bedevilled by misfortune. When, in 1791, power looms were adopted by a Manchester cotton firm, the mill was destroyed by a hostile hand-loom weaver. Then in 1793 Cartwright found himself in financial difficulty and was forced to close his Doncaster factory. He eventually retired to a farm in Kent on the strength of a Parliamentary grant.

(iii) It took some time to perfect the power loom. A big improvement came in 1803 when William Horrocks of Stockport constructed a metal power loom. This model was further improved into a practical factory machine by Richard Roberts in 1822. By the end of the 1820s the number of steam-powered weaving mills began to increase, but hand-loom weavers stayed in business until the 1840s when their numbers declined rapidly (see section 4.7).

(f) Improvements in other textile processes

(i) The preparation of the raw cotton was quickened by the invention of the *cotton gin* by Eli Whitney in 1793. This machine was able to sever the seeds from the cotton fibres and therefore opened the way for larger quantities of cheap raw cotton to be supplied to Britain.

(ii) Finishing processes were improved as follows:

- Thomas Bell invented a machine in 1783 which was able to print patterns on cotton cloth by means of revolving copper cylinders. Previously the cloth was laboriously hand-printed using engraved plates.
- James Watt introduced the use of chlorine for bleaching cotton cloth. This method was much quicker than leaving cloth to bleach itself under the sunlight.
- Charles Tennant, a Glaswegian, produced a powder for bleaching cloth, made from chloride of lime (1798).
- Methods of dyeing cloth were improved by the discovery of mineral and chemical dyes which gradually replaced the use of vegetable dyes.
- In 1805 the *jacquard loom* was invented, which was capable of weaving coloured patterns.

4.7 WHY WAS FACTORY WEAVING SLOW TO ESTABLISH ITSELF?

Once the water frame and mule had been invented, factory spinning developed rapidly. The same cannot be said of the weaving process; despite the invention of the power loom, domestic weavers were not put totally out of business until about 1850. A number of reasons have been suggested for this:

● When factory spinning was initially introduced before the power loom, hand-weavers found themselves very much in demand. For a time they were prosperous and had plentiful supplies of yarn. They were reluctant to relinquish such prosperity.

● Hand-loom weavers were, by nature, a resilient group and they resisted the introduction of new machinery, often using violence.

● Until the power loom was perfected it was difficult to install in a factory and also expensive, needing a considerable investment of capital. It was cheaper for yarn to be put out to hand-weavers and some fabrics were best suited to hand-weaving.

● A further factor was a trade depression between 1811 and 1821 which made factory owners reluctant to buy expensive power looms. One advantage of employing hand-loom weavers was that they could be laid-off during such periods.

From the 1820s power looms began to be used in greater numbers and hand-loom weavers found it progressively more difficult to make a living. Sometimes separate weaving mills were built, but it was more usual for existing spinning mills to be extended to become 'integrated', that is, they could cope with all the manufacturing processes on the same site. As with spinning, it was the cotton industry which was the first to adopt factory weaving. In 1834 there were some 100 000 power looms in the cotton industry as opposed to about 2000 in the woollen industry.

4.8 WHY DID THE COTTON INDUSTRY BECOME CONCENTRATED IN SOUTH-EAST LANCASHIRE AND CENTRAL SCOTLAND?

In 1835, according to figures produced by R. Burn, Lancashire had 683 cotton mills employing 122 415 people. Central Scotland was next in importance with 159 mills and 32 580 workers. There were good reasons for this predominance.

Lancashire had a number of advantages which made it an ideal location for the cotton industry:

- The climate is relatively wet and this provided a damp atmosphere which meant that the cotton thread was less likely to break when stretched on the machines.
- The port of Liverpool was ideally located to receive supplies of raw cotton which, from the late eighteenth century onwards came predominantly from the West Indies and America.
- The western slopes of the Pennines provided soft water for washing the cotton and powering the early mills.
- The Lancashire coalfield was able to supply abundant fuel when the steam-engine became the main source of power in the mills.
- The labour force possessed the necessary skills.

In Scotland, the Clyde valley provided almost identical advantages. Glasgow was perfectly situated as a port to receive raw cotton from across the Atlantic Ocean and coal was available for power. Paisley had been important as a cotton centre when the cotton was based on water but with the introduction of steam-power the industry moved to Glasgow. In 1839 there were 98 mills in Glasgow and Renfrewshire.

4.9 WHAT CHANGES TOOK PLACE IN THE WOOLLEN INDUSTRY?

The woollen industry followed the same path as the cotton industry, but about 30 years behind in time. The West Riding of Yorkshire which had fast-flowing streams and coal deposits became the centre of the woollen industry (particularly worsteds) at the expense of East Anglia and the West Country which went into decline. The spinning jenny was not adopted in Yorkshire until 1785 and it took until 1787 for the first spinning mill to be opened (at Addington near Skipton). From the 1790s mules began to be used in mills in Bradford and Leeds, but it took until the 1840s for the power looms to be adopted. The most enterprising manufacturer in Yorkshire was Benjamin Gott who opened a large mill at Bean Ing near Leeds in 1792. He machine-manufactured both worsteds and woollens obtaining lucrative contracts to supply the British Army during the French Wars. Other important towns which developed were Halifax, Huddersfield, Dewsbury and Wakefield.

4.10 HOW IMPORTANT WAS THE ROLE OF THE COTTON INDUSTRY IN THE CONTEXT OF INDUSTRIALISATION?

Rostow's assessment is that the role of cotton was crucial, as it led Britain through the stage of industrial take-off, setting the example to the other industries. An examination of cotton's rapid growth and achievements lends support to this viewpoint – the imports of raw cotton increased from almost 1 million kilos in 1760 to 113 million kilos in 1830.

● By 1835 there were (according to Burn's statistics of the cotton trade, 1847) 221 169 workers employed in cotton factories in Britain.
● In 1830 the cotton trade accounted for half the total value of British exports.
● Handsome profits were made by the cotton magnates and much of this was re-invested in order to promote further expansion (for example, by Arkwright).
● Cotton was the first industry to organise itself on a factory basis (firstly using water-power and then steam) with powered machinery and mass production.
● The growth of the factory system in the cotton industry led to the development of large urban areas. It also stimulated the iron and coal industry and increased the demand for cheap, quick transport (for example, the Liverpool-Manchester railway, 1830).

These achievements are impressive but Phyllis Deane is correct to warn of the dangers of seeing the industrial revolution purely in terms of the growth of the cotton industry. It is more appropriate to judge cotton as an integral part of much wider changes, that is, one link in a chain of development.

4.11 CONCLUSION

(a) The changes in the textile industry can be seen on three levels:

(i) The first level was the development of spinning machines and the move from domestic industry to rural factories powered by water.

(ii) The second level was the development of weaving machines powered by steam which meant that factories became located in towns.

(iii) Cotton pioneered these developments, wool followed, but silk and linen remained relatively minor textile industries.

(b) The changes may be summarised in diagrammatic form:

CHANGES IN THE TEXTILE INDUSTRY

	Organisation	Power	Location	Output + Distribution	Skill/ Expertise
1750	DOMESTIC SYSTEM	Hand Animal Water (for fulling)	Rural Cottages	Small Output Localised Markets	Traditional hand skills in operating spinning wheels and looms. Skills passed down through generations
1850	FACTORY SYSTEM	(a) Water Power (b) Steam Power	Pennine Streams (rural mills) Coalfields (urban mills)	Mass Production National and Export Markets	Erosion of traditional skills to 'machine-minding'

QUESTIONS

1. **Objective 1**

'There is a danger . . . of overstressing the social advantages of the [domestic system] and, in particular, of idealising the conditions of labour'. (T. S. Ashton)

(a) Describe the various forms of organisation used under the domestic system in the textile industry during the early eighteenth century. (12 marks)
(b) How far do you agree or disagree with the opinion of T. S. Ashton? Give reasons for your answer. (8 marks)

2. **Objective 1**

(a) Describe **three** of the following textile inventions:

● Kay's flying shuttle
● Hargreaves's spinning jenny
● Arkwright's water frame

- Crompton's mule
- Carwright's power loom. (12 marks)

(b) Assess the importance of the three inventions you have described above. (8 marks)

3. **Objectives 1, 2 and 3**

The year is 1800. You have just retired from your job at a spinning mill in Manchester. Describe the changes you have witnessed during the 40 years you have worked in the cotton industry. (20 marks)

4. **Objectives 2 and 3**

(a) Why was cotton the first textile industry to adopt the new inventions? (6 marks)
(b) Why did the hand-loom weavers manage to survive until the 1840s? (6 marks)
(c) 'Cotton was the most important industry during the Industrial Revolution'. How far do you agree with this statement? (8 marks)

5. **Objectives 1, 2 and 4**

Study Sources A to C and then answer the questions which follow:

Source A (courtesy of Mansell Collection)

Source B (courtesy of John R. Freeman (Photographer) Ltd

Source C

Exports of cotton cloth – yearly averages in millions of yards

Year	Yards
1810–19	227
1820–29	320
1830–39	553
1840–49	978
1850–59	1855
1860–69	2375
1870–79	3573
1880–89	4575
1890–99	5057

(a) What are the differences in the working conditions of the women in Source A from those in Source B?   (5 marks)

(b) By comparing Source A and Source B say what mechanical advances had been made in spinning.   (5 marks)

(c) Why were mills built for the textile industry?   (5 marks)

(d) Explain the growth in cotton cloth exports between 1810 and 1859, as shown in Source C.   (5 marks)

(e) In what ways were the textile mills of the mid-twentieth century like those in Source B, and in what ways were they different?   (5 marks)

(f) What additional evidence would you need before deciding that the textile industry *as a whole* was in decline during the twentieth century up to 1975?   (5 marks)

(Southern Examining Group)

6. **Objective 4**

Study the source below and then answer the questions:

Friday, Nov. 29, 1782.

THE following incendiary Letter was this Day received by Mr. *Richard Arkwright* :

(C O P Y.)

Mr. Arkwright, at Mr. Brocklehurft's, Manchefter.

Sir,   Man. 28th Nov. 1782.

I am very forry to hear that you ftill do all you can to diftrefs the trade of Manr: after you had loft the Caufe in London this town thought you would then have been eafy the remainder of your Time in the patent out. but you ftill keep doing all you can and not only that but you have been heard to fay that you was determin'd to ruin every perfon that enter'd into that Bufinefs, the purport of this is to advife you that if you d'not withdraw all your profecutions before Dec. is out I am determin'd to lay in wait for you either in this town Nottingham or wherever I moft likely to find you. I will afhure fhute you as your name is what it is dam you do you think the town muft be ruled by fuch a Barber as you. take notice if you are in town on Saturday next I will make an end of you meet you wherever I can. I am not yours, but a friend to the town of Manchefter.

Now I do hereby promife a Reward of ONE HUNDRED GUINEAS to any Perfon or Perfons who fhall difcover or give Information of the Author or Writer of the faid Letter, fo that he os the may be profecuted thereon.

RICH. ARKWRIGHT.

N. B. The above Letter was put into the *Manchefter* Office, on *Thurfday* Evening the 28th *November* 1782, after the fix 'o'Clock Poft was fent off.—Now if the Perfon who put it into the Offrce will give proper and fufficient Proof who he received it from, he fhall for fuch Information receive Fifty Guineas Reward, by applying to me

RICHARD ARKWRIGHT.

(*courtesy of Manchester Central Library*)

(a) Briefly explain what the letter is about.   (4 marks)

(b) Why do you think the letter was written?   (4 marks)

(c) What is significant about the reference to Nottingham?

                                (2 marks)

(d) How did Arkwright react to the contents of the letter?

(4 marks)

(e) How far does this source prove that Arkwright was an unpopular man? (6 marks)

THE LUDDITES

5.1 INTRODUCTION

The Luddite Riots occurred during 1811–12 and again in 1816 with the counties of Nottinghamshire, Yorkshire, Lancashire and Cheshire being affected. The riots involved the smashing of machinery and, in some areas, setting fire to mills. Most of the standard texts present the Luddites as industrial hooligans, smashing machines which they thought were a threat to their jobs. This view, however, has recently been challenged by writers such as E. P. Thompson and Norman Longmate. There is more to Luddism than at first meets the eye.

5.2 WHAT WERE THE ORIGINS OF THE TERM 'LUDDITE'?

(a) Machine-breaking was not 'invented' by the 'Luddites' of 1811–12. It dated back to the eighteenth century at least, when it was used as a tactic by the workers to get the employers to agree to certain demands (such as wage-levels). For this reason, machine-breaking has been referred to as 'collective bargaining by riot'.

(b) The machine-breakers of 1811–12 adopted the name of Luddites. Threatening letters to mill-owners were signed by Ned Ludd or General Ludd and the word was used in all the counties affected by machine-breaking at this time. 'General Ludd' was a label; such a leader did not exist. The word Luddite could have come from a framework-knitter called Ludlam who smashed one of his father's machines in a fit of temper or it may have derived from a wayward Leicester apprentice called Ned Ludd. All we can say for certainty is that it was a phrase which became synonymous with machine-breaking at this time.

5.3 THE LUDDITE COUNTIES AND MAIN EVENTS OF THE MOVEMENT

(a)   Luddism started in March 1811 in the lace and hosiery industry of Nottinghamshire. Here, the targets for the workers were the wide-frames which had been introduced for making stockings. This involved the production of large pieces of material which were cut up and stitched to produce a stocking inferior in quality to those made on the traditional narrow-frames. From Nottinghamshire machine-breaking spread to Yorkshire in January 1812. Here the croppers attacked gig-mills and shearing-frames. The croppers' traditional craft was to raise the nap (rough threads) on woollen cloth and trim it with large shears to give the material a smooth finish; gig-mills (machines for raising the nap) and shearing-frames (for cutting off the nap) were being introduced on a wide scale. Finally, by March 1812 the movement had reached Lancashire and Cheshire where steam-driven power looms were the target.

(b)   On 11 March 1811 a crowd gathered in the centre of Nottingham to complain about the general economic situation. This escalated into a march to the outlying village of Arnold where some 60 wide stocking frames were destroyed. In 1811 *The Gentleman's Magazine* reported an orgy of rioting in Bulwell, Sutton, Basford, Kimberley, Mansfield, Ollerton, Retford and Hucknall. The most serious incident was at Bulwell where a Luddite named John Westley of Leicester was 'killed while tearing down the window-shutters'. By the end of February 1812 the rioting abated with an estimated 1000 frames destroyed at a cost of a possible £10 000. In March 1812, at Nottingham Assizes, seven Luddites were sentenced to transportation. In 1816 Luddism resumed with an attack on Heathcoat and Buden's mill at Loughborough. This resulted in the execution of Jem Towle.

(c)   In January 1812 Oatlands Mill near Leeds was set on fire. This was followed by widespread smashing of gig-mills and shearing-frames through the West Riding. The most violent incidents involved the croppers of the Spen Valley around Huddersfield. On 11 April a force of 150 men marched on Rawfolds Mill owned by William Cartwright, who had defended his building with nine men. In the ensuing battle two Luddites, Samuel Hartley and John Booth, were killed and the attack was called off. After this, the croppers and other workers closed ranks refusing to divulge information to the authorities which would have led to the arrest of the leaders of the attack on

Cartwright. After this 'defeat', the Yorkshire Luddites changed their tactics slightly and turned their attention to individual mill-owners. On 18 April they tried, unsuccessfully, to murder Cartwright. They did, however, succeed in shooting William Horsfall, a mill-owner who had publically denounced the Luddites. In January 1813 Yorkshire Luddism was effectively ended with a special trial of Luddites at York Assizes. George Mellor, William Thorp and Thomas Smith were found guilty of murdering Horsfall and were hanged on 8 January. Fourteen men were hanged for their part in the Rawfolds incident and five were sentenced to transportation for 'administering unlawful oaths'.

(d) Between February and April 1812 a number of attacks took place in Lancashire, mainly aimed at power looms. The most serious incident was an attack on a power-loom factory at Middleton on 20 and 21 April 1812. Five Luddites were killed on the initial assault. The rioters regrouped and staged a second attack and this time six were killed. In May 1812 at Chester Assizes 47 Luddites were tried, and concluded with 12 hangings and 8 sentences of transportation.

5.4   WHAT CAUSED LUDDISM?

Several explanations have been forwarded:

- Luddism must be viewed in the context of the time. A series of bad harvests had resulted in high bread prices at the same time as a general depression in the textile trade. In 1810 the Government imposed a ban on trade with the continent in retaliation to the Napoleonic blockade. This in turn resulted in widespread redundancies and wage-cuts in the hosiery and textile industry. Coupled with the continuing use of the truck system, the workers protested by rioting and machine-breaking. It would appear that a number of hosiers deliberately introduced wide-frames in this period and employed 'colts' (apprentices) at low wages in order to produce stockings quickly to capture what trade there was on offer.
- There was concern among the workers that wide-frames and shearing-frames reduced the quality of the final product and 'cheapened' their craft. It is also possible that the workers feared the factory system which brought a reduction in skill and disciplined hours.

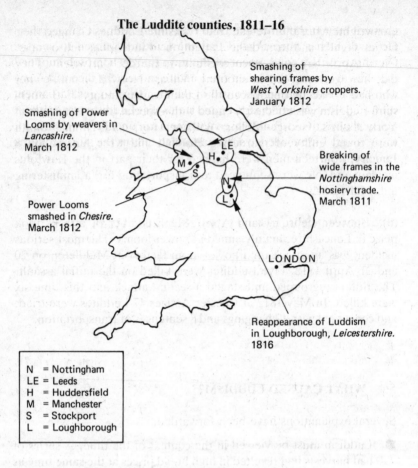

The Luddite counties, 1811–16

Smashing of shearing frames by *West Yorkshire* croppers. January 1812

Smashing of Power Looms by weavers in *Lancashire*. March 1812

Breaking of wide frames in the *Nottinghamshire* hosiery trade. March 1811

Power Looms smashed in *Chesire*. March 1812

LONDON

Reappearance of Luddism in Loughborough, *Leicestershire*. 1816

N = Nottingham
LE = Leeds
H = Huddersfield
M = Manchester
S = Stockport
L = Loughborough

● In his book *The Making of the English Working Class*, E. P. Thompson advances an alternative theory about the cause of Luddism. He argues that Parliament was no longer interested in protecting the old traditional crafts or laying down regulations about the way masters should conduct their businesses. *Laissez-faire* gave the masters 'carte-blanche' to do as they pleased, and this led the worker to feel insecure and vulnerable. Hence, the attacks on machinery.

5.5 HOW FAR DID LUDDISM HAVE POLITICAL AIMS?

Traditionally, it is believed that Luddism only had industrial and social aims (that is, the regulation of the trade, reasonable wages and maintenance of high standards of workmanship). Even a number of eminent men at the time, like Lord Fitzwilliam, were of this opinion. However, it has been argued that the Luddites wanted to see the overthrow of the government of the day. E. P. Thompson supports this view by saying that when the Luddite movement died out many of its adherents became involved in the campaign to get Parliament reformed. R. J. White disagrees and states that Luddism was 'without political objectives'. Both these viewpoints can only be conjecture for there is very little evidence surviving which tells us the story from the Luddite angle.

5.6 HOW AND WHY DID LUDDISM FADE AWAY?

(a) Luddite activity had little long-term effect. Masters continued to use shearing-frames. This probably served to discourage interest in Luddism.

(b) The tactics of the authorities helped to defeat the Luddites:

- Troops were deployed on a wide scale.
- The sentences handed out by the judges at the Assizes at York, Lancaster and Chester were harsh enough to deter further Luddite activity.
- Government spies (*agents provocateurs*) were employed to bring Luddite plots into the open.
- An Act, passed in February 1812, made machine-breaking a capital offence.

(c) Once trading conditions improved after 1813 and work became regular again the labourers lost interest in Luddism.

5.7 CONCLUSION

Luddism appears almost to raise more questions than it answers. The causes, motives and effects of the movement are all open to argument. One point, however, which historians agree on to some degree is that Luddism has to be seen in the widest context of working-class protest against authority, and as such was a forerunner of trade unionism. It was in the words of Malcolm Thomis 'a successful exercise of working-class solidarity'.

QUESTIONS

1. **Objective 3**

(a) As a Nottingham stocking-maker in 1812, write a letter to the *Nottingham Review* in which you explain your grievances.
(10 marks)
(b) As a Nottingham magistrate, write a reply to the above letter in which you give your opinion on Luddism and the measures which the authorities should take against it. (10 marks)

2. **Objectives 1 and 2**

(a) What were the causes of Luddism? (6 marks)
(b) Describe the main events in Luddite history from 1811–16.
(8 marks)
(c) How far was Luddism successful? (6 marks)

3. **Objective 4**

Study the following sources and then answer the questions:

Source A

An artist's impression of Ned Ludd
(courtesy of BBC Hulton Picture Library)

Source B

A Handbill issued in Nottingham (courtesy of Nottinghamshire County Council, Local Studies Library)

WHEREAS,

Several **EVIL-MINDED PERSONS** have assembled together in a riotous Manner, and **DESTROYED** a **NUMBER** of

FRAMES,

In different Parts of the Country :

THIS IS

TO GIVE NOTICE,

That any Person who will give Information of any Person or Persons thus wickedly

BREAKING THE FRAMES,

Shall, upon **CONVICTION**, receive

50 GUINEAS

REWARD.

And any Person who was actively engaged in **RIOTING**, who will impeach his Accomplices, shall, upon **CONVICTION**, receive the same Reward, and every Effort made to procure his Pardon.

☞ Information to be given to Messrs. **COLDHAM** and **ENFIELD.**

Nottingham, March 26, 1811.

G. Stretton, Printer, Nottingham

Source C

An example of a Ned Ludd letter

> *To Mr. Smith of Huddersfield*
> SIR,
> Information has just been given that you are a holder of those
> DETESTABLE SHEARING MACHINES. You will take notice
> that if they are not taken down by the end of next week I shall
> attach one of my Lieutenants to destroy them . . . and if you have
> the impudence to fire at any of my men they have orders to murder
> you and burn all your housing,
> Signed,
> Ned Ludd (Sherwood Forest Office)

(a) What conclusions is it possible to draw from Source B about authority's attitude to the Luddites? (2 marks)

(b) What conclusions is it possible to draw from Source C about:
  (i) the attitude of the Luddites.
  (ii) the view that the Luddites were 'unintelligent hooligans'? (4 marks)

(c) 'Source C proves that Ned Ludd existed'. Do you agree? (4 marks)

(d) Study Source A. 'The fact that this is an artist's impression of Ned Ludd makes it totally unreliable'. Do you agree? (5 marks)

(e) Does Source C support or contradict Source A? Explain your answer. (5 marks)

CHAPTER 6

THE COAL INDUSTRY
1700–1850

6.1 INTRODUCTION

In 1700 Britain produced about 2.5 million tonnes of coal: in 1854, the first year that official figures became available, the output had risen to 64.7 million tonnes. This increase reflects the importance of coal in the industrialisation of Britain. It formed a vital link with many parts of the economy and provided the platform for the expansion of many industries, particularly the iron industry. During this period mines became deeper and miners faced hardship and increasing danger in winning the 'black diamond'.

6.2 HOW WAS COAL MINED IN 1700?

(a) Professor Nef has pointed out how the production of coal had been increasing since the sixteenth century. This increase was achieved without having to sink deep shafts; the deepest mines in 1700 were about 165 feet (50 metres). Most coal was obtained by working relatively near to the surface by one of the following methods:

- *Open-cast mining*. This was where the surface soil was scraped away to reveal a layer of coal.
- Where a seam of coal outcropped on the side of a hill, a *drift mine* was opened up. This was a tunnel dug into the side of the hill.
- Where the coal was about 30 feet (10 metres) down, a bell pit would be dug, so called because of its shape. This method was common in the Forest of Dean.

The most important mining area at this time was in the north-east of England in the valleys of the Tyne and Wear. This area had a lucrative trade with London. Coal was loaded onto colliers and transported via the North Sea to the capital, hence its title of 'sea coal'. Most of this coal was used on domestic fires.

(b) Surface coal mining was satisfactory as long as the demand did not exceed the supply of surface seams. In the late eighteenth century the demand for coal did, in fact, increase, and it was obvious that deeper mines would have to be opened up if the demand was to be satisfied.

6.3 WHY DID THE DEMAND FOR COAL INCREASE AFTER 1750?

- The growing population of Britain meant that more coal was required for domestic use. This was also due to the fact that wood was becoming scarcer and more expensive.
- Coal was needed in a multitude of traditional industries: glass-making, sugar-refining, brewing, brick-making, soap-boiling and the production of nails and cutlery.
- Coal was also used in smelting industries such as lead, tin and copper. It was the iron industry, however, which demanded the greatest quantity of coal for the smelting of iron ore and the forging of wrought iron, following the work of Abraham Darby I and Henry Cort (see chapter 7). The demand for coal in these industries coincided with the scarcity of charcoal as a fuel.
- In the last quarter of the eighteenth century the steam-engine was improved and perfected by James Watt. The invention of rotary motion meant that the steam-engine could be used to drive machinery in numerous industries. Coal was used to raise the steam. As more steam-engines were manufactured so the demand for coal increased.
- By 1810 William Murdoch had successfully pioneered the production of coal gas. This gradually became used for street lighting in many of Britain's industrial towns.
- The development of the steamship and the locomotive in the early nineteenth century also required great quantities of coal.

82

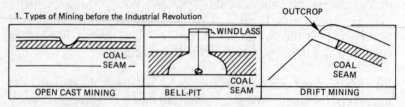

1. Types of Mining before the Industrial Revolution

OUTCROP

COAL SEAM

OPEN CAST MINING | BELL-PIT | DRIFT MINING

WINDLASS

COAL SEAM

COAL SEAM

2. Vertical Shaft Mining

SURFACE

COAL SEAM · 300 m · Shaft · PITPROPS

Danger of Shaft Mining	Solution by 1840
Flooding	Steam Engine
Foul Air	Exhaust Fan
Methane (Explosions)	Safety Lamp
Subsidence	Pine Pit Props
Bring Coal to the Surface	Wire Ropes and Steam Haulage

3. Coalfields in 1800

1 = Lanarkshire
2 = Northumbria
3 = Cumbria
4 = Yorkshire, Derbyshire, Nottinghamshire
5 = Lancashire
6 = North Wales
7 = Shropshire
8 = Staffordshire
9 = Warwickshire
10 = South Wales

6.4 THE GROWTH OF BRITISH COALFIELDS

(a) With the increased demand for coal it was necessary to dig vertical shafts to reach the rich seams deep below the surface. Mines soon went down to about 980 feet (300 m) and by the 1830s a pit in Staffordshire, Apedale, had reached a depth of some 1960 feet (600 m).

(b) The coalfields developed during this period were the North-East (Tyne and Wear), the Central Lowlands of Scotland (Ayrshire,

Lanarkshire, Stirling, Fife and Midlothian), Cumberland, Lanca-shire, Yorkshire, Derbyshire and Nottingham, North Wales (Flint and Denbigh), North and South Staffordshire, Shropshire, the Mid-lands (Warwickshire and Leicestershire), the Forest of Dean, Bristol, North Somerset and South Wales.

The sinking of new pits was often at the initiative of private landowners who were eager to make a profit and were therefore prepared to risk their capital.

To save transport costs, coal-using industries became located 'on' the coalfields. Around the industrial factories large urban areas grew up, for example, Manchester, Newcastle and Sheffield.

6.5 WHAT WERE THE DANGERS OF DEEP SHAFT MINING AND HOW DID THE MINING INDUSTRY ATTEMPT TO OVERCOME THEM?

Inevitably deeper mines brought increased dangers and hazards to the miners.

(a) The problem of drainage

(i) All mines need to be drained of water. The deeper the mines became, the greater the problem, as water percolated from the surface through the rocks into the workings. Flash storms could also produce instant flooding in the mine and drown the miners without warning.

(ii) One of the simplest attempts to drain drift mines was the digging of an adit or 'sough'. This was a channel dug at an angle to the main passage which would allow water to flow away under the force of gravity. In vertical shaft mines, endless chains of buckets operated by a horse gin were used; this proved too slow and incapable of dealing with sudden floods and excessive rain.

(iii) In 1698 Thomas Savery invented a steam-engine which he called 'the miner's friend'. This was a pump to raise water from mines. Savery, however, could not perfect his engine and it proved unreliable. His work was followed up by Thomas Newcomen, an ironmonger from Dartmouth. Newcomen un-derstood the urgent need for a reliable pump to drain the Cornish tin mines. He produced an atmospheric pump capable of lifting ten gallons (45.5 litres) of water with each stroke. The first Newcomen engine was installed at Dudley Castle, near Tipton on the Staffordshire coalfield, in 1712. Although the engine was more reliable than Savery's it was expensive to buy and operate. Nevertheless, it was adopted in Warwickshire, Flintshire and the north-east. The great advantage of the steam-engine was that it was capable of draining very deep mines, thus making accessible huge deposits of coal. In 1769 James Watt constructed a steam-engine that was more economical in coal consumption. This slowly replaced Newcomen's engine as many mine-owners were prepared to invest capital in the best available technology.

(b) The problem of foul air

(i) Obnoxious gases presented a serious problem in most shaft mines. It was not necessary to go very deep before **chokedamp** was encountered. This gas is composed of carbon-dioxide and, if not dispersed quickly, results in suffocation.

   If this gas threatened, the miner's candle would dim; small amounts of the gas could be dispersed by wafting the air. Sometimes canaries were used as an 'indicator'. Deeper down lurked a more lethal gas – **methane** or **firedamp**. This gas is highly explosive should it come into contact with the naked flame of a candle. In desperation, miners used fish skins to try to provide a dim light. In some mines 'firemen' were sent with the purpose of trying to explode small pockets of firedamp by using a candle on the end of a long pole. This pole was poked into the crevasses in the coal seam. This was of course, highly dangerous and very limited in efficiency. As the numbers in mining increased and the mines reached increasing depths, the problem of gases demanded an effective solution.

(ii) The answer to the problem lay in finding an efficient method of ventilating the mines combined with a safe means of providing light. Good ventilation would rid the mines of dangerous gases, provide a flow of fresh air and reduce the temperature of the galleries.

   The first attempts at ventilation were rather crude. Two shafts were dug into the ground. The downcast shaft was used to lower and raise miners, whilst at the bottom of the upcast shaft a furnace was installed. This had the effect of heating the foul air and making it rise upwards out of the mine. The heat from the furnace, however, could quite easily ignite any pockets of firedamp that were present in the air. Around the middle of the eighteenth century, Spedding of Whitehaven introduced the system known as 'air-coursing'. By the use of partitions and trapdoors, fresh air was made to travel all round the underground passages in the mine. In 1807 Buddle built an exhaust fan and installed it at Hebburn colliery. The fan sucked foul air out of the mine but was not capable of producing the same powerful ventilation currents as a furnace. In 1835 the first centrifugal fan was built. As this was capable of creating powerful currents of fresh air, it was the most effective means of ventilation yet invented. It took until 1860 for this device to be developed. The most efficient was the Guibal fan which was made in Belgium.

(c) The problem of lighting the mines

(i) For a total remedy of the problem of gases, a safe method of lighting was required as well as efficient ventilation. Even where the ventilation was effective, a naked flame would still ignite any methane which was present. Spedding experimented with a steel mill in an effort to produce an alternative method of lighting to the candle. This produced a stream of sparks when turned. The light produced was inconsistent and, of course, the mill had to be turned by someone else other than the miner. The sparks were also capable of igniting firedamp.

(ii) On 25 May 1812 a terrible explosion occurred at the Felling colliery, claiming the lives of 90 miners. The local incumbent, the Revd John Hodgson, was devastated, and he was instrumental in the formation of the *Sunderland Society for the Prevention of Accidents in Coal Mines*.

In August 1815 the Society contacted Sir Humphrey Davy to ask for advice on the lighting of coal mines. Davy took a sample of firedamp from Hebburn colliery and went away to study the problem. By November 1815 he had come up with his answer – a safety lamp. The scientific principle behind the working of the lamp was explained in a pamphlet called 'On the Fire-Damp of Coal Mines and on Methods of Lighting the Mine so as to Prevent its Explosion'. The flame of the lamp was protected by a wire gauze which kept the heat in and prevented it from coming into contact with any methane on the outside.

In addition if the gas was present the flame would change its colour slightly affording the miner a warning of the danger.

(iii) This invention provoked a storm of controversy. George Stephenson claimed that he had, in fact, produced a safety lamp before Davy. The two men became involved in a bitter quarrel. It is possible, however, that both men were outdone by Dr Clanny of Sunderland who, it is claimed by some sources, invented a safety lamp as early as 1813.

(iv) *How successful was the safety lamp?* The lamp did provide more light to work by, but it was far from perfect. In some instances mine-owners believed the lamp to be infallible and opened up deeper galleries. However, in the deepest mines strong currents of air were capable of forcing the flame outside the gauze, thereby putting it in contact with any methane which was present. The lamp, therefore, did help to increase output but it did not completely eliminate the risk of explosion. This was particularly true if the mine did not have an effective system of ventilation. Two disasters in 1866 at Ardsley Oaks, Barnsley and Talk o' the Hill in Staffordshire claimed 350 and 91 lives respectively. There were many cases of miners actually lifting the top off the lamp to expose the naked flame. If discovered they were subject to fines or even a spell in prison. In some areas safety lamps were not even adopted, and the miners continued to work by the light of a candle.

However, on the whole the safety lamp was invaluable. It must be remembered that the numbers employed in mining were increasing (300 000 by 1815) and the deaths from explosions were reduced in percentage if not in absolute terms. The lamp also enabled output to be increased.

(d) The problem of moving coal from the face to the surface

(i) With deeper and larger mines, the coal face could be as far as four kilometres away from the shaft bottom. In some mines women or children had to drag the coal along in baskets called corves. A more humane method was for the coal to be hauled in small waggons along cast-iron rails. By 1804 the steam-engine was being employed at the base of the shaft to haul the coal from the face by means of a system of ropes and pulleys. Underground haulage using the steam-engine was first used in

Lancashire and Scotland. By 1850 engines operated by means of compressed air were being installed in mines.

(ii) Getting the coal up the shaft to the surface was another problem to be overcome. In Scottish mines, women and children climbed ladders with baskets of coal on their backs. The prevalence of this method was illustrated in the 1842 'Report of Children's Employment Commission'. Horse gins and water gins were also widely used to wind coal up to the surface. Gradually, however, steam-engines were installed to lift the coal. With the introduction of round iron wire ropes in the 1840s it was possible to lift coal from much greater depths than before – and in relative safety. A further improvement was the gradual adoption of an iron cage which was hauled up and down the shaft within guide rails. Full tubs of coal could be loaded directly into the cage, wound to the surface, emptied and returned. This system was first used at South Hetton colliery in Durham in 1834, and was the brainchild of Y. T. Hall. The cage was also used to raise and lower the miners.

(e) The problem of subsidence

The deeper the mines became, the greater the danger of the roof collapsing became. Usually the gap left after the coal had been hewn was progressively filled with stone (goaf) as the face advanced. Immediately behind the miners a passageway was left which was supported with wooden pit props. In wet conditions these were liable to rot and collapse, bringing the roof down with them. Between 1837 and 1842 over 1000 deaths were recorded in the south Staffordshire coalfield, and half of these were down to mines caving in and burying the miners. This problem was not really solved during the nineteenth century.

6.6 HOW FAR DID TECHNIQUES OF CUTTING COAL IMPROVE?

The actual task of hewing the coal at the face remained very much the same throughout the period up to 1850. The coal was hewn by hand, with the miners' basic toolkit, consisting of a pickaxe, wedge, crowbar and shovel. From 1825 gunpowder was used for the blasting of coal seams. This was obviously dangerous with the potential presence of firedamp. It was also found that the small particles of dust caused by blasting hung in the atmosphere for some time and were liable to cause explosions. Mechanical cutters began to appear from the mid-nineteenth century but they were only adopted gradually and mining remained a hard, demanding job.

6.7 CONCLUSION: HOW IMPORTANT WAS THE CONTRIBUTION OF THE COAL INDUSTRY TO THE PROCESS OF INDUSTRIALISATION?

(a) The following figures illustate just how much coal was demanded by the economy:

Uses of coal, 1840
(figures in percentages of UK tonnage)

Iron	25.0
Coal-mines	3.0
Steam navigation	1.5
Gas	1.5
General manufacturing	32.5
Domestic	31.5
Export	5.0

The main feature revealed by these figures is the decline of domestic consumption and the increase in the industrial use of coal.

(b) The coal industry also formed a vital link in the chain of factors which brought about industrialisation:

- More coal was required by a growing population and industry.
- The coal mining industry responded. More coalfields opened up and output increased.
- Transport was stimulated as coal had to be moved to the main industries which used it.

In the words of Christopher Harvie, 'the use of coal was...an integral part of the technologies of other industries, as a substitute for other fuels, raw materials and sources of power, and as an essential part of new industries, like chemicals'.

QUESTIONS

1. **Objectives 1 and 2**

(a) Why did the demand for coal increase in the second half of the eighteenth century? (6 marks)
(b) What were the dangers of deep shaft mining and how were they overcome? (14 marks)

2. **Objective 3**

Write a letter to *The Times* lending your support to either Humphrey Davy, or George Stephenson, in the 'safety-lamp' controversy.

(20 marks)

3. **Objective 4**

Study the source below and then answer the questions which follow:

Have you any calculations of the number of men and ships employed on the two rivers [Tyne and Wear]? – I have made a summary; there are, seamen 15 000, pitmen and above ground people employed at the collieries 21 000, keelmen, coal boatmen, casters and trimmers 2000, making the total number in what I call the Northern coal trade, 38 000. Do you think that the particular accidents by explosions, which you have decided, have been much lessened by the introduction of Sir Humphrey Davy's safety lamp? – They have, I conceive. If we had not had the Davy lamp, these mines could not now have been in existence at all; for the only substitute we had, and that was not a safe one, was what we called the steel mills. They were completely superseded by the Davy lamp of the simplest construction; it costs only about 5 or 6 shillings...[The lamp] introduced quite a new era in coal mining, as many collieries are now in existence, and old collieries have been reopened, producing the best coals, which must have lain dormant but for the introduction of the Davy lamp. (Taken from the Select Committee on the State of the Coal Trade 1829 – Evidence of J. Buddle. Quoted in *Documents on British Economic and Social History 1750–1850* by Peter Lane.)

(a) What kind of a source is this? (2 marks)
(b) Why was this document written? (3 marks)

(c) How far would you say this source was biased?   (4 marks)

(d) What information does it provide us with about the coal industry? How much is fact and how much is opinion?

(6 marks)

(e) How accurate and reliable do you think this source is?

(5 marks)

THE IRON INDUSTRY
1700–1850

7.1 INTRODUCTION

Historians of the industrial revolution such as T. S. Ashton and
Phyllis Deane, rightly emphasise the 'key role' played by the iron
industry in the industrialisation of Britain between 1780 and 1850. In
1700 the British iron industry was in the doldrums and facing a
number of problems which prevented it from progressing. During the
course of the eighteenth century the industry expanded on such a
scale that it was able to supply a host of industries and contribute to
the export market. The transformation was due to a series of
technical improvements in the manufacturing processes (which were
rapidly adopted) and the existence of a group of ironmasters not
afraid to risk their capital.

7.2 WHAT WERE THE MAIN PROCESSES INVOLVED IN THE MANUFACTURE OF IRON IN THE EARLY EIGHTEENTH CENTURY?

(a) In 1700 the raw materials used were:

● Iron-ore (stone which contained veins of iron).
● Charcoal (produced by the controlled burning of timber).
● Limestone (used as a 'flux' to draw off impurities in the iron).

(b) Smelting

Iron-ore and limestone were loaded into a blast furnace, which was
fired using charcoal as the fuel. A blast of cold air was blown into the
furnace by a set of bellows which were driven by a water-wheel. The

heat generated melted the iron in the iron-ore which collected at the base of the furnace, whilst the impurities and gases (slag) floated on the top of the molten iron. At this stage the iron was drained off into trenches coated with sand and allowed to set; this was pig iron (so called because the trench resembled a sow lying on her side) which was impure and brittle. The molten iron could, however, be poured immediately into moulds of the required shape (for example, cannons). This was **cast iron** which was high in carbon; although very hard, it could snap very easily and this limited the uses to which it could be put. Sometimes cast iron was produced in a **foundry**, which involved melting down pig-iron ingots and then casting the liquid iron into whatever shape was wanted.

(c) Forging

The most adaptable type of iron was **wrought** (or **bar**) **iron**. This was manufactured in a forge; the technique involved reheating pig iron in a furnace using charcoal as fuel, and then hammering it to drive off the impurities. The effect of this process was to reduce the amount of carbon in the iron. This wrought iron could now be worked quite easily into the required shape; its drawback, however, was that it was soft. In 1700 producing wrought iron was a very slow process and only small quantities were produced. Wrought iron was widely used in the manufacture of nails – a vital commodity at a time when wood was the dominant building material.

(d) Steel production

Steel is, in effect, purified wrought iron; it is both hard and flexible. In 1700, however, ironmasters had only the technology to produce it in minute quantities (see section 7.7).

7.3 WHY WAS THE IRON INDUSTRY UNABLE TO INCREASE ITS OUTPUT IN THE EARLY EIGHTEENTH CENTURY?

At this time Britain produced under 20 000 tonnes of pig iron, not sufficient to fulfill the increasing demand from other industries. Output, however, could not be increased as long as four interlocking barriers remained:

(a) Limited location

The industry was tied to sites where iron-ore and timber were readily accessible (charcoal for smelting was needed in large quantities). Thus, the iron industry was widely spread throughout the country, usually where forests were to be found, for example, the Scottish Highlands, North-East England, Cumbria, Forest of Dean, Shropshire (the Wrekin area), Staffordshire and the Wealden area of West Sussex, Surrey and Kent. It was also the tendency for ironworks to be disintegrated, that is, blast furnaces were located away from the forges.

(b) Limited transport

The industry was also hampered by the fact that it was difficult to convey bulky iron-ore, timber or finished products over long distances. Roads at this time were poor and there were few navigable rivers which could be used for transport.

(c) Dependence on water-power

Iron works needed water to drive the bellows of the blast furnaces and the hammers in the forges. Total reliability on this type of power posed a risk as streams tended to dry up in summer and freeze over in winter. There could also be the competition from other concerns for the use of the water, for example, corn mills.

(d) Declining supplies of charcoal

Wood was used to build houses and ships as well as being the main form of domestic heating. It took large amounts of timber (estimates vary) to make limited amounts of charcoal and, as a result, Britain's forests were receding at an alarming rate and a crisis was fast approaching the iron industry – a lack of fuel for smelting. If the industry was to maintain, let alone increase its output, a suitable new fuel had to be found. The obvious answer was **coal** – but there were problems. Coal contains sulphur which was absorbed into the iron, making it most impure. Experiments with coal-smelting had been taking place since the early seventeenth century, notably by Dud Dudley in 1619, but no ironmaster had managed to perfect the technique so that iron could be produced which equalled the quality of charcoal iron. Poor quality iron was as much of a problem as no iron at all. This was the problem needing the most urgent attention.

7.4 WHAT CONTRIBUTION DID THE 'DARBY DYNASTY' MAKE TO THE DEVELOPMENT OF THE IRON INDUSTRY IN THE EIGHTEENTH CENTURY?

(a) In 1709 Abraham Darby (1677–1717) became the owner of a blast furnace at Coalbrookdale in eastern Shropshire.

(b) Coalbrookdale was virtually the ideal site for an ironworks:

● The River Severn provided transport.
● Iron stone was available from Wenlock Edge and limestone from Benthall Edge.
● Timber was to be found on the nearby hills.
● Coal measures were also present.
● There were several other ironworks in the area and there was a supply of skilled labour.

(c) Darby began experimenting to see if it was possible to smelt iron using coal as the fuel. He was fortunate in that the local 'clod' coal contained only a small amount of sulphur and if the coal was coked before being charged into the furnace, the sulphur was removed altogether. Using this method the coal became a suitable fuel for smelting. It was obviously a vital discovery as it meant that iron-smelting would no longer be dependent on the diminishing supplies of charcoal; the door was open to expansion.

(d) Darby, however, appears to have kept his discovery quiet. No one is totally sure why, although a variety of explanations have been offered:

 (i) Darby may not have been totally confident that his method was reliable. The pig iron turned out was not good enough in quality for turning into wrought iron in the forge; it was only suitable for use in casting.

 (ii) It is generally believed that Darby's Quaker religion would have prevented him from advertising his breakthrough. Quakers have a reputation for determination, persistence and modesty. Darby appears to have had all three of these qualities in abundance.

 (iii) It may also have been that Darby had no time or desire to publicise his methods, concentrating instead on making

Coalbrookdale into a large foundry capable of supplying a wide range of domestic utensils. The process of coke-smelting took the best part of 50 years to permeate the industry.

(e) Darby's son Abraham Darby II (1711–63) took control of the Coalbrookdale Works in 1732. Under him the following developments took place:

- Expertise in casting parts for the steam-engine was built up, cylinders being produced for Newcomen's steam-engine.
- Further experiments took place with coke-smelting and it appears that Darby II managed to produce limited amounts of good quality pig iron which could be turned into wrought iron.
- He improved the means of producing coke by using coking-ovens.

(f)

(i) On the death of Darby II the Coalbrookdale Company was managed by his son-in-law Richard Reynolds (1735–1816). In 1767, Reynolds, keen to develop tramways from the local ironfields to the furnaces, succeeded in manufacturing the world's first cast-iron rails. He was quick to see the potential of the rotary steam-engine, reputedly ordering the first one from Boulton and Watt. The following year Abraham Darby III (1750–91), who was the son of Abraham Darby II, took over the Company and worked closely with the expert Reynolds.

(ii) In 1779 construction of the world's first iron bridge began. The parts for the bridge were cast at Coalbrookdale and it was finished in 1781. It was 25 feet (7.5 m) wide and 295 feet (90 m) long with a single arch. The bridge improved communications in the area and stimulated the growth of the small town of Ironbridge. The bridge attracted many visitors, being a 'wonder of the age' and was also the prototype for other iron bridges.

(iii) By 1785 the Coalbrookdale Company had become a very large concern. It had a number of furnaces and forges along the length of the Severn Gorge. The Coalbrookdale site had 8 blast-furnaces and 9 forges (linked by railway), and there were 16 steam-engines employed. It was, in fact, the first 'integrated' ironworks. Pig-iron production had been gradually increasing, from about 30 000 tonnes in 1750 to 68 000 tonnes in 1788. By 1806 the output stood at 272 000 tonnes. Most of this pig iron was coke-smelted.

(g) The 'Darby Dynasty' made a vital contribution to the British iron industry and therefore to the industrial revolution. Trevor Rowley claims that 'the Darbys and the Coalbrookdale Works acted as a catalyst for other industrial innovation…and laid the foundation of industrial development throughout the world'.

7.5 WHAT IS THE IMPORTANCE OF HENRY CORT IN THE MASS PRODUCTION OF IRON?

(a) Despite the developments in coke-smelting of pig iron, the manufacture of wrought iron remained a slow and expensive process. It was still necessary to use charcoal in the forge to reheat the pig iron before the impurities were hammered out; it could take up to 12 hours to produce a single tonne of wrought. By the mid-eighteenth century, the demand for good quality wrought was increasing – which the home manufacturers could not supply. Britain was, therefore, dependent on imports of wrought from Sweden and Russia which was considered undesirable – particularly during a time of war (Britain was involved in the Seven Years War 1756–63). A much quicker method of producing wrought iron in large quantities was desperately needed.

(b) Ironmasters applied themselves to solving this problem. In 1766 Thomas and George Cranage, employees of the Coalbrookdale Company, succeeded in producing wrought iron using coal in a 'reverberatory furnace'. For some reason their discovery was not publicised and the credit for producing cheap wrought iron is traditionally given to Henry Cort.

(c) **Henry Cort's** (1740–1800) job as a Navy agent was to supply the navy with ammunition and equipment. Cort was frustrated at the poor quality of the British wrought iron and felt that positive improvements could be made. In 1775 he bought an ironworks at Fontley (near Fareham) in Hampshire, and by 1783 he had worked out a process for producing wrought iron. This involved the use of a 'reverberatory' furnace which had two compartments separated by a 'fire bridge'. In one side raw coal was loaded and in the other

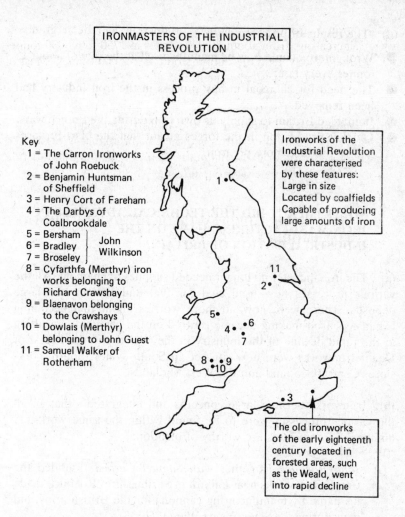

IRONMASTERS OF THE INDUSTRIAL
REVOLUTION

Key
1 = The Carron Ironworks
of John Roebuck
2 = Benjamin Huntsman
of Sheffield
3 = Henry Cort of Fareham
4 = The Darbys of
Coalbrookdale
5 = Bersham
6 = Bradley   John
7 = Broseley   Wilkinson
8 = Cyfarthfa (Merthyr) iron
works belonging to
Richard Crawshay
9 = Blaenavon belonging
to the Crawshays
10 = Dowlais (Merthyr)
belonging to John Guest
11 = Samuel Walker of
Rotherham

Ironworks of the
Industrial Revolution
were characterised
by these features:
Large in size
Located by coalfields
Capable of producing
large amounts of iron

The old ironworks
of the early eighteenth
century located in
forested areas, such
as the Weald, went
into rapid decline

ingots of pig iron were loaded. The coal did not, therefore, come into direct contact with the iron which was heated by flames 'rebounding' off the roof of the furnace and over the bridge. A door in the front of the furnace was opened and the liquid iron was stirred or **puddled** with long rods. During this process the iron was 'de-carbonised' and purified by the oxygen passing through it. Puddling went hand-in-hand with the **rolling** process, which Cort patented in 1784. Once the stirring was completed the iron was allowed to partially cool and then it was drawn into large lumps (blooms). The blooms of iron were then passed through different sets of grooved rollers which resulted in whatever shape the ironmaster required – plates, pipes, rails, sheet-metal, etc.

(d) The results of puddling were:

- Wrought iron could now be manufactured at the rate of about 15 tonnes every hour.
- The need for charcoal in any process in the iron industry had been removed.
- It enabled Britain to supply its own iron during the French wars.
- Quicker production in the forges meant that the blast-furnaces had to produce more pig iron.

7.6 WHAT IMPACT DID THE TECHNICAL ADVANCES IN IRON-MANUFACTURING HAVE ON THE INDUSTRIALISATION OF BRITAIN?

(a) The iron industry no longer needed supplies of charcoal. All the various processes now used coal for fuel and Britain had large deposits. There were now no more worries about fuel becoming exhausted. Iron-making became centred on the coalfields, resulting in the rapid decline of the industry in the Weald and the Forest of Dean. Ironworks were now situated in South Wales, South Yorkshire, Central Scotland and the West Midlands.

(b) Ironworks became large concerns and integrated – that is, all the various processes were to be found within the same works. A number of ironmasters are worthy of mention:

(i) *John Roebuck* (together with *Samuel Garbett*) founded the Carron Ironworks near Falkirk in Stirlingshire. Roebuck made his name by manufacturing cannons for the British army and navy during the Seven Years War (1756–63).

(ii) *John Wilkinson (1728–1808)* – 'Iron-Mad' – had great drive and energy, building up a number of large concerns. At Bersham, in Clywd, Wilkinson perfected the process for boring cylinders; this was a vital part for the steam-engines of Boulton and Watt. He then opened a large forge at Broseley in the Severn Gorge where he quickly introduced steam engines for operating the bellows of the furnace and the hammers in the forge. Wilkinson was well known for supplying weapons and ammunition to the British army and produced iron boats which transported goods along the Severn. Wilkinson also owned a works at Bradley in South Staffordshire, where he manufactured cast-iron pipes for the Paris water-supply system. In 1779 he played a significant part in the construction of the first iron bridge (see Section 7.4(f)(ii)). Wilkinson also had works at Willey, Hadley and Snedshill and he was a prolific maker of coins – some commemorative and some for tokens.

(iii) In south Yorkshire, *Samuel Walker* was responsible for the establishment of a large ironworks at Masborough, near Rotherham. Walker also provided the army with large guns, and between the mid-eighteenth century and 1815 he ran a very lucrative business. Later ironmasters were able to expand the iron industry in Yorkshire using Walker as their inspiration.

(iv) The largest ironworks were built in South Wales, where the puddling process was adopted immediately it was developed. There was a movement of ironmasters from Shropshire to Gwent and Glamorgan where coal and iron ore were readily available. *John Guest*, originally from Broseley, started the Dowlais Ironworks in the later 1760s. The *Homfrays*, also from Broseley, set up in business at Cyfarthfa before moving to Penydarren. The Cyfarthfa iron works at Merthyr were later taken over by the *Crawshay* family and became a massive concern. In 1806 Richard Crawshay had 6 blast-furnaces and employed 2000 men; by 1850 his grandson, William, had 11 blast-furnaces, 10 iron-mines and 8 coal-mines. The Crawshays also had works at Blaenavon in Gwent.

(c) Iron became the principal building material, replacing wood and stone. It was used to make machinery, bridges, locomotives, ships, piping, rails and machine tools. The 'age of iron' heralded the start of engineering.

(d) The improvements in iron manufacture also meant that parts for the steam-engine could be accurately made – and mass produced.

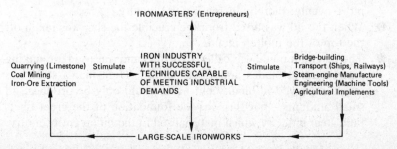

7.7 WHY WAS STEEL PRODUCED IN SMALL QUANTITIES IN THE EIGHTEENTH AND EARLY NINETEENTH CENTURY?

Until the 1850s wrought iron was the dominant metal in British industry. Steel is a superior form of metal but it took a long time for ironmasters to devise a method for its mass production. Steel is a mixture of iron and a small amount of carbon, with all other impurities removed. Mild steel has a low carbon content (less than one per cent) whilst hard steel has about 1.4 per cent. By a process of alternate heating and cooling, steel becomes very hard but is also flexible. Before the 1850s steel was produced by two methods.

(a) The cementation process

This probably dated from the seventeenth century and involved a process of purifying bars of wrought iron enclosed in a clay receptacle. The bars were separated by layers of charcoal which added carbon to the iron when heat was applied in the furnace. After about two weeks the bars were covered with swellings; they were then heated and hammered to produce the steel (sometimes known as 'blister' steel because of the swellings). The end product was mediocre in quality as the carbon only permeated the surface of the iron and could only be produced in very small quantities.

(b) The crucible process

This was devised in 1740 by *Benjamin Huntsman (1704–76)*, a Doncaster clockmaker. He required better quality steel for manufacturing the parts of his clocks and moved to Sheffield in search of an answer. His process involved the following stages:

- Blister steel or high quality wrought and a small amount of charcoal were put into clay pots called crucibles.
- The crucibles were heated in a furnace fuelled by coke.
- This had the effect of spreading the carbon through the steel more evenly, thereby increasing the quality.
- When the lid was lifted from the crucible the slag was taken off the top of the molten metal.
- The resultant metal was called cast-steel and was used for making cutlery, razor-blades and clock springs. Huntsman's steel was much improved in quality but again could only be produced in small amounts – but this was the foundation of the great Sheffield steel industry which materialised in the nineteenth century.

7.8 CONCLUSION

The success of the eighteenth-century ironmasters was a vital element in the industrialisation of Britain. Technical advances in the iron industry came relatively quickly after 1780 and permitted other industries to develop. Phyllis Deane's words cannot be bettered when she says that the iron industry 'provided cheaply and abundantly, the commodity on which . . . modern industry was to depend for its essential equipment . . . [and furthermore, enabled] continuous industrialisation [to take place in Britain]'.

QUESTIONS

1. Objective 1

Study the map below and then answer the questions:

The Iron Industry in the Eighteenth Century

GLASGOW
CARRON

E

D

SHEFFIELD • ROTHERHAM

AREA C

MERTHYR AREA B

AREA A

FONTLEY

(a) Name Areas A and B – two centres of the iron industry in 1700.
(2 marks)

(b) Why was the iron industry located in these two areas at this time? (2 marks)

(c) Name the two countries, represented by the arrows D and E, from which bar iron was imported in 1700. (2 marks)

(d) Name two important ironmasters who were based in Area C. (2 marks)

(e) Outline briefly the importance of these two ironmasters. (4 marks)

(f) Name the ironmasters who had large works at Carron, Merthyr and Rotherham. (3 marks)

(g) Name the man who perfected the process of 'puddling' at Fontley in 1783. Why was this an important discovery? (4 marks)

(h) What method of making steel was used by Benjamin Huntsman in Sheffield in the eighteenth century? (1 mark)

2. Objectives 1 and 2

(a) *Assess the importance* of **two** of the following the the history of the iron industry between 1700 and 1800:

● The Darby Family
● John Wilkinson
● Henry Cort. (12 marks)

(b) Why was steel still only produced in small quantities during this period? (8 marks)

3. Objective 3

The year is 1783. Henry Cort, having gone bankrupt, is hopeful that he will be granted a government pension in recognition of his work.

(a) As an associate of Cort's, write a letter to William Pitt, the Prime Minister, explaining why you believe the government should give the ironmaster a pension. (10 marks)

(b) As a member of the Treasury, keen to save money, write a memorandum to Pitt explaining why you think Cort does not qualify for a pension. (10 marks)

4. Objective 4

Study the sources and then answer the questions which follow them:

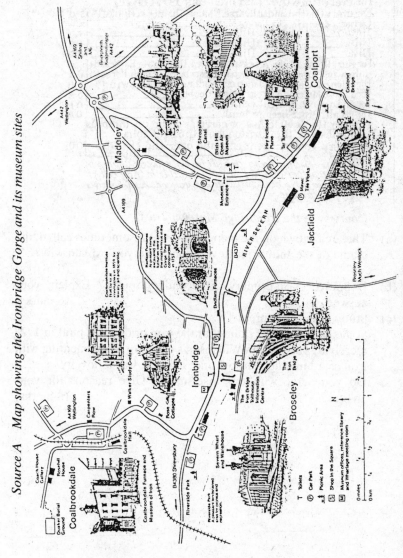

Source A   Map showing the Ironbridge Gorge and its museum sites

(courtesy of the Ironbridge Museum Trust)

Source B   A table of tolls displayed on the toll-house of the world's first iron bridge, 1778, in Shropshire

• **TABLE of TOLLS**. •
For every time they pass over this BRIDGE.

For every Coach, Landau, Hearse, Chaise, Chair, or such like⎱ Carriages drawn by Six Horses, Mares, Geldings, or Mules ___⎰	8 d
Ditto _____ by Four Ditto _____	2.0
Ditto _____ by Two Ditto _____	1.6
Ditto _____ by One Ditto _____	1.0
	0.6
For every Horse, Mule, Ass, pair of Oxen, Drawing or Harness'd ⎱ to draw any Waggon, Cart, or such like carriage, for each Horse&⎰	0.3
For a Horse, Mule, or Ass, laden or unladen and not drawing,	0.4½
For a Horse, Mule, or Ass carrying double, _____	0.2
For an Ox, Cow, or neat cattle_____	0.1
For a Calf, Pig, Sheep, or lamb _____	0.0½
For every Horse, Mule, Ass, or carriage going on the roads and not over the Bridge, half the said tolls.	
For every Foot passenger, going over the Bridge	00½

N.B. This Bridge being private property, every Officer or Soldier, whether on duty or not, is liable to pay toll for passing over, as well as any baggage waggon, mail-coach or the Royal Family.

(courtesy of the Ironbridge Museum Trust)

(a) The area shown on the map (Source A) is sometimes called 'the cradle of the Industrial Revolution'. Can you explain why?
(6 marks)

(b) Is Source A a primary or secondary source? Explain your answer.
(6 marks)

(c) Study both the sources:
Some history books claim that the iron bridge was built in 1779 merely to satisfy John Wilkinson's craze for experimenting with iron as a building material and, as such, was a novelty.
Do you agree with this assessment? Give reasons for your answer.
(8 marks)

THE POTTERY INDUSTRY
1700–1900

8.1 INTRODUCTION

Prior to the eighteenth century, the quality of British pottery was very basic. It consisted of wares which were brown, black or dirty yellow in colour. The nobility preferred to use pewter mugs whilst the poor ate from wooden plates. In the early eighteenth century the location of the pottery industry was widespread and scattered. Wherever there were deposits of suitable clay, pottery was made. Bristol, Derby, Worcester, Glasgow and North Staffordshire were all important local centres. The organisation was, however, very much based on a domestic system. A common pattern was for a farmer and his family to make pottery as a 'sideline'. Many farmers had their own kiln and they sold their wares at the nearest local market. From about 1750 changes began to take place in the British pottery industry which resulted in it becoming a major factory-based industry. Most of the changes were inspired by Josiah Wedgwood in North Staffordshire.

8.2 HOW AND WHY DID NORTH STAFFORDSHIRE BECOME THE MAIN CENTRE OF THE BRITISH POTTERY INDUSTRY?

(a) North Staffordshire, like the other local centres, possessed the basic raw materials for making pottery. There were deposits of red clay and supplies of coal for firing the kilns. Wood and water supplies were also available as was a wealth of skilled labour.

(b) In 1794 W. Pitt wrote, 'the manufacture of the potter's ware in the north of the county is very extensive and important . . . The potteries consist of a number of scattered villages, occupying an extent of about ten miles'. By 1800 there were an estimated 20 000 people engaged in the North Staffordshire pot-banks. This expanding activity also gave rise to the growth of a number of 'service' industries such as crate-making, colour-making and lathe-making. The pot-banks had become centred around the six settlements of Tunstall, Burslem, Hanley, Stoke, Fenton and Longton. There were many notable potters within this area but one in particular, Josiah Wedgwood, was the leading light. He was a man of flair, intelligence and imagination. Wedgwood was ever ready to experiment and devise new methods and he possessed a great deal of business sense. He set the pace and others followed his lead.

THE POTTERIES

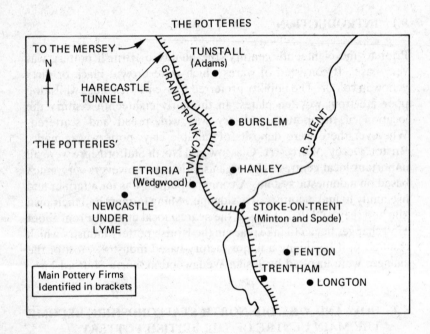

(c) The expansion of the pottery industry, in general, was stimulated by a combination of factors which emerged in the second half of the eighteenth century:

● People began to drink more tea and coffee. In London the professional classes frequented the tea houses to discuss the affairs of the day. Here was a ready made market for good quality pottery.

● The increase in the population created a bigger demand for pottery in general.

(d) With canal-building, and the perfection of the steam-engine, the Staffordshire pottery industry was able to satisfy the changing fashions and increased demand. Couple these factors with the genius of Wedgwood – born in the right place and at the right time – and the emergence of North Staffordshire as the dominant area of pottery manufacture is explained.

8.3 JOSIAH WEDGWOOD (1730–95)

(a) Etruria

(i) Wedgwood's first factory was at the Bell Works in Burslem where he perfected the production of cream-ware, a light-coloured earthenware. In 1766 Wedgwood purchased the Ridge House Estate which was located about half-way between Hanley and Newcastle under Lyme. Here he proceeded to build a new factory together with houses for the workers and a large hall. The new works was given the name of 'Etruria' after the ancient Etruscan artists of central Italy.

(ii) Etruria had been carefully planned. One half of the works, 'The Big Yard', concentrated on the production of useful (functional) ware and the other half, 'The Black Bank' specialised in ornamental (elegant) ware. Around the outside of the yards were the bottle-ovens used for firing the ware. Etruria heralded the start of the factory system in the pottery industry. Symbolic of this was the installation of a Boulton and Watt steam-engine in 1782, which was used for grinding flint stones. Pottery was manufactured at Etruria until 1950.

(b) Why was Wedgwood so successful?

(i) *Wedgwood produced a wide range of wares*

- Wedgwood was quick to perfect cream-ware. This was attractive and, at the same time, functional. Queen Charlotte was impressed enough to buy a tea-service in cream-ware in 1765, and from this date the product was dubbed 'Queensware'. In the 1770s Catherine the Great, Empress of Russia, purchased a dinner-service in cream-ware. The pieces had a variety of English viewscapes painted on them. Wedgwood's reputation was enhanced by this success.

● Wedgwood was very keen to cater for those people who wanted to have ornamental pottery in their homes. This motivated him to carry out numerous experiments which resulted in the production of a product called Jasper-ware. This was produced in a variety of colours – blues, greens and yellows were all possible. Superimposed on to the body of the ware were white images – pattern designs or figures. Many of the designs had a classical theme in keeping with the tastes of eighteenth century society.

● Another type of decorative ware perfected by Wedgwood, in 1768, was Black Basalt. The fact that Wedgwood sought to produce such a wide range of products was a major factor in his success. Other potters copied Wedgwood's products but they were unable to capture the same percentage of the market as Wedgwood.

(ii) *Marketing techniques*

Whilst in Liverpool in 1762, Wedgwood met Thomas Bentley. The two men quickly established a rapport and went into partnership in 1769. Bentley took charge of the marketing side of the business. A catalogue of products was published and showrooms were opened in a number of cities. Wedgwood's products were also advertised in Europe and an export trade was developed. So confident was Wedgwood of the excellence of his pottery that he offered a 'money-back' guarantee.

(iii) *Personal contacts*

Wedgwood's outgoing personality meant that he became nationally known. He was a member of the Birmingham Lunar Society and was also very active in the General Chamber of Commerce. Many talented and well-known individuals were among his acquaintances, including James Watt, Matthew Boulton, Joseph Banks and George Stubbs. The fact that Wedgwood was prominent in so many different walks of life helped to promote his own products and also the potteries of North Staffordshire. He was an ambassador in the fullest sense of the word.

(iv) *Organisational expertise*

At Etruria Wedgwood found, like other factory owners of the day, that the work force had to be educated into a routine. He organised the factory using 'division of labour' where workers specialised in one part of the manufacturing process, a method still used today. Workers were paid on 'piece-rates' so that high wages could be earned and output maintained at a high level. Wedgwood demanded the highest standards of his work force and nothing but perfect workmanship would suffice. The workers were expected to operate according to a set of rules and those who offended were subject to a range of fines. In return for being disciplined and loyal the workers were provided with housing and schooling. It took some time, however, before a code of discipline was firmly established. Many took time off to go to sporting events and, in 1783, there were riots at Etruria caused by high bread prices. Wedgwood's reaction to the riot was to lecture his workers in a pamphlet called, 'An Address to the Young Inhabitants of the Pottery'. These events were merely minor setbacks and the general smooth operating of Etruria was another factor in Wedgwood's success.

(v) *Enterprise*

A vital part of Wedgwood's make-up was his determination to find solutions to any problems which threatened to prevent the development of his firm. For example, he was most concerned that, at a time when he wanted to expand his business, he was thwarted by the lack of good communications. To rectify this he became involved in schemes to have turnpike roads constructed. Wedgwood was also quick to see the potential of canals, following the success of the Duke of Bridgewater in 1761 (see Section 11.4). He helped to petition Parliament for permission to dig a canal to link the Trent with the Mersey, thereby facilitating the import of china clay from Cornwall and the export of finished pottery. Wedgwood put up a deal of the necessary capital and the canal was started in 1766. When opened, in 1777, it had the immediate effect of reducing transport costs. An arm of the canal went directly to the Etruria works.

8.4 WHAT WAS LIKE LIFE FOR A POTTERY WORKER IN THE NINETEENTH CENTURY?

(a) The industrial landscape of the Potteries in the nineteenth century was a grim sight. Hundreds of coal-fired bottle-ovens filled the skyline, belching out thick smoke. As with other factory-based industries, the workers were required to work long, hard hours. Twelve hours a day and above were common practice. Child labour was widespread. Children were employed to light fires, turn the jigging machines and fetch and carry moulds. As late as 1862 it was estimated that there were 11 000 children at work in the Potteries.

(b) Wages were paid according to a worker's trade. Throwers earned the highest wages, possibly 25 shillings per week (£1.25) in the 1850s. A lathe-treader could earn up to ten shillings (50p) and children would receive two shillings (10p). The methods of payment varied from factory to factory. Piece-work was widely adopted but the worker would only be paid for items of ware which were judged as 'good'. The truck system was also used with workers having to accept at least part of their wages in token or kind. So unpopular was the method of payment that riots occurred in the 1830s. Only slowly, as the century progressed, did the working conditions improve.

(c) Housing conditions were extremely spartan. The terraced houses lacked adequate sanitation, water-supply and drainage. Raw sewerage was allowed to drain into cesspools or direct into the River Trent. Disease was prevalent in such conditions, particularly cholera, dysentry and typhoid. Linked to this many workers were prone to industrial diseases. Those who worked in the flint crushing mills suffered from pneumonoconiosis. Ventilation of the mills was almost totally absent. In addition, the people of the Potteries lived with the most appalling atmospheric pollution.

8.5 CONCLUSION

By the nineteenth century pottery had become a large factory-based industry producing ware which catered for all tastes. North Stafford-shire emerged as the main centre and this was due, in the main, to the enormous contribution made to the industry by Josiah Wedgwood. There can be no doubt that his role was crucial.

QUESTIONS

1. Objectives 1 and 2

'[Wedgwood] devoted himself to his work for its intrinsic interest and for the sake of achievement rather than for private gain'. (Alison Kelly).

(a) What contribution did Josiah Wedgwood make to the development of the pottery industry? In your answer use the following guidelines to aid your assessment:

- His motives.
- His personal qualities and skills.
- His importance and overall impact. (14 marks)

(b) How far was Josiah Wedgwood a 'product' of his environment? (6 marks)

2. Objective 4

Read the following source carefully and then answer the questions which follow:

> I have been twenty years manager and foreman here . . . Boys are principally employed in running moulds and turning the jigger. The average age for boys beginning to turn jigger and run moulds would be ten or eleven . . . I think a child of nine or ten is old enough for this work; nor have I ever found that children have been injured by it . . . The wages of a child of nine or ten would be 2s or 2s 6d. Jigger turning is turning the wheel which turns the whirler on which the potter makes plates, saucers, and cups.
> Mould running is carrying the plates, saucers, and cups and some dishes, on the moulds, into the drying house or stove, and there placing it on the shelves to dry . . .
> . . . I never heard of children or of their parents complaining either of their work being too hard or paid too little. Perhaps, but very rarely, I have heard of children who happen to have a bad master being badly treated . . .
> . . . The lads always have their half hours for breakfast and their hour for dinner, which is spent in play. I do not know a single case where a man has prevented his children having their hours for their food and play . . .
> The mould runner also assists in wedging the clay for the man. It is throwing or beating the clay to drive out the air. I consider [this] a

healthful exercise. The children come in the morning to light the fires. They seldom come before six . . .

. . . Boys are also employed by the dippers. Their age would generally be from 12 to 14. Their work is carrying baskets full of ware, handing the ware to the dipper, and then carrying it away. Little boys are not so much employed in this work, because care is required.

(Children's Employment Commission 1862, 'The Evidence of John Lawton of Ashworth's Earthenware Manufactory, Hanley')

(a) Is this a primary source or secondary source? Explain your answer. (2 marks)

(b) What evidence does the source provide about the jobs undertaken by child labour in the pottery industry? (6 marks)

(c) In 1862 a group of pottery masters complained that 'the employment of children . . . stunts their growth and . . . distorts their spine'. Does the evidence of John Lawton support or contradict this statement? Give your reasons. (4 marks)

(d) How reliable is Lawton's evidence? (4 marks)

(e) How useful would you say this source is to the historian? (4 marks)

3. **Objective 2 and 4**

Study the source below (*courtesy of Mary Evans Picture Library*) which shows Etruria:

(a) What is the building in the centre background of the picture? What impression does this building convey about the owner of the Etruria works? (4 marks)

(b) What evidence is there in the picture to tell us about how pottery was fired. (2 marks)

(c) What date do you think this photograph was taken? Explain your answer? (4 marks)

(d) Why was Etruria a successful pottery works in the late eighteenth and nineteenth century? (10 marks)

4. **Objective 3**

(a) Why did the pottery workers of Stoke-on-Trent appear to accept their squalid conditions so readily? (10 marks)

(b) How would a member of the upper classes have viewed the working conditions of the potters? (10 marks)

CHAPTER 9

THE DEVELOPMENT OF POWER 1700–1850

9.1 INTRODUCTION

The development of steam-power was arguably the most vital element in the industrialisation of Britain; in the opinion of T. S. Ashton, 'steam was the pivot on which industry swung into the modern age'. Certainly, to be able to mass-produce goods in factories a reliable form of motive power was needed – and steam supplied this need. Just how rapid was the development of the steam-engine is a matter of conjecture. Recent research suggests that the transformation from traditional forms of power (wind, water and animals) was relatively gradual and took some time to come about.

9.2 TRADITIONAL FORMS OF POWER

(a) Water-power

Water-power had been used for many centuries and involved utilising the force of water to drive a large wheel which in turn drove a piece of machinery. By the mid eighteenth century water-power was being used for a variety of purposes including the grinding of corn, the fulling of cloth, driving bellows and forge-hammers in ironworks, and providing the motive power for the spinning frames in the first cotton mills. Water-power could, in fact, be very efficient and it continued in use long after the steam-engine had been perfected.

(b) Wind-power

Windmills were widely used for the grinding of corn and pumping water. The wind drove large sails which in turn operated millstones or other machinery. However, windmills were inefficient, being dependent on the wind blowing. If the conditions were calm the sails simply did not turn, no matter how much work there was to be done!

(c) Animal power

Animals have been used by man since prehistoric times to provide power, oxen for ploughing and pack-horses for carrying goods being two examples. Horses were widely used in industry to operate gins which were used for lifting coal and draining mines. Horse gins, however, were slow and very limited.

9.3 WHAT ROLE DID THOMAS SAVERY PLAY IN THE DEVELOPMENT OF STEAM-POWER?

(a) Savery (1650–1715) came from Cornwall and was aware of the urgent need for an improved method of pumping water out of tin and copper mine shafts. In 1698 he built a steam-pump called 'The Engine for Raising Water by Fire' for which he obtained a patent which was to last, in one form or another, until 1733. Savery's engine had a number of deficiencies – it was capable of lifting water only modest heights and when in operation there was a high risk of explosion.

(b) Savery's steam-pump provided a platform for other inventors to build on, and his engines gained fame outside Cornwall (a Savery engine was still working in a London waterworks as late as the 1820s). At the same time, however, Savery held back the development of the steam-engine. This was because he held the patent for 35 years (even beyond his death) and this prevented improvements from taking place more rapidly (see Section 9.4(a)).

9.4 WHAT ROLE DID THOMAS NEWCOMEN PLAY IN THE DEVELOPMENT OF STEAM-POWER?

(a) Newcomen (1663–1729) was also motivated by the drainage problem in the Cornish tin mines to design a functional steam-engine to pump water. The first engine built by Newcomen (erected at Dudley Colliery in Staffordshire in 1712) took six years to build and was capable of lifting 110 gallons (500 litres) of water every minute from a maximum depth of 165 feet (50 metres). Although Newcomen was a skilful craftsman the technology did not exist at the time to manufacture the cylinders accurately. Newcomen's engine was, strictly speaking, an atmospheric engine. Its motion was provided by the force of atmospheric pressure and not the power of steam. Newcomen must have felt frustrated by the fact that Savery held the patent of **all** 'fire engines' as it denied him the opportunity of trying out new ideas.

(b) Newcomen's engine needed large amounts of coal to work efficiently. Despite the expensive running costs, Newcomen's engines were widely used in collieries; by 1775 there were 100 at work on the north-east coalfield alone. The engine was also used in London to pump water from the river Thames to private houses. The other limitation of Newcomen's engine was that it was only capable of lifting water out of mines. If the steam-engine was to be used to drive machinery a more versatile type of motion would have to be devised.

9.5 JAMES WATT (1736–1819)

(a) **Why is James Watt's background an important factor in the development of the steam-engine?**

Watt was born in Greenock near Glasgow. In 1757 he was appointed to a post at Glasgow University to make and repair scientific instruments. Watt had taken a keen interest in the early steam-engines and had studied them closely. It was chance, however, which provided Watt with the opportunity to put his learning to practical use when, in 1763, he was given a model of a Newcomen engine to repair. He swiftly identified the weaknesses in the engine's design and he set about devising an improved version.

(b) **What initial improvements did Watt make to the steam-engine?**

(i) Watt was concerned with the large amount of fuel consumed by the Newcomen engine. This was due to the fact that between each stroke of the engine the cylinder had to be heated and then cooled. Watt came up with the idea of having a second cylinder called a **condenser** where the steam could be cooled independently; the main cylinder could thus be kept permanently hot, thereby reducing fuel consumption. If this idea could be incorporated into a working engine, steam-power would become a very attractive proposition to industrialists.

(ii) Watt was short of money to build such an engine and, as yet, no one had been able to manufacture the various parts with the necessary precision. Help came from Professor Joseph Black, a chemist at Glasgow University. Black took an interest in Watt's work and introduced him to John Roebuck, the owner of the Carron Ironworks. Roebuck gave Watt financial support which resulted in a new steam-engine being produced and patented in 1769. Watt, though, was not totally satisfied and lost interest. When Roebuck went bankrupt in 1773 it appeared to be the end for James Watt.

9.6 HOW IMPORTANT WAS WATT'S PARTNERSHIP WITH MATTHEW BOULTON?

There can be little doubt that the partnership of these two men was the reason why the steam-engine was perfected and made into a viable commercial proposition. R. A. Buchanan believes that 'the conversion of the steam engine from a rather rough and ready piece of smithy-work into a product of precise engineering was the achievement of Boulton and Watt'.

(a) Matthew Boulton was the owner of the expanding Soho Hardware factory near Birmingham, and he was prepared to give Watt the financial backing he required. In 1774 Watt left Scotland for Birmingham, and by the following year he had rebuilt his engine. This time he was more successful as he was able to incorporate accurately bored cylinders which were produced by John Wilkinson. The first 'improved' engine was installed at Blomfield Colliery near Tipton in 1776. The new firm of Boulton and Watt quickly won a good reputation among industrialists.

(b) Boulton realised that there was a ready market for a steam engine which was capable of driving machinery in factories and mills. He actively encouraged Watt and William Murdoch (the foreman at the Soho Works) to modify the engine.

(i) In 1781 Watt and Murdoch constructed an engine with 'sun and planet' gears which produced rotary motion. On the flywheel a cog-wheel was built on (the sun). Attached to this was the connecting rod which had a second cog (the planet) at the end of it. When the beam went up and down the gears turned the flywheel; this was then harnessed, by means of a belt, to a machine. The first commercial rotative engine of this type was built for Wilkinson to operate a hammer in one of his forges.

(ii) A further improvement came in 1782 when **double-action** was added. This allowed steam into the cylinder at both ends via two valves. Now the piston could be motivated from both above and below. With single motion steam could only drive the piston by forcing it down from above.

(iii) By 1784 Watt had patented parallel motion. This was a small rod which joined the piston to the beam, where a chain had been used previously. This was safer and more efficient as the piston rod was kept in a vertical position.

(iv) Finally, in 1788 Watt added a centrifugal governor which had the effect of keeping the engine running at an even speed.

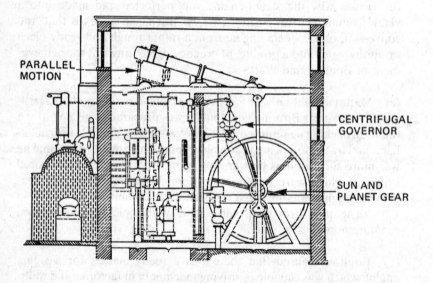

(c) Once Watt had perfected the steam-engine it still had to be marketed. This was where the enterprise of Boulton played a part. Watt's inventiveness had given Boulton an excellent product:

● The engine was relatively cheap to run compared to Newcomen's engine.
● Rotary motion opened up a wide field of prospective buyers as now the steam-engine could be used in a variety of industries.

Between 1775 and 1800 the firm of Boulton and Watt manufactured and sold some 500 engines. The parts of each engine were individually built for the customer. The company supplied drawings, plans and a foreman to supervise the erection of the engine on the site; the customer had to supply the workers. In 1795 Boulton and Watt opened a new foundry in Birmingham which was purpose-built for the manufacture of steam-engines. The partnership of Boulton and Watt displayed the best of 'organising ability and inventiveness'.

9.7 CONCLUSION: WHAT IMPACT DID THE STEAM-ENGINE HAVE ON THE BRITISH ECONOMY?

The steam-engine made an indelible impact on the British economy;

(a) With the invention of rotary motion, steam could now be harnessed, not only to drain mines, but also operate bellows and hammers in ironworks, drive machinery in textile mills, flour mills, paper mills, distilleries and breweries. By means of pulleys, belts and flywheels, one steam-engine could drive a number of different machines in one factory.

(b) The 'triumph of steam' was a gradual phenomenon. Research shows that it was not until the mid nineteenth century that steam was the dominant source of power. For a time before 1820 it was probably on a par with water-power. One reason for this was that steam-engines were individually made, not mass-produced. Not until the 1840s were steam-engines mass-produced with standardised parts.

(c) The need to manufacture accurate parts for the steam-engine (for example, pistons and cylinders) stimulated the growth of a class of mechanical engineers. Such men developed from the traditional craftsmen of the eighteenth century – the millwrights, locksmiths, blacksmiths and wheelwrights. Outstanding engineers like William Murdoch, Henry Maudslay and James Nasmyth came to the fore. From here engineering evolved into a number of specialist branches, for example, civil, electrical and marine engineering.

(d) To buy and install an early steam-engine was a risk. It was expensive and capital needed to be raised. A number of men were willing to do this and, with the steam-engine being a success, others were encouraged to show enterprise in other fields of industrial activity. The steam-engine illustrated that many different types of risk had to be taken if progress was to be made.

(e) After 1800 experiments began with high-pressured engines, which eventually led to the development of the locomotive and steamship. Steam-power also served to stimulate the coal industry and the iron industry.

(f) The adoption of the steam-engine as the main source of power also had a wide-reaching social impact. Industry gradually became located on the coalfields around which large urbanised areas mush-roomed. Steam was also a major factor in the establishment of the factory system which transformed the working habits, attitudes, values and lifestyle of the labour force.

Even though the adoption of the steam-engine was a gradual process, there is no doubt that its impact was monumental. R. A. Buchanan states that 'The steam engine was the greatest single British invention of the Industrial Revolution period and [became] widely adopted in virtually all industrial processes during the nine-teenth century'.

QUESTIONS

1. **Objectives 1 and 2**

Assess the parts played by Thomas Savery, Thomas Newcomen and James Watt in the development of the steam-engine. Why was steam-power such an important invention? (20 marks)

2. **Objectives 1 and 2**

Assess the role of James Watt in history. Use the following guidelines for your assessment:

● Give relevant biographical details.
● How far was Watt helped in his work by outside factors?
● How successful was Watt?

Credit will be given if you use precise quotations to support your analysis. (20 marks)

3. **Objectives 1 and 4**

Study the figures below and then answer the questions:
Fig. 1

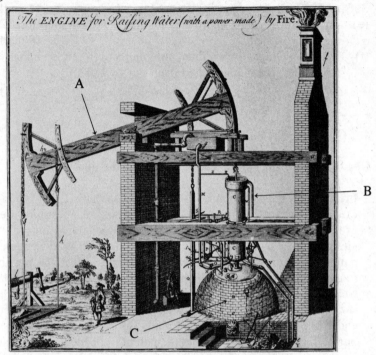

(courtesy of BBC Hulton Picture Library)

Fig. 2

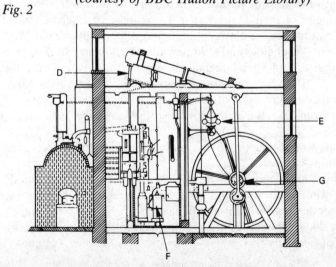

(courtesy of the Science Museum)

(a) Who invented the type of engine shown in Figure 1? (1 mark)
(b) Who patented the improvements shown in Figure 2? (1 mark)
(c) Name the parts labelled A, B and C in Figure 1.   (3 marks)
(d) Name the parts labelled D, E, F and G in the improved engine of Figure 2.   (4 marks)
(e) Explain how these improvements made the engine more efficient and versatile.   (8 marks)
(f) List three uses, other than pumping water out of mines, to which the steam-engine had been put by 1800.
(Oxford Board.)   (3 marks)

4. **Objective 4**

Read the following source and then answer the questions:

From 1755 onwards James Watt and Matthew Boulton, in a classical partnership of technical inventor and businessman, were producing new-type steam engines which solved the serious loss of energy in the earlier Newcomen machines. In 1782 Watt went on to patent . . . rotary motion. From this time onwards it was possible to use the steam engine as the means of motive power in factories. Necessity was certainly the mother of this invention. A year earlier Boulton had written to Watt, 'the people in London, Manchester and Birmingham are steam mill mad. I don't mean to hurry you but . . . ' By continuing to hold the patent until 1800, Boulton and Watt were at the centre of the new industrial scene, selling, in Boulton's picturesque phrase, 'what all the world wants – Power'. A catalogue of their customers is a catalogue of England's most active enterprise . . . between 1775 and 1800 Boulton and Watt turned out 496 engines and their new foundry, opened in 1795, was the largest and best managed engineering works in the world' . . . Both inventiveness and organising ability must be given prominence in any study of the Industrial Revolution.
(Taken from *The Age of Improvement* by Asa Briggs)

(a) What, would you say, is the author's opinion of Boulton and Watt?   (2 marks)
(b) Is this source opinion or fact? Give your reasons.   (2 marks)
(c) For whom, do you think, was this source written? Has the author any reason to distort the facts?   (3 marks)
(d) Why do you think the author claims that rotary motion was born out of necessity?   (3 marks)

(e) What evidence is there in the source that Boulton was a highly-motivated business man? (3 marks)

(f) Study the last sentence of the source. Use your wider historical knowledge to say whether you agree or disagree with the statement. (4 marks)

(g) What other sources of evidence could you use to check the accuracy of the above passage? (3 marks)

5. **Objectives 2 and 3**

(a) Which group of people might have welcomed the perfection of the steam-engine? Explain.

(b) Would anyone have opposed the steam-engine? Explain.

(c) 'The steam engine was a turning point in the industrial history of Britain'. How far is this true?

(Total = 25 marks)

CHAPTER 10

ROAD TRANSPORT

10.1 INTRODUCTION

This chapter traces the improvements that took place in the quality of British roads between 1750 and 1830. In the early part of the eighteenth century British roads were in an appalling condition. It was due to the development of the Turnpike Trusts and civil engineering that some of the road network was improved to meet the economic and social needs of the country. An attempt will also be made to assess the importance of developments in road transport in the context of the whole process of industrialisation.

10.2 WHAT WERE ROADS LIKE IN PRE-INDUSTRIAL BRITAIN?

(a) The evidence provided by contemporary writers suggests that the roads were in a state of total decay. Daniel Defoe and Arthur Young both wrote at length on the conditions. Defoe wrote that, 'sometimes a whole summer is not dry enough to make the roads passable' and he described scenes of coaches being dragged through quagmires by oxen in the winter months. A coach journey between London and Edinburgh was a major undertaking which, in the winter, could take up to two weeks. The worst roads were those that passed over the heavy claylands of the Midlands. Defoe commented that these roads were 'plow'd so deep' that they were beyond repair – yet they had to carry a large amount of traffic into London.

(b) Coach travel must have been a dreadful experience. Carl Moritz described a journey from Leicester to Northampton in which he 'feared for his life'. He finished the journey bruised, tired and 'shaken to pieces'. Freight was carried by pack-horse trains or by heavy, lumbering stage-waggons. Livestock were driven along the roads by drovers to be sold in the markets of the larger towns. Apart from the appalling conditions, travellers also had to contend with highwaymen and robbers.

10.3 WHY WERE BRITAIN'S ROADS IN SUCH POOR CONDITION?

The simple answer to this question is **maladministration**. British roads had been in decline since the end of the Roman occupation and no attempt was made to improve them until the reign of Mary I. In 1555 an Act was passed which put each parish in charge of its own roads. The main landowners in the parish had to provide tools and equipment, whilst the ordinary labourers had to work six days (unpaid) each year on the local roads. This was called **statute labour**. Parish administration, however, was inefficient for the following reasons:

● Forced, unpaid labourers obviously gave their services grudgingly, and were not interested in making a good job of road repairs.
● Parishes often felt resentful that they had to repair roads often for the benefit of strangers as they passed through on a long journey.
● Some parishes on important routes had a much more exacting task in maintaining their roads than those parishes off the beaten track.
● With some 15 000 parishes, the administration was cumbersome and the unpaid parish overseers did the job with varying degrees of efficiency.

In addition, until the late eighteenth century there were very few skilled engineers with the necessary knowledge to repair and maintain a road properly. For decades, therefore, road maintenance amounted to no more than filling in pot-holes with gravel.

10.4 WHY WAS AN IMPROVEMENT IN THE QUALITY OF THE ROADS ESSENTIAL AFTER 1750?

As the population started to grow after 1750, so too did the towns. Better roads were needed to transport food from the local farms to the townspeople. The growing industries of this period also needed better links to the ports and markets. Raw materials were needed by many industrial regions that were located away from a river. Coal, in particular, needed to be moved. It became clear that an improved road network for the country as a whole would be a great advantage but the government, by and large, clung to the outmoded Tudor administration.

10.5 GOVERNMENT ATTEMPTS TO IMPROVE THE ROADS IN THE EIGHTEENTH CENTURY

In keeping with the philosophy of *laissez-faire* there was no direct government intervention in the situation. Legislation was minimal and, without exception, ineffective: attempts were made to limit the amount a waggon could carry, three tonnes being set as a maximum. This was still a sufficient amount to cause damage to the poorly-constructed roads. There were also difficulties in weighing a load exactly:

- In 1753, Parliament passed a **Broad Wheel Act**. The increase in wheeled traffic was the main cause of road surfaces disintegrating. This Act was an attempt to spread the waggon's load over a greater surface area by setting 22 centimetres as the minimum permissible width of a wheel rim.
- In 1776 parishes were allowed to install a paid road surveyor. Any such appointment had to have the backing of at least two-thirds of the ratepayers.

10.6 WHAT WAS THE ROLE OF THE TURNPIKE TRUSTS AND HOW SUCCESSFUL WERE THEY IN IMPROVING BRITAIN'S ROADS?

(a) The idea of a turnpike road dated back to 1663 when a group of JPs from the adjacent counties of Huntingdonshire, Cambridgeshire and Hertfordshire agreed to set up gates along part of the Great North Road and to charge a toll for using the road. The toll would be used to maintain the condition of the road and the idea was put into operation by an Act of Parliament.

(b) In 1706 the idea was taken a step further when Parliament sanctioned the first **Turnpike Trust**. Such a trust was made up of a group of local men who were keen to improve a stretch of road in their locality. They were usually motivated by self-interest rather than wishing to provide a service to the community. Once such a group had decided to form a trust they had to apply to Parliament to obtain an Act giving them the legal right to proceed. The Act empowered the trustees to raise turnpike gates along the nominated road and to collect tolls to help pay for repairs. They also had to appoint a surveyor, a clerk and a treasurer. The trustees usually took out a loan of money to pay for the trust's legal fees, the building of the toll-keeper's house and the cost of the initial work required to bring the road up to standard. The tolls that were collected from the travellers had to pay for a variety of expenses such as interest on the loan and the salaries of the officials. Only after these expenses had been met was anything spent on maintaining the road. The Act was only to last for 21 years, when the trust was obliged to apply for a renewal.

(c) There was a rapid acceleration in the number of Turnpike Trusts as the eighteenth century progressed, so that by 1830 there were 1100 looking after about 22 000 miles (35 200 km) of Britain's roads. Just exactly where Turnpike Trusts were established rested entirely on local initiative and in no way was a national network in operation. Most minor roads were left untouched; in fact, approximately 80 per cent of the nation's roads remained very much as before.

(d) On balance the trusts did good work but there were still a number of disadvantages:

(i) As the trusts were set up on local initiative it had the result of creating discontinuity along the major routes. If a traveller was going from London to Edinburgh turnpike roads would be interspersed with roads that had not been improved.

(ii) Undoubtedly those trusts which were well organised and efficiently run did provide a good road surface. Some, however, had such heavy expenses that they only had a limited amount of money left to spend on the road. In addition, some of the early surveyors did not do a good job. Whilst Defoe was generally enthusiastic about the turnpikes, Young was more guarded in his comments and was quick to remark on any deficiencies. 'I know not, in the whole range of language, terms sufficiently expressive to describe this infernal road' was his forthright comment on the Wigan to Preston turnpike.

(iii)   Turnpikes were also not universally welcomed. Local people could find themselves paying a toll to travel a short distance within their own district. This led to people evading the toll by jumping over the gate or simply refusing to pay. Quarter Session Minute books contain numerous entries where such miscreants were brought to justice. In Huntingdonshire the records show that a fine of up to 40 shillings (£2) was the penalty for toll evasion. In some areas local feeling ran so high that the toll-gates were smashed down as at Bedminster in 1749, and during the so called 'Rebecca Riots' of 1842–3 in South Wales. In conclusion, it must be said that the turnpikes did valuable work on the main trunk routes but their importance should be kept in perspective.

10.7   WHAT WAS THE CONTRIBUTION OF 'THE GREAT ROAD ENGINEERS' TO ROAD IMPROVEMENT?

(a) General Wade improved some of the roads in the Scottish Highlands during the Jacobite Rebellion of 1745, but this was purely to give the English army the mobility to crush the rebels.

(b)   John Metcalfe (1717–1810) was the first road engineer of any real note during this period. He was responsible for the construction of 180 miles (288 kilometres) of road in Lancashire, Yorkshire and Cheshire, coping with some of the most difficult terrain in the country. Metcalfe's formula for success was to lay a foundation of heather and brushwood and to ensure the surface of the road had good drainage. Once built, his roads were so solid that no repair work was needed for several years. Metcalfe was blind and his achievements, therefore, are all the more remarkable.

(c)   Thomas Telford (1757–1834)

(i)   Telford's first attempt at road building was in his native Scotland, having been commissioned by Parliament to improve the roads in the Highlands in 1802. Telford carried out this task with great zeal – surveying, writing reports and employing contractors. The contractors had to carry out the work to the stringent requirements of Telford and they were closely watched by a supervisor who had been carefully trained. Telford built some 900 miles (1440 kilometres) of road in Scotland including the trunk road from Glasgow to Carlisle.

(ii) Telford's reputation was now made, and in 1815 he was once again commissioned by Parliament to improve the main road between Shrewsbury and Holyhead. Since the 1801 Act of Union with Ireland, Irish MPs had campaigned for a better link between Dublin and Westminster, and finally Parliament gave way to their demands. Between London and Shrewsbury the road was reasonable, with 29 Turnpike Trusts along the route. From Shrewsbury onwards the road quickly deteriorated as it passed over the mountainous terrain of Snowdonia. Telford was granted £750 000 to improve this stretch of road and the money was used to reduce gradients, straighten out bends and improve the drainage. To take the road over the Menai Straits Telford constructed a magnificent suspension bridge and it was opened, amid great enthusiasm in 1826. When the road was completed, travelling time from London to Holyhead was reduced from three days to just over one day.

(iii) Telford developed a method of roadbuilding which required a foundation of heavy stones. The road was then built up with a layer of stones, with gravel for the surface. The surface was cambered to facilitate drainage. This method made for a road of excellent quality but it was expensive on materials and labour. The vast majority of trusts could not afford to adopt this method with only limited funds at their disposal (it should be remembered that Telford had the backing of Parliamentary funds).

(d) John Loudon Macadam (1756–1836) made, arguably, an even greater impact on the improvement of the roads than Telford. He devised his own method of road construction after a number of years of meticulous experimentation. His method was publicised in a number of essays one of which 'The Present State of Road-Making' went into five editions. Macadam disagreed with Telford about the need for a heavy foundation to the road. Macadam's method was:

● Ensure that the 'native sub-soil' was dry. This was, he argued, sufficient to carry the weight of the traffic.
● The soil was then to be covered with layers of angular stones, preferably granite.
● The surface was to be cambered for drainage.

The weight of the wheeled traffic on the surface of the road would grind the stones down to make a smooth surface. This method was successful and it also had the advantage of being cheap on materials and labour. The majority of Turnpike Trusts adopted Macadam's method when they repaired or constructed roads. Macadam was made Surveyor-General of the roads in the Bristol area in 1815 and, in 1827, Parliament appointed him to the position of General-Surveyor of Roads. He also was the consultant engineer for numerous Turnpike Trusts nationwide.

10.8 WHAT WERE THE BENEFITS OF ROAD IMPROVEMENTS DURING THIS PERIOD?

(a) Improved roads led to quicker and more reliable stage-coach services. Journey times were considerably reduced and coach companies grew in size and number. Competition was stimulated with companies trying to claim to be the quickest and most efficient over the main trunk routes. There was an atmosphere of confidence and the phrase, 'God Willing' was omitted from the handbills and advertisements. Examples of how travelling times were reduced are legion. Suffice it to say that the journey from London to Edinburgh in 1830 took just 36 hours. In 1750 a stage-coach took two days to travel from London to Cambridge; by 1820 times of just seven hours were the norm.

(b) Between 1810 and 1830 the coaching business enjoyed a period of unparalleled prosperity, with over 3000 stage-coaches in use. This provided employment for coach-drivers, innkeepers, blacksmiths, ostlers, grooms and wheelwrights. The increased use of the roads was mainly for passenger travel. It should be noted, however, that coach travel was too expensive for the poorer classes who had to walk or use the freight waggons. Some of the rich people often preferred to travel by post-chaise. Freight haulage by road did not increase so rapidly because of the competition from the canal companies.

(c) In 1784, on the recommendation of *John Palmer* of Bath, the Royal Mail was carried for the first time by coach from Bristol to London. Palmer argued that armed mail-coaches would be much quicker and more dependable than the post-boys. He was proved to be correct and his idea was a great success. Within the Post Office, *Thomas Hasker* was an enthusiastic supporter of mail-coaches, and he did all he could to encourage an efficient service. He ensured that the highest standards were maintained by the drivers and guards. In time most of the main towns in the country were linked to London by a mail-coach route. These coaches also carried passengers, often the representatives of firms trying to spread their markets farther afield.

10.9 WHY DID THE COACHING ERA COME TO AN END?

The advent of the railways in the 1830s was a serious event for the coaching companies. Initially they tried to compete by undercutting the railway fares. When it became painfully obvious that the railways were far quicker, turnpike trusts and coaching companies recognised 'defeat' and went out of business, sometimes selling out to the railway company. In 1839 a Select Committee of the House of Commons inquired into the state of the Turnpike Trusts. One witness was Edward Sherman, a well-known stage-coach proprietor. He said he had lost 15 coaches daily on the northern routes out of London due 'entirely' to the competition of the railroad. He forecasted that, in the near future, coach companies would be unable 'to get a living'. He was completely accurate! A cartoon of the time drawn by George Cruickshank showed a group of shabby coach-drivers whose livelihood had been 'smashed by them railway chaps'. Gradually the Turnpike Trusts folded up. Coach travel only managed to survive in more rural areas which were not touched by the railways until the late nineteenth century. Finally in 1888 the Local Government Act gave the newly-created County Councils the task of maintaining the nation's roads.

10.10 CONCLUSION: HOW FAR DID ROAD IMPROVEMENTS 1750–1830 CONTRIBUTE TO THE INDUSTRIALISATION OF BRITAIN?

Roads played a less important part in the industrialisation process than the canals and railways. The roads had a social effect in that they put people in touch with each other and helped to break down regional differences. They also helped to spread news more quickly via the mail-coaches. They did not, however, play a large part in the transportation of raw materials and finished products; they were unable to compete with the bulk carried by the canals or the speed of the railways. In conclusion, the roads served a purpose in the short term only to be made obsolete by the railways. Their day was to come again with the internal combustion engine.

QUESTIONS

1. Objective 1

Study the source below and then answer the questions:

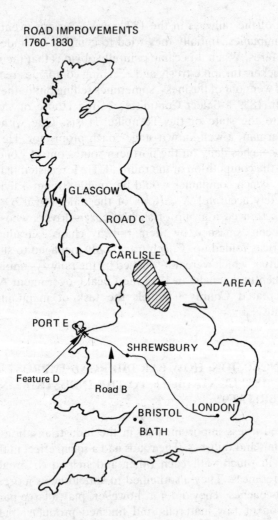

ROAD IMPROVEMENTS
1760-1830

(a) Identify the following:

   (i) The builder of roads in Area A.
   (ii) The builder of roads B and C.

(iii) Feature D.

(iv) Port E.   (Total = 5 marks)

(b)   Why was road B improved after 1815?   (2 marks)

(c)   Why was this road an engineering challenge?   (2 marks)

(d)   Which idea originated in Bath in 1784? Name the person responsible.   (2 marks)

(e)   Who held the position of Surveyor-General of Roads in Bristol in 1815?   (1 mark)

(f)   Describe the organisation of a typical Turnpike Trust (4 marks)

(g)   Compare the three methods of roadbuilding employed by the three engineers featured in Source A. Which method was the most popular? Why?   (4 marks)

2.   **Objective 4**

Study the sources below and then answer the questions:

Source A

A banging of the coach doors, a swaying of the vehicle to one side as the heavy coachman and still heavier guard climbed into their seats . . . "Off she goes!" . . . amidst a loud flourish from the guard's horn and the calm approval of all the judges of coaches and coach-horses congregated at the Peacock . . . [The guard] having now exhausted his usual topics of conversation, folded his arms as well as he could in so many coats, and falling into a solemn silence, looked carelessly at the familiar objects which met his eye on every side as the coach rolled on . . . The weather was intensely and bitterly cold: a great deal of snow fell from time to time, and the wind was intolerably keen . . . The night and the snow came on together and dismal enough they were . . . They were little more than a stage out of Grantham, or about half-way between it and Newark, when Nicholas . . . was suddenly aroused by a violent jerk which nearly threw him from his seat. Grasping the rail, he found that the coach had sunk greatly on one side, though it was still dragged forward by the horses . . . he hesitated for an instant whether to jump or not, the vehicle turned easily over . . . flinging him into the road.

(Taken from the novel, *Nicholas Nickleby* by Charles Dickens, 1839)

Pub.by Tho.McLean 26 Haymarket Aug 31st 1835

Travelling in England, or a peep from the White horse cellar.

(courtesy of BBC Hulton Picture Library)

Source B

Source C

Good roads, by diminishing the expense of the carriage, put the remote parts of the country more nearly upon a level with those in the neighbourhood of the town . . . They encourage the cultivation of the remote . . . They are advantageous to the town . . . they open many new markets to its produce.
(*The Wealth of Nations* by Adam Smith, 1776)

Source D

About half a century ago, the heavy goods passing through Leicester to London . . . did not require more than one daily broad-wheeled waggon each way . . . At present there are about two waggons, two caravans and two fly-boats daily . . . from Leicester for London . . . There are at least six weekly waggons to Birmingham . . . to Bristol three times a week and the same to Stamford, Wisbech and the eastern counties . . . and at least 250 country carriers to and from the villages, many twice a week.
(*Tour through the United Kingdom 1828* by Phillips)

(a) What impressions do Sources A and B convey about stage-coach travel in the early nineteenth century?   (6 marks)
(b) In what way does Source D support the claim in Source C that 'good roads encourage the cultivation of the remote'?

(2 marks)
(c) How did the roadbuilder, Thomas Telford, 'encourage the cultivation of the remote'?   (2 marks)
(d) Why is the reference to 'broad wheels' in Source D significant?

(2 marks)
(e) 'Improved roads had a greater effect on the social life of Britain than the economy.' Examine this statement in the light of the sources above.   (4 marks)
(f) 'Source A is taken from a novel and, therefore, is of no value to the historian'. How far do you agree with this statement? Give reasons.   (4 marks)

3. **Objective 4**

Read the following source and answer the questions which follow:

At a meeting of the Trustees of the Bowes and Sunderland Bridge Road held at the house of Mrs. Brunskill Innkeeper in Staindrop on Saturday 7th day of May 1836.

. . . A letter received from the Chairman of the South West Durham Junction Railway was..read . . . in which it is stated that Mr. Pease (of the said railway) asserted before . . . the Committee (of the House of Commons) "that he had leave from the General Surveyor (of this Trust) to lay a railroad across the above Turnpike road. [Also read] was a letter . . . from the General Surveyor to Mr. Pease which is as follows "Dear Sir, I was much surprised to find . . . that you should assert in such Committee that you had obtained my leave to lay a railroad across the Turnpike road leading from Bowes to Sunderland Bridge near Saint Helen's Auckland. In the first place I had not authority to give such leave, in the next, I never was applied to either by yourself or any other person for such leave. You will therefore oblige me stating on what authority you made such assertion. I am Dear Sir, Yours respectfully John Trotter." [It was further stated] that this meeting . . . feels satisfied from the confidence they have in their General Surveyor that no such leave had been given and again express their regret that Mr. Pease should have made such assertion without more correct information. The Trustees cannot allow the present meeting to separate without expressing their determination not to allow any Railroad to pass over their Trust without endeavouring to protect the interests and safety of the public and compel the owners of such Rail Roads to submit to such terms as the Trustees consider proper.

R. M. Dinsdale
(Chairman)

(Durham County Record Office. Document contained in *Archive Teaching Units* compiled by D. R. Brenchley and C. Shrimpton)

(a) Is this a primary or secondary source? Explain your answer.
(4 marks)

(b) What is the event which has caused such great concern?
(4 marks)

(c) The Mr. Pease in question was the son of Edward Pease. How had the Pease family gained fame in the north-east dating back to the 1820s? (4 marks)

(d) How reliable do you think this source is as evidence of the workings of a Turnpike Trust? How could you find out the outcome of this dispute? (8 marks)

4.   Objective 3

Study the material on pages 138–9.

You are the Treasurer of the Newcastle to Buckton Burn Turnpike Trust. The year is 1840. Write a speech you are to deliver to the Annual General Meeting of the Trust. You need to comment on the following:

(i)   An explanation of the accounts for the year just ended.

(ii) The future prospects of the Trust.

(iii) Any other points of which you think the meeting should be informed.   (Total = 20 marks)

GENERAL STATEMENT of the Income and Expenditure
Newcastle upon Tyne, to the Town of Belford, and fro
between the 31st. Day of March,

EXPENDITURE.	£.	s.	d.
To Balance due from the Trustees to the Surveyor of the Northern District of the Road	3	18	2
To Surveyors' Accounts of Day Labour, between the 31st. day of March, 1829, and the 1st. day of April, 1830, for Maintenance or Repair of Roads	591	2	2
To Surveyors' Accounts of Team Labour, between the 31st. day of March, 1829, and the 1st. day of April, 1830	841	7	8
To Surveyors' Accounts for Work done by Contract, viz. for Winning and Breaking 2421 Tons of Stones, at from 6d. to 3s. 4d. per Ton	945	0	5
To the Treasurer's and Surveyors' Accounts for Repairs, or Maintenance, or Building of Houses, Gates, or Bridges	192	6	9½
To the Treasurer's and Surveyors' Accounts for Damages done	27	12	6
To the Treasurer's and Surveyors' Accounts for the Rent of Quarries	0	2	6
To Salaries and other Payments of Clerk, Treasurer, Surveyors, or other Officers	336	0	3
To Printing, Advertizing, and Stationary	21	8	0
To Interest of Debt	126	8	0
To Incidental Charges	70	8	4½

	£.	s.	d.			
Balance in the Treasurer's Hands	902	1	7¼			
Balance in the Hands of the Surveyor of the Northern District of the Road	7	7	3			
	909	8	10¼			
Deduct Balance due to the Surveyor of the Southern District of the Road	8	12	6½	900	16	4¼

	4056	11	2¼

General Statement

	£.	s.	d.
An Account of the Amount of Debt bearing Interest	3210	0	0

(Signed) By Order of the Trustees.

D. W. SMITH, *Chairman.*

Alnwick. 26th. April. 1830

(Courtesy of Public Research Office, Durham)

of the Turnpike Road leading from the Cow-Cawsey, near the Town of
n thence to Buckton Burn, in the County of Northumberland,
1829, and the 1st. Day of April, 1830.

	£.	s.	d.
RECEIPTS			
By Balance in Treasurer's Hands on the last Settlement - - - -	873	7	11¾
By Balance in the Hands of the Surveyor of the Southern District of the Road	4	0	0¼

By Amount of Rents received from the Lessees, or Tolls received from the Gatekeepers, between the 31st. day of March, 1829, and the 1st. day of April, 1830 as follows :—

	£.	s.	d.		£.	s.	d.
Gosforth Gate	1131	0	0	Brought up	2307	0	0
Morpeth South Gate	673	0	0	Alnwick South Gate	424	0	0
Morpeth North Gate	503	0	0	Heckley Gate	239	10	0
Carried up	2307	0	0	Belford Gate	160	15	0

	£.	s.	d.
	3131	5	0

By Amount of Statute Labour, between the 31st. day of March, 1829, and the 1st. day of April, 1830, as follows :—

	£.	s.	d.		£.	s.	d.
The Township of Coxlodge	1	6	9	Brought up	11	12	9
- - North Gosforth	0	10	0	Cawsey-Park	0	5	8
- - Weetslet	3	5	8	West Thriston	0	19	6
- - Plessey & Shotton	0	5	2	Cannongate	1	1	0
- - Stannington	3	8	1	Belford	5	19	6
- - Bullersgreen	1	2	0	Acton and Old Felton	3	0	0
- - Highlaws	0	19	4	Alnwick	10	0	0
- - Hebron	0	7	2	Alnwick South Side	0	14	0
- - Cockle Park	0	5	0	Newton on the Moor	0	9	9
- - Fenrother	0	0	9	Rock and South Charlton	0	4	0
- - Earsdon	0	2	10	Felton	3	7	0
Carried up	11	12	9				

	£.	s.	d.
	37	13	2
Incidental Receipts - - - - - - - - - - -	10	4	6
	4056	11	2¼

of Debts and Credits.

	£.	s.	d.
Balance of Cash in the Hands of the Treasurer - - - - -	902	1	7¾
Balance of Cash in the Hands of the Surveyor of the Northern District of the Road - - - - - - - - - -	7	7	3
	909	8	10¾
Balance due to the Surveyor of the Southern District of the Road - -	8	12	6¼
	900	16	4¼
Vested in the 3 per Cent. Consolidated Annuities as a Sinking Fund - -	1080	12	0

CHAPTER 11

CANALS

11.1 INTRODUCTION

From about 1760 to 1830 a widespread network of canals was built in Britain. This was a staggering achievement and one which was vital for the industrialisation process. Without canals the movement of huge volumes of heavy goods would not have been possible. Canals answered a need at a crucial time.

The canal age also provided a base for future transport developments, such as railways, for it allowed men to gain a wealth of experience in solving engineering problems. Brindley, Telford and Rennie were just three individuals who played vital roles in canal-building, not to mention the thousands of 'navigators' who provided the labour.

11.2 WHAT FORMS OF WATER TRANSPORT WERE AVAILABLE BEFORE THE MID-EIGHTEENTH CENTURY?

(a) Coastal shipping had been a feature of domestic trade for centuries. Coal was transported from Newcastle to London and some manufacturers of woollen cloth received their supplies of raw wool via this form of transport. It was also common for passengers to travel on coastal ships, particularly during the summer months.

(b) Navigable rivers were also used to move goods. The main rivers used were the Thames, Humber, Mersey, and Severn. Since the sixteenth century Parliament had passed Acts which permitted rivers to be made more navigable.

11.3 WHY WERE CANALS NEEDED?

(a) Although rivers were a useful mode of transport they had a number of shortcomings:

- They were liable to droughts and floods.
- They were not always suitable for navigation nor could they be easily 'improved'. Such rivers were too fast flowing in their upper reaches and had too many sweeping bends near their estuaries.
- There was often competition for the use of their water ranging from millers to fishermen. Arguments and disputes abounded on such rivers.
- Many rivers had no towpath and the constant wear and tear of horses' hooves made the banks unsafe.
- The course of a river is dictated by nature and, as such, they do not always flow conveniently where they are needed!

(b) With the increase in population and consequent increased demand for industrial and agricultural products rivers were simply not adequate to deal with a similar increase in trade. This would still have applied even if vast sums of money had been invested to improve their navigability. Furthermore, in the mid eighteenth century, the roads were still in an atrocious condition (see chapter 10) and totally unsuitable for the movement of industrial goods. Thus, the demands of industry requiring a reliable and efficient method of transport (particularly for bulky commodities like wood, stone and coal) led to the start of the canal era.

11.4 HOW DID THE CANAL NETWORK DEVELOP IN BRITAIN BETWEEN 1760 AND 1830?

(a) The first real canal of this era was the Sankey Brook Navigation, built by John Eye and opened in 1757. The canal joined the town of St Helens to the river Mersey and was used principally, to transport coal to Liverpool.

(b) However, it is the building of the Worsley Canal, 1759–61, which traditionally takes the credit for sparking off the age of canals in Britain.

Francis Egerton, the third Duke of Bridgewater (1736–1803), had large deposits of coal on his Worsley estate. He transported the coal the 10 miles (16 kilometres) into Manchester by pack-horse, but he was far from satisfied with this method of carriage. It was expensive, and the roads were muddy and narrow. He successfully applied to Parliament for an Act to build a canal between Worsley and Manchester. The Duke instructed his agent, John Gilbert, to organise its construction. Gilbert employed a Derbyshire millwright, James Brindley (1716–72), to survey a suitable route and construct the waterway. Brindley took the canal over the river Irwell into Manchester by means of an aqueduct at Barton. When complete the canal reduced transport costs and, hence, the price of coal to the Manchester residents. This encouraged the Duke to extend the canal from Manchester to Runcorn in 1767. The Duke also permitted other traders to use the canal, charging them tolls and making a handsome profit.

The Worsley Canal illustrated the tremendous advantages canals would bring to industrialists and, in turn, the nation's economy.

(c)   The canal network grew in a 'piece-meal' fashion with no overall plan ever being conceived by the central government. The only 'plan', as such, was based on a idea of Brindley's that became called 'The Cross'. The intention was to link the four major ports and rivers of England by a network of canals and navigable rivers. Thus Liverpool (the Mersey), Hull (the Humber), Bristol (the Severn) and London (the Thames) would be linked by waterways which intersected at Birmingham in the Midlands.

(d)

(i)   One component of 'The Cross' was the Grand Trunk Canal (the Trent and Mersey Canal) started in 1766 by Brindley and completed in 1777. A leading figure in the initiation of this waterway was the Staffordshire potter, Josiah Wedgwood (see chapter 8). Building the canal presented Brindley with a number of engineering challenges, but it provided a direct cross-country route linking the Mersey with the Trent and, in turn, the Humber. The actual length of the waterway was 93 miles (149 kilometres).

(ii)   'The Cross' was completed with the opening of a number of canals in quick succession. In 1772 the Staffordshire and Worcestershire Canal was opened, linking the Grand Trunk Canal to the River Severn at Stourport. The Birmingham Canal, also opened in 1772, linked the growing industrial city to the Staffordshire and Worcestershire Canal and thus to the Mersey. The final arm of 'The Cross' was completed in 1790 with the opening of the Oxford Canal and the Coventry Canal which, between them, linked the River Thames with the Grand Trunk.

(iii) By this time the canal 'bug' had taken a grip and the years 1791–4 are traditionally known as 'canal mania'. During this period over 40 canals were authorised and built. Some of them were built in agricultural areas and were commercial failures – the classic example being the Basingstoke Canal, which linked the Hampshire market town to London via the River Wey.

(iv) In the early years of the nineteenth century a number of important canals were opened. Among them were:

- The Grand Junction Canal 1805 (a direct link between Birmingham and London, engineered by Barnes and Jessop).
- The Ellesmere Canal 1805.
- The Kennet and Avon Canal 1810.
- The Huddersfield Canal 1811.
- The Grand Union Canal 1814.
- The Worcester and Birmingham Canal 1815.
- The Leeds-Liverpool Canal 1816.

By 1830 the canal network in Britain totalled some 4,000 miles (6400 kilometres).

(v) Much discussion has taken place about the piece-meal manner in which the canal network developed. Canals came about in Britain because of an abundance of men willing to risk capital and the engineering genius of men like Brindley and Telford. It has been pointed out that if the government had planned the network several advantages would have accrued. For example, capital would not have been wasted on over-ambitious schemes and all canals would have been built to a uniform width. This may well have been so, but canals were built during a time when the economic climate was one of *laissez-faire* and this made direct government intervention unlikely.

11.5 WHAT DIFFICULTIES FACED ENGINEERS IN CONSTRUCTING CANALS?

(a) The building of a canal was a massive undertaking, which involved the shifting of vast amounts of earth. The labour and muscle power was provided by men called 'navigators'. These men were tough and hardened to the demands of physical work. Many were Scottish, Irish or men who had had experience digging drainage cuts in the Fenlands of England. The 'navvies' lived a nomadic life, moving about the country to work on different projects. They gained a reputation for rowdy behaviour, heavy drinking and violence. It was common for them to be paid in tokens which could be exchanged for goods at specified shops or alehouses along the route of the canal.

(b) Canals also produced a class of engineers. They had no previous experience to guide them and, as a result, they had to deal with each problem as and when it arose. The main engineers were James Brindley, Thomas Telford, John Rennie, James Barnes and William Jessop. They were employed by canal companies and had the responsibility of surveying the route (usually by walking the terrain) and overseeing the work of the various contractors employed to dig the canal. Surveying was very much a 'hit and miss' affair; there were no Ordnance Survey maps and geological maps showing the dominant underlying rocks in the area were also not available at the time.

(c) In the actual construction of a canal one of the major concerns was to overcome gradients.

(i) If the way was barred by a small hill it was usual for pound locks to be employed to take the boats up or down a level. Sometimes, in hilly areas, a number of locks were built in succession to form a flight or a staircase. A flight was a group of locks with a short piece of water between them. A staircase was where a series of locks ran directly into one another such as the famous Bingley Five Rise on the Leeds-Liverpool canal. Their great drawback was the amount of time it took the boatmen to negotiate them.

(ii) In later years other devices were constructed for lifting boats up steep gradients. One of the most famous was the Inclined Plane at Foxton in Leicestershire on the Grand Junction Canal (see photo p. 146). The Inclined Plane was opened in 1900 and it was capable of lifting a boat from the lower level of the canal to the higher level in 12 minutes, compared to the 45 minutes it took to negotiate the adjacent flight of locks. However, the lift was expensive to operate and, in 1911, the Grand Junction Canal Company reverted back to using the locks.

(iii)   If a very large hill had to be negotiated it would necessitate the building of a tunnel. This was a costly and dangerous operation and would not be embarked on unless all other alternatives had been ruled out. Perhaps Brindley's greatest achievement was the building of the Harecastle Tunnel on the Trent and Mersey Canal. The tunnel took 11 years to build between 1766 and 1777 and was 2880 yards (2633 m) in length. It was originally built without a tow-path and this led to the practice of legging boats through the tunnel. Men laid on 'legging boards' and propelled the boats through by walking their feet along the side or roof of the tunnel. In 1827 Thomas Telford was employed to build a second Harecastle Tunnel, this time with a tow-path.

(iv)   Another major problem for the engineer was taking a canal over a river valley. Brindley set the example by building the Barton Aqueduct, but an even greater achievement was the construction of the Pontcysyllte aqueduct which carried the Ellesmere Canal over the River Dee in North Wales. This was the work of Thomas Telford and his able assistant, Matthew Davidson. The aqueduct was built of stone with a cast-iron trough of four metres containing the water of the canal. It is some 120 feet (37 m) high and 1000 feet (310 m) long. It is still in use and is a truly magnificent sight viewed from the side of the Dee Valley.

(v)   Apart from the engineering problems the building of a canal also meant the construction of wharves, warehouses, offices and lock-keepers' cottages. This involved the employment of bricklayers, stonemasons and carpenters.

(d)   The second major concern of an engineer was to ensure that the canal was kept supplied with water and that the canal was watertight. Sometimes the water was pumped from a nearby river as with the Kennet and Avon Canal at Crofton. The most common method of water-supply was to build large reservoirs, if possible above the summit level of the canal. The reservoirs were supplied by streams which were dredged at regular intervals. Canals were made water-tight by lining the bottom and sides with 'puddled' clay – clay mixed

Inclined plane on Grand Junction Canal

(courtesy of British Waterways Board)

with water. Men donned puddling boots and worked the water into the clay. Again this was an idea first demonstrated by Brindley when he built the Worsley Canal.

(e) Brindley's canal-building strategy differed from the later canal engineers. He kept his canals on the same level by following the contours; in doing this he wished to avoid large numbers of locks, tunnels, cuttings, embankments and aqueducts. This reduced the cost of the canal but also resulted in long twisting routes. After Brindley's death canals were built in a more direct line between two places. Telford (1757–1834) employed numerous cuttings and embankments. Although more expensive, it proved to be a successful method and subsequently some of Brindley's canals were straightened. Telford was also responsible for building the Caledonian Canal in Scotland, linking the Atlantic Ocean to the North Sea, which was opened in 1802.

11.6   HOW WERE CANAL COMPANIES STARTED AND FINANCED?

(a) The starting point was for a group of local men, usually businessmen and merchants, to join together to promote a scheme for building the canal. Meetings were held to put forward the arguments in favour of the proposed canal. Then an Act of Parliament had to be obtained. This involved drawing up a petition and putting the case before a Committee of the House of Commons. This was expensive as legal and parliamentary fees had to be met. If there was any opposition to the scheme the cost would increase. Opposition from Turnpike Trusts, rival river navigations and landowners could be fierce.

(b) Once the Act was passed the canal company had the power to purchase land and raise capital. The company, in its preparations, would have estimated how much the canal would cost to build. It was usual for a sub-clause to be included in the Act which gave the company the power to raise further capital if it was needed – and this was often the case. Some canals were abandoned before they were completed because of lack of funds; such was the fate of the Southampton to Salisbury Canal.

(c) It has been estimated that some £20 million was invested in building canals between 1760 and 1830. Where did this money come from?

(i)   On some occasions a local landowner or businessman, realising the need for a canal, took the lead and put up most of the money for the canal. The classic examples were Francis Egerton and Josiah Wedgwood.

(ii)   In most cases, however, the Canal Company raised capital by selling shares to anyone willing to invest their money. Shares varied in cost from about £50 to £200. Once the canal was built the company charged tolls aiming to make an operating profit each year. The shareholders were then paid a dividend from the profit. Shares sold easily, particularly during the years of the 'mania' and a number of investors used the canal boom to speculate, hoping to earn a quick return on their capital.

(d) In reality few canals managed to pay high dividends to their shareholders. The most profitable canals proved to be the Oxford Canal, the Forth-Clyde Canal, the Coventry Canal and the Grand Junction Canal. In the agricultural south the canals never paid high dividends. In fact the best profit ever made by the Basingstoke Canal Company amounted to just one and a half per cent for a year's trading.

11.7 WHAT BENEFICIAL RESULTS DID CANALS HAVE FOR THE BRITISH ECONOMY?

(a) For all their deficiencies the canals played a vital part in the early industrialisation of Britain. They enabled heavy industrial goods to be moved in large amounts at costs lower than road transport. Furthermore, finished products could be easily moved to ports for export.

(b) Perhaps the most important commodity conveyed on the canals was coal – the fuel which formed the corner-stone of the industrial revolution. Other heavy commodities conveyed easily by canal were building-stone, pig iron, clay, timber, cotton and wool. The canal network played a vital part in supplying the increased demand for industrial products in the period 1760–1830.

(c) The industrial areas which benefited most from the building of canals were inland with no navigable rivers in close proximity. The iron industry of the Black Country and South Wales, the metal-working industries around Birmingham, and the pottery industry of Staffordshire all fall into this category.

(d) Although canals built in agricultural areas were generally un-successful, some farmers were able to benefit from canals. Grain and livestock could be transported via canal to the industrial cities, and fertilisers such as marl, manure and lime could be brought back.

(e) Some canals helped to stimulate the growth of towns. Leicester, Stourport, Goole and Runcorn are three examples of towns which grew as a result of being located on a canal.

(f) Canals also provided employment for vast numbers of men.

11.8 WHEN AND WHY DID CANALS DECLINE?

(a) It is usually accepted that the canals started to decline in the 1840s, but of course this is a sweeping generalisation. Some canals continued to be successful for many more years and it is interesting to note that the Leeds-Liverpool and the Leicester Navigation carried their peak tonnages in the late 1840s. On the other hand some canals were in decline before the 1840s.

(b) The main reason why canals started to lose trade was the development of the railways. In comparison with the railways, canals were very slow. In addition, railway companies deliberately set out to buy out the river canals so as to kill competition. Much bitterness ensued as canals passed into railway ownership. Railways also had the advantage of being able to convey passengers in greater numbers. Apart from a few exceptions, such as the Forth-Clyde, canals were never popular as a means of passenger transport.

(c) It is usually assumed that the decline of canals was hastened by the lack of uniformity in the system. This prevented 'through' traffic and, it is argued, helped the railways take over. As canals were built by individual companies widths, lock-sizes and depths all varied. With different canal dimensions boats also varied in size. Wide craft used on the wider canals such as the Kennet and Avon were just over 10 feet (3 m) wide and about 60 feet (18 m) long, whereas the narrow boats were 69 feet (21 m) long and only just over 6 feet (2 m) wide.

(d) Finally it can be argued that the canal companies did not fight their corners with much determination. In some cases they more or less accepted that the railway would buy them out and they merely set about obtaining as much compensation as possible. What they really needed was a man with strong leadership qualities willing to engineer canal amalgamations which would have brought greater uniformity. Unfortunately such a figure did not emerge.

11.9 CONCLUSION

For a period, canals played a crucial role in the growth of the British economy. Pauline Gregg sums up their value when she writes, 'Though canal transport had the disadvantages of slowness and troublesome transhipment . . . they were the arteries which carried the coal and iron which was the life-blood of industrialism . . . It was largely their initial service which gave life to the early stages of the Industrial Revolution'.

QUESTIONS

1. **Objectives 1 and 2**

(a) Why did a canal network develop in Britain in the late eighteenth century? (6 marks)

(b) Which of these causal factors do you consider to be the most important and why? (6 marks)

(c) Why did canals decline in importance? Could their demise have been prevented? Explain your answer. (8 marks)

2. **Objectives 1 and 2**

Assess the importance of James Brindley in the development of canals. Make a reference to:

● His personality.
● How far external factors played a part in his actions.
● Why his success was important. (20 marks)

3. **Objectives 1 and 4**

Read the following source and then answer the questions which follow:

Manchester
30th September 1763

Dear Sir,
I have lately been viewing the artificial wonders of London and the natural wonders of the Peaks, but none of them gave me so much pleasure as the Duke of Bridgewater's navigation in this area . . . At Barton bridge . . . a navigable canal in the air [has been erected] for it is as high as the tops of the trees . . . On this I must confess I dared hardly venture to walk as I trembled to behold the large river beneath me across which this navigation is carried by a bridge . . . The navigation begins at the foot of some hills near a small village. In these hills the Duke's coals are dug, from whence a canal is cut through rocks, which daylight never enters. By this means large boats are hauled to the innermost parts of those hills and are there filled with coal . . .
From Barton I steered my course towards this place and in my way sometimes saw the navigation carried over public roads and in one place over a huge bog, but generally it proceeds by the side of the

hills . . . All in these parts are in high praise of the navigation and contemplate the forthcoming winter with a calm spirit their pockets not being as much emptied as in the past . . .
(*Annual Register* 1763)

(a) Who built this navigation? What evidence is there in the source to back this up? (3 marks)
(b) What had been erected at Barton? Why did the writer view it with such awe? (3 marks)
(c) Assess the importance of this 'navigation' in the context of the development of the canal network. (8 marks)
(d) How reliable is this source as historical evidence? (6 marks)

4. **Objective 3**

You are the secretary of a company planning to build a canal in an industrial area of England in the year 1804. You are to address a public meeting about your company's proposal. Prepare the speech you intend to deliver, bearing in mind you expect to encounter some opposition. In your speech you should reconstruct the historical situation and context. Make reference to some or all of the points below:

● Where the canal is to be built.
● Anticipated engineering problems and how they will be overcome.
● The advantages of building this particular canal.
● The projected cost and how the company intends to raise capital.
● The opposition you encounter and your reply.

(20 marks)

5. Objectives 1 and 2

Study the map below and then answer the questions which follow:

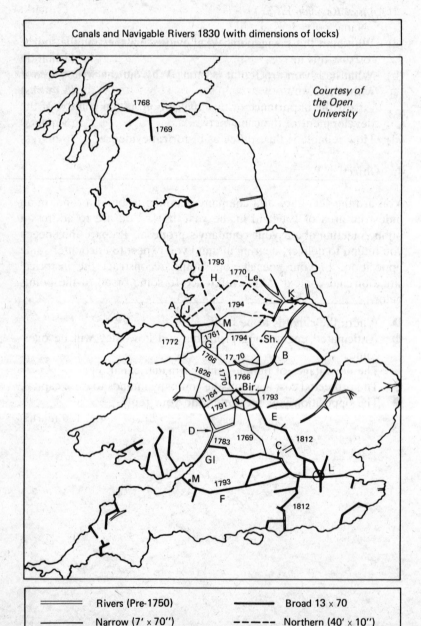

Canals and Navigable Rivers 1830 (with dimensions of locks)

Courtesy of the Open University

Rivers (Pre-1750) Broad 13 × 70

Narrow (7' × 70'') Northern (40' × 10'')

Dates of Authorisation of Canals Given

(a) Name rivers A, B, C, D.   (2 marks)
(b) What disadvantages did rivers have as a method of transport?
                                                      (3 marks)
(c) Name canals E, F, G, H.   (2 marks)
(d) Name ports J, K, L, M.   (2 marks)
(e) With reference to the map explain the theory behind Brindley's
     'Cross'.   (4 marks)
(f) What was the significance of the fact that some canals are shown
     as 'broad' and others as 'narrow'? How far was this a factor in
     the demise of canals as a major form of inland transport?
                                                      (7 marks)

6. **Objective 4**

Study the sources below:

Source A
John Telford to Thomas Telford 1804:

> Last Saturday was pay day and a very disagreeable one it
> was . . . the men were all informed when you was here that those
> upon day's wages would only receive 1s 6d per day; they refused to
> take it . . . they threatened much and were on the point of using
> violence several times.

Source B

> Let us for a moment reflect upon the advantages which result from
> employment of between one and two hundred workmen, all
> natives of Sussex. In the usual method of cutting canals, these men
> are a constant nuisance to the neighbourhood, and the terror of all
> other descriptions of people. But in Lord Egremont's canal, the
> men are all drawn from amongst his own workmen, and have none
> of that turbulence and riot with which foreign workmen are
> inspired . . . the expenses of the job are much less to the
> employer, whilst the weekly wage of the men in this business,
> instead of 8s or 9s rise up to 14s or 15s.
> (From *A General View of the Agriculture of Sussex 1808*, quoted in
> *Roads and Canals* by R. Tames (OUP, 1970))

Source C

(courtesy of Hampshire County Museum Service)

(a) The sources suggest that navvies were paid in at least three different ways. What were they? (6 marks)

(b) How does the writer of Source A differ from the author of Source B in his attitude towards the navvies? What is the possible explanation? (6 marks)

(c) How does Source C differ in nature from Source A and B? (2 marks)

(d) Compare Source A with Source B:
● How reliable is each source.
● Which is more useful to the historian?
(6 marks)

RAILWAYS

12.1 INTRODUCTION

Although railway lines, plateways, waggon-ways or tramways had been used in Britain since the seventeenth century, it was not until the early nineteenth century that 'modern railways' were developed. This was when the locomotive – a steam-engine on wheels – was invented, to haul carriages along a track. It took the early locomotive designers some time to solve the technical problems but once they had been overcome, the potential of the 'modern' railway was quickly seen by businessmen and industrialists and the growth of the railway network between 1825 and 1875 was astounding.

12.2 HOW AND WHERE DID RAILWAYS ORIGINATE?

(a) During the seventeenth century it became common in the mining areas of the Black Country and the North-East to build a wooden waggon-way to enable horses to pull the coal from the pithead to the nearest wharf. Here the coal was loaded on to boats and transported to the towns. In 1731 Somerset landowner, Ralph Allen, built a wooden railway to carry stone from his quarries to the nearby River Avon. This operated on a self-acting incline. In 1758 a railway was authorised for the first time by an Act of Parliament. The Act permitted a railway line to be built connecting Middleton Colliery with Leeds – thus an important precedent was set, for after this it became general practice to obtain an Act before constructing a railway.

(b) Wooden rails had their limitations. They rotted quickly or were soon damaged by the heavy waggons. In 1767 rails made entirely from cast iron were produced at Coalbrookdale, and in 1820 *John Birkinshaw* of Bedlington designed a rail made out of wrought iron. In 1803 the Surrey Iron Railway was opened between Wandsworth and Croydon. Engineered by William Jessop, the line was the first to be built for public use. Horses pulled varying materials along the line and the public could make use of the facility on payment of a toll.

12.3 WHO WERE THE INVENTORS OF THE EARLY LOCOMOTIVES?

(a) Steam-engines had been used in mines and factories for several years, either for pumping or driving machinery. Until 1800 the patent for the steam-engine was held by Boulton and Watt. Once the patent expired, greater scope was given to men trying to devise a steam-engine on wheels – a locomotive. Such an invention depended on the use of high-pressure steam.

(b) A Cornishman, *Richard Trevithick (1771–1833)* pioneered the development of the first steam-locomotives. After designing a steam-carriage to run on the road, he built a high-pressure locomotive for Samuel Homfray, proprietor of the Penydarren Ironworks near Merthyr Tydfil. The locomotive was partly successful in that it hauled iron and passengers a distance of some 9 miles (14 km) to Abercynon. In 1808 Trevithick demonstrated a locomotive called the *Catch-Me-Who-Can* running on a circular track at Euston and the public were invited to ride in a carriage behind the locomotive. Trevithick was, however, dissatisfied with his achievements, and he abandoned his work with locomotives. He had shown that it was possible to construct a steam-engine which could drive itself along and in running his locomotive on rails he had conceived the notion of the modern railway.

(c) After this the centre of locomotive development became the Wylam Colliery in County Durham. Here in 1813 William Hedley and Timothy Hackworth built the *Puffing Billy* and the *Wylam Dilly*. Slowly engineers began to recognise that the traction of smooth wheels would be facilitated if the track was level.

(d) In 1814 *George Stephenson*, the engine-wright at Killingworth Colliery, built his first locomotive, *The Blucher*. Stephenson, with his son Robert, was to become the most important engineer in the early history of the railways. Stephenson possessed the determination which Trevithick had apparently lacked. His mind was constantly occupied with the problems of producing an efficient locomotive. *The Blucher* was no better or worse than its predecessors, hauling about 30 tonnes of coal at four miles (6.5 km) per hour. Within 16 years, however, Stephenson was to prove beyond doubt that the steam-locomotive was superior to all other available modes of propulsion.

12.4 THE STOCKTON TO DARLINGTON RAILWAY 1825

(a) Why was a railway built between Stockton and Darlington?

The Stockton to Darlington railway was opened on 27 September, 1825 but the idea for the line had been formulated some eight years earlier by a Quaker businessman, Edward Pease. He believed that a railway would provide the best means of transport for coal from the Witton Park Colliery (nine miles west of Darlington) to the River Tees at Stockton. An Act of Parliament was passed in 1821 authoris-ing the construction of the line and Pease deserves credit for advocating the railway despite much cynical opposition – many felt that it would be better to build a canal. Quaker friends put up the money.

(b) What part did Stephenson play in the building of the Stockton and Darlington line?

Pease invited Stephenson to be the surveyor and engineer for the line. Stephenson built the track with a gauge of 4 feet 8.5 inches (1.5 m) and rails made of wrought iron. At first the Stockton to Darlington company had envisaged horses being used on the line. Stephenson, however, argued enthusiastically for steam-locomotives and in 1823 a second Act was passed allowing locomotives to haul coal waggons. Passengers were still to be conveyed by horses. Stephenson built his *Locomotion No. 1* for use on the Stockton and Darlington. It still had a plain boiler, however, and could not provide enough steam for speeds over five miles (8 km) per hour when hauling heavy goods.

(c) What was the importance of the Stockton and Darlington railway?

The line was opened amid scenes of great enthusiasm – a locomotive was still very much a novelty. The opening ceremony was publicised locally and the *Durham County Advertiser* estimated that some 40 000 to 50 000 people 'witnessed the proceedings of the day'. Historians have made various assessments as to the importance of this railway although many of them have been exaggerated. Trevor May claims that the opening of the railway was not at all well known outside Teeside. The general public most probably did not appreciate the importance of the event. Up to 1825 no public railway in the world had employed steam-locomotives – even then this was only because of the determination of George Stephenson. The real importance of the Stockton and Darlington railway is that it provided a springboard for future railway construction. The line proved to be beneficial to the coal-mining industry; in 1822 1224 tons (1204 tonnes) of coal were supplied from Stockton – by 1835 this had risen to 704 781 tons (693 504 tonnes). It also carried, from 1833, an increasing number of passengers.

12.5 THE LIVERPOOL TO MANCHESTER RAILWAY 1830

(a) Why was the line proposed? By 1825 South-East Lancashire was a very important cotton manufacturing area. Supplies of raw cotton came into the port of Liverpool and were transported by pack-horse and water inland to the Manchester textile mills. The population of both cities increased dramatically and the whole area was a hive of industrial activity. A group of industrialists from the two cities were unhappy about the monopoly of the Bridgewater Canal, River Mersey and Irwell Navigation, in transporting their goods. They wanted a faster, cheaper, more efficient means of transport. There was enough support to form a committee and petition Parliament to pass a Bill authorising a railway to be built between the two cities.

(b) **What part did the Stephensons play in its construction?**

(i) In 1824 George Stephenson was engaged by the Committee as the chief engineer. When he surveyed the route he had to face tremendous opposition. Lord Derby and Lord Sefton did their utmost to stop the survey taking place. The Bridgewater Canal Company spread propaganda about the dangers that locomotives would bring. Stephenson refused to give in and pressed ahead, finished his survey, and calculated that it would cost £400 000 to build the line.

When the Bill was put before Parliament George Stephenson was insufficiently prepared and was made to look inade-

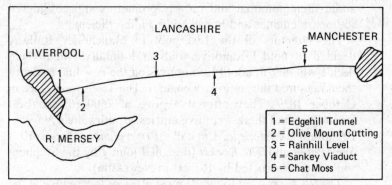

Engineering Problems on the Liverpool to Manchester Railway

quate under cross-examination. As a result the Bill was not passed. Stephenson was dismissed and the line re-surveyed by John Rennie. He put the estimated cost at £500 000 but his plans were very thorough and in 1826 the Bill was passed in Parliament. The Liverpool-Manchester railway was, at last, authorised. However, John Rennie demanded a salary and conditions which the Company refused to meet and thus they re-appointed George Stephenson as the engineer. A lucky break one might argue!

(ii) *Engineering problems*

The construction of the line presented a real challenge to Stephenson. He built a tunnel on the outskirts of Liverpool – The Edgehill Tunnel, 2240 yards (2036 m) long. Then a huge cutting was blasted through Olive Mount and a superb viaduct took the line over the Sankey Viaduct. Stephenson's greatest achievement was in successfully taking the line over a huge swamp called Chat Moss on the outskirts of Manchester. He did this by building a raft of heather and brushwood upon which the line floated. Stephenson worked long hours on the construction of the line and it was a tribute to his determination and perseverance.

(iii) *The Rainhill trials*

In 1827 Robert Stephenson began work at his Newcastle Works planning and designing locomotives. The locomotive still had many faults and little progress had been made since 1814; not surprisingly the general public were unconvinced about their potential and railway promotors still considered stationary engines and horses to be more efficient.

The directors of the Liverpool to Manchester Railway decided to hold locomotive trials at Rainhill to help them decide whether to adopt locomotives on the new line (most of them favoured the stationary engine). The Trials took place in October 1829. They offered a prize of £500 for the best locomotive and there were five entries: Braithwaite's *Novelty*, Brandreth's *Cyclopede*, Burstall's *Perseverance*, Hackworth's *Sans Pareil* and *The Rocket* (designed jointly by the Stephenson's and constructed by Robert in Newcastle).

The Rocket proved to be the most efficient locomotive at the trials. It ran for 70 miles (112 km), without mechanical failure, achieving a top speed of 27 miles (43 km) per hour. No other locomotive was able to match this and the Stephensons received the £500. The potential of the steam-locomotive had been displayed to the public.

(iv) *The success and importance of the Liverpool-Manchester railway*

The Liverpool-Manchester line was opened on 15 September 1830. It can be safely argued that with the opening of this line, Britain had entered into the 'Railway Age'.

● The line was an unqualified success in the conveyance of goods and, to the surprise of the directors, passengers. The following figures illustrate this success:

	1831	1832	1833	1834	1835
Passengers carried	445 047	356 945	386 492	436 637	473 846
Merchandise carried (Tonnes)	98 089	126 169	138 090	142 099	155 562

● By 1838 the company was paying an annual dividend of 10 per cent to its shareholders.
● The 'Railway Boom' followed and Stephenson's work had been vindicated. Suddenly he was a national figure, but

how different it could have been had John Rennie accepted the post of engineer in 1826!

12.6 HOW QUICKLY DID THE RAILWAY NETWORK GROW?

The success of the Liverpool to Manchester line sparked off a nationwide railway boom – often referred to as railway 'mania'. The mania hit three high points – 1836–7, 1840 and 1844–8. In 1838 the first inter-city line was opened between London and Birmingham (the work of Robert Stephenson). Birmingham in turn was linked to Liverpool by the Grand Junction in 1840 (the work of George Stephenson). By 1843 London had been connected with Bristol – the Great Western Railway, Southampton, Brighton and Dover. In 1850 there was a choice of two routes from London to Scotland, only the hilly areas of South-West England and Mid-Wales had not been subject to the mania. The growth of the network can only be described as phenomenal as these figures illustrate:

Railways opened (miles and (km))

1825–29	51 (82)
1830–34	246 (397)
1835–39	666 (1075)
1840–44	1256 (2026)
1845–49	3670 (5918)

The above figures do not reveal the full story; many more kilometres were authorised by Parliament but were never built. With the opening of the Carlisle-Settle line in 1876 most of the major lines in Britain had been completed, and just before the outbreak of the First World War the railway network had a total length in excess of 23 000 miles (36 800 kilometres).

12.7 WHAT PROBLEMS WERE ENCOUNTERED BY THE PROMOTERS WHEN ESTABLISHING A RAILWAY COMPANY?

There were great problems in forming a company but the early railway promoters persevered and managed to overcome most of them.

(a) Writing the prospectus

The first step was to write a prospectus setting out the promoters' arguments for the projected railway. At this stage the promoters would have formed a committee which would have made a preliminary survey of the route and made an estimate of the total costs involved.

(b) Finance

(i) Capital was raised by *selling shares*. Many people were anxious to buy shares in the hope of making money (the company would pay annual dividends out of their profits). Railways were, therefore, a form of speculation. Some railways proved to be very profitable, paying handsome dividends but the average dividend in 1850 was only 3.3 per cent.

(ii) *Expenses*

A railway was an expensive undertaking; buying the land, and constructing the track were costly, but so too was obtaining an Act of Parliament. The company had to have a Bill prepared which was then debated in Parliament before going before a committee. Here the company had to argue its case and opponents had the chance to raise objections to the railway. This involved a considerable amount of money in legal costs – lawyers and solicitors had to be paid. Often the railway company underestimated the amount of money required to construct the railway. It only needed a tunnel undertaking to present engineering problems for the cost to rise considerably. The estimated cost of the Settle-Carlisle line was put at £2.25 million but the contractors met many troublesome problems and the final cost was £3.50 million.

(c) Opposition

A railway company could meet fierce opposition both with the general public and at the committee stage. In the early days people opposed railways through 'fear of the unknown'. Fears regarding frightened livestock and hayricks being set on fire were founded on ignorance. Whole towns, like Abingdon and Northampton refused to have the railway coming into their vicinity. Fears about accidents probably had greater foundation. Sabbatarians were opposed to the railways as they were against Sunday travel. Canal companies, however, had good reason to oppose the building of a railway as they would lose business. The railway companies did not always act honourably in overcoming this particular objection – they merely bought out the canal company and left the canal to go derelict. Turnpike trusts feared a loss of revenue in tolls and stage-coach companies also objected strongly to the railways, more so when it became clear that they were popular with passengers. There were occasions when landowners initially would not allow a railway to be built on their land but later relented, selling the required acreage at a high price. Surveyors were on occasions shot at by the landlord's men as they attempted to walk the proposed route of the railway.

(d)   The Act of Parliament

Finally, if the company was unsuccessful in raising capital and overcoming opposition, their Bill would be written into the Statute Book as an Act. The company now had the authority to buy land, issue shares, build and operate the line.

12.8   WHAT PROBLEMS WERE ENCOUNTERED IN THE CONSTRUCTION OF RAILWAY LINES?
(See diagram on p. 164)

(a)   At first engineers did not agree on the gauge (width) of the track. Most companies adopted the gauge of 4 feet 8.5 inches (1.5 metres) which was used by George Stephenson; Isambard Kingdom Brunel preferred the wider gauge of 7 feet (2.15 metres) and his Great Western railway (GWR) was built to this specification.

(b)   The engineers soon realised that it was best to build their line level, avoiding gradients as far as possible. This involved the building of embankments, the construction of viaducts, the blasting of tunnels and the excavation of cuttings. This work was done by the 'railway navvies' (see Section 12.9).

(c)   Tunnels

Robert Stephenson was forced to excavate the Kilsby Tunnel on the London-Birmingham line. This was a monumental achievement; the tunnel had to be constantly pumped to prevent flooding and took two and a half years to complete, at a cost of £300 000.

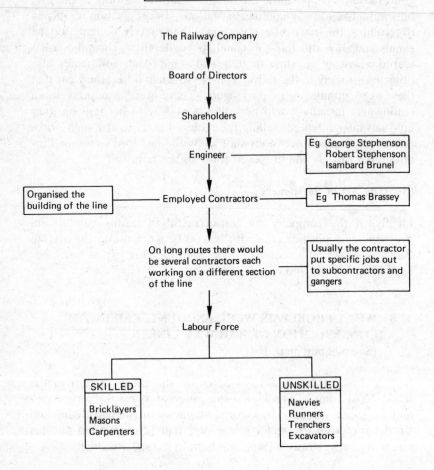

BUILDING A RAILWAY LINE

The Railway Company

Board of Directors

Shareholders

Engineer ——— Eg George Stephenson
                   Robert Stephenson
                   Isambard Brunel

Organised the
building of the line ——— Employed Contractors ——— Eg Thomas Brassey

On long routes there would
be several contractors each
working on a different section
of the line ——— Usually the contractor
put specific jobs out
to subcontractors and
gangers

Labour Force

SKILLED

Bricklayers
Masons
Carpenters

UNSKILLED

Navvies
Runners
Trenchers
Excavators

(d) Cuttings

When digging a cutting such as the one at Tring (on the London-Birmingham) the navvies would construct planks running from the bottom of the cutting to the top. They filled their barrow with soil and then ran up the plank with their load. This was not as dangerous as tunnelling but it was very demanding physically. (Barrow Run races helped to take the tedium out of the long day.)

(e) Viaducts

Many magnificent viaducts and bridges were also constructed at this time. The Ribblehead Viaduct on the Settle-Carlisle line is a superb example of Victorian engineering but it took four years to complete it and the navvies had to cope with snowstorms and fierce Pennine gales. When it was finished it had 24 arches and was 165 feet (50 metres) high. Brunel displayed his immense engineering talent in the building of the Albert Bridge at Saltash which took the GWR over the River Tamar.

12.9 HOW FAR DID THE NAVVIES DESERVE THEIR NOTORIOUS REPUTATION?

The navvies are traditionally portrayed as a bunch of 'wild heathens' who would terrorise the local population. At the height of the mania some 250 000 navvies were employed on the railways tackling such enormous projects as those mentioned in Section 12.8. They were physically strong and durable, capable of moving 20 tonnes of earth in a day. Many drank heavily in their leisure time as a means of escape from the exhausting demands of their work. A navvy lived a nomadic existence, moving from one undertaking to the next. They built crude shanty towns at the side of the line. Some priests spoke out against the sub-culture of the navvies, but others were brave enough to try and convert them to the Christian religion. In 'defence' of the navvies it may be said:

- They were, on occasions, exploited by the contractors who paid up to three-quarters of their wages in tokens (under the truck system). This forced the navvies to buy provisions (which were sometimes tampered with) from the contractor's shop.
- Working and living conditions were terrible – not many men could have stood them.
- They would receive no insurance or compensation if they were injured in carrying out their dangerous work.

Thus any criticism of the behaviour of the navvies should be put into the context of their working conditions.

12.10 WHY DID AMALGAMATIONS TAKE PLACE?

(a) The railway network was the product of the work of numerous individual companies each of which had obtained its Act of Parliament to build a stretch of line. Some companies like the London and South-Western were large concerns, but companies owning very short stretches of line were far more common. The network, therefore, had inbuilt problems. A long journey would involve travelling on lines belonging to different companies, thus entailing passengers to change carriages. In 1842 the Railway Clearing House was set up to deal with the problem of through travel. This enabled a through-ticket to be bought by the passenger so that he could travel on the lines of several companies. Greater efficiency followed if railway companies merged or amalgamated.

(b)   The first person to put amalgamation into practice on any real scale was George Hudson, a draper from York and a close friend of George Stephenson. In the space of a few years Hudson built a huge railway empire and was referred to as the 'Railway King'. In 1849 he was in charge of lines stretching from London to Bristol and through the Midlands via Sheffield to York and Newcastle. Hudson's first big amalgamation was that of the Midland railway with the Birmingham and Derby railway. Both companies had previously provided two different routes between Rugby and Derby. Hudson went on to buy enough shares to give him control of numerous other companies; he also vehemently opposed any scheme which was contrary to his own interest. He founded the North-Eastern railway centred on York, and in 1846 had 1000 miles (1600 kilometres) of railway under his wing. Hudson's financial dealings were put under scrutiny by a number of shareholders at a meeting of the Midland railway in 1849. Shortly afterwards Hudson resigned and an investigation was carried out. The outcome was that Hudson had 'indulged in fraudulent use of shareholders' money', one of his misdemeanours being the payment of dividends out of capital. Hudson fled to Paris owing shareholders thousands of pounds.

12.11   WHAT WAS THE ROLE OF THE GOVERNMENT IN THE GROWTH OF THE RAILWAY NETWORK?

(a)   The railways boom took place at a time when the doctrine of *laissez-faire* was held in high esteem. As with many other spheres of life, the government did not show any inclination to plan the growth of railways directly; its association with the railways was more one of supervision. As the network developed in a piecemeal fashion, numerous mistakes were made, but the right of individuals to compete freely in business was the dominant principle.

(b) William Gladstone (President of the Board of Trade 1843–5) was keen for the Government to have some control over the railway boom of the 1840s:

(i) He formed a railway board (within the Board of Trade) to co-ordinate all proposed railway schemes so that capital was not wasted having two rival routes between the same towns. Such co-ordination proved to be beyond the realms of possibility as the Board was inundated with so many 'proposals' between 1844 and 1847 that it literally could not cope with the administration. The railway board was allowed to lapse, leaving the Parliamentary Committees with the final say in railway affairs.

(ii) In 1844 Gladstone instigated the passing of the **Railways Act**. The Act stated that:

- The government would have the legal power to buy up railway companies after 21 years of existence, dating from 1844.
- 'Parliamentary Trains' should be introduced, whereby each company was obliged to run one third-class train per day on its line at a fare which did not exceed 1d (0.4p) per mile. This measure was intended to make railway travel possible for the labouring classes, but many companies ran their 'Parliamentary Trains' at inconvenient times.

(c) As the railway network grew, so did the problem of operating them safely (both locomotive brakes and signalling systems were inadequate to cope with the increase of railway traffic).

In 1846 an Act was passed which stated that Railway Companies were liable in the event of passengers being injured or killed in any accident.

As time went on it became clear that many railway companies paid insufficient attention to safety. As traffic increased so did accidents; 65 passengers were killed on the railways in 1865. It took a serious disaster in 1889 to press the government into decisive action. On 12 June a train carrying a Sunday School outing crashed at Armagh, killing 80 people and injuring over 250. This was the worst railway accident to date and in September 1889 *The Regulation of Railways Act* was passed which made block signalling, continuous brakes and interlocking points compulsory – thus making railways much safer.

(d) In 1846 The Gauge Act was passed. Parliament recognised that if companies were allowed to choose their own gauge, through traffic of passengers and freight would be chaotic. Gloucester Station illustrated what happened where a broad gauge (in this case Brunel's GWR) met the 4 feet 8.5 inch (1.5 m) gauge of the Midland company. This entailed passengers and freight changing trains. Brunel had argued that the broad gauge was safer and would permit faster speeds. The Gauge Act, however, stated that the standard gauge on the railway network was to be 4 feet 8.5 inches (1.5 metres). It was not until 1892 that the GWR was converted to this gauge.

(e)   Railway comfort

In the early days on the railways the comfort of passengers was not very high on the list of priorities. As the network increased, railway companies started to compete using passenger comfort as a yardstick of their standard of service. As the companies amalgamated, standards tended to become more unified.

Third class carriages were originally open to the elements. In 1872 the Midland railway set an example to the other companies by providing third class carriages on all of its trains.

First and second class carriages became more luxurious with upholstered seating and, from 1884, steam heating. In 1873 sleeping cars were adopted by the larger companies, and in 1879 the restaurant car was brought into use by the GWR. Other improvements included corridor trains and toilet provision.

12.12   WHAT WERE THE SOCIAL EFFECTS OF RAILWAY GROWTH?

(a)   The railways enabled all classes of people to be mobile. For the first time people could travel speedily over long distances; the growth of passenger travel was a phenomenon.

1838	5.4 million
1851	79.7 million
1870	336 million
1880	603 million
1890	817 million
1901	over 1100 million

The implications of this were that a labourer could move away from his home town or village seeking enhanced employment prospects. Travelling broadened the labourer's experience and brought him into contact with more people. Members of the middle and upper classes were now able to reside in the countryside and commute daily to work in cities such as London. A number of companies, following the example of the Great Eastern Company, ran special artisan's trains into the city in the morning and back in the evening. Cheap day excursions became a central feature of British social life. Weekend leisure habits changed as townspeople were able to travel into the countryside for walks and picnics. The British Almanac and Companion of 1852 said that 'the excursion trains of the Great Eastern were never before equalled either in numbers or magnitude'. It goes on to say that one GWR train from Bristol and Bath contained more than 5000 people. Thomas Cook was the first to see the potential of excursions, organising trips to the Great Exhibition of 1851 (his first excursion had run from Leicester to Loughborough in 1841). He then went on to organise Grand Railway Tours of France, Italy and Switzerland.

James Thorne writing in 1866 claimed that 'the cheap day excursions are . . . encouraged by railway directors, because they return an enormous profit at little additional cost'.

Such were the number of commuters converging on London by railway the streets became very congested. People still had to walk some distance to work from the station. This led to the building of the underground system. The Metropolitan Line was constructed on the 'cut and cover' method, linking Paddington to Farringdon Street. The first 'tube' was the City and South railway opened in 1890 powered by electricity.

(b) The growth of seaside resorts was also a product of the railways. The arrival of railways at coastal towns sparked off the rapid growth of the population making them into holiday resorts serving the closest industrial area. Kelly's Directory of 1899 hinted at the ways the railway had benefited Bournemouth:

'The London and South-West Railway Company's direct line, opened in 1888, reduced the distance from London to 107 and a half miles [172 Km] . . . the town has increased rapidly and contains many capacious and elegant mansions'.

As these resorts grew they provided facilities for the trippers and trade prospered.

Resort	Arrival of railway	Population		Area Serving
		1841	*1901*	
Brighton	1841	65 569	123 478	London
Weymouth	1857	7 708	11 970	West Midlands
Skegness	1873	300	2 200	East Midlands South Yorkshire

(c) Railways enabled news to be disseminated far more quickly. Newspapers were distributed from London to all parts of the country; the son of W. H. Smith saw the potential and established newspaper stands on all mainline stations. Railways speeded up the delivery of the mail aided by Rowland Hill's Penny Post in 1840. Special mail coaches were designed so that mail could be sorted en route (such a coach is superbly preserved at Didcot in Oxfordshire).

(d) Before the railways, time in Britain was not standardised, for example, Reading, west of London, was four minutes behind in time. With the growth of the railway network it was soon obvious that standardised time throughout the nation was a necessity for the successful compilation of timetables. This brought about the adoption of Greenwich Time in 1852 – all the country's clocks being set at the same time as London.

(e) Political propaganda was also spread by the railway. The Anti-Corn Law League sent its message and speakers via the railway in 1840s. Without the railway their task in putting over their argument to the workers would have been virtually impossible. Later in the century Gladstone introduced the practice of 'Whistle-Stop Tours' during his Mid-Lothian campaign of 1879.

   All in all, the railways brought the nation closer together – the first step in shrinking the work. The 'British Almanac' said 'the passenger traffic . . . stimulates the energies, widens the sphere of observation, [and] sharpen[s] the intelligence'.

12.13 WHAT WERE THE ECONOMIC EFFECTS OF THE RAILWAYS?

(a) The railways provided a large amount of employment. Initially a large army of navvies was kept busy during the 'hungry' 1840s constructing the lines; once the railways were established, employment was in the form of operational staff and those working in allied industries.

(b) Numerous industries were stimulated by the development of the railway network. The iron industry had to supply the tracks and the rolling-stock; not just for the home market but also for foreign railways. With the large-scale production of steel in the 1850s and 1860s, iron tracks became outmoded and were replaced. Steel rails were stronger and able to withstand greater pressure. The brick industry (around Bedford and Peterborough) had to expand to supply the railway contractors with the bricks to build viaducts and line tunnels.

(c) Railway engineering became a large industry and a number of 'railway' towns grew up – amongst them were Crewe, Swindon and Eastleigh. One excellent example of railways stimulating the growth of a town is Peterborough, which became important as a junction between the Midlands, East Anglia and the North-South lines. The population grew rapidly:

	Peterborough
Year	Population
1851	8 000
1871	18 000
1901	30 000

In 1853 the Great Northern Railway established large locomotive sheds at Peterborough. Close to the sheds the company built a township – New England to house their workers. As well as terraced housing the company provided a church, chapel, mechanics institute, public houses, schools and recreation grounds.

(d) The railways carried passengers in large numbers right from the start but it took some time before freight was carried in large amounts. The canals continued to be used until the Railway Clearing House was organised to facilitate through traffic. Coal and minerals were the two most important cargoes.

By the 1860s farmers were using the railways to transport livestock to market. Previously drovers had to drive the animals along the roads which was tedious and slow. Railways were quicker and, of course, the animals did not lose weight between leaving the farm and arriving at market. The British Almanac of 1864 even quotes statistics of the transport of animals for England and Wales as follows:

Horses	226 439
Cattle	2 123 833
Sheep	6 076 908
Pigs	1 270 561

British farmers benefited from the railways in other ways. New markets further afield were now in reach. As Britain became a nation of town-dwellers they could be easily supplied with fresh food from the countryside. Milk, vegetables, flowers and fresh meat were transported quickly by the railway. The fact that farmers could now supply towns some distance away meant that food prices were reduced (farmers living near towns lost their monopoly). Similarly, urban areas could be supplied with fresh fish from coastal ports such as Aberdeen, Hull, Grimsby and Lowestoft. The diet of the nation was consequently improved.

(e)   Railways encouraged people to invest in joint-stock companies. At one time 10 per cent of the nation's income was tied up in the railway network; this helped the growth of the London Stock Exchange. Eventually as the railways proved themselves, turnpike trusts, coaching companies, and canals, went into a gradual decline; they just could not compete with the speed of the railways.

12.14   CONCLUSION

The story of railway growth in Britain is a vast subject: there are many aspects mentioned in the above chapter which could be developed. The rapid mushrooming of the network illustrates the initiative of Victorian private enterprise. Despite the mistakes and frauds, the railways transformed the economic and social life of the nation. The story also threw up a number of determined individuals such as the Stephensons, Brunel, and the unknown navvies. On the other side of the argument, however, one is left to ponder what might have happened if the railways had been subject to greater government scrutiny; it probably would have meant the slow growth of the system which would in turn have retarded the process of industrialisation. Trevor May indicates the dilemma:

> Parliament was wedded to the Private Bill procedure, whereby each projected line was treated on its merits, and while this system undoubtedly spread the railways more rapidly than would otherwise have been the case, the result of virtually unrestricted private initiative was the absence of a nationally planned network.

QUESTIONS

1. **Objective 1**

Assess the role of George Stephenson in the growth of the railway network in the nineteenth century. You should consider the following:

- How far Stephenson was a product of his environment.
- Any personal qualities Stephenson had which allowed him to succeed.
- How far his career was decided by 'outside' factors.
- His overall importance.

(Total = 30 marks)

2. **Objective 3**

What do you think would have been the viewpoints of the following towards the coming of the railways?

(a) A clergyman
(b) A turnpike trust
(c) A canal company
(d) A landowner

(Total = 20 marks)

3. **Objective 1, 3 and 4**

Read the source below and then answer the questions:

> There was little government control. This helped lead to some duplication of routes, when competing companies built their own separate lines to link the same towns. There were different gauges, the Great Western only finally adopting the standard gauge in 1892.
>
> In 1844 the government of Sir Robert Peel finally passed an Act. This Railway Act laid down some safety regulations. It also included the famous clause which led to the 'Parliamentary Trains', making it possible for ordinary people to enjoy the benefits of railways.
>
> (Adapted from *The British Revolution 1750–1970* by M. Parker and D. Reid.)

(a) (i) Why did the Great Western use broad gauge until 1892?
   (ii) Describe the problems which resulted from this difference of gauge.
(b) The 1844 Railway Act 'laid down some safety regulations'. Why was it necessary to pass this Act?
(c) Explain as fully as you can the benefits brought to 'ordinary people', as stated in the second paragraph.
(d) (i) Using this passage *only*, describe the attitude of the government to the railways.
   (ii) How could you check whether the authors were correct in what they have written about the government's attitude?

(Total = 25 marks)
(Southern Examining Group)

4. **Objective 2**

(a) How important were railways to people living in the late nineteenth century?
(b) How important are railways to people living in the late twentieth century?

Your answer should be reasoned.   (20 marks)

5. **Objectives 3 and 4**

Study the following sources and then answer the questions:

Source A

The opening of the Stockton to Darlington railway in 1825 (courtesy of BBC Hulton Picture Library)

Source B

The Opening of the Stockton to Darlington Railway. September 27th 1825. The Stockton and Darlington railway was formally opened for the use of the public . . . The novelty of the scene, and the fineness of the day, had attracted an immense concourse of spectators, the fields on each side of the railway being literally covered with ladies and gentlemen on horseback, and pedestrians of all kinds . . . Tickets were distributed to the number of near 300, but such was the pressure and crowd, that both loaded and empty carriages were instantly filled with passengers. The signal being given; the engine started off . . . and such was its velocity that, in some parts, the speed was frequently 12 miles [19 km] an hour, and in one place 15 miles [24 km] an hour.
(John Sykes, *Local Records . . . of Northumberland and Durham 1866*)

Source C

An extract from a letter which appeared in *The Times* on Friday 3 January 1845.

RAILWAY GRIEVANCES

SIR, – We are now so completely at the mercy of the railway companies, that our only chance to is to make known our grievances through the public press . . . On Saturday last, the 28th December, I travelled by the Grand Junction train which should have reached Chester by ten minutes past 10 a.m. with the intention of going to Liverpool. Owing, however, to the weather we were behind our time, and when we arrived at Chester, the train for Birkenhead had left . . . instead of having waited until we came in . . . This was mishap the first.

I returned by the 4 p.m. train from Birkenhead to Chester. The train was an extremely heavy one, and when we were halfway through the tunnel we came to a stop . . . the whole train then began to move backwards . . . The confusion was extreme – guards and officials shouting and running about, ladies shrieking and gentlemen getting out . . . mishap the second . . .

Even if the Chester and Birkenhead Company have quarrelled with the Grand Junction, why should the public suffer? . . . All public support should be withdrawn from [these two companies],
Your obedient servant,
CIVILIS.
Whitchurch, Shropshire. Jan 1st.

Source D

The railway navvies (courtesy of Mansell Collection)

NAVVY IN HEAVY MARCHING ORDER.

'In 1845 there were 200 000 [navvies] working on about 3000 miles [4800 km] of new line. In the eighty years from 1822 onwards millions of navvies made 20 000 miles [32 000 km] of railways in Britain'. (Terry Coleman, *The Railway Navvies*, 1968)

Source E   Railway lines opened each year

1830	47 [75 km]
1835	40 [64 km]
1840	528 [845 km]
1846	634 [1029 km]
1848	1253 [2005 km]

(a) Study Source B. Why do you think such a large crowd attended the opening of the Stockton to Darlington railway?

(b) How far does Source A support Source B?

(c) According to Terry Coleman (Source D) the navvies were vital to the building of the railway network. Why, then, did many contemporaries fear them?

(d) Source C suggests that railway travel in the 1840s was hazardous. Source E shows that railway construction increased dramatically in the 1840s. How can this apparent contradiction be explained?

(Total = 30 marks)

6. **Objectives 1 and 3**

What problems might have faced a railway company in constructing and operating a railway line? You could consider:

● Raising capital.
● Opposition.
● Constructing the line.
● The daily operation of the line.
● Amalgamations.

Give specific examples wherever possible.

(20 marks)

THE DEVELOPMENT OF

SHIPPING

1800–1939

13.1 INTRODUCTION

As we have already seen, an industrial country needs an efficient system of transport to convey raw materials to the factories and finished products to market. In the nineteenth century Britain's economy stimulated the development of roads, canals and railways for internal transport. The import and export of goods, however, depended on ships and, predictably, the period 1800–1939 saw the gradual improvement of shipbuilding and design. This trend involved a change from wood to iron and steel as the main shipbuilding material, the adoption of steamships instead of sailing ships, and the production of sophisticated marine engines.

13.2 FROM WOOD TO STEEL

(a) Why was wood replaced by iron and steel as the main shipbuilding material?

Before the nineteenth century timber was the traditional shipbuilding material but this was to change gradually over a period of about 120 years; by 1900 iron and steel ships were more the norm. This transformation was inevitable given the circumstances at the time:

(i) By 1820 timber suitable for shipbuilding was becoming a very scarce commodity in Britain – much of it had to be imported from the Baltic.

(ii) Wood had disadvantages as a shipbuilding material. Ships could only be built up to a length of about 328 feet (100 metres) and to a weight of 1500 tonnes; any larger and they would just break up in heavy seas. In addition, there was a tendency for the hulls to go rotten after a time.

(iii) From the late eighteenth century the technology was available for ships to be built of iron following the development of puddling and rolling; by 1870 more ships were being constructed of iron than wood.

(iv) Three inventions in the mid-nineteenth century made the mass production of steel possible – Bessemer's 'Converter' (1856), Siemen's and Martin's 'Open Hearth' (1867) and Gilchrist-Thomas's 'Basic Processes' (1879).

(v) Iron and steel were both far superior to wood. They were stronger and facilitated the building of large ocean-going ships. Despite these advantages iron and steel were not immediately accepted by shipbuilders who feared that the metal would interfere with the functioning of the ship's compass and they stated that the metal would pollute cargoes, particularly foodstuffs.

(b) Which vessels, in particular, were important in the transformation from wood to iron and steel?

The answer is provided by the following diagram:

Year	Vessel	Comment
1747	*The Trial*	An iron barge built by John Wilkinson.
1821	*The Aaron Manby*	The vessel managed to sail across the Channel to Le Havre under the captaincy of Sir Charles Napier. She then served as a cargo vessel on the rivers of Eastern France.
1827	*Anglaria*	Built of iron by David Napier and employed as a river vessel on the Clyde.

1843	S.S.*Great Britain*	A major development in the use of iron, she was built by Brunel. She weighed about 3500 tonnes, the biggest iron ship constructed up to that date. In 1846 she was grounded off the coast of Ireland. It took eleven months to refloat her. Even after such a long time she had suffered no structural damage and illustrated the strength of iron.
1855	*Persia*	Constructed for Cunard by Robert Napier. An iron vessel with accommodation for 250 passengers.
1858	*Great Eastern*	The brainchild of Brunel. Even larger than S.S. *Great Britain* weighing over 19 000 tonnes. Although unsuccessful as a commercial liner she illustrated the suitability of iron as a shipbuilding material.
1881	*The Servia*	The first ocean-going liner to be built of steel, owned by the Cunard line. She was built on Clydeside and accommodated 1250 passengers. She showed steel to be a better shipbuilding material than iron.

13.3 THE DEVELOPMENT OF THE STEAMSHIP IN THE NINETEENTH CENTURY

(a) Who were the early pioneers of the steamship?

Although the steam-engine had been perfected in 1781 by James Watt, its application to shipping was relatively slow to come about.

(i) The first successful steamship to be constructed was William Symington's *Charlotte Dundas*. She had a Boulton and Watt engine driving paddle-wheels and, in 1804, managed to pull two heavy barges along the Forth-Clyde canal for a distance of 19 miles (30 kilometres).

(ii) One spectator watching the *Charlotte Dundas* in action was an American from Pennsylvania, Robert Fulton. He returned to America full of enthusiasm for the steamship and determined to build his own ship. Using a Boulton and Watt engine imported from Britain, he constructed *The Clermont* in 1807. The ship had two paddle-wheels and travelled a distance of 87.5 miles (140 kilometres) on the Hudson River.

(iii) Henry Bell, a Scotsman, designed *The Comet* in 1812. Based upon the ships of Symington and Fulton she was 16 metres long and successfully operated a ferry service on the River Clyde between Greenock and Glasgow. There were still doubts, however, about whether a steam ship would be able to negotiate a *long ocean* voyage.

(iv) These doubts appeared to be justified by the performance of the American vessel *The Savannah*. She managed to make the crossing over the Atlantic, taking $27\frac{1}{2}$ days, but relied mainly on the winds. Her steam-engines were used for only a period of 55 hours during the journey.

(b) What contribution did Isambard Kingdom Brunel make to the development of the steamship?

(i) At this point a breakthrough was required – it was necessary for someone to construct a steamship capable of making long journeys without the aid of sails. After building the Great Western Railway between London and Bristol, Brunel suggested to the company directors that they should build a steamship to carry passengers to New York; an ambitious scheme but one that appealed to them. The resulting vessel was the steamship *Great Western*, built of wood and driven by paddle-wheels; she was built at William Patterson's shipyard in Bristol to a length of 236 feet (72 metres) and a weight of 1300 tonnes. The *Great Western* was big enough to take on enough coal to make an Atlantic crossing with plenty to spare. However, the Great Western Company had a competitor. The British and American Steam Navigation Company was also anxious to stake a claim to the Atlantic route and decided to try to beat the *Great Western* to New York with *The Sirius*. She left

Cork on 4 April 1838 and arrived in New York on 22 April in a time of 18 days 10 hours, with her coal bunkers almost empty. The *Great Western* left Bristol on 8 April 1838 and reached New York on 23 April in a time of 15 days 5 hours and with plenty of coal left. This was a great 'propaganda' victory for the Great Western Company and between 1838 and 1846 their vessel crossed the Atlantic on 67 occasions.

(ii) In 1843 Brunel launched the S.S. *Great Britain*. This vessel was built of iron and was driven by a screw propeller (the invention of Francis Smith and John Ericson). The screw propeller was more powerful than paddles and enabled a vessel to cope better with heavy seas. In 1846 the *Great Britain* sailed from Liverpool to New York in 14 days 21 hours. After 1847 she was used on the Liverpool to Melbourne route, illustrating the excellence of the screw propeller.

(iii) In the meantime Brunel aimed to construct the largest steamship to date. Under the auspices of the Eastern Steam Navigation Company, work was started on the *Great Eastern*. She took three years to build and was dogged by misfortune from the start. At the launching at Millwall, in November 1857, she became stuck in the mud of the Thames; the slipway simply could not cope with a ship of such size. Eventually she was launched in January 1858. She was 700 feet (215 metres) long, about 19 000 tonnes in weight, and was powered by a combination of propeller, paddles and sails. Unfortunately, the enterprise took its toll on Brunel who died from paralysis in September 1859. The *Great Eastern* started service on the Atlantic route but her size made her commercially unviable; she was too coal-hungry and would not attract enough fare-paying passengers (she had accommodation for 4000 people). In the end she became an ocean cable-laying vessel before being scrapped in 1888.

(c) What was the importance of Samuel Cunard?

In the 1830s steamships plying the Atlantic had to carry so much coal that they had little room for passengers who would have brought in much-needed revenue. Profits could be made, however, by carrying mail, but who would secure the contract from the Admiralty?

(i) *Cunard (1787–1865)*, a Canadian, first came to Britain in 1838 to try to secure the mail-carrying contract in the face of competition from the St George Steam Packet Company and the Great Western Company. Cunard guaranteed the Admiralty that he would provide a twice-monthly service from Liverpool to Halifax, Boston and Quebec. As a result he was given the contract for a price of £55,000 per year. In 1839 he had four ships built by Robert Napier on the Clyde and established the British and North American Royal Mail Steam Packet Company. In 1840 the paddle steamer *Brittania* made the first Royal Mail crossing to North America in a time of 15 days. Cunard managed to keep the Admiralty contract by offering competitive prices that his rivals could not match.

(ii) In the mid-1860s Cunard started to carry large numbers of emigrants across the Atlantic. His success was derived from the fact that he placed great stress on a 'reliable service'. The Cunard line later was to have great success as a passenger-carrying organisation (see Section 13.8).

13.4 WHY WERE SAILING SHIPS ABLE TO COMPETE WITH STEAMSHIPS FOR SO LONG?

(a) It was not until the 1870s that steamships managed to gain the upper hand over the sailing ship. This was partly because of design improvements in sailing ships that took place between 1800 and 1840:

(i) In the early part of the nineteenth century the American shipbuilding yards led the world in the construction of sailing ships. They designed their ships with long, lean hulls and the fastest vessels were able to complete the eastbound journey across the Atlantic in about 23 days, making full use of the predominant westerly winds. The British shipbuilders did their best to emulate the American yards and they designed the 'Blackwall Frigates' which were capable of high speeds given favourable winds.

(ii) The fastest of all sailing ships were the 'Clippers'. These were first designed in America and the first clipper *The Rainbow* was launched in New York in 1845. Between 1850 and 1869 the clippers (so called because they 'clipped' the journey times) dominated the oceans. The American-built *Lightning* sailed from Boston to Liverpool in 14 days which matched the performance of any steamship. The clippers, however, were most effective on the long run to the Far East and Australia. On the outward-bound journey they sailed via the Cape of Good Hope and they returned via Cape Horn, thus utilising the westerly winds. The clippers brought wool from Australia and tea from China.

(iii)   The American Civil War of 1861–5 enabled the British to take the lead in the construction of clippers. By now the hulls were composite in design, having an iron frame covered with wood. In 1866 two British tea clippers, the *Ariel* and the *Taeping* raced each other to London from China; they arrived virtually neck and neck in 99 days.

(b) From 1870 a number of factors weakened the challenge of the sailing ship as can be deduced from the graph below:

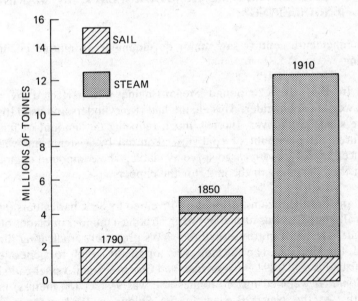

- Sailing ships were obviously dependent on the wind blowing. Fast speeds one day could be followed by days of calm.
- They were not really suitable for conveying passengers as they rolled about in heavy seas. Steamships, once established, afforded passengers a degree of luxury and comfort.

● Initially, sailing ships could carry more cargo than a steamship which needed vast amounts of coal, thus limiting cargo space. But after 1870 more powerful engines meant less coal was needed on board, thus releasing valuable space for cargo (see Section 13.5). Furthermore, coaling stations were established at convenient points on all the major shipping routes (Aden and Gibraltar were two).

● The opening of the Suez Canal in 1869 was the final nail in the coffin for the sailing ship. The canal, 165 kilometres long, linked the Red Sea to the Mediterranean Sea, thereby allowing steamships a short cut between Asia and Europe; there was no longer the need to sail round the Cape of Good Hope. The canal, however, was not suitable for sailing ships. They would have to be towed through the canal by steamships and, furthermore, the winds of the Mediterranean were not suitable for fast travel.

13.5 WHAT DEVELOPMENTS TOOK PLACE IN MARINE ENGINEERING?

The nineteenth century saw major developments in marine engineering:

(a) In 1854 the Compound Steam-Engine was perfected by a Glaswegian, John Elder. This engine had two cylinders and used the same steam twice over, thereby much reducing the amount of fuel required. The amount of coal now required by a steamship was reduced, making more cargo space available. The compound engine spelt the 'beginning of the end' for the clippers.

(b) In 1884 the Steam Turbine was invented by Sir Charles Parsons at Wallsend. This was turned by steam striking a number of blades on a shaft. The shaft in turn drove the ship's propeller, eradicating the need for pistons. The turbine was originally used to generate electricity but in 1894 Parsons installed one in a small vessel called *Turbinia*. It weighed just 40 tonnes and was 98 feet (30 metres) in length. At the Naval Review in the Solent in 1897 it made a spectacular appearance achieving a speed of 34 knots. Subsequently the Admiralty placed an order for a number of turbine-driven destroyers.

13.6 WHAT PART DID PARLIAMENT PLAY IN THE DEVELOPMENT OF SHIPPING?

Parliament took only a supervisory role; in keeping with the *laissez-faire* tradition, developments came about through the efforts of private firms and individuals. The legislation that was passed was concerned mainly with safety regulations.

(a) The *Merchant Shipping Act 1850* gave the Board of Trade the power to train ship's officers and to insist that they had to be fully qualified to work on board a ship. The Act also introduced a code of standards so that the crew was not exploited (for example, in their living quarters and food provision).

(b) Many shipping companies overloaded their ships in order to make large profits out of one journey. This sometimes resulted in the ship sinking and the owners claiming the insurance money. Sometimes old ships were deliberately overloaded so they sank; the insurance was again claimed. A Member of Parliament, Samuel Plimsoll (1824–98), introduced a bill into Parliament proposing that ships should have a line marked on their side which would disappear below the water line if the ship was overloaded, thus allowing the port authorities to detect any dishonest companies. Plimsoll's idea was adopted and enforced by the *Merchant Shipping Act 1876*. A loophole, however, was that the Act did not state where the line had to be placed on the ship's hull and owners could, therefore, sidestep the Act. This was eventually corrected in 1890.

(c) The *Merchant Shipping Act 1893* codified all previous legislation and laid down minimum requirements for lifeboat provision on ocean-going vessels.

13.7 WHAT EFFECTS DID THE STEAMSHIP HAVE ON THE BRITISH ECONOMY?

(a) British agriculture was one section of the economy which suffered from the advent of the steamship. From the 1880s large cargoes of North American grain were conveyed across the Atlantic at cheap rates, as well as frozen meat from the Antipodes. Such cargoes entered Britain free of duties and provided fierce competition for the domestic farmer. This was a contributory factor in the agricultural depression of 1875–1914 (see Section 23.5).

(b) In all other respects, however, the British economy benefited from the development of the steamship:

(i) Britain emerged as the world's premier shipbuilding country. New shipyards grew up on the wide estuaries of the Mersey, Clyde and Tyne at Birkenhead, Glasgow and Newcastle respectively. Barrow and Belfast also became important shipbuilding centres. Gradually the old yards in the south of England, originally located near to the timber supplies (for example, Buckler's Hard, Hampshire) were abandoned. The new shipbuilding centres were near to iron and coal supplies, and between 1880 and 1914 enjoyed tremendous prosperity and hardly had a foreign competitor.

(ii) As a result, shipbuilding became one of Britain's staple industries (along with coal, iron and steel, and textiles). Between 1910 and 1914 British yards built three-fifths of the world's ships.

(iii) Britain came to possess the world's largest mercantile marine, which by the end of the nineteenth century carried half the world's trade. Britain's large Empire and advantageous position for the Atlantic route also helped her to develop this business, bringing in much needed 'invisible earnings'.

(iv) With the growth of cargo and passenger traffic there was a corresponding growth in the size of British ports; new docks and harbours had to be constructed. Bristol and Liverpool, two ports which had been important in the Triangular Trade (see Section 20.2) of the eighteenth century, had new docks and warehouses built to cope with the increased business. Southampton (important for passengers), Glasgow and London also grew in importance.

(v) The advance in shipbuilding acted as a stimulant to the coal industry as the steamships required large amounts of coal. The South Wales coalfield, in particular, benefited. Cardiff and Swansea grew as coal-exporting ports, the coal being transported to the coaling stations around the world. Iron and steel was also in greater demand for shipbuilding. Apart from agriculture, the whole of the British economy profited from the steamship. In the words of W. H. B. Court 'the rapid growth of... shipbuilding did much to give a special shape to the national economy'.

13.8 THE AGE OF THE PASSENGER LINER

(a) By 1914 oil was being used as the fuel in some ships to produce the steam for the turbine; diesel fuel also became popular. Both these fuels were cleaner than coal and eradicated the need to replenish at the coaling stations.

(b) There were signs in the years immediately before the First World War that Britain's lead in shipbuilding was being threatened by America and Germany. Britain's response was to start building huge luxury liners powered by steam turbine engines:

(i) In 1907 Swan and Hunter's Yard at Wallsend built the *Mauretania* for the Cunard Line. She was a giant 800 feet (243 metres) long and capable of carrying 3000 passengers across the Atlantic in $4\frac{3}{4}$ days. Her weight was 31 488 tonnes and she held the Blue Riband (awarded to the fastest liner on the Atlantic route) between 1907 and 1929. Another liner, however, the *Titanic*, did not enjoy such a long career. She sank on her maiden voyage in April 1912 with a catastrophic loss of life.

(ii) In 1934 the Cunard Line launched the *Queen Mary* weighing 79 704 tonnes and she was followed in 1938, by the *Queen Elizabeth* (81 672 tonnes). This latter vessel was built by John Brown and Company on the Clyde and had accommodation for 2288 passengers. These purpose-built liners were the ultimate in luxury and gave years of excellent service.

13.9 CONCLUSION

The British shipping industry was a tower of strength in the economy between 1870 and 1914, providing jobs for thousands of workers; inherent in this strength was a deep reservoir of skills and expertise. The First World War, however, changed this picture. During the war Britain lost 16 million tonnes of shipping and then, after 1920, a slump hit the shipbuilding industry. Sidney Pollard reveals how in

1938 the tonnage launched in Britain's yards had dropped to 5 per cent of the 1920 level (which stood at 2 million tonnes) and adds a comment which gives some indication why the shipbuilding industry has never recovered, when he writes that 'in the mid 1930s . . . some British owners began to place their orders abroad'. This lost trade was never recovered.

QUESTIONS

1. **Objectives 1 and 2**

(a) What changes took place in the building and method of propulsion of ocean-going vessels during the nineteenth century? (12 marks)
(b) Why has the importance of the passenger liner declined in the twentieth century? (8 marks)

2. **Objective 2**

The design and method of propelling ships changed very little over many centuries up to 1800. From this date developments in shipping were much quicker and rapid progress was made. Why was this the case? (20 marks)

3. **Objectives 1 and 2**

Assess the role of Isambard Kingdom Brunel in the development of shipping in the nineteenth century. Consider:

● What made him 'tick'.
● Outside factors which enabled him to further his career.
● His overall importance. (20 marks)

4. **Objective 2**

How did the following events affect Britain and British shipping:

● The opening of the Suez Canal in 1869.
● The invention of refrigerated holds.
● The establishment of shipyards in Britain located on river estuaries? (20 marks)

5. **Objective 3**

As an Irish person emigrating to America in 1850 describe your voyage across the Atlantic Ocean. (20 marks)

6. **Objective 4**

Study the following sources and then answer the questions:

Source A

The 'Titanic' (courtesy of BBC Hulton Picture Library)

Source B   Reports from the Daily Mirror 16 April 1912.

EVERY ONE ON BOARD WORLD'S GREATEST LINER SAFE AFTER COLLISION WITH ICEBERG IN ATLANTIC OCEAN.

TITANIC'S WIRELESS SIGNAL BRINGS VESSELS TO SCENE.

46,000-Ton Ship, with 2,300 Abroad, in Peril.

EVERYONE SAFE.

Morning of Suspense Ends in Message of Relief.

PASSENGERS TAKEN OFF.

Helpless Giant Being Towed to Port by Allan Liner.

The White Star liner Titanic, the greatest ship the world has ever known, has met with disaster on her maiden voyage.

She left Southampton on Wednesday last and carried about 2,300 passengers and crew on board, with 3,400 sacks of mails.

On Sunday she came into collision with an iceberg, and immediately flashed out wireless messages for help.

Many steamers rushed to her aid, but her fate and that of the thousands on board remained in doubt on both sides of the Atlantic for many hours.

It was at length known that every soul was safe, and that the vessel itself was proceeding to Halifax (Nova Scotia), towed by the Allan liner Virginian.

All her passengers had by that time been taken aboard two of the liners that hurried to the scene in reply to the wireless message.

DRAMATIC TELEGRAMS OF DISASTER

So many and so conflicting were the reports that reached London yesterday concerning the fate of the Titanic that until detailed and definite tidings come to have it is difficult to establish much more than the one important and outstanding fact that—

Every man, woman and child on the great liner is safe.

PASSENGERS TRANSHIPPED

MONTREAL, April 15.—It is now confirmed here that the passengers of the Titanic have been safely transhipped to the Allan liner Parisian and the Cunarder Carpathia.

The Virginian is still towing the Titanic towards Halifax.—Exchange.

NO LIVES IN DANGER.

NEW YORK, April 15.—The White Star officials here state that the Virginian is standing by the Titanic and that there is no danger of loss of life.

A wireless telegraph message to Halifax states that all the passengers were safely taken of the Titanic at 3.30.

Mr Franklin, vice-president of the White Star Company, states that the Titanic is unsinkable. The fact that she was reported to have sunk several feet by the head was, he said, unimportant. She could go down many feet at the head as the result of water filling the forward compartments and yet remain afloat indefinitely.—Exchange.

Source C

The 'Titanic' of 46 000 tons, built at Belfast, with the newest
separate 'watertight' bulkhead construction, sank within three
hours of hitting an iceberg on her maiden voyage in 1913, with a
loss of 1500 lives. 'God himself could not sink this ship' one of her
passengers had been told at Southampton.
(*Britain 1851–1945* by Richards and Quick: Longmans, 1967)

(a) Is Source B a primary or a secondary source? Explain your
     answer.
(b) What does Source A tell us about the British shipbuilding
     industry in the early twentieth century?
(c) Does Source C support or contradict Source B?
(d) We now know that the *Titanic* actually did sink. Why does the
     Daily Mirror claim that this was not the case?
(e) Here we have sources which contain apparent inaccuracies.
     What conclusions can we draw from this?

(20 marks)

CHAPTER 14

FACTORY REFORM

14.1 INTRODUCTION: THE FACTORY SYSTEM

(a) What is meant by 'the factory system'?

The question is probably best answered by the diagram below:

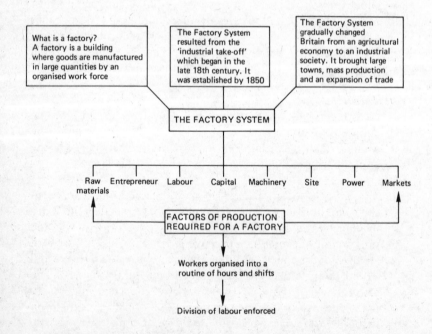

(b) What are the origins of the factory system in Britain?

The inventions adopted by the textile industry were instrumental in bringing about a factory-based economy in Britain. The very first factories were established in rural areas, where fast-flowing streams provided the power to drive the machinery. The factory buildings were modelled on the silk mill erected by the Lombe brothers in 1720 and Arkwright's Cromford Mill (1771). With the perfection of the steam-engine in the 1780s, textile factories became located on the coalfields. This, in turn, led to the growth of the large northern manufacturing towns such as Manchester and Leeds. According to Mitchell and Deane the number of people working in the cotton industry increased from 93 000 in 1806 to 439 000 in 1862.

14.2 WHO WERE THE 'FIRST GENERATION' OF FACTORY WORKERS?

About 75 per cent of the factory work force was made up of women and children. Women were cheaper to employ than men, whilst children were ideally suited to carrying out a number of tasks peculiar to spinning and weaving, for example, mending broken threads. Whilst conditions for adults were extremely harsh, the real scandal was the extensive use of child labour which came from two sources;

(i) *Parish apprentices* – The parish Poor Law authorities used the factories to off-load orphaned children. They would bind the children to a factory for a period of apprenticeship. The arrangement was that the factory-master would give the apprentices food and lodgings in return for his labour.

(ii) *Free labour* – Many parents in the manufacturing towns sent their children to work in the mills as they needed the extra income to run the household. In many factories it was the practice for the spinning operative to 'employ' his own team of child labourers. He would pay them out of his own wages and would extract full value of the children for his money. The children would have to sweep up, oil and clean machinery (whilst it was working) and mend broken threads. Accidents on the unfenced machines were frequent. Cobbett wrote, 'the notorious fact is that . . . children [are] decrepit and deformed, and thousands of them are slaughtered by consumption before the age of 16' (Political Register, 24 November 1824). Some contemporary observers, however, argued that the children's work was far from laborious and they received excellent training, humane treatment and useful incomes.

(iii) A point worthy of note is that child labour was not introduced by the factory system; it had been used for many years in the domestic system where the children were expected to carry out set tasks (for example, combing and carding) in the processing of raw wool or cotton.

14.3 WHAT DIFFICULTIES FACED THE FIRST GENERATION OF FACTORY-OWNERS? HOW DID THEY ENFORCE A CODE OF DISCIPLINE?

(a) Before making unqualified judgements about the cruelty of factory-masters it is necessary to bear in mind that they had a number of difficulties to overcome:

● They had no experience to draw on to help them manage their factories. Many were naïve in terms of man-management and therefore resorted to establishing a harsh regime to achieve discipline among the workers.
● The early mills were crudely constructed with inadequate ventilation and lighting. This probably did not aid the creation of a 'harmonious' working atmosphere.
● For a factory to function efficiently regular attendance and hours were essential as was a set of rules. This was not easy to enforce when the first generation of factory-workers had been brought up on the old traditions of the domestic system where irregular hours were accepted. The workers were liable to go absent without leave if there was a special occasion, for example, race-days. Many workers were also used to consuming alcohol whilst working.

(b)

(i) Apart from a minority of 'progressive' factory-owners (see Section 14.3(c)) harsh methods were usually adopted to produce a disciplined work force. Corporal punishment was used for children in many factories. The Report of the *Royal*

RULES
TO BE OBSERVED
By the Hands Employed in
THIS MILL.

RULE 1. All the Overlookers shall be on the premises first and last.

2. Any Person coming too late shall be fined as follows:—for 5 minutes 2d, 10 minutes 4d, and 15 minutes 6d, &c.

3. For any Bobbins found on the floor 1d for each Bobbin.

4. For single Drawing, Slubbing, or Roving 2d for each single end.

5. For Waste on the floor 2d.

6. For any Oil wasted or spilled on the floor 2d each offence, besides paying for the value of the Oil.

7. For any broken Bobbins, they shall be paid for according to their value, and if there is any difficulty in ascertaining the guilty party, the same shall be paid for by the whole using such Bobbins.

8. Any person neglecting to Oil at the proper times shall be fined 2d.

9. Any person leaving their Work and found Talking with any of the other workpeople shall be fined 2d for each offence.

10. For every Oath or insolent language, 3d for the first offence, and if repeated they shall be dismissed.

11. The Machinery shall be swept and cleaned down every meal time.

12. All persons in our employ shall serve Four Weeks' Notice before leaving their employ; but L. WHITAKER & SONS, shall and will turn any person off without notice being given.

13. If two persons are known to be in one Necessary together they shall be fined 3d each; and if any Man or Boy go into the Women's Necessary he shall be instantly dismissed.

14. Any person wilfully or negligently breaking the Machinery, damaging the Brushes, making too much Waste, &c., they shall pay for the same to its full value.

15. Any person hanging anything on the Gas Pendants will be fined 2d.

16. The Masters would recommend that all their workpeople Wash themselves every morning, but they shall Wash themselves at least twice every week, Monday Morning and Thursday morning; and any found not washed will be fined 3d for each offence.

17. The Grinders, Drawers, Slubbers and Rovers shall sweep at least eight times in the day as follows, in the Morning at 7½, 9½, 11 and 12; and in the Afternoon at 1½, 2½, 3½, 4½ and 5½ o'clock; and to notice the Board hung up, when the black side is turned that is the time to sweep, and only quarter of an hour will be allowed for sweeping. The Spinners shall sweep as follows, in the Morning at 7½, 10 and 12; in the Afternoon at 3 and 5½ o'clock. Any neglecting to sweep at the time will be fined 2d for each offence.

18. Any persons found Smoking on the premises will be instantly dismissed.

19. Any person found away from their usual place of work, except for necessary purposes, or Talking with any one out of their own Alley will be fined 2d for each offence.

20. Any person bringing dirty Bobbins will be fined 1d for each Bobbin.

21. Any person wilfully damaging this Notice will be dismissed.

The Overlookers are strictly enjoined to attend to these Rules, and they will be responsible to the Masters for the Workpeople observing them.

WATER-FOOT MILL, NEAR HASLINGDEN,
SEPTEMBER, 1851.

J. Read, Printer, and Bookbinder, Haslingden.

(courtesy of Helmsham History Society, Helmsham, Lancashire)

Commission on the Employment of Children published in 1833, contained statements such as 'the boys were often severely strapped', 'the overseer carries a strap' and 'the overseer struck him in the eye with his clenched fist'. Sheer fatigue was often a problem. Working anything up to 14 hours a days would result in small children literally falling asleep towards the end of the day. Overseers would resort to shaking or beating the offending child in order to keep him awake.

(ii) Some factory masters adopted a system of 'shaming' their employees. Offenders were made to carry cards round their necks. In some cases a heavy stone had to be worn around the neck: both practices served to humiliate the offender and was intended to 'shame' him enough so as not to repeat the offence.

(iii) With adults, in particular, a system of fines was rigorously enforced. The extract on page 197 from a list of Rules at Water-Foot Mill near Haslingden in 1851 shows the rigid discipline and fines payable for various offences.

(c) Progressive factory-owners

A minority of factory-owners adopted a more enlightened approach in running their factories. Into this category come Richard Arkwright, Robert Owen, Jedediah Strutt, the Ashworths of Bolton, Matthew Boulton, Benjamin Gott, Robert Peel Senior, John Fielden (author of *The Curse of the Factory system*, 1836) and Samuel Oldknow. Consideration of one of the these owners will illustrate their methods:

● *Robert Owen* (see diagram opposite for full details of his life) bought the New Lanark Mills from David Dale, his father-in-law, in 1800. He ran his factory based on incentives and rewards rather than fear and shame. He provided the factory children with free education and did not employ anyone under the age of 10. The working day was $10\frac{3}{4}$ hours with a total of $1\frac{1}{4}$ hours given for dinner and breakfast. Employing children at an earlier age would in Owen's opinion 'be injurious to the children and not beneficial to the employers'. Owen also provided housing and benefit funds. He was also keen to discourage drinking among his workers. A visitor to the New Lanark Mills commented that 'the [children] live with their parents in neat comfortable habitation, receiving wages for their labour . . . The regulations here to preserve health of body and mind, present a striking contrast to those of most large manufactories in this kingdom' (*Gentleman's Magazine*).

Owen's Theories	(1) People should be encouraged to work in harmony and co-operation, sharing the proceeds of their labour. (2) The environment was all-important in forming a person's character, particularly in the early years of life. A good education and caring parents were essential. 'Man's character is made for him and not by him.' (3) Capitalism resulted in greed and competition. Owen believed that people should have an equal share of wealth. (4) Owen's beliefs were set out in a book 'A New View of Society', published in 1813.
	ROBERT OWEN (1771–1858) 'The Founder of British Socialism'
How Owen attempted to put his theories into practice	(1) As a factory master. Owen was co-owner of the model NEW LANARK MILLS and was a 'progressive' in his approach. (See 14.3) (2) He established the London Co-operative Society (1824) which ran a number of co-operative shops – an idea later taken up the 'Rochdale Pioneers' (See 21.9) (3) Owen tried out his idea of people working together by establishing a community called 'New Harmony' in Indiana (USA) in 1825. The experiment failed. (4) In 1829 he established a Labour Exchange in London – a producer's co-operative (See 21.9) (5) Owen made an attempt to organise the labouring classes into one large trade union (the GNCTU) with the aim of overthrowing the capitalist society and establishing a Socialist country (See 21.2)
	'SOCIALISM' A system whereby 'the means of production . . .should be owned . . .by the people, everyone should be given an equal opportunity to develop his talents, and the wealth of the community should be fairly distributed' (FLORENCE ELLIOTT)

(d) Factories such as New Lanark tended to be in the minority; generally speaking, working conditions were appalling. Even at the time, observers were critical of such conditions. A Leeds surgeon, Charles Thackrah, saw the factory system producing 'a degenerative race, human beings stunted, enfeebled and depraved'. A Parliamentary Select Committee of 1816 also produced evidence to show how harsh the conditions were in many factories. G. A. Lee, a Manchester factory-owner, had a 76-hour working week and he notified the Committee with a degree of resolution that he had 'no intention to make any alteration whatever', even though he had heard the damning evidence given by other witnesses. Lee felt that shorter working hours 'would [not] improve the condition of the people'.

14.4 WHAT EARLY ATTEMPTS WERE MADE AT FACTORY LEGISLATION AND WHY WERE THEY UNSUCCESSFUL?

(a) In 1802 Robert Peel (Senior), the employer of 1000 apprentices, managed to have a measure passed called *The Health and Morals of Apprentices Act*. It dealt only with apprentices in textile mills and stated:

● Night work was forbidden.
● The hours of apprentices were limited to a maximum of 12 per day.
● Mills were to be adequately ventilated and kept clean by being white-washed every six months.
● Male and female apprentices were to have separate sleeping quarters.
● Apprentices were to be given basic schooling in reading, writing and arithmetic. They were also to be instructed in the Christian faith.
● Mills were to be inspected by the local Justices of the Peace (JPs) or their representatives.
● Mill-owners who were found ignoring the Act would be fined.

(b) In 1815 Peel and Robert Owen began a campaign for a further measure to be introduced and eventually the *Factory Act of 1819* was passed. It applied to cotton mills only and said:

● Children had to be at least nine before they could be employed.
● Young persons under 16 could work no more than 12 hours a day.

● Meal breaks were to be an hour for dinner and half an hour for breakfast.
● Mill-owners who contravened the Act would be fined.

(c) The Acts of 1802 and 1819 had inbuilt deficiencies which made them ineffective. The most serious of these was that they did not make any real provision for inspection. The JPs were often sympathetic to the factory-owners and in a number of cases possessed their own mill. The 1802 Act applied solely to apprentices, but this method of employment was on the decline; it did not apply to 'free labour'. There was also no method of birth registration so that it was difficult to prove the age of a child.

(d) It was difficult to get legislation passed at this time because of the dominant economic philosophy of *laissez-faire*, the idea that the state should not interfere with the rights of the individual (things should be 'left alone'). The factory-masters allied themselves to this philosophy which provided them with a powerful argument. Their beliefs were further backed up by the writings of the 'Political Economists' such as Adam Smith (*The Wealth of Nations*, 1776), Thomas Malthus (*Essay on the Principles of Population*, 1798) and David Ricardo (*Principles of Political Economy*, 1817). These men argued that the laws of economics (supply and demand) should be left alone and not tampered with by Parliament.

14.5 THE STRUGGLE TO REFORM THE FACTORIES

(a)

(i) *The origins of the 'ten hours movement'*

During the mid-1820s a small number of factory-masters in Yorkshire and Lancashire made it known that they believed that 10 hours should be the maximum working day. In September 1830 Richard Oastler, a land steward from Fixby Hall near Huddersfield, wrote a strongly worded letter to the *Leeds Mercury*. Oastler had been moved into action after discussing the issue of child labour with John Wood, a worsted manufacturer from Bradford. His letter was headed *Slavery in Yorkshire* and it had a resounding impact on public opinion. 'Gentlemen', he wrote, 'thousands of our fellow creatures and fellow subjects, both male and female . . . are at this moment existing in a state of slavery more horrid than are the victims of that hellish system "Colonial Slavery" '.

(ii) Throughout the textile areas of Lancashire and Yorkshire, *Short-Time Committees* were established. They consisted of factory operatives and were usually led by a local personality who sympathised with their cause. The 'Ten Hours Movement' began to gain more momentum during 1831. The movement contained both landowning Tories, and working-class Radicals – an unusual mixture. The 'cause' was so strong that in the words of Ursula R. Q. Henriques 'the political differences of Tory and Radical did not prevent their combining against the . . . social laissez-faire which constituted the gospel of cotton kings'. The Parliamentary leaders of the Ten Hours Movement were Michael Thomas Sadler, a Tory banker, Lord Shaftesbury, a Tory landowner, and John Fielden, a Radical factory-master. Other prominent members of the movement, apart from Oastler, included John Doherty (a Trade Unionist), Robert Owen (a Socialist), William Cobbett (a Radical) and George Bull (a Church of England parson).

(b) The Campaign for the 'Ten Hour Day' in the period 1831–3

(i) Sadler introduced a Bill in December 1831, proposing that textile workers between the ages of 9 and 18 could only work 10 hours a day. He also wanted factory-owners to keep time books and the workers to have age-certificates. The Whig Government decided that the whole matter should be investigated by a Parliamentary Select Committee under the Chairmanship of Sadler. The Committee examined 89 witnesses (including operatives) and the Report of the Minutes, published in August 1832, revealed the appalling conditions in the textile mills (see extracts in the Questions section). In December 1832 Sadler lost his seat in Parliament when he was defeated in an election at Leeds. For a time the movement lost some of its momentum.

(ii) George Bull then persuaded Lord Shaftesbury to take over Sadler's role in the Commons. Coming from the agricultural south, Shaftesbury knew nothing about the north of England, let alone the textile industry. However, he had been shocked by the Report of Sadler's Committee and he agreed to take on the position. Shaftesbury was a conscientious, determined man, and he made several visits to the north to see the conditions for himself. This served to deepen his convictions.

What motivated Shaftesbury? The answer probably lies in a combination of the following factors:

- Having experienced an unhappy childhood himself he was possibly able to empathise with the factory children.
- His deep-rooted 'evangelical' beliefs made him anxious to save the factory children from what he saw as a state of 'moral degradation'. He feared that their lack of education and depressing work environment would breed juvenile criminals.
- He may have believed that the factory reform issue would enable him to make a name for himself in national politics.

(iii) In February 1833 Shaftesbury re-introduced the Ten-Hours Bill into Parliament. Shaftesbury proposed that the minimum age for employment should be nine and that those aged between 9 and 18 should work a maximum of 10 hours a day (and 8 on Saturday).

(iv) There was great opposition to this Bill, with the factory-masters counter-attacking with a number of arguments:

- Foremost was the argument that the doctrine of *laissez-faire* dictated that Parliament had no right to interfere with private enterprise. Contracts of employment between master and worker had nothing to do with the legislature.
- Shorter working hours would result in less production, lower turnover and thus lower wages. Furthermore, prices would have to be increased and this would put the textile industry under threat from foreign imports.
- Factories had huge running overheads and the masters only began making a profit in the final hour of the day. Nassau Senior developed this argument in a letter to Parliament declaring 'if the hours of working were reduced by one hour a day, net profit would be destroyed . . . if they were reduced by an hour and a half, even gross profit would be destroyed'.
- Some masters claimed that working long hours kept children off the streets and prevented them leading a life of crime.
- Many masters were angry at the Report of Sadler's Committee and pointed out that it was biased and exaggerated.

(v) In early 1833 the government appointed a 'Royal Commission of Enquiry into the Employment of Children in Factories'. Within months a Report was published which concluded that there was 'a case . . . for the interference of the legislature on behalf of the children employed in factories'. The government now put forward its own Bill under the sponsorship of the leader of the House of Commons. Lord Althorp. The Bill became law in August 1833.

(vi) *Althorp's Factory Act 1833* had the following terms:

- No child under nine could be employed in a textile factory.
- Children between the ages of 9 and 13 were to work a maximum of 9 hours a day and 48 hours a week.
- Young persons between 13 and 18 were to work a maximum of 12 hours per day and 69 hours in a week.
- Night work for those under 18 was not permitted.
- Children up to the age of 13 'shall attend some school'.
- There were to be four inspectors to ensure that the terms of the Act were obeyed.

The Short-Time Committees were disappointed with the Act as it was not as far-reaching as they wanted. It had not achieved the ten-hour day for young people between 13 and 18 and adult hours remained unchanged. Shaftesbury was philosophic and realised that it was probably the best they could have achieved at that time. The Act was, in fact, a minor breakthrough:

- It applied to all textile mills, except lace-manufacturing.
- It firmly established the fact that *laissez-faire* was not sacrosanct and that Parliament was prepared to interfere with private enterprise.
- It provided a basis for the fight to be continued.
- It provided, at least, *some* independent inspectors.

(c) The struggle continued 1834–53

(i) For a time the issue of Factory Reform faded. Fielden and Oastler became involved in opposing the New Poor Law, whilst others devoted their energy to Chartism, which gained momentum after 1838. In the meantime, Shaftesbury was involved in reforming the conditions of the collieries (see Section 14.6).

In the early 1840s the agitation for Factory Reform picked up again. In 1844 Peel's Tory Government passed a Factory Act (*Graham's Act*) which had the following terms:

- Children between the age of 8 and 13 could work up to 12 hours per day.
- Young persons between 13 and 18 and women could work up to 12 hours per day.
- It was to be compulsory for textile machinery to be fenced.
- Cleaning of moving machinery was banned.

The Act still fell short of the Ten Hour Day but it was now easier to determine the exact age of a child since the *1836 Registration of Births Act*. The clause on fencing machinery was the result of pressure exerted by Leonard Horner and his team of factory inspectors.

(ii) By now *The Times* was lending its support to the Ten Hour Movement. In January 1846 Shaftesbury began to promote a new Ten Hours Bill. Progress, however, was halted as the Irish Potato Famine and the question of repealing the Corn Laws dominated the politics of the day. Shaftesbury, in fact, resigned his seat in Parliament over the matter. He was in favour of repealing the Corn Laws but as he represented a farming county (Dorset) he felt duty bound to resign; he was unable to put the views of the Dorset farmers who were desperate for the Corn Laws to be retained. John Fielden now took over the Parliamentary leadership of the Ten Hours Movement and he succeeded in getting a Ten Hour Bill passed in 1847 – *Fielden's Act*. It stated:

- As from 1 May 1848 the maximum length of the working day for young people under 18 was to be 10 hours and the working week was not to exceed 58 hours.
- The same regulations would also apply to women workers.

This appeared to be the culmination of the struggle but the factory owners found a loophole. The Act said nothing about the hours of men so, by working women and young people in relays, the factories could be kept operating for up to 14 or 15 hours per day. For example:

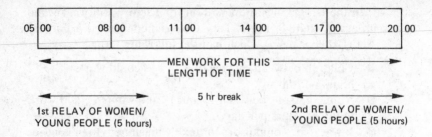

(iv) The system of relays was declared 'legal' under the terms of the 1847 Act by the Court of Exchequer. Shaftesbury was now back in Parliament as MP for Bath; he recognised that the only way out of the dilemma was to make a compromise. He declared that he would be in favour of working $10\frac{1}{2}$ hour days provided the hours were worked between 6.00 a.m. and 6 p.m. (6.00 a.m.–2.00 p.m. on Sundays). As a result Shaftesbury was dubbed a traitor to the Ten Hour Movement by many of the Short-Time Committees but Shaftesbury argued that there was no other way round the problem of relays. In 1850 (*Grey's Act*) was passed which stated that women and young persons were to work a maximum of $10\frac{1}{2}$ hours a day which had to be between the hours of 6.00 a.m. and 6.00 p.m.

(v) *Further legislation* – Gradually other factories and workshops were regulated:

● *The Lace Works Act (1861)* made the lace industry subject to the previous factory legislation.
● *Acts of 1860 and 1861* made bleaching and dyeing subject to Factory Law.
● *An Act of 1864* brought domestic fustian workers under the terms of factory legislation.
● *Disraeli's Factory Act (1878)* enforced a maximum 10-hour day ($56\frac{1}{2}$-hour week) in **all** factories and workshops with more than 50 employees.

14.6 WHY AND HOW WAS THE MINES ACT (1842) PASSED?

(a) Reference has already been made in chapter 6 to the working conditions in British coal-mines. Agitation for reform in this industry lagged behind – collieries did not figure in the brief of the Ten Hours

Movement. In 1840, after Shaftesbury had exerted considerable pressure, a Royal Commission was set up to investigate the working conditions of children in coal-mines and manufactories. The Commissioners, one of whom was Dr Southwood Smith, sent assistant commissioners to all the British coalfields. Their findings (Mines Report, 1842) revealed the full horror of the conditions:

- In Derbyshire children were employed at the age of 6 to carry coal in wooden baskets which contained up to 28 kilogrammes.
- In West Yorkshire Elizabeth Eggley (aged 16) said that 'we go to work between four and five in the morning . . . we come out at four, five or six at night'. The wages for this labour were ten shillings per week (50p).
- Where the seams of coal were thin children had to drag coal along on their hands and knees. George Dyson, a coal-miner owner told the sub-commission that:

  the lads hurry with a belt and chain on all fours. Thirty-eight years ago they had no belt and chain, but used to run along on one hand and feet, and pull the corves with the other hand; that was much worse for them.

- In the East of Scotland coal was taken out of the mine up a series of ladders by women laden down with baskets on their backs . . . 'It is not unfrequently . . . the load falls upon those females who are following'.
- In the West of Scotland the sub-commissioner commented on the work of the 'trappers' who were five or six years old.

  Their chief occupation is to open and shut doors . . . by which a current of air is kept in its proper course for the due ventilation of the . . . mine . . . The trapper has to sit often exposed to damp completely in the dark and in silence.

There were also many comments about the poor health of the mining community. Many miners suffered from 'stunted growth', 'deformities', 'crippled gait' and 'curvature of the spine'. Dr Thompson from Ayr observed that 'a collier at fifty generally has the appearance of a man ten years older than he is' and a sub-commissioner noted the 'emaciated' look of a man compared with the 'robust' and 'hearty' constitution of a farm labourer. Other diseases referred to were skin irritations, heart disease, ruptures, asthma, bronchitis and rheumatism.

(b) Southwood Smith had employed artists to go underground with the commissioners to make sketches of the workers. These drawings appeared in the Commissioners' Report which was published in 1842. They were graphic and immediate and public opinion was noticeably shocked. Shaftesbury drafted a Bill which went rapidly through the House of Commons, but it met opposition in the Lords. However, towards the end of 1842 the *Act to Prohibit the Employment of Women and Children in the Mines and Colliers* became law. It had the following clauses;

- Employment of women underground was illegal.
- Boys under 10 could no longer work underground.
- Parish apprentices between the ages of 10 and 18 could continue to work in mines.

There were no clauses relating to hours of work and inspection could only take place on the basis of checking the 'condition of the workers'. Ironically many women were annoyed that they could no longer earn much needed money. When they lost their jobs they received no 'redundancy' money. In 1850 a further Act widened the authority of colliery inspectors; they could now check on the state of the condition of the machinery.

14.7 THE CLIMBING BOYS

(a) Industrialisation brought a rapid increase in the size of towns; housing was rapidly built to accommodate the factory-workers. With coal-burning fires, chimneys needed to be regularly swept clean of soot. Perhaps the most scandalous use of child labour during this period was that of the 'climbing boys'. These youngsters were made to climb up the flues, many of which were irregular in shape, to clean them. There are many recorded cases of the dangers of such work:

- Children being badly burned.
- Bruised knees and elbows caused by the narrowness of the chimneys.
- Dust and soot being inhaled into the lungs.
- Suffocation.
- Some children became physically jammed in chimneys.

The Children's Employment Commission (1863) included several cases of climbing boys being killed.

(b) Attempts to stop the use of climbing boys had been made since 1785 when Jonas Hanway wrote a book entitled *The Sentimental History of the Chimney Sweepers in London and Westminster* in which he put forward proposals for abolishing the trade. Dickens also made pointed references to the climbing boys in *Oliver Twist* (many of the boys were obtained from the Parish overseers). Little (if any) notice was taken of attempts at legislation and in 1840 Lord Shaftesbury became involved in the campaign and an Act was passed prohibiting children from climbing chimneys. It was only partially successful. In the 1850s he unsuccessfully sponsored a number of Bills to deal with the problem. An Act was passed in 1864 but, again, it failed to have the desired effect, mainly because no one was given the powers to enforce the regulations. In 1863 the life of a climbing boy was depicted in *The Water Babies*, a novel written by Charles Kingsley. Finally in 1875 an Act was passed which required a chimney-sweep to obtain a licence annually from the police. If it was found that a chimney-sweep was employing climbing boys his licence was withdrawn.

14.8 CONCLUSION

The advance made in factory legislation had been made in the face of determined opposition from mill-owners, colliery-owners and political economists. That this was at least partially overcome was due in no small measure to individuals like Lord Shaftesbury, Michael Sadler, Robert Oastler, John Fielden and Robert Owen. On the positive side the following had been achieved:

- The principle that the state had responsibility to help and protect its citizens, thus weakening the doctrine of *laissez-faire*.
- Linked to this was the establishment of the Factory Inspectorate, the only certain way of enforcing the regulations.
- Gradually factory-masters came to realise that shorter working hours did not reduce their profits.

However, much remained to be done:

- There was no regulation of the so-called 'sweated industries'.
- Hours in collieries were still unlimited.

In attempting an assessment of factory legislation, one line of judgement would be to criticise the government's overall reluctance to interfere in the organisation of privately-owned industry. This argument, however, lacks conviction in that it really displays the strength of *laissez-faire*. Such deeply-rooted beliefs are extremely difficult to break down. A more realistic judgement would probably be that of Ursula R. Q. Henriques who argues that 'the factory acts provided a precedent for state action in a 'free' economy . . . which made subsequent interventions that much easier'.

QUESTIONS

1. **Objectives 1 and 3**

Lord Shaftesbury has been described as 'a member of the aristocracy who was more familiar with rural life and agriculture than the lives of the northern factory operatives'.

(a) Describe the contribution Shaftesbury made to the reform of factories and collieries.   (12 marks)
(b) In view of the quotation above what do you think motivated Shaftesbury to devote himself to the reform of working conditions in factories?   (8 marks)

2. **Objective 3**

You are a child who has experienced working in a coal-mine. The year is 1842 and you have been called to give evidence to the Parliamentary Commission investigating the conditions in collieries. Write an account of the interview.   (20 marks)

3. **Objective 3**

Read the following sources and then answer the questions:

Gets many a good beating.
The overseer carries a strap.
The overseer struck him in the eye with his clenched fist.
The common hours of labour were from six in the morning till half past eight at night.
(Evidence from the Commission on the Employment of Children in Factories 1833)

(a) You are a child working in one of the first cotton mills. Write an account of the conditions under which you work.

(b) As a factory-owner in 1820 write a letter to the *Leeds Mercury* justifying the treatment of your child labour.

(c) As a humanitarian anxious to obtain factory reform make out a case for the ten-hour day.

(Total = 30 marks)

4. **Objectives, 1, 3 and 4**

Study the following sources and then answer the questions:

Source A

When I was nine years old (in 1840) my work consisted of continually carrying about 40 pounds of clay upon my head from the clay heap to the table where the bricks were made. This I had to do without stopping for thirteen hours a day.

(Memories of a child labourer written down at the end of the nineteenth century)

Source B
A mid-nineteenth century engraving showing child labour in a brickyard (*courtesy of Mansell Collection*)

Source C

In 1841 S. R. Bosanquet conducted a survey of the poor. His findings were written up in a publication called *The Rights of the Poor*. This is an extract from his work:

> Elizabeth Whiting is a 40 year old widow with four young children . . . Does charring and brush-making . . . She pays three shillings a week rent [15p] . . [She] earned nothing this week; last week three shillings; the week before about 5s 8d. [28p] . . . She owes £1. 13s. [£1.65p] . . . [She] had five four-pound loaves this week from the parish.

(a) Is Source A a primary or secondary source? Explain.

(b) The 1834 Poor Law Amendment Act stated that an able-bodied person had to enter the workhouse to obtain poor relief. Source C reveals that Elizabeth Whiting received help from the parish whilst, apparently, living in her own house. How do you account for this?

(c) What do you think Elziabeth Whiting would have felt about sending her daughter, aged 10, to work in a brick-works like the one in Source B?

(Total = 25 marks)
(Adapted from the Southern Universities' Joint Board)

5. **Objective 4**

Study the two sources of evidence below and then answer the questions:

Source A (*courtesy of Mansell Collection*) first appeared as a contemporary print, 1836.

Source B first appeared in a publication called *Michael Armstrong – Factory Boy* written in 1840 by Frances Trollope:

(courtesy of Mansell Collection)

(a) What differences and similarities do you detect in the two sources?

(b) What leads you to believe that Source B is biased?

(c) 'Biased sources of evidence are of no use to the historian'. How far do you agree?

(d) What other sources would you require if you were to produce a balanced history of factory conditions in the early nineteenth century?

(Total = 20 marks)

6. **Objectives 1, 2, 3 and 4**

Study the sources below and then answer the questions.

Source A Taken from the Mines Report, 1842, pp. 436, 448, respectively (*courtesy of Ford Collection, Southampton University Library*)

Janet Cumming, eleven years old, bears coals, and says:
'I gang with the women at five and come up at five at night; work *all night* on Fridays, and come away at twelve in the day. I carry the large bits of coal from the wall-face to the pit-bottom, and the small pieces, called chows, in a creel. The weight is usually a hundred-weight; does not know how many pounds there are in a hundred-weight, but it is some weight to carry; it takes three journeys to fill a tub of four hundred-weight. The distance varies, as the work is not always on the same wall; sometimes 150 fathoms, whiles 250 fathoms. The roof is very low; I have to bend my back and legs, and the water comes frequently up to the calves of my legs. Has no liking for the work; father makes me like it. Never got hurt, but often obliged to scramble out of the pit when bad air was in'.

The following represents an older girl carrying coals.

Isabella Read, twelve years old:
'I am wrought with sister and brother; it is very sore work. Cannot say how many rakes, or journeys, I make from pit-bottom to wall-face and back, thinks about thirty or twenty-five on the average; distance varies from 100 to 250 fathoms. I carry a hundred-weight and a quarter on my back, and am frequently in water up to the calves of my legs. When first down, fell frequently asleep while waiting for coal, from heat and fatigue. I do not like the work, nor do the lassies, but they are made to like it.' When the weather is warm, there is difficulty in breathing, and frequently the lights go out.'

216

(courtesy of the Ford Collection, University of Southampton)

Source B

The floors of the cottages inhabited by colliers are composed generally of beaten earth . . . The bedstead is generally covered with dust, and with innumerable fly-marks. In summer, bugs in multitudes may be seen, more, especially at night, when the light of a candle is suddenly thrown upon the bedstead. The odour of these apartments is most offensive and sickening, from the long continued presence of human impurities.

(Parliamentary Papers 1842. Quoted in *Human Documents of the Industrial Revolution* by E. Royston Pike)

Source C

328.LANCASHIRE AND CHESHIRE. The work of a trapper. This occupation is one of the most pitiable in a coal-pit, from its extreme monotony. Exertion there is none, nor labour, further than is requisite to open and shut a door. As these little fellows are always the youngest in the pits. I have generally found them very shy, and they have never anything to say for themselves. The whole time is spent in sitting in the dark for twelve hours, and opening and shutting a door to allow the waggoners to pass. Were it not for the passing and repaying of the waggons it would be equal to solitary confinement of the worst order.

330. but far the greater number of children and persons employed in coal-mines are engaged in propelling and drawing tubs laden with coal, from the face to the pit-eye, or the main levels in those pits where they have horses. This is done by placing the hands on the back of the waggon, and propelling it forward with as great velocity as the inclination of the mine, the state of the road, and the strength of the waggoner admit of.

Agnes Kerr, fifteen years old, coal-bearer, dryden Colliery: 'Was nine years old when commenced carrying coals; carry father's coal; make eighteen to twenty journeys a day; a journey to and fro is about 200 to 250 fathoms; have to ascend and descend many ladders: can carry $1\frac{1}{2}$ cwt.

(Mines Report, 1842)

(a) Why did early nineteenth-century society accept conditions such as the ones described in the sources? (5 marks)

(b) Why was nothing done about reforming these conditions for so long? (5 marks)

(c) Why did Parliament eventually pass the 1842 Mines Act? (5 marks)

(d) Take each source in turn and describe how the 1842 Mines Act would have changed the conditions described. (5 marks)

SOCIAL AND ECONOMIC CONDITIONS IN BRITAIN 1793–1822

15.1 INTRODUCTION: BACKGROUND

In 1789 the French lower and middle classes, dissatisfied with their conditions and the absolute rule of the monarch, rose in rebellion. France was plunged into chaos which culminated in the King, Louis XVI, being guillotined by his own subjects in 1793; this was the French Revolution. European countries with monarchies were horrified at these events and declared war on France, including Britain. Eventually, Napoleon, the French Emperor, was beaten in the Battle of Waterloo in 1815. Thus, Britain was at war with France for a period of 22 years, with a brief gap of six months' peace in 1801–2. Although no fighting took place on British soil, the war inevitably had economic and social effects for the nation. The immediate post-war years between 1815 and 1822 brought a period of 'distress and discontent' and growing demands for the reform of Parliament.

15.2 WHAT WERE THE ECONOMIC AND SOCIAL EFFECTS OF THE FRENCH WARS (1793–1815)?

(a) Finance

(i) *Paying for the war*: As well as having to finance her own war effort, Britain lent out £57 million to enable her allies to maintain the fight against Napoleon. Initially, William Pitt (Prime Minister in 1793) raised extra funds by borrowing from the Bank of England, but later he raised money by increasing indirect (purchase) tax on everyday consumer items and, in 1799, income tax. This was set at a rate of two shillings (10p) in the £ for everyone who earned over £200 per year. By 1815 this tax was raising £15 million for the Exchequer, one-third of the government's annual income.

(ii) *Inflation*: Prices showed a tendency to increase, as normal everyday commodities were in short supply. In particular, wheat prices spiralled, pushing up the cost of bread. The situation was made worse in 1797 when the government stopped the banks paying out gold coins (cash). This in turn, meant that the banks printed more paper money to compensate. Too much paper money in circulation resulted in inflation (see also Section 23.2(a)).

(iii) At the end of the war the *National Debt* stood at £876 million (it had amounted to £240 million in 1793). The country suffered as a result of having to pay off large amounts of interest each year.

(b) Trade

(i) In 1805 Nelson's fleet defeated the French Navy in the Battle of Trafalgar, thus giving the British control of the high seas. Napoleon, realising a direct invasion of Britain was no longer feasible, embarked upon a policy of economic warfare in the hope of starving the British into surrender. This policy was implemented by the Berlin Decree (1806) and Milan Decree (1807), otherwise known as the *Continental System*. Under this policy:

● France and her allies would refuse to import British products.
● British vessels were banned from any country under the control of the French government.

Britain's reply was to issue 'Orders in Council' in 1807 which imposed a complete blockade on France and those countries co-operating with Napoleon. Ships taking vital goods into Napoleonic Europe were intercepted and the cargoes confiscated. As Britain's Navy was supreme, the blockade proved to be successful, although it did lead to war with the USA (1812–14) as the Americans objected to their ships being intercepted by the British Navy.

(ii) The impact of his economic warfare was as follows:

- The war with America meant a shortage of raw cotton for the Lancashire factories.
- The worst years for trade were 1810–12. Factories closed or went on short time causing widespread unemployment (Luddism was at its height – see chapter 5).

(c) Industry

(i) Some industries expanded during the war:

- The chemical industry had to supply explosives.
- Shipbuilding was boosted with increased orders from the Navy.
- The iron industry had to supply the demand for cannons, armaments, chains and anchors.
- The woollen industry benefited by obtaining lucrative service contracts for uniforms and bedding.
- More steam-engines were needed as a result of the boom in the iron and woollen industries.

(ii) The cotton industry did not particularly benefit from the war, and in fact suffered a setback in 1813–14 because of the difficulty in obtaining raw material. The pottery industry lost much of its European market and underwent a war-time recession.

(d) Agriculture

The home farmers experienced a period of prosperity (see Section 23.2) whilst agricultural labourers suffered from the high prices and, from 1795, were subjected to the Speenhamland System (see Section 16.3).

(e) Public opinion

(i) The French Revolution reverberated around Europe and stimulated many authors to publish books and pamphlets offering their opinion.In 1790 Edmund Burke wrote *Reflections on the Revolution in France* in which he expressed his 'disgust and horror'. Burke feared that the French Revolution would lead to an attack on the institution of Parliament. Tom Paine viewed the Revolution differently. In 1791 he published *The Rights of Man* in which he stated that he thought the French Revolution had struck a blow for the right of the ordinary people to rule themselves. Paine forecast that such democracy would lead to a wide range of social legislation (for example, pensions). Corresponding Societies were founded to communicate with the revolutionaries in France (the most prominent was the London Corresponding Society under the leadership of Thomas Hardy).

(ii) After the execution of Louis XVI and the declaration of war against France, attitudes changed, and the government became nervous at the thought of revolutionary ideas penetrating British society. It, therefore, responded with a number of **repressive measures**:

- Corresponding Societies became targets of suspicion and were either disbanded or forced to operate in secret.
- In 1795 it became illegal to organise meetings of over 50 people.
- In order to 'gag' the popular press the stamp duty (a tax) was raised on political broadsheets making them too expensive to enjoy a wide circulation.
- In 1799 and 1800 the Combination Laws stopped Trade Union activity (see chapter 21).

15.3 WHAT CAUSED THE DISTRESS AND DISCONTENT AMONG THE LABOURING CLASSES IMMEDIATELY AFTER THE FRENCH WARS IN THE PERIOD 1815–22?

These years saw a great deal of suffering among all sections of society (see section 23.2 for the hardship encountered by farmers) but the labouring classes had the hardest time for a number of interrelated reasons:

(a) Unemployment was high in both urban and rural areas

(i) The return of 250 000 servicemen from the war. The government made plans to stagger the demobilisation of troops which were unsuccessful, and as a result, they saturated the labour market *en masse*.

(ii) There was a trade recession after the wars with the demand for British goods in decline. European countries which had been involved in the war entered a period of austerity in an effort to stabilise their war-exhausted economies. Furthermore, woollen manufacturers and ironmasters no longer had to supply the army with their products.

(iii) Agricultural labourers and the hand-loom weavers were particularly hard hit. The decline of the small farmer meant redundancies in the countryside and the weavers had to compete against the increasing adoption of the power loom.

(b) High taxation also affected the labouring classes

(i) The Corn Laws, reintroduced in 1815, tended to keep the price of bread higher than it might have been had foreign imports been allowed into the country.

(ii) The government abolished the unpopular income tax in 1816. To compensate, purchase tax was increased and this hit the labourers with low wages more than the upper classes (see Section 23.3(b)).

(c) Exploitation of labour

Even those labourers in employment found life hard:

● Factory discipline was extremely harsh and the hours were long. No effective Factory Act had been passed at this time (see chapter 14).
● Agricultural labourers in work still had to put up with the humiliation of the Speenhamland System (see Section 16.3) which continued in force until 1834.

15.4 IN WHAT WAYS WAS THE PARLIAMENTARY SYSTEM OUTDATED?

By 1815 Parliament had become unbalanced in its composition and was generally unrepresentative of the population. The electoral system had originated during the Middle Ages and had not changed in unison with the process of industrialisation.

(a) Parliament was dominated by the landowning classes who were anxious to protect their own interests, hence the passing of the Corn Laws in 1815.

(b) The right to vote was a privilege afforded to just 3 per cent of the population, mainly from the upper and middle classes. No working man had the franchise and, therefore, could not use his vote as a protest.

(c) The growing industrial towns in the north of England, for example, Manchester, Leeds, Bradford, Sheffield, had no seats in Parliament.

(d) The agricultural south, with a smaller population than the north, had more than half the total number of MPs in the House of Commons. The south was, therefore, over-represented. Other anomalies included the fact that the largest and smallest counties in England (Yorkshire and Rutland) both had the same representation, that is, two MPs. Also the southern counties of Hampshire, Wiltshire, Dorset, Devon and Cornwall collectively had more MPs than the whole of Scotland.

(e) Elections were a farce. Votes were bought and sold on the 'open market'; a voter sold his vote to the candidate bidding the highest amount of money. As voting was not carried out by a secret ballot, candidates could 'check' that voters had kept to their word. Sometimes voters were threatened with physical violence.

(f) Some boroughs (towns) were owned by one man. He instructed his tenants who to vote for, putting them under the threat of eviction. Such boroughs were called 'pocket boroughs' as the voters were 'in the pocket' of the landowner.

(g) There were also a number of 'rotten boroughs'. These were towns which had been prosperous in the Middle Ages but, by 1815, had declined so much that hardly anyone lived there, yet they retained their representation in Parliament. One example was Dunwich in Suffolk. It had once been a thriving coastal town but gradually over the decades it had 'disappeared' into the North Sea due to the erosion of the cliffs; it still retained two MPs.

15.5 WHO WERE THE RADICALS AND WHY WERE THEY PROMINENT IN THE PERIOD 1815–22?

(a) Given the state of affairs described above, a number of men campaigned for the reform of Parliament. These men were called 'radicals' (they wanted to get at the root of the problem) and, rather than being a homogenous political party, they consisted of a variety of individuals and groups who operated independently of each other. In the period 1815–22 the campaign for reform became intensive, with the radicals using the distressed conditions as a means of pushing their ideas. R. J. White argues that they 'harnessed economic discontent to the cause of political reform'.

The radicals, in general, did not favour violence, and concentrated instead on persuading people to petition Parliament, and addressing mass-meetings. According to the *Northern Liberator*, the radicals were 'for democracy . . . universal suffrage . . . and vote by ballot'.

(b) Individuals included:

(i) *Henry Hunt (1773–1835)* gained a reputation for his powerful public speaking. He was nick-named 'The Orator' and was prominent at Spa Fields in 1816 and St Peter's Fields in 1819.

(ii) *William Cobbett (1763–1832)* favoured parliamentary reform using his weekly *Political Register* (started in 1802) to voice his point of view. He also published *Rural Rides* which described rural England in this period. The descriptions were interspersed with satirical comments attacking the authorities of the day.

(iii) *Samuel Bamford (1788–1872)* wished to see an improvement in the living conditions of the labourers. He published *Passages in the Life of a Radical*.

(iv) *John Wade*, the author of *The Black Book*, which attacked the electoral system as having 'no rational principle of either population, intelligence or property'.

(c) Radical clubs

(i) *The London Hampden Club* was established in 1812 by Major John Cartwright (1740–1824) and Sir Francis Burdett (1770–1864) with the objective of campaigning for the reform of Parliament by means of peaceful methods. Similar clubs were established outside London.

(ii) *The Spencean Society*: The Spenceans were disciples of a bookseller, Thomas Spence (1750–1814). His main platform was that all farmland should be owned by the parish. The farmers would pay a rent, part of which would go to the central exchequer. Spence maintained that this 'single tax' would be sufficient to finance the nation's spending.

(iii) *The Westminster Committee*: In 1807, Burdett became the MP for Westminster and he sat in the House of Commons with a small group of radicals who dubbed themselves 'The Westminster Committee'.

(iv) *The Philosophic Radicals* were followers of Jeremy Bentham and J. S. Mill. They wanted the secret ballot and votes for all men over the age of 21. J. S. Mill published an essay 'On Government' which echoed the views of Bentham. In Parliament the philosophic radicals were supported by Burdett. From this base developed the philosophy of Utilitarianism or Benthamism (see chapter 16).

15.6 WHAT ACTION DID THE LABOURING CLASSES TAKE TO PROTEST AGAINST THEIR DISTRESSED CONDITION?

(a) The Ely and Littleport riots (1816) (see Section 23.3(c)).

(b) The Spa Fields riots 1816

In an atmosphere of unemployment and trade recession the Spencean Society and Hampden Club organised a meeting at Spa Fields for 15 November 1816. The crowd heard an address by Hunt in which he called for the lowering of taxes and the reform of Parliament. Subsequently, Hunt attempted to deliver a petition to the Prince Regent but he was rebuffed by the authorities. A second rally was called for 2 December 1816 to discuss the petition. Unfortunately this meeting became violent when a group broke into shops and marched on the Tower of London. The rioters were soon brought under control and the main instigators arrested. The incident was viewed with disgust by the majority of radicals as it was a breach of their 'non-violence' policy.

(c)   The march of the Blanketeers

The early months of 1817 were particularly hard. A group of industrial workers decided to march to London from Manchester to petition the Prince Regent requesting him to do something to improve conditions. On the appointed day, 10 March, the military turned back most of the marchers after only a short distance. The term 'Blanketeers' was derived from the fact that the marchers carried blankets to bed down *en route* to London.

(d)   The Derbyshire Rising (or Pentrich Revolution) 1817

(i)   In the Midlands an *agent provocateur* named W. J. Richards (with the pseudonymn 'Oliver') spread stories that the government in London was about to fall the victim of an armed rising.

In the East Derbyshire villages of Pentrich and South Wingfield the workers felt encouraged enough to plan a march on Nottingham Castle from where they would journey south to the capital. The marchers were led by Jeremiah Brandeth and consisted of stockingers, quarrymen and ironworkers.

(ii)   The march, numbering about 250 men, began on the evening of 9 June 1817 in wet, miserable weather. They did not get very far as, on the outskirts of Nottingham, they were intercepted by a small patrol of soldiers. Most of the men fled but a number of arrests were made. The authorities, informed by Oliver, had known all the time. Brandeth and two accomplices, Isaac Ludlam and William Turner, were publicly hanged outside Derby jail; 14 other men were transported.

(e)   The 'Peterloo Massacre' – August 1819

(i)   A mass meeting was arranged for Monday 16 August 1819, to take place on a large open area called St Peter's Place, Manchester. *The Times* of 19 August 1819 carried a vivid report of the event. A crowd of approximately 80,000 assembled, including women and children; many had travelled into Manchester from the outlying villages. A number of banners were carried with slogans such as 'Vote By Ballot' 'Annual Parliaments', 'No Corn Laws' in evidence. There was no hint of violence and the crowd was in good humour.

At approximately 1.30 p.m. Orator Hunt arrived to address the meeting. The National Anthem was played and the crowd settled to listen to Hunt's speech. Within a few minutes the

Yeomanry rode through the crowd, surrounding the platform and arrested Hunt. The Orator did not resist and was led off to face the magistrates. After this the Yeomanry rode through the crowd with sabres drawn; in the resulting mayhem 11 people were killed and over 400 were injured, some sustaining fractured skulls.

(ii) *The Times*, the mouthpiece of the ruling aristocracy, condemed the events complaining that a number

> of the King's unnamed subjects have been sabred by a body of cavalry in the streets of a town of which most of them were inhabitants, and in the presence of those magistrates whose sworn duty it is to protect and preserve the life of the meanest Englishman.

The newspaper also conceded that the actions of the authorities were unjustified in view of the fact that the meeting was not an unlawful assembly. The authorities had, therefore, overreacted.

(iii) The incident was quickly given the title of 'Peterloo', which rekindled the image of the Battle of Waterloo. Its immediate effect was to polarise opinion; the radicals closed ranks even more determined to campaign for parliamentary reform whilst the government quickly passed further repressive measures to make such large gatherings illegal (part of the Six Acts, see Section 15.7(c)).

Public indignation at the massacre was high and the broadside writers of the popular press had a field-day satirising Lord Liverpool's government.

(f) The Cato Street conspiracy 1820

In the loft of a house in Cato Street London, a group of men led by Aruthur Thistlewood hatched a plot to kill all the members of the Tory Cabinet whilst they dined at the Earl of Harrowby's residence in Grosvenor Square. They planned to establish a democratic republic.

Unfortunately for them, one of their number was an *agent provocateur* named George Edwards; he fed information to the Home Secretary. On 23 February 1820 the Cato Street house was raided by a group of Bow Street Runners and the conspirators were arrested.

Five of the men (including Thistlewood) were executed and the other six were transported.

(g) 'The Radical War' in Scotland 1820

In the Glasgow area there were rumours that the country was on the brink of a revolution, most probably originating from *agent provocateurs*. In an atmosphere of unemployment a number of men took the bait and decided to attack the Carron Ironworks. Troops stopped the march and arrested the ringleaders. As a result 2 rebels were executed and 18 transported.

15.7 WHAT MEASURES DID THE GOVERNMENT TAKE TO DEAL WITH THE DISTURBANCES?

The Tory government, under Lord Liverpool, took a number of repressive measures:

(a) The suspension of habeas corpus 1817–18

'Habeas corpus' means 'let us have the body'. When in operation suspects in the custody of the magistrates had to be charged and brought to trial within a reasonable time span. With this law suspended it meant that subjects could be held indefinitely without a trial. The aim was to take trouble-makers out of circulation.

(b) The Seditious Meetings Act 1817

This outlawed meetings exceeding 50 people unless a minimum of seven ratepayers inserted a signed advertisement in a local paper. Rate-payers were likely to be middle-class and not inclined to 'revolutionary' behaviour.

(c) The Six Acts 1819

Passed in December 1819, they were a response to 'Peterloo'. Collectively, they forbade the possession of arms, banned military training and prevented the spread of 'seditious literature'. All protest – peaceful or not – was seen as a threat to the government.

15.8 WHY DID THE GOVERNMENT ADOPT A REPRESSIVE ATTITUDE?

A number of possible explanations have been put forward:

(a) A Report of a House of Commons Secret Committee 'on the disturbed state of the country' in February 1817, stated that the 'labouring . . . classes of the community are at present involved to induce . . . a total overthrow of all existing establishments'. There appears to be some justification to support the view that the government feared a 'French' type revolution in Britain. Hence they wished to put down marches and protests before they escalated.

(b) The government did not understand the distress suffered by the labouring classes. Most of the Cabinet had no idea of the life and conditions of a northern industrial worker. They were located in the South of England and did not have sympathy for the industrial classes. Furthermore, a number of Tory politicians believed that providence dictated the conditions of the poor, their lives were pre-ordained by God and could not be changed. This attitude was also reflected within the Church of England where many clergymen did not encourage the poor to attend church fearing that their 'fleas and vermin' would drive away the pew-renting upper classes.

(c) Even if the government had empathised with the labouring classes, they would probably have been unable to help them. One way of reducing the protests would have been to remove the causes of economic distress; they did not have the knowledge to do this.

(d) Many government ministers including Lord Sidmouth and Lord Eldon (the Lord Chancellor) felt their privileged position threatened. There was no regular police force and the maintenance of law and order depended on county Lord Lieutenants and the magistrates. Hence, they passed measures which strengthened the powers of these authorities.

(e) There was also a school of thought believing that demands for parliamentary reform had to be repressed in the country's interest. *The Quarterly Review* stressed that 'the present system had proved itself to be the best which ever stood the test of experience, and . . . [under it] the nation had attained . . . the highest degree of glory, prosperity, wealth and liberty'.

15.9 WAS BRITAIN CLOSE TO REVOLUTION IN THIS PERIOD?

The word 'revolution' may be interpreted as a series of violent events which culminates with the system of government being overthrown and replaced by an alternative government. It is possible to justify the opinion that revolution, in this sense, was never a serious threat between 1816 and 1820, even if some of the ruling class feared this.

(a) The French Revolution had involved all social classes wanting to see Louis XVI overthrown, in Britain only the labouring classes were protesting.

(b) The radicals only wanted to see reform, not the overthrow of the system. They wanted to participate in government policies and the radical leaders, Hunt, Cobbett, Place, Burdett were not violent and did not wish to see a revolution.

(c) The government also kept its nerve. There was never a hint that they had lost control and they maintained military support.

(d) The protests and marches were localised and there was no 'national leader' to draw the strands of protest together. The radical groups never merged.

(e) There is no evidence to suggest that Lord Liverpool was over-concerned about the disturbances. He was preoccupied by foreign policy in the aftermath of the defeat of France.

15.10 CONCLUSION

(a) In the 1820s there was a change in the economic and social climate of the country and the working-class demonstrations diminished. A number of factors contributed to the change:

- Trade and the employment situation improved.
- Many of the old ultra Tories disappeared from the government for various reasons. Sidmouth retired in 1821 and Castlereagh, the Foreign Secretary, committed suicide.

New faces appeared in the Cabinet including Robert Peel and William Huskisson. Such men were more flexible and ushered in the period of 'Liberal Toryism'. A number of reforms were introduced – for example, in 1824 the *Combination Acts* were repealed and the Metropolitan Police Force was formed in 1829.

(b) In 1830 the reform of parliament issue re-emerged and in 1832, the First Great Reform Act was passed by Lord Grey's Whig Government. The Act was very limited: it enfranchised the middle classes and abolished the rotten boroughs. The labouring classes, however, were still without the vote and in 1836 they turned their support to Chartism (see chapter 21). Changes in the electoral system were to evolve over the next 100 years.

QUESTIONS

1. **Objectives 1, 2 and 3**

(a) Why was there so much social unrest in Britain in the period 1815–22? (8 marks)
(b) How did the labouring classes protest? (8 marks)
(c) What attitude did the government adopt towards the labouring classes? (4 marks)

2. **Objectives 1, 2, 3 and 4**

Study the cartoon entitled *Manchester Heroes*. Using this souce and your own background knowledge answer the following questions:

(a) What can you tell about the social class of:

  (i) The soldiers.
  (ii) The people attending the meeting? (4 marks)
(b) Why did the authorities attack a peaceful meeting with such violence? (8 marks)
(c) The people who went to the meeting were not protesting about poverty; they were protesting about not having the right to vote. Which was the greater problem at the time? Explain your answer. (8 marks)
(Southern Examining Group)

3. **Objectives 3 and 4**

Study Sources A and B and then answer the questions:

(courtesy of Mansell Collection)

Source A An artist's impression of the Pentrich revolutionaries (courtesy of BBC Hulton Picture Library)

Source B

R. J. White describes the Pentrich Revolutionaries as 'a bunch of "Derbyshire yokels"' who set out on a 'pitiful march' to London led by Jeremiah Brandreth . . . 'Along the march . . . small groups of men were to be seen stealing away across the fields . . . [Brandreth] threatened to shoot the deserters'. (*Waterloo to Peterloo* by R. J. White, 1968.)

(a) What impression is given of the Pentrich Revolutionaries in Source A?   (4 marks)

(b) What impression is given of the Pentrich Revolutionaries in Source B?   (4 marks)

(c) Why should two sources about the same event differ?
                                                        (4 marks)

(d) Brandreth was executed for his part in the Pentrich Revolution. Does this mean that the authorities of the time were callous and cruel? Explain your answer.   (8 marks)

4. **Objective 4**

Study Sources A and B following and then answer the questions:

(a) Is Source B a primary or secondary source? Explain your answer.   (4 marks)

(b) How reliable do you think Source B is? Explain your answer.
                                                        (4 marks)

(c) Study Source A. Identify the figure of Henry Hunt. How is he reacting to the situation?   (4 marks)

(d) Was the author of Source A for or against the Yeomanry? Explain your answer.   (4 marks)

(e) How could you check the accuracy of the events shown in Source A?   (4 marks)

Source A
A view of St Peter's Place
(courtesy of Manchester Public Libraries)

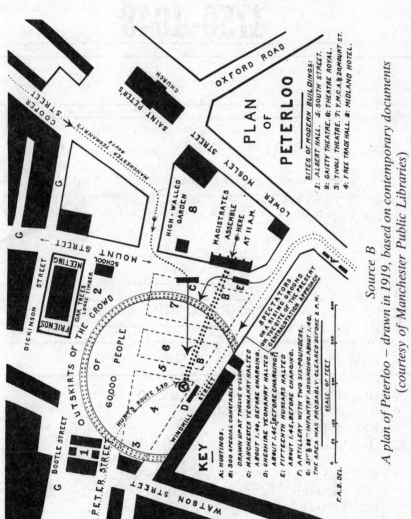

Source B

A plan of Peterloo – drawn in 1919, based on contemporary documents
(courtesy of Manchester Public Libraries)

CHAPTER 16

THE POOR LAW
1750–1948

16.1 INTRODUCTION

The failure to provide the basic necessities of life – food, clothes and shelter – results in a state of poverty. The problem of poverty has long been a thorn in the side of society and this period was no exception.

POVERTY

LACK OF FOOD, CLOTHES, SHELTER

POSSIBLY CAUSED BY	MAY LEAD TO
UNEMPLOYMENT (LAZINESS OR ECONOMIC RECESSION)	MISERY
OLD AGE	DEMORALISATION, RESENTMENT, APATHY
SICKNESS	VIOLENCE
LOW WAGES	CRIME
HIGH PRICES	SQUALOR

In the period under consideration, the poor were subject to the **Poor Law**. The year 1834 is a dividing line in poor law administration. Before this year, historians refer to the Old Poor Law and afterwards to the New Poor Law.

16.2 HOW WAS THE POOR LAW ADMINISTERED BEFORE 1834?

(a) **The Old Poor Law** originated in 1601 and was based on the parish as the principal unit of administration. Such affairs of the parish were supervised by Justices of the Peace. In Elizabethan times England was a rural country with few large towns and it made sense to put poor law administration on a local footing. Each parish was responsible for looking after its own poor. An overseer was appointed each year to collect a poor rate from certain people (usually occupiers of land, houses or tithes) which was used to relieve the poor. The overseer of the poor was an unpaid official and he was expected to look after the poor, as well as his own job. He kept accounts of the amounts paid in, and the money he gave out to help the poor.

(b) An important feature of the Old Poor Law was that distinctions were generally made between various types of pauper. A labourer who was out of work was termed an **able-bodied** pauper, whereas the sick and elderly were called **impotent** paupers. The parish was also responsible for any orphans.

(c) Relief was given in a variety of ways. Outdoor relief was when the poor received help (either in money or in kind). Indoor relief was when the the poor had to enter the parish poor-house or house of correction to receive help. Not all parishes had a poor-house, however, and outdoor relief tended to be more widespread.

(d) During the seventeenth and eighteenth centuries a number of modifications were made to the Poor Law. It soon became evident that some parishes were more sympathetic towards their poor and this tended to result in paupers moving into the area from parishes which were less benevolent. To stop this Parliament passed the *Settlement Act* in 1662. This stated that a person had to have 'a settlement' in order to obtain poor relief from the parish. A settlement could be secured by:

● Birth.
● Marriage (in the case of a woman).
● Having a job in a parish for longer than a year.

If a labourer moved away from his parish of origin in search of work, the JPs issued him with a certificate of settlement. This said that if the labourer fell on hard times his own parish would receive him back and pay for him to be 'removed'. The Settlement Act was later criticised by opponents of the Poor Law who argued that it hindered the free movement of labour. Adam Smith, the political economist, went further and called the law 'an evident violation of natural liberty'.

(e) In 1782 *Gilbert's Act* allowed parishes to join together into Unions for the purpose of building one central workhouse. It appeared sensible for a number of small parishes to pool their resources, but only a minority took advantage of the Act. (By 1834 there were just 67 Gilbert Unions made up from a total of 924 single parishes).

16.3 WHAT WERE ALLOWANCE SYSTEMS? WHY WERE THEY INTRODUCED AND WHAT EFFECTS DID THEY HAVE ON THE POOR?

(a) By the end of the eighteenth century changing economic and social conditions within the country began to put a great strain on the poor law administration. For a start, the population was rising very rapidly and the process of industrialisation was under way. Serious problems emerged in the rural areas where enclosure had taken away the use of the common from a number of labourers at the same time as domestic industry was declining. The rural agricultural labourer found employment harder to come by and those with jobs were paid very low wages. The situation was aggravated by the outbreak of war with France. Prices started to rise rapidly and then between 1793 and 1795 a succession of poor harvests put wheat in short supply, making bread very expensive. Wheat was 49s 3d. (£2.46) per quarter, but by 1795 had reached 78s. 7d. (£3.93).

(b) At Speen near Newbury (Berkshire) the situation was desperate enough for the local JPs to meet at the Pelican Inn in May 1795. Adopting a humanitarian approach to the situation they discussed ways of helping the labourers in their locality. The outcome was a scale of allowances or subsidies that would be paid to a labourer according to the price of bread and the size of his family. His wages would thus be 'made up' by the parish to an agreed subsistence level. Such an idea became known as the Speenhamland or Allowance System; it was adopted by many other parishes throughout the South and East of England. JPs made up their scales of allowances to suit their own locality.

(c) The *effects* of the allowance system on the labourer are contentious. Those who are critical stated:

 (i) Farmers tended to keep wages down as they were fully aware that the parish would 'make up' the labourers' pay to subsistence level.

(ii) The Poor Law Commissioners of 1832 argued that the allowance system was a 'bounty on indolence and vice'. By this they meant that many labourers would do the minimum amount of work in the knowledge that they would have their wages subsidised by the parish. Conversely, the honest, conscientious labourer was degraded by the system – it did not matter how hard he worked he would still have to rely on the parish for at least part of his earnings. His independence was, thus, taken away from him.

On the other hand, however, it has been argued that the allowance system saved a number of families from starvation and destitution in some parishes during the 'years of scarcity' of the mid 1790s.

16.4 WHY WAS A ROYAL COMMISSION OF INQUIRY INTO THE POOR LAWS APPOINTED IN 1832?

(a) The views of contemporary writers

In 1797 Frederick Morton Eden published a booked called *The State of the Poor*, in which he attacked the administration of the poor law. He was strongly against the allowance system. The labourer, he argued, should be taught to fend for himself by spending his money carefully and adopting an alternative staple diet to bread – 'domestic economy'. Eden referred to the northern labourer as a good example in this respect.

(b) Ratepayers became alarmed at the rising cost of administering the poor laws

The cost of relief spiralled from £2 million in 1784 to £4 million in 1803 and in 1813 to £6.5 million. This was partly due to war-time inflation and the rising population – two factors which escaped the attention of the rate-payers. Attitudes began to harden towards the poor and as a result greater attention was paid to the theories of

Thomas Malthus who, in 1798, published his *Essay on the Principle of Population* (see chapter 1). Malthus advocated the abolition of the poor laws. He was particularly critical of allowance systems, which he argued encouraged early marriages and large families. The labourer, he argued, should not get married until he had enough money to support a family.

The pessimistic views of Malthus gained widespread support, especially amongst the ranks of the political economists such as David Ricardo (who favoured *laissez-faire*) and the academic journals of the period. *The Edinburgh Review*, for example favoured the argument of Malthus.

(c) The change in attitude towards the poor in the 1820s was reflected by *the work of the so-called 'Nottingham Reformers'*, George Nicholls of Southwell and the Reverend Robert Lowe of Bingham. Both men, alarmed at the amounts spent on poor relief in their parishes, set out to reduce the expenditure. By eliminating the allowance system and imposing harsh discipline in the workhouse they succeeded in their aim. They made the workhouse an object of fear and a deterrent to the poor. At Southwell Nicholls reduced poor law expenditure from £1884 (in 1821–2) to £786 (1823–4).

(d) In late 1830 the *Swing Riots* occurred in the agricultural counties of South and East England (see chapter 23). The government immediately noticed that the counties where the rioting had taken place were 'Speenhamland' counties. The riots were seen as a breakdown in the traditional bond of paternalism between the labourers and the local gentry – a harsher attitude towards the poor was demanded.

(e) The rising concern about the Poor Law led the Whig Government to set up a *Royal Commission of Inquiry* in February 1832. The Poor Law Report followed in February 1834. It was mainly the work of Edwin Chadwick and Nassau Senior. Chadwick wanted to improve the administration of the poor laws; he had been deeply influenced by the views of the utilitarian Jeremy Bentham. The utilitarians believed that all laws should operate for the 'greatest happiness of the greatest number'. The Report was highly critical of the Allowance System and it also highlighted the amateurish administration and lack of uniformity in the way the Poor Laws operated in different parishes. In its conclusion the Report came out in favour of reform of the Poor Laws rather than abolition; this was mainly due to the influence of Edwin Chadwick.

16.5 WHAT WERE THE TERMS OF THE POOR LAW AMENDMENT ACT 1834?

The Report was written with conviction and the Whig Government acted swiftly on its recommendations. A Bill was introduced into the House of Commons in April 1834 and by August 1834 the *Poor Law Amendment Act* was in the Statute Book. Its main terms were as follows:

(i) Outdoor relief to continue for the aged and infirm.

(ii) Outdoor relief for the able-bodied was to be abolished. In future if an able-bodied man wanted poor relief he had to go into the workhouse (this was called the Workhouse Test).

(iii) Conditions in the workhouse were to be 'less eligible' (less comfortable) than the conditions of the lowest paid labourers in work. The idea was to make the workhouse a feared institution so that the able-bodied would apply for relief only as a very last resort. The harsh attitude demanded by the farmer-ratepayer had been heeded. The Act, however, failed to recognise that a man could become destitute as a result of being thrown out of work by a trade depression. Not all paupers were necessarily indolent.

(iv) There was to be a central Poor Law Commission with its headquarters at Somerset House, London. Three commissioners were to oversee the administration of the poor laws throughout the country. They had the responsibility of imposing a degree of uniformity nationwide.

(v) Parishes were to join together to form Poor Law Unions. Each union was to share one central workhouse which would be governed by an elected **Board of Guardians**. The Guardians employed a full-time Master and Matron to be responsible for the day-to-day running of the workhouse. (Each parish would continue to levy a poor rate which would go into the funds of the Union.)

(vi) The Act thus ensured that the Poor Law would be efficiently administered by professional officials rather than by indifferent amateurs. The ideas of Bentham, rather than Malthus, had clearly influenced the government in the formulation of the Act.

THE ADMINISTRATION OF THE NEW POOR LAW
– as introduced in 1834 –

Three Poor Law Commissioners
based at Somerset House, London
(Secretary: Edwin Chadwick)

↓

ASSISTANT POOR LAW COMMISSIONERS
Supervised and inaugurated Poor Law
Unions. Each Assistant Commissioner was
designated an area to deal with

↓

Each Poor Law Union had a
BOARD OF GUARDIANS who
were elected by the ratepayers.
The Guardians met twice a month

↓

Each Union had one central
Workhouse managed by a Master
and Matron

↓

Inmates inside the Workhouse were
subject to rigid rules and discipline

16.6 HOW DID THE CENTRAL POOR LAW COMMISSION PUT THE ACT INTO OPERATION?

(a) The three commissioners appointed to put the Act into operation were George Nicholls, Thomas Frankland Lewis and John George Shaw Lefevre. Much to his chagrin, Chadwick was not invited to be a Commissioner – but he did obtain the post of Secretary to the Poor Law Commission.

(b) The Commission sent out a small team of Assistant Commissioners to all parts of the country. Their role was to group parishes into Unions, explain the terms of the new Act and help to establish a Board of Guardians. To do this they would call a meeting of the magistrates and property-owners in the locality. The Assistant Commissioner had to work extremely hard for a miserly salary. The Act proved difficult for the local authorities to understand and Chadwick had to issue a number of circulars explaining the details.

(c) If, when a Union had been created, there was not an existing workhouse to use, the Assistant Commissioner had to advise the Board of Guardians how to set about building a new one. Usually the new workhouses were built according to plans drawn up by Sampson Kempthorne, a London architect.

(d) The Poor Law Commissioners drew up diet sheets and lists of rules and regulations to be adopted in the Union Workhouses. The Board of Guardians had to keep minutes of all their meetings and were expected to send annual returns to London giving details of the number of paupers that had been in the workhouse during the year and the expenditure. Punishment Books were also kept. Many of these documents still survive and can be seen in County Record Offices.

(e) By 1839 most of the country's 15 000 parishes had been grouped into a total of 600 Poor Law Unions and 350 Kempthorne Workhouses had been built at a considerable cost. This was a staggering achievement and was due, in the main, to the energies of the Assistant Commissioners.

16.7 HOW DID THE NEW POOR LAW WORK IN PRACTICE?

(a) Under the New Poor Law, when an able-bodied man became destitute, if he wanted relief, he had no option but to apply to the workhouse. He was obliged to take his family with him. He was interviewed by the workhouse authorities as to the reasons for his destitution and, once admitted, he was separated from his family. Men and women were housed in separate blocks of the workhouse. Children were only permitted to see their mother for a short time each day. All paupers wore a standard uniform.

(b) The workhouse undoubtedly humiliated the inmate. The rules, discipline and strict regulations (not forgetting the uniforms) all combined to provide a regimented existence; the workhouse gained the nickname of 'bastille' in many areas. Some workhouses, however, were worse than others – much depended on the character and personality of the Master in charge.

(c) In most workhouses work was provided for the inmates and, in some, education was given to the children. As it was almost impossible for the Assistant Commissioner to regularly inspect the workhouse (twice a year was usual) there was a considerable amount of freedom for the Master to run his institution according to his own wishes. Some masters tried to show a degree of humanity (within the law), others ran harsh regimes. Such was the case at Andover, where a 'scandal' was revealed in 1845. Here the female inmates were at the mercy of the Master, Colin McDougal, an ex-military man and a drunkard. Inmates were made to crush bones to make fertiliser as part of their work. In 1845, it became public that paupers were gnawing the bones for extra sustenance and the Poor Law Commission had a national scandal on its hands. (A Select Committe of Inquiry was established in 1846 to investigate.) Such scandals obviously did not promote the type of image required by the Commissioners. Doubtless other incidents in other workhouses did not make the news.

16.8 HOW FAR WAS THE POOR LAW AMENDMENT ACT ACCEPTED?

(a) In the South the new Act was put into operation quickly and without any protests from the labourers. It was a different story in the North of England. The act was strongly opposed in the industrial counties of Lancashire and West Yorkshire. Opposition came not only from the labourers but also from a number of magistrates who believed that the new centralised administration of the Poor Law reduced their influence.

(b) The industrial North was subject to a series of trade depressions between 1838 and 1848. Large numbers of workers were thrown out of work through no fault of their own. In theory, the only way to obtain poor relief was to enter the dreaded workhouse but his could not be achieved in practice as there simply was not room in the workhouses. The Act appeared to be a travesty of justice and Anti-Poor Law Committees were set up to campaign against the Act. William Cobbett, Richard Oastler, John Fielden and the Chartist, Joseph Rayner Stephens, were prominent in leading the opposition to the New Poor Law. Riots took place at Todmorden, Preston and Stockport and the Poor Law was not really established in the North until the 1860s. It is worth noting that the Reform of the Poor Law had primarily been a response to conditions which had prevailed in the agricultural South of England.

(c) *The Times*, owned by John Walter II (a Tory MP), was bitterly opposed to the New Poor Law from the start. This newspaper, a champion of *laissez-faire* did not like the central administration and it had very little time for Chadwick and his passion for efficient administration. Day after day articles appeared condemning the New Poor Law and the Commissioners. Other opponents included the writer Charles Dickens who patronised the Poor Law in his novel *Oliver Twist*, although it is clear that he overexaggerated.

16.9 HOW SUCCESSFUL WAS THE NEW POOR LAW?

(a) On the positive side, the New Poor Law did reduce the cost of poor relief in many areas. This was enough for many contemporaries (especially ratepayers) to be extremely pleased with the Act. Certainly, the Poor Law Commissioners claimed great success for the Act, particularly in the South where they believed the labourer had regained his pride and self-respect. Their comments, based on the testimonies of the Assistant Commissioners were published in the Annual Reports. It is highly likely, however, that these Reports highlighted the 'successes' and played down any failings.

(b) It can be argued that the basis of the New Poor Law administration stood the test of time. Its framework with some modifications remained until 1948.

(c) In a number of ways, however, the New Poor Law did not work in practice:

(i) It was impossible to enforce the principle of less eligibility and the workhouse test. Consequently, relief for the able-bodied continued to be given outside the workhouse. There was just not enough space in the workhouse to accommodate destitute labourers who applied for relief during a trade depression.

(ii) It took a long time for all parishes to be brought under the 1834 Act. Areas with 'Gilbert Unions' managed to stay independent of central control for well into the 1860s and 1870s.

16.10 WHAT OTHER CHANGES WERE MADE IN POOR LAW ADMINISTRATION AFTER 1834?

(a) Despite the New Poor Law, the parish continued to play a part in the administration of the Poor Law for a number of years. Parish Overseers still collected the poor rates and kept the Account Book.

In 1865, however, the Union Chargeability Act, made the Union the unit for rating and in doing so eradicated the parish's role.

(b) The Poor Law Commission survived until 1847 when, as part of the backlash to the Andover scandal, it was replaced by the Poor Law Board (which had representation in Parliament). This in turn was replaced by the Local Government Board in 1871.

(c) In 1905 a *Royal Commission on the Poor Law and Unemployed* was set up to examine the existing laws. It took four years to complete its work and then, unable to agree, issued two Reports:

● The Majority Report recommended that Boards of Guardian should be abolished and their duties handed over to the new County and County Borough Councils. It also suggested minor changes such as outdoor relief being renamed 'Home Assistance': other than this it maintained the framework of the Poor Law as per the 1834 model.

● The Minority Report was mainly the work of Sidney and Beatrice Webb and it recommended the sweeping away of the Poor Law. Instead it wanted a Ministry of Labour and Local Authority Committees to deal with the poor.

Both these reports were ignored and nothing came of their suggestions. Consequently it was left to the Liberal Government (1906–14) to make a direct attack on poverty, old age and unemployment. In 1929 the Poor Law Guardians were abolished, but it was not until 1948 that the last traces of the Poor Law were removed by the Welfare State measures of Clement Attlee's Labour Government.

16.11 CONCLUSION

The Poor Law Commissioners of 1834 adopted a severe attitude to the poor, assuming that all poverty was caused by laziness. This simplistic approach overlooked the profound problems which industrialisation had brought. Population growth, the decline of domestic industry and trade depressions were not considered when the Poor Law Amendment Act was passed. In its treatment of the problem of poverty the Act left much to be desired.

On the other hand the Act helped to establish important principles for future reforms and administration. The practice of setting up Royal Commissions of Inquiry prior to the passing of an Act of Parliament was widely copied after 1834. The New Poor Law also helped to establish the idea of a central authority working in conjunction with local bodies. This arrangement is the basis of Local Government administration today.

QUESTIONS

1. **Objectives 1 and 2**

Assess the role of **Edwin Chadwick** in the reform of the **Poor Law** and **Public Health**.
It may help you to consider the following questions:

● What sort of a character was Chadwick? What were his motives and attitudes? What made him 'tick'?
● How far were events determined by Chadwick's own personality?
● How far were Chadwick's actions determined by impersonal/ external factors?
● How important was Chadwick's contribution to the reform of the Poor Law and Public Health?
● How successful was the work of Chadwick?

(Total = 30 marks)

2. **Objectives 1 and 2**

Study the extracts below, both of which come from *The Report of the Royal Commission into the Poor Laws 1834*:

Extract A

'We recommend, therefore, the appointment of a Central Board to control the administration of the Poor Laws, with such Assistant Commissioners as may be found requisite'.

Extract B

We recommend that the Central Board be empowered to cause any number of parishes which they may find convenient to be incorporated for the purpose of workhouse management, and for providing new workhouses where necessary to declare their workhouses to be the common workhouse of the incorporated district.

(a) Describe the main feature of Poor Law administration **before** 1834. (6 marks)

(b) Why was the Royal Commission set up in 1832 to inquire into the Poor Laws? (4 marks)

(c) In what ways did Jeremy Bentham influence the thinking of the Royal Commission? (5 marks)

(d) The main recommendations of the Commission were embodied in the Poor Law Amendment Act of 1834.

  (i) Name the two main persons involved in producing the Report. (1 mark)

  (ii) What was to be the function of the Central Board? (3 marks)

  (iii) How was the recommendation described in Extract B put into practice? (3 marks)

  (iv) Briefly describe the other terms of the Poor Law Amendment Act. (3 marks)

3. **Objective 3**

Study the source material below and then answer the questions:

Source A

Another decision taken by the Andover Guardians . . . was their choice of master and matron. They placed advertisements in various newspapers . . . for applications from suitable candidates at an annual salary of £80. Out of twelve replies they called Sergeant-Major Colin McDougal. At two o'clock on Christmas Eve 1836 Colin McDougal arrived for interview. He was 44, short and fair, with a slight limp from active service . . . Both he and his wife, Mary Ann, made an excellent impression with the Guardians and were appointed as master and matron.

(Taken from *The Scandal of the Andover Workhouse* by Ian Anstruther, 1973)

Source B

In 1845 *The Times* reported a scandal at the Andover Workhouse with paupers being made to crush bones and, at times, actually eating the raw meat on them . . . Such was the outcry that an Inquiry was set up and witnesses were interviewed to ascertain the facts.

(a) As Colin McDougal, write a letter to the Andover Guardians applying for the post of Workhouse Master.

(b) As a reporter working for *The Times* write an article revealing the conditions in the Andover Workhouse.

(c) The year is 1846. Colin McDougal has been called by the Inquiry to give evidence. What do you think he would have said in his own defence?

(Total = 30 marks)

4. **Objective 4**

Study the following source carefully and then answer the questions:

Hammersmith
Jaunery 5th 18012

Gentlemen My duty to you all to Let you no that I am in Great Distrest I should be veary Glad to have a Little Helpe from you for my famely is very hard Everything is very Deare half a years Rent Wich is £3.10s.0d and I Have not the Money to pay and my Landlard says the money he most & Will Have for he Will tack my

THE TRAVELS OF JOSEPH BAILEY

HAMMERSMITH

BROCKENHURST

Hampshire

HAMMERSMITH TO BROCKENHURST
= about 130 km

goods from me and then I most send my famley Down to you for pay the Money I am Not able to pay I have fore Childerins nobody to Earin nothing Bot my Selfe My Name is Joseph Bailey I Wase Down With you Febery the 1 1807 I worked at Hethedilton for Meger generl popem & for Mr Admere and we Was in the porehouse ratfard was the Loocken over that time you Simd to think that Brockhurst was Not my parish Bot it is and no othern if you do not think to Relive me I Shal loos my goods the I & my fameley most Com down and you most find me Som I do not Want to troubel you no forthern My Landlords name is Mr Elliott hangyard Hammrsmith Middsex so no more at present . . . from your Homlel Sarvent Joseph Bailey

Let me no Whethen you Will Send an no Wen you Send Direct for me

Near the six Bells on to the Landlard.

(A Letter in the Hampshire Record Office)

(a)   Comment on the following:
    ● The tone of the letter.
    ● The date at the top of the letter.   (4 marks)

(b)   Who or what was the 'Loocken Over'?   (2 marks)

(c)   Why has Joseph Bailey written this letter?   (4 marks)

(d)   Suggest reasons why Bailey was living in Hammersmith when Brockenhurst appeared to be his home parish.   (2 marks)

(e)   How reliable would you regard this letter?   (4 marks)

(f)   How could you find out what happened to Joseph Bailey?
    (4 marks)

LAW AND ORDER

1700–1900

17.1 INTRODUCTION

The methods of law enforcement were established during the Middle Ages and the reign of Queen Elizabeth I; the authorities dealing with the maintenance of law and order were amateur in status and, as with the Old Poor Law, the parish was used as the basic unit for administration.

By 1815 such methods were outdated and this realisation led to the formation of an organised police force. Attitudes also began to change regarding punishment of offenders. Prisons, for example, were administered by a number of different authorities and the majority were in an appalling state. During this period individuals like John Howard and Elizabeth Fry made progress towards reforming prisons and the government began to take a more active role in the prison system.

17.2 WHO KEPT LAW AND ORDER DURING THE EIGHTEENTH CENTURY? HOW EFFECTIVE WERE THEY?

(a) Magistrates (Justices of the Peace)

Since the Middle Ages a magistrate had been the person traditionally in charge of law and order in a particular area. Although this was an unsalaried position members of the local gentry were often keen to do the job because of the prestige and power it carried. All aspects of law enforcement were part of the magistrate's duty including the arrest of suspects and punishments. JPs could hold 'Quarter Sessions' in their area where they dealt with administrative, legal and criminal matters.

(b) Parish constables

Most parishes elected a parishioner (unsalaried) to carry out the duties of constable usually for a year at a time. The constables acted as assistants to the magistrates, their duties included catching law-breakers, supervising the local public houses, keeping watch, and generally maintaining order in the parish. The constable needed to be literate as he was required to keep a record of his activities for the Quarter Sessions.

(c) Watchmen

These were appointed in many towns to help the parish constables. Such men were unpaid, often elderly, and they generally demanded little respect from the population. They were frequently goaded as they sat in their 'sentry-boxes' and appear to have had little effect. They collectively earned themselves the name of 'Charlies'.

(d) Troops

When law and order broke down and rioting occurred the military could be called out to restore calm. From the eighteenth century the magistrates would usually inform the Lord Lieutenant of the County when rioting was occurring; the Lord Leiutenant then ordered out the local yeomanry or militia. This system was used during the Luddite Riots of 1811–12 and the Swing Riots of 1830.

(e) Private citizens

For many centuries criminals had been apprehended by the method of 'raising the hue and cry', showing that all members of the community were responsible for the upkeep of law and order. However, during the eighteenth century the government began to encourage private individuals to enforce the law by offering rewards for the capture of criminals. This resulted in widespread abuse and the practice of 'professional thief-taking'. Thief-takers were men making a living out of catching criminals or framing people and then claiming the reward. One notorious thief-taker was William Payne of London, who was something of an expert in this trade.

Thus law enforcement was both ineffective and totally *laissez-faire* in organisation and an increase in crime would demand an improved system (see Section 17.4).

17.3 WHAT IMPROVEMENTS IN LAW-ENFORCEMENT TOOK PLACE DURING THE EIGHTEENTH CENTURY?

The increase in crime was most marked in London where the population grew rapidly in the late eighteenth century. Some improvements in law-keeping did, therefore, come about but they were mainly through the work of individuals rather than the government.

(a) The Bow Street magistrates

(i) In 1739 a London magistrate, Colonel Le Veil, opened an office in Bow Street so that he was able to deal with offenders on the spot. His work was followed up when in 1748 Henry Fielding (1707–54), the Chief Magistrate for Westminster, moved into Bow Street. In 1753 he set up a small group of constables to patrol the area; this 'élite' group was paid a modest salary by courtesy of a grant from the government and in time were named 'The Bow Street Runners'.

(ii) Henry Fielding died in 1754 and was succeeded by his half-brother, John Fielding. A number of innovations followed, including the establishment of the Bow Street Horse Patrol in 1753. The Horse Patrol wore scarlet waistcoats and carried handcuffs and truncheons. This uniform was important in helping to establish the notion of a group of law-enforcers distinct from other people. John Fielding also sought the co-operation of the public by publishing information about 'wanted men' in a pamphlet called *The Weekly Pursuit*.

(iii) In 1782 law and order became the responsibility of the Home Secretary, and in 1792 Parliament passed 'The Middlesex Justices Act'. This was an unprecedented step and it brought into being seven more offices (on Bow Street lines) each manned by three salaried magistrates and six paid constables.

(iv) By the end of the eighteenth century pilfering of cargoes in the port of London had become a major problem. The worst group to suffer, the West Indian merchants (who imported rum, sugar and tobacco) protested, and this led to the setting up of the River Thames Police (1798) to patrol the river.

17.4 WHAT FACTORS HIGHLIGHTED THE NEED FOR A REGULAR POLICE FORCE?

(a) The industrial towns were rapidly built without much planning. Slum areas soon developed, streets were unpaved and unlit, and in most towns there was no effective policing. Such conditions encouraged crime. London's East End was particularly bad with theft, assault, prostitution and drunkenness part of daily life.

(b) There were a number of riots in the late eighteenth century which resulted from either political or economic unrest:

● In 1780 the Gordon Riots took place. These were whipped up by General George Gordon who objected to some anti-Catholic laws being abolished. After a week of rioting troops managed to gain control, but the incident showed the need for an effective police force.
● Hunger Riots were also common during this time coinciding with periods of inflation.

(c) Along the south coast of England, smuggling was endemic during this period. This was encouraged by the heavy custom duties placed on goods, particularly liquor from France. Again there was no force to deal with the problem; it was left to revenue officers who were largely ineffective.

(d) The aftermath of the French Wars in 1815 brought a period of social unrest, demonstrations and marches (see chapter 15). At this time imprisonment, fines, transportation and the death penalty were widely used by magistrates. Within the Penal Code 223 offences, ranging from the very trivial to murder, were punishable by the death sentence.

17.5 IN VIEW OF THE GROWING LAWLESSNESS WHY WAS A REGULAR POLICE FORCE NOT ESTABLISHED UNTIL 1829?

For a number of years before 1829 leading magistrates had advocated the setting up of a regular police force. The idea of a regular police force was, therefore not new but there were numerous reasons why it took so long to materialise:

- Cost was a major consideration. A large salaried police force would be expensive. The only way to cover the cost was by levying a rate; governments appeared reluctant to do this.
- There was a deep-rooted fear that a regular police force would be an unacceptable infringement on traditional freedoms.
- Finally many people thought that a 'police force' would merely be 'troops' in disguise. Given the unpopularity of the militia at the time, governments were uncertain about how a police force would be accepted by society.

17.6 WHAT CONTRIBUTION DID ROBERT PEEL MAKE TO THE REFORM OF LAW AND ORDER?

(a) Peel had a more enlightened approach to law and order than many of his Tory colleagues at the time. He was quick to see that the Penal Code was inappropriate, and managed to get the list of capital offences reduced by over one hundred. Peel should only be given part of the credit for this improvement as the early campaigning against the Penal Code had been carried out by the barrister Sir Samuel Romilly (1757–1818). The gradual reform continued until by 1861 only murder, treason, piracy on the high seas, and the destruction of the Crown's Dockyards carried the death penalty.

(b) The Metropolitan Police Force 1829

 (i) Peel was keen to see the formation of a single police force with the emphasis on the 'prevention of crime' and, worried by the increased crime rate in London, decided that it was high time the Metropolis had such a unit. He had the right pedigree to push through such a measure, for as Chief Secretary for Ireland in 1812 he had overseen the formation of the 'Peace Preservation Police'.

 (ii) Peel knew he would encounter opposition and was accordingly very careful in framing the Metropolitan Police Bill in 1829. The main features of his Bill were that the proposed force would be under the ultimate authority of the Home Secretary, would wear a uniform and be controlled from central headquarters. Peel left the City of London out of the Bill and thus removed his most serious opposition. The Bill became law in July 1829. (The City of London formed its own police force ten years later.)

(c) The organisation of the Metropolitan Police Force

(i) Peel appointed two commissioners to put the Act into operation. They were Colonel Charles Rowan (1783–1852) and Richard Mayne (1796–1868). They were both Irishmen and in many ways the perfect blend, Rowan having a military background and Mayne a legal training. Rowan was an acquaintance of Edwin Chadwick and was motivated by a belief in Utilitarianism and Christian principles.

(ii) The two commissioners split London into 17 Divisions, each one coming under a superintendent on a salary of £200 per annum. Next in the structure came four inspectors (£100 per annum) and then four sergeants (£58 per annum). Each division initially had a complement of 36 constables who were paid £54 per annum. Promotion throughout the ranks was favoured to ensure continuity of expertise.

(iii) Building up discipline in the force took time. Some of the first recruits came from the ranks of the unemployed, others possibly joined for the challenge of the job. The pay, however, was not very good. Added to this, the police constable had to bring prosecutions personally to court. If he failed in the prosecution he had to pay the costs out of his own pocket. The work was also very demanding with constables walking the beat for 12 hours at a time. Many left the force after a short time; others were sacked for breaching discipline (for example, drinking on duty).

(iv) It took time for the police to be accepted by the general public. They were initially treated with great suspicion, gaining the nickname of 'Peel's Bloody Gang'. Magistrates were also resentful at the fact that the police deprived them of some of their powers. Rowan and Mayne, however, put a high priority on public relations and gradually the Police were accepted. One event which helped in this respect was when they successfuly dealt with a riot at Cold-Bath Fields in London (1853).

17.7 HOW WERE POLICE FORCES EXTENDED OVER THE COUNTRY AS A WHOLE?

(a) Modifications in the Metropolitan Police Force (MPF)

(i) In 1839 the Marine Police became the Thames Division of the Metropolitan Police.

(ii) Also in 1839 the Bow Street Runners were abolished with the MPF taking over their duties.

(iii) In 1842 a detective branch was established based at Scotland Yard, consisting of two inspectors and six sergeants, whose task it was to detect crime. They wore plain clothes and eventually became the Criminal Investigation Department (CID) in 1878.

(b) The establishment of Provincial Forces

(i) The 1835 *Municipal Corporations Act* gave boroughs the power to establish police forces paid for out of the rates. The Act was not obligatory and progress was slow.

(ii) In 1836 a Royal Commission recommended that there should be a nationwide police force organised on a county basis, with a central authority to guide the overall policy.

The *County (Rural) Police Force Act (1839)* only partially recognised the Report's proposals. This Act allowed County Magistrates to set up a police force if they wished. As such a project was expensive, only a few counties took advantage of the Act; by 1853 22 had responded.

(iii) In 1856 the *County (Rural) Police Act* became law; this Act was obligatory. It stated that:

- All counties and boroughs without a police force were to set one up as soon as possible. (It took six years for all counties to meet this requirement.)
- Counties and boroughs were given the freedom to organise their force in the manner they wished (many followed the example set by the Metropolitan Police Force).
- A grant of up to 25 per cent was available to those forces who made annual returns on crime statistics in their area and received an acceptable report from the inspectorate.

● For the first time inspectors were to be appointed to check the work and conduct of both the County and Borough Police Forces who received the government grant.

This Act had the effect of filling the gaps so that the whole nation was protected by a local police force (see map below).

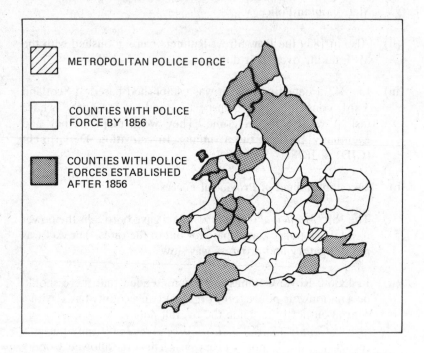

METROPOLITAN POLICE FORCE

COUNTIES WITH POLICE FORCE BY 1856

COUNTIES WITH POLICE FORCES ESTABLISHED AFTER 1856

(iv) In 1888, as part of the local government re-organisation, County Constabularies came under the newly-constituted County Councils. Borough forces remained 'independent' of this arrangement.

17.8 HOW EFFECTIVE WERE THE POLICE?

There is no clear way of measuring the success of the police, although we can refer to a few pointers which suggest that they were effective:

● The 1830s saw a widespread dispersal of criminals out of London into the provincial cities. This showed that they feared arrest by the Metropolitan Police; their presence in other cities led to the establishment of Borough Police Forces!

- There were occasions when the Police kept calm and prevented violence, for example, the Chartist Meeting of April 1848.
- Statistics can lie but figures produced by the Metropolitan Police pointed towards a fall in criminal activities in the ten years between 1825 and 1835.

At least one citizen in London was rapidly convinced of the success of the police force and he wrote to *The Times* on 6 October 1829 expressing thanks to Mr Peel for the 'quietness of the streets' and the 'overthrow of the old plan of watching'.

17.9 WHAT WERE PRISON CONDITIONS LIKE IN THE EIGHTEENTH CENTURY AND EARLY NINETEENTH CENTURY?

Prison administration was haphazard. The government had virtually nothing to do with the administration of prisons during this period; this task was left to a variety of local authorities and individuals:

- There were Town Gaols, County Gaols (under the authority of the County Sheriff) and in some areas gaols were run by private individuals.
- In some areas there were prisons specifically for debtors as in London (The Fleet and Marshalsea). Usually, however, debtors were put into ordinary gaols and detained side by side with hardened criminals.
- The day to day running of the prisons was undertaken by unsalaried staff. Gaolers and warders ('turnkeys') gained a living by charging the prisoners fees (for example, for liquor, bedding, food). The 'system' was open to widespread abuse.
- Most prisons had a 'mixed' population of inmates. Apart from some of the larger prisons like Newgate there was no attempt to classify the inmates as to the kind of offence they had committed. Thus, murderers and robbers mixed with those who had committed trivial offences or those who had not been convicted of a crime and were waiting for a trial.
- There did not appear to be any purpose to prison life; there was certainly no attempt at 'character-reforming' or rehabilitation. A number of prisons had a chaplain, but he found most prisoners hostile to any religious teaching. In addition, most prisons lacked proper sanitation or ventilation and disease was rife, particularly typhus.

17.10 WHAT WAS TRANSPORTATION?

As the population increased, and with it the crime rate, prisons were unable to cope. Magistrates, therefore, increasingly used 'transportation' as a way of dealing with criminals. At first such criminals were taken to America where they worked on penal settlements. After the American War of Independence, Australia was used for this purpose. In all, some 160 000 prisoners were taken either to New South Wales or Van Diemen's land (Tasmania). After sentence prisoners were kept on board large ships called 'hulks' which were in effect floating prisons whilst waiting to be taken to the colonies. The hulks were anchored in the estuary of the Thames and Portsmouth harbour. There was a feeling that transportation was advantageous to all; it cleared the country of convicts who in turn had the opportunity of a 'fresh start'. Transportation could be imposed for a variety of offences including poaching and rioting. Thus many 'Swing Rioters' suffered this fate as did the 'Tolpuddle Martyrs' in 1834 and the Chartist rioters of 1842.

Transportation ended in 1852 when the Australian Government protested and said that no more British convicts would be accepted.

17.11 WHAT STEPS DID JOHN HOWARD AND ELIZABETH FRY TAKE IN AN ATTEMPT TO REFORM PRISON CONDITIONS? HOW SUCCESSFUL WERE THEY?

(a)

(i) *John Howard (1726–90)* became the Sheriff of Bedfordshire in 1753. As part of his duties he inspected Bedford Gaol; so appalling were the conditions that he undertook a study of prisons both in this country and Europe. His observations were published in 1777 in *The State of the Prisons in England and Wales with Preliminary Observations and an Account of Some Foreign Prisons*. The detail in his book is quite remarkable and provides us with a vivid picture of prisons in this period. He remarked that, 'Debtors crowd the gaols with their wives and children . . . increasing the danger of infection and corrupting the morals of children'. He rated the Tolbooth in Inverness as the 'most . . . offensive prison that I have seen in Scotland'. Howard was generally critical of the poor standards of hygiene and sanitation. Magistrates were blamed for the poor conditions as many did not bother to inspect the prisons in their locality.

(ii) Howard as an individual, could do little to change the system, but none the less he made a list of recommendations to the authorities on prison reform including:

- The abolition of fees for gaolers.
- A reasonable diet of food (including meat).
- Clean clothing twice a week.
- Clean bedding.
- An improvement in the morals of the inmates (for example, no fighting, swearing or gambling).
- Baths for inmates.
- Classification of prisoners.
- Better buildings with good ventilation.
- Prisons to be administered by local authorities.

(iii) Howard's work met with little success during his life although his campaign did much to publicise the appalling conditions; he was probably in advance of his time.

(b)

(i) *Elizabeth Fry (1780–1845)* was a devout Quaker and the daughter of John Gurney. Her humanitarian principles were derived from her religious belief. She first became involved with prison reform in 1817 when she visited Newgate Prison in London.

Mrs. Fry was shocked by what she saw and became a regular prison visitor hoping to improve the conditions for women prisoners in particular. She also undertook a long tour of prisons in the north of Britain (1818) with her brother Joseph Gurney. As a result a report was published in 1819 called 'Notes on the Prisons in Scotland and the North of England' in which they recommended an improvement in 'our system of discipline . . . by which there may be rendered schools of industry and virtue, instead of the very nurseries of crime'.

(ii) At Newgate Mrs Fry tried to reform the inmates, preferring this to any system of punishment. She occupied the women with embroidery, bible readings and schooling. She persuaded the authorities to appoint a female matron to supervise the women. She drew up a list of rules for the female inmates which bore some resemblance to the recommendations made by John Howard. Mrs. Fry's rules included:

- Suitable employment to pass the time.
- Daily bible readings.
- Proper supervision of any children who had been forced into prison with their mothers.
- No immoral activities (gambling, begging, etc.)

(iii) Robert Peel listened to the arguments of Mrs. Fry and in 1823 passed *The Gaol Act* which listed the following measures:

- Regular prison visits by a chaplain and surgeon.
- Gaolers to be paid a living wage; fees to be abolished.
- Prison inmates should be 'reformed'.
- Gaols to be cleaned regularly.
- Female staff for female inmates.
- No inmate to be put in irons without the prior knowledge of the magistrates.

As with previous legislation, this act had little real effect; once again no provision had been made for an inspectorate.

(iv) In 1835 the Prison Act rectified this fault and in the following year the first Annual Inspection of Prisons took place.

(v) Mrs Fry's work did not bring radical improvements to prison life but she did succeed in bringing the issue to the attention of the public. She should also be given some credit for the fact that prison inspectors were eventually appointed – a vital step forward in terms of prisons obeying legislation. Mrs Fry was probably ahead of her time in that she was against a system of punishments in prisons believing instead that there should be an attempt to reform the criminal using religion as a motivating force.

The general attitude, however, was that prisons should be places of correction and that criminals should be made to pay for their wrong doings.

17.12 WHAT WERE PRISONS LIKE IN THE MID-NINETEENTH CENTURY?

(a) By 1840 the government recognised that it had to provide more prisons and several institutions were built or modified including Millbank (1841), Pentonville (1842), Winchester (1846) and Dartmoor (1850). In all, over 50 new prisons were opened during this period.

(b) The new prisons followed the design of Pentonville and their main features are illustrated in the photograph below:

Winchester Prison (courtesy of the Hampshire Chronicle)

They had:

- A radial design, that is, a central hub from which a number of wings radiated. From the 'hub' a warden could view all the wings.
- Separate cells.

- Punishment sheds (housing treadmills and oakum-picking booths).
- Exercise yards.

Most of these prison buildings are still in use today.

(c) By this time two 'regimes' had become adopted in British prisons:

(i) *The separate system*: This was an American idea where the prisoner was detained in solitary confinement for the initial period of his sentence. The theory was that the criminal would mull over his sins and realise that he had to change his ways. He would eventually break down and be willing to have his character reformed by the prison chaplain. The system was opposed by many people at the time, including the inspectors, who in 1842 reported, 'that in the last year eight prisoners were sent from [Millbank] to Bethlehem Hospital in a state of raving madness' (quoted in *The Times*, 1 December 1842). In fact the system led to cases of suicide. Under this system, however, the inmates were given work which had some purpose, such as gardening and woodwork. At the time this system was thought to be 'progressive'. It was condemned as cruel at the end of the nineteenth century.

(ii) *The silent system*: Here prisoners were forbidden to talk under any circumstances. The theory was that they would pass on criminal tendencies to each other if allowed to talk. Prisoners were set to work on monotonous meaningless tasks such as the treadmill, oakum-picking and turning the crank-handle of a wheel or a capstan. The treadmill was particularly tiring and, given the poor prison diet, such exercises led to prisoners becoming physically exhausted. It was believed that the severity of these conditions would result in the inmates avoiding crime on their release for fear of a return to prison.

 For breaches of prison discipline an inmate could be confined to a dark cell or even flogged. Flogging probably was declining by this time, but the executioner at Newgate had written into his contract that he would receive five shillings (25p) for each flogging administered.

(iii) By 1860 all wardens were uniformed.

17.13 OTHER LEGISLATION AND MEASURES

(a) In 1853 the Home Secretary, Lord Palmerston, passed the Penal Servitude Act. With the end of transportation, there would be a problem in accommodating all the convicts in British prisons. The Act:

● Reduced the maximum sentences for many offences.
●. Said that a prisoner who had a record of good conduct could obtain a 'a ticket-of-leave', that is, they were released 'on probation'.

Many people opposed this Act believing it to be too lenient. Palmerston was forced to compromise to some extent by reiterating that prisoners should be subject to hard work during their sentence.

(b) In 1854 Lord Shaftesbury established the Prisoners' Aid Society which aimed to lend support to prisoners on their release. He also supported Palmerston in setting up Reform Schools for young offenders to protect them from the harsh primitive regime of the prisons.

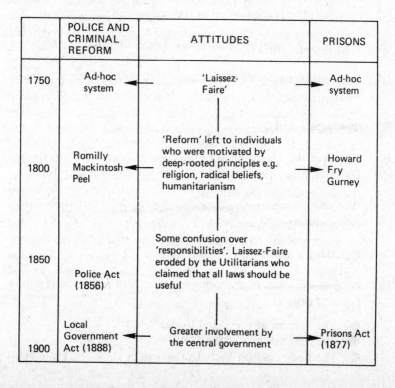

	POLICE AND CRIMINAL REFORM	ATTITUDES	PRISONS
1750	Ad-hoc system	'Laissez-Faire'	Ad-hoc system
1800	Romilly Mackintosh Peel	'Reform' left to individuals who were motivated by deep-rooted principles e.g. religion, radical beliefs, humanitarianism	Howard Fry Gurney
1850	Police Act (1856)	Some confusion over 'responsibilities'. Laissez-Faire eroded by the Utilitarians who claimed that all laws should be useful	
1900	Local Government Act (1888)	Greater involvement by the central government	Prisons Act (1877)

(c) In 1877 the Prisons Act put all British prisons under the direct control of the Home Secretary.

(d) In 1898 and 1899 the use of the crank and treadmill was banned in British prisons.

17.14 CONCLUSION

By 1900 it would be safe to say that the 'modern' system of enforcing law and order had been established – but why did it take so long?

The probable answer is that it took the government until then to accept its responsibility. The diagram on page 267 summarises the pathway to reform.

QUESTIONS

1. **Objectives 1 and 2**

(a) How was the law enforced in the eighteenth century?
(8 marks)
(b) Why was the Metropolitan Police Force set up in 1829?
(6 marks)
(c) What problems faced the Metropolitan Police Force in its early years? (6 marks)

2. **Objectives 1 and 2**

(a) How was the Metropolitan Police Force organised? (8 marks)
(b) Describe how other areas of Britain set up their own forces.
(8 marks)
(c) Why did it take so long for police forces to be established on a national basis? (4 marks)

3. **Objectives 1 and 4**

(a) Give descriptions of the following aspects of nineteenth century law and order:

   ● The reform of the Penal Code.
   ● Transportation.
   ● The design of mid-Victorian prisons. (12 marks)

(b) If you had to research a topic on 'Law and order in the nineteenth century' what sources of evidence would you consult? (8 marks)

4. **Objectives 1 and 2**

(a) Describe prison conditions in the eighteenth century.(8 marks)
(b) *Assess* the work of John Howard and Elizabeth Fry in reforming prison conditions. (12 marks)

5. **Objective 3**

(a) As a supporter of the **solitary system** in 1845 write down your arguments as to why this system should be adopted in British prisons. (10 marks)
(b) As a supporter of the **silent system** in 1845 write out your arguments as to why you believe that this system should be used in British prisons. (10 marks)

6. **Objectives 3 and 4**

Study the sources below and then answer the questions:

Source A

Number of prisoners in 1776

Area	Debtors	Felons	Petty offences	Total
London	1274	228	194	1696
39 counties (England)	752	617	459	1828
Wales	67	122	–	189
Town Gaols	344	122	–	466
Totals	2437	994	653	4084

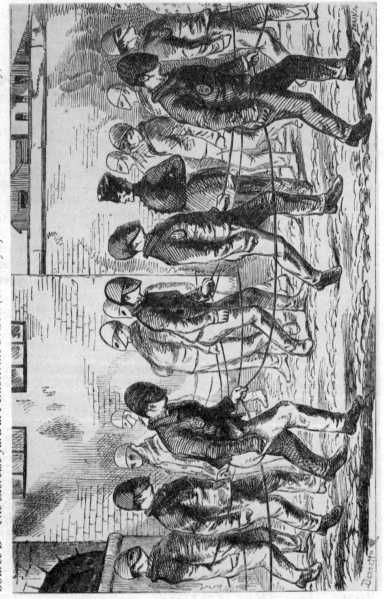

Source B   The exercise yard at Pentonville Prison (courtesy of BBC Hulton Picture Library)

Source C Picking oakum (courtesy of Mansell Collection)

Source D   Women prisoners at Tothill Fields Prison (courtesy of BBC Hulton Picture Library)

Source E Young offenders at Tothill Fields Prison (H. Mayhew) (courtesy of BBC Hulton Picture Library)

(a)   What can be deduced from Source A?   (2 marks)

(b)   What is happening in each of the Sources B, C and E?
                                                            (3 marks)

(c)   Explain the reasoning behind each of the activities shown.
                                                            (5 marks)

(d)   Study Source D more closely. Why would we today regard this scene with dismay? Why was this apparently 'normal' in the nineteenth century?   (5 marks)

(e)   What similarities and differences can you detect between Sources B and D?   (4 marks)

(f)   What would a person living in the nineteenth century have thought about the scenes in Sources B, C, D and E?
                                                            (6 marks)

(Questions adapted from the Southern Regional Examinations Board)

7.   **Objective 4**

Study the sources below and then answer the questions:

Source A
General Instructions to the Metropolitan Police (quoted in *The Times*)

> 'September 29th 1829. Police Constables . . . are particularly cautioned not to pay attention to any ignorant or silly expression of ridicule.
> June 3rd 1830. The Commissioners have to draw the attention of the whole force to the frequent recurrence of charges of 'obstructing police officers in the performance of their duty' . . . A constable who allows himself to be irritated by any language . . . shows that he has not a command of his temper.
> November 1st 1830. [Constables should] do their duty with every possible moderation and forbearance.

Source B (*courtesy of Metropolitan Police*)

A View of the Brutal Attack
ON AN UNARMED, RESPECTABLE, AND PEACEABLE MULTITUDE
OF BOTH SEXES, AND ALL AGES, MADE BY A
DESPOTIC POLICE,
IN HYDE PARK, ON SUNDAY, JULY 1st, 1855,
DEDICATED TO LORD G———R AND ALL THE SAINTS,

Source C
Letter sent to applicants to join the Metropolitan Police 1834

'If . . . who has applied for a situation as a constable in the Police
will attend at Westminster on Tuesday next at eleven o'clock in the
forenoon precisely he will be examined as to his fitness for such an
employment. He need not attend and will not be appointed if he
cannot read or write; if he is above 35 years or age; if he is under 5
feet 7 inches high without his shoes, nor unless he is free from
every bodily complaint, is of a strong constitution and generally

intelligent, as he will have to pass the strict examination of the surgeons.

(Salaries: Superintendant – £200 pa; Inspectors – £100 pa; Constables – £54.)

Source D
Advertisement in the Leeds Press 19 March 1836

BOROUGH OF LEEDS
WANTED IMMEDIATELY

Twenty men for the purpose of a Day Police to be composed under the following heads and at the following salaries:-
– A Chief Officer at £250 a year
– A Superintendent at £100 a year
– Four Inspectors at £75 a year
– Fourteen men at £46.16s a year.

In reference to the men, each applicant will be expected to be not less than 21 nor more than 35 years of age. He must be at least 5ft.7inches in height. He must be able to read and write with facility and must be well recommended for Command of Temper, Sobriety, Honesty, Activity and Intelligence.

Source E
An Extract from *Oliver Twist* by Charles Dickens. Oliver was apprehended by a member of the public for pickpocketing. Dickens commented:

'He might have attempted [to run away] . . . had not a police officer (who is generally the last person to arrive in such cases) at that moment made his way through the crowd, and seized Oliver by the collar'.

(a) What conclusions can you draw from Sources A and B?
(b) What similarities and differences can you detect between Sources C and D?
(c) What does Source E suggest about Dickens' attitude towards the police?
(d) As Source E originates from a novel, does this make it worthless to the historian?
(e) Which of these sources do you think contains the most bias? How far does this detract from its value as a source of evidence?

(Total = 30 marks)

EDUCATION

1750–1944

18.1 INTRODUCTION

(a) Most children today are educated in state schools with only a small minority paying to attend schools in the private sector. The state, therefore, plays a direct and influential role in the position of education. State education policy is formulated at the Department of Education and Science in London.

(b) The day-to-day running, staffing and financing of state schools is the work of Local Education Authorities. These schools and colleges are financed partly from the local rates and partly from the rate-support grant handed out by the central government (see below).

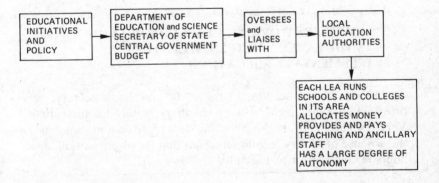

(c) Although the state provision of schools is something of a 'hotch-potch', there is a distinguishable pattern in the education of the nation's children between the ages of 5 and 16:

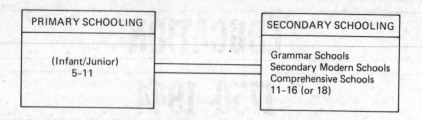

At the age of 16 a pupil may leave or stay on to study in the Sixth Form. At the age of 18 higher education (University, Polytechnic or College of Higher Education) is available for those who wish to go further.

(d) The modern system has evolved slowly, and sometimes painfully, since the early nineteenth century. In 1800 the state played no part at all in providing education adopting the *laissez-faire* attitude advocated by the political economists of the day. The state gradually became involved in education, firstly on a **supervisory** basis between 1833 and 1870 and then on a more direct **interventionist** basis from 1870 onwards.

(e) It is helpful to appreciate that during the nineteenth century the phrase 'elementary education' meant basic schooling for children from working-class backgrounds whereas 'secondary education' was provided by the Public Schools and Grammar Schools. The latter was only available to children from the upper and the middle classes.

18.2 HOW WERE WORKING-CLASS CHILDREN EDUCATED IN THE EARLY NINETEENTH CENTURY? (ELEMENTARY EDUCATION)

(a) Elementary education, in the early nineteenth century, was provided on a piecemeal basis by voluntary groups and individuals. Very few children from the labouring class received any schooling as the absence of factory legislation meant that they were working long hours in collieries or textile mills.

(b)

(i) Some children attended Dame Schools where they received a very basic education – a little reading and writing and little else. These schools were run by elderly women who charged a small fee for their services but in reality they were little more than child-minders.

(ii)   In some areas Sunday Schools had been established. Robert Raikes, a printer from Gloucester, introduced such schools in 1780. Walking through Gloucester one Sunday, when the factories were closed, he noticed the large numbers of children playing in the street. Raikes, a religious man, believed that these children would be far better off learning the three 'Rs' and having the Bible read to them. Raikes' idea spread so that in 1795 an estimated 250 000 children were attending Sunday Schools. Although somewhat limited, Sunday Schools took children irrespective of their religion or place of settlement and did at least attempt to instil a code of conduct.

(iii)   In some areas Charity Schools were in existence. These were financed by wealthy individuals for the purpose of teaching the three Rs and some vocational skills. Some Charity Schools were under the auspices of the Society for the Promotion of Christian Knowledge.

(iv)   Individual evangelicals and humanitarians came to realise that it was important to spread education if the poor were to lift themselves out of degradation. Two such men were Andrew Bell, a Church of England minister, and Joseph Lancaster, a Quaker, who both claimed the credit for the introduction of the **monitorial system**, where one teacher could teach up to 200 children by employing older pupils called monitors. Bell used the system when he was working in an orphanage in Madras in India (in 1797) and a teacher shortage led Lancaster to use monitors in his school in Southwark. The monitorial system was mechanical but cheap as only one teacher's salary had to be paid (see below).

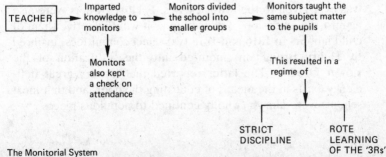

The Monitorial System

The work of Bell and Lancaster led to the formation of two rival religious groups which aimed to provide schools and education for poor children. In 1811 the 'National Society for Promoting Education of the Poor in the Principles of the Established Church throughout England and Wales' was formed. The Society set out to provide schools which taught the three Rs and the Catechism of the Church of England (that is, the Established Church). The monitorial system was employed. Meanwhile, Lancaster had already established the Royal Lancastrian Society in 1808 which, in 1814, was renamed 'The British and Foreign Schools Society'. This society aimed to provide schools which taught the three Rs and non-denominational religion; it attracted the support, therefore, of non-conformist groups. Samuel Whitbread, Owen and Wilberforce all backed the society.

(v) Both societies, in the absence of state participation in education, had a degree of success. It was the National Society which had the upper hand, being supported by the Anglican Clergy and Oxford and Cambridge Universities. Rivalry with the British and Foreign Society was intense. Apart from their religious differences both claimed to have introduced the monitorial system.

(vi) The two religious societies just did not have the necessary resources to provide education for all the nation's children. Many areas of the country remained without any schools at all. Only the state could provide elementary education on a nationwide basis. Even at this time a few voices expressed such an opinion but *laissez-faire* was firmly established and also the ruling classes were fearful of what might happen if education was ever given to the lower classes. Factory owners were also against the extension of education as it would deprive them of child labour. In 1816 and 1818 two select committees, inspired by Henry Brougham, inquired into the 'Education of the Lower Orders'. The latter reported that 'a very great deficiency exists in the means of educating the poor' and that most schools were almost 'wholly confined to populous places'.

18.3 WHAT MEANS OF EDUCATION WERE AVAILABLE FOR THE MIDDLE AND UPPER CLASSES IN THE EARLY NINETEENTH CENTURY? (SECONDARY EDUCATION)

As with elementary education, the state played no part in providing schooling for this section of society.

(a) Children of squires and parsons would often be educated in their home by a private tutor or governess. The Census Returns of the nineteenth century often reveal a governess living with the local rector's family.

(b) Middle-class children could choose to be educated at one of the old endowed grammar schools. These schools were founded in the late Middle Ages and Tudor period by a benefactor who endowed a sum of money for the education of the local children. As part of the charter laying down the terms of the endowment, the schools were to be 'free' and to cater for all classes. They were to teach the classical subjects of Latin and Greek. By 1800 the grammar schools were in sharp decline. Many had started to charge fees and accommodate boarders (thus going against their original charter). Moreover, with the onset of industrialisation their curriculum was obsolete; middle-class parents began to demand less emphasis on the classics.

(c) Some middle-class children attended private schools run by individuals – sometimes clergymen. These establishments varied in quality. A few offered a wider curriculum than the grammar schools but more were of the Dotheboys Hall type portrayed by Dickens in the novel *Nicholas Nickleby*. The masters were ill-educated themselves and merely interested in making some money from the fees they charged.

(d) Some of the grammar schools which started to charge fees and take boarders became known as Public Schools – among their number were Eton, Harrow, Winchester and Shrewsbury; they catered for the upper class. The Public Schools were, however, under a cloud in the early part of the nineteenth century. Bullying, flogging and even rioting were a part of life in these schools.

(e) In Scotland, Ayr town council took the lead in establishing Academies from the mid eighteenth century. Anxious to prepare pupils for the changing world of industrialisation the Academies offered a broad curriculum which mixed classical subjects with practical subjects such as science.

18.4 WHAT DEVELOPMENTS TOOK PLACE IN ELEMENTARY EDUCATION BETWEEN 1833 AND 1862?

(a) In 1833 Althorp's Factory Act made it illegal for children under nine to be employed in textile mills, thus providing more potential pupils for the schools. In 1833 the government provided a grant of £20 000 to be shared between the two religious societies. This was hardly enough, but at least the state had recognised that it had some kind of duty to educate the poor. Unfortunately the division of the money between the two societies helped to kindle further the jealousy and rivalry between them. The amount of the grant was increased to £30 000 in 1839. A further development in 1839 was the creation of the Committee of the Privy Council on Education with Dr James Kay-Shuttleworth as its secretary.

(b) Kay-Shuttleworth made a significant contribution to the development of elementary education. He was not impressed with the monitorial system, and in the workhouse school at Norwood he experimented with a system he had seen in Holland where older pupils acted as 'apprentices' to the teacher. This was the origin of the famous 'pupil-teacher' system.

In 1840 Kay opened the Battersea Teachers' Training College. It was a Church of England college which trained pupil-teachers and adults (between the ages of 20 and 30). The trainees were given a sound grounding in teaching methods and also had to study a wide range of subjects to broaden their own personal education. In 1843 the National Society took over the running of the college and opened several more on the same lines. By 1845 there were 23 colleges under the auspices of the National Society with 540 students. In 1846 the pupil-teacher system was formally introduced. A potential pupil-teacher had to be intelligent and at least 13 years of age before he could commence his training. He would assist the teacher in the classroom during the day and then study in the evenings. His apprenticeship lasted for five years, at the end of which, on the passing of an examination, he entered a Teacher Training College. (Successful candidates were awarded a grant called the Queen's Scholarship to finance their studies at Training College.) Those pupil-teachers who did not pass the examination would become assistant teachers.

(c) The Committee of the Privy Council also introduced inspectors, following the precedent set by Althorp's Factory Act of 1833. Any school receiving money via the government's grant was eligible for inspection. The Church of England was bitterly opposed to this idea as it resented the state interfering into the organisation of National Society Schools. As a result, a concordat was agreed in 1840 between the Church and State. Before an inspector could be appointed to a National Society School both the Archbishops of Canterbury and York had to be consulted.

(d) Despite the interest shown by the state in elementary education, individuals continued to take important initiatives. A Portsmouth shoemaker, John Pounds, founded a school which catered for the poorest children in the city. He taught them reading and writing and practical skills. This led to the Ragged Schools Union being formed in 1844; by 1858 the Union overviewed some 192 schools with a total of about 21 000 children. The Ragged School Movement was inspired by Lord Shaftesbury in England and Dr Guthrie in Scotland.

(e) The Newcastle Commission

(i) The government grant to elementary education grew steadily up to the middle of the nineteenth century: in 1846 £100 000 was given to education, and in 1858 the amount was £663 435. By this date the public were beginning to question the increasing education grant, particularly in view of the fact that £78 million had been spent on fighting the Crimean War (1854–6). Amid this concern the government appointed the Newcastle Commission (chaired by the Fifth Duke of Newcastle, Henry Pelham, and with Naussau Senior as one of its members) to 'inquire into the present state of Popular Education in England, and to consider . . . what measures . . . are required for the extension of sound and cheap elementary instruction to all classes'.

(ii) Their report, published in 1861, revealed some interesting information: – one in eight children of the poor population were going to school, albeit on a rather casual basis:

● Most children had left by the age of 10 to find work.
● Teachers were generally only interested in teaching the gifted pupils.

The Commission commented that the general teaching standard failed to 'secure a thorough grounding in the simplest but most essential parts of instruction'. Most of the Commissioners agreed that the government should continue to give public money for the 'assistance of education' together with a grant from the local county rates. However, these grants would only be paid if the pupils attended school regularly and passed annual examinations (in other words, payments would be according to results).

(f) The Revised Code

(i) In 1856 the Committee of the Privy Council had become the Department of Education. In 1862, Robert Lowe, the Vice-President of the Department, introduced the Revised Code which embodied a system of payments by results, but not in the exact form recommended by the Newcastle Commission. Lowe ignored the idea of a local county rate and decided to keep to the present system of grants being paid from Central Government funds. Lowe faced considerable opposition to this Revised Code and he was forced to justify his proposals in the House of Commons: 'I cannot promise the House that this system will be an economical one and I cannot promise that it will be an efficient one, but I can promise that it shall be one or the other.'

(ii) Lowe's scheme stated that schools could claim annually four shillings (20p) for each pupil who had a satisfactory attendance record. Another eight shillings (40p) was available if a pupil passed examinations set in reading, writing and arithmetic. The examinations were to be graded from Standard I to Standard VI. If a pupil failed in any one of the three Rs 2s.8d. (13p) would be deducted from the schools grant. The examinations were to be supervised by the inspectors who were issued with rigid instructions.

(iii) The most immediate effect of payment by results was a reduction in the education grant from £813 441 in 1862 to £636 806 in 1865. The schools made a greater effort to enforce regular attendance. However, the system stifled imaginative teaching and produced anxiety and tension amongst both teachers and pupils. Inspectors were seen as 'ogres' and were feared by the teaching staff. Payment by results lasted until 1897.

18.5 WHAT IMPROVEMENTS TOOK PLACE IN PUBLIC SCHOOLS AND GRAMMAR SCHOOLS IN THE MID-NINETEENTH CENTURY? (SECONDARY EDUCATION)

In the early part of the nineteenth century the numbers attending Public Schools and Grammar Schools rapidly declined (see Section 18.3). Their fortunes were revived by three interacting forces:

(a) Progressive headmasters

(i) *Samuel Butler* became the headmaster of Shrewsbury in 1798, a post he held until 1836. He reformed the teaching methods at Shrewsbury, abandoning rote learning. Butler was an imaginative and gifted teacher, always seeking to encourage and reward his pupils. He used a system of prefects giving the older boys a degree of responsibility. Shrewsbury's reputation was duly enhanced and provided a model for other Public Schools to follow.

(ii) In 1828 *Thomas Arnold* became the headmaster of Rugby School. Arnold instilled a moral code into his scholars and insisted that the classics were of value. Arnold also broadened the curriculum, however, by teaching science and humanities. His whole philosophy originated from his deep Anglican religious beliefs. Before long Arnold's drive and initiative had revitalised Rugby. Without doubt he made an important contribution in rebuilding the reputation of the Public School. He died in 1842.

(iii) A third headmaster in a similar mould was *Edward Thring* of Uppingham in Leicestershire. He built Uppingham up from a run-down Grammar School in 1853 to a greatly respected Public School with boarding facilities. Thring believed that all pupils had talent in at least one area of the curriculum; thus he provided a wide range of subjects. The morning was taken up with academic study and the afternoon was put aside for organised games and practical subjects. Uppingham had a gymnasium, workshops and a swimming pool. Thring believed in hard work and good organisation: his motto was 'Honour the work, and the work will honour you'.

(b) The work of the 'reforming headmasters' coincided with other developments. The Industrial Revolution produced a class of businessmen and industrialists who were anxious to give their sons and daughters a good 'character forming' education away from home. With the construction of the railways, children were able to travel away to school with ease. Thus the Public Schools were given the incentive to improve their reputations. The Grammar Schools were aided by the Municipal Corporations Act of 1835 which abolished the old town corporations and ended their influence. This opened the way for local trustees to provide grants to develop the Grammar School. In addition the Grammar Schools Act of 1840 said that it was no longer binding to keep the original charter. Thus new subjects (other than classics) could be introduced into the curriculum.

(c) The Clarendon Commission was appointed in 1861 'to inquire into the state of Public Schools'. Its report, published in 1864, recommended that classical subjects should remain at the hub of the curriculum but that other subjects should be introduced. The report was generally favourable to the Public Schools, praising the prefect system and the discipline. In 1864 the Schools Inquiry Commission was set up under the chairmanship of Lord Taunton. Its purpose was to investigate schools which had not come under the terms of reference of the Newcastle Commission and Clarendon Commission, that is, endowed schools, private schools and proprietary schools. The report (published in 1868) was critical of the Grammar Schools and advocated that secondary education should be provided for a greater proportion of the population.

The government's response was to pass the Endowed Schools Act in 1869. This established the Endowed Schools Commission which sat from 1869–74 – its duties were then taken over by the Charity Commission. The commission was given the brief of providing more secondary education for girls and reallocating endowments. A start was made in the mid nineteenth century to provide Girls' Secondary Education. Miss Frances Buss founded the North London Collegiate School in 1850, and this was followed by the opening of Cheltenham Ladies' College in 1858 under the principal, Miss Dorothea Beale. In 1872 The Girls Public Day School Trust was formed, and soon 33 schools had been opened catering for 7000 girls.

18.6 WHY WAS THE ELEMENTARY EDUCATION ACT OF 1870 PASSED AND WHAT WERE ITS TERMS?

(a) By the late 1860s there was increasing pressure for the state to intervene directly into elementary education. The Manchester Education Society (1864) and the Birmingham Education League (1869) campaigned vigorously for state education.

(i)   British industrial supremacy was being challenged, particularly by Germany and America. Contemporary critics were quick to point out that Germany had a state system of education.

(ii) The 1867 Second Reform Act gave the urban working-class man the vote. It was recognised that these men needed literacy if they were to use their vote correctly. Robert Lowe said that after the passing of the Reform Act 'I would believe it will be absolutely necessary [to] . . . prevail on our future masters to learn their letters'.

(iii) The population continued to increase rapidly and the voluntary societies could not provide enough school places, for example, in Birmingham and Leeds only 45 000 children out of 141 000 received any education. The Victorians were aware that education was vital in an industrialised society such as Britain.

(iv) There was also concern about the amount of alcoholism in society. This was put down to ignorance.

(b)   In 1868 the Liberals, under W. E. Gladstone, came to power. They recognised the problem but knew that any direct state intervention into elementary education would have to be a compromise in order to pacify the two religious societies, both of whom were frightened that they would lose a lot of influence. W. E. Forster was given the job of framing the Act. He based the proposed legislation on the suggestion that state schools could run side by side with church schools – the so called **dual system**. The state would provide schools in areas where the church groups had not developed. On 17 February 1870 Forster introduced the Bill to the House of Commons and said 'How can we cover the country with good schools? Our object is to complete the present voluntary system, to fill up gaps.'

(c)   The Elementary Education Act had the following terms:

1.   The present voluntary societies were to continue and would receive an increased grant from the government.
2.   The voluntary societies were given **six months** to build schools in the areas which had insufficient educational provision.

3. After six months a school board was to be elected to build Board Schools in areas where the provision was deficient.

4. The school boards had the power to levy a local rate for the building of schools in the area. (Finance would also come from government grants.)

5. The school board could charge a small weekly fee – up to 4p – but poor children were exempt.

6. School boards were given the power to make attendance compulsory – but this was left to the discretion of the local board.

7. To overcome the religious problem the Cowper-Temple Clause was included in the Act (named after the MP who proposed it) which said that 'no religious catechism . . . which is distinctive of any particular denomination, shall be taught in the school'. In addition parents could withdraw their child from religious lessons if they wished.

18.7 WHAT DID THE 1870 EDUCATION ACT ACHIEVE?

(a) The Act was a breakthrough in that it heralded the dawn of a new era where the state was to play a direct leading role in the position of education (up to 1870 the state's role had been one of 'overseeing' and supervising).

(b) Ironically, the Act inspired the voluntary societies to even greater efforts. Between 1870 and 1876 they provided a further one million places, and even in 1900 were actually responsible for the education of more children than the Board Schools.

(c)

(i) The Board Schools, introduced by the 1870 Act, still made a significant contribution to the system. For the first time there was provision for **all** children, no matter what their class or religion. Therefore children from non-church-going families now had the chance to go to school.

(ii) Furthermore, the Board Schools had better financial resources as they were supported by the local rates. They generally had better equipment and furniture than the voluntary schools, and attracted the more able teachers, although some had large classes.

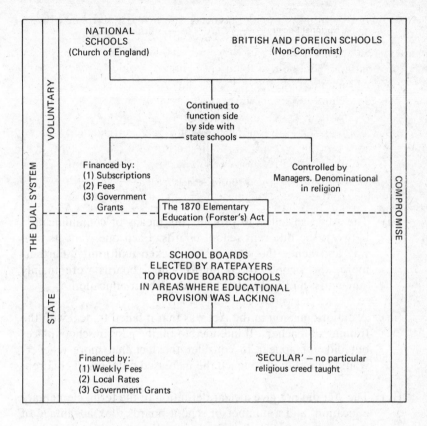

(iii) By 1876 at least half of the school boards had introduced a bye-law as they were entitled to in the Act, making education compulsory in their schools but the voluntary schools did not have the statutory power to make attendance compulsory.

(d)

(i) It must be remembered that the Act was a compromise. This inevitably brought criticism from all quarters. To the radicals in the National Education League the Act did not go far enough as it failed to make education free and compulsory. Many people still favoured the doctrine of *laissez-faire* and claimed that the state had no right to interfere in education. Some Anglican ministers accused the school boards of 'malpractice', saying that they had established themselves in areas where the Church had already satisfied the local needs. The dual system was therefore entangled with bitterness:

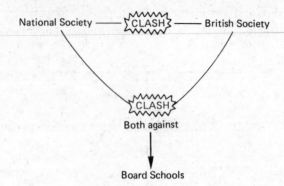

(ii) The Act also failed to provide any means of communication between the different school boards. Each one went its own way and hence the state system lacked uniformity. Furthermore, the people voted on to school boards were mainly 'amateurs' and had little knowledge about education.

(iii) A major omission in the Act was that it failed to deal with the training of teachers. It intended to fill the gaps in school places but did not appear to consider the fact that more teachers would be required to teach the increased numbers of children.

(iv) The Act did not give a clear definition of the term 'elementary education' and a number of school boards took advantage of this and provided Higher Grade Schools out of the rates, where the older, brighter children could be given a more challenging education. This was to have important consequences in later years (see Section 18.8(d)).

(e) Sandon's Act (1876) and Mundella's Act (1880) between them made elementary education compulsory up to the age of 10. In 1893 the school leaving age was raised to 11 years and then in 1899 to 12 years. Meanwhile in 1891 elementary education was made free.

18.8 WHY WAS THE 1902 EDUCATION ACT PASSED? WHAT WERE ITS TERMS AND HOW FAR WAS IT SUCCESSFUL?

(a) Secondary education was in a confused state by the latter decades of the nineteenth century. This type of schooling was still only available to a few children. Furthermore, six different government departments were involved in the administration of secondary education: The Education Department, Science and Art Department, Charity Commissioners, War Office, Admiralty, and Board of Agriculture. These departments did not consult with each other and the result was an administrative 'muddle'.

(b) In 1894 the Bryce Commission was set up to 'consider the best methods of establishing a well-organised system of secondary education in England'. In 1895 the Bryce Report recommended that one single department (controlled by a Minister of Education) should administer elementary and secondary education. Local education authorities, the report went on, should run secondary schools in the form of state Grammar schools (which would be fee paying with some free 'scholarship' places). The Minister of Education should advise the local authorities on teaching methods and inspection rather than issuing rigid regulations and laws. Bryce did not, however, recommend **free** Secondary Education for **all**.

(c) Legislation followed close on the heels of the Bryce Report. In 1899 The Board of Education Act joined together the previous administrative bodies so that secondary education came under the supervision of one central Board of Education. The Board was given the right to carry out inspections of secondary schools.

(d) Controversy lay just around the corner. The idea of joining the elementary sector with the secondary sector seemed logical to many government officials. This would facilitate administration at both national and local level. The school boards, however, were steadfastly against such a plan, wishing to retain their power. Robert Morant, a civil servant in the Education Department in 1895, was anxious to provide a more logical system of administration. He was aware that school boards were providing a form of 'secondary education' in Higher Grade Schools and he knew that this was strictly illegal, as the 1870 Act had stated that school boards only had the power to provide elementary education from the rates. In 1898 T. B. Cockerton, an auditor, challenged the right of the London School Board to provide Higher Grade Schools out of the rates they levied. The Cockerton Judgement of 1901 ruled that such schools were illegal, 'school boards are in the future to be limited to duties connected with elementary education' (Duke of Devonshire).

Thus the government was forced into legislation to straighten out the chaotic situation. In 1902 the Balfour Education Act was passed.

The Act was mainly the work of Robert Morant with Balfour guiding legislation through Parliament. The Act stated:

- School boards were to be abolished.
- They were to be replaced by local education authorities (328 in all) of which were to be two types;

(i) Part II LEAS – these were County Councils and County Borough Councils. They had the right to provide both elementary and secondary education.

(ii) Part III LEAS – these were the smaller borough councils with populations of at least 10,000 and Urban District Councils with over 20,000 people. They were empowered to provide elementary education only (the old board schools became council schools):

   - LEAS were to set up Education Committees.
   - Voluntary schools, now called 'non-provided schools', were to receive further financial aid out of the rates and they were to be supervised by the LEAs.
   - LEAs could, if they wished, provide teacher training colleges.
   (See diagram opposite.)

18.9 HOW WAS THE ACT RECEIVED AND WHAT WAS ITS IMPORTANCE?

(a) There was a great deal of opposition to the Act, particularly from the non-conformists who resented paying rates which would go to support schools where the Anglican Creed was taught.

(b) The Act did not provide secondary education for all children as the powers of the LEAs were permissive in character. Furthermore, no additional secondary school could be provided in areas under the jurisdiction of Part III LEAs. The provision of secondary education varied from area to area. Most working-class children's education was still obtained in an elementary school between the ages of 5 and 13.

(c) On the positive side, Balfour's Act was successful in bringing some kind of order to the previous organisational confusion. It also had the effect of increasing the supply of trained teachers, and it established a framework for future educational organisation, with a central body in London liaising with local authorities.

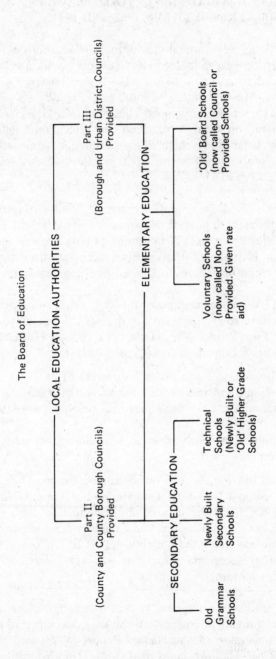

The Board of Education

LOCAL EDUCATION AUTHORITIES

Part II
(County and County Borough Councils)
Provided

Part III
(Borough and Urban District Councils)
Provided

SECONDARY EDUCATION

ELEMENTARY EDUCATION

Old Grammar Schools

Newly Built Secondary Schools

Technical Schools
(Newly Built or 'Old' Higher Grade Schools)

Voluntary Schools
(now called Non-Provided. Given rate aid)

'Old' Board Schools
(now called Council or Provided Schools)

18.10 WHAT DEVELOPMENTS TOOK PLACE IN EDUCATION BETWEEN 1902 AND 1944?

(a) In 1907 the new Liberal Government increased the number of free scholarship places in secondary schools. Working-class pupils would have their fees paid by the LEA if they passed a scholarship examination. Most secondary schools would reserve 25 per cent of their places for scholarship pupils. Thus bright working-class children were given the opportunity to climb 'the educational ladder'. For pupils who failed the scholarship examination some LEAs had 'Central Schools' which provided a practically-biased curriculum between the ages of 11 and 15.

(b) In 1906 The Education (Provision of Meals) Act stated that LEAs had the right to provide daily meals, and in 1907 the Education (Miscellaneous Provisions) Act permitted LEAs to carry out medical inspection in elementary schools. Both these measures were passed partly as a result of pressure organised by Margaret Macmillan.

(c) In 1917 the government was thinking about improving educational provision to compensate for the severe loss of young lives during the First World War. Herbert Lewis and H. A. L. Fisher inspired Fisher's Education Act (1918) which stated:

- The school-leaving age would be raised to 14.
- LEAs should provide nursery classes and also day-continuation classes for adolescents (on a part-time basis) between the ages of 14 and 18.
- A committee on teachers' salaries would be formed (the Burnham Committee).

The Act had brave intentions but became a victim of the post-war depression. Many LEAs did not respond to the Act and a shortage of money did not help; the idea of day-continuation classes was not realised. Fisher's Act, however, had a number of inbuilt weaknesses: the main one was that it did not abolish Part III LEAs and therefore in some areas secondary education was very scarce. Secondary education for all remained a dream.

(d) Very gradually a national system of education was evolving. major developments in educational thinking developed in the 1920s with the publication of the **Hadow Report** (1926) and the **Spens Report** (1928). Hadow, concerned with 'The Education of the Adolescent' recommended a break in the education process at the age of 11. The stage up to 11 should be called Primary (not elementary) Education. After 11 the pupils would begin the secondary stage of education suiting their ability and needs, which would last until the age of 15. Hadow's thinking was very influential at the time, and the Spens Report continued in the same vein. Spens suggested that pupils should be transferred to a secondary school at the age of 11 plus, according to their performance in a selection examination. These recommendations reflected the thinking of psychologists at the time who stated that children's innate intelligence could be measured by an intelligence test. The Norwood Report of 1943 made a very clear statement as to the organisation of education in the future when it recommended the **tripartite system**:

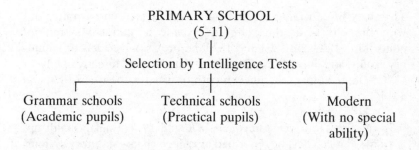

PRIMARY SCHOOL
(5–11)

Selection by Intelligence Tests

Grammar schools	Technical schools	Modern
(Academic pupils)	(Practical pupils)	(With no special ability)

At the time, doubts were expressed about the fairness of selecting children at the age of 11. Were IQ (Intelligence Quotient) Tests accurate and reliable? These doubts were to play a part in the development of education in the 1950s and 1960s when Comprehensive Schools were set up in large numbers.

(e) In 1944 Butler's Education Act was an important step forward and achieved the ideal of 'secondary education for all'. The terms of the Act were:

- Part III LEAs were swept away and the number of LEAs was reduced from 315 to 140.
- Education was to be provided free for all children between the ages of 5 and 15 (the school-leaving age would be raised to 16 as soon as possible).
- Free milk and medical inspection.
- The Board of Education became the Ministry of Education.
- Education was to be provided in three stages, primary, secondary and further.

How to select children at 11 plus was left to the LEAs. Most of them opted to administer the 11+ examination which placed children in one of the three kinds of secondary school.

Thus the tripartite system was put into operation, although the Act did not refer to such a system by name:

● Religious instruction in state schools was to be non-denominational and compulsory but parents were given the right of withdrawing their children.
● Public schools and private schools were permitted to remain independent from the state and to continue charging fees.

18.11   CONCLUSION

The story of education up to 1944 is complicated and synonymous with the efforts of the state to provide a 'national system of education'. Between 1800 and 1870 the provision was left to voluntary groups and only from 1870 did the state become directly involved. H. C. Dent captures the uneven path of progress between 1870 and 1914:

In the forty four years between 1870 and 1914, England built up, from what can best be described as ragged chaos, statutory systems of elementary and secondary education . . . The twenty years between 1918 and 1939 were to be a period of gestation rather than action. Not until 1944 was rapid advance resumed.

QUESTIONS

1.   **Objectives 1 and 2**

(a)   What provision was there for the education of working-class children before 1870?   (8 marks)
(b)   Why was the Elementary Education Act passed in 1870?
                                                                (4 marks)
(c)   What changes did this Act make to the education system?
                                                                (8 marks)

2.   **Objectives 3 and 4**

Study the source opposite and then answer the questions:

(courtesy of BBC Hulton Picture Library)

(a) Describe the main features of the monitorial schools in the early nineteenth century.

(b) Explain (i) why some people were in favour of such schools, and (ii) why other people were against them.

(c) Do you think the person who drew the illustration (above) was a supporter or an opponent of monitorial schools? Give reasons for your answer.

(Total = 25 marks)

(Southern Examining Group)

3. **Objectives 2 and 4**

Study the following extracts which are taken from School Log Books and then answer the questions. The school in question was a National Society School opened in 1840 situated in a small rural village:

Extract A
'1863 – It was agreed that the master should be paid a salary of £56 per annum. This would be paid in monthly instalments by the Rector'.

Extract B
'July 16th 1866 – Today the school's grant was announced. It amounted to £19.15s, made up of £10.8s for examinations and £9.7s for attendance'.

Extract C
'September 16th 1892 – School visited by the Rector who gave a Scripture lesson'.

Extract D
'May 24th 1907 – Empire Day. The timetable will not be followed this morning. Lessons will be given on the Empire. Opened school by singing the National Anthem'.

Extract E
'September 5th 1908 – Sydney Smith was caned today for scrumping apples out of the Rector's garden on his way home from school'.

Extract F
'April 25th 1918 – Received a circular letter from the Director of Education on "The War and its Meaning"'.

Extract G
Name on the village War memorial: 'Sydney Smith – killed in action on the Somme. July 20th 1916'.

Extract H

We all attended the village school from the age of three. The infants' room was a gallery. At the front was a small space for the teacher's desk, a blackboard, a cupboard for our slates and the coke stove. The rest of the room was taken up by a wide staircase which stretched from wall to wall. Wooden tables with iron legs were screwed to each step and the infants sat on the step above the floor, the youngest at the front, and it was only when we advanced to be a 'big' infant and sat at the top of the gallery that we could see out of the windows . . . When the boys were ten they moved to the Higher Grade School three miles away in the town. My brothers walked in and out daily . . . We girls never went to the Higher Grade . . . We had none of the frills of modern education, but we all learnt the 3Rs and how to hand sew.
(Recollections of an elderly resident on her schooldays in 1906, written in 1972)

(a) Explain why the rector played a role in the running of this school.   (2 marks)
(b) Explain how the grant (Extract B) was worked out and under which piece of legislation.   (3 marks)
(c) What evidence is there that this school was affected by national events?   (3 marks)
(d) How would this school have been affected by Balfour's Act of 1902?   (2 marks)
(e) Is Extract H a primary or secondary source? Explain your answer?   (3 marks)
(f) How has education changed compared with the description given in Extract H?   (7 marks)

4. **Objective 3**

The year is 1861. You have just started at a famous Public School. Write a letter to your parents describing life in your new school.
                                                                                        (20 marks)

5. **Objectives 1 and 2**

(a) Describe the following aspects of education:
- Acts passed by the Liberals in 1906 and 1907
- 1918 Fisher's Education Act
- 1926 The Hadow Report
- 1944 Butler's Education Act. (15 marks)

(b) How important were these events? (5 marks)

PUBLIC HEALTH IN BRITAIN 1750–1900

19.1 INTRODUCTION

'Public Health' is the notion that **all** the people in a country should be fit and healthy. Such a notion can only be realised if all people live and work in a clean environment, have a balanced diet and a high standard of medical care. In the early nineteenth century none of these preconditions applied to the population of Britain with the exception of the upper classes. The main reason for this was that the industrial take-off brought the rapid growth of towns. Such was the growth of the urban population that proper drainage, sanitation and water-supply were ignored and the housing accommodation was 'jerry-built'. Disease was rife and death rates were alarmingly high.

Progress towards a Public Health System in Britain was only gradual and it contained two phases:

- Firstly, the provision of a clean living environment by efficient sanitation (preventative measures).
- Secondly, an attack on the causes of individual diseases which developed with the science of bacteriology from about 1865 (curative measures) (see Section 19.9).

19.2 WHAT WERE THE MAIN ENVIRONMENTAL PROBLEMS OF THE GROWING TOWNS IN THE FIRST HALF OF THE NINETEENTH CENTURY?

(a) Housing

(i) The standard of housing in the towns was extremely poor. Builders were unscrupulous and out to make huge profits.

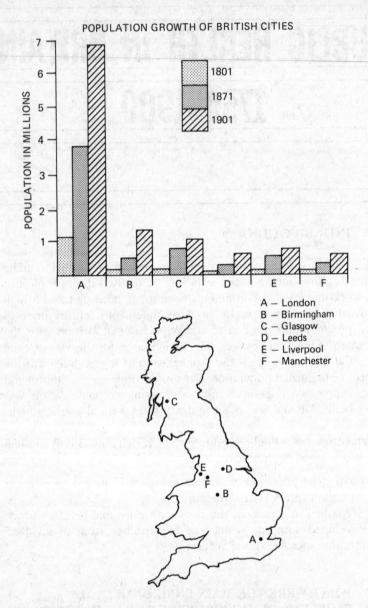

POPULATION GROWTH OF BRITISH CITIES

A — London
B — Birmingham
C — Glasgow
D — Leeds
E — Liverpool
F — Manchester

James Hole, describing housing in Leeds, claimed that the builders wanted 'immediate sales and hence put as little material and labour into them' as they possibly could. As housing was in such great demand small areas of land were subject to high-density houses which were built as quickly as possible. Row upon row of 'back to back' terraces were constructed. There were no gardens, and privies were at the end of the street. In many cities houses were constructed around a courtyard, 'cul-de-sacs' which had one entrance. Such courtyards were dismally dark, devoid of sunlight and subject to poor ventilation, allowing obnoxious smells to linger. Into the courtyard domestic refuse of every conceivable type was deposited. In Edinburgh some of the houses had more than ten storeys; the top was usually filthy as people could not be bothered to carry water up to the top. The interiors were damp as a result of the inhabitants having windows bricked in so as to avoid the payment of the hated window tax.

(ii)   As the population continued to increase at an unprecedented rate, there were simply not enough houses to go round. The result of this was widespread 'cellar-dwelling'. Edwin Chadwick's *Report on the Sanitary Condition of the Labouring Classes* published in 1842 revealed the overcrowding in graphic detail. Cellars were subject to flooding – often with effluent from the street above, and they were often shared by large numbers of people. Dr Duncan Howard investigated the working-class areas of Manchester on behalf of Chadwick and estimated that there were '8000 inhabitant cellars in Liverpool . . . [with] . . . 35 000 to 40 000 occupants'. He goes on to describe how he visited a family of 13 'twelve of whom had typhus fever, without a bed . . . , without straw or timber shavings . . . '. Furthermore, cellars were often occupied by a miscellaneous collection of individuals – to find perhaps two or three families together with seamen, pedlars and whores was commonplace. In Manchester 40 people were found to be living in one cellar. Such conditions resulted in sexual promiscuity, with perhaps married couples sharing their bed with their children and the lodger. Cases of incest were regularly brought to the courts.

(iii) The large towns had a number of 'Common Lodging Houses' which were usually overcrowded and filthy. They were run by 'keepers' intent on extracting as much as possible in charges from the various lodgers. Before 1851 these Lodging Houses were totally unregulated – thus they were poorly furnished, badly ventilated and overcrowded. A Northumbrian miner, William Eddy, described a lodging house 'which [was] not to be fit for a swine to live in . . . there was 16 bedsteads . . . and 50 occupied these beds at the same time . . .

often three at a time in the bed and one at the foot'. In London, the Metropolitan Police Force found 29 seamen in six tiny rooms. In one of the rooms the body of a dead seaman had been left, covered with a dirty blanket.

(b) Sanitation and street pollution

Most towns had totally inadequate systems of drainage and sewerage disposal. Where sewers did exist, they were incapable of dealing with the large volume of effluent. Sewers tended to be square in shape and built of porous brick. They constantly became blocked and men had to descend into them to shovel out the sludge which had deposited. This sludge ('night-soil') was left in a pile in the street. Some of the wealthier residents of the towns had water closets, but these were generally not connected by pipe to the sewer: instead the waste was fed into the nearest river or ditch. The vast majority of people had to share outside privies, which were cleaned out infrequently and emitted a terrible stench. In many cases the contents of the privy drained into a cesspit or an open gutter or ditch. Some of the streets were cleaned by 'scavengers' but the alleyways and courtyards had large deposits of domestic refuse and human excreta decomposing in large heaps. Many people kept pigs which were allowed to search the 'dung-heaps' for pickings. In addition, slaughter houses filled the open sewers with offal and blood and factories pumped in waste products. Chadwick stated that 'of 687 streets inspected [in Manchester], 248 were . . . unpaved, 112 ill-ventilated [and] 352 [had] stagnant pools, heaps of refuse, etc.'

(c) Water-supply

Fresh running water in the towns was at a premium – only available to the wealthier classes. Most townspeople had obtained their water from stand pipes in the streets, wells or butts which collected rain water. The water was supplied by private water companies who competed fiercely. The taps or pumps were turned on for a limited period during the day and people had to queue to fill up buckets. Water was rationed carefully and it was common to use it twice over, once for cooking and then for washing pots. London's water came from the River Thames which was where the city's sewage was deposited. Michael Faraday described this river as an 'opaque pale brown fluid'.

(d) Graveyards

As the towns expanded the churchyards and burial grounds could not cope with the larger numbers of dead. The problem was made worse by the thousands who died during the cholera epidemics. Bodies were buried above each other and sometimes human bones actually poked out from the ground. Often bodies could not be buried immediately and they began to decompose, giving off a repugnant stench.

19.3 WHAT WAS THE HEALTH OF THE PEOPLE LIKE IN THE CITIES?

Not surprisingly, the general health of townsfolk, particularly the labourers, was poor: disease was rife. Susceptibility to disease was increased by poor diet and the appalling environmental conditions. The death-rate increased alarmingly in some cities from 1820 onwards.

(a) Diet

Most working people existed on a diet of potatoes, bread and dripping, and porridge. Very little fruit or fresh vegetables were consumed. Furthermore, a large percentage of the weekly income was spent on alcohol. Food was often adulterated by profit-seeking shopkeepers: for example, tea-leaves were dried out and resold, salt was added to beer, chalk was added to milk and flour.

(b) Disease

(i) Disease was regarded as part and parcel of life at this time and people generally adopted a philosophical attitude, particularly to endemic (as opposed to epidemic) disease. Diptheria and scarlet fever struck young children in the cities, and typhus claimed about 4000 victims every year, mainly from the labouring classes. Dysentry, typhoid and smallpox, whooping-cough and measles, were also a threat to life. There were four major outbreaks of typhoid from 1830 to 1836 and despite the introduction of the smallpox vaccination, there were still people dying from this disease. In 1848 the *Illustrated London News* commented that 'the extent to which vaccination is neglected . . . is deplorable and inconceivable'. It reported that out of 140 deaths in East Sunderland in the first quarter of

1848, 47 were smallpox victims. The 'white plague' or tuber-culosis (TB) was another widespread disease consistently accounting for a large number of deaths.

(ii) It was generally accepted at this time that there was a correlation between dirt and disease. It was thought that refuse and decomposing matter resulted in the air becoming contaminated by a poisonous gas or 'miasma' – this brought the spread of disease. This filth and decay resulted in the spontaneous generation of germs. Chadwick, himself, was led to comment that 'all smell is disease'. No one, as yet, fully understood that germs caused disease which was then passed between people via contaminated water, food, or a carrier (human or animal). There was, however, a growing belief in the contagion theory – that disease was spread from person to person. Again no-one really understood how: it was mainly a hunch.

(iii) It was *Asiatic Cholera*, however, which caused the most consternation. This disease appeared in India in 1818 and gradually spread north-westwards through Europe. Two doctors, Russell and Barry, were despatched to St Petersburg to study the effects of the disease. It was evident that it was only a matter of time before cholera reached Britain. The doctors' report confirmed the government's fears about the devastating effects of the disease and a Central Board of Health was set up as a contingency measure. Many towns established *ad hoc* Boards of Health and began to issue information and advice about cholera. In October 1831 the first case of cholera in Britain was reported in the seaport of Sunderland. The authorities imposed a quarantine order on the port arousing great anger among sea merchants and tradesmen who objected to their trade being disrupted. The disease spread rapidly, and by mid-1832 had resulted in 52 000 deaths, including 10 000 in Edinburgh and Glasgow alone. Cholera actually frightened people and for a time the casual attitude of 'accepting' disease was undermined. This infection appeared to strike at all sections of society – not just the labourers; it also struck with alarming speed. The local Boards of Health tried desperately to control the epidemic. Houses were whitewashed with chloride of lime and barrels of burning tar were placed in the streets to 'disperse the miasma'. Instructions were issued to the effect that victims should be speedily buried. In retrospect we can see that most of these measures were based on a total misunderstanding of how the disease was spread. However, at the time, they were seen as sensible as they genuinely believed disease to be spread by miasma.

When the epidemic abated, the Boards of Health were disbanded and the old attitudes reappeared. Some people, like Robert Baker, a Leeds surgeon, recognised that cholera 'prevailed [most] in those parts of the town where there is often an entire want of sewerage, drainage and paving'. Baker reported 702 deaths in Leeds between May and November 1832, and he suggested that Leeds should be provided with a proper system of paving, drainage and sewerage disposal. Despite this advice, little was done immediately in Leeds or across the country. Further cholera epidemics struck Britain in 1848–9 (70 000 deaths), 1853–4 (30 000 deaths) and 1866 (18 000 deaths).

(c) Life-expectancy

In 1842 Edwin Chadwick's *Report on the Sanitary Conditions of the Labouring Classes* showed that city-dwellers had a much lower life-expectancy than those living in rural areas; furthermore, social class was shown to be a factor in determining how long a person would live. The following figures, taken from the report, are for the years 1839–40:

	Average age at death					
Social class	*Liverpool*	*Leeds*	*Manchester*	*Bolton*	*Kendall*	*Rutland*
Gentlemen and professional persons	35	44	38	34	45	52
Tradesmen (including farmers in rural areas)	22	27	20	23	39	41
Labourers/operatives, mechanics and servants	15	19	17	18	34	38

Statistics were also quoted which indicated a high rate of infant mortality in the cities. Chadwick commented 'It is an appalling fact that of all who are born of the labouring classes in Manchester, more than 57% die before they attain five years of age'. Chadwick attributed the differences in life-expectancy to the filthy living conditions in the towns. The investigator, Mr J. R. Wood – of the Statistical Society of Manchester, said that he found 'instances of the squalid misery so frequently in large towns . . . extremely rare' in Rutlandshire, a rural agricultural area. Chadwick also suggested that the badly-ventilated factories and long working hours (see chapter 14) were a contributory factor towards an early death.

19.4 WHY WAS SO LITTLE DONE TO IMPROVE LIVING CONDITIONS IN THE FIRST PART OF THE NINETEENTH CENTURY?

(a) Inefficient administration

(i) Today services like sewage disposal, street lighting and paving are provided by **one** authority called the Local Authority. Before 1835, many of the growing industrial towns did not possess a Royal Charter and therefore did not have a Town Council. Where councils did exist they were often corrupt and inefficient; furthermore, they were self-perpetuating rather than elected and they did not have to account for the way they spent the rates. In some towns, power was in the hands of the parish vestry which was elected by property owners.

(ii) The *1835 Municipal Corporations Act* tried to rectify this situation:

- Town councils were to be elected by the ratepayers every three years.
- Rates could be levied for street-lighting, pavements, fresh-water-supply and sewage disposal, but this required a local Act of Parliament.

(iii) In view of the situation in (i) a number of *ad hoc* bodies had developed since the mid eighteenth century. These were called *Improvement Commissions*. Usually they each dealt with one aspect of health – water-supply, drainage, paving, etc.; duties therefore overlapped and there was total confusion. The commissions often competed with each other and indulged in nuisance tactics in order to prevent a rival body gaining an advantage. For example, the two drainage commissions in Lancaster refused to integrate the drainage system for the town as a whole. London was a total muddle. In the words of Finer, London had '300 parishes, improvement commissions and boards of trustees, operating under 250 local Acts'. Such chaos obviously militated against reform: the whole system needed rationalising, but vested interests were so strongly ingrained that change would not be easy to achieve.

(b) Self-interests

Water companies and builders were in search of profit and they were against any interference in the status quo. Water companies, for example, only supplied water to those areas of a town where the householders could afford their fees. Builders exploited the excessive demand for housing by building dwellings rapidly, taking little notice of drainage, ventilation or water-supply. Furthermore, private landlords were reluctant to pay for sanitary improvements stating that they were not prepared to subsidise the cleanliness of the labouring class.

(c) Lack of scientific knowledge and ignorance

Knowledge of town planning was limited and this was a contributory factor to the jerry-building. There is also evidence to suggest that many middle-class people were ignorant of the living conditions of the labouring classes. Middle class areas contained 'Gothic' style villas built on the edge of the town and were worlds apart from the inner-city slums.

(d) The philosophy of *laissez-faire*

This is often quoted as the main reason why nothing was done to improve conditions; the government, in keeping with *laissez-faire* attitudes did not see it as their responsibility; and therefore did nothing. Prior to 1870 the government had to be goaded into taking action by a number of individuals who were passionate in their demands for reform.

19.5 WHY AND HOW DID THE 'SANITARY REFORM MOVEMENT' ORIGINATE IN THE MID-NINETEENTH CENTURY?

(a) The Sanitary Reform Movement

This Movement originated from the Poor Law Commission established in 1834, (see chapter 16). As secretary to the Commission, Chadwick did not relate to the other Commissioners (Frankland Lewis in particular) and became increasingly disaffected. He began to diversify his interests and, motivated by his Utilitarian education under Bentham, turned his attention to the health of the labouring classes. Chadwick was out to stop waste and was aware that the poor rates were being used to provide medical care for paupers. He set out to investigate living conditions with the idea that if the conditions of the cities were improved it would, in the long run, cost the poor law authorities less money.

(b) In 1838 living conditions in London were investigated by Dr Neil Arnott, Dr James Kay (later Sir J. Kay-Shuttleworth) and Dr Southwood Smith. Two reports were produced as a result of their inquiries, one had particular reference to the areas of Bethnal Green and Whitechapel. Both reports drew attention to the abysmal conditions already referred to in Section 19.2. The Bishop of London put forward a motion in the Lords that a nationwide investigation was now necessary. The motion was carried and Chadwick was charged with the task. The inquiry was nominally under the Poor Law Commission but Frankland Lewis was far from happy about it. Chadwick mobilised poor law medical officers and assistant commissioners to interview people and make personal visits to towns in search of evidence. They started in 1839 and the *Report on the Sanitary Conditions of the Labouring Class of Great Britain* was published in 1842. Its author was Chadwick. The Poor Law Commission disassociated themselves from the report as they feared a backlash from the numerous bodies Chadwick had criticised. The impact of the report was devastating (see Section 19.2), some 30 000 copies being initially printed.

(c) Chadwick recommended preventative measures in the report. He had no time for curative theories or for doctors, declaring that sanitary 'engineers were needed for the task at hand not the medical profession'. Among his recommendations was the **arterial system** which was an integrated plan for the removal of filth. First and foremost a regular supply of clean water was needed in towns. This would provide drainage from houses into a main sewer which would carry waste away from the town. He then favoured a system whereby the liquid manure would be directly supplied to the farmer's fields.

The arterial system

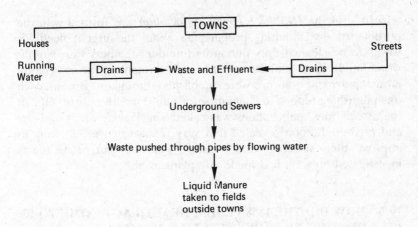

- Chadwick stated that sewerage systems should be built using cylindrical earthenware pipes which enabled the action of water to push along solid waste. Chadwick's view on this matter came from the influence of John Roe, who was the sanitary engineer for the Holborn Commission of Sewers. Before long Henry Doulton of Lambeth was manufacturing earthenware drainage pipes in large quantities.
- Chadwick anticipated the question – 'Who would pay for such a system?' by stating that the cost would be minimal if towns borrowed money which was paid back by householders over a period of 30 years.
- Finally, as one would expect from Chadwick, he was anxious to improve the administration of towns. He wanted the *ad hoc* bodies to be abolished and replaced by one authority which would be responsible for drainage, paving, water-supply and street cleaning. Such a suggestion was to arouse much opposition, particularly from the vested interest groups in London.

(d) The report on intra-mural interments, December 1843

This was an appendix to the 1842 report written by Chadwick at the request of Graham (Home Secretary). In it Chadwick recommended the opening of public cemeteries on land on the outskirts of towns and he also wanted the cause of death confirmed by the medical officer. In 1852 the Home Secretary was given the power to close overcrowded cemeteries in London. In 1853 this legislation was enforced on a national basis; in addition parishes could now buy land for burial purposes outside towns.

(e) In 1844 the *Health of Towns Association* was formed with the purpose of disseminating propaganda about the urgent need for towns to be cleaned up. Among its founder members were Southwood Smith, Lord Shaftesbury and Lord Normanby. The association grew rapidly and branches were established throughout Britain, each one publishing reports and agitating for public health reform. One of the associations' publications was called *The Weekly Sheet of Facts and Figures*. It soon revealed that very few towns were looking to improve their sewerage and drainage systems. Out of 67 towns investigated only six had made any plans at all.

19.6   HOW DID THE 1848 PUBLIC HEALTH ACT COME TO BE PASSED AND HOW EFFECTIVE WAS IT?

(a)   In 1847 William Duncan became the Medical Officer for Liverpool, the first such appointment in Britain. This was directly due to the influence of the Health of Towns Association. By now the public health debate had polarised into those in favour of reform, 'The Clean Party' and those against, 'The Dirty Pack' (or 'Muckabites'). After a fierce debate in the Commons the *1848 Public Health Act* was passed (see the diagram opposite).

(b)   Alongside the Act was passed the *Nuisance Removal Act* which made provisions for combating the imminent cholera outbreak.

(c)   The Public Health Act at least, helped to break down the attitude of *laissez-faire*. It also provided some 182 smaller towns with local Health Boards, many of whom had arterial systems installed under the supervision of the skilled engineer, Robert Rawlinson. The system was shown to be workable, illustrated by the fact that many townspeople wrote to Chadwick to express their satisfaction. However, the Act had several weaknesses. For example:

● The lifespan of the Central Board was limited to five years, almost a probationary period.

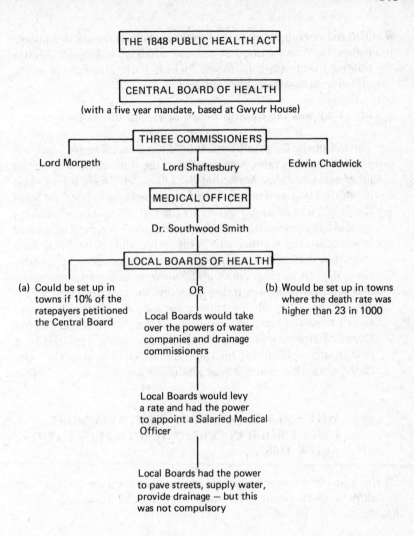

THE 1848 PUBLIC HEALTH ACT

CENTRAL BOARD OF HEALTH
(with a five year mandate, based at Gwydr House)

THREE COMMISSIONERS

Lord Morpeth   Lord Shaftesbury   Edwin Chadwick

MEDICAL OFFICER

Dr. Southwood Smith

LOCAL BOARDS OF HEALTH

(a) Could be set up in towns if 10% of the ratepayers petitioned the Central Board

OR

Local Boards would take over the powers of water companies and drainage commissioners

(b) Would be set up in towns where the death rate was higher than 23 in 1000

Local Boards would levy a rate and had the power to appoint a Salaried Medical Officer

Local Boards had the power to pave streets, supply water, provide drainage — but this was not compulsory

- The Act was permissive in character. Many towns did not bother to take advantage of the Act. The large cities by-passed the Act by keeping the old system of obtaining a private Act of Parliament to carry out any improvements (thus keeping matters on a local level and avoiding any centralised interference).
- The Act was based entirely on preventative measures and as such was narrow in outlook. Undoubtedly, such measures did bring improvement but Chadwick refused to pay any attention to contagionist theories or curative measures and thus alienated the medical fraternity.

● The Act did not legislate for London which remained an administrative nightmare. London became administered by the Metropolitan Commission of Sewers which took 17 years to install
effective drainage in the capital.

(d)   Why was the Central Board of Health disbanded?

The life of the Central Board should have ended in 1853 but was
granted a year's extension because of the third cholera epidemic
(1853–4). Chadwick knew that the Dirty Party were intent upon
his destruction and he published a propaganda 'report' on what
the board had achieved during its time of office. Unfortunately,
he could not resist criticising the vested interest groups again and
in doing so, put another nail in his own coffin. A hostile debate
ensued in Parliament in which Chadwick came under heavy fire.
He was seen by *The Times* and *Punch* as truculent, obnoxious
and someone who was trying 'to bully' the country into cleanliness. Eventually, the pressure took its toll and Chadwick resigned from the Central Board. On 12 August 1854 the Central
Board of Health was officially abolished – it was replaced by a
new Board of Health. This came under Sir Benjamin Hall and
lasted until 1858 when it was abolished for good.

19.7   WHY DID THE GOVERNMENT PLAY A MORE DIRECT ROLE IN PUBLIC HEALTH LEGISLATION AFTER 1865?

By the mid-1860s a number of developments forced the government
to adopt a more positive approach in terms of providing public
health:

(a)   Great concern was caused by a fourth cholera epidemic in 1866;
it was clear that the 1848 Act had only partly succeeded and its
permissive nature had allowed many towns 'off the hook'.

(b)   By this time Pasteur was beginning to demonstrate 'The Germ
Theory of Disease', that is, the belief that germs caused disease. It
was therefore essential to remove dirt if disease was to be controlled
and *The Lancet* disseminated the new ideas.

(c)   Dr John Snow's work in Soho in 1854 also became well known.
He was able to show by careful observation that cholera was spread

by the contaminated water issuing from a pump in Broad Street. In the light of this new knowledge it was obvious that only direct involvement by Parliament could enforce efficient drainage and water-supply in all British towns. The philosophy of *laissez-faire* was dying.

(d) In 1867 the Second Reform Act gave working-class urban males the vote. For the first time they could directly influence their living conditions by voting in MPs willing to support Public Health reform.

(e) In 1858 Public Health provision came under the joint juris-diction of the Privy Council and the Home Secretary. Sir John Simon, a surgeon and Medical Officer for London 1848–55, was appointed Medical Officer of Health for the Privy Council, and he provided more data and statistics about the nature of disease. Simon went a stage further than Chadwick, being very keen to combine curative and preventative measures to ensure a healthy population, and instigating numerous inquiries.

19.8 WHAT LEGISLATION WAS PASSED BETWEEN 1866 AND 1900 TO IMPROVE PUBLIC HEALTH?

(a)

(i) In 1866 the Sanitary Act was passed which forced towns to appoint sanitary inspectors who were to check that water-supplies and drainage were adequate.

(ii) Such was the volume of information gathered by Sir John Simon on diseases and public health, the government ap-pointed a Royal Sanitary Commission in 1869; it was particu-larly concerned that public health was administered by a wide range of bodies whose work often overlapped. The commission published its report in 1871 and as a result the *Local Govern-ment Board Act* was passed; this placed public health and the poor law in the hands of the Local Government Board. This was followed by the *1872 Public Health Act* which split the country into 'sanitary areas' each of which had to appoint a Medical Officer of Health. The combined effect of these two Acts was to tighten up the administration of public health.

(iii) *The Times* of 25 August 1875 commented 'that no less than 29 sanitary measures have been enacted since . . . 1846 . . . These Acts . . . [have been] made at different times, by various hands and with different objects'. In 1875 another *Public Health Act* was passed to rectify this confusion. It rationalised all the previous Acts into one piece of legislation. Local authorities were to be responsible for:

- Street-lighting.
- Lodging houses.
- Water-supply.
- Drainage and disposal of sewage.
- Provision of pure food.
- Public parks.
- New housing.
- Public toilets.

Furthermore, all authorities were compelled to employ health inspectors and medical inspectors to ensure that the Act was enforced.

(iv) Despite these measures, Sir John Simon resigned his post, embittered by the fact that an individual Ministry of Health had not been created. Simon always plays second fiddle to Chadwick in the 'public health story' – but we should not underestimate his contribution. In many ways he was more forward-looking than Chadwick, believing that public and private health were complementary. He deserves credit for his unstinting energy and his role in improving the administration of public health.

(b) Housing

(i) There still remained vast areas of slums in Britain. Little attention had been paid by Parliament to this aspect of the environment. A few individuals had campaigned for better housing taking the initiative in local schemes:

- *Prince Albert* took an interest in housing and had some 'model dwellings' built at his own expense in Hyde Park in 1851 to coincide with the Great Exhibition.
- *George Peabody (1795–1869)*, an American, provided money to build houses for the poor in North London.

● *Octavia Hill (1838–1912)* sponsored a number of projects to provide housing and recreation parks in city areas. She was a founder member of the National Trust (1895).

These were praiseworthy efforts but they were only scratching the surface of what was a huge problem. Government action was needed.

(ii) *The Torrens Act of 1868* was a step in the right direction but still very limited. It gave local authorities the power to demolish individual dwellings which had no drainage or water-closet. Next, in 1875, Richard Cross passed *The Artisans' and Labourers' Dwellings Improvement Act*. This enabled local authorities to place compulsory purchase orders on substandard areas of housing, knock them down and rebuild new dwellings for renting out. Few authorities used the Act because it involved them in heavy costs; one notable exception was Joseph Chamberlain, Mayor of Birmingham, who rebuilt large areas of the city.

(iii) Public opinion remained indignant about the poor state of Britain's poor housing. In response to this the Liberal Government appointed a Royal Commission of Inquiry in 1884. It confirmed in its report that much of Britain's inner-city housing was in a state of decay and recommended urgent action. As a consequence, the *Housing of the Working Classes Act* was passed in 1890. It restated the power of local authorities to purchase slum areas and construct new houses. Once again few town councils took advantage of the legislation; not until 1919 were large council house estates built.

19.9 MEDICAL ADVANCES

(a) What factors hindered medical progress in 1800?

In 1800 medical practice was still based mainly on theories and treatments which dated back to the Middle Ages. Among the factors holding back medicine were:

(i) Lack of knowledge about the causes and cure of disease. Although doctors knew that germs existed they believed that they resulted from disease (rather than causing it). This was the 'theory of spontaneous generation' which was rigidly adhered to by most doctors. Cures which originated from the belief that the body was made up of four humours of liquids were still prevalent, for example, purging and blood-letting. Herbal remedies were also widely used.

(ii) Doctors were hindered by a lack of equipment to help them carry out research. The microscope was in its infancy and there were no technical aids such as X-ray machines. In addition, the sciences of physics and chemistry had not been developed.

(iii) Surgery was still very primitive. Internal operations could not be carried out successfully because of the risk of infection; there were no antiseptics and surgeons did not realise that cleanliness was necessary for successful surgery. Operations were carried out in unhygienic conditions and the surgeons wore their everyday clothes with an apron to protect them from blood-stains. Instruments had wooden handles which harboured bacteria and they were not sterilised. The 'operating table' was more like a butcher's block. Blood-loss was also a problem. Although William Harvey had established that blood circulated the body (and, therefore, there was a fixed volume of blood), surgeons did not realise that there were four blood groups which had to be matched for successful transfusions. In addition, the instruments and syringes used in attempts to transfuse blood were usually infected. Finally, there were no anaesthetics apart from alcohol, and drugs such as mandrake and opium. Operations were, therefore, extremely painful, with many patients dying from surgical shock. The mark of a good surgeon was the speed with which he could carry out an amputation.

(b) Why was progress made in medicine between 1800 and 1900?

The number of factors of change combined to produce rapid progress (see opposite diagram).

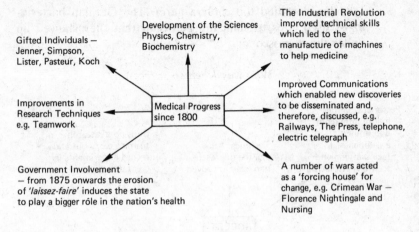

Gifted Individuals — Jenner, Simpson, Lister, Pasteur, Koch

Development of the Sciences Physics, Chemistry, Biochemistry

The Industrial Revolution improved technical skills which led to the manufacture of machines to help medicine

Improvements in Research Techniques e.g. Teamwork

Medical Progress since 1800

Improved Communications which enabled new discoveries to be disseminated and, therefore, discussed, e.g. Railways, The Press, telephone, electric telegraph

Government Involvement — from 1875 onwards the erosion of 'laissez-faire' induces the state to play a bigger rôle in the nation's health

A number of wars acted as a 'forcing house' for change, e.g. Crimean War — Florence Nightingale and Nursing

A number of factors of change combined to result in rapid progress

Medical progress, however, was on occasions obstructed by those who wanted to keep things as they were, fearing change. Jenner, Pasteur, Simpson and Lister all had to face scathing criticism from the medical world.

(c) Who were the pioneers of bacteriology?

(i) *Louis Pasteur (1822–95)*

In 1865 Pasteur, a French chemist, proved beyond doubt that the air was full of tiny micro-organisms which caused decay and disease ('The Germ Theory of Disease'). He gave several public demonstrations of an experiment using a swan-necked flask to illustrate this discovery. Pasteur had to face a torrent of criticism and abuse from the spontaneous generationists led by Dr Charlton Bastian.

(ii) *Robert Koch (1843–1910)*

He was a German scientist who built on the foundations established by Pasteur. Koch was able to show that specific micro-organisms were the cause of specific diseases in humans and animals. Once the micro-organism had been identified (and this was the real problem), methods of destroying it could be found. Koch initially discovered the bacterium which caused animal anthrax; in 1882 he discovered the TB germ, and in

1883 he identified the cholera germ. The German bacterio-logist used dyes to stain the germs so that they showed up under the microscope:

Why was Koch so successful?

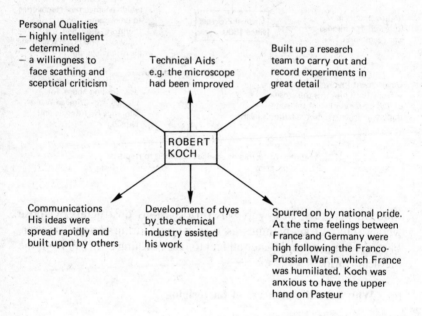

Personal Qualities
— highly intelligent
— determined
— a willingness to face scathing and sceptical criticism

Technical Aids e.g. the microscope had been improved

Built up a research team to carry out and record experiments in great detail

ROBERT KOCH

Communications His ideas were spread rapidly and built upon by others

Development of dyes by the chemical industry assisted his work

Spurred on by national pride. At the time feelings between France and Germany were high following the Franco-Prussian War in which France was humiliated. Koch was anxious to have the upper hand on Pasteur

Following the work of Pasteur and Koch, bacteriology deve-loped rapidly, and other micro-organisms were discovered (for example, diphtheria (1884), tetanus (1884), pneumonia (1884), and bubonic plague (1894).

(d) What developments took place in preventing and curing disease?

(i) *Vaccination*

This may be defined as 'the injection of weakened infectious matter into a healthy body, to provide immunity against the particular disease' (Ritchie Calder)

● *Edward Jenner (1744–1823)*: In the early 1790s Jenner observed that dairymaids did not appear to contract the killer disease smallpox. Frequently, however, they were victims of cowpox, a milder form of smallpox, which they caught from the cows; their hands and arms were covered in sores. In 1796 Jenner took cowpox matter from Sarah Nelmes, a local dairymaid, and inserted it via two tiny incisions into the arm of a young boy, James Phipps. Two weeks later, smallpox matter was inserted into the boy's arm. Jenner watched and waited, and as he suspected, the boy did not contract smallpox. However, Jenner did not understand the process (which he called 'vaccination' – from the Latin word for cow, *vacca*). His discovery was, therefore, treated with a deal of scepticism; Gilray produced a cartoon which suggested that people who received a vaccination against smallpox would develop cows' horns and cows' heads would protrude from their arms and limbs.

● *Louis Pasteur and vaccination*:
It was some years before the idea of vaccination was accepted. Once germs had been successfully identified, however, it was realised that vaccines could be developed to prevent diseases. In 1880 Pasteur, along with his associates Charles Chamberland and Emile Roux, discovered a vaccine against chicken cholera. In 1881 he produced a vaccine to prevent anthrax and then in 1882, a vaccine against rabies. The first human to be vaccinated against rabies was a young boy from the province of Alsace, Joseph Meister.

● *Other developments* included the discovery of an anti-toxin against diptheria (Emile Behring, 1890) and a vaccine against TB (Albert Calmette and Camille Guerin, 1906).

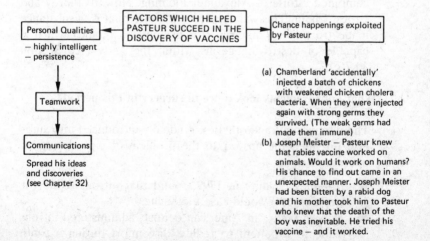

Personal Qualities
— highly intelligent
— persistence

FACTORS WHICH HELPED PASTEUR SUCCEED IN THE DISCOVERY OF VACCINES

Chance happenings exploited by Pasteur

Teamwork

Communications
Spread his ideas and discoveries
(see Chapter 32)

(a) Chamberland 'accidentally' injected a batch of chickens with weakened chicken cholera bacteria. When they were injected again with strong germs they survived. (The weak germs had made them immune)

(b) Joseph Meister – Pasteur knew that rabies vaccine worked on animals. Would it work on humans? His chance to find out came in an unexpected manner. Joseph Meister had been bitten by a rabid dog and his mother took him to Pasteur who knew that the death of the boy was inevitable. He tried his vaccine – and it worked.

(ii) *Drugs*

A drug is a substance produced from plants or chemicals which is used to cure disease.

Developments in the manufacture of chemical drugs came slowly. The pioneer in this field was another German, Paul Ehrlich (1854–1915). He originally worked with Koch and Behring, but in 1896 he established his own practice. Ehrlich felt that chemically-produced compounds might be able to kill certain bacteria within the blood without damaging the rest of the body. With this hypothesis in mind, he carried out an intense programme of research, concentrating on arsenic compounds, hoping to find one which would kill the syphilis germ. He and his team tried over 600 compounds without success. In 1908, a newcomer to the research team, Sahachiro Hata, retested some of the previously rejected compounds. This resulted in the discovery of Salvarsan (compound number 606), which Hata showed was able to find and destroy the syphilis germ if it was present in the blood-stream. Ehrlich referred to it as a magic bullet because it homed in on its target without harming the rest of the patient's body.

Ehrlich's work opened the door for a revolution in the production of chemical drugs. In 1934 Gerhard Domagk discovered that a red dye called Prontosil would destroy the germs which caused wounds to turn septic. Following this, a whole range of sulphonamide drugs were produced which were successful in killing a number of germs.

Between 1928 and 1943 penicillin was pioneered by the combined efforts of Alexander Fleming, Howard Florey and Ernest Chain. This was the first antibiotic, that is, a substance made from living material (for example, a mould) which is capable of destroying germs within the body (see Section 30.7(c)).

(e) What improvements took place in surgery in this period?

(i) The discovery of anaesthetics, gradually introduced into surgery, provided the answer to the problem of pain during an operation:

- *Humphrey Davy*, in 1799, found that nitrous oxide (or laughing-gas) would ease toothache.
- *Horace Wells*, an American dentist, administered nitrous oxide to a patient to reduce discomfort during a tooth

extraction (1845). Watching colleagues were not impressed.

- Ether was used as an anaesthetic by *William Morton*, an American surgeon, when removing a tumour on the neck of Gilbert Abbott (1846).
- A few days later Robert Liston emulated Morton when carrying out a leg amputation at University College, London. His patient, Frederick Churchill, was given ether.
- Ether had unpleasant side-effects. James Young Simpson (1811–70) was of the opinion that a more suitable substance existed. He carried out a number of experiments and, in 1847, found that chloroform rendered a person unconscious without the irritation which ether caused to the skin and lungs.

(ii) Initially, the use of anaesthetics was regarded with suspicion by both society and the medical profession. Their fears were increased when a small number of patients died after being given overdoses of anaesthetic. Eventually anaesthetics became generally accepted after it was known that Queen Victoria had given permission for the royal doctor to use chloroform during the delivery of Prince Leopold. In addition, anaesthetics became safer once surgeons became experienced about how much could be safely administered.

(iii) Infection remained a problem. In the early nineteenth century the mortality rate for surgical operations was as high as 85 per cent in some hospitals. Patients often survived the operation only to die when the wounds turned septic. Improvements in surgical cleanliness were slow to be accepted.

In 1847 a Hungarian, Ignaz Semmelweis, insisted on doctors in his hospital washing their hands in chloride solution before examining patients. His request was treated with amusement, even though the death rate from infection in the hospital was reduced. Semmelweis had no concrete evidence to support his idea – Pasteur's work on the Germ Theory did not occur until 1865.

Once Pasteur had shown that bacteria were present in the atmosphere, the way was open for the development of antiseptic surgery. The pioneer in this field was Joseph Lister (1827–1912), who designed a carbolic acid spray for use in operating theatres. The idea was to spray the atmosphere and instruments with a mist in order to kill germs. His methods were successful but he was attacked fiercely by the medical profession who accused him of having 'a mania for cleanliness'.

(iv) The successful transfusion of blood during an operation became possible in the early years of the twentieth century. In 1901 blood groups were identified (O, A, B, AB), and in 1914 sodium citrate was first used to stop blood coagulating in the syringe.

(f) Florence Nightingale and surgery

Before the work of Florence Nightingale (1820–1910) in the Crimean War, nursing was regarded with disdain and certainly did not rank as a profession. During the Crimean War (1854–6) Nightingale read the reports of *The Times* war correspondent, W. H. Russell, which told of the horrific condition in the British military hospitals. She organised a team of 38 nurses who travelled to the Crimea to care for the injured soldiers at Scutari. The improvements made were immediate:

- Sanitary conditions were cleaned up.
- The nurses cared for the soldiers in a compassionate and professional manner.
- Nightingale made the government spend more money on medical supplies.

The work of Nightingale was reported by W. H. Russell and, as a result, nursing gained status. She illustrated that good nursing was a vital component of medicine. Doctors, too, came to recognise the value of nurses, whereas previously they had viewed them with distrust. In 1860 the Nightingale School of Nursing was opened in St Thomas' Hospital, London. Others followed, and by 1900 there were over 60 000 trained nurses in British hospitals.

19.10 CONCLUSION

By 1900 considerable progress had been made in Public Health. In particular, the state had come to accept that it had an important role to play in maintaining a clean environment. There was still, however, much work to be done with regard to private health – vaccination campaigns, medical services, care of the elderly, the removal of poverty and the provision of unemployment insurance still had to be addressed. The Liberal Government of 1906–14 was to attack a number of these problems.

QUESTIONS

1. **Objectives 1 and 2**

(a) Describe the conditions in Britain's industrial cities in the early nineteenth century. (8 marks)

(b) Why was nothing done to improve such conditions before 1848? (4 marks)

(c) How successful was the Public Health legislation passed in the period 1848–75? (8 marks)

2. **Objectives 3 and 4**

Study the sources below and then answer the questions.

Source A

Courts and Cul-de-sacs exist everywhere . . . In one cul-de-sac in Leeds there are 34 houses, and in ordinary times there dwell in these houses 340 persons, or ten to every house. The name of this place is Boot and Shoe Yard, from whence the Commissioners removed, in the days of Cholera, 75 cartloads of manure which had been untouched for years. For the most part these houses are built back to back . . . A house of this description will contain a cellar, a house and chamber . . . To build the largest number of cottages on the smallest possible space seems to have been the original view of the speculators. Thus neighbourhoods have arisen in which there is neither water nor offices.

(Taken from *An Inquiry into the State and Condition of the Town of Leeds* by Robert Baker, 1842)

Source B   Plague spot near the London Gas-works, South Lambeth c.1840 (courtesy of BBC Hulton Picture Library)

PLAGUE SPOT NEAR THE LONDON GAS-WORKS, SOUTH LAMBETH

Source C   Shepherd's Buildings

Shepherd's Buildings consists of two rows of houses with a street seven yards wide between them; each row consists of what are styled 'back and front' houses, that is two houses placed back-to-back. There are no backyards; the privies are in the centre of each row, about a yard wide . . . each house contains two rooms . . . In one of these houses there are nine persons belonging to one family . . . There are 44 houses in the two rows, and 22 cellars, all of the same size. The cellars are let off as separate dwellings; these are dark, damp, and very low, not more than six feet between the ceiling and floor. The street between the two rows is seven yards wide, in the centre of which is the common gutter, or more properly sink, into which all sorts of refuse are thrown; it is a foot in depth. Thus there is always a quantity of putrefying matter contaminating the air. At the end of the rows is a pool of water very shallow and stagnant, and a few yards further, a part of the town's gas works. In many of these dwellings there are four persons in one bed.

(Taken from *The Report on the Sanitary Conditions of the Labouring Population, 1842*)

Source D

'We had rather take our chance of the cholera than be bullied into health by Mr. Chadwick'. (*The Times*)

Source E

'Not until the 1875 was the first really effective piece of Public Health legislation passed'.

(a)   What similarities can you detect between Sources A and C?
(b)   How far are Sources A and C reliable?
(c)   Source B has been drawn by an artist. Does this reduce its value as a piece of historical evidence?
(d)   Why did Chadwick face such hostility as depicted in Source D?
(e)   Why did it take so long for effective legislation to be passed – despite the filthy conditions and cholera epidemics?

(Total = 30 marks)

3.   **Objective 3**

Write a letter to *The Times* stating:
(a)   Why you deplore the newspaper's attack on Chadwick.

(b)   Why you support what Chadwick is trying to achieve.

(Total = 20 marks)

4.   **Objectives 1 and 2**

Explain why such rapid progress has taken place in medicine over the last 180 years. You might like to consider the following factors:

● Individual brilliance.
● Social attitudes.
● The Industrial Revolution.
● The development of communications.
● War.
● Chance.
● The development of science.

(Total = 20 marks)

5.   **Objectives 1 and 2**

(a)   Briefly describe the achievements of **two** of the following individuals in medical history:

● Louis Pasteur
● Robert Koch
● Florence Nightingale
● Joseph Lister.

(b)   Out of the two individuals you have chosen which do you think made the most valuable contribution to medical progress?

(Total = 25 marks)

6.   **Objectives 2 and 4**

Study the sources below and then answer the questions:

Source A   An eighteenth-century amputation (courtesy of BBC Hulton Picture Library)

Source B   Lister's carbolic spray c.1870 (courtesy of BBC Hulton Picture Library)

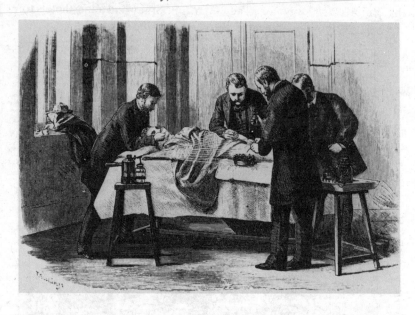

Source C   A modern operation (courtesy of BBC Hulton Picture Library)

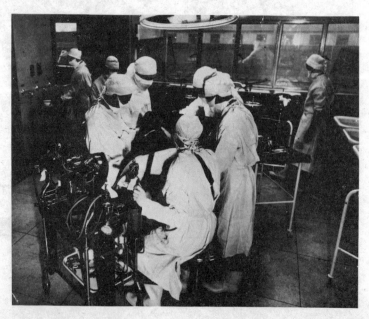

(a) How do these three sources illustrate progress in surgery between 1750 and the present day?

(b) It took some time for Lister's Carbolic Spray and anaesthetics to be accepted by surgeons. Why was this the case?

(Total = 20 marks)

7. **Objectives 1 and 2**

(a) What is the role of the central government today in the provision of public health? Give examples in your answer.

(10 marks)

(b) How do the attitudes of today towards public health differ from those of the nineteenth century? (10 marks)

CHAPTER 20

TRADE AND TRADING POLICY SINCE 1750

20.1 INTRODUCTION

(a) This chapter deals with the general trading policy adopted in Britain over the last 250 years or so. In 1750 Britain's trade was regulated and her industries protected under the 'mercantilist system', but by 1860 she had developed a policy of 'free trade'. After this there was, by 1932, a return to 'protection', which has been reversed, with Britain joining the European Economic Community (EEC) in 1973.

(b) A brief glossary of terms will be useful. According to the Oxford Dictionary, 'trade' entails 'the exchange of commodities [goods] for money or other commodities . . . [between] different countries'. When a country places a custom duty (tariff) on incoming goods from abroad, that country is following a policy of 'protecting' her own industry from foreign competition. Conversely, when a country allows goods in without imposing any customs duties, a policy of 'free trade' is in operation. For example:

PROTECTION

COUNTRY X ⟶ Exports Cloth ⟶ Country Y puts a
to country Y at Customs Duty of 5p per
10p per metre metre on the incoming
cloth, making the price
15p

In the shops therefore
foreign cloth (15p) is at a
disadvantage when home
cloth is priced at 10p, i.e.
it has been
PROTECTED.

FREE TRADE

COUNTRY X ⟶ Exports Cloth ⟶ Country Y, following a
to country Y at   policy of free trade, im-
10p per metre   poses no customs duty.
Foreign cloth and home
cloth sell at the same
price.

(c) An 'at a glance' chart (see overleaf) will provide a useful point of reference:

20.2 WHAT WERE THE MAIN FEATURES OF BRITAIN'S TRADING POLICY IN THE EIGHTEENTH CENTURY?

(a) The mercantilist system

This system originated in the Tudor period and it consisted of a collection of laws designed to protect industry, and boost the home economy. The mercantilist system remained in operation, with a number of modifications, until 1776 when it was challenged by the political economist, Adam Smith.

(i) The *aims of mercantilism* were threefold:

- To ensure that more goods were exported than imported so that there was always an abundant stock of bullion (gold and silver) in the treasury. It was believed that such wealth would guarantee the strength of the country.
- In order to control imports and stimulate exports a number of regulations were imposed. Tariffs (customs duties) were placed on incoming goods to make them more expensive on the home market – particularly manufactured products. Some commodities such as Indian cotton were outlawed from Britain. Some areas of the economy were given 'bounty payments' as an incentive to export goods. Farmers, for example, were paid for exports of corn. In addition, it was made an offence to export machinery (which would have helped foreign industry) and also raw wool.
- To ensure that home shipping, including the navy, was powerful enough to earn money and protect the country from foreign invasion.

Trading policy	Year/Period	Main events
Protection	1651 and 1660	Navigation laws passed
	C17th & C18th	The mercantilist system in use
	1776	*The Wealth of Nations* published (Author: Adam Smith)
	1786	William Pitt the Younger started to move towards free trade
	1815	Corn Laws reintroduced (a protectionist measure)
	1823	Huskisson followed a policy of reducing tariffs and introduced 'colonial preference'
	1839	Anti-Corn Law League formed
Free Trade	1842 1845 }	Two 'free-trade' budgets introduced by Robert Peel
	1846	Famine in Ireland. Corn Laws repealed
	1852–5 1859 }	Gladstone continued to abolish duties
	1860	The Cobden-Chevalier Treaty made Britain a free-trade nation. This policy was beneficial to Britain at a time when she was the 'Workshop of the World'

Free Trade Challenged	1881	The Fair Trade League formed – called for a return to Protection
	1903	Tariff Reform League formed by Joseph Chamberlain
Protection	1915	The McKenna Duties introduced
	1921	Safeguarding of Industries Act
	1932	Import Duties Act – embodied Imperial Preference
	1947	General Agreement on Tariffs and Trade (GATT). Idea of Free Trade re-established
Free Trade	1957	European Economic Community (EEC) established under the Treaty of Rome
	1973	Britain became a member of the EEC

(ii) *The navigation laws 1651 and 1660*

These laws were enacted at a time when the English merchant fleet was being challenged by the Dutch who were increasingly carrying more of Europe's trade. Consequently, these laws aimed to protect the home fleet from this competition by stating that all imports had to be conveyed in English ships or in vessels belonging to the country of origin. These laws were revered and considered to be the basis of the nation's prosperity. They were not finally abolished until 1849.

(b) The role of the empire

(i) During the course of the eighteenth century Britain built up a number of overseas possessions:

- The East India Company established a number of trading posts in India in the early part of the century. Robert Clive then acquired more Indian territory in 1763 after the Seven Years War.
- Until 1783 Britain controlled the 13 colonies of North America.
- Canada was acquired from the French in 1763 after the Seven Years War.
- By 1815 Britain had added Australia, Cape Colony (South Africa), Trinidad (1802), Tobago (1803), St Lucia (1815), Tasmania (1803).

(ii) Initially Britain saw the colonies as possessions to exploit to the full. This attitude is often referred to as *the old colonial system* and it was in keeping with the mercantilist doctrines of the time. Under this system, rules were imposed which were designed to keep the economies and commercial development of the colonies in check, so that they did not challenge British products in world markets:

- The colonies were ordered to supply British industry with raw materials and products (for example, cotton and tobacco) which were not produced in Britain.
- The colonies had to buy British goods.
- The colonies were not allowed to develop trading links with other countries.
- The colonies could not build up industries which already existed in Britain (for example, pottery).

Obviously such a restrictive system was bitterly resented by the colonies – particularly the Americans who rose in revolt and defeated Britain in the War of Independence (1776–83). Subsequently Britain relaxed the old colonial system and removed the restrictive rules. However, the Empire as a whole still remained a vital element in Britain's commercial development as a source of raw materials, and as a market-place for her manufactured products.

(c) The Triangular Trade

(i)   This was an important element of Britain's trading activity in the eighteenth century, and it involved the trading of slaves. British ships left Liverpool, Bristol and London with cargoes of metal goods (nails, chains, etc.) and manufactured articles bound for trading posts on the West African coast. On arrival, they sold these products and took on board negro slaves. These unfortunate people had either been captured by slave-traders raiding their village, or else they had been taken prisoner during a clash with a rival tribe and sold to the slavers. From Africa the ships made the five-week voyage across the Atlantic Ocean to the West Indies and America. Here they were auctioned to the owners of sugar and cotton plantations. (The experience of one negro Kunta Kinte, is told in Alex Hailey's book, *Roots*). After this, the ships' captains returned to Britain with cargoes of cotton, rum, sugar and tobacco. The whole business was an immense money-spinner and huge fortunes were made. Profits made from the slave-trade were invested in large mansions and the purchasing of seats in Parliament; the slave-traders thus became a very powerful lobby in the eighteenth century:

(ii)   The treatment of the slaves was appalling. For the middle passage they were packed into the ships and chained to the deck. Conditions were filthy, the food was inadequate and the suffering beyond imagination. Probably a third to a half of the negroes would die of disease. The others received little exercise or fresh air. On top of this the voyage would have been extremely rough as the ships were always sailing against the prevailing south-westerly winds. Those who survived the journey would be auctioned, like cattle, with the highest prices being obtained for young 'bucks' (men in their early twenties) who would give a plantation owner full value in the cotton

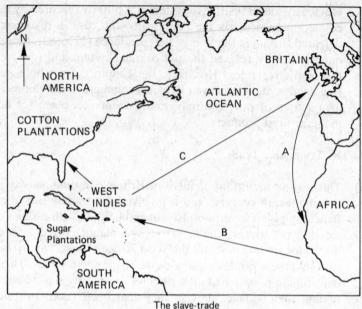

The slave-trade

Ports
1 = Liverpool
2 = Bristol
The three legs of the
journey involved these
'commodities'
  A Britain to Africa — hardware and
                     manufactures
  B Africa to W. Indies — slaves
     and America
     (Middle Passage)
  C W. Indies to Britain — cotton, sugar,
                          tobacco, rum

fields. The treatment of the slaves on the plantations varied but, generally, the slaves lived in the most basic of conditions. Their diet would probably consist of salted fish and cornmeal, sometimes supplemented by vegetables grown on the truck patch (land set aside for this purpose by the plantation owner). Accommodation was nothing more than wooden huts which were inadequately furnished and overcrowded.

(iii)   Towards the end of the eighteenth century agitation to abolish the slave-trade became vociferous both in the country and in Parliament.

(iv) The wider campaign against slavery within the British Empire was spearheaded by the evangelicals of the Church of England. The evangelicals objected to slavery on moral and humanitarian grounds and they attacked the system with great conviction. William Wilberforce and Thomas Clarkson were the two individuals who have been give most of the credit for the anti-slavery campaign

The anti-slavery movement met dogged opposition from the slave-traders who were well represented in Parliament. They believed in their case arguing that:

● Black negroes were inferior and were little better than savages.
● Conditions on the plantations were better than those they had in their native countries.
● If they did not use slave labour they would not be able to make ends meet and would be forced out of business.
● Slave labour kept down the price of sugar and cotton.

Wilberforce (MP for Hull) made a series of powerful speeches in the House of Commons in which he argued that economic arguments for slavery were irrelevant in the face of the human suffering and degradation involved in the system. In 1789 he prepared a *Bill to End the Slave Trade* which, predictably, was defeated. The agitation continued until, in 1807, an Act was passed which made it illegal to carry slaves on British ships. Half the battle had been won. Now there was the problem of freeing the slaves who were still working on the plantations. In 1833, Parliament passed the *Emancipation of Slaves Act* which stated that:

● Plantation owners would receive government compensation to the tune of £20 million.
● The freeing of slaves was to be phased over a period of seven years. During this period a slave had to devote three-quarters of a working day to his owner and spend the rest of his time preparing for his freedom.

Wilberforce died after the Act reached the Statute Book. Recent work on the slave-trade has pointed out that the role of Wilberforce on the anti-slavery movement has been exaggerated. John Kent, writing in 1967, suggests that 'less than their due significance [has been] attached to Charles Grant, Henry Thornton, James Stephens and other Evangelicals'.

(d) Trade and trading patterns 1700–1815

(i) During this period Britain's trade grew steadily, apart from temporary reverses in the 1740s, 1780s and the period of the French Wars (1793–1815). Robert Owen, writing in *Observations on the Effect of the Manufacturing System* in 1815 was sufficiently impressed to comment 'that . . . [from 30 or 40 years ago] . . . to the present day the home and foreign trade have increased in a manner so rapid and extraordinary as to have raised commerce to an importance which it never previously attained'. In 1700 the total value of imports into Britain amounted to between £3.5 million and £5 million whilst exports were worth about £7 million; by 1800 these figures had increased to £28 million and £40 million respectively.

(ii) As well as a growth in trade there was also a fundamental change in the pattern of trade. In 1700 the bulk of Britain's business was with the continent of Europe:

- From Scandinavia came hemp, timber, pitch and wrought iron.
- From Russia came wrought iron.
- From France came lace, wine and brandy.

Britain's imports from other parts of the world included spices and tea from the East Indies, and cotton and sugar from the West Indies. Britain in return exported woollen garments, manufactured metal products, salt and wheat.

By 1800 the Empire was playing a much bigger role in Britain's trade, with Europe declining as a trading partner. Britain now was an importer of wheat, rather than an exporter as she had been in 1700, and exports of cotton goods were predominant over wool.

(iii) The British re-export (entrepôt) trade continued to flourish and expand. Figures given by Phyllis Deane put the value of this trade at £3.5 million in 1750, increasing to £9.5 million in 1790 and £18.5 million in 1800.

(iv) After the French Wars (1793–1815) 'invisible' exports became a major money earner in the British economy. Such exports were made up of the following items:

- The export of money (capital). As Britain industrialised

she created enough wealth to be able to lend money to other countries for engineering projects such as railway construction. The interest on this money constituted 'an invisible export'.

- The provision of banking facilities for overseas countries for which fees were charged.
- The conveyance of goods for other countries which lacked a mercantile marine.

Invisible exports became increasingly vital in putting Britain's balance of trade in 'the black'.

(e) The relationship between trade and industry

Britain's increasing trade was bound up with the process of industrialisation:

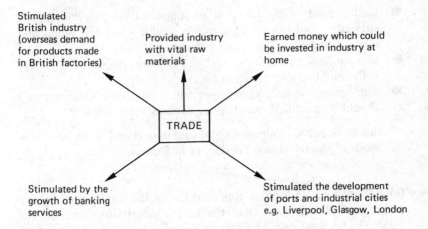

20.3 **HOW DID THE FREE-TRADE MOVEMENT ORIGINATE?**

(a) In the late eighteenth century the mercantilist system came under fire as merchants realised that it hindered their activities. In particular the system had become very difficult to interpret. For example, there were well over 1000 different tariffs placed on various commodities entering Britain which made the job of customs officials something of a nightmare. Some of these tariffs were intended to protect home products from competition whilst others were imposed to raise money for the government. It was becoming clear, however, that the amount raised by some of the tariffs was negligible – in fact, it sometimes cost more to carry out the various stages of administration. Smuggling became a 'boom industry' along the coves of the south coast as goods were brought into the country, secretly so as to avoid paying tariffs.

(b) In 1776 Adam Smith (1723–90), the Professor of Economics at Glasgow University, published *An Inquiry into the Nature and Causes of the Wealth of Nations*, a book which rapidly went into five editions, so widely was it read. In his treatise Smith outlined why he believed 'mercantilism' to be obsolete, and he put forward the notion of 'free trade' between nations. He wrote that 'taxes imposed with a view to prevent or even diminish importation, are . . . destructive . . . of the freedom of trade'.
Smith argued that:

● Each country should be left to concentrate on developing its strengths – individuals best create wealth when left alone and allowed to pursue their own objectives.
● Government restrictions, such as customs duties, would only stifle initiative and hinder trade.
● The navigation laws were important to the nation's defence and should be modified gradually as circumstances allowed.

Smith's book proved to have a significant impact and it helped to sow the seeds of the free-trade movement in Britain.

(c) *The Wealth of Nations* appeared just at the right point. By the end of 1815, Britain was well on the road to industrialisation, and had established a lead over the rest of the world. As she had no real competitors a policy of free trade would benefit British industry. She could purchase raw materials cheaply and turn them into manufactured products for both the domestic and foreign markets: there was nothing to fear from foreign competition, whilst she was in such a dominant position. In addition, free trade would permit the importation of cheap food for the urban factory workers. In this atmosphere, Smith's arguments were readily accepted by industrialists and merchants. Gradually, between 1783 and 1860, Britain became a free-trade nation.

20.4 WHAT POLICIES WERE ADOPTED BY WILLIAM PITT AND WILLIAM HUSKISSON TO HELP TRANSFORM BRITAIN INTO A FREE-TRADE NATION?

(a) William Pitt the Younger (1759–1806)

Pitt was Prime Minister on two occasions, first between 1783 and 1801 and then from 1804–6. He came into office after the American War of Independence and his first task was to initiate a programme of economic recovery. Having read *The Wealth of Nations*, part of Pitt's strategy was the adoption of a number of free-trade measures:

(i) Anxious to reduce the high rate of smuggling, Pitt reduced the duties on a number of commodities notably tea and brandy. Tea carried a duty of 119 per cent. Pitt slashed this to 12 per cent.

(ii) Pitt continued and extended the number of bonded ware-houses. Imported goods were stored in such warehouses and duties only became payable when they were required for the home market. If the goods were released in consignments, duty would be paid in appropriate instalments. Furthermore, if the goods were stored pending re-export no duty was payable at all, which helps to explain the increase in this trade (see Section 20.2(d)(iii)).

(iii) Before 1783 duties payable had been calculated on percentages which often meant customs officers made errors, and it was also extremely tedious. In response Pitt introduced, in 1787, a revised *Book of Rates* which simplified the procedure and set out the amount payable on each item.

(iv) In 1786 Pitt negotiated a reciprocal treaty with France (the so-called *Pitt-Vergennes Treaty*) which resulted in Britain reducing duties on French brandy and wines in return for France allowing in British metal goods and textiles at favourable rates.

The outbreak of the French Wars made this Treaty obsolete but, nevertheless, Pitt had set an example, and illustrated that free-trade measures could be successfully introduced.

(b) William Huskisson (1770–1830), President of the Board of Trade

In 1820 a Select Committee of the House of Commons reinforced the ideas of Adam Smith when it argued that the complicated systems of tariffs stifled 'the operations of commerce . . . and the growth of opulence'. It went on to conclude that Britain's prosperity would be enhanced if merchants were allowed to operate with 'unlimited freedom'.

These views were fully accepted by William Huskisson who was President of the Board of Trade from 1823–7. From this point onwards David Thomson (in *Britain in the Nineteenth Century*, Penguin) states that economic policy was seen 'in terms of promoting national wealth by untrammelled private enterprise'.

Aided and abetted by Frederick 'Prosperity' Robinson (Chancellor of the Exchequer from 1823–7), Huskisson made a number of reforms which pushed Britain a little nearer to the status of a free-trade nation:

(i) Widespread reduction of protective customs duties

Huskisson argued that lower tariffs on imported goods would mean lower prices for consumers and higher profits for manufacturers; this in turn, would stimulate employment and increase trade. He consequently brought down the duties payable on a number of commodities including wood, copper, lead, tin, zinc, raw silk, coffee, cocoa and paper. The size of the reductions varied – some raw materials were subject to a duty of only 10 per cent whilst the maximum duty now to be charged was set at 30 per cent.

(ii) Restrictions on exports were lifted

For the first time Huskisson permitted the export of British machinery – subject to government approval and the issuing of a licence. In addition, skilled workers were permitted to leave Britain and work in other countries; this had previously been viewed as undesirable because it would denude Britain of talented craftsmen.

(iii) The Reciprocity of Duties Act (1823)

This Act allowed the government to negotiate trading terms with individual nations on a similar basis to the Pitt–Vergennes Treaty. In the ensuing years a number of agreements were made with European and South American countries, encouraging the flow of trade and helping international relations.

(iv) *The Navigation Acts*

These were altered by Huskisson in 1825 with the purpose of allowing trade to flow more freely. He was reluctant to remove these Acts altogether as, like Adam Smith, he felt they were important for national defence. Huskisson's measure were:

- To allow foreign ships to bring trade into Britain.
- To reduce the charges made to use port facilities.
- To remove trading restrictions on the colonies which had been inherent in 'the old colonial system'.

However, Britain's trade with the colonies was still to be carried exclusively in British ships.

The Navigation Acts were eventually wiped away in 1849. Although a Tory, Huskisson was sceptical about the relevance of the Corn Laws. He felt that they kept the price of bread high and believed that they were too rigid. Removal of these laws was impossible as the landowning class still dominated Parliament.

Huskisson, therefore, devised a sliding scale of duties on imported corn. When the home price of corn was high, duty on foreign corn was reduced; when corn prices were low, the duty on imported corn was increased. This proposal was bitterly opposed and Huskisson felt strongly enough about the issue to resign from the Cabinet in 1827. (Ironically, in 1828, the Duke of Wellington introduced a sliding scale which was based on Huskisson's proposals.)

Huskisson's work was generally successful in that trade and industry were stimulated.

20.5 THE ACHIEVEMENTS OF SIR ROBERT PEEL (1788–1850) – TORY PRIME MINISTER FROM 1841 TO 1846

(a) What free-trade measures did Peel enact via his budgets?

(i) Peel faced several difficult problems on becoming Prime Minister in 1841. Since 1837 the country had been in the grip of a trade recession and the outgoing Whig government had left the Exchequer with a deficit. After a lull, the free-trade question once again came to the fore. In 1840 The Select Committee on Import Duties reiterated the previous arguments in favour of free trade. Peel used his Budgets to put his free-trade policy into action.

(ii) *The Budget of 1842*

This 'great budget' introduced the following measures:

- Duty on manufactured goods was set at a ceiling of 20 per cent.
- Duty on partially-manufactured goods was set at a maximum of $12\frac{1}{2}$ per cent.
- Duty on raw materials was set at a maximum of just 5 per cent. The theory was that cheaper raw materials would result in cheaper finished articles. Industrialists would therefore sell more, make larger profits and expand their factories, taking on a bigger labour force. This measure did, in fact, have the desired effect.
- To cater for the anticipated drop in revenue, Peel reintroduced income tax at the rate of 7d. (2.9 pence) in the pound on incomes over £150 per annum. As it turned out, revenue from customs duties did not decrease as the volume of trade went up after the Budget. Smuggling, on the other hand, became a less attractive occupation. In 1843 Peel lifted all restrictions on the export of machinery.

(iii) *The Budget of 1845*

This continued the free-trade policy. Peel repealed the import duties on some 520 items as well as getting rid of all export duties (which made British goods cheaper abroad). After this Budget meat, sugar, cheese, butter and potatoes were all cheaper to the British consumer. In 1846 Peel removed the duty on virtually all the raw materials which entered the country.

Despite all this activity there was still one fly left in the free-trade ointment – the Corn Laws.

(b) The repeal of the Corn Laws 1846

(i) *How did the Anti-Corn Law League come into existence? What arguments did it utilise?*

Opposition to the Corn Laws had been evident ever since they were reintroduced in 1815. Petitions were presented to Parliament and Anti-Corn Law Associations were formed in a number of towns (for example, Birmingham, Nottingham and London) from 1833 onwards. In 1838 an Anti-Corn Law Association was set up in Manchester and this developed into the *Anti-Corn Law League* in March 1839. The League was a predominantly middle-class pressure group made up of northern industrialists. Although there is evidence to suggest that it did have some initial links with the Chartists, the League operated in competition with Chartism and there was a degree of hostility between the two groups (see chapter 21). (These two would indulge in sabotaging each other's meetings.) The specific objective of the League was to see the Corn Laws repealed and to this end they employed a catalogue of arguments:

- The League claimed that the Corn Laws were outmoded and only the large landowners and farmers derived any benefit from them. It was, they argued, selfish for the landowners to utilise their parliamentary muscle in order to maintain the Corn Laws.
- The Corn Laws kept bread prices higher than they needed to be; Richard Cobden said they were 'a bread tax . . . levied upon the poorest classes'. After buying food the labouring masses had no money left to buy industrial products.
- Industrialists were forced to pay higher wages than they could really afford so that their work force could afford to feed their families.
- The League pointed out that the removal of protective duties had worked to the advantage of industry and the same should apply to agriculture.
- If foreign countries were allowed to import corn into Britain without having to pay duty, they would make money which they would spend on British industrial products. This would provide cheaper food and enhance employment prospects.
- The League finally employed a moral argument which is best illustrated by the slogans which appeared in 1843 on a 'free-trade hat' designed to be worn by supporters of the League. Around the rim were the words 'God will prosper the righteous efforts of men leagued against tyrants who

witold food from the labourer'. The design of the hat depicted a poor family saying 'Give us this day our daily bread' and underneath was shown how a family would benefit from duty-free bread. Large loaves of bread were prominent on the dining table accompanied by the line 'We thank thee O Lord for what thou hast so bountifully provided?' The overall implication was that protection was immoral and scorned by God.

(ii) *Who were the leaders of the League?*

Among the early Anti-Corn Law campaigners were J. B. Smith, Archibald Prentice, George Wilson and Ebenezer Elliott, who wrote Anti-Corn Law poems. The two men who dominated the League, however, were Richard Cobden and John Bright who made a formidable team. Both these men gave total commitment to the cause, making public speeches to put over the arguments of the League.

Cobden (1804–65) became the owner of a calico printing factory in Manchester and in 1841 he became the MP for Stockport. He was often scathing in his attack on the large landowners and felt that the issue of the Corn Laws was a battle between the farming aristocracy and the emerging industrial class of factory-owners. He was also in favour of free trade in general and saw the abolition of the Corn Laws as part of a campaign to get rid of 'every monopoly'.

Bright (1811–89) was a cotton manufacturer from Rochdale who was invited to join the League by Cobden in 1841. Bright was a Quaker and tended to adopt the moralistic argument when speaking at public meetings. He was a superb orator 'capable of holding large crowds for several hours'. He entered Parliament in 1843 as the member for Durham.

(iii) *What tactics did the League adopt?*

Cobden and Bright spearheaded a powerful propaganda campaign to obtain the repeal of the Corn Laws. Being a middle-class group, money was no object and funds were raised very speedily. In 1844 alone, the League managed to raise £90,000, a very substantial amount. Propaganda was disseminated in a number of ways:

● Numerous pamphlets and leaflets were published, as well as pottery and clothing bearing Anti-Corn Law slogans.

- The League had its own newspaper – *The Anti-Corn Law Circular*.
- Public meetings were held throughout the country; even groups of farmers were addressed, to try and convert them to free trade.
- The distribution of literature and movement of speakers was facilitated by the introduction of the Penny Post in 1840 and the growth of the railway network.
- In addition, the League used its funds to finance candidates at elections and this enabled the Anti-Corn Law viewpoint to be promulgated in the House of Commons.

(iv) *Who opposed the League?*

The League faced fierce opposition from several quarters:

- *The Times* openly attacked Cobden accusing him of 'recklessly and unceasingly labouring to direct . . . odium personally . . . on the Minister' [Peel]. The newspaper also called members of the League 'a parcel of quacks' who were prepared to use 'threats of violence' to achieve their objects. *The Times* had traditionally represented the farming lobby but an attempt on Peel's life motivated the newspaper to print these particularly vitriolic articles against the League.
- The bulk of the Tory Party was made up of landowners who were against repeal; they wished to maintain their position and rejected the argument that agriculture was becoming secondary to industry in creating the nation's wealth. They claimed that the industrialists wanted cheaper bread prices so that they could reduce wages and make higher profits. A more emotive opinion was expressed by a landlord who described the League as 'the most cunning, unscrupulous . . . body of men that ever plagued this . . . country'. The hard line opposition in the Tory party was led by Benjamin Disraeli.
- The oppostion of the landowners was channelled by the Duke of Richmond into the Central Agricultural Protection Society, formed in 1844. Its aim was to maintain the Corn Laws.

(v) *What events brought the eventual repeal of the Corn Laws?*

Peel gradually decided that the Corn Laws had to go. He agreed with many of the points made by the League but he faced a dilemma. He represented, in theory, the landowning classes; if he repealed the Corn Laws he would be seen as a traitor and would probably be forced to resign.

Peel was finally forced into action by the Irish potato famine of 1845–6. A wet summer had caused potato blight rendering the crop inedible; thousands of Irish people starved to death and thousands more left for America. The same conditions also ruined the wheat crop in England. By October 1845 Peel had decided to repeal the Corn Laws. The Whig leader, Lord John Russell, pledged his party to repealing the Corn Laws if he was asked to form a government.

Peel, however, was unable to convince all the members of his cabinet that the Corn Laws should go and he resigned as Prime Minister. The Whig leader, Russell, was invited to form a government but he was unable to do so; the Whig party was also split on the issue.

In December 1845 Peel returned to power with a newly-constructed Cabinet, and set out to repeal the Corn Laws. A realignment of groupings in the Commons ensured that the Corn Laws were repealed on 26 June 1846, with 'Peelites', Irish Members, League MPs and the majority of the Whigs voting for the Bill. Opposition came from the 'Old' Protectionist Tories and a minority of the Whig MPs.

(vi) In the short term, repeal came too late to help the Irish. The famine had already taken its toll, and together with the effects of emigration, the population of Ireland was reduced from 8.2 million to 6.6 million.

By the 1850s Britain entered into a period of prosperity. Bread prices came down, employment increased and the standard of living for the masses improved. Predictably, Cobden and Bright attributed this to the Anti-Corn Law League.

British agriculture did not suffer immediately from the effects of foreign competition. Farmers responded to the challenge by adopting the policy of 'High Farming' (see chapter 23). After 1873, however, cheap foreign grain did challenge the home farmers.

Robert Peel's political career was terminated. He resigned from office after being defeated in an attempt to pass a Coercion Bill to prevent rioting in Ireland on 29 June 1846. He spent the last four years of his life in opposition haunted by the words of the Duke of Wellington who stated that Peel 'had been put in his damned fright . . . [by] rotten potatoes'.

20.6 WHAT CONTRIBUTION DID WILLIAM GLADSTONE (1809–98) MAKE TO THE ACHIEVEMENT OF FREE-TRADE?

(a) Gladstone was the Chancellor of the Exchequer from 1852–5 and from 1859–65. Having been President of the Board of Trade in Peel's Government (1841–6) he was totally committed to completing the free-trade policy. By the early 1850s this policy was almost universally accepted by British politicians and public opinion. This was shown by:

● The publication of John Stuart Mill's *Principles of Politcal Economy* (1848), which was yet another book confirming the views of Adam Smith.
● The fact that the 'Old Tories' under Disraeli had accepted that, for the time being at least, free trade was what the nation wanted.
● The Great Exhibition (1851) which was seen as a symbol of Britain's strength under the free trade umbrella.

Gladstone set about removing most of the remaining duties using the Budget as the instrument of policy.

(b) Gladstone's Budgets

(i) *1853* – Gladstone reduced the revenue duties on eggs, butter, fruit, tea and cocoa, abolishing altogether those on soap. He also scrapped duties on most semi-manufactured goods. Gladstone had also hoped to abolish income tax but the outbreak of the Crimean War in 1854 forced him to raise it to 1s.2d. (6p) in the £.

(ii) *1860* – A further 371 duties were swept away including those on dairy products and fruit. Less than 50 duties now remained with the intent of bringing in revenue, rather than protecting home manufacturers from foreign competition.

(iii) *1861* – Gladstone abolished the duty on imported paper, thus removing, in his own words, 'the tax on knowledge'. This reduced the price of newspapers, books and journals stimulating interest in politics.

(c) The Cobden-Chevalier Treaty 1860

In 1860 Anglo-French relations were at a low point and Gladstone felt that a reciprocal trade agreement would reduce the tension. Richard Cobden travelled to Paris and negotiated a treaty with Napoleon III's government which said:

- France would admit British machinery, coal, textiles and iron, charging no more than 30 per cent in duty.
- Britain in return would allow in French wine, brandy and silk at reduced rates of duty.

Free trade was, at last, a reality.

20.7 FREE TRADE CHALLENGED

(a) For 20 years Britain enjoyed a spell of great prosperity. She was the leading industrial nation, and whilst she had no serious competitors, free trade served her well. The policy brought in cheap food and raw materials which suited the urban populations of the country. The general public, therefore, was imbued with the benefits of free trade.

(b) From about 1880 some sections of society began to speak out against free trade, advocating a return to some form of protection. The main reason for this was increasing foreign competition:

- By now farmers were feeling the effects of imports of North American wheat and meat products from the Antipodes. Farmers, therefore, would have liked tariffs to be imposed on these products as a means of protection.
- Factory-owners were also having to face a stern challenge from the emerging industrial countries of USA, Germany and France. These countries were beginning to gain a larger share of the world markets at the expense of British manufacturers. This, in turn, was causing a tide of rising unemployment and it was argued that only the healthy state of Britain's invisible exports was keeping the economy afloat:

1870	Exports	£244m
	Imports	£303m

Invisible exports	£112m
Excess balance	£153m

(Figures from Bagwell and Mingay, *Britain and America 1830–1939* Routledge, 1970)

● It was further pointed out that Britain's industrial competitors had not adopted free-trade policies. Instead they utilised tariffs to protect their industries from foreign competition. For example, in 1890 USA introduced the McKinley Tariff, whilst France, Russia and Germany had imposed tariffs on foreign imports in the later 1870s.

(c)   What was the Fair Trade League of 1881?

A number of northern businessmen felt that it was 'unfair' that foreign countries could get their products into Britain free of charge while charging duties on British commodities. The fair Trade League advocated a policy of 'tit for tat' tariff reform to even out the competition. Any country charging tariffs on British goods should have similar duties imposed on their products entering this country. The proposals of the League made little headway. The Royal Commission of Trade and Industry (1886) was of the opinion that free trade was still the best policy for Britain. Furthermore, John Bright spoke out strongly against the League, restating the benefits free trade had brought. 'If you inquire as to . . . wages . . . you will find them . . . nearly doubled . . . whilst the price of food and the hours of labour have diminished'.

(d)   The Tariff Reform League 1903–6

(i)   *Background*

The inspiration behind the Tariff Reform League was Joseph Chamberlain (1836–1914), the Colonial Secretary from 1895–1903. He was a committed imperialist and saw the reintroduction of tariffs as a vehicle to strengthen the British Empire. If protective duties were brought back, colonial countries would be granted imperial preference and this would help to keep the Empire united. Chamberlain was obsessed with maintaining the Empire, and his views were reinforced by the Boer War (1899–1902) which almost resulted in a humiliating defeat for Britain. Unfortunately, Chamberlain was unable to persuade the Conservative Cabinet that his proposals were right for the country. Many Conservatives were, in fact, free traders and Balfour (Prime Minister in 1903) would not give a lead either for or against tariff reform. As a result, Chamberlain resigned as Colonial Secretary on 14 September 1903 and determined to fight his case via the Tariff Reform League.

(ii) *The Tariff Reform Campaign 1903–06*

Chamberlain travelled the country making a number of major speeches to spread his ideas. He was supported by some manufacturers who were suffering from foreign competition and people who wished to see a strong Empire. An additional point was that money raised from tariff would be utilised by the government to finance social insurance schemes.

(iii) *Who opposed Chamberlain – and why?*

Chamberlain met a great deal of opposition and for a variety of reasons – the bulk of the British population favoured free trade as it guaranteed cheap food. Tariff reform would inevitably make food more expensive – even if imperial preference was given to food products from the Empire:

- Many factory-owners were used to obtaining cheap raw materials. This meant that they could keep their prices down, sell more and make higher profits. If tariffs were brought back – even with imperial preference – raw materials would cost more which would lead to higher prices. This would make it more difficult to compete with other countries.
- A number of Empire countries were against Chamberlain's policy. Canada, for example, imposed duties on imports of British machinery and some manufactured products. If 'colonial preference' was introduced, Britain would expect these duties to be reduced in return for giving Canada reduced rates of import duty and this would harm Canadian industry.
- Many argued that the reimposition of tariffs would severely damage Britain's extensive entrepôt trade which was at that time a big money-earner.

(iv)   *What was the result of the Tariff Reform Campaign?*

Chamberlain's campaign had one far-reaching effect:

Tariff reform divided the Conservative Party but, at the same time, unified the Liberals, after a period of disarray. The vast majority of the Liberals agreed that free trade was still beneficial. Tariff Reform was one of the main issues in the General Election Campaign of January 1906. The Liberals exploited the situation to the full claiming to be the party of the 'free trade loaf', which was said to be much larger and cheaper than the 'protectionist loaf'. The Conservatives, whether they liked it or not, were dubbed the party of protection and thus expensive food. The outcome was a landslide victory for the Liberals. For a time the call for a return for protection was silenced.

20.8   WHAT EVENTS LED TO PROTECTION RETURNING?

● During the First World War the Chancellor of the Exchequer, Reginald McKenna, wanted to ensure that cargo-carrying space in British merchant ships was used for essential supplies of food. In 1915 he introduced the McKenna Duties which imposed tariffs on luxury items from abroad (for example, watches and motor cars).
● By 1921 Britain had entered a trade recession and the protectionist lobby began to be heard once again. Many foreign countries took advantage of Britain's free-trade status to 'dump' goods on the home market. To stop this, the government passed *The Safeguarding of Industries Act* which imposed duties on a range of commodities. Even so, free trade remained virtually intact.
● Protection was eventually brought back by the national government at the height of the Great Depression in 1932 with the passing of the *Import Duties Act* and the *Ottawa Agreements* (see Section 29.6). The wheel had turned full circle since 1776 and *The Wealth of Nations*.

20.9   BRITAIN'S TRADING POLICY SINCE 1945

Since the Second World War Britain has gradually returned to a policy of free-trading (which has been a general world trend). This has come about via the following sequence of events:

(a) By signing the *General Agreement on Tariffs and Trade* in 1947 (GATT), Britain committed herself to fostering the principle of free trade. This has resulted in the gradual removal of tariffs throughout most of the world as the signatories of GATT are responsible for 80 per cent of the volume of world trade.

(b) In 1960 Britain became a member of the *European Free Trade Association* (EFTA), which was pledged to remove tariffs. EFTA was formally constituted under the Stockholm Convention in November 1959 and by a series of gradual tariff reductions reached a position of free trade within the association in 1967. The founder members of EFTA were Austria, Denmark, Norway, Portugal, Sweden, Switzerland and the United Kingdom.

(c) On 1 January 1973 Britain joined the European Economic Community (EEC) which had been established in 1957 under the Treaty of Rome. The expressed aim of the EEC was 'to establish a common market and . . . a customs union for all their goods . . . and to devise common policies for agriculture, the movement of capital, labour and transport'. The original members of the EEC were West Germany, France, Italy, Netherlands, Belgium and Luxembourg; Eire and Denmark joined in 1973, and Greece in 1981, followed by Spain and Portugal in 1986.

(d) Britain's trading policy in 1986 has the following salient features:

- There are no tariffs at all on good admitted from EEC countries.
- As a member of the EEC Britain has reciprocal trading treaties with EFTA countries.
- Trading agreement with Commonwealth countries are regulated by the Convention of Rome (1975).
- There are a large number of agreements with other foreign countries under the auspices of GATT.
- Only 7 per cent of Britain's imports have a tariff imposed on them (for example, textile goods, fire-arms).
- Only a few exports have any government regulations placed upon them (exceptions are military arms, livestock and some alcoholic drink).

The general policy, therefore, is one of free trade.

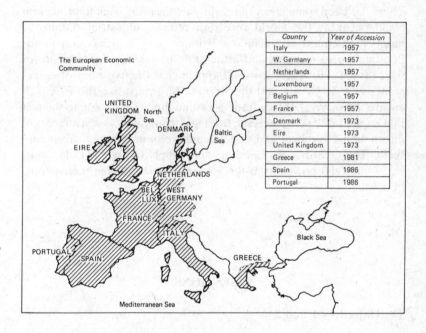

Country	Year of Accession
Italy	1957
W. Germany	1957
Netherlands	1957
Luxemburg	1957
Belgium	1957
France	1957
Denmark	1973
Eire	1973
United Kingdom	1973
Greece	1981
Spain	1986
Portugal	1986

The Organisation of the EEC

Aims of the EEC	The Institutions of the EEC
Free trade between member states	European Parliament. There are 434 members of the European Parliament representing the member states
Peaceful development of nuclear energy	The European Commission does the paper work for the Community. It supervises the implementation of treaties
Free movement of labour between member countries	The Council of Ministers is made up of Senior Ministers from the member states. Takes the main decisions
To aid countries in their agricultural, industrial and economic development	The Court of Justice is made up of 12 judges. Deals with countries and individuals who break the laws of the EEC

20.10 CONCLUSION

There has been some concern recently that a swing back to protection could occur as the world recession reduces industrial output. A number of countries (including Britain) have criticised Japan for flooding world markets and attempting to take an unfair share of world trade. However, it would appear that the existence of agreements such as GATT and the strength of groups like the EEC will ensure the survival of free trade for some time. This is due to the fact that present-day politicians see trading communities as instruments of international goodwill and understanding: an insurance against conflict. The words of Cobden still apply: 'Free Trade must . . . snatch the power from the governments to plunge their people into wars'.

QUESTIONS

1. **Objectives 1 and 2**

(a) What contribution did the following politicians make towards the adoption of a free-trade policy in Britain?

- William Pitt
- William Huskisson
- Robert Peel
- William Gladstone   (12 marks)

(b) Assess the importance of Adam Smith's book, *The Wealth of Nations*, in the free-trade movement.   (8 marks)

2. **Objective 3**

What views might the following have had about the Corn Laws in 1845:

(a) A member of the Tory party who was a large landowner
(b) A member of the Anti-Corn League
(c) A Chartist?

(Total = 30 marks)

3. Objectives 1 and 2

Britain's trading policy between 1750 and the present day has fluctuated between 'protection' and 'free trade'. Explain why this has been the case.   (20 marks)

4. Objective 4

Study the sources below and them answer the questions:

Source A   A cartoon from Punch (1846) (courtesy of Mansell Collection)

THE MAID OF ALL WORK IN TROUBLE.

" WELL, Richard Cobden! they've been and given me warning, and I shall lose my place thro' talking to you!"

Source B   A cartoon from Punch (1846) (courtesy of Mansell Collection)

THE DEAF POSTILION.

A POLITICAL PARODY, AFTER GEORGE CRUIKSHANK.

Source C   The 'Free Trade Hat' (courtesy of BBC Hulton Picture Library)

PRINT INSERTED IN THE CROWN OF THE "FREE TRADE HAT."

Source D   A cartoon from Punch (1850) (courtesy of Mansell Collection)

THE BRITISH LION IN 1850;

Or, THE EFFECTS OF FREE TRADE.

Source E

Throughout the 1830s hatred of the Corn Laws grew. The landlords and the Tory Party supported them because they protected
agriculture but the manufacturers maintained that if they were
repealed people would get cheaper bread and that countries from
which we bought wheat would in turn buy our industrial products.
As Britain changed from being an agricultural to a manufacturing
country these arguments became more important. In 1839 the
Anti-Corn Law League was formed. The League was an organisation with which the manufacturers set out to defeat the landlords.

Brilliantly led by two Lancashire manufacturers, Richard Cobden and John Bright, cleverly organised and well financed, the Anti-Corn Law League became a powerful force in the 1840s. The manufacturers spent hundreds of thousands of pounds employing professional writers and issuing almost 9 million pamphlets. They made great use of the penny post which had been founded by Rowland Hill in 1840, and their speakers were able to travel widely on the growing railway.

(Taken from *Machines, Money and Men* by D. P. Titley, 1969)

(a) Sources A and B are making the same point. Explain what they are saying.

(b) Which group would have issued Source C?

(c) Why is this source useful?

(d) In June 1846 the Corn Laws were repealed. What, according to Source D, was the effect of this?

(e) What might a landowner have said about Source D?

(f)   (i)   Study Source E. Pick out two statements which are fact and two which are opinions.

     (ii) Source E is the only secondary source. The other sources are primary but all appear biased in some way. Which of the sources do you consider to be the most reliable and trustworthy?

(g) If an historian was trying to write a balanced history of how and why the Corn Laws were repealed what types of sources would he need?

(Total = 30 marks)

5. Objective 3

(a) As a Liberal candidate in the 1906 General Election campaign, write a speech in favour of free trade.

(b) As a member of the Tariff Reform League in 1906 write a speech outlining the arguments why Britain should return to a policy of protection.

(Total = 20 marks)

6. Objectives 1 and 2

(a) Describe the origins of the EEC.   (6 marks)

(b) Give an account of the main administrative organs of the EEC.
                                                          (10 marks)

(c) Why did Britain not join the EEC at its inception in 1957?
                                                          (4 marks)

7.   **Objective 4**

Study the sources below and then answer the questions:

Source A   Caught Napping (Punch) (courtesy of Mansell Collection)

CAUGHT NAPPING !

THERE WAS AN OLD LADY AS I'VE HEARD TELL, | SHE WENT TO MARKET ON A MARKET DAY | BY CAME A PEDLAR—GERMAN—AND STOUT,
SHE WENT TO MARKET HER GOODS FOR TO SELL, | AND SHE FELL ASLEEP ON THE WORLD'S HIGHWAY. | AND HE CUT HER PETTICOATS ALL ROUND A

*Source B   History Reverses Itself (Punch) 1903 (courtesy of Mansell
Collection)*

PUNCH, OR THE LONDON CHARIVARI.—December 16, 1903.

PAPA COBDEN TAKING MASTER ROBERT A FREE TRADE WALK.

HISTORY REVERSES ITSELF;

OR, PAPA JOSEPH TAKING MASTER ARTHUR A PROTECTION WALK.

Papa Joseph. " COME ALONG, MASTER ARTHUR. *DO* STEP OUT ! "
Master Arthur. " THAT'S ALL VERY WELL, BUT YOU KNOW I CANNOT GO AS FAST AS YOU DO."

Source C   Election poster (courtesy of Mansell Collection)

Source D

'I'm not for Free Trade and I'm not for Protection.
I approve of them both, and to both have objection'.
(Wilfred Lawson on the views of A. J. Balfour, 1904)

(a) Estimate the date that Source A was published. Explain your
     answer.
(b) What viewpoint is Source A expressing?
(c) Study Source B.
   (i) Identify the two central characters in this source.
   (ii) Explain the viewpoint it is expressing.
(d) Study Source C.
   (i) Which political party would have issued Source C?
   (ii) What is this source telling the public?

(e) Does Source D support or contradict Source B? Explain your answer.

(f) 'Source C is so blatantly biased that it is of little use to the historian'. Do you agree? Give reasons for your answer.

(Total = 30 marks)

CHAPTER 21

WORKING-CLASS MOVEMENTS

21.1 INTRODUCTION

Before the 'industrial take-off' a homogeneous 'working class' did not exist in British society. Instead workers were divided into trades and crafts each with their **own** particular interests at heart and, as such, it is more accurate to refer to the 'labouring classes'. By 1900, however, this situation had changed. Industrialisation and the factory system had eroded the traditional bonds between employer and employee and the result was the emergence of a uniform working class – conscious of the need to defend itself against the strength of the employers. This class-feeling originated through a number of different organisation and groups which collectively constitute 'the working-class movements'. They were:

- Trade Unions
- Chartism
- The Labour Party
- Friendly Societies
- The Co-operative Movement

This chapter will trace the development of each of these movements.

21.2 THE ORIGINS OF THE TRADE-UNION MOVEMENT 1789–1850

(a) What is a trade union?

Sidney and Beatrice Webb defined a trade union as 'a continuous association of wage-earners for the purpose of maintaining or improving the conditions of their employment' (quoted by Coates and

Topham in 'Trade Unions in Britain'). Although the improvement in working conditions is the main concern of a union, it may also branch out by participating in education and politics and providing 'benefits' to its members.

(b) How did early trade unionism come into existence?

 (i) During the Middle Ages industrial society was dominated by the trade guilds. These were based on a particular craft and were composed of master craftsmen, journeymen and apprentices. Within such an organisation both master and employee had the same interests and relations were generally harmonious.

 (ii) The state also played a significant role at this time. In 1563 Elizabeth I's government passed **The Statute of Artificers**. This empowered local JPs to adjust wages in order to maintain living standards and also required them to supervise the entry of apprentices into the trades. The statute assured that apprentices worked to a high standard and included a list of punishments which could be imposed if either a master or an employee broke their contract of employment. The measures were seen as necessary protection for all those involved in a craft.

 (iii) In the late eighteenth century the theory of *laissez-faire* led to the masters resenting the state's interference in their businesses. In addition, the growing population was putting great pressure on industries to increase output; gradually the master-employee relationship became impersonal as businesses became larger. Each now had a different outlook and began to separate. The state formally abdicated its protective role in industry when the Statute of Artificers was repealed in 1813.

 (iv) The workers reaction to the changes was as follows:

   ● They began to form trade clubs or associations to look after their interests. They were composed of skilled workers in the same trade and initially their main purpose was to pay out benefits to those in needs (for example, for sickness). Many trade clubs were based at a local public house.

- Workers would 'petition' Parliament directly when they had a grievance against the master. Such petitions usually concerned complaints about wages.

(v) By the end of the eighteenth century trade clubs were joining together into larger 'combinations' and became more aggressive in their demands, rather than just paying out benefits. They now became concerned with trying to achieve improved working conditions and higher wages, and thus took on the role of a 'trade union'. Some combinations resorted to striking when their demands were refused by the employers and some used the tactic of 'collective bargaining by riot' (see Section 5.2).

(c)   What were the Combination Acts (1700–1800) and why were they passed?

(i) A variety of factors persuaded Parliament that action was required to deal with the increasing number of combinations who were claiming higher wages:

- The ruling classes associated 'combinations' with revolutionary activity, a feeling reinforced by the French Revolution and the naval mutinies at Nore and Spithead (1797).
- In 1799 the government received a petition from the master millwrights of London asking that legislation should be passed to abolish a recently formed combination of workers.

(ii) Parliament's answer was the Combination Acts of 1799 and 1800 which together stated that:

- '[combination of workmen] . . . for obtaining an advance of wages . . . or altering their . . . usual hours of . . . Working . . . shall be illegal, null and void'.
- The penalty for breaking this law was three months imprisonment or two months hard labour.
- Workmen who were prosecuted could, if they wished, appeal to the local Quarter Sessions (this amendment was made in 1800).

(d)   How and why were the Combination Acts repealed in 1824?

(i) The Acts were not very successful: rather than eliminate combinations, some historians, including E. P. Thompson, claim that the number of trade unions actually increased during 1800–24. Unions found loopholes in the Acts by claiming to be friendly societies, which had been made legal by an Act passed in 1793. Some combinations operated in secret, employing passwords and secret oaths.

(ii) In the 1820s the government adopted a more liberal attitude towards the workers and a campaign to get rid of the Combination Acts came into existence. Francis Place, a master tailor from Charing Cross, argued that the Acts did more harm than good and, in practice, produced bad feeling between master and workman. Place was influenced by Bentham's utilitarian motto that 'all laws should be useful' and the Combination Acts according to him did not fit this description.

(iii) Place acquired the support of Joseph Hume MP who was successful in having a Parliamentary Committee of Inquiry established to investigate the effectiveness of the Combination Acts. Place had planned his tactics and vetted a large number of witnesses before they appeared before the Committee. This work paid off as the witnesses gave all the 'correct' answers to the questions. The Select Committee's Report (1824) recommended the repeal of the Combination Laws. Parliament duly obliged and combinations were legalised providing that they did not 'resort to any form of violence during industrial action'.

(iv) Immediately there was a deluge of strikes throughout the country; an improvement in trade and higher employment, together with their newly-acquired freedom, gave workmen the confidence to take on the masters. As a result an *Amending Combination Act* was passed in 1825 which stated:

● Combinations of men were to remain legal 'for the sole purpose of consulting upon and determining the rate of wages . . . or hours . . . '
● 'Molesting', 'intimidating' and 'obstructing' fellow workers and/or masters would be an offence, and would carry a penalty 'not exceeding three calendar months'.

The Act left Trade Unions in a rather ambivalent position. Although they could exist, their powers to stage an effective strike were much reduced: it depended on the discretion of a judge as to the interpretation of phrases such as 'molesting'. Furthermore, fund-boxes were not given legal protection under this Act.

(e) How successful were the first attempts to form large national trade unions?

(i) The concept of forming a large powerful general union of all workers over a wide area originated in the 1820s. John Doherty was enthusiastic about the idea of forming a large union which would put fear into the employers. He summoned a conference in the Isle of Man in 1829 and formed the *Grand General Union of Operative Spinners of Great Britain and Ireland*. The idea mushroomed, and in July 1830 Doherty founded *The National Association for the Protection of Labour* which was to consist of 'organised Trades throughout the kingdom'. This union was far too ambitious and by 1832 had broken up. Its failure was explained by the inadequate communications at the time, which meant that co-ordinated action was almost impossible to organise.

(ii) In February 1834 the GNCTU was formed (*Grand National Consolidated Trades Union*). Instrumental in its birth was Robert Owen (see chapter 14 for his biographical details). Owen hoped that a large national union would achieve his dream of a socialist society. Within months of its formation the Union had 500 000 members, but this claim has been questioned. There was, in fact, no accurate record of the membership, and it is believed that there were just 16 000 paid-up subscribers.

(iii) The GNCTU had a number of weaknesses and it did not succeed because:

- Such a large organisation did not have a realistic chance of success given the lack of communications at the time: it was almost impossible to co-ordinate any action.
- Owen's tactics differed from the rank and file; he believed that his ideas were so sensible that they would inevitably materialise. The workers, distraught by the imminent introduction of the New Poor Law, and the savage treatment of the Swing Rioters (1830), generally favoured more militant action.
- An attempt to organise a General Strike (or Sacred Month), which would (theoretically) cause the collapse of industry and allow the workers to take over the means of production, never got off the ground. Only a number of uncoordinated local strikes materialised.

- The employers took decisive action against the GNCTU which helped to bring about its demise. Many used the tactic of locking out their workers unless they signed 'The Document' renouncing the GNCTU and pledging that they would never join it. The lock-out was an effective weapon, as eventually workers were forced to give in because of starvation.

- Another tactic of the employers was to compile a list of union 'trouble-makers' and mutually agree not to employ them.

(iv) *The case of the 'Tolpuddle Martyrs'* dealt the final death blow to the GNCTU. The Whig Home Secretary, Lord Melbourne, was determined to crush the GNCTU at the first possible opportunity. In February 1834 six labourers from Tolpuddle (Dorset) decided to form a lodge of the GNCTU in an effort to resist a decrease in their wages. The local magistrate, James Frampton, reported the matter to Lord Melbourne, who gave orders for the immediate arrest of the six men on a charge of taking unlawful oaths (under an Act of 1797 which had been passed to deal with the naval mutinies). The men were tried at Dorchester and sentenced to seven years' transportation. There was a large measure of protest but the sentences were carried out. The men – George Loveless, James Loveless, James Hammett, James Brine, Thomas Standfield and John Standfield – became known as the 'Tolpuddle Martyrs'. On passing sentence in 1834, the judge commented that he was obliged to impose a harsh sentence to serve as 'an example and warning'. He was totally successful. Support for the GNCTU rapidly declined with workers fearing the same fate as the Tolpuddle men. By August 1834 the GNCTU had folded.

(f) How much trade union activity was there between 1835 and 1850?

The traditional view of this period is that trade unionism virtually 'disappeared' as the workers invested their efforts into other movements such as Chartism, short-time committees and co-operative shops. This, however, is oversimplifying the picture. Trade unionism among the skilled trades did, in fact, continue to make headway during these years.

Estimates put total union membership in the early 1840s at about 100 000 – small, but not negligible.

21.3   NEW MODEL UNIONS 1850–80

(a)   How did the new model unions originate and what features did they possess?

(i)   In 1851 William Allan of Crewe and William Newton of London took the lead in combining a number of unions into the *Amalgamated Society of Engineers, Machinists, Smiths, Millwrights and Pattern-Makers*; it was the first so-called **new model union**.

(ii)   Gradually the ASE developed the following features:

- A full-time secretary with headquarters in London.
- Membership limited to skilled engineers only.
- High subscription of one shilling (5p) per week.
- Payments for funeral expenses, pensions and sickness benefits and emigration.
- A **moderate** policy towards strikes. Industrial action was only to be taken after consultation with the central executive in London. No unofficial strikes would receive the support of the union.
- Unlike the GNCTU, the ASE had no desire to overthrow the existing form of government. It aims were purely economic and social – not political.

By 1867 the ASE had 33 000 members and 308 branches throughout the country with total assets of £140 000.

(iii)   Other unions followed the format pioneered by the ASE, the most important one being the *Amalgamated Society of Carpenters and Joiners* (ASCJ) led by Robert Applegarth. In 1866 it had 8,000 members and 187 branches. Like the ASE the subscriptions were one shilling a week (5p), with sickness benefit of six shillings per week (30p), emigration grant of £6 and pensions up to eight shillings a week (40p). To become a member of the ASCJ a man had to 'be in good health, have worked for five years at the trade, be a good workman, of steady habits, of good moral character, and not more than 45 years of age'. The Model Unions were anxious to gain a respectable public image.

(iv)   *The Junta*: By the 1860s trade councils were being set up in the major cities of Britain. The most well known of these councils was the London Trades Council, otherwise known as 'The Clique' (by it opponents) or 'The Junta'. It consisted of the secretaries of the main new model unions – Allan, Applegarth, Edwin Coulson of the *Operative Bricklayers Society*, George Odger of the *Boot and Shoe-makers* and Daniel Guile of the *Iron Founders*. The idea behind the Junta was that it would co-ordinate trade union policy across the country, seeking to limit strikes and using arbitration to settle disputes. To many unionists, the Junta was far too moderate in its approach.

(v) The Junta has been criticised by left-wing historians, such as E. P. Thompson and the Webbs, who argue that it only served the needs of the 'labour aristocracy' – the skilled artisans. Although the living standards were improved for this section of the work force, the vast majority of workers remained unorganised.

(b)   What setbacks were suffered by the trade unions in this period?

(i) *The 'Sheffield Outrages'*: In 1866 it became evident that non-unionists in the cutlery trade were being intimidated and threatened by union members. The practice of 'rattening' (stealing a blackleg's tools) increased and violence was being used, with one group of cutlers actually blowing up a blackleg's house. The effect of the 'outrages' was to tarnish the 'responsible' image which the new model unions had given to the movement.

(ii) *Hornby* v. *Close*: In 1867 the secretary of the *Bradford Boilermakers' Society* absconded with £24 out of the fund box. The union believed that its fund-box was insured under the 1855 Friendly Society Act and took the official to court to get its money back. The Lord Chief Justice, however, ruled that although the *Boilermakers' Society* did perform duties akin to those of a friendly society (for example, payment of sickness benefit), it also acted 'in restraint of trade' (went on strike) and, as such, was **not** covered by the 1855 Act. The implications were clear: union fund-boxes all over the country were now at risk.

(iii) Parliament, concerned at the above incidents, appointed a Royal Commission of Inquiry into Trade Unions. The Commission's Report was generally favourable to the unions, although comments were made expressing doubts about the legality of picketing. Legislation followed in 1871 (see Section 21.3(e)).

(c) Why and how did the TUC originate?

(i) In 1867 George Potter called a *Conference of Trades* in London and from this came the idea of holding a national conference of trade union delegates to discuss policy. The first meeting took place in 1868 in Manchester and was attended by 34 delegates who represented about 100 000 members — this body became known as the TUC (Trades Union Congress). The TUC came to meet annually and by 1875 was attended by 153 delegates representing over one million members.

(ii) A further development was the formation of the TUC Parliamentary Committee in 1871. It original object was to act as a 'watch-dog' with regard to the Trade Union Bill (see Section 21.3(e)) which was then being debated in Parliament. Hereafter the Parliamentary Committee broadened its outlook, and as well as trying to influence Parliament it took an interest in factory conditions and later became known as the General Council of the TUC.

(d) Trade union legislation 1871–5

In 1871 two Acts were passed by Gladstone's Liberal Government in response to the Royal Commission:

(i) *Trade Union Act 1871*

This Act was favourable to the unions in that it gave them the right to register under the 1855 Friendly Societies Act, which meant that they could now sue any official who stole from the fund-box. In addition the Act afforded Trade Unions legal acceptance in so far that 'the purpose of any trade union shall not, by reasons merely that they are in restraint of trade, be deemed to be unlawful'.

(ii) However, trade unionists joy was short-lived for the very same day (29 June) the Liberals passed the *Criminal Law Amendment Act* with the intention of preventing any repeats of episodes like the Sheffield Outrages. The Act imposed a penalty of three months' imprisonment for **any** form of 'molesting' or 'intimidation' during a strike. The words used could be widely interpreted and even peaceful picketing would be a risk. This was proved when some agricultural labourers went on strike in Chipping Norton in 1873. Seven wives of the labourers were convicted for merely shouting insults at black-legs during the strike.

(iii) The Liberal Government was to pay for the passing of this Act at the 1874 General Election. Urban workers (who had been given the vote in 1867) protested by voting for the Conservatives under Disraeli.

(iv) In gratitude to the workers, in 1875 Disraeli passed the *Conspiracy and Protection of Property Act* which restored the strike weapon to the trade unions. The Act permitted picketing on the condition that no violence was used.

(v) Trade unions were also unhappy about the regulations which covered **breach of contract**. If a worker broke his contract it was considered a criminal offence, carrying a penalty of imprisonment. For an employer, the same action was only a civil offence punishable by a fine. The situation was rectified in 1875 with the *Employers and Workmen Act* which made breach of contract for both worker and employer a civil offence.

(e) Why did the trade union movement not make more rapid progress in the years immediately after 1875?

The newly-acquired legal status did not bring the expected progress to the trade union movement, and in fact it suffered further setbacks in the second half of the 1870s.

(i) The unions were still primarily concerned with the skilled worker and as such were not concerned with fighting for the large mass of unskilled men. This attitude prevented the extension of trade unions.

(ii) The unions were also adversely affected by the industrial and agricultural depression which started to bite into the economy about 1873. This weakened the position of the unions. With more workers available than jobs the employers could sack men as they wished.

(iii)   The adverse effects of the depression on trade unionism is exemplified by the attempt to organise the agricultural labourers in 1872. The initiative came from a Warwickshire labourer, and Methodist lay preacher, called Joseph Arch. In February 1872 he addressed a meeting of farm workers at Wellesbourne and formed a union which immediately struck for a wage increase (without success). The workers, however, were still enthusiastic and in March 1872 Arch founded the *Warwickshire Agricultural Labourers Union* at Leamington Spa. Then in May 1872 the *National Agricultural Labourers Union* (NALU) was established which grew to a membership of 100 000.

After some initial success the union found itself up against some determined opposition from the farmers. They adopted a policy of locking-out and evicting unionists from cottages. Perhaps the union could have fought this in normal circumstances, but in 1874 the agricultural depression caused the membership to drop rapidly; by 1880 the NALU had virtually evaporated.

(iv)   Another factor was the moderate leadership of the Parliamentary Committee of the TUC between 1875 and 1889. The Secretary of this body was a Liberal – Henry Broadhurst – and he was more concerned with conciliation; it is argued that he did not push the claims of the trade unions hard enough.

21.4   GROWTH OF THE NEW UNIONS 1880–1900

(a)   What was 'new unionism' and why did it gain a foothold in the 1880s?

'New unionism' was the name given to the organisation of the ranks of the **unskilled** workers. These unions:

- Charged minimal subscriptions and adopted a much more militant stance towards the employers.
- Did not seek to exclude workers and were organised across whole industries rather than individual crafts.

(b) Why did they develop in this period?

(i) *Fundamental changes in society were taking place*

Industrialisation had created a large rift between employer and employee. The employers saw themselves as part of the 'middle class' with a common need to defend themselves against the rising tide of organised labour.

The workers had also become more class conscious and they, too, believed they had to fight to obtain a higher standard of living. Such (class) feeling was waiting to be tapped; the new unions proved to be the outlet.

(ii) *The workers were slowly acquiring some political power*

By 1884 the agricultural labourer had been given the vote and there was a spirit of determination among the workers to campaign for favourable legislation in Parliament. There was a growing sense of confidence within working people.

(iii) *The revival of socialism*

This was also important in the rise of the new unions, with a number of individual socialists inspiring a number of strikes during the 1880s (see also Section 21.8).

(iv) *Successful strikes*

The Match Girls 1888

In 1888 Annie Besant investigated the working conditions of female labour at Bryant and May's factory in East London. They found low wages, girls suffering from phosphorus poisoning, and a harsh regime of rules and regulations. Mrs Besant publicised her findings in an article in the journal *The Link* under the headline 'White Slavery in London'. Charles Bradlaugh MP raised the matter in Parliament. Mrs Besant organised *The Match-Makers Union* which came out on strike. Eventually the girls won an increase in wages and some of the factory's rules were relaxed. Nothing was done, however, about phosphorus poisoning, and girls continued to suffer the horrible effects of 'phossy-jaw' – a disease which caused the jaw to rot away. The success of the match-girls encouraged other new unions to take on the employers.

The London Gasworkers

In 1889 Will Thorne, a member of the Social Democratic Federation, assisted by Eleanor Marx, formed the *Gasworkers' and General Labourers' Union* which very rapidly had over 20 000 subscribers. He organised a strike at the Becton Gasworks and demanded a working day of three 8-hour shifts as opposed to two 12-hour shifts. The employers, the South Metropolitan Gas Company, agreed to the demand together with an increase in wages.

The London Dock Strike 1889

The greatest struggle, however, occurred in the summer of 1889 in London's dockland. The dockers were badly paid and demoralised until Ben Tillett organised them into making a number of demands of the employers including an increase in pay from 5d. (2.08p) to 6d. (2.5p) per hour (The Dockers' Tanner), the abolition of piece-work, work periods of at least four hours and 8d. per hour for overtime. Tillett prepared for a long strike, and he was joined in the leadership by John Burns and Tom Mann. The strike began on 12 August and virtually all the various dock trades (porters, trimmers, warehousemen, stevedores and general labourers) came out. At Tower Hill, Tillett gave daily speeches to the men and the public rallied in support of the dockers. Herbert Champion wrote articles for the press publicising the dockers' case. Money was sent from all parts of Britain to keep the men and their families in food; an amazing £30 000 arrived from Australian trade unionists. The strike lasted for five weeks until Cardinal Manning and the Lord Mayor of London called called a conciliation meeting between the two sides at the Mansion House. The result was victory for the Dockers; they received the 'tanner' and 8d. (2.8p) per hour for overtime. After the strike the *Dock, Wharf, Riverside and General Labourers Union* was formed under the leadership of Tillett and Mann; within two months it had a membership of 30 000 men.

The immediate effect of these three strikes was a rapid growth in the trade-union membership and an increase in the number of disputes as the unions tested their strength. Trade unions grew in membership from 750 000 in 1888 to 2 000 000 in 1900. One large union formed during this period was the *Miners' Federation of Great Britain* (MFGB).

(c) How did the employers react to new unionism?

(i) The employers, faced with increasing foreign competition, were determined that the new unions should not dictate terms to them and used the 'lock-out' as a tactic.

(ii) An employers' 'counter-attack' was deliberately conceived with the organisation of *Employers' Federations* such as that of the shipping merchants which drew up a register of seamen that were acceptable as employees. Employers' federations also co-ordinated lock-outs to defeat strikes.

(iii) In 1877 the Employers' Parliamentary Council was formed with the objective of arguing the employers' case and trying to influence Parliament. It issued pamphlets and propaganda arguing that the new unions were doing untold damage to the strength of the British economy.

(iv) In 1893 William Collison set up the *National Free Labour Association* (NFLA) with the object of supplying employers with blackleg labour during a strike.

(v) A number of employers tried to make the best of a bad job realising that the new unions had established a foothold and they were here to stay. Thus they adopted an attitude of trying to settle disputes by using the various items of arbitration and conciliation machinery. The 1896 Conciliation Act strengthened this machinery by allowing the Board of Trade to intervene directly into disputes and to appoint conciliators. This proved to be quite a successful measure (see Section 21.6).

21.5 WHAT LEGAL SET-BACKS DID TRADE UNIONS SUFFER IN THE PERIOD 1880–1910?

(a)

(i) *Lyons v. Wilkins*

In 1896 the *Amalgamated Trade Society of Fancy Leather Workers* was involved in a dispute with a leather-manufacturing firm owned by Mr Lyons. The union placed picket lines on the workshop and the owner gained an injunction to stop the workers picketing. The union, believing itself to be in the right under Disraeli's Act of 1875, appealed to the High Court – but in 1898 the judge ruled that the injunction should stand. This was a serious blow to the trade unions as once again their right to picket was in doubt before the law.

(ii) The Taff Vale Case 1900–01

On Monday, 20 August 1900, a strike was called by the *Amalgamated Society of Railway Servants* (ASRS) against its employer, the Taff Vale Railway Company. The Taff Vale was an important line, transporting coal from the valleys to the port of Cardiff for export. The strike had a number of causes:

● The ASRS, in the eyes of the company, did not have the right to indulge in collective bargaining for wage increases. The union regarded this as a slight.
● Despite a period of good trade, the Taff Vale Company had not granted a wage increase.
● The company instructed John Ewington, an active member of the ASRS, to move to a new job on another part of the line. He objected and this was the spark which brought the union out on strike.

The day-to-day running of the strike was organised by James Holmes, the area convenor, and Richard Bell, the General Secretary of the ASRS. There were a number of acrimonious exchanges with the company, including a threat from the union that they were ready to back the strike to the tune of £250 000. The company's manager, Mr Ammon Beesley, called on the NFLA and was supplied with blackleg labour. He also gained an injunction to stop the ASRS picketing this labour. On 31 August 1900 the dispute was 'settled'. The union achieved neither a wage increase or recognition. The strike was a humiliation for the ASRS leadership. The company did not even give way on the position of Ewington, merely agreeing that the Board of Trade 'should investigate the matter'.

Once the dust had settled, the company took the ASRS to court and sued for damages to compensate for loss of revenue during the strike. They were duly victorious and the ASRS had to pay the company £23 000 and the costs of the case. This was a crushing blow to trade-union aspira-

tions: future strikes in any industry could suffer the same
fate.

(iii) *The Osborne case and judgement 1908–9*

In 1908 a member of the ASRS (W. V. Osborne) objected to
part of his union subscription being contributed to the funds of
the Labour Party. Osborne, a Liberal, gained the support of
the right-wing press and was provided with legal aid so that he
could put his case before the courts. The case went as far as the
House of Lords who, in 1909, ruled in favour of Osborne. The
basis of the judgement was that nowhere in the various
trade-union legislation did it make provision for trade-union
funds to be used for political purposes. The implications of the
case were clear: how would the voice of trade unionists be
heard in Parliament, if their mouthpiece, the Labour Party,
was devoid of funds to allow it to develop?

(b)   How were these setbacks overcome?

(i) In 1906 the Liberal Government, under pressure from the 29
Labour Party MPs, and lobbied by the Parliamentary Committee of the TUC, revoked the Taff Vale Judgement by passing
the *Trade Disputes Act*. The Act stated that:

- 'It shall be lawful for any one or more persons to peacefully persuade any person . . . to abstain from working'
(this once again made picketing a legal activity).
- 'An action against a Trade Union . . . in respect of . . .
damages . . . shall not be entertained by any court' (thus
the 'cloud' of Taff Vale was removed).

(ii) The effects of the Osborne Judgement on the successful
development of the Labour Party were nullified by two Acts:

- *1911 Payment of Members Act* – MPs were to receive an
annual salary of £400. Although this did not mean that the
Labour Party could receive donations from trade unions,
at least working men could now become MPs and support
their families.
- *1913 Trade Union Act* – this stated that a trade union
could divide its subscriptions into a political fund and a
social fund, providing the membership gave their approval
in a ballot. Furthermore, any union member not wishing to

pay into the political fund could 'contract out' so that 'contribution to [it] . . . shall not be made a condition of admission to the union'.

21.6 INDUSTRIAL DISPUTES 1910–14

(a) What were the main disputes during these years?

These years were littered with hostile disputes, violence and long drawn-out strikes, particularly in the transport and mining industries. A brief catalogue of events illustrates this point:

(i) The start of 1910 saw strife in the Northumberland and Durham coalfield with the miners striking against the introduction of three 8-hour shifts a day. They were defeated after three months.

(ii) In November 1910 there was a bitter dispute in the Rhondda Valley, when the miners refused to work difficult seams without extra pay. The owners refused what the miners were asking and the result was a 10-month strike which spread to other collieries with an estimated 30 000 idle. Blackleg labour was employed by the owners and there were many ugly scenes on the picket lines as the miners fought with the police. Eventually the miners were defeated and forced to return to work.

(iii) In 1911 the Southampton dockers refused to handle the departure of the liner *Olympic*, asking for an increase in wages. They won and their victory triggered off disputes in other ports – including Hull, London and Liverpool.

(iv) In August 1911 the four main railway unions – (*General Society of Signalmen's and Pointsmen's Union, ASRS, Associated Society of Locomotive Engineers and Firemen, General Railway Worker's Union*) – tired of not being recognised by the employers, called a national strike. The government intervened and got the employers to agree to a Conciliation Board being established to negotiate a settlement. This was enough to bring a return to work.

(v) On 1 March 1912 a national strike was called by the MFGB demanding a minimum national wage of 25p per shift for men and 10p for boys. The owners refused. They were against a national wage agreement, preferring to make local settlements. The government passed the *Coal Mines (Minimum Wages) Act* (see Section 25.6) which brought the dispute to an end.

In the end it was only the outbreak of war in 1914 which brought an end to the industrial strife.

(b)   Why was there so much industrial tension in these years?

A number of factors contributed to bring about the industrial turmoil:

(i)   The trade unions felt strong enough to take on the employers; trade was good and employment was high. Workers were confident of winning concessions, particularly with numbers growing rapidly (four million plus by 1914).

(ii)   Many employers were provocative, refusing to recognise the Unions (for example, the railway companies) and employing blackleg labour. Furthermore, they tended not to grant wage increases even though trade was prosperous.

(iii)   Trade unions came to believe that if they were to get any concessions from the employers they would have to gain them by industrial action. This view was brought about by the failure of the Labour Party to make any tangible progress between 1907 and 1910 (see Section 21.8(e)).

(iv)   *The growth of syndicalism*: This was a movement which had its origins in the writings of Daniel de Leon (an American Marxist) and the French Socialist, Georges Sorel. The basic tenets of syndicalism were:

1.   Labour should be organised in huge industrial unions.
2.   The overthrow of capitalism by means of a general strike.
3.   Workers' control of industry.

These ideas were promulgated in Britain in 1910 by Tom Mann. He published the *Industrial Syndicalist* each month, in which he argued the militant approach. How much influence syndicalism had is hard to assess. It definitely gained ground in South Wales among the miners. Its influence can also be seen in the growing trend towards the amalgamation of unions. This brought about the formation of the **Triple Alliance** in 1912 (consisting of the National Transport Workers' Federation, the NUR and the MFGB) which introduced the concept of 'unity is strength' and hinted at sympathy striking. It is probably more exact to say that the syndicalists rather than sydicalism inspired the industrial strikes of this period; the workers were far more concerned with winning better living conditions than they were with the overthrow of the existing order of society.

21.7 CHARTISM

(a) What was Chartism?

(i) It is almost impossible to arrive at a foolproof definition of Chartism; it was a complex phenomenon and one which still provokes a great deal of debate among historians. In very basic terms Chartism may be defined as 'a working-class movement to obtain representation in Parliament'. This would then result in economic and social reforms being made. In 1838 Joseph Rayner Stephens, a Chartist agitator in the North of England, referred to the movement as 'a knife and fork question, a bread and cheese question' meaning that political power was only the means to achieving better living conditions for the working people and not merely an end in itself.

(ii) Between 1838 and 1848 the main objective of the movement was to get the six points of 'The People's Charter' made law; after this date the nature of the movement changed and adopted a 'socialist' attitude (see Section 21.7(f)). The Charter was the work of William Lovett, Henry Hetherington and, to a lesser degree, Francis Place. All three were members of the *London Working Men's Association* (LWMA) a group of skilled craftsmen who recognised the need to gain political representation for the working classes. After discussing the issues with Thomas Attwood's *Political Union* in Birmingham, the six demands were made public in May 1838. *The People's Charter* demanded:

1. Manhood suffrage – all men over 21 to have a vote.
2. Voting by secret ballot.
3. Abolition of the property qualification rule for men wishing to stand for Parliament.
4. Members of Parliament to receive a salary.

5. Voting districts (constituencies) which were the same size.
6. Parliament to be elected annually.

All the points were political in nature; if achieved they would enable working men to become MPs and bring about legislation which would deal with the social issues of the time, for example, the Poor Law and factory hours.

(b) What caused Chartism to be popular in the period 1838–48?

People probably supported Chartism for different reasons and motives but overall the following factors appear to have encouraged working people to support the movement:

(i) *Disappointment with the 1832 Reform Act*

In 1832 the working class had combined with the middle class to pressurise Parliament into passing the above Act, believing that they would obtain the vote. However, the extension of the franchise, under the Act, turned out to be very limited: only an estimated 700 000 people were given the privilege, and they were all from the middle ranks of the society. Many working people harboured resentment and felt that they had been double-crossed. If working men wanted the vote they would have to achieve it by their own efforts. Chartism was seen as the answer.

(ii) *Factory legislation was a disappointment*

The 1833 Factory Act had failed to achieve the 10-hour day and left many workers resentful (see chapter 14).

(iii) *Bitterness towards the 1834 Poor Law Amendment Act*

The harsh attitude towards the able-bodied unemployed contained in this Act caused feelings to run high, particularly in the North of England. Anti-Poor Law Committees were formed in the textile towns of Yorkshire and Lancashire to campaign against the 'cruelty' of the Act. Richard Oastler believed that the government had 'made poverty a crime'. The situation was made worse as the decision to accelerate the building of new union workhouses (bastilles) coincided with a trade depression and high unemployment at the end of the 1830s. The Anti-Poor Law agitators viewed Chartism as a vehicle which would add weight to their cause.

(iv) *The suppression of trade unionism*

Although trade unions could exist, their powers to hold a successful strike were in doubt. The treatment of the Tolpuddle labourers undoubtedly discouraged working men from subscribing to unions. Chartism, therefore, appeared to be the panacea for improving the lot of the working man.

(v) *Fluctuations in trade*

The years of 1838–9, 1842, and 1847–8 were ones of trade recession and high unemployment, with thousands of working families in poverty and despair. Such conditions, it is traditionally argued, made people support the Chartist movement. Historians have usually applied 'economic determinism' to the Chartist movement pointing out that the years of recession were the ones when Chartism attracted the most interest; in the words of Halevy, Chartism was the 'blind revolt of hunger'. Once trade improved, interest in Chartism subsided.

Recent writers have argued that the traditional view about the causes of Chartism outlined above has been overstated. The most up-to-date analyses of Chartism put greater emphasis on the belief that it was inspired by 'the continuing concern of ordinary men and women to maintain or regain control over their own lives' (Edward Royle). This standpoint infers that working people had come to realise that as a *class* they were down-trodden by the middle and upper classes and that working people needed to unite to improve their status.

(c) Who were the Chartist leaders? What methods did they advocate?

(i) *William Lovett (1800–77)* believed that the working man could gain greater political freedom by 'peaceful evolution' with debate and argument winning over the ruling powers (this was **moral force**). At the high point of the Chartist violence, in August 1842 (see Section 21.7(e)) he disassociated himself from the movement, claiming that 'violent words do not slay the enemies but the friends of our movement'.

(ii) *Henry Hetherington (1792–1847)* was a colleague of Lovett in the LWMA and an advocate of moral force. He wrote the

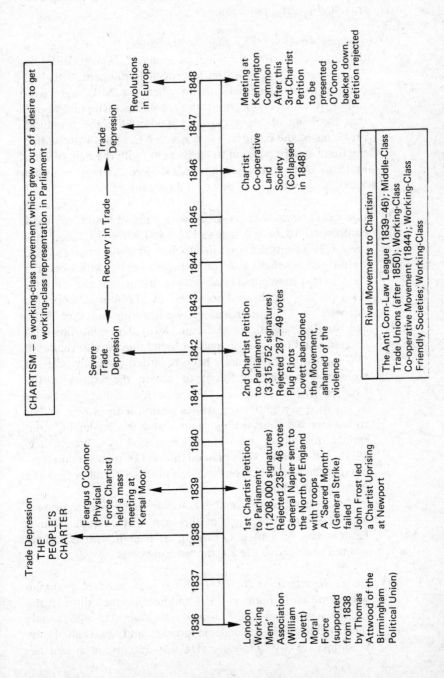

CHARTISM — a working-class movement which grew out of a desire to get working-class representation in Parliament

Trade Depression
THE PEOPLE'S CHARTER

Feargus O'Connor (Physical Force Chartist) held a mass meeting at Kersal Moor

Severe Trade Depression ← Recovery in Trade → Trade Depression

Revolutions in Europe

1836 | 1837 | 1838 | 1839 | 1840 | 1841 | 1842 | 1843 | 1844 | 1845 | 1846 | 1847 | 1848

London Working Mens' Association (William Lovett)
Moral Force (supported from 1838 by Thomas Attwood of the Birmingham Political Union)

1st Chartist Petition to Parliament (1,208,000 signatures)
Rejected 235—46 votes
General Napier sent to the North of England with troops
A 'Sacred Month' (General Strike) failed
John Frost led a Chartist Uprising at Newport

2nd Chartist Petition to Parliament (3,315,752 signatures)
Rejected 287—49 votes
Plug Riots
Lovett abandoned the Movement, ashamed of the violence

Chartist Co-operative Land Society (Collapsed in 1848)

Meeting at Kennington Common
After this 3rd Chartist Petition to be presented O'Connor backed down.
Petition rejected

Rival Movements to Chartism

The Anti Corn-Law League (1839–46); Middle-Class
Trade Unions (after 1850); Working-Class
Co-operative Movement (1844); Working-Class
Friendly Societies; Working-Class

Twopenny Dispatch and, in the early stages of the movement, travelled widely, publicising the Charter.

(iii) *Thomas Attwood (1783–1856)* was a banker by profession and the founder of the *Birmingham Political Union* (BPU) in 1829, which believed in the reform of Parliament. Attwood became involved with Chartism when the BPU were consulted by Lovett concerning the six points. Attwood hoped that the issue of paper currency would solve the economic problems of the country. He was given the job of presenting the first Chartist petition to Parliament (with the help of John Fielden). Attwood believed in moral force claiming he would 'wash his hands . . . of any . . . physical force'.

(iv) *Feargus O'Connor (1794–1855)* was, without doubt, the most controversial Chartist figure. He was Irish and trained as a lawyer at Trinity College in Dublin. In November 1837 he started the *Northern Star* (published in Leeds) which became the Chartist newspaper with outlets throughout the country. Also in 1837 he helped to found the London Democratic Association. O'Connor had an awe-inspiring presence and a charisma to match. He was capable of delivering powerful speeches and the working people found him easy to relate to. O'Connor has traditionally been regarded as an advocate of violence (or physical force) to obtain the points of the Charter. In 1847, however, O'Connor denied that he believed in violence saying 'I have always been a man of peace'. His co-leaders were suspicious of him and the leadership constantly quarrelled and were never united as a group. The *Illustrated London News* blamed this on O'Connor, commenting that 'he was dangerous . . . but more to his party than the community at large'.

Recent work on O'Connor, however, has tended to present a more sympathetic view of the man. For example, James Epstein has presented O'Connor as a man who genuinely wanted to improve life for the working class.

(v) *James Bronterre O'Brien (1805–64)* was another Irishman who came to London in 1839 and became the editor of the radical newspaper *Poor Man's Guardian*. He was widely respected for his journalistic powers and was called 'the schoolmaster' by O'Connor. He was initially an ardent believer in physical force but later modified his views. He also quarrelled with O'Connor over a number of issues.

(vi) *George Julian Harney (1817–97)* was co-founder of the London Democratic Association. He gained a reputation for militancy, once writing in the *Northern Star* that 'the musket is unanswerable'. Harney maintained his interest in Chartism into the 1850s when he tried to forge a link with the trade unions.

(vii) *Henry Vincent (1813–78)* joined the LWMA in 1836 and had connections with Chartists in Bath and Hull. He initially favoured violence and inspired the Newport Rising (see section 21.7(e)). He later became a Christian, leading him to renounce violence.

(viii) *Ernest Jones (1819–78)* helped O'Connor to set up the 'Chartist Co-operative Land Company; in 1846, and he became a prominent leader of the movement in the 1850s. Like Harney be believed that Chartism should become socialist in its approach.

(d) Why were the Chartists divided over tactics?

(i) Physical force tactics appeared to be most prominent in the industrial north, where working conditions were the worst. Wool-combers, for example, who worked in appalling conditions, were known for their militancy. The Scottish Chartists, on the other hand, tended to favour moral force. It has been suggested that this was because the workers were not subject to the New Poor Law, and the worst jobs were given to Irish immigrants. There may be some truth in this but it would be dangerous to apply it in every case. There were probably some physical force Chartists in good jobs and vice versa.

(ii) The Chartists disagreed as to how much support they should seek from the middle classes. Lovett argued that their support would be an advantage to the movement. He teamed up with the Birmingham Quaker, Joseph Sturge, the founder of the 'Complete Suffrage Movement'. Sturge's idea was that the middle class and working class should work together 'for the extension of the franchise'.

O'Conner and O'Brien were opposed to any merger with the middle classes. They hated the Anti-Corn Law League and dismissed the argument that the abolition of the corn laws would reduce the price of bread for the workers (see Chapter 20). O'Brien believed that lower bread prices would mean bigger profits for the industrialists as it would provide them with the excuse to keep wages low. Richard Cobden later commented that the failure of the Chartists to join forces with the Anti-Corn Law League (ACLL) was a fundamental factor in its downfall.

(e) What were the main events of the Chartist movement 1838–48?

(i) The First Petition 1839

After the publication of the Charter it was decided by the three most prominent Chartist leaders – Lovett, Attwood and O'Connor, that a petition should be presented to Parliament with as many signatures as possible. In autumn 1838 'elections' were held to select delegates to attend the National Chartist Convention. The Convention met in London in February 1839 with the objective of deciding on the course of action should the petition be rejected by Parliament. The debate was highlighted by a wide divergence of opinion and no clear agreement was reached. A number of delegates favoured a General Strike (or Sacred Month) accompanied by a period of civil disobedience where the Chartists would not pay taxes.

The petition, with 1 208 000 signatures, was presented by Attwood on 14 June 1839 and, predictably, was rejected by 235 votes to 46. Parliament was still dominated by the landowners who had an inborn fear of losing their privileged position.

(ii) The Newport rising

The idea of the 'Sacred Month' did not materialise; calls to go on strike were not heeded and the National Convention was dissolved in September 1839. This was a period when the movement, at national level, lost its sense of direction and the local groups took their own steps. Violence broke out in some areas and the government reacted by arresting a number of the Chartists leaders (including Henry Vincent) and sending troops under General Napier to the North of England.

The worst incident occurred at Newport in Gwent. John Frost, an ex-delegate at the National Convention, led an ill-planned demonstration into the town on 3 November 1839, believing that his action would coincide with similar displays of Chartist force in other parts of the country. A small group of troops garrisoned at the Westgate Hotel opened fire, killing 24 Chartists. Frost was sentenced to death but this was later reduced to transportation.

The aftermath of the Newport Rising was the further arrest of leading Chartists, including O'Connor and O'Brien. At York Assizes, O'Connor was given an 18-month prison sentence for 'seditious libel' to run from 11 May 1840. O'Brien was given a similar sentence.

(iii)   *The second Chartist petition 1842*

Between 1840 and 1842 Chartist activity was not so intense. Trade had improved and more people were in employment. One notable development was the establishment of the National Charter Association which aimed to bring tighter co-ordination to the movement; by 1842 there were about 400 local branches and some 40 000 members. In some areas marches and torch-light parades were held and the *Northern Star* continued to publish Chartist propaganda. In autumn 1841 the Chartist leaders had been released and they each tried to reassert their authority on the movement. The result was public disagreement and bickering.

With trade declining in spring 1842 there was once again a resurgence in interest in Chartism. A second petition was prepared, this time with 3 315 752 signatures. It was presented to Parliament by Mr T. Dancombe, who pointed out the gross inconsistencies in the electoral system. This time the petition was rejected by 287 votes to 49.

(iv)   *The plug riots August 1842*

The rejection of the petition coincided with the worst weeks of the recession, and widespread rioting and strikes broke out in Yorkshire, Lancashire, Scotland, the West Midlands and South Wales. In many towns factories were brought to a standstill as mobs removed the plugs from the steam-engine boilers. At Bury 33 mills were idle, and it was reported at Rochdale that 'operatives of every description for miles around have ceased to work'. At Stockport there 'was an attack on the

New Union Workhouse . . . where the mob . . . commenced to help themselves to . . . no fewer than 672 seven pound loaves . . . and about £7 in copper'. Eventually order was restored by troops and offenders were punished by the court. The rank and file lost interest in the movement as full employment returned in 1843. Furthermore, the leadership was now totally estranged. Lovett broke with the movement, leaving O'Connor as the main personality. From 1844 the co-operative movement began to attract some support from the workers, and in 1846 there was a revival in the fortunes of the *Short-Time Committees* (see chapter 14). Chartism had reached a low point but it was not finished.

(v) *O'Connor and land reform*

O'Connor now became obsessed with the formation of a 'Chartist Land Company' assisted by Ernest Jones. He per-suaded the National Convention to support him and in 1846 'The Chartist Co-operative Land Company' was founded, later to become 'The National Land Company'. The idea was to collect money from sympathisers and buy units of land that could be divided up into small plots and rented out. For a time the Land Scheme looked like being successful. Five estates were bought, including one at **Snig's End** (Gloucestershire) and another near **Watford**. In the end the scheme collapsed as many families could not afford the rent and moved away. In 1848 the scheme was investigated by Parliament on the grounds that O'Connor had been embezzling the funds. This was found to be untrue; in fact, O'Connor had lost a great deal of his own money financing the venture.

(vi) *The third national petition 1848*

1847 saw an upturn in O'Conner's fortunes when he was elected MP for Nottingham. Then in late autmun yet another trade recession hit British industry and unemployment re-turned. Interest in Chartism was revived and it was decided to present a third petition to Parliament. A Chartist Convention made plans to hold a large demonstration on Kennington Common from where a procession would walk to Westminster to present the petition to Parliament. The authorities were dismayed, their concern being fuelled by the revolutionary atmosphere that was then prevalent on mainland Europe (there were revolutions in France, Hungary and Prussia). The government made hurried plans to 'defend' London. Queen Victoria was despatched to the Isle of Wight and the elderly Duke of Wellington was put in command of the troops. Thousands of special constables were appointed. *The Times* reported that 'artillery will be stationed . . . on both Waterloo and Blackfriar's Bridges . . . There appears to be no doubt that the most extensive and detailed preparations will be made . . . to put down . . . any outbreak which may be attempted on the part of the mob'. Local Chartist groups also called meetings around the country; in the same edition of *The Times* reports were carried of gatherings in Manchester, Blackburn, Leeds, Coventry, Liverpool, Birmingham and Leicester.

April 10 arrived to pouring rain, and an enthusiastic crowd of approximately 20 000 gathered on Kennington Common, far fewer than expected. O'Connor was approached by the Metropolitan Police Commissioner, Mayne, and told that the meeting could proceed but a procession would not be allowed over Blackfriar's Bridge to Westminster. O'Connor told the crowd that he would personally present the petition (containing, 5 700 000 signatures) to Parliament. The crowd dispersed somewhat bemused but there was no violence. The whole affair has been dubbed a 'fiasco' and O'Connor has been accused of 'losing his nerve'. However, at the time he probably made the right decision – had the crowd advanced to Westminster there may have been bloodshed. Furthermore, the argument used by O'Connor to justify his decision did have some sense, namely that by dispersing peacefully the Chartists would illustrate to Parliament that they were responsible and worthy of the vote. The petition was delivered to Parliament in three cabs and was examined by a special committee who discovered that only 1 975 496 signatures were genuine. Furthermore 'Your Committee . . . observed the names of distinguished individuals . . . who can scarcely be supposed to concur in its prayer . . . Victoria Rex . . . , Duke of Wellington . . . Sir Robert Peel . . . and names which are . . . fictictious, such as "No Cheese" . . . "Big Nose" and "Flat Nose". The petition was rejected amid great hilarity by 222 votes to 17.

(f)   What happened to Chartism after 1848?

Chartism as a mass movement was never to revive but it remained in a different format until 1860.

(i)   In the summer of 1848 there were minor riots in the provinces and a number of offenders were imprisoned including Ernest Jones. The punishments meted out by the courts were enough to discourage any further trouble.

(ii)   'Little Chartism' was started in 1848 with a watered-down version of the original charter. It wanted each householder to have a vote and for Parliament to be elected every three years. The movement, founded by John Bright and Joseph Hume, never won much support.

(iii)   O'Connor became increasingly unstable and was declared 'insane' in 1852 after delivering a torrent of abuse at Beckett Denison MP across the floor of the House. He spent most of the remainder of his life in Chiswick Lunatic Asylum. He died in 1855.

(iv)   The survival of Chartism was now in the hands of Harney and Jones. They became the dominant figures in the National Charter Association but they now had different priorities. The Six Points faded away and, instead, the emphasis was put on evolving a socialist society. Jones and Harney, however, did not get on well and were never in total agreement. The National Charter Association was abandoned in 1860.

(g) For what reasons did Chartism fail?

A number of factors interacted to bring the downfall of Chartism as a mass movement.

(i)   *Inherent weaknesses within the movement*

Chartism, on a national level, was difficult to co-ordinate. It was made up of local organisations, but many of them had different hopes and aspirations depending on local factors, for example, some groups were of craftsmen, some contained factory-operatives and others domestic workers. It proved difficult to knit these groups together. Poor communications and lack of funds made the problem worse.

(ii)   *Poor leadership*

As we have already seen in Section 21.7(c), the movement's leadership was at odds and this had a detrimental effect.

(iii) *Lack of middle-class support*

The mutual distrust and suspicion between the middle class and the Chartist leadership meant that they stayed poles apart. It has been argued that if they had combined Chartism would have been a much more effective movement. Once violence started many of the middle classes scorned any association with Chartism. This lost the movement potential funding. Instead the middle classes threw in their lot with the Anti-Corn Law League, which achieved a much greater degree of success.

(iv) After the 1840s trade improved and Britain entered the age of *Mid-Victorian prosperity*. Wages were increased, employment was high and people generally lost interest in political movements. Although this is a crude argument it cannot be denied that Chartism was most volatile during times of recession, particularly 1842 and 1848. When economic conditions improved, Chartism declined and the workers preferred to place their confidence in trade unionism and the co-operative movement.

(v) *Government tactics*

The government (both Whigs and Tories) showed themselves in no mood to tolerate the slightest hint of violence. Heavy punishments were given to the Newport men (1839) and the plug rioters in 1842. Troops, special constables, and *agent provocateurs* were used in troubled areas. The government showed themselves to be more than a match for the Chartist. An interesting point, however, is that the government seemed to be prepared to allow peaceful meetings to go ahead and they also made no attempt to gag the Chartist newspapers.

(h) Was Chartism a total failure?

(i) Although the government appeared anxious to crush any disorder, it also adopted a slightly more progressive attitude towards the condition of the working people during the Chartist period which is reflected in some of the legislation of the period:

1839 Education Grant
1842 Mines Act
1844 Graham's Factory Act

1847 Fielden's Ten Hour Act
1848 Public Health Act

How far this was directly due to the pressure exerted by the presence of Chartism is difficult to say. Other groups had been pushing for these reforms for some time (for example, Short-Time Committees, Benthamites) so would they have happened anyway?

(ii) Over the years five out of six of the Chartist's demands have become law

- Abolition of property
   qualification   – 1858
- Secret ballot   – 1872
- Equal constituencie   – 1885
- Payment of membe   – 1911
- Universal suffrage   – 1918
- Annual Parliament has not become law and probably never will. It would be impractical and too costly to hold an election every year and it would also mean a lack of continuity in running the country.

(iii) Historians of the Labour Movement see Chartism as the forerunner of the socialist revival of the 1880s and as such it is important in the 'development of a working class'. F. C. Mather, for example, argues that 'the class-consciousness of Harney and Jones passed into the Labour traditions' and he also points to thefact that some elderly survivors of the Chartist period helped to form the SDF in the 1880s. How seriously this argument is to be taken probably depends on one's political viewpoint. There may well be some mileage in it but even Mather warns his readers that it should not be overstated.

21.8 THE GROWTH OF THE LABOUR PARTY

(a) What reforms were made in the electoral system which paved the way for a Labour Party?

For the greater part of the nineteenth century there appeared to be no need for a separate political party to represent the interests of working men; indeed for a long time political conditions made such a body impossible. Those who had the right to vote had a straight choice between Conservative and Liberal. However, circumstances gradually changed, and in 1900 the Labour Representation Committee (or Labour Party) was officially formed. This was made possible by changes in the electoral machinery.

(i) In 1858 the regulation requiring prospective members of Parliament to be owners of property was abolished. It was now possible for a working man to put himself up for election.

(ii) In 1867 the Second Reform Act was passed which gave the vote to every householder in urban areas and in addition to any male who was paying £10 a year in rent. This, in effect, extended the franchise to the urban working class and meant that both the Tories and Liberals would have to take this into account when formulating their policies.

(iii) The 1872 Secret Ballot Act meant that bribery and corruption would no longer be possible at elections. Working men could no longer be threatened with eviction if they did not vote for their landlord's choice.

(iv) The Third Reform Act of 1884 further extended the franchise: now all householders and £10 per annum lodgers were able to vote irrespective of whether they lived in an urban or rural area. The effect of this was to give the vote to the rural labourer, whether he was employed in agriculture or industry. These changes now made the political structure conducive to the formation of a Labour party – should the need arise.

(b)   Who were the Lib-Labs?

(i) From the mid-1860s working men in general, and trade-unionists in particular, began to take more interest in politics. In 1865 the National Reform League was set up by the *Junta* as a pressure group to bring political changes favourable to working men (for example, manhood suffrage). This was followed in 1869 by the Labour Representation League (LRL). This group aimed to get local Liberal associations to foster working men as their candidates; it was not very successful and quietly folded up in 1881.

(ii) In the 1870s the only way a working man could enter Parliament was if he received Liberal backing. In 1874 Thomas Burt and Alexander Macdonald were elected to Parliament as members for Morpeth and Stafford respectively. They sat with the Liberals and were known as Lib-Labs. At this time the trade unions and workers did not think there was any need for their own party. One of the staunchest Lib-Labs was Henry Broadhurst, MP for Stoke in 1880 (see Section 21.3(f)). In 1885 there were were 12 Lib-Labs in Parliament.

(c) What factors strengthened the idea that working men needed a separate political party?

Lib-Labism was widely accepted until the late 1880s when a number of factors combined to bring a greater political awareness to the workers.

(i) The revival of socialism

Little had been heard of 'socialism' since the 1830s, but now it re-emerged as a potent political philosophy. Two books inspired this revival – Karl Marx's *Das Kapital* and *Progress and Poverty* by Henry George. Both works advocated socialist ideas, although recently it has been argued that *Das Kapital*'s influence has been overstated. Two main socialist groups were formed:

- The *Social Democratic Federation* (SDF) was founded by a stockbroker, H. M. Hyndman, in 1884. This group attracted the support of H. H. Champion, William Morris (the poet), Tom Mann and John Burns. Its overall objective was the overthrow of the existing order and the means of production being put into the hands of the work force. Hyndman, however, was a dogmatic leader, and this led to the formation of a splinter-group *The Socialist League* run by Morris, and Eleanor Marx (Karl Marx's daughter). In 1888 Burns, Mann and Champian left the SDF as they were disillusioned with Hyndman's autocratic leadership.
- The *Fabian* society was also formed in 1884. This was a group of middle-class intellectuals who wanted to see socialism achieved by 'evolution' rather than revolution. Among the early members were Annie Besant, G. B. Shaw, H. G. Wells and Sidney Webb; their policy has been described as 'establishing democratic socialism in Britain' by 'permeating' the Liberal and Conservative Parties with

'socialist ideas'. After 1900, they threw in their lot with the Labour Party.

Although these two groups were mainly middle class, they both preached that the working man should have a share of the wealth that his labour had created. The influence of the socialists in bringing about new unionism and the successful strikes of 1888–9 have already been mentioned (see section 21.4). The overall effect was that the workers began to realise that they needed stronger representation in Parliament, even though the TUC was initially not convinced and, in many ways, feared socialism.

(ii) *Concern about living standards*

The studies of Rowntree in York and Charles Booth in the East End of London illustrated that, despite Britain's powerful position in the industrial world, many people were still living in appalling slums. Socialists pointed out how unfair this was. In addition wages did not increase as rapidly as prices. The effects of industrial competition from the 1880s onwards were being felt in a number of the staple industries, for example, ships, textiles and mining. Workers genuinely became concerned about their lot and looked to improve their living conditions.

(iii) *Changing attitudes about the role of the state*

In the middle of the nineteenth century the principle of *laissez-faire* was dominant and working men had tackled this divide by concentrating on 'self-help' and investing their energy in trade unions, co-operatives and friendly societies in order to improve their conditions. Now, however, came a fundamental change in attitude. Already the state had intervened into some areas (for example, Public Health and Education) and passed legislation. It increasingly became the view of working people that the state should take some responsibility in dealing with the problem of poverty. A separate party for workers would campaign in Parliament for such intervention.

(iv) *Loss of confidence in the Liberal Party*

Given the above changes, it became patently clear that the Liberal Party was doing nothing for the working man. Since the

1880s social reforms had been conspicuous by their absence and things did not look like changing.

(v) *The attack on the unions by the employers* (see section 21.4(c) for details)

These factors overlapped and interlocked to have the effect of creating a working-class consciousness and a notion of a separate party was firmly cemented (see diagram below).

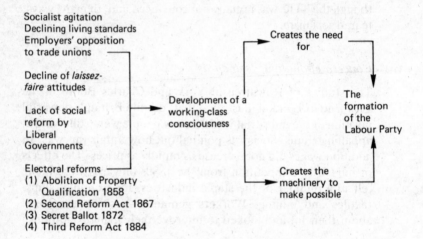

The birth of such a party was, however, to prove to be a complicated one.

(d) What was the role of James Keir Hardie (1856–1915) in the foundation of the Labour Party?

(i) Keir Hardie's background was an important formative influence on the views he came to adopt throughout his life. He was born in Legbrannock, a village near Glasgow. He endured a harsh upbringing and worked as a trapper in a Hamilton coalmine: from an early age Hardie knew what hard physical work was all about. As a teenager Hardie read widely and he became a socialist, believing that a man's labour was totally under-valued by the capitalist society. In 1879 he was dismissed by the colliery owners when he spoke out against a proposed wage-cut. This was a turning point in Hardie's life; he now worked as a journalist and became the secretary of the *Ayrshire Miners' Union*.

(ii)   Hardie soon developed a hard-line socialist philosophy and was not prepared to compromise his principles. To him 'Lib-Labism' was <u>anathema</u> and at the Trades Union Congress he made a savage attack on Broadhurst for his moderate policies, virtually accusing him of being a traitor to the Labour movement. In 1888 Hardie failed miserably to be elected as an independent Labour MP for Mid-Lanarkshire. The same year he helped to form the Scottish Labour Party which adopted a socialist programme of reform. In England H. H. Champion (now an ex-member of the SDF) began a newspaper *The Labour Elector* which urged the creation of an Independent Labour Party.

(iii)   Events in Bradford in 1891 were to provide Hardie with an opportune boost. Samuel Lister's huge woollen mill in Manningham Lane suffered a drop in sales and the wages of the operatives were immediately reduced. The outcome was a five-month strike. The workers received little support from outside their ranks and they blamed it on the fact that the Bradford political scene was dominated by the Liberals – even many of the unions backed Lib-Labism. After the strike the *Bradford Labour Union* was formed with the express purpose of achieving a national independent Labour Party; other local areas followed the example of Bradford. Encouraged by these developments Hardie, John Burns and Havelock Wilson stood as independent Labour candidates in 1892 at West Ham South, Battersea and Middlesborough respectively: all three were victorious. Hardie campaigned on a broadly socialist programme advocating full employment, the 8-hour day, and improved housing and rent reform.

(iv)   Partly on the initiative of Hardie the various socialist groups agreed to hold a conference in Bradford in January 1893. The outcome was the establishment of the **Independent Labour Party** (ILP); a programme was drawn up which included 'The collective ownership of the means of production'. Even at this stage, however, there were differences between the various factions. The SDF believed that the new party was too moderate, whereas the Fabians thought the Liberal Party could adequately represent the working man in Parliament. In the 1895 General Election all 28 ILP candidates were defeated.

(v)   Hardie and his supporters continued the fight, arguing that the ILP needed to forge a closer liaison with the TUC. In 1899 T.R

Steels of the Doncaster Branch of the ASRS proposed that there should be a conference of the TUC and socialist groups, to discuss how working men should be represented in Parliament.

(vi) The proposed conference took place at the Memorial Hall, Farringdon Street, London on 27 February 1900. Represented were the ILP, the SDF, the Fabians and the Parliamentary Committee of the TUC; 129 delegates in total. As expected there was wide-ranging discussion and much disagreement. Eventually the Conference agreed to form the **Labour Representation Committee** (LRC).

The following decisions were taken:

● Ramsay MacDonald of the ILP was nominated as the Secretary. The objective was reported by *Reynold's Newspaper* to 'establish a labour group in Parliament . . . ready to co-operate with any party which for the time being may be . . . promoting . . . the direct interest of Labour' (this hinted that the LRC was prepared to co-operate with the Liberals whilst it established a firm foundation to work on its own).

● The LRC would be financed by groups paying an affiliation fee of 50p per 1,000 members.

(vii) In the 1900 General Election the LRC succeeded in winning two seats – Hardie at Merthyr Tydfil, Richard Bell (Secretary of the ASRS) at Derby. Bell later defected to the Liberal benches. In the 1906 General Election Labour candidates won 29 seats out of 50 contested. This obviously represented a marked upturn in fortunes but the success, to some extent, had been artificially created by MacDonald. He had agreed in 1903 with Herbert Gladstone, that the Liberals would not fight certain seats where the LRC had a candidate. The pact was later dropped. In 1906 the LRC finally adopted the title of **The Labour Party**.

(e) Why did the Labour Party experience difficulties between 1906 and 1914?

Initially the new Labour Party appeared to be on the threshold of great success. It influenced the passing the Trade Disputes Act (1906) which reversed the Taff Vale decision. It also increased its number of

MPs to 42 in 1910. Such success, however, was on the surface: it did not disguise the difficulties the party faced.

(i) It had to fight for an identity in Parliament as the Liberal Government (1906–14) embarked on a programme of wide-scale social reform which helped to maintain the vote of many working-class men (see chapter 25).

(ii) There was a great deal of internal arguing over policy between the various groups. The invasion of syndicalist ideas after 1910 caused some people to 'tarnish' the Labour Party with the same brush; it was seen by some as a party of 'revolution'.

(iii) It proved very difficult to set up the administrative machinery of a new Parliamentary Party; mistakes were made. One such error was the decision to change the chairman by ballot each year instead of having a permanent leader.

(iv) The biggest headache was the Osborne Judgement (1909) which, in effect, deprived the new party of its financial support. Eventually the Payment of Members Act and the Trade Union Act reversed Osborne. The First World War now intervened and provided some space for the new party to collect its thoughts.

21.9 SELF-HELP MOVEMENTS: FRIENDLY SOCIETIES AND CO-OPERATIVES

Self-help groups were in abundance during the greater part of the nineteenth century, finding their origin from the *laissez-faire* philosophy which dominated the period. Frederick Morton Eden and Malthus were both of the opinion that the labouring classes should take care of themselves, and this theme was reinforced by Samuel Smiles, the author of *Self-Help* (1859) and *Thrift* (1875).

(a) What were friendly societies and how did they originate?

Before the introduction of National Insurance in 1911, friendly societies provided a workman with protection against unemployment and sickness. They catered mainly for the skilled workers and worked on a contributory basis thus:

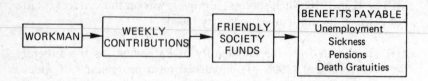

The friendly societies provided social occasions and friendship. The origins of this type of society was to be found in the medieval Guild system. When the Guilds declined, friendly societies took over their role.

(b) How successful were friendly societies in the nineteenth century?

For a time friendly societies enjoyed immense success aided by the fact that they were quickly given Parliamentary support. A number of Acts gave them respectability and legal status. The most important of these were:

(i) *The 1793 Roses Act* said that friendly societies could be established. They were required to draw up a proper constitution with rules and regulations and have them examined by local magistrates.

(ii) *1855 Friendly Societies Act* – Parliament recognised that many societies were in charge of huge amounts of public money. Some societies from 1817 had deposit accounts in savings banks, but there was a need for greater protection of funds from the law. The Act required friendly societies to place their names on a government register adminstered by the Registrar, who had to make regular reports. Most important of all, the Act stated that a society could sue any official who pilfered the fund-box.

(iii) *1875 Friendly Societies (Consolidating) Act* – this drew various Acts together and put them under one piece of legislation. This stated that:

● Societies had to be certified by the Registrar.
● Accounts and Reports had to be published.
● Rulebooks had to be published and adhered to. Changes could not be made without reference to the Registrar.

- Societies' funds were protected by the law of the land.
- Societies were not required to pay stamp duties.

The Act overall confirmed the respected position of friendly societies.

(iv)   Given this 'framework of acceptability' friendly societies flourished. Estimated membership went from 0.7 million in 1801, to 4 million in 1874, to 6.5 million in 1913. Large friendly societies came into existence, for example, The Oddfellows and The Order of Foresters. Such large concerns were 'Affiliated', meaning that they had branches (or lodges) nationwide. Usually there was a certain amount of pomp and ceremony – new members were sworn in, a chain of office was worn by the President and strict secrecy was upheld about the affairs of individual members. Friendly societies stayed a force until the Welfare State schemes were introduced and now their role is very much a supporting one.

(c)   What were producer's co-operatives and why did they fail?

(i)   The idea of producer's co-operatives involved a group of people working together to realise a saleable item from which they shared the profits equally. Robert Owen first put the theory into practice and hence the phrase 'Owenism' is sometimes applied. In 1825 Owen started the settlement of New Harmony in Indiana, America; this consisted of about 1,000 people who collectively cultivated the soil aiming to feed themselves and sell surplus crops on the market. The experiment only lasted three years: it lost money and appeared to be too idealistic to succeed.

(ii)   Owen returned to England in 1829 and tried a new venture – that of 'Equitable Labour Exchanges'. The theory was that goods should be exchanged on the basis of the amount of time it had taken to make them. Paper-notes were produced which had varying values of 'hours-worked'. Again the outcome was a brief flourish followed by abject failure. The main reason for this was the lack of variety in the goods available for exchange and a buyer had to take a producer's word for the number of hours he had spent on the item. The idea fizzled out in 1833 and Owen turned his attention to trade unionism (section 21.2(e)(ii)).

(d) **What were consumer co-operatives? How did they develop and why were they successful?**

(i)   The basic notion of a consumer co-operative is as follows:

THE CO-OPERATIVE SHOPS BUYS GOODS FROM WHOLESALER	→	GOODS SOLD AT PRICES WHICH ALLOW FOR A LOWER PROFIT MARGIN	→	MEMBERS OF THE CO-OPERATIVE SHARE IN THE PROFITS

(ii)   The first successful consumer co-operative was started by a group of flannel-weavers who adopted the grandiose title of 'The Rochdale Society of Equitable Pioneers'. They each put up £1 towards the opening of a shop in Toad Lane, Rochdale (21 December 1844). The 'pioneers' encouraged people to join the co-operative by paying a minimal subscription each week (the equivalent of 'shares') which gave them the privilege of buying food from the Toad Lane Store. The advantage to them was twofold:

● The food would be guaranteed to be 'pure'.
● The price would be reasonable as no attempt would be made to profiteer.

After the first year of trading (there were 74 members) the profits were calculated and divided among the members – the so called 'dividend'. The success of the 'pioneers' motivated others to try the idea; in 1851 there were approximately 140 similar societies and by 1875 the number had increased to 1,266.

(iii) Consumer co-operatives have been extremely successful for a number of reasons:

● Working people could escape the evils of the 'tommy' shops or truck system.
● They were allowed to develop without hindrance from the government. In fact, they were a perfect example of the self-help principle and they enjoyed identical legal protection to the friendly societies.
● Members liked the idea of the dividend and receiving interest on their shares.
● Co-ops invested some of their money in promoting education schemes, as well as buying property and other assets.

- They developed their own manufacturing plants to produce a whole range of goods, for example, biscuits.
- They became nationally co-ordinated via the Co-operative Wholesale Society (CWS) (1863) and Scottish CWS (1868). This made bulk purchases for all the co-operative stores thereby reducing cost prices.

21.10 CONCLUSION

The nineteenth century proved to be a long struggle for the working people of Britain in which they had to fight for industrial, political and social rights. At the end of the century a working-class consciousness was firmly rooted in British society, and the various individual activities described in this chapter could rightfully claim to have a single title 'The Labour Movement' which in the words of Tony Benn 'arose directly from the twin struggles by the British people to control Parliament through the popular vote and to gain the right to organise free trade unions'.

QUESTIONS

1. **Objectives 1 and 2**

(a) Why were the Combination Laws passed in 1799 and why were they repealed in 1824?   (8 marks)
(b) What attempts were made to form large 'national' unions in the period 1825–35? Why did they fail?   (12 marks)

2. **Objective 3**

(a) As one of the Tolpuddle Martyrs write an account justifying your actions in attempting to form a trade union.
(b) As a magistrate, write an article for the local newspaper in which you justify the penalty of transportation.
                    (20 marks)

3. **Objective 1**

Write an outline account of the growth of trade unions in the period 1850–75. You may use any of the following material which you feel is relevant:

- Formation of the Amalgamated Society of Engineers
- The Junta
- The Sheffield Outrages
- The TUC
- Hornby v Close
- Royal Commission on Trade Unions
- 1871 Trade Union Act
- 1871 Criminal Law Amendment Act
- The National Agricultural Labourers' Union
- 1875 Conspiracy and Protection of Property Act

(20 marks)

4. **Objectives 1 and 2**

(a) How did the 'new unions' of the 1880s differ from the 'new model unions' of the 1850s?

(b) Why did new unionism grow so rapidly in the period 1880–1914? How successful were the new unions in improving the lot of the working man?

(20 marks)

5. **Objectives 1 and 2**

Assess the role of James Keir Hardie in the formation of the Labour Party. You should try to cover the following aspects:

- How far Hardie was a product of his environment.
- Any personal qualities Hardie might have possessed which enabled him to become a national figure.
- Any outside factors which influenced Hardie's action.
- His overall importance in the Labour Movement.

(20 marks)

6. **Objectives 1, 2 and 4**

Source A

The vast bulk of the labour employed at the docks was casual, so casual that no-one was even sure how many men regarded themselves as being primarily 'dockers', rather than members of another trade filling in between jobs. Charles Booth estimated that in Bethnal Green, around the three main docks alone, the casuals numbered 10 000, and the future Mrs. Beatrice Webb, one of his investigators, found 700 'royals' at the West and East India Docks, against 1655 casuals without 'tickets' and at the London and St. Katharines Dock 450 'preferred' men, compared to 3250 others. On the Surrey side of the river conditions were different again, since the trade was largely in wool, timber and grain, for which rates of pay were higher, and the demand for men more regular. The dock as a whole, it was believed, provided a living of some kind for about 100 000 people, of whom a high proportion were ticket-less casuals, uncertain of any income from one day to the next. (Taken from *Milestones in Working Class History* by Norman Longmate)

Source B   *Parade of coalheavers during the Great Dock Strike of September 1889 (courtesy of BBC Hulton Picture Library)*

Source C

The strike will remain a most significant event in the relations between capital and labour. There is first the fact that the despised labourers possessed of no special skill or strength, have been able to combine – combination hitherto having being considered as a weapon only available for the skilled labourer. But even this was by no means the most remarkable phenomenon of the strike. If the labourers and their employers had been left alone to fight it out, the labourers could not have held out a week. The hard case of the men gained the sympathy of all riverside workers. More than that, the case of the labourers took a powerful hold upon public opinion. It drew sympathy and material support from all quarters.
(Leader from *The Times*, 16 September 1889)

(a) How does Source A help us to understand why the dockers came out on strike in 1889?

(b) What does *The Times* claim to be the main reason why the dockers won?

(c) In what ways does Source B support Source C?

(d) If you had been asked to write a balanced account of the London Dock Strike and had been given these three sources to work from what comment would you make?

(20 marks)

7. Objectives 1 and 2

What was the importance of the following in trade union history in the period 1900–14?

(a) The Taff Vale case 1900–01.

(b) The Osborne case and judgement 1908–9.

(c) Syndicalism.

(20 marks)

8. Objectives 1 and 2

(a) Why did 'Chartism' originate in the late 1830s?   (8 marks)

(b) What methods did the Chartists adopt in an effort to get their objectives fulfilled?   (8 marks)

(c) How far was Chartism a failure?   (4 marks)

9. Objective 4

Read the following source, which was written by a Chartist from Leicester, and then answer the questions which follow:

> When we get the Charter we will repeal the Corn laws and all other bad laws. But if you give up your agitation for the Charter to help the Free Traders, they will not help you to get the Charter. Don't be deceived by the middle classes again. You helped them to get their votes – you swelled their cry of 'The bill, the whole bill, and nothing but the bill!' But where are the fine promises you made? Gone to the winds! They said when they had gotten their votes, they would help you to get yours. But they and the rotten Whigs have never remembered you . . . And now they want to get the Corn laws repealed – not for your benefit – but for their own. 'Cheap bread!' they cry. But they mean 'Low wages!' Do not listen to their cant and humbug. Stock to your Charter. You are slaves without your votes!
> (Thomas Cooper, *The Life* London, 1872)

(a) Is this a primary source or a secondary source?

(b) Is this source fact or is it an opinion/judgement on an event? Give reasons for your answer.

(c) How far would you consider this to be a reliable source of evidence? You might like to take account of some of the following criteria:

- Why was it written?
- Has the author any good reason to twist the truth?
- Does it contain any bias – if so does the bias detract from its value as a source?
- On what grounds are we testing it for reliability?

(d) What other sources would be needed to obtain a balanced picture of the Chartist movement?

(20 marks)

10. Objectives 1 and 2

Co-operative Festival: Study the quote from *The Times*, 14 August 1900, and answer the questions:

> The annual Co-operative Festival is being held this week at the Crystal Palace, and today the exhibition of goods produced in

co-operative workshops, which has been organised by the Labour Association, will be opened by Major-General Sir J. P. Maurice . . . The exhibition is one of the principal features of the festival week. The Labour Association, which brings it together, has for its object the promotion of co-operative production based on the co-partnership of the workers . . . there has been a seven and a half per cent increase in the number and the trade of the societies, their capital has gone up more than ten per cent, the losses have fallen to half what they were in 1898, the profits have increased by 43 per cent, and the amount of profit paid to employees as a divided upon their wages has grown by 45 per cent.

(a) What is meant by a 'consumer's co-operative'? (2 marks)

(b) Who were the 'Rochdale Pioneers' and what was their importance? (6 marks)

(c) What was the CWS and why was it established? (4 marks)

(d) Why was the co-operative movement so successful? (8 marks)

INDUSTRIAL DEVELOPMENTS 1850–1914

22.1 INTRODUCTION

(a) This period as a whole saw the continued growth of the staple (or basic) industries which had been at the centre of the 'industrial take-off' of the late eighteenth century; these industries included coal, textiles, shipbuilding and iron and steel. From the 1880s newer light industries began to emerge and this has been described by some historians as 'the second industrial revolution'.

(b) Between 1850 and 1873 Britain enjoyed a period of unprecedented economic prosperity. She was the world's leading industrial power and the often-used description 'workshop of the world' was fully justified. In the judgement of David Thomson, Britain could boast 'a growing material prosperity, and a level of industrial production and foreign trade which set [her] far ahead of all other countries'. This economic strength coincided with the heyday of the philosophies of free trade and *laissez-faire*.

(c) In contrast to this, the years from 1873–1914 saw Britain having to face strong opposition from a number of foreign countries who began to develop their industrial capacity at a faster pace. So noticeable was this 'chill wind of competition' after years of being 'top dog' that economists of the day began to use the phrase 'Great Depression' to describe the change in Britain's circumstances. This, however, was probably going too far and the issue has been the subject of fierce debate among historians.

22.2 WHAT WAS THE IMPORTANCE OF THE GREAT EXHIBITION?

Between May and October 1851 the *Great Exhibition of the Works of Industry of all Nations* was held in Hyde Park, London. Not only was it a large commercial success, but also a symbol of the awesome strength of British industry at that time.

(a) The origins of the Great Exhibition

(i) The Great Exhibition was the brainchild of the Prince Consort, Albert, and Henry Cole, the chairman of the Royal Society of Arts. Together they had organised trade fairs on a small scale but they were keen to stage a much larger exhibition similar to ones that had been held in Paris. Having given the idea great thought, they decided 'to go for broke' and set up a huge international exhibition in London which would outstrip any other previous event. The objectives of such an event were seen as twofold:

- To show off the industrial achievements of all nations (worldwide).
- To encourage international peace and friendly relations between countries.

It was clear however, that British industry would be the showpiece of the Exhibition and thus, would gain substantial prestige and publicity.

(ii) A Royal Commission was established in 1849 with the brief of organising the Exhibition. A site of 26 acres (10.5 hectares) was acquired within Hyde Park, and capital for the venture was raised by donations from individuals and sponsorship from companies. Many leading politicians of the day stated their support for the Exhibition, including Lord Derby, Robert Peel and William Gladstone.

(b) Organising the Great Exhibition

The Commission faced a number of problems in organising the Great Exhibition between 1849 and 1851:

- Many people expressed their doubts and opposition. In particular *The Times* conducted an anti-exhibition campaign, claiming that it would attract criminals to London and destroy the beauty of Hyde Park.

● The most formidable problem facing the Commission was the design of the building to stage the Exhibition. The problem was eventually solved by Joseph Paxton, the head gardener of the Duke of Devonshire. He proposed to build a prefabricated structure of iron and glass to the dimensions of 622 yards (569 metres) in length and 137 yards (125 metres) in breadth. *Punch*, a supporter of the Great Exhibition from the outset, called the building the 'Crystal Palace'.

● The sheer volume of work in bringing almost 14 000 exhibitors from all over the world to one location in London was a great feat of organisation. It should be remembered that communications were still relatively limited, despite the advent of the railways, penny post and electric telegraph. Prince Albert admitted that he was 'more dead than alive from overwork'.

(c) The staging of the Exhibition 1 May–15 October 1851

(i) The Great Exhibition was opened on 1 May by Queen Victoria who was unashamedly proud of the achievements of her 'dearly beloved' Albert. Within the Crystal palace there were over 7000 British exhibitors and some 6000 from overseas. The west nave housed the products of British industry with machinery on the ground floor and lighter articles on the upper level. The east nave was reserved for foreign exhibits. Separating the two naves was the central transept, built so as to enclose a number of large elm trees, which Colonel Sibthorp said should not be cut down.

(ii) In all, a total of 6 200 000 people visited the Exhibition. Some had season tickets, but the vast majority of visitors were ordinary people from all over Britain, who saved up to visit London on excursion trips organised by 'travel agents' such as Thomas Cook and the railway companies. From Mondays to Thursdays admission could be obtained for one shilling (5p). The record attendance on any one day was a staggering 109 915, and over the six months that the Exhibition was opened £522 000 was taken in admission charges.

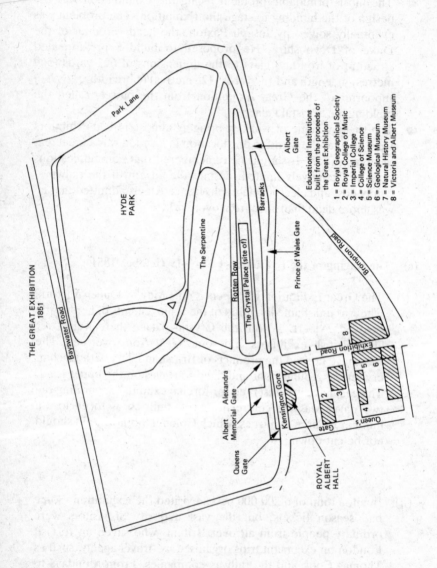

THE GREAT EXHIBITION
1851

Park Lane

HYDE PARK

The Serpentine

Bayswater Road

Rotten Row

The Crystal Palace (site of)

Barracks

Albert Gate

Brompton Road

Prince of Wales Gate

Alexandra Gate

Albert Memorial Gate

Kensington Gore

Queens Gate

Queen's Gate

Exhibition Road

ROYAL ALBERT HALL

Educational Institutions built from the proceeds of the Great Exhibition

1 = Royal Geographical Society
2 = Royal College of Music
3 = Imperial College
4 = College of Science
5 = Science Museum
6 = Geological Museum
7 = Natural History Museum
8 = Victoria and Albert Museum

(d) The importance and significance of the Great Exhibition

(i)   The Exhibition realised a profit of £186 500 which was used to further cultural, educational and scientific learning. A large tract of land (87 acres – 35 hectares) was bought to the south of Hyde Park in Kensington, and over the following 50 years a number of important institutions were developing including:

> The Victoria and Albert Museum
> The Albert Hall
> The Science Museum
> The Natural History Museum
> The Royal College of Music
> Imperial Collge of Science and Technology

All of these still play an important role in the cultural life of the nation (for example, the Science Museum attracts about 3 million visitors each year).

(ii) At the time, the Great Exhibition appeared to symbolise the strength of British industry, and invoked a mood of optimism among the British population. The Exhibition had brought Britain international prestige and had given the nation a great lift. Although poverty and hardship were still present, the next 20 years were to be ones of great progress for the British economy.

22.3 WHY DID BRITAIN ENJOY PROSPERITY BETWEEN 1850 AND 1873?

(a)   A cameo of economic statistics for this period will illustrate the powerful performance of British industry:

(i)   *An increase in output in the staple industries*

- Coal output increased from 60 million tonnes in 1855 to 109 million tonnes in 1870.
- Pig iron production increased from 2.9 million tonnes in 1855 to 5.9 million tonnes in 1875.
- The value of cotton cloth produced rose from £46 million in 1851 to £105 million in 1871.
- The amount of railway track increased from 5890 miles (9,500 km) in 1850 to 13 640 miles (22 000 km) in 1875.

- The size of the merchant fleet increased in tonnage from 2.9 million tonnes to 4.9 million tonnes (1875).
- In 1870 industrial growth was estimated to be running at about 3.5 per cent per year.

(ii) *An expansion of trade*

Britain followed a policy of free trade and, whilst she was the world's leading industrial producer, this proved to be extremely beneficial. Trade expanded as follows:

- Imports went up in value from £100 million (1850) to £300 million (1870), whilst exports rose in the same period from £71 million to £200 million.
- Invisible exports such as banking and insurance facilities and fees for shipping also showed a healthy increase. Earnings from this source counterbalanced the deficit in visible trade. For example:

Trade balances

(£m)	Visible	Invisible	Net
1851–5	−33	+41	+8
1871–5	−64	+139	+75

(iii) *An overall rise in the standard of living*

Although it is true to say that poverty and hardship remained a fact of life for many (as shown by the comments of Henry Mayhew in London and Frederich Engels in Manchester), overall there was a rise in the standard of living during this period. This was characterised by:

- A falling level of unemployment from 12.5 per cent in 1858 to 7 per cent in 1867.
- Real wages went up by about one-third over the period as a whole, with prices increasing at a slower rate mainly because of the free-trade policy allowing cheap raw materials and food into the country.

Rousseaux price (1865 = 100)		Money wages	Real wages (1850 = 100)
1850	95	100	100
1874	121	155	136

(Real wages = wages in comparison with prices – thus if wages increase by 10 per cent and prices increase by 2 per cent in a given year, real wages have increased by 8 per cent.

● Savings deposits increased. In 1861 the Post Office Savings Bank had deposits to the tune of £18 million.
● Cheaper foods meant better diet and higher consumption of protein foods such as meat and fish.
● For the first time industry became the dominant wealth-earning sector of the economy, displacing agriculture. This is borne out by comparing statistics from the 1851 and 1871 Census returns:

	1851		1871
Agricultural labourers	1 904 687	falls to	1 423 854
Coal-miners	193 111	rises to	315 398
Iron and steel	95 350	rises to	191 291
Cotton	414 998	rises to	508 715
Engineering/ shipbuilding	80 528	rises to	172 948

(b) The reasons for this prosperity were numerous:

(i) Britain had sufficient deposits of vital raw materials such as coal and iron ore, to serve her well-established industries. In Rostow's terminology Britain's economy had entered the phase of 'maturity'.

(ii) Britain's expanding population (20.8 million in 1851; 26.1 million in 1871) provided both a source of labour and a sizeable domestic market.

(iii)   A stable democratic government and the fact that Britain avoided war during this period (except for the Crimean War of 1854–6) provided a firm basis for economic growth. Potential competitors, such as America, Germany and France had their economies dislocated by major wars (American Civil War 1861–5 and the Franco-Prussian War 1870–71).

(iv)   Britain's growing Empire, brought closer to the 'motherland' by the developments in steamships and railways, provided a source of cheap materials and a market for manufactured goods.

(v)   There was also a favourable climate for obtaining credit and loans. Gold was discovered in California (1849) and Australia (1859), and this helped to strengthen world currencies. In Britain, London was emerging as the financial centre of the world providing loans and capital for projects overseas. In 1870 Britain's investments abroad totalled £900 million; Europe, the Americas, India and Australia were all able to benefit from British capital.

(vi)   The atmosphere of *laissez-faire* and the policy of free trade together with the *Limited Liability Acts* of 1855 and 1862 promoted individual initiative and enterprise. These Acts gave better security for industrial firms should they encounter financial difficulties. From now on if a company went bankrupt, shareholders' liability to pay off debts was limited to the amount they had invested in shares. Thus, individuals felt more willing to invest their capital in shareholdings.
   Developments in engineering were also vital:

●   Improved techniques were invented for the manufacture of iron and steel (see Section 22.4).
●   The machine-tool industry improved considerably. In the early days of industrialisation, parts for machines such as the steam-engine had to be individually made, and different companies made screws to different specifications. By the mid nineteenth century machine parts and screw-threads were standardised, allowing machinery to be mass-produced. This was mainly due to three pioneering engineers as illustrated in the following diagram:

Name	*Joseph Bramah* (1748–1814)	*Henry Maudslay* (1771–1831)	*Joseph Whitworth* (1803–87)
Biographical detail	Trained as a carpenter	Worked under Bramah	Worked under Maudslay
Achievements	Developed a lock which was made up of standardised parts. He built a hydraulic press and an improved water closet.	Devised a lathe for cutting screws. Perfected a slide-rest which enabled metals parts to be made accurately on milling machines.	Made screws and bolts to a standardised size (e.g. threads). He also devised machine tools which could make parts accurately.

Britain's supremacy, founded on her staple industries, appeared to be unassailable – she truly was 'the workshop of the world'.

22.4 OUTLINE DEVELOPMENTS IN THE STAPLE (BASIC) INDUSTRIES BETWEEN 1850 AND 1914, REFERRING TO COAL, TEXTILES, AND IRON AND STEEL

(a) Coal

(i) Coal was the most important of the staple industries and during this period was in great demand:

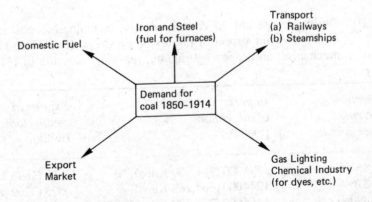

(ii) The British coal industry was able to respond to this demand and both output and exports increased steadily:

Year	Output (m.tons)	% exported
1850	49.4 (48.6 tonnes)	6.8
1870	110.4 (108.6 tonnes)	13.4
1900	225.2 (221.6 tonnes)	25.9

In 1913 a record output was recorded, a total of 287 million tons (282 tonnes).

(iii) Amazingly, these impressive figures were achieved without the mines undergoing mechanisation. In 1900 only 1.5 per cent of Britain's coal was machine-cut compared with 25 per cent in America. The coal was hand dug by miners, often working in difficult seams. Shafts over 656 yards (600 metres) deep were sunk to open up new seams. Some new coalfields were also opened up including South Yorkshire, Nottinghamshire and Kent, but efforts to improve safety standards (such as exhaust fans and wire cages) did not prevent a number of mining accidents (see chapter 6). Private owners were often reluctant to plough their profits back into the collieries by investing in up-to-date technology, but an increase in exports stimulated the growth of ports on the South Wales coast – Cardiff, Newport and Swansea.

(b) Textiles

(i) During this period the cotton industry maintained its position as the most important of the textile products. It continued to mechanise, and expanded rapidly, reaching its zenith in 1914:

Annual average per decade	Imports of raw cotton ('000 lb)	Exports of cotton cloth (million yd)
1850–9	795000 (361,000 Kilos)	1855 (1696 m)
1870–9	1244000 (564,269 Kilos)	3573 (3269 m)
1890–9	1556000 (705,790 Kilos)	5057 (4624 m)
1910–9	1864000 (845,497 Kilos)	5460 (4993 m)

(ii) A number of new machines were introduced into the industry:

- From about 1830 self-acting mules (an improved version of Crompton's original invention) were introduced into spinning mills.
- In the 1840s ring spinning machines (invented by Thorpe in America in 1828) were imported into some British mills. These could spin yarn rapidly and continuously, but their general adoption took about 50 years.
- Power looms were also introduced, and by the 1860s only a few handloom weavers were left. The Northrop loom (another American invention) was gradually adopted from 1892 onwards which made weaving a continuous process.
- Finally, in 1905 electricity was first used to power spinning machines in Manchester. This new form of power spread slowly and steam remained predominant in the British cotton industry.

(iii) The cotton industry did, however, suffer a temporary set back when the American Civil War (1861–5) resulted in a cotton famine. Work on the American plantations was disrupted and supplies of raw cotton dwindled rapidly. British cotton mill-owners had to pay high prices for a limited amount of imported American cotton.

The result was unemployment, with mills closing, but Lancashire recovered from this setback in the 1870s. Some of the Scottish mills never reopened, but Glasgow and Paisley remained as important cotton centres.

(iv) The woollen industry also made progress but more slowly. Mechanisation came gradually:

- From about 1850 wool-combing machines, invented by Samuel Lister and James Noble, were introduced.
- Power looms were adopted extensively from about 1870.

(v)   The British woollen industry depended on imports of raw wool mainly from Australia and South Africa. West Yorkshire was the centre of the woollen industry producing worsted, shoddy and carpets. There were, however, several areas of minor importance – Stroud (Gloucestershire), Wilton (Wiltshire), Kidderminster (Worcester), Kendal (Cumbria) and the Scottish Borders.

(vi) Other minor textile industries which existed included:

- Jute (Dundee)
- Hosiery (Nottingham, Leicester and Derby)
- Linen (Belfast, Newry, Armagh, Dundee)
- Silk (Derbyshire, Cheshire, Staffordshire)
- Flannel (Montgomeryshire)

(c) Iron and Steel

(i) Two improvements were introduced during the early part of the nineteenth century:

- In 1828 the manager of the Glasgow Gas Works, J. B. Neilson (1792–1865), initiated the *hot blast* for heating furnaces. Neilson discovered that if air was pre-heated, less fuel was needed to manufacture pig iron. His idea was widely adopted in Central Scotland but it was several years before it spread to England.
- In 1850 Parry of Monmouth developed the hot-blast process a stage further. He closed in the top of the blast-furnace and removed the carbon monoxide gases through pipes. This gas was then used to heat steam-engine boilers or the air in stoves which was blasted into the furnace. This gas had previously been burnt off and wasted.

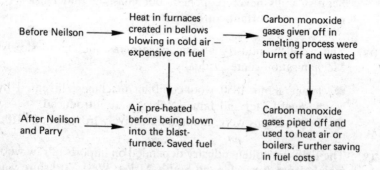

- In 1839 James Nasmyth (1808–90) invented the *Steam-hammer* for shaping wrought iron, after being approached by Brunel who required a wide range of iron products for his many engineering projects. Nasmyth's steam-hammer was an ingenious invention. It could transform huge iron ingots into bars and girders as well as shaping much smaller items.

(ii) In 1850 the most useful metal produced in quantity, by puddling, was wrought iron. Steel, a harder more malleable metal, could only be produced in small amounts (by the crucible process) at a time when such a product was in great demand from many industries. An improved method for making cheap steel in large amounts was urgently needed. In 1856 *Henry Bessemer (1813–98)* and *Robert Mushet (1811–91)*, invented a converter for manufacturing steel. The diagram below illustrates how the process worked:

Molten pig iron was poured into the convertor (a special container) → Air was blown into the converter driving away impurities and refining the iron → Mushet showed that if a small amount of manganese was added the steel was not brittle

● Bessemer's *Converter* produced steel quickly (3 tonnes per hour) and cheaply. The cost of a tonne of steel was halved. One result of Bessemer's invention was the development of Barrow-in-Furness as a steel-making town. However, the converter was only effective if non-phosphoric iron ore was used in the blast-furnace stage; typically the majority of Britain's iron ore deposits contained phosphorus!

(iii) In 1867 William Siemens (1823–83) and Pierre Martin jointly invented the *Open-hearth Process*. Again it could only deal with iron which had been made from non-phosphoric ore. Its main advantage over Bessemer's method was that it could convert scrap-iron into steel:

Pig iron or scrap metal were placed in a hearth or trough → Hot air was blown over the molten metal driving away impurities, thus producing steel → The waste gases were then used to heat the air blast

(iv) In 1879 the *Basic Process* was invented by Sidney Gilchrist Thomas and Percy Gilchrist. This was a major breakthrough, allowing iron ore containing phosphorus to be used in producing steel. Dolomite limestone was put inside the furnace, which reacted with the phosphorus making it float on top of the molten liquid. This phosphorus was drawn off and used for fertiliser, and the molten iron could be converted to steel. This invention had a number of important results:

- New steel-making centres grew up 'on' phosphoric iron fields. In the 1880s Middlesborough became a boom town as steel furnaces opened up using local phosphoric iron ore and limestone from the Cleveland Hills.
- The huge phosphoric iron deposits of Pennsylvania and Alsace-Lorraine were opened up stimulating a rapid growth in the steel production of America and Germany.
- Steel replaced wrought iron as the dominant building material and was used to manufacture machinery, locomotives, ships and bridges (for example, the Forth Bridge 1882–9).

22.5 WHAT 'NEW' INDUSTRIES WERE DEVELOPED IN THIS PERIOD?

In the latter years of the nineteenth century Britain was heavily dependent on the staple industries for her wealth, but a number of new lighter industries were beginning to emerge.

(a) Electrical engineering

In the late nineteenth century several developments enabled electricity to be generated and distributed on a larger scale.

(i) The first power-station was built at Godalming (1881); others followed in the large cities, each owned by a private company.

(ii) Charles Parson's steam turbine (1884) was an important breakthrough as it could generate electricity in large amounts.

(iii) By 1900 electricity was being transported along a grid of cables from the private power stations to both domestic and industrial consumers.

(iv) In 1878 and 1879 Thomas Edison in America and Joseph Swan in Britain invented the incandescent lamp, thus making it possible to have electric street and house lighting. Among the early electrical firms was Sebastian de Ferranti, established in 1876.

(v) Electric power was also adapted to trams, railways and wireless telegraphy, the latter being invented by Marconi in 1901.

(b) Motor-car industry

(i) In 1875 Siegfried Manus succeeded in inventing a petrol driven internal combustion engine but he did not develop his idea commercially. In 1885 Carl Benz and Gottlieb Daimler began to design petrol-driven motor vehicles. They were followed by Emile Lavassor in France and F. W. Lancaster in Britain.

(ii) The development of motor-car manufacture in Britain was hindered by the *Red Flag Act* (1865) which had been passed to curb the dangers of the steam-carriage. This ruled that any mechanically-driven vehicles were to be limited to a speed of 4mph (6.5 kmph) and had to be preceded by a person carrying a red flag as a warning to other road users. Not until this Act was repealed in 1896 did the motor-car industry become established. By 1914 there were 132 000 cars on British roads, all of them were individually built. Among them was the *Silver Ghost* manufactured by C. S. Rolls and F. M. Royce in 1907.

(c) Developments in the chemical industry

(i) The chemical industry was important for producing a wide range of products, including explosives, dyes, fertilisers, coal bi-products, soap and bleach.

(ii) The major development in this period was the Solway ammonia process for producing soda (named after a Belgian chemist). This proved to be much quicker than the traditional process devised by the Frenchman Nicholas le Blanc in 1791. Britain continued to use Le Blanc's method as it produced the bi-products of bleach and hydrochloric acid. Meanwhile Germany and America quickly adopted Solway's process and, as a result, established a lead over the British chemical industry.

(d) The bicycle industry

The earliest 'bicycles' were called hobby-horses and were propelled by the rider's feet. The next development was the Penny-farthing which had the pedals attached to the large front wheel. Not until Lawson invented the endless steel chain in 1879 was the modern bicycle born. One of the earliest cycle manufacturers was James Stanley of Coventry. In 1885 the Stanley Company produced the safety bicycle which had wheels of the same size and later had pneumatic tyres – invented by J. B. Dunlop in 1888. Other companies which manufactured bicycles soon followed, including British Small Arms, Rudge, Humber and Raleigh. By 1913 Britain was exporting 150 000 bicycles worth over £2 million to the economy.

22.6 WHY WAS BRITAIN'S INDUSTRIAL SUPREMACY CHALLENGED IN THE LAST QUARTER OF THE NINETEENTH CENTURY?

(a) During this period conditions were such that America and Germany, two sleeping giants, were able to exploit vast resources to the full. Once this occurred they presented formidable opposition to British manufacturers who were unable to do anything at all to stem the tide. The following reasons explain the industrial development of America and Germany:

(i) *Large populations*

Between 1871 and 1911 Britain's population increased from 31.8 million to 45.3 million. These figures, however, were dwarfed by America and Germany whose populations expanded in the following proportions:

	1871	1911
America	38.5 m	91.7 m
Germany	41.0 m	64.9 m

America's population was boosted by an influx of immigrants from Europe from the 1880s, including Poles, Italians, Austrians and Hungarians. Thus both America and Germany possessed a large labour force and an extensive domestic market.

(ii) *Relative stability in politics*

Although domestic politics in America were far from peaceful she had at least started to recover from the ravages of the Civil War (1861–5). Germany's many states had been 'unified' in 1870–1 under the leadership of Otto von Bismarck. Both countries were now in a position to build up their industrial base.

(iii) *Vast resources*

Both countries had large deposits of coal and iron-ore and furthermore, the Basic Process of Gilchrist Thomas allowed both nations to open up the ironfields containing phosphoric ore. Pauline Gregg explains that 'America pushed out her railways to link her coal and iron . . . the coal of Pittsburgh was thus joined to the iron of Lake Superior'.

(b) Retardation in some aspects of the British economy

It has been argued that Britain laid herself open to foreign competition by not adjusting to the changed circumstances. The following points have been made to support this premise:

(i) Britain maintained a policy of free trade whilst all her main competitors adopted tariff barriers. Whilst this is true, however, other considerations have to be taken into account, namely, that the growing British electorate had become used to cheap imports of food.

(ii) Britain was slow to develop new industries and allowed her competitors to outstrip her in a number of ways;

- It was America who first mass-produced motor cars.
- In the chemical industry, Britain clung to the Le Blanc process whereas America and Germany adopted the Solway method. In 1913, therefore, Britain was a poor third in this industry.
- Other countries took the lead in the manufacture of typewriters, sewing-machines and locks. In general Britain

tended to stress the older staple industries, and in doing so failed to respond to the changing circumstances of the late nineteenth century.

(iii) Britain's industrial plant was based on steam-power and there was a reluctance to invest capital in electrical machinery. America and Germany, by virtue of their late start, were able to take advantage of the developments in electrical engineering, therefore building up a reservoir of expertise in this industry more rapidly than Britain.

(iv) Britain's colliery owners did not invest in up-to-date technology and, as a result, mechanisation in the coal industry was almost unknown in this country. It has been argued that two possible reasons may explain this:

- The will to change and adapt did not exist; there was a 'conservative' attitude among industrialists.
- Between 1873 and 1896 profits were lower than for many years, and thus industrialists may have considered it a financial risk to sink capital in new technology.

(v) British industry, it has been claimed, was slow to reorganise its structure. There were far too many small, family-run businesses which lacked the resources to invest in new technology. Furthermore, their presence encouraged a lack of uniformity and inefficiency. In America and Germany, however, industry was organised into 'cartels' or 'combines' which had two basic kinds of structure:

- Those with horizontal integration where several firms in the same industry amalgamated into one large company.
- Those with vertical integration where a number of processes within one industry were controlled by one large firm (for example, an iron and steel company controlling all the processes involved – from mining the raw material, manufacturing the steel and marketing the product).

Not until the 1890s was there any real move towards larger industrial firms in Britain, for example, United Alkali Company (1891), The English Sewing Cotton Company (1897), and the Imperial Tobacco Company (1901).

(vi) Britain also suffered because of her backwardness in scientific research and technical education. In 1895 the Bryce Commission (see Section 18.8(b)) commented on the emphasis given to scientific training in other countries and this was reflected by the fact that in 1913 Germany produced six times as many science graduates as Britain. In addition, both America and Germany had established state systems of education: Britain lagged well behind in this respect.

22.7 HOW FAR IS IT TRUE TO SAY THAT BRITAIN SUFFERED A 'DEPRESSION' IN THIS PERIOD?

(a) The years 1873–96 have traditionally been labelled 'The Great Depression'. Randolph Churchill speaking in 1884, claimed that Britain's trade was stricken with 'a mortal disease'. In 1886 a Royal Commission on the Depression of Industry and Trade was appointed to investigate Britain's apparent decline. Among the features noted were:

- Industrial products were fetching lower prices and, therefore, industrialists were making smaller profits.
- There appeared to be more unemployment (although no accurate statistics were kept).
- The threat of foreign competition in the form of Germany worried British industrialists. It was from this time that demands for fair trade and protection began to be made.

A number of pamphlets were written on this subject with *Made in Germany* by E. Williams (1896) taking the line that Britain was becoming submerged in products made in German factories.

(b) Was this view justified?

The issue has been hotly debated by historians. However, a number of factors need to be balanced out before arriving at a conclusion:

(i) Britain's industrial output continued to grow during these years but not at the same pace as those of America and Germany. These statistics support this point:

Steel production (m. tons)

	GB	USA	Germany
1880–4	2 (1.9 tonnes)	1.5 (1.47 tonnes)	0.25 (0.24 tonnes)
1910–14	7 (6.88 tonnes)	31.0 (30.5 tonnes)	13.00 (12.8 tonnes)

Railways ('000 miles (km))

	GB	Germany	France
1880	17.9 (28.8)	21.0 (33.8)	14.3 (23.1)
1900	21.8 (35.2)	32.1 (51.7)	23.6 (38.1)

% Increase in coal output

	GB	Germany	France
1880–90	23.5	50.8	34.5
1890–1900	24.0	67.4	28.0

Pig iron production (m tons)

	GB	US	Germany
1871	6.5 (6.39 tonnes)	3.9 (3.83 tonnes)	1.5 (1.47 tonnes)
1910	10.0 (9.84 tonnes)	27.7 (27.2 tonnes)	14.8 (14.5 tonnes)

Given the enormous resources of America and Germany it was not surprising that their industry should grow at a faster rate. Britain's production in the staple industries at least, was still creditable. In some industries, for example, shipbuilding and textile-machinery she was still the outstanding nation.

(ii) Where Britain did suffer was that her share of world markets started to show a decline. It was now more difficult for her to export to Europe and this led to her trying to open up more markets in Africa and the Far East.

(iii) For the ordinary *worker* the period 1873–96 was quite prosperous. Although his wages did not increase, the fall in prices meant that his money went further. He also benefited from cheap food imports. Not until the period 1900–14 did the working man feel the pinch when prices recovered and wages remained static.

(iv) There were signs of a shopping revolution. New stores opened, for example, Lipton's Stores (245 in 1898), Maypole, Home and Colonial Stores, and Boots. Mass advertising also took off during this period.

The general view now accepted by historians is that the 'Great Depression' was a 'myth'. It was more a case of changing circumstances: Britain remained relatively prosperous and 'a major industrial power' (Brian Murphy).

22.8 CONCLUSION

In 1914 the writing was on the wall that Britain was being challenged and she could no longer expect to dominate world trade. There were a number of worrying features about Britain's attitude such as her over-reliance on the staple industries and her lack of progress in the new industries. These trends were to be highlighted after the First World War when British industry was forced to adapt to the new conditions that prevailed. In the words of R. B. Jones, 'The stability and prosperity of mid-Victorian [Britain] rested on [her] virtual monopoly of world industrial production and trade . . . By the 1880s these bases were challenged and a new and very different age was dawning'.

QUESTIONS

1. **Objective 3**

(a) What arguments would
   (i) A supporter
   (ii) An opponent
   of the Great Exhibition have used to justify their opinions?

436

(b) How would an ordinary member of the public have viewed the Great Exhibition?

(Total = 30 marks)

2. **Objectives 1 and 2**

(a) Briefly outline the developments which took place in the 'staple' industries in this period. (12 marks)
(b) Why was Britain the world's leading industrial power at this time? (8 marks)

3. **Objectives 1 and 2**

Read the following source and then answer the questions:

Thirty years ago England had almost a monopoly of the manufacturing industries of the world. She produced more of everything than she needed; other countries produced very little. The rest of the world had to buy from Britain because it could not buy anywhere else. Well, that was thirty years ago. Now France and America have got machinery – our machinery. Each year they sell an increasing amount of their goods here in Britain. On the other hand, year by year, these countries are closing markets to our exports'.
(Edward Sullivan, 1881).

(a) What factors had allowed America, France and Germany to compete with Britain?
(b) Is it correct to say that Britain experienced 'a depression' in industry in the 1880s?

(Total = 20 marks)

4. **Objectives 1 and 2**

(a) What improvements took place in the manufacturing of iron and steel between 1850 and 1880? (12 marks)
(b) What were the results of these improvements? (8 marks)

AGRICULTURE IN BRITAIN 1815–1914

23.1 INTRODUCTION

British agriculture experienced mixed fortunes between 1815 and 1914 and, overall, declined in importance within the economy compared with the industrial sector. Its gradual demise may be illustrated by reference to the numbers employed in agriculture (see below):

Year	% of adult male work force in agriculture
1851	20
1881	16
1911	5

In order to survive at the end of the century, farming was forced to be flexible and adapt to the changing economic conditions. The story of agriculture is clearly definable into three distinct periods.

1815–c.1850 – A period of distress
1850– 1873 – The 'Golden Age of Agriculture'
1873– 1914 – Agriculture depression

This chapter will examine each period in turn.

AGRICULTURAL DISTRESS 1815–50

23.2 THE LANDOWNERS AND FARMERS

(a) Why had farmers enjoyed a period of prosperity during the French Wars (1793–1815)?

The war helped to produce freak economic conditions which bene-fited the farmers (but not the labourers). The increase in population at the end of the eighteenth century created a demand for more food, and farming responded by enclosing land in order to be more efficient. The war restricted the import of corn and, together with a number of meagre harvests (particularly between 1809 and 1812), this meant an increase in the price the farmers could demand for their produce. The price of wheat reached an all-time high in 1812 – 126s.6d. (£6.33) per quarter (see figure below). This inflation was also fuelled by the fact that William Pitt (Prime Minister) suspended cash payments from the banks. Customers could no longer withdraw gold; instead paper currency was issued. The issuing of paper money produced high prices, particularly as the country banks put no limit on the amounts they were willing to loan. Large sums of money were borrowed by farmers at high rates of interest.

Average wheat prices 1786–1830 (per quarter)
(In quinquennial year groups)

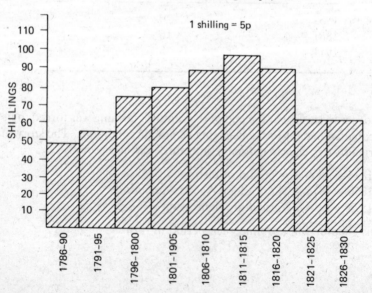

Conditions were 'booming'. Although costs also increased, farmers were able to absorb them because of the abnormally high prices. Furthermore, farmers were willing to invest their profits into enclosing more land and tenants were prepared to take on farms at inflated rents on long leases. They did not appear to foresee an end to this prosperity nor did they appreciate the artificiality which the war had brought to economic conditions. The bubble was soon to burst. The war ended in 1815 with Wellington's victory at Waterloo.

(b) Why did the farmers suffer 'distress' after 1815?

(i) *Falling prices*

The first indication that things were about to change came when improved weather in 1814 and 1815 produced bumper harvests to the extent that supply exceeded demand. Wheat prices plummeted (see table below):

Average price of wheat per quarter

Year	shillings/pence
1813	109/9 (£5.49)
1814	74/4 (£3.72)
1815	65/7 (£3.28)

A number of landowners began to complain and a number of speeches were made in Parliament which had 'agricultural distress' as their central theme. Charles Western, for example, stated in 1816:

> that during the last twenty years agriculture has advanced. The full effects of all our improvements has just been completely realised and two or three good harvests together with continued imports . . . have occasioned such a surplus in the market as accounts . . . for the first depression of the price.

Apart from the renewal of imports, farmers also lost government contracts to supply the armed forces with grain. Prices never recovered their wartime levels and continued to drop rapidly after 1817, reaching a low point of 44s7d. (£2.23) per quarter for wheat in 1822.

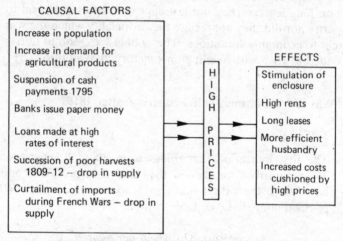

CAUSAL FACTORS

Increase in population

Increase in demand for agricultural products

Suspension of cash payments 1795

Banks issue paper money

Loans made at high rates of interest

Succession of poor harvests 1809–12 – drop in supply

Curtailment of imports during French Wars – drop in supply

HIGH PRICES

EFFECTS

Stimulation of enclosure

High rents

Long leases

More efficient husbandry

Increased costs cushioned by high prices

THE WARTIME AGRARIAN ECONOMY (1793–1815)

(ii) *Costs remained high*

Although prices fell, the farmers' costs remained at wartime levels, for example:

- Rents remained at the same levels because they were part of long-lease agreements which did not account for fluctuations in economic conditions.
- Taxation became more of a burden. Profits were down but the government continued to charge high land taxes.
- The interest on loans taken out during the war had to be paid.

(iii) *Cost of Poor Law and tithes*

As well as all this, farmers were faced with numerous local 'taxes'. The cost of Poor Law relief increased as soldiers returned from the war and found employment almost impossible to obtain in rural areas. The allowance system in the South of England put an additional strain on the poor rates. In addition, there was the church rate to be paid and the rector still demanded the tithe.

(iv) *Depression in industry*

The depression in industry during 1815–20 meant that there was a fall in demand for agricultural produce: the factory workers were having to face lower wages and unemployment.

(c) How widespread was the distress?

(i) In general it appears that many small farmers who had managed to make a living during the war now had great difficulty in making ends meet. William Cobbett claimed in 1821 that 'nothing can be clearer than that the present race of farmers . . . must be swept away by bankruptcy if they do not . . . make their bow and retire'. Many small farmers did, in fact, sell out to large landowners and a number did go bankrupt making for 'large tracts of uncultivated land'.

(ii) In 1816 The Board of Agriculture made an attempt to invest-igate the extent of the distress and sent out a questionnaire. They received just over 300 replies which make interesting reading.

QUESTION	ANSWER	
	YES	*NO*
Are any farms in your neighbourhood unoccupied by tenants?	168 (53%)	127 (40%)
Have any tenants given notice to quit their farms at Ladyday?	REPLIES – MANY – (103) 32% TO SEVERAL – (107) 34% LETTERS NONE – (71) 22% SAYING:	
Is the distress greater on arable farms?	'Distress greater on arable farms' – General reply	

(d) What action did Parliament take and how effective was it?

The expectation that Parliament would help the farmers was based on the fact that the landowning class dominated Parliament and were, therefore, in a position to influence the passing of legislation. Some action was forthcoming.

(i) *1815 Re-introduction of the Corn Laws*

The farmers began to campaign for the return of the Corn Laws in 1813, arguing that protection from foreign imports would lead to a fall in supply-levels at home, and therefore help to maintain the high prices they required to operate their businesses. On 3 March 1815 the Corn Laws were passed. The laws stated that foreign corn would only be allowed on to the market if the domestic price reached 80 shillings (£4) per quarter, or over. This, in theory, guaranteed the British farmer a satisfactory return for his produce.

(ii) *Parliamentary Relief 1816*

The government responded with some reluctance to the findings of the Board of Agriculture's Inquiry and allowed three tax concessions to farmers:

● Duties payable on malt were abolished.
● The property tax (which amounted to 10 per cent on incomes from land) was abolished.
● The tax on farm horses was brought down.

Beyond this, however, the government said it was unable to help. Despite one or two reasonable years, distress continued.

(iii) *Return to Gold Standard 1821*

The government was of the opinion that there was too much currency in circulation because of the increased printing of paper notes by the country banks. In 1821 the currency was put back on the Gold Standard which meant that notes could be again exchanged for gold. This reduced the amount of paper money in circulation and caused deflation (that is, a fall in prices).

(iv) *Tithe Commutation Act 1836*

The tithe, a tax where the farmer had to give 10 per cent of his produce to the local rector, was bitterly resented. This Act changed the method of payment to an annual amount of money calculated by averaging out the price of cereals over seven-year periods. The tithe payment for the parish was divided up according to how much land a farmer possessed or occupied.

(v)   It would appear that government action was not very successful in relieving the distress of the farmers. Why was the Government reluctant to take further measures, given that it was dominated by the landowning class? One possible answer is that the farmers were still relatively well off and merely wanted to maintain wartime profits – thus, there was no need for Parliament to give them much help. Chambers and Mingay have another answer. They argue that distress was only felt in certain areas and was not a general feature of agriculture at this time; an opinion supported by the findings of the Board of Agriculture's investigation of 1816.

23.3   THE AGRICULTURAL LABOURERS

(a)   What were the general living conditions like for an agricultural labourer in this period?

Contemporary writers give a vivid impression of the general degradation of the rural labourer. Cobbett described the homes of Leicestershire labourers in these terms:

> look at these hovels, made of mud and straw, bits of glass or of old cast off windows, without frames or hinges frequently . . . Enter them and look at the bits of chairs or stools; the wretched boards tacked together to serve for a table; the floor of pebble, broken brick or the bare ground'.

A Poor Law Overseer in Hampshire, Arthur Octavius Baker, described the labourer as 'reduced to a state of hopeless misery and servility'.

Such conditions went back to the 1790s; unlike the farmer, the war brought no benefits to the labourer and his suffering continued after 1815.

(b)   Why were the labourers in a 'distressed' condition?

(i)   *A surplus of labour*

There were too many labourers chasing too few jobs; this was brought about by a combination of factors:

● The general increase of population.
● The return of 250 000 soldiers from war service.

- The decline of domestic industries. This was particularly felt in East Anglia.
- The apparent reluctance of labourers to move away from the countryside.

Rural unemployment was, therefore, high.

(ii) *The decline of living-in*

During the eighteenth century it had been common practice for labourers to 'live-in' with their employer; this formed a strong bond between master and servant and brought stability to the countryside. Now with a large amount of labour available this practice declined and casual employment increased and led to more men being dependent on the parish poor fund. The farmers had, therefore, abdicated a traditional 'social welfare' role and left the labourer to fend for himself.

(iii) *The Corn Laws*

Whilst these laws may have been of some benefit to the farmers, they had the opposite effect for the labourer. They tended to keep the price of bread – the staple food for the labourer – abnormally high.

(iv) *Low wages*

Agricultural wages failed to keep pace with the increasing prices and the general tendency was for them to fall. In Wiltshire, wages in 1817–18 averaged about 8 shillings (40p) per week, but contemporaries have suggested that a realistic living wage for a labourer would be about 12 shillings (60p) per week.

(v) *The Speenhamland system*

The detrimental effects of this system on those labourers who were conscientious are explained in section 16.3.

(vi) *Indirect taxation*

The government's policy of abolishing the income tax in 1817 had no consequence for the labourers as they earned below the threshold at which payments began. However, to balance the book, purchase tax was increased on 'everyday items' – and this put many goods beyond the reach of the labourer. Once again Cobbett observes:

> A widower with three children and his pay was 18d. (8p) per day, that is to say, about three pounds of bread each day for six days in the week; nothing for Sunday and nothing for lodging, washing, clothing, candlelight or fuel.

(c) How did the labourers react to these conditions and what measures did the authorities take?

The labourers had no vote and could not register their disapproval of the government in an election. They had to use other methods:

(i) *Crime*

Eric Hobsbawm and George Rudé have shown how the labourers' distress was manifested in an increase in the incidence of crime, particularly poaching. They have calculated that between 1817 and 1820 there were 149 indictments for poaching, rising to 177 between 1821 and 1825 and 281 between 1826 and 1829. In the 1820s 50 per cent of the prisoners in Hampshire prisons were convicted poachers. The fact that the game laws carried savage sentences (14 years transportation in 1828) did not appear to deter the labourers from poaching game – probably a measure of their desperate poverty.

(ii) *Emigration*

There was a steady increase up to the mid-1830s in the number of people who saw emigration as the answer to their difficulties:

	Emigration figures
1815–19	97 799
1820–24	95 030
1825–29	121 084
1830–34	381 956
1835–39	287 356

At least the prospect gave them the opportunity to make a fresh start in life: their present circumstances made it worth the risk involved.

(iii) *Rioting 1816 and 1830*

● *East Anglia 1816*

Disturbances of various kinds were widespread in May and June in the counties of Essex, Suffolk and Norfolk, but the most serious rioting involving agricultural labourers occurred in Ely and Littleport in Cambridgeshire in May 1816. A special trial was held in Ely in June 1816 and five men were sentenced to death for 'diverse robberies'. They were hanged on 28 June 1816. Ten more labourers were transported. There was no attempt to understand or sympathise with the harsh living conditions of such men. Such an attitude, however, has to be put into the context of the times; the ruling classes genuinely feared that the country as a whole was on the point of an armed rebellion.

● *The Swing Riots 1830 (the last labourers revolt)*

In 1829 the harvest failed and there was continuing hardship among the labouring population. The atmosphere was uneasy in the agricultural counties and Cobbett warned the farmers 'to be well with their work-people'. As well as the factors mentioned in Section 23.3(b), the widespread introduction of threshing-machines alarmed the labourers greatly. Rioting started in Kent in June 1830 and by November had spread into Sussex, Hampshire, Dorset, Wiltshire, Berkshire and north into the Midlands and East Anglia. The protest took various forms – robberies, hayricks and farm buildings burned, threshing-machines smashed and attacks on rectors or unpopular poor law officials. There was no real pattern to the riots and they were not orchestrated by some 'central body'. They appear to have been more of a spontaneous protest against the desperate living conditions. In a number of counties the labourers sent threatening letters signed by a Captain Swing (a fictitious leader): 'Sir, This is to acquaint you that if your threshing machines are not destroyed by you directly we shall commence our labours. signed on behalf of the whole, Swing'.

The rioters were quelled by an alarmed government. In November 1830 Lord Melbourne (the Home Secretary) sent out a circular to County Lieutenants and magistrates referring to 'open acts of violence and the secret and malicious destruction of property'. He implored the magistrates to use their powers to the full in dealing with the offenders; 'any inactivity . . . will necessarily incur His Majesty's severest Displeasure'.

The courts were once again severe in the punishments they handed out. According to Hobsbawm and Rudé, 19 labourers were executed, 505 transported, 644 imprisoned, seven fined, one whipped and 800 bound over.

(iv)   *Why did the rioting occur in some villages and not others?*

It has been suggested that rioting was more liable to occur in 'open' parishes than 'closed' ones (an open parish had several landowners; a closed parish had one main landowner). This

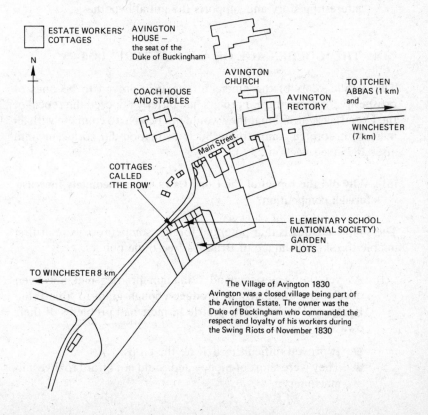

The Village of Avington 1830
Avington was a closed village being part of the Avington Estate. The owner was the Duke of Buckingham who commanded the respect and loyalty of his workers during the Swing Riots of November 1830

statement can be tested by examining events in 1830 in the village of Avington in Hampshire.

All the land in Avington was part of the estate of the Duke of Buckingham and Chandos. There is much evidence to suggest that the Duke took good care of his labourers. Reports in the *Hampshire Chronicle* tell of large feasts of beef and ale in Avington House each Christmas and of his wife, Lady Anne, helping in the village school. The labourers here certainly appeared to be better off than some of their counterparts in other villages. On 22 November 1830 a gang of labourers approached the village from Winchester intent on wrecking the Duke's threshing machines. The rioters were, however, confronted by the Duke's labourers who were led into battle by Reverend Wright of nearby Itchen Abbas. Several of the rioters were captured and held in Avington House whilst soldiers arrived to escort them to Winchester Prison. The Duke of Buckingham and Chandos related this incident in a letter to the County Lieutenant, the Duke of Wellington – it is an interesting story and supports the initial hypothesis.

23.4 THE 'GOLDEN AGE OF AGRICULTURE' 1850–73

The middle years of the nineteenth century proved to be ones of prosperity for agriculture. Farmers had bitterly opposed the repeal of the Corn Laws, afraid that they would not be able to compete with an increase in foreign competition. Such a situation did not occur until after 1875 (see Section 23.5).

(a) Why did the repeal of the Corn Laws not immediately increase foreign competition?

The simple answer is that potential foreign competitors were at first unable to take advantage of Britain's free-trade policy.

(i) As yet the American and Canadian prairies had not been developed sufficiently to produce enough grain to 'flood' the European markets. The prairie farmers had problems of their own:

- It proved difficult to irrigate the crops.
- They were short of money and could not afford to invest in machinery.

- There were boundary disputes with neighbours. Not until barbed wire was invented could they keep livestock off their cereal crops.
- They had to face the opposition of the Red Indian tribes.
- The disruption caused to the American economy by the Civil War of 1861–5.

Not until the 1860s and 1870s did the North American farmers get to grips with these problems.

(ii) Transport was also not fully developed – thus for a time it was physically impossible to send huge amounts of grain to Europe:

- The railway network was not completed until the 1870s and thus it was sometimes difficult to get grain to the eastern seaports.
- Transport acorss the Atlantic Ocean was still dominated by sailing ships. Not until the 1870s were the quicker and more competitive steamship routes fully operative.

(iii) As a result of the above factors, Russia and France still provided the main competition to the British farmer. But these two countries had problems:

- Russia's agriculture was severely disrupted by the Crimean War 1854–6.
- France too was engaged in the Franco-Prussian War (1870–71) which interrupted her export trade.
- Both countries, like Britain, had growing populations and intially needed to satisfy the home market; they did not, therefore, have large amounts of grain to export.

Only after 1875 did Britain become dependent on foreign suppliers.

(b) What factors stimulated British agriculture during this period?

British farmers were not hindered by the problems outlined in (a); instead a number of factors encouraged the expansion of agricultural output:

(i) The population continued to grow providing a ready-made market.

(ii)   The rapid development of the railway network allowed the British farmer to transport his produce quickly and cheaply to the urban areas.

(iii) The mid-Victorian industrial prosperity meant that the economy was healthy, and industrial workers were able to afford to buy fresh farm produce.

(c)   What was 'high farming'?

British farming rose to the challenge and a number of improvements were made to make it more efficient. The initial spur came from a booklet called *High Farming – the best Substitute for Protection*, written by James Caird in 1849. Caird (1816–92) argued that British farmers could overcome the threat of foreign competition by becoming more business-like and progressive – that is, they should practice 'high farming'. He later followed this publication up with two books – *English Agriculture* (1851) and *The Landed Interest and the Supply of Food* (1878). Caird's work had considerable influence.

(d)   How was 'high farming' put into operation?

(i)   *More attention was paid to 'agricultural education'*

British farmers came to realise that one way of achieving good husbandry was to provide prospective farm-owners with specialised education. In 1846 the Royal College of Agriculture, which provided a two-year course at a total cost of £60, was established at Cirencester.

Before this, in 1838, the Royal Society of Agriculture had been formed to foster interest in farming and to encourage progressive methods. Annual agricultural shows were promoted like the one at Oxford which boasted 406 stands. 7852 separate exhibits and a catalogue of over 500 pages. Also during this period, farmers were able to read an increasing number of publications dealing with agricultural practice.

(ii) *The development of chemical fertilisers*

In the early nineteenth century farmers had depended on natural manure or marl to fertilise the soil; both had the limitation that they could not be produced in large quantities. In the mid-1830s guano manure was imported from Peru (this was bird droppings which contained phosphates). The production of chemical or artificial fertiliser was pioneered by Justus von Liebig, a German chemist. In 1840 he published *Organic Chemistry in its Application to Agriculture* in which he advocated the use of phosphates as a manure to replace nutrients in the soil. His work was followed up in Britain by John Bennet Lawes and J. H. Gilbert who, with the moral support of the Royal Society of Agriculture, founded an Experimental Station at Rothamsted (Hertfordshire). Here they carried out numerous trials and developed the use of superphosphates as a fertiliser. Their work was warmly praised by Caird who stated that 'continous corn-cropping was now possible and profitable, without injury to the land'. Also during this period sodium nitrates were imported in large quantities from Chile. Caird warned farmers that 'the old plan of relying on the resources of the farm by depending on the manure made upon it . . . will not answer now'.

(iii)   *Improved drainage*

Well-drained land was an essential requirement for efficient farming and some improvements were made in drainage techniques during this period:

● In 1831 James Smith of Deanston pioneered the use of shallow trenches filled with stones dug to a depth of about 36 in (90 cm). He wrote a book called *Remarks on Thorough Drainage and Deep Ploughing*.
● Josiah Parks developed the use of clay-pipes laid to a depth of 48 in (120 cm).
● In 1845 Thomas Scagg invented an extruding machine which could make clay pipes cheaply and quickly. Drainage pipes were made cheaper still when the government abolished the tax on them in 1850.

(iv)   *Improvements in agricultural machinery*

New machinery was now more readily accepted than it had been in the past:

● In about 1850 Obed Hussey and Cyrus McCormick, two Americans, perfected a reaping machine which was a big improvement on an earlier model built by Andrew Bell (1826). After this other advances were made such as the string-binder produced by the Johnston Company in the late 1870s. Caird commented that such machines could 'do the work of ten men'.

- Steam-power was effectively harnessed to agricultural machinery. Fowler pioneered the use of steam-ploughing and steam-power was also used to thresh corn, grind cattle-cake and cut straw. Such machines, however, were expensive, and were only adopted on the larger farms.
- A multiplicity of other machines appeared during this period including turnip-slicers, clod-crushers, improved seed-drills, harrows and ploughs. Two large agricultural machinery companies – Ransomes of Ipswich and Garretts of Leiston – made their mark from the 1840s onwards.

(v) *Cropping and livestock*

Cereal yields generally improved during this period and root crops were grown more widely (mangolds, swedes, turnips) as part of rotational systems. Livestock breeding was also improved. The Shorthorn became the dominant breed of beef cattle, with Amos Cruikshank doing important work. In Scotland the Aberdeen Angus was perfected by McCombie. If anything, there were signs of pastoral farming becoming more important than arable farming.

(e) **What weaknesses did British farming have?**

(i) Caird, in his book *The Landed Interest and the Supply of Food* (1878), was of the opinion that British farming had improved greatly during the period 1851–75 and he quoted numerous farms where he had observed excellent husbandry, including Mr Hudson of Castleacre (Norfolk), Mr Philip Pusey (Bedfordshire) and George Hope of Fentonbarns in Scotland. These men used all the up-to-date methods and kept their farm buildings in good repair. Caird also argued in 1878 that 'the general condition of the agricultural labourer was probably never better than it is at present'.

(ii) Despite 'high farming' methods, Caird also drew attention to a number of deficiencies in agriculture which were due to be significant in the years of the depression (see Section 23.5):

- He complained that the state did not do enough for agriculture; in keeping with the political doctrine of *laissez-faire* landowners, tenants and labourers were left to their own devices and the free-market economy. There was no government department directly responsible for agriculture (except for the Inclosure Commission which had limited powers).

● He drew attention to the fact that agricultural progress was often thwarted by insecure tenancies. Long leases for example were not common in England; it was now more common to let farms on an annual basis. This practice did not provide a tenant with the incentive to adopt new methods or invest in improving farm buildings (see Section 23.5(f)(iii)).

● Caird also claimed that some farmers kept to the old methods and he also rued the lamentable state of management on many English estates. According to Caird, land management was far more advanced in Scotland and he believed that training for estate owners should be introduced.

Caird's remarks were relevant and, in the period 1873–1914, these weaknesses were to reveal themselves.

23.5 AGRICULTURAL DEPRESSION 1873–1914

The years between 1873–1914 brought hardship to British farming compared with the prosperity of the 'Golden Age' although not all farmers suffered from the depression; some livestock farmers continued to prosper. The changing conditions of the period, however, did bring about a readjustment in the way in which the land was utilised.

(a) Royal Commissions of Inquiry into the Agriculture Depression

During these years two Royal Commissions were appointed to inquire into the reasons for the agricultural depression. They were the Richmond Commission (1879–1882) and The Royal Commission on Agriculture (1894–8). Although both Commissions were very thorough in their deliberations they were unable to suggest any real remedies.

(b) What factors caused the agricultural depression?

(i) *Short-term causes*

The Richmond Commission was of the opinion that the main cause of the farmers' hardship was the atrocious weather between 1875 and 1882. The run of bad weather started with the very wet autumn of 1875, followed by a wet winter in 1876–7. This made it difficult for farmers to plough the land and livestock was rife with disease. Sheep suffered from foot rot and there were outbreaks of foot-and-mouth disease. The spring of 1878 brought heavy snow in some areas and then flooding ensued when the thaw set in. If this was not enough the spring of 1879 was very cold with heavy frosts and the summer was once again extremely wet. With such adverse growing conditions arable yields were very low and crops suffered from mildew, mould and blight. The years from 1880–82 saw snow in the winter and cold, wet summers. The Richmond Commission was correct to blame the weather for the hardship suffered by the farming fraternity but when climatic conditions improved in the late 1880s the depression continued, so it was clear that other factors were affecting agriculture.

The wet cold weather brought down cereal yields in the arable areas of Lincolnshire and East Anglia. Prices and profits fell. Wheat in 1870–4 fetched 55 shillings (£2.75) per quarter on average but by 1895–9 the average price had dropped to 28 shillings (£1.40) per quarter.

The livestock population also fell dramatically. In June 1878 British farms carried a sheep population of 18.4 million, but by June 1882 the figure had dropped to 14.9 million. Prices for wool, meat and livestock also fell. Meat prices between 1870 and 1895 fell by 20 per cent. Farmers were left in a perplexed frame of mind.

(ii)   *Long-term causes of the depression*

In 1846 farmers had warned that the repeal of the Corn Laws would bring ruin as now cheap foreign foodstuffs would be allowed into the country. They were slightly premature in their prediction. By 1880, however, their opinion was well founded. It took some 30 years for the right conditions to blend together abroad to produce this threat to British farmer.

In America the prairies had now been opened up by the railroads and the perfection of reaping machines allowed vast acreages of wheat to be cultivated. Steamships now conveyed the grain across the Atlantic in increasing quantities. Freight charges became lower and lower as Steamship Companies competed for business.

The British arable farmer could not produce his grain as cheaply, and without the protection of the Corn Laws he began to suffer. Even when the home harvest was poor his prices did not increase as the shortage was overcome by simply importing more foreign grain.

The British livestock farmer also felt the pressure of cheap foreign imports. The steamship, together with the invention of refrigerated holds, combined to flood the British market with large quantities of frozen foreign meat and dairy products (butter and cheese in particular). The severest competition came from New Zealand lamb and Argentinian beef. By 1895 one-third of the meat consumed in Britain was imported.

(c) What were the effects of the depression?

(i) *On arable farming*

Without doubt the arable farmers of Lincolnshire and East Anglia suffered the most in the face of the changing conditions of these years. They were unable to compete with cheap foreign grain imports and they were faced with the prospect of changing the way they used their land or reducing costs as far as they could. Converting arable land to grassland was very costly and so the majority of arable farmers opted to reduce their costs. They achieved this in a variety of ways:

- General farm maintenance was ignored. Fences were left unrepaired, drainage ditches were not cleaned out regularly and hedgerows were not trimmed.
- Wages were pegged and in some cases even reduced. Farmers argued that this was necessary because they were no longer allowed to employ cheap boy labour, following the Education Acts of 1870, 1876 and 1880. In Norfolk agricultural wages rose by just 6d (2½p) between 1881 and 1891, from 13s.5d to 13s.11d. (67p to 69.5p).
- Farmers tended to reduce their labour forces. The young men of the parishes therefore had to look elsewhere for a job. Some moved into the towns, others took their chance and emigrated to Australia or Canada. It is estimated that some 300 000 workers left the land during this period.
- Farmers did not replace stock that died as a result of disease and they tended not to spend so much on fertiliser. A greater number of fields were left fallow and allowed to become rough pasture.

● Farmers with the foresight and money reduced their labour by investing in a new self-binding reaper (perfected by McCormick in 1882). This meant that workers were not required to bundle the individual stalks of wheat into sheaves. According to W. Fream in *Elements of Agriculture* (1897), labour costs for cutting, tying and stooking were between 7 and 10 shillings per acre (35–50p), binder cutting costs were between 3 and 4 shillings (15–20p) per acre. The farmer could therefore cut back on the use of casual labour in particular. He could also reduce labour in ploughing if he invested in a new plough which could plough two furrows at once but only needed one ploughman as opposed to the previous two.

(ii) *On livestock farming*

Despite the increasing amount of frozen meat coming into Britain, the livestock farmers were able to withstand the effects in a far more durable manner than the arable farmers. The British people were still keen to purchase fresh meat as opposed to frozen meat. Thus the home livestock farmer could continue to supply fresh meat to the urban markets without fear of foreign competition. The livestock farmers of the northern counties and the West Country actually did benefit from the low cereal prices. In Lancashire livestock output actually increased by a third. In Britain as a whole the number of cattle and pigs increased:

	1880	1890	1895
Cattle	9 871 153	10 789 858	10 753 314
Pigs	2 863 488	4 362 010	4 238 870

Animal foodstuffs were, as a result, cheaper. Bread prices in the towns also fell, and so the industrial workers had money available to spend on other foods – dairy products in particular. Dairy farmers, in fact, were probably least affected by the depression as they were still able to sell their milk in urban centres.

Although farm labourers' wages were generally low (in some cases below the poverty line) a comparison of wages in different areas of Britain shows how the dairy and livestock areas were relatively better off than their counterparts in the arable districts.

Wages in arable districts
Eastern counties (Bedfordshire, Cambridgeshire, Hertfordshire, Huntingdonshire, Lincolnshire, Norfolk, Suffolk)

1881 Average weekly wage of men   13s.4d (67p)
1891 Average weekly wage of men   13s.9d (69p)

Wages in livestock districts
North and North-West counties (Cheshire, Cumberland, Derbyshire, Lancashire, Northumberland, Shropshire, Staffordshire, Yorkshire)

1881 Average weekly wage of men   16s.9d (84p)
1891 Average weekly wage of men   17s.9d (89p)

The above figures help to illustrate that the effects of the depression varied in severity from region to region.

(d) Given the increase in foreign competition, why did the government maintain a free-trade policy?

On the face of it the British farmer would have benefited from a return to protection. However, social and economic conditions had changed to such an extent by the 1880s that a reversal of trading policy was just not viable. The landowning class no longer dominated Parliament and industrial male workers now had the right to vote. Britain was now an industrial nation with a large urban population who enjoyed the cheap food prices brought by a free-trade policy. Any government reverting back to protection would have been voted out of power.

(e) In what ways did British agriculture readjust during the Depression?

(i) With cereal prices so low it became uneconomic for farmers to grow vast acreages of grain – and consequently the amount of land under cereal cultivation, particularly wheat, was drastically reduced:

	1880	1890	1895
Wheat	3 065 895 (1 241 253 ha)	2 483 595 (1 005 504 ha)	1 456 200 (589 554 ha)
Barley	2 695 000 (1 091 093 ha)	2 300 994 (931 576 ha)	2 346 367 (949 946 ha)

(*figures in acres*)

In 1914 the home farmer grew just 20 per cent of the cereals required by the British market.

(ii) Many farmers turned to a more favourable type of farming – usually dairying. Despite the cost and risks involved a number of arable farmers laid down much of their land to pasture; between 1871 and 1901 pasture land increased from 11.4 to 15.4 million acres (4.6 to 6.2 hectares).

(iii) There was a growth of intensive farming in the form of market gardening in areas near to large cities (for example, The Vale of Evesham serving Birmingham, Kent serving London and Cambridgeshire serving the East Midlands). These areas supplied the towns with fresh fruit and flowers. In turn, industries associated with market gardening such as jam-making and canning were established, to add to the traditional manufacture of agricultural implements.

(iv) There is also evidence to suggest that many farmers saw the need to improve techniques and become as efficient as possible in face of the competition from abroad. More scientific experimentation was being carried out at Rothamsted and the Agricultural Notebook for 1897 is packed with information and tips for farmers wishing to achieve the best results on their farms. The results of experimentation were also publicised in periodicals like *The Farmer and Stockbreeder*. More agricultural science courses were being provided by schools and universities.

(f) What did the government do to help the farmers?

(i) The government took little direct action to alleviate the effects of the depression. The two Royal Commissions were inconclusive in their reports. One important development, however, was the setting up of a Board of Agriculture in 1889 which later became the Ministry of Agriculture.

(ii) A number of Acts were passed during this period dealing with smallholdings and allotments. For a number of years there had been a campaign to obtain a larger number of allotments for agricultural labourers. This would allow the labourer to supplement his meagre income. *The Smallholdings Act of 1893* empowered County Councils to provide smallholdings, but few authorities acted upon it. The 1908 *Smallholders and Allotments Act* was more successful with 14,000 holdings being provided by local authorities by 1914.

(iii) The *1875 Agricultural Holdings Act* was passed in an effort to give tenant farmers greater security and encouragement to carry out any improvements like drainage of the land, erecting new buildings or improving roads. In the past tenancies had been subject to 'customs' rather than the statute book and a tenant could be dismissed without receiving any compensation for any improvements he had made. This particular Act stated that an outgoing tenant had a legal right to compensation. However, the Act was permissive and this allowed landlords to escape paying the compensation if he so wished. In 1883 the Act was made compulsory: landlords now had to pay compensation whether they liked it or not. A further Act of 1883 permitted tenants to shoot the landlord's game if it damaged his crops.

(g) How did the status of the landowning class change during this period?

For many years the landowners had been the dominant social class in Britain. As industrialisation increased the status of the landowner was bound to decline. They had been used to serving as JPs, sitting on the Poor Law Board of Guardians and generally 'getting their own way'. The Local Government Act of 1888 established County Councils to run local affairs. Landowners, like anyone else, now had to be elected to the council if they wished to have their say. The landowners also felt the effects of the depression. Some of them, like the Duke of Bedford, coped well, but many went bankrupt or were forced to make drastic economies. For example, running their large mansions proved to be expensive and one economy was to 'let' the house on an annual lease along with the fishing and shooting rights. The decline in status of the landowners was symptomatic of the changes taking place in British industry and agriculture. Their privileged position had been badly eroded.

(h) How did the agricultural labourer cope with the depression?

As indicated in Section 23(c)(iv), some labourers fared better than others. In the north and north-west the farmers had to compete for their labour with the industrial towns and therefore had to keep their wages at a reasonable level. Judged in general, however, the life of the labourer remained hard. (The novels of Thomas Hardy vividly describe these conditions.)

In open villages the housing was appalling. Farm cottages were left in a state of disrepair as the farmers made economies. Some cottages were pulled down and not replaced. Water-supply and sanitation left much to be desired. Although some legislation was passed in an attempt to aid the situation, no tangible improvements were achieved.

In the 1890s there was a revival in trade-union activity in the countryside. Encouraged by the success of the Match Girls' Strike and London Dock Strike, agricultural labourers began to take a fresh interest in union affairs. Even so many areas were still without a union branch. The labourer, as he had always done, was left to make the best of the prevailing conditions.

23.6 CONCLUSION

British farming remained in a depressed condition until 1914, although there was a slight improvement in prices during the early years of the twentieth century. Farmers had been confronted with conditions they could not control and they had to readjust and change in order to survive. Some went out of business but the ones who were prepared to be flexible managed to overcome the adverse conditions. British agriculture in 1914 was much changed. It was a much smaller industry employing far fewer people and farmers had been forced to come to terms with the fact that Britain was now primarily an industrial country. There was to be no return to the halcyon days of the 'Golden Age'.

QUESTIONS

1. **Objectives 1 and 2**

(a) What were the possible causes of the distress experienced by farmers in the period 1815–40? (8 marks)

(b) Which of these causal factors would you consider to be the most important? (4 marks)

(c) Identify (i) the long-term and (ii) the short-term causal factors. (4 marks)

(d) Why was Parliament, apparently, reluctant to take any action to help the farmers? (4 marks)

2. **Objectives 3 and 4**

Study the sources below and then answer the questions.

Source A   (courtesy of Mansell Collection)

THE HOME OF THE RICK-BURNER.

Source B

The *Magistrates* in the Hundreds of *Tunstead* and *Happing*, in the County of Norfolk, having taken into consideration the disturbed state of the said Hundreds and the Country in general, wish to make it publicly known that *it is their opinion* that such disturbances principally arise from the use of Threshing Machines, and to the insufficient Wages of the Labourers. The Magistrates therefore beg to *recommend* to the Owners and Occupiers of Land in these Hundreds, to *discontinue the use of Threshing Machines, and to increase the Wages of Labour* to Ten Shillings a week for able bodied men, and that when task work is preferred, that it would be put out at such a rate as to enable an industrious man to earn Two Shillings per day.

The Magistrates are determined to enforce the Laws against all tumultuous Rioters and Incendiaries, and they look for support to all the respectable and well disposed part of the Community; at the same time they feel a full Conviction, that *no severe measures will be necessary*, if the proprietors of Land will give proper employment to the Poor on their own Occupations, and encourage their Tenants to do the same.

(A notice issued by Norfolk magistrates, November 1830)

(a) What does Source A suggest was the motive for rick-burning?
(b) The Norfolk magistrates (Source B) were mainly landowners. These magistrates, as well as farm labourers, wished to stop the use of threshing-machines and to raise the farm labourer's wages. What reasons would the magistrates have for this?
(c) The government in London wanted to punish the Swing rioters severely. Why was the view of the government different from that of the local magistrates?

(Total = 20 marks)
(Southern Examining Group)

3. **Objective 3**

(a) Write a letter from a prominent landowner to the Home Secretary, dated 23 November, 1830. In the letter describe:

● The rioting taking place in your area.
● The attitude of the landowners towards the labourers.
● Your thoughts on the punishments which should be given to the rioters.

(b) Write an account of the possible thoughts of a labourer awaiting execution for his part in the Swing Riots of 1830. You should consider:

- An explanation of why he took part in the riots.
- An explanation of his attitude towards the landowners, magistrates and the government.
- Whether he regrets his actions.

(Total = 20 marks)

4. **Objectives 1 and 2**

(a) How did J. L. Caird influence the thinking of British farmers in the period 1850–75? (8 marks)
(b) Why, despite the repeal of the Corn Laws, did British agriculture experience a 'Golden Age' in this period? (12 marks)

5. **Objectives 1 and 2**

(a) Why was British farming in a 'depressed state' during the period 1880–1914? (8 marks)
(b) How did British farming readjust to meet the changed circumstances? (6 marks)
(c) 'Without doubt, all rural villages suffered during the agricultural depression'. Test this hypothesis against the available evidence. (6 marks)

6. **Objective 4**

You have been given the task of writing a brief history of a rural village in the period 1850–1900.

(a) What possible sources of evidence would be available to you and where would you obtain them?
(b) Which of these sources would be the most useful?
(c) How would you deal with any sources which were inaccurate, incomplete or biased?

(Total = 20 marks)

CHAPTER 24

THE EMANCIPATION

OF WOMEN

24.1 INTRODUCTION

Whether women today have equality with men in society is very much a 'live issue'. A brief synopsis of the present position of women may be of use:

- In 1971 The Equal Pay Act was passed, an effort to give women pay comparability with men.
- In 1975 The Sex Discrimination Act made it illegal to discriminate between men and women in employment (amongst other things).
- In 1981 40 per cent of the work force was female.
- Women are now able to enter the professions without too many 'eye-brows being raised'.
- Women are able to vote at the age of 18 on equal terms with men and without a property qualification.

On the surface quite an impressive list, but many would argue that women are still treated as 'second-class' citizens and have some way to go before they achieve equal status with men. This may well be true but it remains a fact that the status of women is immeasurably better now than it was 100 years ago. The progress of women towards emancipation (or liberation from male domination) will be charted and discussed in this chapter.

24.2 WHAT WAS THE POSITION OF WOMEN IN 1850?

In Mid-Victorian society beliefs about the role of women were firmly fixed. A woman was considered to be very much inferior to the male and was looked upon as his 'property'. The husband was the head of the household and had the final word.

(a)   In a middle-class household the wife was seen as a child-bearer and was allowed to have no career. She spent her day in genteel pursuits, for example, embroidery and knitting – household chores would be done by servants. Furthermore she had hardly any legal rights. Any property or money she had owned when single, automatically became the possession of her husband on marriage. In law the children of the family were also the property of the husband.

Middle-class girls received a basic education, usually given at home by a 'governess'. The governess was untrained and taught the 3Rs (Reading, Writing and Arithmetic) with some History and a foreign language. Being a governess was one of the few 'jobs' to which a middle-class girl could aspire. A governess, however, would command a very meagre salary: anything above £30 a year would have been respectable and even then this was about half the amount which could be earned in a cotton mill.

(b)   Life in a working-class family was desperately hard for the wife. She was expected to bear children, bring them up and go out to work. Families of seven or eight were commonplace. The working-class wife also had to endure the same lack of rights as her middle-class counterpart. The working-class female would be most likely to enter domestic service, work as a factory-operative, or be an agricultural labourer.

(c)   Finally, women were unable to enter the professions (for example, medicine or law) at this time and they were excluded from public life and voting in any form of election. The role of the Victorian woman was neatly summed up by the *Saturday Review* which claimed that 'married life is a woman's profession'.

24.3   WHAT IMPROVEMENTS IN THEIR STATUS DID WOMEN ACHIEVE DURING THE NINETEENTH CENTURY?

Women made a number of advances to improve their status during the century, often due to persistence and determination of individual females.

(a) Progress in education

(i)   In 1848 Queen's College, London, was opened by F. D. Maurice with the purpose of training governesses, entry being possible from the age of 13 upwards; a second training institution, Bedford College, was opened in 1849.

(ii) Schools for girls were non-existent until the nineteenth century when Frances Buss opened the North London Collegiate School for Girls (1850) and Dorothea Beale started the Cheltenham Ladies' College (1858) (see Section 18.5).

(iii) Some progress was also made in University education for women. A prime mover in this sphere was Emily Davies: she succeeded in establishing Girton College in 1873 as a female college within Cambridge University. A second female college, Newnham, was opened three years later. In 1878 London University admitted female students awarding them full degree status.

These events could hardly be described as 'revolutionary' but they did have the effect of helping to change Victorian attitudes towards the education of women, not least the erosion of the belief that they did not have the intellectual capacity to cope with a high level of study.

(b) Legal progress

(i)   In 1792 *A Vindication of the Rights of Women with Strictures on Political and Moral Subjects* was written by Mary Wollstonecraft. She claimed that women should be treated as human beings and not objects. All women should have the same rights as men before the law. Her book was inspired by the ideas of liberty associated with the French Revolution and the politician Tom Paine's *Rights of Man*. Mary Wollstonecraft made a number of telling points but it took a full century for women to achieve an improved legal status.

(ii) A number of Acts improved the legal status of women:

● Caroline Norton campaigned to get the 1839 *Custody of Infant's Act* which stated that if the parents separated, the wife should legally be able to claim custody of those children under seven. Furthermore, if older children were taken by the husband, the mother could claim access.

- *The Matrimonial Causes Act of 1857* abolished the need for a private Act of Parliament in order to obtain a divorce. Now there would be Divorce Courts and women were allowed to sue for divorce if they could prove two of the following charges; cruelty, desertion or adultery. The husband however, could divorce if he was to prove one of these offences. The number of divorces slowly increased but it still carried a social stigma.

- *The Married Woman's Property Acts of 1870 and 1882* had the combined effect of making it legal for women to keep their money and property when they married.

- In 1878 *The Matrimonial Causes Act* made it possible for a wife to separate from her husband on the grounds of cruelty; furthermore she was legally entitled to claim maintenance and custody of the children. This was extended by *The Married Woman's Act of 1882* which enabled the wife to claim maintenance on the grounds of desertion. The granting of maintenance payments saved many 'injured' wives from the union workhouse or even prostitution.

- From 1891 following a test case, it was possible for a wife to move out of the matrimonial home and live separately from her husband.

- In 1877 Annie Besant and Charles Bradlaugh campaigned for the wider adoption of birth control (see Section 1.3(b)).

By the end of the nineteenth century the status of the married woman had improved to some extent. At least wives were no longer objects to be 'possessed' in totality by their husbands. However, the attitude that the male was automatically 'head of the household' remained firmly intact.

(c) Progress in employment opportunities

Here again a picture of gradual advance is evident.

(i) Through the work in the hospital at Scutari during the Crimean War (1854–6), Florence Nightingale made nursing a 'desirable' profession. During the early part of the century nursing was ridiculed by Charles Dickens and it was a job which no respectable female would even consider entering. By 1900, however, a number of nursing schools had been opened (for example, St Thomas' Hospital) and there were over 60 000 trained nurses (see Section 19.9).

(ii) In the middle of the nineteenth century women were barred from being general practioners (GPs). Elizabeth Garrett (later Elizabeth Garrett-Henderson) was responsible for changing this situation. She was determined to be a doctor but was unable to obtain a place at a medical school. She studied on her own and in 1867 gained the right to practise under the auspices of the 'London Society of Apothecaries. In 1869 Sophia Jex-Blake and four female associates obtained places at Edinburgh University to study medicine. This caused a great deal of controversy and they were finally expelled as it was considered that the university did not have the right to accept female students. Jex-Blake, together with Emma Pechey, pioneered the opening of The London School of Medicine (1874) which was to award women students medical degrees. Despite the door being opened, the world of medicine remained male-dominated.

(iii) The professions apart, employment opportunities for women in 1851 were severely limited. According to the Census there were one million women in service, 520,000 in textile mills, and 380,000 in the clothing trade (seamstresses, etc.). Working conditions were hard with many women working in 'sweat shops'. The life of a domestic servant was hard. This advert from *The Times* (1913) shows how much was expected:

WANTED, TWO SERVANTS: one as Servant of All-work. Must understand cooking. Wages £10 a year; the other to attend on the children, the youngest six years old, and to work at her needle, and making herself generally useful. Wages £6 a year. Apply at Mr. Scott's, confectioner, 6, Bishop's-road. Westbourne-terrace, Paddington.

WANTED, a SITUATION as HOUSEKEEPER in a tradesman's family, by a person respectably connected, who would not object to do the lighter part of the household work, and could also assist in a business if required. Unexceptable reference can be given to the party whom the advertiser has just left. The country not objected to. Address to N. M., (before the 14th instant,) at Mr Duffield's, bookseller, &c. Hackney-road.

Conditions in all the industries were only gradually improved but from the 1880s greater numbers of jobs were open to women, which gave them a degree of independence and possible job-satisfaction. The typewriter (invented in the 1860s) revolutionised office work and there was a bigger demand for typists. Another step forward was the appointment of the first female Factory Inspector in 1892. By 1900 many women had obtained jobs in telephone exchanges, and thousands more were employed as shop assistants. Despite the advances, the women's jobs were still considered menial and less important than those of men: this was reflected in the low rates of pay. The attitude that the female was subservient to the male in the field of employment proved difficult to break down.

(d) Progress in politics

Women had few opportunities to play a part in political affairs in the nineteenth century (the reasons for this are explained in Section 24.6; their participation was limited to local government.

(i) The *Municipal Corporations Act of 1869* gave single women the right to vote in municipal elections. A court case which followed this Act rule that married women were excluded from voting.

(ii) Following *Forster's Elementary Education Act of 1870*, women ratepayers could be elected to, and vote on, School Board elections. Women were permitted from 1875 to be elected to the Board of Guardians of the local union workhouse. In *1888 the Local Government Act* created County Councils and County Borough Councils, making provision for women to vote in the respective elections. From 1894 women were able to serve as Parish and District Councillors (on Urban and District Councils). Finally, an Act of 1900 gave married women the right to vote in elections for London County Council. Despite all this women still could not vote in Parliamentary elections. Thus developed the 'Women's Suffrage Movement' (suffrage meaning the 'right to vote').

24.4 HOW AND WHY DID THE SUFFRAGE MOVEMENT ORIGINATE?

(a) A few women possessed the franchise (vote) during the Middle Ages but this right had gradually faded with time. The 1832 Reform Act specifically stated that only 'male persons' could vote. The use of this phrase made it perfectly clear that women could not vote – even if they happened to meet the required property qualification of being a 40 shillings per annum (£2) freeholder. It was from this time that women were inspired to seek the vote – it was to take the best part of a century to obtain it.

(b) Early political awareness amongst women was embodied in organisations like Anne Knight's 'Sheffield Women's Political Asso-cation', formed in 1851. The issue was then highlighted by the philosopher John Stuart Mill who became the MP for Westminster in 1865. He wrote an article called 'Representative Government' stating that women were the equal of men and should have the franchise. During the debate on the second Reform Bill in 1867, Mill presented a petition to Parliament urging an amendment to the Bill which would give women the vote but it was predictably defeated. Almost immediately the London Society for Women Suffrage was formed (1867) and this set the example for similar groups to be set up in Birmingham, Bristol, Edinburgh and Manchester.

(c) What arguments were forwarded in favour of female suffrage?

The arguments were numerous and evolved during the length of the period:

- During the nineteenth century the male franchise was based on the ownership of property. It was argued that women owned property, and therefore, should be entitled to vote. This argu-ment was strengthened after the Married Women's Property Act 1882.
- Women said that they were liable to the same law as males and therefore should have identical privileges (that is, the right to vote).
- Another argument was that like men, women paid rates and taxes – surely they should have a say in electing Parliament?
- Women also made a vital contribution to the nation's economy (working in factories, etc.) and should be rewarded with the vote.
- Throughout history the country had been headed by a host of Queens. Surely if a woman was considered fit to undertake the role of the monarch, females should be entitled to vote.
- Women should have the vote to force Parliament to pass laws which would give social equality and protection to women.
- Finally, women drew attention to the anomalies of the male franchise qualifications. For example, lunatics and convicts were not allowed to vote and women felt that they were put on the

same level. Also after 1884 agricultural labourers were given the vote.

This led to a situation in many villages where educated upper-class women could not vote whilst illiterate labourers had the right to choose who governed the country. Such anomalies were increasingly resented by women. After the *Corrupt Practices Act (1888)* which stopped political parties paying election helpers, women were to have some involvement in Parliamentary elections by volunteering to canvass and prepare policy leaflets. The Conservatives used *The Primrose League* to organise female volunteers and the Liberals had *The Women's Liberation Foundation.*

24.5 WHICH GROUPS MADE UP THE 'WOMEN'S SUFFRAGE MOVEMENT'?

The Women's Movement evolved so that by the early twentieth century there were two distinct groups, each of which divided further into a number of subfactions. By 1912 the whole movement was a complex web of such groups. The following explanation is necessarily simplified:

(a) The NUWSS

(i) *Origins*

In 1872 the suffrage societies described in Section 24.4(b) came under the direction of The Central Committee for Women's Suffrage. In these early days a leading figure amongst the suffragists was the conscientious Lydia Becker (1827–90) who put forward the woman's viewpoint in the *Woman's Suffrage Journal.* In 1897 the societies merged to form the *National Union of Women's Suffrage Societies (NUWSS)* under the leadership of Millicent Fawcett, the younger sister of Doctor Elizabeth Garrett Anderson, and the wife of Henry Fawcett the Liberal MP. By 1913 the NUWSS had 400 societies which were split between 19 federations covering the country. By 1914 the NUWSS had 500 000 members and an annual income of £45 000.

(ii) *Tactics*

The NUWSS women were 'constitutional suffragists', believing in peaceful methods to achieve their objectives. Their tactics centred around drawing-room discussion, public meetings, processions (for example, The Mud March on 7 February 1907, so called because of the atrocious weather), publishing their views in a newspaper *The Common Cause* and petitioning Parliament.

The NUWSS used the ploy of asking sympathetic MPs to sponsor 'Private Members' Bills' in Parliament and between 1870 and 1914 almost 30 such Bills were introduced. However, without government backing they had little chance of success as they could only be debated after official government Bills had been dealt with. The NUWSS did have some contact with other suffragist organisations such as the WSPU (see below) but abhorred the use of violence to achieve the vote. The NUWSS felt that peaceful methods would strengthen their case by displaying women as rational beings who would be capable of using the franchise. In 1912 the society made it official policy to back Labour Party candidates in elections as it was the only political party which had female suffrage as part of its programme.

(b)   The WSPU

(i)   *Origins*

In 1872 a 14-year-old girl, Emmeline Goulden, attended a suffrage meeting addressed by Lydia Becker. In 1879 the same girl married a leading Manchester lawyer, Richard Pankhurst, and gave birth to four children – Christabel, Sylvia, Henry and Adela. The two elder girls and their mother were to become prominent figures in the Suffrage Movement. Emmeline Pankhurst held public office as a Poor Law Guardian and Registrar of Birth and Deaths. She was widowed in 1898, by which time she had become a committed socialist. Her work as a Poor Law Guardian in the words of Piers Brendon 'brought her into close contact with the squalid wretchedness of working-class life [and] sweated labour'. Emmeline Pankhurst, spurred on by Christabel, formed *The Women's Social and Political Union (WSPU)* at her home 62, Nelson Street, Manchester. She was assisted by Christabel and Sylvia. In the early days Christabel was a more committed suffragist than her mother, who according to H. M. Hyndman was 'a socialist first, a suffragist afterwards'. The aim of the WSPU was declared to be obtaining the vote for women 'on the same terms which it is, or may be, granted to men'. In 1905 the WSPU moved its head-quarters to Clement's Inn, London. Other prominent members at this time were Annie Kennedy, a cotton-mill worker, and Mr and Mrs Pethick-Lawrence (introduced to Mrs Pankhurst by the Labour MP, Keir Hardie) who edited the WSPU publication, *Votes for Women*. By 1910 the WSPU had a reputed membership of 36 000, and an annual income of £35 000.

(ii) *Splinter-groups from the WSPU*

In 1907 Mrs Charlotte Despard and Mrs Teresa Billington-Grieg established *The Women's Freedom League (WFL)*, a breakaway group from the WSPU. The WFL had the specific intention of evading the Inland Revenue, saying that they would not pay any taxes until they had the vote, and in 1911 they refused to co-operate with the Census. Another reason for the split was that they disliked the fact that WSPU was totally dominated by the Pankhursts, who were now dictating WSPU policy.

In 1912 the Pethick-Lawrences left the WSPU and established their own organisation *The Votes for Women Fellowship*. Finally, in 1914, Sylvia Pankhurst formed the *East London Federation*. She had become disillusioned with the WSPU because it had become middle-class orientated and had apparently abandoned working women.

(iii) *Tactics*

At first, the WSPU adopted similar tactics to the NUWSS – to seek to educate the public on female suffrage. In 1905, however, the Pankhursts witnessed a Private Members Bill on Women's Suffrage deliberately 'talked out' by MPs in the House of Commons. Their anger at this treatment caused them to reconsider their tactics. It was obvious, they argued, that men would not listen to their case and they decided that more militant action was necessary. 'Deeds not words' became official WSPU policy. They adopted tactics such as heckling government ministers at meetings, obstructing government ministers at by-elections, and holding an annual 'Woman's Parliament'. In October 1905 Christabel and Annie Kennedy heckled Edward Grey at a Liberal Party rally in Manchester's Free Trade Hall. They were removed from the Hall and imprisoned – this was the first militant act of the WSPU. In

1906 the *Daily Mail* labelled members of the WSPU 'suffra-gettes' in view of their militant stance, thus distinguishing them from the moderate suffragists of the NUWSS.

In 1912 Mrs Pankhurst declared 'war' and sanctioned attacks on property in the cause of winning the vote (see Section 24.7).

(iv) *The radical suffragists*

In a recent book called *One Hand Behind Us*, two historians, Jill Liddington and Jill Norris, give a new view of the women's suffrage movement. They argue that the traditional view gives too much credit to the militant tactics of the WSPU and the role of the Pankhursts. This, they say, ignores the vital contribution made by the 'Radical Suffragists'. These were the female cotton-workers in Lancashire who objected to the violent tactics of the WSPU and the domination of the NUWSS by middle-class ladies. The Radical Suffragists were, in essence, a breakaway faction of the NUWSS. They were closely allied to the trade-union movement and believed fer-vently in winning the vote for the working-class woman by means of a 'grassroots diplomacy'. Prominent in this move-ment were the unsung heroines of the suffrage move-ment – Esther Roper, Eva Gore-Booth, Cissy Foley and Ada Nield Chew. The Radical Suffragists allied themselves pol-itically with the Labour Party. They were in favour of full womanhood suffrage which they perceived as the gateway to improving the social conditions of working women, such as equal pay and acceptance of birth control – they opposed female suffrage based on a property qualification as it would only enfranchise upper- and middle-class women.

24.6 WHAT WERE THE ARGUMENTS USED AGAINST THE WOMEN'S SUFFRAGE MOVEMENT?

Many of the arguments against female suffrage were born out of prejudice and the social attitudes of the time. It is also worth noting that not all women wanted the vote. Queen Victoria referred to women's suffrage as 'wicked folly' and in 1908 Mrs Humphrey Ward went as far as to form the *National Anti-Suffrage League*. Arguments against the Suffragists included:

● A widely-held belief that women tended to be temperamental and prone to outbursts of emotion; how could such beings be trusted with the franchise? The militant tactics of the WSPU in the period 1905–14 did much to reinforce this viewpoint.

- Many men believed that women were 'the weaker sex' and would not be able to cope with the 'hurly-burly' of elections. This view originated in the days prior to the Secret Ballot Act (1872) when voting was 'open' (a suffragist would, therefore, have deemed this objection to be irrelevant).

- It was further claimed 'the voter, in giving a vote pledges himself to uphold the consequences of his vote at all costs . . . women . . . are physically incapable of this pledge'. The argument went on that if, for example, women voted to go to war they would not be physically strong enough to fight the enemy.

- Another view was that if adult suffrage was granted there would be about one and a half million more women voters than men. Thus the government would reflect female views and as women were 'less virile' than men it would result in Britain and the Empire being weakened.

- The Anti-Suffrage League argued that the vote was overvalued. Even though some men had the vote there was still poverty, unemployment and low wages! Thus it must not be assumed that female suffrage would solve all the problems of women.

- Women should keep out of the political arena. Their strength lay within the family providing support, inspiration, and rearing children. If the vote was given to females it might cause political disagreements with the husband and consequently accelerate the breakup of the family. A League member, speaking in 1909, claimed that:

> the family is the keystone of social and domestic life . . . it rests on concord, and on the due fulfilment of man and woman alike of the duties assigned to each by Nature herself . . . If we confuse those duties . . . it will bring destruction.

What stance did the political parties take against the suffragists?

It is not easy to pinpoint the attitudes of the political parties as they were constantly in a state of flux. However, in general terms, the following opinions predominated:

(i) *The Liberal Party*

The Liberals were in power during the whole period of WSPU militancy, from 1906–14. Henry Campbell-Bannerman, the

Prime Minister from 1906–8, probably sympathised with the suffragists but merely advised them 'to keep pestering'.

H. H. Asquith, Prime Minister from 1908–16, was against women having the vote, and was the brunt of much harrassment. He undoubtedly feared the fact that if women received the vote based on a property qualification it would enfranchise many upper-class women who would vote for the Conservatives.

A number of Asquith's colleagues actually favoured female suffrage – Grey, Haldane and Lloyd George among them. They were, however, reluctant to go against the Prime Minister when it came to voting on suffrage Bills in the House of Commons.

Eventually the WSPU, incensed by the intransigence of the Liberal Government, declared that they would oppose all Liberal candidates during elections (this was probably a mistake as it alienated many Liberals).

The Liberals had a number of other problems and saw 'women's suffrage' as a side issue.

(ii) *The Conservative Party*

Most back-bench Conservatives were against women having the vote; in contrast some of the more prominent Tories, such as A. J. Balfour, were sympathetic. There was a fear amongst the Tory opposition that adult suffrage would be granted, thus giving the vote to working men and women. This they felt would upset the balance of the electorate and work against them.

(iii) *The Labour Party*

During this period the Labour Party was in its infancy, and its main priority was to represent working men. Votes for women, therefore, was a secondary issue.

Prominent Labour Party members who supported the women were George Lansbury, Ramsay MacDonald, Philip Snowden and Keir Hardie – who was probably their strongest advocate. By 1912 womanhood suffrage had become official Labour Party policy, as long as the vote was extended to all men at the same time.

From 1907 the WSPU became middle class in character and Mrs Pankhurst, in particular, moved towards the 'right' gradually disassociating herself with the Labour Party. It now appeared that her aim was limited suffrage for women; she had deserted working-class women.

24.7 WHAT WERE THE MAIN EVENTS OF THE SUFFRAGE MOVEMENT BETWEEN 1905 AND 1914?

- On 7 February 1905 the NUWSS held the 'Mud March' in London to draw public attention to their cause.
- In October 1905 Christabel Pankhurst and Annie Kennedy were imprisoned, after disrupting the Liberal Rally in the Free Trade Hall, Manchester. Shortly afterwards the WSPU moved to London (see Section 24.5).
- On 21 June 1908 a huge demonstration was held in Hyde Park with an estimated attendance of 250 000 and much pageantry.
- In October 1908, Christabel, Emmeline and Mrs Flora Drummond were arrested for 'obstructing' when a group of suffragettes tried to march on the Houses of Parliament. They received three months' imprisonment in Holloway.
- In July 1909 Marion Wallace Dunlop went on hunger-strike in prison, protesting that she was being treated like a criminal, rather than a political offender. (Members of the WSPU were made to disrobe publicly, followed by a bath and issue of prison clothing.) The reaction of the prison authorities to Miss Dunlop's refusal to take food was to force-feed her – pouring liquid down a rubber tube which was pushed down the throat via the nostrils. This treatment caused a public outcry, but the government continued to sanction such methods rather than risk the death of a suffragette who would be made into a martyr by the WSPU.
- Hunger-striking was copied by many other imprisoned suffragettes including Emmeline Pankhurst. She now publicly advocated attacks on private property.
- In 1910 the government was at last stirred into action and an all-party Conciliation Committee introduced the *First Conciliation Bill* into Parliament, which proposed to give female householders the vote. The Bill was defeated and, to show their disgust, a large suffragette demonstration took place outside Parliament on 11 November 1910. A running battle took place with the police – the suffragettes dubbed the incident 'Black Friday'.
- Following this the WSPU called a truce whilst a *Second Conciliation Bill* was debated during 1911. However, it was once again defeated, leaving the militant suffragettes outraged.

- On 1 March 1912 suffragettes went on the rampage in London's West End, smashing shop windows and causing thousands of pounds worth of damage. Emmeline and the Pethick-Lawrences were arrested. Christabel fled the country and went to Paris.
- In early 1913 the government introduced its *General Electoral Reform Bill* into Parliament which proposed to give all men over 21 the vote. Asquith said that there would be a free vote on the Bill. An amendment was moved to the effect that women should also receive the vote. The Speaker, however, ruled that the amendment was out of order and the whole Bill was dropped. The WSPU were incensed and stepped up their action. Arson and bombing now became the chief weapons. Empty houses were burnt down, including a residence newly built for Lloyd George into which he was waiting to move. Emmeline Pankhurst took responsibility for this deed (she most likely did not do it) and was sentenced to three years' imprisonment in March 1913. In her 'defence' she said 'I have no sense of guilt. I look upon myself as a prisoner of war'. Once imprisoned she went on immediate hunger-strike.
- In April 1913 the government, concerned at the large numbers of hunger-strikers passed the *Prisoners' Temporary Discharge Act (The Cat and Mouse Act)*. This Act permitted the authorities to release a suffragette on licence so that she could regain her strength. She would then be rearrested.
- 4 June 1913 brought a major incident. During the Derby at Epsom, Emily Wilding Davison (a member of the WSPU) ran on to the course as the horses rounded Tattenham Court. She collided with the King's Horse *Anmer* and died four days later in Epsom Cottage Hospital. *The Times* called the incident 'reckless fanaticism' and claimed that such incidents could only damage the cause of the women suffragists. We will never know Miss Davison's real motives – did she intend to collide specifically with the King's horse? Was she merely trying to stop the race in search of publicity? However, the WSPU claimed her as a martyr saying that she had sacrificed her life for the cause. The funeral was 'stage-managed' to gain as much publicity as possible. Still no progress.
- On 4 August 1914 Britain declared war against Germany and the militant campaign was called off. Mrs Pankhurst was released from prison and she encouraged women to contribute to the war effort. Sylvia, however, carried on the campaign setting up 'The Women's Suffrage Federation'.

24.8 DID MILITANT TACTICS FURTHER THE CAUSE OF THE SUFFRAGISTS?

Much debate has taken place on this question, but in hindsight, the evidence suggests that militant tactics did more harm than good to the suffrage movement.

In the 'early days' it would appear that the women had quite a lot of public sympathy. In 1908 a reporter in the *Daily News* claimed that 'the feeling of the people in general . . . is coming round to the side of the suffragettes'.

It is quite likely that the public would still have sided with the suffragettes if their militant tactics had meant heckling ministers and ceremonial marches. It was after the campaign became violent and destructive of private property that the public turned against the suffragettes. Lloyd George, for example, claimed that violence 'antagonised' and 'poisoned' both the public and the government.

It is interesting to note also that the biggest suffrage group, the NUWSS, did not support any form of violence. However, it has been suggested that violence was the only way to get the government to listen to them: meetings, leaflets and argument did not work. Piers Brendon claims that 'Mrs Pankhurst's . . . great achievement had been to make women's suffrage a major national issue, something forty years of constitutional agitation had failed to do'. Even accepting this, he continues, Mrs Pankhurst 'failed to perceive that her violence was back-firing'.

24.9 HOW FAR IS IT TRUE TO SAY THAT THE WORK OF WOMEN DURING THE FIRST WORLD WAR (1914–18) BROUGHT THEM THE VOTE?

In simple terms there is much to support this argument; there is little doubt that women played an important role in the war and that this was one factor in gaining the vote in 1918.

(a) It took some time for women to be employed in industry in large numbers. Mrs Pankhurst, anxious that women should play their part, conducted a 'right to serve' campaign. Not until conscription was made law in 1916 were women recruited in large numbers into industry as more men went off to fight in the trenches:

● In July 1917 there were 500 000 women working in ammunition factories making shells, etc.

- In 1917 there were 60 000 women working in banking and commerce, and almost half a million in Local Government. Women also joined the Women's Auxillary Army Corps and in 1917 there were 40 000 nurses serving in France and Belgium.
- In 1918 there were 120 000 bus conductresses.
- By 1918 there were 18 000 working in the Women's Land Army.

Women also worked in iron and steel, chemical and rubber industries and as plumbers and electricians. The war made it easier for them to join the medical profession.

The number of women in domestic service dropped from one and a half million to one and a quarter million in 1918. Women enjoyed higher wages in the factories even if the work was hard and sometimes dangerous. For example, the munition girls put their health at risk handling explosives such as TNT. One side effect was 'toxic jaundice' which caused the skin to turn yellow. This could actually result in death in extreme cases.

(b) However, there were other factors at work which helped to bring the franchise in 1918.

The war showed the shortcomings of the property qualification for men to have the franchise. Those who had been fighting at the front for over a year lost this qualification (as the law then stood), and therefore could not vote. This anomaly, together with the fact that so many men had been killed in action, made a revision of the Electoral Register essential before another election could be held. It was, therefore, considered an opportune moment to consider giving women the vote. In 1916 a Conference under the auspices of the Speaker was set up to investigate the form of a new Electoral Register. The Conference reported in 1917 and recommended that a limited number of women should be given the vote. In February 1918 *The Representation of Peoples Act* became law. Its terms were:

- All males over 21 should have the vote.
- Women who were householders or wives of householders, and over 30 could vote.
- Female graduates over 30 could vote.

This obviously was a breakthrough, but critics of the Act have pointed to the fact that many women who contributed to the war effort were under 30! Why had not they received the vote? In the words of Martin Pugh, it was 'an unspectacular victory'.

24.10 CONCLUSION

What further developments took place in the emancipation of women after 1918?

(a) Political

 (i) In 1919 the first woman took her seat in the Commons. She was Nancy, Lady Astor, who was the new MP for Plymouth Sutton.

 (ii) In 1928 the franchise was extended to all women over the age of 21; thus now there was full universal suffrage.

(iii) In 1929 Margaret Bondfield, the Labour MP, became the first female Cabinet Minister. Other women to achieve a similar status include Ellen Wilkinson (1945–7), Florence Horsburgh (1951–5), Barbara Castle (1964–70), Judith Hart (1968–70), Shirley Williams (1974–9) and Margaret Thatcher (1970–74).

 (iv) In 1979 Margaret Thatcher became the first woman Prime Minister.

 (v) In 1958 female peers were accepted in the House of Lords for the first time.

(b) Social

Since 1918 women had achieved a degree of social emancipation. Attitudes towards fashion have become more 'liberal', and during the 1920s and 1930s it became accepted to wear make-up. The growing invasion of labour-saving devices into the home has also given women more time to pursue careers. Furthermore, there is now a trend for the husband to take a more active role in the household. Some families have actually had a reversal of roles with the wife earning the living and the male adopting the role of househusband. It is becoming increasingly common for girls to study subjects previously regarded as the domain of boys (for example, Craft Design and Technology – CDT). Progress has been made.

(c) How much further is there to go?

We have come full circle and returned to the premise expressed in Section 24.1, namely that women feel there is still much progress to be made before they achieve full equality with men. Furthermore, they would probably claim that what has been achieved so far is the result of 'blood, sweat and tears', witness the efforts of the women's suffrage movement. The 'lack of equality' can be illustrated by the fact that the 1983 General Election resulted in just 23 women being returned to Parliament out of a possible 650 MPs! The present position is neatly summed up by Frances Gibb, writing in *The Times* in 1981, when she says, 'The depressing conclusion is that despite some breakthroughs . . . there is still a long way to go . . . [for example] . . . It is still almost impossible for women to combine a career and run a home'.

QUESTIONS

1. **Objectives 1 and 2**

(a) How did the tactics and policies of the WSPU differ from those of the NUWSS? (8 marks)
(b) How far were 'violent' methods successful? (6 marks)
(c) Did the First World War (1914–18) help women to obtain the vote? Explain your answer. (6 marks)

2. **Objectives 1 and 2**

Assess the role of **three** of the following in the suffrage movement:

● Millicent Fawcett
● Emmeline Pankhurst
● Christabel Pankhurst
● Syliva Pankhurst
● The Liberal Government

(Total = 20 marks)

3. **Objective 3**

A large meeting has been called at the Manchester Free Trade Hall to discuss the question of women's suffrage.

(a) As a member of one of the female suffrage groups write a speech outlining your views about why women should be given the vote. (10 marks)

(b) As a member of the Anti-Suffrage League make an address to
the audience explaining why women should not be given the
vote.   (10 marks)

4. **Objectives 1 and 4**

Study Sources A, B, C and D and then answer the questions:

Source A

Source B

Source C   (courtesy of BBC Hulton Picture Library)

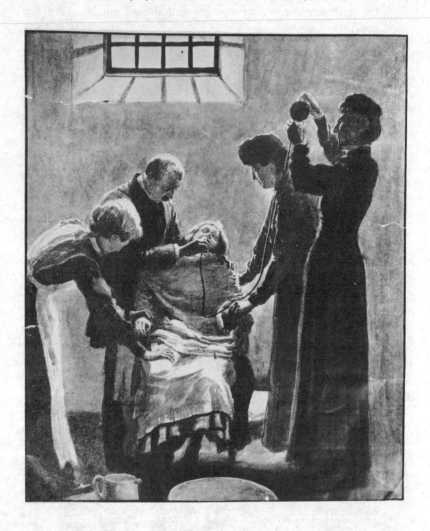

(a) What point is being made in Source A? Why was it necessary to produce this poster? (3 marks)
(b) What qualifications did a man need to have the vote at this time which is not referred to in Source A? (1 mark)
(c) Why does the cartoonist refer to 'Militant Suffragist' in Source B? (2 marks)
(d) What is the attitude expressed towards suffragists by Source B? (2 marks)

Source D   (*courtesy of Mansell Collection*)

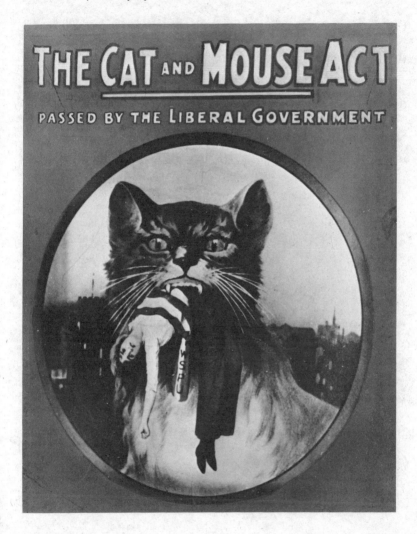

(e)   Explain the link between Sources C and D.   (4 marks)

(f)   In what ways could Source D be described as propaganda?

(2 marks)

(g)   Show how subsequent events altered the social and economic status of women up to 1928.   (6 marks)

(London and East Anglian Examinations Group)

5. **Objective 2**

(a) How far has the status of women changed in the last 100 years?
(12 marks)

(b) How much further is there to go before women have true equality with men?
(8 marks)

6. **Objective 4**

Study Sources A and B and then answer the questions.

Source A   Excelsior! (Punch, 13 July 1910) (courtesy of Mansell Collection)

EXCELSIOR!

(a) What does Source A suggest about the attitude of Parliament to women's suffrage?
(4 marks)

(b) How far would you agree with the suggestion implicit in Source A? Give evidence to support your answer.
(6 marks)

(c) In Source B identify:
   (i) The person playing the violin.
   (ii) The person with the 'pro' arm-band.
   (iii) The significance of the banner.
(4 marks)

(d) Explain the background to Source B.
(6 marks)

Source B *Rag-time in the House (Punch, 29 January 1913) (courtesy of Mansell Collection)*

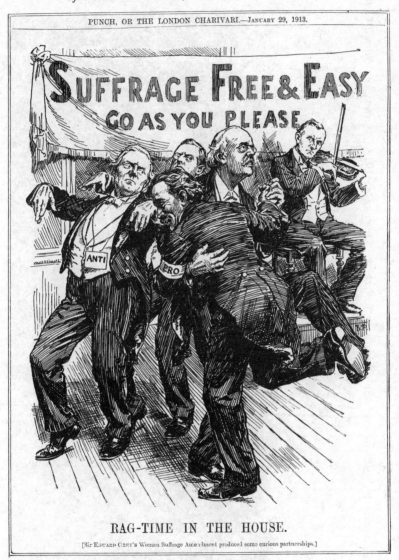

PUNCH, OR THE LONDON CHARIVARI.—January 29, 1913.

RAG-TIME IN THE HOUSE.

[Sir Edward Grey's Woman Suffrage Amendment produced some curious partnerships.]

488

7. Objective 4

Study the sources below and then answer the questions: *Source A   Derby Day 1913 (courtesy of Mansell Collection)*

Source B

'The incident . . . had a disconcerting effect on the other jockeys who turned around in their saddles at the untoward occurrence'.
'Captain Henry Jocelyn Davison R.N. (retired) said that his sister, Miss Davison, was 38 years of age'.
'P.C. Eady found inside her jacket . . . a half return ticket from Epsom to Victoria'. (*The Times*, 11 June 1913)

Source C

'Most of the horses had passed, but there was about three still to come'.
'Her object was not thought [to be] to take her own life.' (The Coroner recorded a verdict of 'death by misadventure'.) (*The Times*, 11 June 1913)

Source D

'As she became worse she was operated on on Friday to relieve pressure on the brain, but she never regained consciousness and died on Sunday afternoon'. (*The Times*, 11 June 1913)

Source E

'Captain Davison could only think . . . that it was with the object of calling attention to the suffrage movement. He felt perfectly certain it was an accident'. (*The Times*, 11 June 1913)

Source F

'Inquiries at the Epsom and Ewell Cottage Hospital yesterday showed that Miss Davision, the Suffragist, who caused the accident had rallied during the day. She had been conscious since the previous afternoon, but was still unable to speak. She was able to take some nourishment'. (*The Times*, Friday 6 June 1913)

Source G

'The WSPU propose to give a public funeral on Saturday to Miss E. W. Davison . . . [At yesterday's meeting] Mrs. Mansell said that she desired to make it perfectly clear that Miss Davison went out with the express purpose of stopping the King's horse'. (*The Times*, 9 June 1913)

Source H

'The jockey's injuries consisted of slight concussion, cuts and bruises on the head and body, and an injury to the arm'. (*The Times*, 5 June 1913)

Source I

'Horse and Jockey were unhurt'. (Taken from *Unshackled* by Christabel Pankhurst)

Source J

'The climax to the Suffrage Movement came when the Suffragette, Emily Davison, threw herself under the King's horse, "Anmer", at the 1913 Derby. "The Cause", she said "needs a martyr".' (Taken from *Modern Britain* by James Hagerty, 1980)

(a) Study Sources A, B and C. What similarities and differences can you detect?
(b) How does:
   (i) Source I contradict Source H?
   (ii) Source D contradict Source F?
(c) 'Emily Davison went to the 1913 race to commit suicide for "the cause"'.
   (i) Use the sources above to present evidence for and against this statement.
   (ii) What overall conclusions can you draw?
(d) What evidence is there in the sources that the WSPU used the occasion to gain publicity?
(e) 'These extracts reveal beyond doubt that primary sources are much more valuable than secondary sources'. Do you agree?

(Total = 30 marks)

THE SOCIAL REFORMS OF THE LIBERAL GOVERNMENT 1906–14

25.1 INTRODUCTION

In January 1906 the Liberals were returned to power with a landslide majority. The full result of the General Election was:

Liberals 377 **seats**
Irish Nationalists 83 **seats**
Labour & Sympathisers 53 **seats**
Conservatives 157 **seats**
Liberals Overall Majority 84 **seats**

Despite being one of the world's leading industrial nations, poverty was still a serious problem in Britain. During the latter part of the nineteenth century governments had made some progress in extending elementary education, strengthening trade unions and in providing public health, but a number of social evils still remained. Winston Churchill suggested that casual labour, unemployment, undernourishment and poverty were the most urgent problems the Liberals should attack.

The notion that it was time for the barriers of *laissez-faire* to be lowered and for the state to play a more active role in supporting its citizens was held by a number of 'new' Liberals. They had been influenced in their thinking by the investigative studies of Charles Booth in London and Seebohm Rowntree in York. Both men concluded that about a third of the people in each city lived in appalling poverty. The Fabian Society and the Salvation Army also highlighted the terrible conditions in which many people lived in the large cities of Britain. In addition to this the politicians had been profoundly shocked when it was discovered that half the men who volunteered to fight in the Boer War were unfit and suffering from malnutrition.

Social evils remaining in 1906

1800–1850	1851–1900	Situation in 1906
Ideas of *Laissez-faire* and Self-help dominant	Some legislation passed 1870 Elementary Education Act 1875 Public Health Act Artisan's Dwelling Act 1875 Conspiracy and Protection of Property Act (Trade Unions)	No State Insurance Cover for Workers No State Help for the Elderly Poverty still a major problem

The 'new' Liberals argued that if they did not tackle the problem of poverty they would lose the working-class vote to the rapidly-emerging Labour Party. The newly-appointed Liberal Cabinet in 1906, however, contained a majority of old-school Liberals who still believed in individual freedom and *laissez-faire*. Progress in tackling the nation's social problems was therefore, very slow at the outset. The death of the Prime Minister, Campbell-Bannerman, in 1908 provided the opportunity for the two 'new' Liberals to come to the fore. These men, David Lloyd George and Winston Churchill, were both strong willed and they recognised that it was time for the Liberals to adopt a more adventurous policy in attacking social evils. Herbert Asquith, the new Prime Minister, was concerned about the poor performance of the Liberal Party in recent by-elections. He sensed that social evils should be eradicated and consequently he let Lloyd George and Churchill 'have their heads'. He was careful, however, to keep hold of the reins to prevent the horse from bolting.

Thus it is from 1908 that the Liberals made a determined effort to push through a programme of social legislation. Although by modern-day standards their reforms were limited, in the context of their own time the achievements of Lloyd George and Churchill were quite substantial. At times they had to overcome fierce opposition and only their determination carried the day. This is particularly true with reference to the *National Insurance Act* of 1911.

25.2 WHO HELD THE MAIN CABINET POSTS BETWEEN 1908 AND 1914?

Position	Minister
Prime Minister	Herbert Asquith
Chancellor of the Exchequer	David Lloyd George
President of the Board of Trade	Winston Churchill

25.3 WHAT DID THE LIBERALS DO TO HELP CHILDREN?

(a) The Education (Provision of Meals) Act 1906

By 1906 elementary education had been made compulsory in Britain. It was obvious from the reports of teachers that many children were suffering from malnutrition and disease associated with inferior diet. A Labour MP had drawn up a Private Members Bill to deal with this problem and this prompted the Liberals to pass the *Education (Provision of Meals) Act*.

The Act gave local authorities the right to levy a rate to finance school meals for those children in need of them. Although a step in the right direction – by 1914 150 000 children were benefitting – the Act was limited. It was not obligatory for a local authority to provide meals and in many areas the problem of malnutrition amongst the school population remained as serious as it had ever been.

(b) The Education (Administrative Provisions) Act 1907

This Act introduced annual medical inspections in elementary schools. Some credit for this measure should be given to Robert Morant, Secretary to the Board of Education. He was constantly reminding those in authority of the need for children to be fit and healthy if they were to benefit from their schooling.

Despite the good intentions of the government, the Act was not well received in some quarters. A letter to *The Times* conveyed the fear that 'nothing could be more lamentable than that the use of the rates should drive away the army of volunteer workers who have laboured devotedly for many years . . . recognising the unhappy home conditions of many children' (Saturday, 2 January 1909).

(c)   The Children's Act 1908

This Act is sometimes referred to as the 'Children's Charter'. It introduced a number of measures designed for the protection of children:

- Juvenile courts and borstals were set up to deal with young offenders.
- Shopkeepers were not to sell alcohol and tobacco to juveniles.
- Limits were set on the hours children were allowed to work in part-time jobs.
- Parents were deemed to be responsible for bringing up their children and penalties could be imposed for negligence.

These measures in themselves may not be regarded as being particularly radical, but the principle of *laissez-faire* had been dealt a blow as the state could be seen as interfering directly with family life.

25.4   THE ELDERLY

(a)   Why did the old people need helping? What measures did the Liberals take to support the elderly?

With improved medical knowledge people were living longer, yet nothing had been done by the state to cater for the elderly. Old people were dependent on sympathetic relatives or the regulation of the workhouse. Many, however, became destitute and helpless.

In 1908 the Liberals passed the *Old Age Pensions Act*, a much needed piece of legislation.

- Old people over the age of 70 were to receive five shillings a week (25p), providing their income from other sources was below 12 shillings (60p). Pensions were to be non-contributory in nature.
- Pensions would be paid from 1 January 1909.

The Act had a number of loopholes, particularly the details relating to applying for a pension. The Liberals met with a deal of public debate on the issue. One point of contention was exactly how pensions would be financed.

(b)   How did the Liberals raise the money for Old Age Pensions? What opposition did they encounter?

Asquith had helped to pass the Old Age Pensions Act but it was Lloyd George, as Chancellor of the Exchequer, who had the problem of raising the necessary money. At the same time he had to finance the building of eight new 'Dreadnought' battleships. His solution was to tax the rich 'to wage war against poverty and squalor'. Lloyd George's 1909 Budget was dubbed the 'People's Budget':

- He proposed to increase taxes on alcohol and tobacco, and to introduce a new motor-car licence.
- Income tax was to be increased from one shilling (5p) to 1s.2d. (7p) in the £ for those earning above £3000 per year.
- Addition super-tax of 6d. (2.5p) for those with an income of more than £5000 per year.
- An increase in death duties.
- Profits made from the sale of land to be taxed.

The rich were totally against these proposals and their opposition was manifested by the peers in the House of Lords where the Conservatives had a large majority. They rejected the Budget and, in doing so, precipitated a major constitutional crisis. The struggle culminated in the power of the Lords being reduced by the *Parliament Act of 1911*.

The Old Age Pension Act itself also produced criticism from members of the Labour Party who felt the measures were a dilution of what was really needed, and they argued that the Act should have been far more radical in outlook. Lloyd George was obliged to meet several deputations from the trade unions worried about a variety of aspects of the Act. Some Conservative MPs were even of the opinion that pensions would be 'profoundly demoralising . . . and weaken the moral fibre . . . of the nation' (report in the *The Times*, 17 December 1909).

The Liberals, for their part, could at least argue that they had made a start.

25.5   WHAT DID THE LIBERAL GOVERNMENT DO TO HELP WORKERS WHO WERE EXPLOITED?

(a)   Sweated industries

As late as 1909 there were still a large number of workers who were not covered by the terms of the various Factory Acts. The people concerned were employed in the so-called 'sweated industries'; among such industries were dressmaking, hosiery, lacemaking, cardboard-box manufacture and nail-making. Often the work was farmed out and done in the homes of the workers. Long hours had to be worked for pitiful wages. As the workers were dispersed it proved difficult to organise them into trade unions. John Burnett's *Report to the Board of Trade on Sweating in the East End of London* (1888) estimated that:

> There must be at least two thousand sweaters in the East End of London, and of these, not one third can be known to the factory inspectors, hidden as their shops are in the garrets and backrooms of the worst kinds of East End tenements.

Pressure groups such as the Anti-Sweating League also drew attention to the extent of the problem. In 1906 the *Daily News* sponsored an Anti-Sweating Exhibition but still no legislation was forthcoming.

Finally, in 1909 Winston Churchill inspired the passing of the *Trade Boards Act*:

- Four occupations were to come under the terms of the Act; box-making, tailoring, lacemaking and chain-making.
- 200 000 workers were to be covered.
- For each of these industries a Board was to be established, representative of the employers, the workers and the government.
- The Boards were given the power to establish minimum wages and regulate conditions of work.

In 1913 six more trades and a further 170 000 workers were brought under the Act.

Although the Act was a limited measure it illustrated that the Liberals were willing to intervene in industry to fix minimum wages and improve working conditions.

(b) Shop assistants

In 1911 the *Shops Act* was passed. It stated:

- Shop assistants should be granted a weekly half-day.
- There should be regular meal-breaks during the working day.

The Liberals had intended to reduce the hours of shopworkers and outlaw Sunday opening, but lack of time in the Parliamentary session forced them to abandon these proposals. Thus, the Act was a disappointment both to the government and the workers.

25.6 WHAT LEGISLATION WAS PASSED CONCERNING COAL-MINES?

(a) The Coal Mines (Eight Hours) Act 1908

This limited the number of hours a miner could work underground to eight a day. However, this excluded the time taken to reach the coal face and the return journey after the shift had finished. As a result many miners were at the colliery for longer than eight hours in a day. Surface workers, on the other hand, did generally enjoy a shorter day.

(b) The Coal Mines (Minimum Wages) Act 1912

In 1912, a year of widespread labour unrest, the miners called a national strike. In order to get the miners back to work the Liberals passed this Act. In future minimum wages were to be negotiated by local boards in each mining district. Each board was to have a neutral chairman.

Both these Acts can be viewed as bringing some benefit to Britain's miners, but coal-mining remained a hard and dangerous occupation (see Section 21.6(a)).

25.7 WHAT DID THE LIBERAL GOVERNMENT DO TO ASSIST WORKERS WHO WERE INJURED AT WORK OR ABSENT FROM WORK DUE TO SICKNESS?

(a) In 1906 the Liberals passed the *Workmen's Compensation Act* under the terms of which a worker was entitled to compensation from his employer for injuries received at work. This idea had originally been introduced in 1897, but now the provision was extended to cover any workman who was earning less than £250 per year.

(b) Perhaps the most important social reform of the Liberals was the *National Insurance Act* passed in 1911. Up to this time there was no state cover for workers who were forced to be absent from work because of illness. Unskilled workers could not afford to pay the high subscriptions demanded by the friendly societies. In some cases workers became ill through the nature of their work (for example, coal-mining, match-making and flint-grinding in pottery works), yet if they took time off there was no income for their family and the inevitable result was hardship and poverty.

In August 1908 Lloyd George visited Germany to study at first hand the social reforms which had been introduced by Bismarck in the 1880s. He was suitably impressed and on his return he made it clear that he intended to introduce a similar state insurance scheme in Britain as soon as possible. Lloyd George said that the government was coming to 'the rescue of people who were unable to see themselves through troubled times'.

The first part of the *National Insurance Act* was concerned with sickness:

- The terms of the Act applied to all workers between the ages of 16 and 70 in manual trades earning less than £160 per year.
- These workers were obliged to register with an 'approved society' (a friendly society, trade union or designated industrial insurance company).
- The scheme was contributory, with the worker paying 4*d*. (1.7p), the employer 3*d*. (1.25p) and the state 2*d*. (0.8p).
- The total amount paid – 9*d*. (3.75p) was indicated by a stamp stuck onto an insurance card – contributions were payable from 15 July 1912 and benefits were to be paid from 15 January 1913.
- In return for money paid in, the worker was entitled to 10 shillings (50p) per week for up to 26 weeks of the year if he was off work sick and, thereafter he could claim a disablement pension of 5 shillings (25p) per week.
- Simple medical attention was available free of charge from a doctor registered on an approved society panel.
- Special hospital treatment was to be provided for TB victims.
- A maternity benefit of 30 shillings (£1.50) was payable on the birth of a child.
- Doctors would receive 4 shillings (20p) per year (plus 2 shillings for medicine) for each patient treated.

Although an estimated 13 million workers were compulsorily covered by the scheme, it received a deal of criticims and opposition (see Section 25.9(c)).

25.8 HOW DID THE LIBERALS DEAL WITH THE UNEMPLOYED?

(a) The second part of the *National Insurance Act* aimed to deal with the unemployed in certain designated trades:

● Workers earning less than £160 per year in the following trades were covered:
Transport construction (railways, docks and canals)
Shipbuilding
Mechanical engineering
Vehicle construction
Sawmilling.
● Employers and workers participating in the scheme each paid 2.5*d.* (1p) into an unemployment fund.
● In return a worker was entitled to receive 7 shillings (35p) per week for a maximum of 15 weeks in the year if he was out of work. After 15 weeks the worker would have to seek help from the Poor Law authorities if he was still unemployed.

The scheme was rather modest in its objectives – at most 2 250 000 workers were covered – but it did at least provide some state support for those workers most vulnerable to unemployment. It also challenged the *laissez-faire* philosophy and established a platform for more ambitious schemes in the future. The unemployed received their benefits at the newly-opened Labour Exchanges (see Section 25.8(b)).

(b) Winston Churchill, President of the Board of Trade, worked out the details of the *Labour Exchanges Act* passed in 1909. Once again the Liberals used a German idea and the Act was to complement the second part of the National Insurance Act. The country was divided into ten districts, each district being responsible for establishing Labour Exchange Offices. These offices advertised job vacancies in the locality and, from 1911, paid out unemployment benefits. The Liberals saw Labour Exchanges as a solution to the problem of casual labour, a practice which tended to bring an increase in the numbers of unemployed. Lord Hamilton of Dalzell explained the Act:

Its purpose was to set up a network of labour exchanges all over the country at which the man who wanted to buy labour would be put in touch with the man who had labour to sell . . . in other words it would put an end to the present state of things, under which there was a vacancy in one place and a man seeking employment in another. The system would also obviate the necessity of a man tramping about the country in search of work'. (*The Times*, 1909)

By 1914 over 400 Labour Exchanges had been opened. The Act aroused considerable debate but there is no doubt that the Liberals were honestly trying to deal with a 'grave evil' in a practical manner.

25.9 HOW SUCCESSFUL WERE THE LIBERALS AND HOW WERE THE SOCIAL REFORMS RECEIVED AT THE TIME?

On the surface it would appear that the Liberals were very successful in overcoming the grave social evils of the early twentieth century. For the first time the state had made a worthwhile attack on the problems of old age, poverty and the unemployed; this in itself was an achievement as there were many who clung to the old deep-rooted philosophy of self-help and *laissez-faire*. A closer look at each of their main social measures should illustrate the opposition encountered by the Liberals.

(a) Old Age Pensions

The idea of pensions for the elderly was not exclusive to the Liberals of 1906–14. Already, in 1908, there were state pensions in ten countries and the idea had been discussed in Britain as early as the 1880s. Charles Booth had actually drawn up a list of proposals for an Old Age Pension Scheme in 1891. The Liberals were expected by many to introduce pensions and the only surprise was that they had to be pressurised into doing it by backbench MPs.

When the Old Age Pension Act was passed it did bring improvement and benefits to many elderly people; by 1913 there were almost one million pensioners and Lloyd George's claim that the Liberals had lifted 'the shadow of the workhouse from the homes of the poor' was to some extent justified. Yet the measures could have gone much further:

- Pensions were not made universal.
- Only people with an income of less than £21 per year were entitled to benefit.
- Pensions were withheld from lunatics and people who had criminal records.

● The qualifying age was set at 70 and not 65 as had been anticipated.

Even Lloyd George admitted that the Act was only a 'start' and 'an experiment'. There was a deal of criticism from radicals and socialists that the Act was too limited and they felt that the Liberals had missed a golden opportunity to eradicate total poverty amongst the elderly. This was rather an idealistic view and it is reasonable to state that Lloyd George had gone as far as was possible at the time.

(b)   Labour Exchanges Act

In 1906 William Beveridge advocated a system of Labour Exchanges in his book *Unemployment: A Problem of Industry*. The basic idea of having an office which advertised job vacancies made good sense. It would indeed save the casual labourer much time and effort as he would no longer have to walk long distances in search of work.

The Fabian Society and hardline Conservative MPs were critical of the Act, but for different reasons. To the Fabians the Act should have said that an employer could only take on workers by advertising at a Labour Exchange, therefore giving the state effective control of the labour market. Sidney and Beatrice Webb were particularly strong exponents of this point of view. The right-wing element of the Conservative Party, however, rejected this notion and argued that the state had no right to interfere in the free labour market.

William Beveridge adopted a view somewhere between the two arguments. He said that Labour Exchanges should be used by employers on a voluntary rather than compulsory basis. Insurance, however, in certain trades should be compulsory. Labour Exchanges would be most effective, he argued, working hand in hand with an insurance scheme. This was the policy adopted by the Liberal Government.

Despite the criticism the Liberals had at least done something to aid the unemployed.

(c)   The National Insurance Act

The Bill to introduce National Insurance was pushed through Parliament in seven months. Lloyd George introduced the Bill in May 1911; it became law on 16 December 1911. The Chancellor of the Exchequer worked for endless hours on the measure, receiving deputations and framing the various clauses.

Initially the scheme was quite well received, but as time went on it came in for heavy attack. In the end Lloyd George was relieved to see a scheme reach the Statute Book even though he had to admit it was limited in outlook and was only 'the first step'. The opposition to the National Insurance scheme formed a catalogue:

- Lloyd George had originally intended to include widows and orphans in the scheme, but he met with such fierce opposition from industrial insurance companies, like the Prudential, that he was forced to drop the proposal. These insurance companies specialised in the payment of 'death benefits' and they were most reluctant to be faced with opposition from the state. Such was the political influence of the insurance companies that they forced Lloyd George to make his retraction.

- Lloyd George could only pacify the opposition of the friendly societies by making them responsible for administering the Act as 'approved societies'.

- A number of trade unions who ran their own insurance schemes opposed the Act. Lloyd George nullified their opposition by granting them state supplements to enhance their policies.

- Socialist groups and the Labour Party were annoyed that Lloyd George had made the scheme contributory. They mocked his catchphrase 'Ninepence for Fourpence' and posed the question 'Why not fivepence for nothing?' Keir Hardie argued that the whole cost should be covered by the state.

- Many workers were indignant about having to pay part of their wages into the scheme. Their feelings were channelled into propaganda campaigns organised by the Northcliffe press. The *Daily Mail* championed the so-called 'mistresses and maids' campaign and frequently published letters and articles attacking the National Insurance Act. Lloyd George was seen as a 'thief' and a 'cheat' rather than a politician who was trying to introduce social reforms to the benefit of the working class.

- The British Medical Association, representing the nation's doctors, was very hostile to the whole idea of National Insurance. They resented being employed by 'approved societies'. Being on the panels of such societies, they argued, would take away their independence and would lead some doctors receiving more work than others. It would also take away the freedom of the patient in choosing their own doctor to treat them. Lloyd George tried hard to talk the BMA round but their opposition remained strong.

Lloyd George had to do some 'wheeling and dealing' to see the National Insurance Bill safely through Parliament. Even he, however, was worried about how the Act would work in practice. This led to a massive publicity campaign designed to familiarise the people with the scheme. Leading Liberals were despatched to all corners of the country to explain the Act at countless public meetings. It is true that the Act did have weaknesses and it was limited but, on the other hand, it was amazing that anything at all reached the Statute Book in view of the strong opposition that was mounted at the time. Lesser men than Lloyd George may well have given up the scheme.

25.10 CONCLUSION

How far were the social reforms of the Liberals the start of a Welfare State?

A 'welfare state' is one which supports its citizens 'from the cradle to the grave', providing a wide range of social services. Taking this definition at face value the Liberal reforms must be regarded as a starting point towards a welfare state. The Liberals must be credited with taking a number of difficult steps with great determination. They had recognised the nation's social problems, and from 1908 in particular, had made a concerted attack on them.

The Liberal reforms were not universal and they provided the minimum rather than the optimum of state care. To be fair, however, the Liberals may well have achieved more had they not had to step a middle course between the 'extreme' of socialism and right-wing Conservatism.

Thus the reforms may be regarded as the foundation of the modern British Welfare State, not so much in the measures they introduced but more in the way they established the principle of state intervention into the life of the nation. The Liberals had shown the way and illustrated what governments could achieve in terms of social legislation given favourable circumstances and the general support of the electorate. This can be seen as being of benefit to Clement Attlee's Labour Government of 1945–51. It was this government which cemented the Welfare State, introducing welfare measures such as the National Health Service and a comprehensive National Insurance Act. Lloyd George and Winston Churchill had opened the door to such measures with their attack on social evils between 1908 and 1914.

QUESTIONS

1. **Objectives 1 and 2**

(a) 'The Liberals did not really start to attack social evils until 1908'. How far is this statement true? (8 marks)

(b) Why did the Liberal Government attack social evils?
(12 marks)

2. **Objective 1**

Describe the main features of the following pieces of legislation:

Workmen's Compensation Act; Trade Boards Act; Labour Exchange Act; Coal Mines (Eight Hours) Act; Coal Mines (Minimum Wage) Act; Shops Act. (20 marks)

3. **Objectives 1 and 3**

(a) Outline the terms of the Old Age Pensions Act. (5 marks)

(b) How far could pensions be regarded as an idea of the Liberals?
(5 marks)

(c) As a member of the Fabian Society write a letter to *The Times* expressing your views on the Old Age Pensions. (10 marks)

4. **Objectives 1 and 4**

Study the following extracts and answer the questions which follow:

Source A

So much has been said and written about the inauguration of the Act that the age poor entitled to benefit by its provisions were fully informed as to take advantage of it, and the payments were made, as a rule without difficulty or inconvenience . . . to the public . . . or . . . the Post Office.
(*The Times*, Saturday, 2 January 1909)

Source B

One old man at Wimbledon was desirous of drawing four weeks in advance, and it took a deal of explanation to convince him that his application could not be entertained.
(*The Times*, Saturday 2 January 1909)

Source C

In Balham and Tooting some of the old people who were unable to write failed to bring a relative to sign for them, and they were greatly disappointed when told that they could have no money until the order had been signed by someone who knew the applicant. In a few instances the pensioners had overlooked the fact that the signing had to be done in the presence of the 'post office' officials.
(*The Times*, Saturday 2 January 1909)

Source D

Mr. W. J. Davies . . . secretary of the National Society of Amalgamated Brassworkers sent the following telegram to the Prime Minister:-
'Brassworkers wish you and the Chancellor of the Exchequer happiness and prosperity for the New Year. Express gratitude for State recognition of veterans of industry generally . . . on this glorious pensions day'.
(*The Times*, Saturday 2 January 1909)

Source E

At Kettering . . . all the pensioners of the town were entertained at tea and two of them moved . . . a vote of thanks to the Government.
(*The Times*, Saturday, 2 January 1909)

Source F

Taken from *Punch* 13 January 1909 (*courtesy of Mansell Collection*)

O. A. P.

He (filling in claims for himself and wife). "Question Fower—'Sex.' Wot do Oi put there, Missus?"
She. "I dunno wot yer conscience'll allow *you* to put; but ye puts *me* down a Primitive Method."

Source G

Another thing already clear is that the Act as at present framed will produce a large number of anomalies and hard cases; and that there will be a demand for relaxation of its restrictive clauses . . . The disqualification on account of having received Poor Law Relief during the year 1908 will also raise loud protest . . . The Act . . . on the other hand . . . opens the door to a sort of sponging upon the public by persons a great deal better off without pensions than those who have nothing but the pension.
(*The Times* (Editorial Comment), Friday, 1 January 1909)

Source H

The cost of this Act will be a very serious item in the nation's annual Budget.
(*The Times*, Friday, 1 January 1909)

(a) Would you consider the above sources to be primary or secondary source extracts? Explain your reasons. (6 marks)

(b) What do Sources B, C and F indicate about the understanding of the Old Age Pensions Act? You must make direct references to the evidence. (6 marks)

(c) Does Source A support or contradict Sources B, C and F? Explain your answer. (4 marks)

(d) What evidence is there in the above sources to suggest that the elderly were grateful to receive a pension? (4 marks)

(e) Study Source G. What shortcomings does *The Times* believe the Act to have? What 'restrictive clauses' other than the ones mentioned in Source G, did the Act have? (5 marks)

5. **Objectives 1, 2 and 4**

Study the cartoon *Getting into Deep Water* (taken from *Punch*, 11 August 1909) shown overleaf and answer the following questions:

(a) What positions were held in the Liberal Cabinet (from 1908) by Asquith, Lloyd George and Churchill? (3 marks)

(b) How did the 'new' Liberalism differ from 'old-school' Liberalism? (4 marks)

(c) Why, according to the cartoon, are Lloyd George and Churchill making things 'uncomfortable' inside 'the Cabinet'? (3 marks)

(d) What does the cartoon suggest about the convictions and character of Lloyd George and Churchill? What role does the cartoon see Asquith playing in the government? (2 marks)

(e) Choose two social reforms of the Liberals which took them into 'deep water', with either the socialist groups of the time or the Conservative Party. In each case explain the reasons for the controversy and indicate how the Liberals overcame it. (8 marks)

Source *Punch* (11 August 1909)

(courtesy of Mansell Collection)

6.   Objectives 1, 2 and 4

Study Source A *The Doctor* (*Punch*, 14 June 1911) and Source B *The Glorious Fifteenth* (*Punch* 10 July 1912). Answer the questions which follow:

PUNCH, OR THE LONDON CHARIVARI.—JUNE 14, 1911.

THE DOCTOR.
(*With Apologies to Sir Luke Fildes, R.A.*)

PATIENT (*General Practitioner*). "THIS TREATMENT WILL BE THE DEATH OF ME.'
DOCTOR BILL. "I DARE SAY YOU KNOW BEST. STILL THERE'S ALWAYS A CHANCE."

(courtesy of Mansell Collection)

510

NATIONAL INSURANCE A...

CRAVEN HILL

THE GLORIOUS FIFTEENTH.

OUR ST. SEBASTIAN. "AND NOW, LADIES AND GENTLEMEN, AFTER THESE REFRESHING
PRELIMINARIES, LET US GET TO BUSINESS."

(Courtesy of Mansell Collection)

(a) When was the National Insurance Bill introduced into Parliament? When did it become law? (2 marks)

(b) What does Source B suggest about the passage of the National Insurance Bill through Parliament? (2 marks)

(c) Who is the person, shown in both cartoons, responsible for the National Insurance legislation? (1 mark)

(d) In Source A why does the doctor think the treatment will be the death of him? Use the cartoon and your historical knowledge to write a detailed answer. (4 marks)

(e) What other opposition did the government meet over the National Insurance Act? (5 marks)

(f) In what way was the Labour Exchange Act complemented by the National Insurance Act? (3 marks)

(g) Why was the National Insurance Act (Part 2) regarded as a 'limited measure'? (3 marks)

7. **Objective 3**

(a) As a person who qualifies for a pension what is your opinion of the Liberal Government?

(b) As a member of the landed aristocracy, explain why you are opposed to Lloyd George's Budget of 1908.

(Total = 20 marks)

CHAPTER 26

THE FIRST WORLD WAR (1914–18) AND ITS EFFECTS

26.1 INTRODUCTION

(a) Before the First World War (1914–18) Britain's wealth was based on the strength of her basic industries – iron and steel, textiles, shipbuilding and coal-mining. Her people had become used to being regarded as the world's premier industrial country, although this position had been under challenge from America and Germany since the 1880s (see chapter 22). Britain was also the financial centre of the world, providing banking facilities and loaning capital to the developing nations (in 1914 Britain had £4000 million invested overseas). These 'invisible exports' were of vital importance to the British economy, enabling her to have a favourable balance of payments. The basis of international finance prior to the war was the Gold Standard which was designed to keep exchange rates between currencies stable and where money was linked to gold reserves. Sterling was the international currency with London holding gold for the entire world.

(b) After the war British businessmen confidently expected a return to the pre-1914 status quo. Such a viewpoint appeared to be justified when, immediately after the war, countries restocked with commodities which were unobtainable between 1914 and 1918. This so called 'replacement boom' was a temporary phenomenon and it merely served to disguise a changed set of economic conditions. The war had, in fact, broken up the pre-1914 trading patterns, increased the strength of the challenge to Britain's industrial position, and wrecked the system of international finance. From 1921 a trade slump set in which hit the basic industries particularly hard. Unemployment rose to three million and never fell below a million between 1921 and 1939 (see chapter 29).

26.2 WHAT MEASURES WERE INITIATED BY THE GOVERNMENT TO DEAL WITH A TOTAL WAR SITUATION BETWEEN 1914 AND 1918?

(a) When the war broke out in August 1914 it was assumed that business would continue as usual and the conflict would be short-lived. Very few people foresaw a situation where the government would have to intervene and mobilise the resources of the country. Early in the war it was believed that private firms would be able to provide the armed forces with enough weapons and supplies. However, as time progressed it became evident that an economy based on *laissez-faire* could not satisfy the demands of the war. The state, therefore, built up a system of controls, albeit on a piecemeal basis.

(b)

(i) In 1915 the *Defence of the Realm Act* was passed, which gave the government the power to commandeer factories and convert them to any use they wanted.

(ii) At the Battle of Ypres in April 1915 the British Army had found itself short of shells – supplies were not reaching the front. The popular press in Britain, led by Lord Northcliffe, published stories concerning 'the great shell scandal'. The government reacted quickly by passing the *Munitions Act* (May 1915) which set up the Ministry of Munitions under Lloyd George, and gave the state the power to control all aspects of the manufacture of munitions, from the acquisition of raw materials to the distribution of the finished product. By 1918 this Ministry employed over three million people producing shells and guns at the rate required by the army. This was 'state collectivism' in action, with the government 'organising, directing and managing' the economy rather than private firms.

(iii) In 1917 a Ministry of Food was established to distribute food, considering both civilian and military requirements. Rationing was avoided until February 1918 when the full effects of the 'U-boat' attacks on British shipping were felt. Meat, butter, bacon, lard, sugar and ham were rationed by price. At the end of the war the government was purchasing four-fifths of Britain's imports and ensuring that they were shared fairly. In the words of W. H. Beveridge 'The Ministry of Food . . .

accomplished what private enterprise . . . could never have accomplished'.

(iv) Another facet of the war was the need for the state to control and direct manpower. From 1916 this was achieved via the Ministry of Labour, assisted from March 1917 by the Ministry of National Service. These two ministries made sure that essential workers were kept at home; this was achieved by a system of starred (vital) occupations. Conscription from 1916 was also carefully monitored to avoid too many skilled men joining up. (The trade unions generally co-operated with the government, agreeing to 'dilution of labour' in 1915, whereby unskilled men and women were allowed to take on jobs previously done by skilled craftsmen.)

(v) Transport during the war was also directed by the state. In 1914 railways came under the Board of Trade and shipping was directed by a Shipping Controller appointed to oversee that the correct number of ships were distributed between the Merchant Fleet and the Navy according to needs.

26.3 THE ECONOMIC AND SOCIAL EFFECTS OF THE WAR

(a) Did the war alter society's attitude with regard to the role of the state?

After the war the majority of government controls were quickly removed as businessmen called for a return to pre-war conditions. How far, then, can we judge if the economic collectivism of the war had any long-lasting effect on society? Arthur Marwick has studied this question in depth and he believes that the collectivism of the war left an indelible mark – even if the machinery of state control was removed after 1918. He states:

● Society had been introduced to the concept of **full scale** government intervention. Thus society was more prepared to accept state measures during peacetime, for example, the *Unemployment Insurance Act* 1920.

● Marwick goes on to claim that 'precedents had been set, establishing . . . a new measure of tolerance for large scale State intervention'.

Furthermore, society realised that there could be 'no complete return to the *laissez-faire* orthodoxy of 1914'. In the longer term, the experience of society during both World Wars together probably prepared the ground for wide-scale government legislation between 1945 and 1951.

(b) Loss of manpower

Britain had 750,000 men killed in the war and a further 1.5 million were left with physical handicaps and injuries. Society referred to the 'lost generation' as many of these men were between the ages of 18 and 45, and in peacetime would have been the backbone of the nation. Many young men who were lost had talents and skills that the country could ill-afford to lose – scientists, teachers, politicians, craftsmen, etc. However, leading authorities like Medlicott and A. J. P. Taylor claim that the lost-generation factor has been overplayed. For example:

- The so-called lost generation produced three Prime Ministers in Clement Attlee, Harold Macmillan and Anthony Eden.
- The lost generation did not result in a reduction in the labour force as women were trained in large numbers during the war to do important work in agriculture, industry, business and government, which was a factor in deciding to give some females the franchise in 1918 (see Section 24.9).

(c) Loss of confidence

Britain suffered little environmental damage during the war and only 1,500 civilians were killed, most of these suffering in Zeppelin and aeroplane attacks on London towards the end of the war. Nevertheless, the country was left in a state of shock. No one had expected the war to last so long and to result in such catastrophic military losses. People had to overcome bereavements and readjust their lives. The jingoistic mood in which the war had started had been replaced by one of melancholy. In addition, Europe had to face a severe 'flu epidemic between June 1918 and January 1919. It remained to be seen if the promises of 'reconstruction' would materialise. Lloyd George claimed he would make Britain 'a country fit for heroes to live in'.

(d) Capital equipment

Britain lost two-fifths of her merchant fleet (about seven million tonnes of shipping) sunk by the German U-boats. However, as priority was given to maintaining the capacity of the shipbuilding yards during the war, the losses were quickly replaced. On the other hand Britain lost very little machinery or factory plant during the war and, in a sense, this proved to be a disadvantage in the 1929s and 1930s. Britain spent no money updating her factory machinery and this proved to be one reason why she was to lose ground to her industrial competitors.

(e) Financial cost of the war

At the height of the war in 1917, the government was spending an estimated £7 million per day, or approximately £2550 million a year. Over the four years of the war A. J. P. Taylor puts the cost at £9000 million. How did the government cope with such a burden?

● Britain sold £1000 million of her overseas assets (leaving about £3000 million).

● Britain increased her own borrowing to the tune of £1350 million, over half of which came from the USA. At the same time, Britain lent £1825 million to other countries. Money lent to Russia was never paid back. When Lenin seized power from the Tzar in 1917 he immediately declared all Russia's overseas' debts to be null and void.

● The general method of raising money internally was by increased taxation (this raised about one-third of the government's revenue). In 1918 income tax was 30p in the £ for those on incomes over £130 per annum (it had stood at 12.5p in 1914 payable on incomes over £169 per annum). In 1914 1.3 million people paid income tax; in 1918 the number had risen to just under 8 million. The government also established National Savings Schemes as a means of borrowing money from the general public.

On the surface it appeared that the government had managed its finances very well – but underneath, the position of Britain had been weakened:

● Her position as the world's leading financial country was now in question, with America taking on this role (it took some time for this to filter through to British financiers).

● Britain was also to find that a number of important overseas markets had been lost (see chapter 28).
● The war had brought about a network of 'international indebtedness' which was to collapse in 1929, plunging the world, including Britain, into acute Depression.

26.4 ATTEMPTS AT RECONSTRUCTION 1918–22

(a) What Acts were passed to improve social welfare in the years following the war? How successful were they?

(i) In December 1918 Lloyd-George's Coalition Government was returned to power, and was given the task of rehabilitating Britain after the hardship of the war years. In fact, plans for the post-war period were laid as early as 1917 when Dr Christopher Addison was created the Minister of Reconstruction. This Ministry established a wide range of committees to investigate topics such as housing, raw materials, education, transport and scientific research. Ultimately, very little of the Ministry's work came to fruition. One possible explanation for this is that the politicians, like the industrialists, had a fixation with returning to the *laissez-faire* days of 1914, and did not take into account the changes brought about by the war. Most of the Ministry's effective work was concerned with the demobilisation of the armed forces and the transference of labour from wartime jobs into peacetime employment.

(ii) The legislation which took place was piecemeal in origin – there was no overall plan or structure for reform. The following Acts were passed:

Fisher's Education Act 1918 (see chapter 18 for details).

Housing and Town Planning Act 1919
House-building had come to a standstill during the war, leaving Britain short of at least 600 000 dwellings. Two Royal Commissions in 1917 had identified the shortfall, and recommended state intervention to ensure that new houses were built at prices which the mass of people could afford to buy or rent – a task beyond the resources of private contractors. The Act, inspired by the new Minister of Health, Christopher Addison, stated:

- Local authorities were required to survey their areas and report on housing needs.
- Following this, central government would make funds available to assist councils and private firms to construct new houses. The Act had mixed success. It provided 200 000 new houses and 'established the principle that housing was a social service' (A. J. P. Taylor), but the money paid out by the government was far in excess of the initial estimates. In 1922 the Act was terminated as part of the spending economies recommended by Sir Eric Geddes (see below).

Unemployment Insurance Act 1920

This was passed during the 'replacement boom' and was calculated to cope with an unemployment rate of 4–5 per cent. The terms were:

- All workers were included in the scheme except civil servants, agricultural labourers and non-manual workers earning in excess of £250 per year.
- The state, employer, and employee, paid a total of 4p per week into the unemployment fund.
- A worker qualified to receive unemployment benefit after having made 12 payments into the fund.
- Benefits would be paid at the rate of 75p per week for a maximum of 15 weeks in any given year.

The Act was, on the whole, successful, and could once again be considered a legacy of the wartime collectivist mentality. However, when the trade slump began in 1921 unemployment rose to the figure of 10 per cent, and this resulted in a number of alterations being made to the 1920 Act (for example, the period for which benefit was payable was extended to 32 weeks).

(b)   How successful was reconstruction?

The government's attempts to reconstruct society were only partially successful; their plans were sabotaged by changing economic circumstances beyond their control.

(i) *The Geddes 'Axe' 1922*

In 1921 it was evident that the economy was slowing down:

● Unemployment was increasing rapidly, costing the government large amounts of dole payments.
● The export trade had fallen away to half its 1920 figure and Britain was losing much needed revenue.

Lloyd George appointed a Committee under Sir Eric Geddes to examine public expenditure. Geddes reported in February 1922 and suggested swingeing reductions in the amounts spent by the government – an orthodox solution in this period and one which was to be adopted again by the National Government in the 1930s. Geddes proposed to cut back by £75 million but eventually a figure of £64 million was accepted by the government.

(ii) *Who suffered under the 'Axe'?*

● The Education Act of 1918 was savagely cut back. The Day Continuation Schools never materialised, teachers' salaries were reduced, and class sizes increased.
● The Addison Act of 1919 was terminated as the government, it was argued, could not afford to pay out the subsidies.
● Government spending was also reduced on the armed services, welfare provision and agricultural subsidies.
● The Unemployment Insurance Act was modified.

(iii) *What were the effects of the Axe on the economy?*

There was little doubt that Geddes reduced government expenditure but 'the approach was a little naive' (Trevor Lloyd) as it contributed to a domino effect, thus:

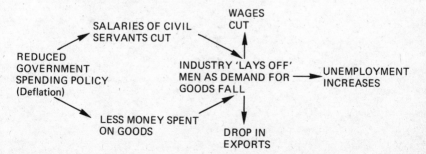

26.5 CONCLUSION

By 1922 the immediate post-war optimism had disappeared. It was now clear that there was to be no lasting policy of reconstruction and that the economy was under pressure. Worse was to come with the Wall Street Crash of 1929 (see chapter 29).

QUESTIONS

1. **Objectives 1 and 2**

(a) What were the economic and social results of the First World War?   (12 marks)
(b) How far did the war change people's attitudes about how big a part the government should play in structuring society?
                                                                          (8 marks)

2. **Objective 1**

(a) Describe the following post-war legislation:

   (i)   Fisher's Education Act 1918.
   (ii) Housing and Town Planning Act 1919.
   (iii) Unemployment Insurance Act 1920.   (12 marks)

(b) Why did the government's attempt at reconstruction fail?
                                                                          (8 marks)

THE TRADE UNIONS
1914–39

27.1 INTRODUCTION

Trade union history in this period was dominated by the General Strike of 1926. A General Strike, in the fullest sense, is a strike by the whole of the labour force at the same time.

The General Strike of May 1926, however, was really a sympathy strike with many workers (but by no means all) coming out in support of a group of fellow workers – the coal-miners. The TUC, in fact, took great care not to call it a General Strike, preferring such terms as 'national strike' and 'co-ordinated action'. This was probably to avoid any suggestion that the strike was an attempt at 'revolution'. Nevertheless, the General Strike did shake British society, and it forms a central part of trade union folklore. Much analysis and assessment has been produced on the strike. Martin Jacques, writing in 1976, saw it as '[a] period of [great] working-class militancy' and Mark Stephens (1981) says it 'marked a watershed' as it created a 'desire on all sides to see less destructive means used to achieve political and industrial ends'.

27.2 THE POSITION OF TRADE UNIONS AFTER THE FIRST WORLD WAR

(a) Why were the trade unions in a strong position in 1918?

Two main factors increased the strength and status of trade unions immediately after the war:

(i) Between 1910 and 1913 there had been a number of strikes in the mines and the docks as organised labour tried to assert itself. During the war, however, the unions co-operated with the government, making a vital contribution to the war effort. There was some industrial trouble on Clydeside in 1915, but this was an exception. The trade unions in general, agreed to the **dilution** of labour (see Section 26.2(b)(iv)). The general agreement to dilution did much to enhance the status of the unions. There was a feeling of 'working together'. The question of how far this co-operation was permanent would be answered after the war.

(ii) During the war the number of people in trade unions steadily increased from 4 150 000 in 1914 to 6 530 000 in 1918. The increase continued in the years immediately after the war to reach 8 350 000 in 1920. The unions had a new sense of confidence and they were in a position to press for increased wages and better conditions. In an effort to build on the wartime boom, a number of amalgamations took place, for example, the Amalgamated Engineering Union in 1920 and the 'giant' Transport and General Workers' Union in 1921.

(b)   What was the attitude of the trade unions after the War?

(i) The idea of working with the government and employers disappeared after 1918 as the unions tried to assert their newly-acquired strength. The pre-war 'militancy' returned and there was a wave of strikes in 1919–20. The unions were keen to see major industries nationalised as they had been during the war. The purchasing power of the pound had dropped from pre-war days and the unions felt that they had the power to push for their rights. This feeling was strengthened when the government failed to carry out its promise of reconstruction after the war (see chapter 26). The government, on the other hand, frightened by the Russian Revolution of 1917, became suspicious of the unions. Some politicians believed that Bolshevik ideas were influencing the work force.

(ii) In April 1920 there occurred the *Jolly George* incident. This was when London dockers blacked a ship called the *Jolly George*, which they suspected was carrying a cargo of commodities to Poland to help them in their war against Soviet Russia.

Later in the year it appeared as if the British Government was considering declaring war on USSR in support of Poland. The Labour movement reacted by forming a *Council of Action* and threatening an all-out strike if the British Government intervened in the war. This incident was significant because for the first time trade unions had used their strength for political rather than industrial motives. It also helped to further the government's belief that the trade unions were becoming dominated by communists and syndicalists.

In October 1920 Lloyd George's Coalition Government, worried by an increasing number of strikes, passed the *Emergency Powers Act*. This gave them authority to maintain vital services, using troops in the event of a strike without permission of Parliament.

The prelude to a clash between the unions and 'the ruling class' had been established, and troubles in the coal industry brought about the eventual confrontation in 1926.

27.3 WHAT CAUSED THE GENERAL STRIKE OF 1926?

The General Strike was the outcome of seven years of industrial strife, mainly between the miners and the government. There were also difficulties in other industries but with coal-mining being the most important industry in the economy, events concerning the miners tended to dictate events in other sectors. Coal was vital to the railways and factories and earned Britain large sums in the export market.

(a) Miners' demands – January 1919

The Miners' Federation of Great Britain (MFGB) made a number of demands of the government who were in control of the mines following the war. They pressed for:

● An increase in wages by one-third.
● A national wage agreement. Wages were fixed from area to area. This resulted in some miners in the less prosperous districts getting lower wages. The MFGB wanted all miners to receive the same wage and proposed a central fund whereby the prosperous mines subsidised those that were not profitable.
● Immediate nationalisation.
● A six-hour day.

The MFGB felt strong enough to make these demands, particularly as the miners made up over 16 per cent of the work force. The government's reponse was to set up a Commission headed by Sir

John Sankey to inquire into the coal industry. The report was made in two stages, in March and June of 1919, and overall its recommendations were:

- Nationalisation.
- A seven-hour day.
- Better housing for the miners.
- 'the principle of state ownership . . . to be accepted'.

At the time, however, trade was healthy and the government was preoccupied with the peace negotiations with Germany. Lloyd George, the Prime Minister, delayed a decision before eventually rejecting nationalisation. The Sankey Report, therefore was not implemented, with the exception of the Seven Hour Day, brought in by the *Coal Mines Act 1919*.

(b)   Black Friday

(i)   In 1920 the trade depression set in and unemployment began to increase. The demand for coal dropped and exports fells. The government announced that the mines would be 'de-controlled' and returned to their private owners on 31 March 1921. The mine-owners insisted that the only way they could operate was for the miners to take a reduction in wages. Predictably, The Miners' Federation rejected any such proposition. The owners then announced that new reduced district wage rates were to come into operation; in South Wales wage cuts of up to 50 per cent were proposed. These proposals went against the MFGB's demand for a **national** wage agreement. In addition, the private owners said that they could not afford to invest in any new machinery.

(ii)   The **triple alliance** was now brought into play. It consisted of the miners, transport workers and railwaymen (see section 21.6). The latter two groups felt that an attack on the miners was a threat to all other workers and they were prepared to come out in support. On 31 March 1921 the miners were locked out by the owners and the NUR and the transport workers said they would help the miners by refusing to move coal as from Saturday 16 April 1921. By Friday 15 April they had changed their minds and they withdrew their support. The miners called it **Black Friday** in view of the fact that they felt let down and betrayed. This lack of unity in the labour ranks made the owners even more determined not to make any concessions to the miners. The miners stayed on strike until July when they were forced to go back on the owners' terms. The sequel to this was recrimination and bitterness within the Labour movement.

(c) There was a minor industrial recovery when the **French Occupied the Ruhr** coalfield in Germany in January 1923 and extracted coal as compensation for the damage the Germans had caused to French industry in the First World War. As a result Britain was able to export to the German market. There was an 'uneasy' peace in the coal industry as the miners won a slight increase in their wages during 1924. Trouble, however, was not far away. At the end of 1924 the coal exports dwindled again as the Ruhr mines recovered production when the French ended their occupation.

(d)   'Red Friday' – 31 July 1925

(i)   In April 1925 Winston Churchill, the Chancellor of the Exchequer, announced that Britain was returning to the Gold Standard. Churchill wanted to see Britain reclaim her position as the centre of world banking, but he overlooked the fact that the measure would put up the price of British exports. In the context of the unfavourable trading conditions at the time, Robert Rhodes James has described this decision as 'an unmitigated disaster'. All British exports would now be harder to sell.

(ii)   In the summer of 1925 the mine-owners stated that the mines could only keep going if the miners took a reduction in wages and increased hours again. The alternative, they said, would be widespread unemployment in the industry. Baldwin, the Conservative Prime Minister, intervened and said that workers should be prepared to make a sacrifice 'to put the industry on its feet'. Such statements were far from popular with the Miners' Federation who now had the support of the TUC. Accordingly the unions said they would refuse to transport coal if the mine-owners locked out the miners for refusing to take a wage cut. A showdown looked imminent. Then on Friday 31 July 1925 the government changed its stance and announced that they would subsidise miners' wages to their present level for a period of nine months. In the meantime, a Commission under *Sir Herbert Samuel* would investigate the industry. The unions proclaimed a 'victory' and called the day *'Red Friday'*. The subsidy had brought a temporary truce.

(e) Events from July 1925 to March 1926

(i) During the period that the Samuel Commission was sitting, the Government was preparing for the future; they anticipated that a General Strike would occur at some point and they wanted to be ready. *The Organisation for the Maintenance of Supplies* (OMS) was formed under the leadership of Sir John Anderson. This made preparations to keep the country supplied with essentials (for example, food) in the event of a strike, by mobilising volunteer labour; it was 'privately run'.

(ii) In addition, the government divided England and Wales into ten regions each under the control of a Civil Commissioner. He was to form a local committee which would deal with the strike when it came. The Civil Commissioner would keep in contact with a group of Senior Civil Servants in London who would have the power to recruit special constables.

(iii) In October 1925 the government arrested 12 leading members of the Communist Party. There was obviously a fear in some government quarters that the communists were subversives and were planning a General Strike for political motives, that is, the overthrow of capitalism. Therefore the arrests were made to take the activists 'out of circulation'. Whether or not Britain was under the threat of a revolution at this time is discussed in Section 27.6.

(iv) The Labour movement was surprisingly inactive; there is no evidence to suggest that preparations were being made for a General Strike. Much hope was pinned on Samuel reporting favourably for the miners so that they could negotiate a settlement. The miners adopted a low profile, not wishing to do anything to aggravate the situation.

(f) The Samuel Report – 6 March 1926

(i) The main proposals of the report were:
- Miners should accept a wage reduction for the time being.
- Longer working hours should not be implemented by the owners.
- The industry should work towards a national wage agreement.

- The coal industry needed to reorganise under the present system of private ownership; nationalisation, therefore, was not recommended.
- The government subsidy was to end.

(ii) The report was in many ways sympathetic to the miners but failed to deliver the goods on 'wage reductions' and 'nationalisation'. A. J. Cook, the secretary of the Miners' Federation stated, 'not a penny off the pay, not a minute on the day'. The owners also rejected the report, refusing to make any concessions. With both the MFGB and the mine-owners refusing to change their stance, the report achieved nothing. Deadlock resulted.

(iii) There followed a period of hasty negotiation with the government and the TUC trying to narrow the gap between the miners and owners before the subsidy terminated. They were unsuccessful; on 30 April 1926 the subsidy came to an end; on Saturday 1 May the mine-owners locked out the miners.

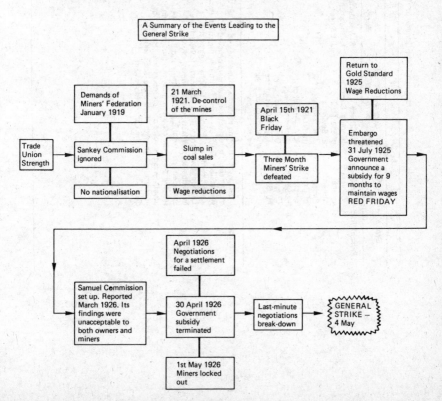

A Summary of the Events Leading to the General Strike

Protagonists in the General Strike 1926

	The Labour Movement			Government and employers	
Group	Miners	General Council of the TUC	Labour Party	Government	Employers
Personalities	A. J. Cook (Secretary of the Miners' Federation of Great Britain) H. Smith (President, MFGB)	W. Citrine (General Secretary of the TUC) E. Bevin J. H. Thomas of the NUR A. A. Purcell of the Furnishing Trades Union A. B. Swales of the Amalgamated Engineering Union	R. MacDonald P. Snowden J. Clynes	S. Baldwin (Prime Miniser) W. Joynson-Hicks (Home Secretary) W. Churchill Lord Birkenhead	About 1400 private coal-mine owners, represented by 'the Employers' Association'
Attitudes		There were differing attitudes within the Labour movement. The extreme left-wingers believed in syndicalism. Both Cook and Smith saw the strike as a 'class conflict'. Those on the right wing of the Labour Movement wished 'socialism' to be achieved in gradual steps. MacDonald, Thomas, Clynes and Snowden fell into this group. Citrine and Bevine were somewhere in the centre of these two groups. Bevin usually was the voice of 'common sense'. He did not, however, get on with MacDonald. Such were the divisions within the Labour Movement		Baldwin, an ex-industrialist, was against the strike. He wanted to win but he also wished to avoid causing bitterness among the workers. Churchill and Joynson-Hicks were right-wingers who wanted a showdown with the unions. They believed the strike had political motives and was an attempt to overthrow the government	Almost to a man the employers were obstinate and hardliners. They were not prepared to bend their entrenched position. Even members of the Conservative Government had little time for them. Most mines were lacking in up-to-date equipment. Lord Birkenhead remarked "I should call the [miners' leaders] the stupidest men in England if I had not previously had to deal with the owners."

(iv) On the same day, at a meeting of trade-union executives in London, it was agreed to support the miners. They agreed that the TUC would act on behalf of all unions and that there would be a General Strike as from midnight on 3 May. The government now put its emergency machinery into operation and the OMS mobilised volunteers and installed the ten Civil Commissioners into their respective areas.

Even at this stage, however, the General Council of the TUC hoped to negotiate a settlement. Mark Stephens claims that Ernest Bevin was on the point of getting all sides to agree to a formula he had drawn up as a basis for a settlement. Then in the very early hours of 3 May Baldwin informed the TUC that negotiations were 'off'. This dramatic decision was brought about because the printers at the *Daily Mail* had refused to print an editorial which was highly critical of the miners. In view of this action, Baldwin said negotiations were untenable. Thus it could be argued that ultimately it was the government which actually provoked the General Strike.

27.4 THE NINE DAYS OF THE GENERAL STRIKE 4–12 MAY 1926

It should be made clear that the strike was not a General Strike in the strict sense of the word, as only selected trades were called out.

(a) The first group of workers who came out were the printers, dockers, railwaymen, metal-workers, power-station workers and road transport workers – in all, some 2 million workers were officially on strike in support of the miners. To begin with the strike was effective. There were very few trains, trams or buses running daily and newspapers were reduced, at most to a single broadsheet. It was an impressive show of working-class solidarity and led A. J. Cook to write in his book *The Nine Days*, 'Tuesday May 4th started with the workers answering the call. What wonderful response! What Solidarity! . . . The workers acted as one. Splendid discipline!'

(b)

(i) The TUC, however, had not made any real preparations for running the General Strike. Within three days the General Council (with Bevin heavily involved) had set up five sub-committees to guide the strike. An example of one such committee was the one which dealt with food supply. This involved permission being given to vehicles to distribute food with posters saying 'By Permission of the T.U.C.'.

(ii)   Around the country groups set up Councils of Action and Strike Committees to co-ordinate the strike on a local basis. Such bodies liaised with the TUC headquarters at 32 Eccleston Square, London, as to the conduct of the strike.

(c)   The government's preparations were swiftly put into operation. Volunteers such as office workers and students were enlisted to do a variety of jobs and a large number of special constables were enlisted. Troops were called in to maintain supplies, moving food from the docks to special distribution depots. Power-stations were also run by troops. The government even stationed warships in the Clyde, Mersey, Tees and other river estuaries, ostensibly to protect the docks from attack by the workers.

(d)   Conduct

Most textbooks present the strike as a 'peaceful', good-humoured occasion with little violence or trouble to be seen. The fact that the police played the strikers at football in several areas (such as the famous match at Plymouth) is often highlighted. Certainly, local strike committees did their best to encourage the workers to organise sporting events during the strike. However, there were violent scenes in London's docks, and buses were overturned in Nottingham. In Glasgow mass-pickets were charged by police wielding batons, and in Manchester some workers were arrested under the Emergency Powers Act for distributing 'seditious literature'. A. J. P. Taylor estimates that 4000 arrests were made altogether, and describes this as 'trivial'. His assessment is difficult to argue with, but on the other hand the image of total 'good-humour' during the strike is not exactly accurate either.

(e)   The media

(i)   With the national newspapers severely restricted, both sides published their own newspapers during the strike. The government's standpoint was put over in *The British Gazette*. Baldwin did not like Churchill's aggressive attitude to the miners, and according to Robert Rhodes James 'neatly removed him from day to day control of the strike' by giving him the editorship of

The Gazette. Churchill called the strike 'unconstitutional' and a 'hold-up of the nation'. He clearly saw the strike as a 'revolutionary threat'. There is little doubt that Churchill was a source of great irritation to Baldwin who was at pains not to alienate the Labour movement completely.

(ii)   The mouthpiece of the Labour side was *The British Worker*. Its object was to keep the strikers in touch with what was happening in various parts of the country. It also constantly denied that the strike was a political one and said that it had nothing to do with bringing down the government. On 5 May it said 'The General Council of the TUC wishes to emphasise the fact that this is an industrial dispute. It expects every member to be exemplary in his conduct'.

In essence the two newspapers fought a propaganda war during the strike.

(iii)   The role of the BBC in the strike has been hotly debated. How far was the BBC neutral and independent during the strike, giving both points of view? Regular bulletins were issued on the strike but the balance appears to have been in favour of the government. When the Archbishop of Canterbury wanted to broadcast proposals for a settlement he was refused permission and Ramsay MacDonald was not allowed to make a statement on behalf of the Labour Party. Any item which the government did not agree with was not broadcast.

27.5 HOW AND WHY DID THE STRIKE COME TO AN END ON 12 MAY 1926?

(a)   Everything appeared to be going well for the workers when on 12 May it was announced that the Negotiating Committee of the TUC had called off the strike. The majority of the strikers were dumbfounded. Many refused to believe the news and continued to strike. Demonstrations and processions were held against the decision. *The British Gazette* (Thursday 13 May 1926) said that it was 'unconditional withdrawal . . . by [the] T.U.C.'. Several factors lay behind the TUC's decision:

● On 6 May Sir John Simon, who had been the Liberal Attorney-General from 1913 to 1915, announced in the House of Commons that 'a decision of the TUC to call out everybody regardless of contracts and without notice is not lawful action at all'. There were some doubts about this opinion from people such as Sir Henry Slesser, but it definitely worried the TUC.

● The General Council was mainly made up of 'moderate' men who were not happy about the conduct of the strike. They did not like being attacked as 'unconstitutional revolutionaries'. They also did not like the Communist Party using the strike to further its own ambitions.

● On 7 May Sir Herbert Samuel offered to act as mediator between the TUC, the miners and the government. A document called the **Samuel Memorandum** was drawn up which reiterated the points made by the Samuel Report of March 1926 and, in addition, stated that the government should renew its subsidy.

● Encouraged by this the TUC decided to terminate the General Strike hoping that the government would reopen negotiations using the Samuel Memorandum as a basis for peace.

The miners, however, were not convinced that the Memorandum had any authority and they rejected it. On 12 May 1926 the Negotiating Committee visited 10 Downing Street and told Baldwin that the strike was off. Baldwin saw this as a surrender and gave no written guarantee to the TUC. Not one concession had been made to the miners. The surrender was indeed 'unconditional'.

(b)   Who was to blame for the 'fiasco'?

Not surprisingly the air was full of acrimony and bitterness after the end of the strike. The miners felt that they had been betrayed; the left wing accused the TUC of a sell out, being afraid to take on the government. So who should take the blame . . . The answer is probably all of the groups involved within the Labour movement:

● The MFGB for not being prepared to shift their ground at all and being completely intransigent (although they countered that the owners were not prepared to move either).

● The left wing for inciting thought of 'revolution' and undermining the position of the TUC.

● The TUC and MFGB also did not clarify who was doing what and on behalf of whom. Was the TUC in charge of the negotiations or did the miners still control their own destiny? Neither side was clear.

● The TUC has to accept blame for failing to achieve any guarantee for the miners when it called the strike off. It would appear that Baldwin somehow 'got away with murder'.

(c)   The immediate aftermath of the strike

- There was a drift back to work by the vast majority of workers, but the miners tended to continue the struggle alone. The General Strike had done nothing to improve their position. Many returning workers were victimised by their employers.
- In July 1926 Baldwin passed *The Eight Hours Act* increasing the working shift in the mines to eight. This did nothing to enhance his claim that he could be trusted. Baldwin came in for a deal of criticism in his handling of the strike, often from his own party. In some quarters he was regarded as being 'too soft' on the strikers. Others said that he was manipulated by the likes of Churchill and Joynson-Hicks, the Home Secretary.
- In November 1926 the miners were forced back to work by starvation and poverty. They had to accept reduced wages and longer hours. Cherished dreams of a national wage agreement were as far away as ever. A number of pits were closed on the grounds of 'unprofitability' and unemployment among miners increased.

27.6   WHAT WERE THE EFFECTS OF THE GENERAL STRIKE ON THE TRADE UNION MOVEMENT?

(a)   The immediate effects were all too obvious:

- Divisions within the Labour movement.
- A financial loss. The strike had cost the trade unions £4 m.
- Humiliation for the unions.
- A startling drop in union membership from 5.5 million in 1926 to under 5 million in 1927.

(b)   In the longer term the government acted to make sure that there could never be a repeat of the General Strike by passing, in 1927, *The Trade Disputes and Trade Union Act*. The Act is generally seen as a sop by Baldwin to the right-wingers in his party. The Act said:

- Trade unionists wishing to contribute to political funds of the Labour Party had to 'contract in' (rather than 'contract out'). This resulted in loss of funds to the Labour Party.
- Civil Service Unions were banned from affiliating to the TUC (Civil servants were vital to the government during a General Strike).
- 'Sympathetic' strikes were to be against the law.

- Mass picketing of factories during a strike was illegal.
- Employees of the local councils were not allowed to strike.

The Act considerably weakened the legal standing of trade unions until it was repealed in 1946 by Attlee's Labour Government.

(c) Was Britain close to a socialist revolution in 1926?

The General Strike was seen at the time (and since) as an attempt to overthrow the existing order and democracy. With hindsight, however, it is possible to show that this could never have happened:

- The moderates 'reformists' held the sway in the TUC. They were as frightened of the revolutionary talk as the government.
- According to Margaret Morris, who has studied the General Strike in depth, the actual influence of the left was grossly exaggerated.
- The final word on this issue is possibly given by Arthur Marwick, who claims that the left wing (that is, the Communist Party of Great Britian – CPGB) 'had no clear idea of how the coal crisis was to be converted into a revolution'.

Thus there was little chance of a revolution in Britain in 1926.

27.7 CONCLUSION: CHANGED ATTITUDES 1926–39

(a) In the late 1920s, in a reappraisal of future strategy, the General Council of the TUC rejected the tactics of a General Strike and decided to follow a policy whereby unions would pursue their industrial aims in a more constructive manner. The left stated that the strike illustrated how working people could fight solidly together but this was very much a minority viewpoint. The moderate approach was strengthened by the changes that were taking place in the structure of British industry. The older staple industries, coal, iron shipbuilding, textiles – the bases for union militancy – were on the decline. The newer lighter industries did not have any trade-union traditions, and as they were prosperous industries, strikes amongst the work force were rare. Ideas of a 'class war' and 'direct action' receded into oblivion.

(b) The changed attitude of the unions – and a number of employers – was encapsuled in the Mond-Turner Talks 1927–30. Sir Alfred Mond, Chairman of ICI, and 21 other employers, wanted to harness the positive side of trade-union expertise to improve conditions in the industries and thereby create a healthy atmosphere for production. They had a series of talks with union leaders led by Ben Turner and Ernest Bevin. They made a number of suggestions which never actually materialised – but the important point about the talks was that they were symbolic of a changed attitude on both sides: there was willingness to work together.

(c) The Labour Party won increased support in the 1929 General Election and, with Liberal support, was able to form a government. The increased vote was a result of trade unionists turning towards Parliamentary means to achieve its objectives.

(d) In the 1930s, during the Great Depression (see chapter 29), the unions accordingly adopted a low-key stance. The TUC encouraged individual unions to provide leisure activities for the men out of work in their area. By the late 1930s the trade-union movement began to recover some of the lost members. In particular, the Transport and General Workers Union grew steadily as did the General and Municipal Workers Union. The majority of the work force was relieved to see a sense of calm return to industrial relations and they felt encouraged by the moderating influence of men like Bevin and Citrine. The government began to consult the TUC over such matters as economic policy and, from 1937, preparations for war. When the Second World War eventually broke out on 3 September 1939 the unions declared their total commitment to the war effort (see chapter 30).

QUESTIONS

1. **Objectives 1 and 2**

(a) What were the causes of the General Strike of 1926? (8 marks)
(b) Which of the causal factors would you judge to be the most important and why? (4 marks)
(c) Why did the General Strike collapse? (6 marks)
(d) What were the consequences of the General Strike for the trade-union movement. How far were these consequences 'intended'? (7 marks)

2. **Objective 3**

(a) As a member of the executive of the Miners' Federation in April 1926 why do you believe that the miners should not give in to the owners?
(b) What might a mine-owner have said in reply to the Miners' Federation?
(c) What might have been the feelings of a miner on strike from May to December 1926?

(Total = 30 marks)

3. **Objectives 1 and 2**

Study the chart below:

Column A	Column B
Personalities in favour of the strike	Personalities against the strike
Walter Citrine	Winston Churchill
Ernest Bevin	Stanley Baldwin
A. J. Cook	

Choose **one** person from *each* column:

(a) Describe their part in the strike. (10 marks)
(b) Which one of the people you have selected do you think played the more influential role in the dispute? Give your reasons.

(10 marks)

4. **Objective 4**

Study the sources below and then answer the questions:

Source A

STAND BY THE MINERS

The General Council's decision to call off the General Strike is the greatest crime that has ever been permitted, not only against the miners, but against the working class of Great Britain and the whole world . . . Instead of responding to the magnificent lead by

a call to every section of organised labour to join the fight against
the capitalists, the General Council have miserably thrown itself
and the miners on the tender mercies of the workers' worst enemies – the Tory Government.

Source B

Mine workers are to be congratulated on their firm struggle against
the dictation of the mineowners.
Stand by your trade unions as other unions are standing loyally and
steadfastly by you.

Source C

ORDER AND QUIET THROUGH THE LAND

Growing Dissatisfaction Among The Strikers.

INCREASING NUMBERS OF MEN RETURNING TO WORK.

Source D

WEDNESDAY EVENING, MAY 5, 1926.

WONDERFUL RESPONSE TO THE CALL

General Council's Message: Stand Firm and Keep Order

The above sources were published by the Miners' Federation, *The British Worker*, The Communist Party of Great Britain and *The British Gazette*.

(a) Identify the correct source of each extract. Give reasons for your choices. (8 marks)

(b) How important were *The British Gazette* and *The British Worker* during the strike? (6 marks)

(c) All the above sources are biased and cannot be relied upon to provide us with evidence about the General Strike. Do you agree with this statement? Give your reasons. (6 marks)

5. **Objective 4**

Study the sources below and answer the questions.

Source A

THE LEVER BREAKS

The Lever Breaks (Punch) (courtesy of Mansell Collection)

Source B   (*courtesy of Glasgow Bulletin, 1926*)

Source C

'The General Council of the Trades Union Congress wishes to emphasise the fact that this is an *industrial* dispute'.
(*The British Worker*)

Source D

SMASH THE CAPITALIST OFFENSIVE
NATIONALISE MINES WITH WORKERS CONTROL
(Communist Party of Great Britain)

Source E   Poverty! (courtesy of BBC Hulton Picture Library)

(a)   What view does the author of Source A take towards the General Strike? Explain as fully as you can.   (3 marks)

(b)   (i)   Which of the other sources supports Source A? Explain.
                                                                  (2 marks)

       (ii)   Which of the other sources contradicts Source A? Explain.
                                                                  (2 marks)

(c)   How useful is Source B to an historian studying the General Strike? Explain your answer.   (3 marks)

(d)   Study Sources C and D

       (i)   In what ways do they differ?   (2 marks)

       (ii)   Both *The British Worker* and the Communist party were on the side of the miners during the General Strike. Why, then, do you think they disagree?   (4 marks)

(e)   Photographs, such as Source E cannot be biased and, therefore, they are more reliable than other sources of evidence. Do you agree? Explain.   (4 marks)

INDUSTRY BETWEEN THE WARS 1919–39

28.1 INTRODUCTION

Industry between the wars presents a two-sided image. The basic industries based on the coalfields suffered a dreadful slump. The new industries, however, established themselves in the area around London and the South-East. After 1934, in particular, these areas enjoyed growing prosperity. This chapter describes the fortunes of each industry and should be studied in conjunction with chapter 29 which examines the depression of the thirties.

28.2 THE BASIC INDUSTRIES 1919–39

For what general reasons did the old basic industries decline between 1919 and 1939?

The interwar years witnessed the continuing relative decline of the basic industries, a trend which had begun before the war. A number of general factors contributed to this decay:

(a) During the war Britain lost markets overseas as countries either developed their own industries or turned to other suppliers.

(b) Most of Britain's competitors protected their industries by tariff barriers; Britain remained a free trade country until 1932. Some countries, like Germany, Italy and USSR, aimed at economic self-sufficiency (autarchy).

(c) Britain's factories and machinery were outdated and in urgent need of replacement. Such modernisation did not materialise.

(d) The return to the Gold Standard for the period 1925–31 hindered Britain by making her exports more expensive. (The Gold Standard had been abandoned at the outbreak of war in 1914).

(e) The basic industries were unable to adapt to the changes in trading conditions which is borne out by the figures below:

Main components of British exports
(% of total value)

Decade	Cotton	Other textiles	Iron & steel	Coal
1900–9	26	12	14	10
1910–9	25	15	12	10
1920–9	24	12	12	8
1930–9	14	10	12	9

(*Source*: Mitchell and Deane, *Abstract of British Historical Statistics* (Cambridge University Press, 1962)).

What problems faced each individual basic industry in this period?

(a) Coal

The coal industry experienced an unhappy period. It faced a number of problems:

(i) British collieries were poorly equipped with outdated machinery. The government refused to nationalise the mines, a move which might have brought greater investment into the industry. As a result there were hostile relations between the private owners and the miners, leading to a number of strikes, and culminating in the General Strike (see chapter 27). Such conditions were hardly conducive to high output.

(ii) The coal industry found it difficult to compete overseas (exacerbated by the return to the Gold Standard in 1925 – see Section 27.3(d)) and, in fact, lost a number of important markets. Poland, Spain and the Netherlands opened up new well-equipped collieries during this period.

(iii) In addition, alternative forms of energy were gaining ground. Oil was used in ships and power stations (it was cleaner), hydro-electric power was being developed in Scotland and Wales. Gas was being used as a domestic fuel.

(iv) The effect of these troubles was to reduce the number of men employed in coal-mining from 1.25 million in 1924 to 1 million in 1930. This meant a drop in output and a drastic fall in exports as these figures show

Year	Output (millions of tons/tonnes)	Exports
1913	287 (282 tonnes)	98 (96 tonnes)
1929	258 (254 tonnes)	77 (96 tonnes)
1933	208 (205 tonnes)	57 (56 tonnes)

(b) Cotton

(i) The cotton industry had played a prominent role in the British economy since the late eighteenth century. In 1900 British manufacturers dominated the world market – two-thirds of all cotton cloth sold in the world was British made. The cotton industry accounted for 26 per cent of the total value of British exports.

(ii) From this position of almost overwhelming superiority the industry underwent an alarming slump:

● During the war export markets were lost as the cotton industry was unable to supply the demand because of a shortage of raw cotton and labour. This spurred India, Japan and America to increase the capacity of their own cotton industries based on the most up-to-date machinery. These countries were able to supply their own needs and also bit into markets which had been previously dominated by Britain (for example, India took over the lion's share of the Far East market).
● Britain also had the disadvantage of being a high-wage economy. Manufacturers in India and Japan paid much lower wages, producing a much cheaper finished article.

● British manufacturers failed to modernise their factories and continued to operate using machines which were made in the late nineteenth century. One problem here was that banks refused to lend money in such unfavourable circumstances.

(iii) The state of this decline can be seen in the fact that by 1938 the cotton industry accounted for just 14 per cent of the total value of British exports and its share of the world market had plummeted to just 28 per cent.

(c) Wool

The woollen industry fared a little better. Wool sold more than cotton in the domestic market and exported far less. Although woollen manufacturers faced more opposition in overseas markets, her sales at home counterbalanced any loss of exports.

(d) Shipbuilding

(i) Before the War British shipyards constructed two-thirds of the world's merchant shipping with Belfast, Clydeside and Tyneside being the main centres. During the war the shipyards had been kept busy replacing ships which were sunk by the Germany U-boats. Immediately after the war (1919–20) the order books were full as shipping companies replaced lost tonnage. After this, as with cotton, the shipbuilding industry underwent a dramatic decline as illustrated by these figures:

Shipping built in British yards ('000 tons)	
1913	1950 (1919 tonnes)
1920	2400 (Replacement boom) (2362 tonnes)
1925	800 (787 tonnes)
1930	680 (669 tonnes)
1939	1000 (Rearmament programme) (9842 tonnes)

(ii) The reasons for the decline make familiar reading:

● During the war British yards had been unable to build ships for foreign customers as they had to concentrate on domestic needs. These customers proceeded to develop their own industries, particularly Sweden, Norway, Japan, America and The Netherlands. They no longer depended on Britain.

● Once the replacement era ended hard times ensued. The slump in world trade meant less goods were transported and consequently the order books were empty. British yards also received fewer orders as they were slow to develop the ability to build the new-style petroleum-driven motor ships which were in the greatest demand.

(e) Iron and Steel

(i) Problems in the iron and steel industry were evident before the war when Britain, although increasing her output, fell behind the Americans and Germans (see Section 22.6). *The Oxford Junior Geography* textbook from the early twentieth century referred to the area south of the Great Lakes in America as having 'the greatest coalfield in the world covered with manufacturing towns . . . Chicago, Cincinnati and Pittsburg'.

(ii) The British iron and steel industry went into a slump between 1920 and 1933:

● Export markets were lost during the war.
● Britain's free-trade policy allowed foreign countries to dump cheap iron and steel on the home market.
● The depression 1929–33 resulted in a drop in demand as iron-and-steel-using industries (for example, shipbuilding) were doing virtually no business. Exports dropped by two-fifths in this period.

28.3 THE NEW INDUSTRIES

(a) What features distinguished the new industries?

The new industries consisted of motor-car assembly, chemicals, electrical engineering and supply, synthetic fibres, plastics and rubber. They were different from the old basic industries in the following ways:

(i) They used oil and electricity for power rather than steam (as was the case with the old staple industries). As they did not need coal they had much more flexibility as to location. The most important factor in their location, therefore, was the proximity to markets and size of market rather than the nearness of raw materials. As a consequence, they were mainly located in the south and south-east around London (with its huge population).

(ii) They were far less dependent on export markets than the staple industries, with the majority of their products being sold at home. This, therefore, reinforced the importance of the market as the main factor of location.

(iii) They tended to be more structured in organisation; using up-to-date methods of mass-production and assembly. Furthermore, greater emphasis was put on the training of personnel both in management and on the shop floor.

(iv) They were much more technologically orientated than the staple industries, with greater attention being paid to scientific research to improve products and production.

(b) What developments took place in the new industries 1919–39?

(i) *Electrical engineering and supply*: The generation of electricity had begun in the 1880s but had a slow rate of growth before 1919. In the interwar years, however, there was a significant upturn. The most important reform was the passing of the *Electrical (Supply) Act of 1926*. Before this Act, electricity had been generated and distributed by a multitude of private firms across the nation. Now, under the auspices of the Central Electricity Board (CEB), there was to be a common voltage, larger power stations and a national grid for the distribution of electricity. The CEB was immensely successful:

● It employed 100 000 workers.
● It increased electricity output to such an extent that Britain could claim to be on a par with all European countries.
● In 1938 two out of every three houses received electricity.
● The number of consumers increased from 730 000 (in 1920) to 2 844 000 (in 1929) to 8 920 000 (in 1938).
● Improved methods of generation and distribution brought the prices of electricity down over the period as a whole.

Once electricity could be efficiently generated and supplied, electrical engineering developed:

- Industry started to use electricity as a source of power (particularly true of the new industries).
- Some railway lines in the Southern Region were electrified.
- Electric street lighting became adopted, replacing gas.
- A whole range of domestic appliances were manufactured including vacuum cleaners, refrigerators, radios, gramophones, washing machines.
- Large electrical firms such as EMI and Associated Electrical Industries grew up.
- By 1938 the electrical engineering industry employed 350 000 workers.
- Exports of electrical products (including transmission cables, generators) were stimulated. In 1937 Britain had a one-third share of the world market.

(ii) *Motor-car assembly*: Before 1914 there were some 200 firms in Britain, most of them small concerns producing motor cars individually and at high prices. The motor industry was stimulated during the war as the Army increasingly relied upon this form of transport. This also helped to build up a reservoir of knowledge in that army personnel gained experience in servicing and repairing motor vehicles. The British motor-car industry underwent a transformation between 1919 and 1939 as shown by these statistics:

Number of motor vehicles produced 1908–1938 (000s)

1908	10	Numbers employed	
1913	34		
1923	95	1923	120 000
1928	212	1938	250 000
1933	286		
1938	445		

There were a number of reasons for this growth:

- The adoption of the assembly-line method of production pioneered in 1908 by the American, Henry Ford. In Britain William Morris of Cowley, Oxford, and Herbert Austin, were the first men to use this method to mass produce motor cars; between them they manufactured three-fifths of British cars in this period. Austin was the originator of the 'Baby' Austin 7, the first vehicle to be mass-produced in Britain.

● There was a tendency to develop larger firms which resulted in greater efficiency and standardisation of components. In 1939 there were only 20 firms making motor cars, including the American-owned Vauxhall Motor Company of Luton, and Fords of Dagenham. A few firms like Rolls-Royce specialised in producing quality cars – only 12 per cent of British car output was exported (there was no real demand for small cars abroad) but this was compensated by heavy demand at home. Assembly methods were quick, components and raw materials fell in price, and the result was that motor cars were built at prices which could be afforded by many (for example, the Morris-Cowley sold for about £130). Furthermore, the home market was protected by a tariff of 33 per cent on foreign imports (imposed in 1915). The car industry escaped the worst effects of the depression of 1929–32.

(iii) *Aircraft manufacture*: During the war aircraft manufacture had been encouraged by the Department of Scientific and Industrial Research (DSIR) and this proved a basis upon which to build between 1919–39. Firms involved in building aircraft included Armstrong-Siddeley and Rolls-Royce; in 1933 some 30 000 were employed in this industry, which was further boosted by rearmament after 1937.

(iv) *The chemical industry*: Britain's chemical industry produced acids and sodas for use in the manufacture of paper, glass, textiles and soaps. During the war the DSIR promoted research into the development of chemicals and progress was made in the 1919–39 era.

A new range of products were manufactured including dyes, gases, plastic, celluloid (used in the growing film industry), drugs, explosives, cosmetics and fertilisers. In 1926 the huge Imperial Chemical Industries (ICI) was established when the firms of British Dyestuffs, Nobel Industries, United Alkali and Brunner-Mond merged together with combined capital assets over £50 million.

The first synthetic fibre, rayon, was also developed. This was made from cellulose which is derived from wood-pulp and sulphuric acid. Courtaulds and British Celanese manufactured most of Britain's rayon during this period, the former having large factories in Coventry and North Wales. Rayon was used in the production of stockings. In 1939 nylon was introduced on a commercial basis. Britain, however, did not progress as quickly as America, Germany and Japan in the production of synthetic fibres and her share of the world rayon market was a miserly 8 per cent.

28.4 WHAT DEVELOPMENTS TOOK PLACE IN BRITISH AGRICULTURE BETWEEN 1914 AND 1930?

(a) From the 1870s the British had grown used to cheap food coming in from abroad under the free-trade policy. In 1914 Britain imported 40 per cent of her meat, 80 per cent of her grain, 80 per cent of her fruit, and all of her sugar. During the war the dangers of depending on foreign food so much were made plain when the German 'U'-boats carried out attacks on the shipping convoys. Slowly the government intervened to encourage British farmers to produce more food.

(i) War Agricultural Committees were set up in each county in 1916 with the task of overseeing farming activity.

(ii) The *Cultivation Production Act (1917)* gave the Agricultural Committee the right to force a farmer to transform pasture land into arable use.

(iii) The *Corn Production Act (1917)* introduced a minimum wage for agricultural labourers and gave farmers a guaranteed price for the grain. This was quite effective with 3 million acres (1.2 million hectares) being converted from pasture to arable cultivation; as a result cereal and potato production increased by three-fifths at the expense of meat and dairy products.

(iv) The government helped farmers to introduce machinery and the *Women's Land Army* provided valuable labour. In addition, the DSIR sought to improve seeds and fertilisers.

(v) These measures represented the policy of 'economic collectivism' and they did help farming to make a vital contribution to the war effort. The precedent of state intervention into agriculture had been firmly set.

(b) As with industry, agriculture was a victim of the interwar slump. Initially there was a brief hint of optimism in 1920 with the passing of the *Agricultural Act*, which restated the policy of guaranteed prices for cereals and gave tenant farmers greater protection by granting them better security of tenure. The rot, however, soon set in.

(i) By 1921 prices on the world cereal market had fallen dramatically (in 1920 wheat was selling at 86s.4d. (£4.32) per quarter; in 1922 it fetched 40s.9d. (£2.04). At the same time the home market was threatened by cheap American grain imports as the prairie farmers had experienced a bumper harvest. Guaranteed minimum prices for the farmer were going to be too costly for a government under pressure to reduce its spending (see section 26.4) and it responded by rescinding the 1920 Act. (This saved the government an estimated £35 million in subsidies.)

(ii) The British farmers responded in a predictable manner; they changed back to pastoral farming, concentrating more on dairying and market gardening. The amount of land under arable acreage dropped by approximately 2,480,000 acres (one million hectares).

(iii) The *Agricultural Wages Board of 1924* brought back the regulations giving agricultural labourers a reasonable wage. In some counties wages went up to 30 shillings (£1.50) per week – still some way behind an industrial worker. Despite this measure a number of labourers left the countryside, some voluntarily, some as victims of dismissal. The numbers employed in farming dropped from 996 000 in 1921 to 711 000 in 1939. The workers who had lived in East Anglia and the southern counties probably found employment in the towns of the developing south.

(iv) Government intervention increased as the farming community continued to suffer. The *Sugar Subsidy Act of 1925* gave farmers money to grow sugar-beet. This was taken up, mainly in East Anglia, wtih 395 000 acres (160 000 hectares) being given over to this new crop. Sugar factories were then developed (for example, at Peterborough, Ely, Spalding, Kings Lynn and Bardney) to process the beet into sugar. The British Sugar Corporation (BSC) was established in 1936 to control and oversee sugar production.

(v) A number of other measures were designed to help farmers, for example, the *Agricultural Rate Act of 1928* freed farmers from having to pay rates on farm buildings and the *Agricultural Credit Act* provided loans for the improvement of farms and the purchase of machinery. During this period the number of tractors in use increased from 6000 in 1921 to 50 000 in 1939. The Agricultural Research Council of 1930 stimulated improvements in pesticides, fertilisers and seeds.

(vi) The slump of 1929–32 hit British farmers a crippling blow with prices falling and farmers going bankrupt. The government again intervened and passed a number of measures to help agriculture (see chapter 29).

28.5 CONCLUSION

The interwar years, therefore, present an image of decay in the old industries contrasted with steady growth in the new industries, particularly after 1934. The pattern for future trends was set with the British economy having to adapt to conditions in a world of rapidly developing technology. No longer could she sit back and rely on the strength of her basic industries.

QUESTIONS

1. **Objectives 1, 2 and 4**

Study the following material (*courtesy Radio Times Hulton*) and then answer the questions which follow:

Motor-car manufacturing

Historically the motor industry developed out of the cycle manufacturers of Coventry. By 1935 the industry had become centred in two main areas, where over 85% of its factories were situated. But during the 1930s Britain faced a critical problem of unemployment. The areas most affected were those that had produced the 'old'

staples of the export trade. The government developed a policy with the primary aim of directing the flow of industries into the depressed areas. The fact that these areas were unattractive to the new industries made it necessary for the government to find means to persuade them.

(Goodwin, *Structure of the Motor Vehicle Industry*)

(a) (i) What production technique is being used in the picture?
(1 mark)
(ii) Who first developed this method for cars? (1 mark)
(iii) What were the advantages of this type of production?
(2 marks)
(b) (i) Where were the 'two main areas' in which the motor industry had developed by 1935? (2 marks)
(ii) Name two of the 'old' staples of the export trade and the areas in which they were situated. (4 marks)
(c) (i) How did the government persuade the motor industry to move to the 'depressed areas'? (1 mark)
(ii) How successful were the government in achieving this aim? (2 marks)
(d) Describe the growth of other new industries in the twentieth century and explain the social and economic changes that resulted. (12 marks)
(Cambridge Board)

2. **Objectives 1 and 2**

(a) Describe the fortunes of the following old industries after the First World War:

● Shipbuilding.
● Cotton and wool. (12 marks)

(b) How far was their decline a direct result of the First World War? (8 marks)

3. **Objective 2**

(a) In what ways did the government interfere in agriculture during the First World War and why? (8 marks)
(b) What difficulties faced agriculture during the 1920s and what measures were taken to overcome them? (12 marks)

THE WALL STREET CRASH

AND THE DEPRESSION

OF THE THIRTIES

29.1 INTRODUCTION: THE INTERNATIONAL BACKGROUND

(a) America emerged from the First World War as a creditor nation, that is one which lent money to other countries. In particular she lent huge sums of money to help European countries recover from the war and this established a complicated interconnected network of 'international indebtedness. For example:

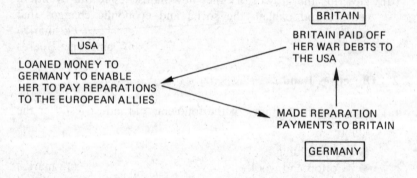

Such a network was operational only as long as America maintained her capacity to make the initial loans (between 1924 and 1928 she lent out an estimated 5.75 million dollars).

(b) Undermining the loans and repayments network was the fact that America chose to adopt a policy of protection and she imposed high tariffs on imported goods under the terms of the *Fordney-McCumber Act of 1922*. This made it difficult for countries to sell their products in America which would have earned them dollars to help repay the sums they had borrowed. The whole financial structure was, therefore, extremely delicate and had the world 'on the edge of a precipice'.

29.2 THE WALL STREET CRASH – THE COLLAPSE OF THE AMERICAN STOCK EXCHANGE

(a) What happened?

On Thursday 24 October 1929 the Wall Street Stock Exchange suffered, in the words of *The Times*, 'a Niagara of liquidation' as people rushed to sell stocks and shares. On this day alone 12 880 000 shares were sold at very low prices; such was the rate of selling that the recording ticker was three hours 'behind the trading'. Worse followed, despite the efforts of American bankers to instill calm – on Tuesday 29 October 1929 16 000 000 shares exchanged hands. People realised that share prices were collapsing and were desperate to sell – even at a loss.

(b) What brought about the crash?

The causes of the 'Crash' are not easy to analyse but the following factors all played a part:

- American society had been extremely prosperous during the 1920s. By this time the vast resources of America had been harnessed by industry and farming and an orgy of production ensued. Consumer goods such as cars, cookers, hoovers and radios were readily available. Many people bought these products on credit terms via hire-purchase agreements or loans. The profits of industrial firms increased rapidly, breaking all records. American industry was able to achieve this because she alone emerged from the war in a strong position. Whilst her European competitors struggled to recover from the war, America built up a huge domestic market. At the same time she insured herself from overseas competition by imposing tariffs.

- Within this atmosphere of 'boom' and 'prosperity' Americans began 'to play' the Stock Exchange, often borrowing money from banks to speculate in the purchasing and selling of shares. Banks, too, used people's savings to buy shares so as to increase their profits. Foreign countries such as Britain also joined in the spree and invested capital in the American economy. Prices on the Wall Street Stock Exchange rose to such high proportions that they bore no relation to the actual value of the shares; returns on shares then started to fall. Panic set in when it was realised that the high prices were artificial. Once this happened confidence quickly drained away and the crash occurred. Banks called in their loans but found that people had no money to pay them back and thus went out of business. Those that survived became much more stringent in their lending.

Much of the speculation was based on 'on the margin' buying whereby it was possible to put a deposit on the purchase of shares with a promise to pay off the remainder in the future – the whole system was vulnerable should confidence begin to decline.

Such was the rapid expansion of the American economy that by 1927 saturation point was soon reached. The demand started to fall away yet production continued at high levels. Over-production made it more difficult for firms to sell their products. Farming was also beginning to suffer in the late 1920s – and not just in America. The reason was over-production. American farmers went on producing vast amounts of grain and cotton which brought a fall in agricultural prices and a slowing down of the American economy in general. Despite this, speculation on the Stock Exchange continued – until eventually the crash occurred.

(c) How did the Wall Street Crash affect the rest of the world?

● In America firms became bankrupt overnight, production declined and mass unemployment set in (12 million by 1932). The Smoot-Hawley tariff raised customs duties further and sparked off retaliatory increases across the world, thereby damaging prospects for world trade further.

● The collapse of the American economy reverberated across the world because of the web of international indebtedness that had built up in the twenties. From 1928 America had been reducing the amount of money she lent to foreign countries and now **all** loans were stopped. This in turn meant that Germany could not make her reparation payments and Britain could not pay off her war debts.

● British and foreign financiers also lost money directly in the crash. They had been lured into speculating capital in the 1920s – but now this capital was gone at a time when it was desperately needed at home. 'The speculative mania diverted capital from urgent and serious purposes' (*The Times*).

- Shrinking world trade led to widespread unemployment in Europe bringing down prices as manfacturers competed for business. Paradoxically, the standard of living did not fall because lower price levels were now operating.
- Countries whose economies were based on primary products (such as food) found that their incomes were reduced and they no longer had the purchasing power to buy products from the industrial nations.

29.3 THE ECONOMIC AND POLITICAL CRISIS IN BRITAIN – 1931

The Wall Street Crash in often seen as the cause of 'the depression' in Britain, the event that heralded industrial decline and unemployment. In fact it is more accurate to see the crash as a symptom of depression. Industrial decline and unemployment were already in evidence, the crash just seemed to exacerbate the situation. Depression continued well into the thirties and 'recovery' was only marginal.

(a) How did the crisis originate?

(i) In May 1931 the biggest bank in Austria, the Credit-Austalt collapsed when France refused to give it loans to remain solvent. At the same time the French withdrew loans to German banks and the German government was unable to meet its reparation payments (remember that loans from America had already stopped). President Hoover sought a solution to the problem by imposing a twelve-month moratorium on reparation payments. This, however, was merely tinkering with a much deeper problem. The collapse of the Central European Banks now put pressure on London. Financiers who had lost money invested in Germany and Austria, now withdrew their gold from London, before any more catastrophes took place.

(ii) Britain's position, however, had also become very weak. With the growing numbers of unemployed (2.5 million in March 1931) the Labour Government was being forced to spend large amounts on dole payments – beyond, in fact, the 'takings' in insurance contributions. The Treasury was having to plough money into the unemployment fund and this meant that there was a shortfall in income over expenditure. The Labour Chancellor of the Exchequer, Philip Snowden, stated that the government had had to borrow £70 million to cover unemployment benefits. He was of the opinion that in 1931 Britain should balance the budget between income and expenditure, otherwise foreign investors would lose all confidence in the British economy and would withdraw funds from London.

(b) The May Committee

In February an Economy Committee was established by Snowden. Its brief was to examine the present financial situation and suggest remedies to the problems. The Committee was under the chairmanship of Sir George May.

During July 1931 the withdrawal of money from London continued giving bankers cause for great concern. A bank loan of £50 million was obtained from Paris and the Federal Reserve Bank of New York to cover the money being withdrawn from London. On 31 July 1931 the May Committee published its report which shocked the nation. It forecasted a budget deficit of £120 million in the financial year 1931–2 (it actually turned out to be £170 million) and proposed a number of economies which amounted to £96.5 million. The full proposals were:

		£'000
Reduction in	Armed Services	2 724
pay of	Police	925
	Teachers	13 150
Savings to	Armed Forces Pensions	190
be made in	Civil Services Gratuities	167
	Defence Budget	954
	Road Building	7 883
	Agricultural Grants	1 053
	Colonial Grants	625
	Unemployment Benefit	66 500
	Health Insurance	1 000
	Other Items	1 329

The Times agreed with the May Report, expressing the opinion that the budget had to be balanced 'at all costs' and that sacrifices 'all round [were] necessary to meet a national emergency'.

(c) The Formation of the National Government

(i) The Labour Prime Minister, Ramsay MacDonald, issued the report to his Cabinet with the instruction that it would be discussed after the summer recess. The MPs duly left London to enjoy their holidays almost in ignorant bliss. Meanwhile, after a brief lull, the pressure on the Bank of England continued. On 7 August 1931 the Bank's Deputy Governor informed Snowden that the situation was becoming 'more serious by the day and immediate action was needed from the Government . . . otherwise bankruptcy would become a reality'. The Cabinet was hastily called back to London to discuss May's proposals. Reductions in unemployment benefits aroused bitter arguments – how could a Labour Government sanction a measure which would hit at the very people who had put it into power? The difficulty now, however, was that the French and American banks were refusing to advance a further loan of £80 million unless the government reduced its expenditure. The Cabinet was split with 11 in favour of the cuts and 8 against.

(ii) On 24 August MacDonald went to see King George V, ostensibly to inform him that the Labour Government could no longer continue in office. What followed, however, was a day of frantic meetings between the King and the other party leaders, Stanley Baldwin (Conservative) and Sir Herbert Samuel (Liberal). The outcome was that MacDonald resigned the Labour Ministry and became the leader of a new National Government which was established for 'the maintenance of confidence' and with the 'sole purpose of meeting the present financial emergency'. The solution of a National Government had been mooted for some time and it is possible that Herbert Samuel convinced the King that it was the right thing to do.

(iii) The outcry against MacDonald from his colleagues in the Labour Party was loud and vociferous. He was judged as a turncoat, a man who had betrayed his class; he was expelled from the Labour Party and was the subject of bitter attack from the TUC. In his defence it must be stated that MacDonald had a very difficult decision to make, and in the end he took the course of action he believed best for the country. A 'National Cabinet' would give foreign countries the impression that Britain was prepared to tackle her problems as 'one' and this would restore confidence in the British banking system. It is also clear that the King handled the situation with great skill and continually boosted MacDonald's ego by declaring that he was 'the man for the job'. MacDonald's most recent biographer, David Marquand, is convinced that the King's 'gruff exhortations had a special resonance [and were] couched . . . in terms to which MacDonald was . . . likely to respond, Patriotism; duty; self-respect'. As for Baldwin, he readily agreed to serve under MacDonald. He had initially been against a National Government but he had now changed his mind. Did he sense that the Tories would enhance their position in the minds of the electorate by helping 'to solve' the problems which had been the 'fault of a Labour Government? In fact the crisis was probably beyond the ability of any government to control – the world economy had behaved like 'an unpredictable drunkard'.

(d) The 'National Cabinet' was made up of the following men:

Labour – Ramsay MacDonald PM; Philip Snowden (Chancellor of the Exchequer); Lord Sankey (Lord Chancellor); J. H. Thomas (Minister for the Dominions and Colonies).
Conservatives – Baldwin (Lord Privy Seal); Neville Chamberlain (Health); Samuel Hoare (Trade).
Liberals – Sir Herbert Samuel (Home Secretary); Earl Reading (Foreign Secretary).

There were a further 18 ministers who were not given Cabinet status, 9 of whom were Conservatives, 6 Liberal and 3 Labour. Thus the official Labour Party and TUC announced that they would have nothing to do with the National Government.

29.4 WHAT IMMEDIATE STEPS WERE TAKEN BY THE NATIONAL GOVERNMENT TO DEAL WITH THE CRISIS?

(a) Snowden's Budget 10 September 1931

The formation of the National Government was sufficient to convince the New York and Paris bankers that it was now safe to advance the loans of £80 million mentioned previously. On 10 September Snowden introduced an Emergency Budget which included the following measures:

- Increase in indirect taxation – beer was put up by 1*d*. (0.4p) a pint, tobacco up by 8*d*. (3.4p) to 9*s*.6*d*. per pound (48p), petrol up by 2*d*. (0.8p) a gallon and an increase in the entertainment tax.
- Direct taxation increased – Income Tax rose from 4*s*.6*d*. (22.5p) in the £ to 5*s*. (25p) in the £. Surtax increased by 10 per cent.
- Unemployment Benefit was reduced by 10 per cent (saving £14 million) and was only payable for 26 weeks. After this the Means Test would be applied.
- Salary cuts were suffered by the armed services (10 per cent), the police (ten per cent), teachers (15 per cent) and MPs – saving £56 million in all.

Snowden made no apologies for the cuts, stating that the nation had to 'face the situation seriously'. Keesing's Contemporary Archive reporting the Budget speech said that Snowden informed the House that there was to be no more borrowing to prop up the Unemployment Fund and that he had used the strategy of combining expenditure cuts with increased taxation in order to balance the budget.

(b) The bank rate was increased from 4.5 per cent to 6 per cent making it more expensive to borrow money.

(c) These measures had little effect; the pressure on the Bank of England continued. On 15 September 1931 there was a naval mutiny at Invergordon, when sailors protested about the cut in their salaries. This soon blew over but it had an adverse effect in that a number of foreign countries actually viewed it as a prelude to a 'revolution'. The result was a further loss of confidence and the withdrawal of yet more money from London (to the tune of £33 million between 16 and 18 September). On 20 September 1931 the dramatic announcement came that Britain was suspending the export of gold: the Gold Standard had been abandoned temporarily it was hoped.

The Bank of England would no longer sell gold at a fixed price. The reasons given were that Britain could no longer afford the drains on her gold reserves. She still had reserves of £130 million which ought to be maintained for the good of the nation. As if to placate the public, the government stated that the decision had been taken with 'the greatest reluctance' and that the 'resources of this country are enormous . . . and the present difficulties will prove only temporary'. This, however, was not to be the case – the difficulties continued throughout the thirties. The immediate effect of coming off the Gold Standard was to devalue the pound by 25 per cent. The exchange rate was now 3.40 dollars as opposed to 4.86 to the pound, which in effect would make British exports cheaper to purchase in the international markets.

(d) It was now decided to hold an election to give the National Goverment a 'doctor's mandate' to tackle the problems created by the depression. Each party issued its own manifesto which was countersigned by MacDonald. The Prime Minster was given a rough ride in defending his seat at Seaham, where he was continuously challenged to justify the cuts in unemployment benefits. The result of the General Election held on 27 October 1931 was:

National Government	554 seats
Labour	52 seats
Independent Liberals (Lloyd George)	4 seats

Out of the National Government's seats 473 were Conservative members. Although MacDonald remained as the Prime Minister the new government was in truth a Conservative ministry; The Labour Party was left in ruins, the electorate's scapegoat for the financial crisis of 1931.

29.5 WHICH AREAS OF BRITAIN WERE HIT MOST BADLY BY THE DEPRESSION AND WHY?

(a) The most seriously affected areas were those where the old staple industries dominated – cotton, textiles, shipbuilding, coal-mining, iron and steel manufacture. These industries were developed during the nineteenth century and were based on the coalfields. Thus the areas left reeling from depression were – Clydeside, Tyneside, Cumbria, south-east Lancashire, Ulster and South Wales. These areas suffered the highest rates of unemployment and distress – why?

- There were no alternative forms of employment in these areas – all the industrial eggs were in one basket.
- The basic industries had been slipping since the 1880s and their decline was hastened by a loss of export markets in the First World War. The depression merely intensified a long-term trend in these industries (see chapter 26).

(b)

(i) In contrast, the Midlands, South and South-East England suffered far less – in fact they enjoyed a degree of prosperity after 1934. These were the areas where the 'new' industries were being established, and even though Britain was slower to develop them than her competitors, they still made their mark (see chapter 28).

(ii) These industries suffered a setback at the height of the depression between 1931 and 1933 but then continued to grow. As prices were lower, the people in these areas were able to enjoy a higher standard of living. Food was cheaper and therefore people were able to spend more on 'luxuries' such as cars, vacuum sweepers, etc. This in turn stimulated demand for these products and created jobs. Towns which grew during this period included Slough, Reading, Oxford, Luton and Dagenham.

29.6 WHAT LONG-TERM MEASURES DID THE NATIONAL GOVERNMENT ADOPT TO ALLEVIATE THE EFFECTS OF THE DEPRESSION?

(a) A return to protection

Immediately after the General Election of October 1931, the National Government set about putting the 'doctor's mandate' into operation. The immediate issue was that of tariffs; Britain was the only major industrial country still pursuing a free-trade policy.

The mere thought of tariffs was anathema to men like Snowden and Samuel but, as the Conservatives now pulled the strings within the National Government, a return to protection was virtually inevitable. Tariffs were reintroduced through a series of measures:

(i) As an interim measure, on 16 November 1931 the *Abnormal Importation Act* was passed. It empowered the Board of Trade to charge customs duties of up to 100 per cent on any foreign manufactured products which were entering Britain in very large (abnormal) quantities. The object of this was to discourage foreign countries dumping goods on the British Market.

(ii)   In December 1931 legislation was passed which allowed customs duties to be put on fruit and vegetables (the *Horticultural Products Act*).

(iii)   In February 1932 the *Import Duties Act* was passed, the work of Neville Chamberlain, the new Chancellor of the Exchequer. It stated that:

- A customs duty of 10 per cent would be charged on most foreign goods.
- No duties would be charged on Empire products for the time being, but discussions were to take place in Ottawa.
- There was to be an Import Duties Advisory Committee to investigate the need of further modifications to these measures. The result was an increase in duties – up to one-third on some goods.

(iv)   In July 1932 the Dominion countries met a British delegation at Ottawa to discuss tariff reform. The Conference turned out to be a frustrating experience for the British, who found the Canadians and Australians, in particular, tough to bargain with. Eventually the *Ottawa Agreements*, which embodied the concept of 'imperial preference', were signed, but Britain had been out-bargained. The measures implemented were:

- A promise by Britain that she would keep her duties on foreign goods until 1937 at least.
- American and European grain to be charged higher duties when entering Britain.
- Four-fifths of the products entering Britain from Empire countries would not be subject to tariffs (imperial preference).
- The Dominions would keep tariffs on British goods at a moderate level.

The Ottawa Conference left a nasty taste in the mouth for many of the British delegates. The hard bargaining of the Dominions showed that, Empire or no Empire, during a depression it was every man for himself.

(v)   Britain also made a number of bilateral trading agreements with other countries, which usually established quotas and tariffs.

(b) Financial measures

(i) Chamberlain's budget of April 1932 was important in that it enabled the government to borrow £150 million to establish an Exchange Equalisation Fund which would be used in an emergency should there be a run on the pound. This would have the effect of keeping the exchange rate steady. In time the amount in the fund was raised to £350 million. Chamberlain commented that the income from tariffs would help to balance the nation's budget, but he felt that 'austerity' was still required and as such no concessions were introduced.

(ii) The Government also brought down the bank rate from 6 per cent to 2 per cent in June 1932. The theory behind this was that cheaper loans would stimulate the growth of industry. This move was more appropriate to the new industries of the South than to the decaying basic industries.

(c) Government assistance to industry and agriculture

(i) *Marketing boards and aid to farmers*

Under the *Agricultural Marketing Act*, from 1931 onwards a number of marketing boards were introduced for a range of agricultural products, for example, milk, hops and potatoes. With milk, the Milk Marketing Board (formed in 1933) paid farmers a 'stable' price and controlled the marketing of dairy products. The overall effect was to subsidise the farmer, guaranteeing a minimum price.

Subsidies were also given to farmers to grow cereal crops and sugar-beet. Farmers were given an acreage allocation which they were not allowed to increase without the permission of the Ministry of Agriculture. This prevented over-production which would have resulted in low prices. The *Wheat Quota Act* of 1932 gave farmers a guaranteed price of 10 shillings (50p) per hundredweight (51 kg).

The overall effect of these measures was to bolster up agriculture and regulate production. Between 1931 and 1937 agricultural output increased by 16 per cent and a steady recovery was ensured. There was also a tendency towards mechanisation on the farms with more tractors being used.

(ii)   *Subsidies to the shipbuilding industry*

In 1934 the government passed the *North Atlantic Shipping Act* which was designed to support the shipping service between Britain and America. Loans totalling £9.5 million were forwarded to build ships for this route; one ship which benefited was the *Queen Mary* launched in 1934.

The policy of loans was extended by the *British Shipping (Assistance) Act (1935)* which made money available for the building of new 'tramp' ships. A 'scrap and build' scheme was also introduced. Shipowners could obtain loans to build new ships if they undertook to scrap obsolete vessels as requested.

(d)   The rationalisation of industry

This involved the closing down of outdated factories operating with obsolete machinery, and amalgamating the remaining factories in search of greater efficiency. The government played a 'supervisory' role in this sphere, supporting the formation of the *National Shipbuilders' Security Ltd (1930)* and the *British Iron and Steel Federation (1934)*. It has been argued that it would have been more humanitarian to keep many firms open and reduce their profits as amalgamation inevitably meant redundancies and the creation of 'ghost towns' in some areas.

The National Shipbuilders' Security Ltd, set up to rationalise the industry, bought out a number of smaller yards, including Palmer's of Jarrow, and generally controlled what remained. The result of this was that Britain's shipbuilding capacity was drastically reduced.

In the final analysis, only the threat of war from 1937 brought back work to the shipyards when the government started to rearm. In 1939 almost one million tonnes of shipping was launched which represented something of a recovery compared with the doldrums of 1935.

The Iron and Steel Federation followed a similar policy. Works at Coatbridge and Dowlais were closed down and new works developed on the Jurassic limestone belt of Northamptonshire and Lincolnshire – Corby and Scunthorpe benefited here. The Federation also negotiated import quotas with Britain's competitors. Steel output increased from 7 million tons (6.88 million tonnes) (1933) to 13 million tons (12.79 million tonnes) (1937). This indeed was a measure of success, but at the cost of how much human misery? (see Section 29.7).

The Cotton Spinning Industry Act of 1936 enabled the cotton industry to be rationalised. Under this Act a Spindle Board paid mills compensation if they scrapped obsolete spindles; in all, six million (12 per cent) spindles were dismantled. In addition to this, 140 mills were bought and closed down by the Lancashire Cotton Corporation. The policy then was to work the remaining factories at profit.

A Coal Mines Reorganisation Commission was set up to amalgamate collieries and phase out unprofitable pits.

(e) The government and unemployment

(i) Unemployment proved to be one of the biggest headaches to the government. Before September 1931 unemployment benefit was payable at the rate of 17 shillings (85p) for a man, 9 shillings (45p) for his wife and 2 shillings (10p) for each child. After the Budget of September 1931 the rate was reduced to 15*s*.3*d*. (76p), 8 shillings (40p) and 2 shillings (10p) and was payable for a period fo 26 weeks only. (Note – The original rate was restored in April 1934.) After this a man had to apply for transitional benefit to be paid directly by the government (rather than out of the Insurance Fund) and had to undergo the hated Means Test to establish how much he should receive (see Section 29.7). Initially, transitional payments were decided by the local Public Assistance Committee (PAC).

(ii) In 1934 the *Unemployment Act* was passed to iron out the anomalies created by the PACs (some paid below the going rate and others even refused to administer the Means Test). The Act established the Unemployment Assistance Board, which had offices throughout the country. The UAB took over the duties of the PACs, and because it was centrally organised transitional payments were standardised – but at a lower rate than some unemployed men had been receiving before. There was a vitriolic debate in Parliament which ended with the *Standstill Act* being passed; this stated that all the unemployed were to receive payments to at least equal what they were getting prior to the UAB. The UAB also had the power to initiate training and welfare schemes but little was achieved on this front.

(iii) Also in 1934 came the *Special Areas Act*. A series of hunger marches organised by the Communist National Unemployed Workers' Movement galvanised the government into action. Investigators were despatched to the distressed areas of the north and their report revealed their miserable conditions. The

568

Act introduced two commissioners (one for England and Wales, the other for Scotland) who were given a derisory £2 million to spend in improving employment prospects in the following areas – Tyneside, Cumbria, South Wales and Scot-

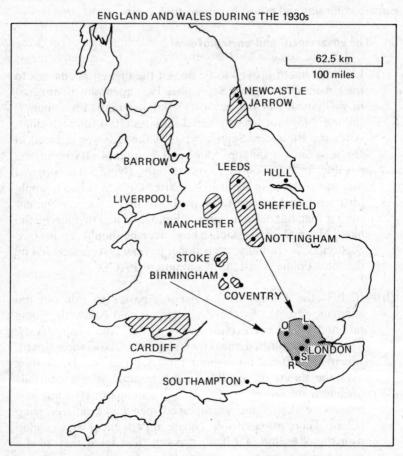

ENGLAND AND WALES DURING THE 1930s

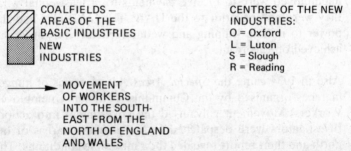

COALFIELDS –
AREAS OF THE
BASIC INDUSTRIES

NEW
INDUSTRIES

CENTRES OF THE NEW
INDUSTRIES:
O = Oxford
L = Luton
S = Slough
R = Reading

MOVEMENT
OF WORKERS
INTO THE SOUTH-
EAST FROM THE
NORTH OF ENGLAND
AND WALES

land. They achieved little as many of their proposals were rejected by the government. Few firms wanted to locate new factories in areas of squalor. Only in 1937 when the government offered tax allowance incentives did the position improve. Part of the Act was to attempt to transfer labour away from the distressed areas to the South where more work was available. The most successful move here was the relocation of Scottish steelworkers in Corby. Overall the tactic of moving labour did not work. Though it reduced the unemployment figures in the distressed areas it split up families and helped to destroy whole communities. Those who remained, tended to be in their forties, and the areas were drained of young talent.

29.7 WHAT WERE THE SOCIAL EFFECTS OF LONG-TERM UNEMPLOYMENT?

(a) For those workers in the depressed areas unemployment was long term; there was little hope of finding work, particularly for the middle-aged. Consequently there was an atmosphere of despair, misery and humiliation. Areas such as Tyneside, South Wales, Clydeside, Lancashire, Cumbria and Ulster became industrial morgues, smelling of decay and desolation. The conditions in these areas was captured by the literature of the time in works such as *The Road To Wigan Pier* (George Orwell), *Love on the Dole* (Walter Greenwood) and *English Journey* (J. B. Priestley).

(b) The humiliation of unemployment was deepened by the Means Test which was bitterly resented. After 26 weeks out of work the test was applied. The amount of benefit entitlement of a family would be reduced if there was other income available. Thus a pension or savings would result in a cut in benefit payments. If younger members of the family had a job their income was set against the amount of benefit payable. The Means Test was hated as:

● It meant families were the victims of incessant prying by officials from the UAB.
● Some unemployed had actually paid insurance contributions since 1911 – but this counted for nothing if you had been out of work for 26 weeks.
● The Means Test was often applied without tact or feeling.
● It could result in the breakup of the traditional extended family as the younger members who were in work often moved away from the area so that the benefit payments would not be reduced.

Unemployment figures (by regions)
(Percentage of insured workers)

Region	1929	1932	1937	Type of industry
London & South-East	5.6	13.7	6.4	New
South-West	8.1	17.1	7.8	New
Midlands	9.3	20.1	7.2	New
North of England	13.5	27.1	13.8	Staples
Wales	19.3	36.5	22.3	Staples
Scotland	12.1	27.7	15.9	Staples
Northern Ireland	15.1	27.2	23.6	Staples

Unemployment in selected towns in 1934

Town	% Unemployed	Region	Main industries
Jarrow	67.8	North of England	Shipbuilding
Merthyr	61.9	Wales	Coal, iron & steel
Gateshead	44.2	North of England	Shipbuilding
Luton	7.7	South-East	New industries
Watford	7.0	South-East	New industries
London	8.6	South-East	New industries

(c) The feelings of the unemployed were often vented in hunger marches, the most famous of which was the *Jarrow March in 1936*. Since the mid nineteenth century Jarrow had been dominated by Palmer's shipyard, which provided the town with work – at its zenith 10 000 men were employed. The yard felt the pinch of depression after the First World War and by 1932 the order books were empty. In 1934 the National Shipbuilding Security Ltd closed down Palmer's yard, putting three-quarters of the Jarrow labour force on the dole. Jarrow's Labour MP 'Red' Ellen Wilkinson was moved to write an article called 'The Town that was Murdered' and she was instrumental in organising the Jarrow March. Two hundred of the town's unemployed walked to London, a distance of 291 miles (466 km), to present a petition to Parliament, hoping something would be done to improve the situation. The march was widely reported, particularly in the *Daily Herald* and gained a good deal of public sympathy. Some of the marchers are still alive and one of their lasting memories of the march is that as they neared London they noticed 'the prosperity . . . apparent on every side'. The marchers drew a negative response from the government, being informed that they should return and seek work for themselves. There was a touch of irony here as Jarrow had tried to secure the opening of a light-steel industry in the town – only to be thwarted by the Iron and Steel Federation who rejected the idea.

29.8 HOW PROGRESSIVE WERE GOVERNMENT POLICIES AND WERE THEY SUCCESSFUL IN BRINGING A RECOVERY?

(a) Initially the government adopted policies which were orthodox and cautious. In 1931 traditional theories were applied to the financial crisis:

- Balancing the budget.
- Cutting public expenditure.
- Attempting to preserve London's 'role' in the international money market.

(b) From 1932 onwards there was a little more imagination shown and attitudes began to change in that the state became more directly involved in industry. A number of Committees were set up to study the economy and the concept of a planned economy with government and private enterprise began to emerge. Symbolic in this was the Political and Economic Planning Group (PEP) which issued a number of discussion documents during the 1930s.

(c) The success of government policies in the thirties is debatable. There was a measure of recovery in that:

- Unemployment fell from 2.7 million in 1931 to 1.4 million in 1937.
- New industries continued to grow – industrial production in 1937 was 25 per cent up on 1929.
- The budget was balanced.
- Agriculture was stabilised.
- The low bank rate stimulated a house-buying boom.

Also the cost of living came down, but part of the reason for this was that imports were cheaper due to a fall in world prices rather than by government action. In the final analysis, however, it must be pointed out that long-term unemployment in the depressed areas was not conquered by the government, and that it was only rearmament and the Second World War that got the nation back to work. The government was too cautious, preferring to make modifications to the existing economic framework rather than instituting bold initiatives. A. J. P. Taylor attributes any recovery to 'increased consumption' by the individuals in work who took advantage of the lower prices to spend their money raising their living standards; this in turn stimulated production in the light industries. However, we should bear in mind David Thomson's assessment when he states that the depression can 'be seen as largely . . . the result of world tendencies . . . the wisdom or folly of the policies which Governments adopt must be judged in awareness of this fact'.

29.9 WHAT ALTERNATIVE THEORIES TO COMBAT THE DEPRESSION WERE SUGGESTED AT THE TIME?

(a) In 1930 Oswald Mosley presented a 'Memorandum' to the Prime Minister, Ramsay MacDonald, in which he advocated widescale government spending to provide employment. His ideas were well thought out and also included earlier retirement as a means to providing jobs for the young people of the nation. His ideas were discussed at Cabinet level but seen as too radical, and rejected. Mosley resigned from the Labour Party and set up the Fascist party in Britain.

(b) The leader of the Transport and General Workers' Union, Ernest Bevin, also published proposals for dealing with the depression. These included;

● Raising the school leaving age to 16.
● A reduction in the working week.
● Higher pensions.
● Retirement at 60 (as opposed to 65).

Bevin put these ideas in an article 'My Plan for 2 Million Workers' (1933). He also wanted to see the unemployed put to work improving Britain's infrastructure (housing, water-supply, etc.). At the time, however, his ideas were rejected by the National Government as they would have involved massive Treasury spending.

(c) The most widely-publicised alternative policy for fighting the depression was that of the economist John Maynard Keynes (1883–1946). In 1936 he published *The General Theory of Employment: Interest and Money*. His ideas were completely the opposite to the traditional policies being followed by the government of the day. Keynes wanted public spending to increase, and saw large-scale public works as the antidote to depression and unemployment. He was advocating full-scale government interference with the economy in terms of planning and direction. The ideas were too revolutionary and bold and were not accepted in the thirties. Keynes, however, pushed his ideas hard, and was totally opposed to the reduction of government spending: he called the May Report 'the most foolish document I have ever had the misfortune to read'

29.10 CONCLUSION

The following points are worth emphasising:

- The thirties had a double-edged picture of long-term depression in the basic industries of the north and prosperity in the new industries of the south.
- Although events showed the government to be somewhat impotent in dealing with depression, lessons were learned. For example, the planned economy became reality in the later 1940s, 1950s and 1960s, with governments following Keynsian policies of public spending and full employment. Such policies were being formulated, if not accepted, during the depression. Labour's victory in the 1945 General Election was in many ways a throw-back to the thirties; memories of the depression were still present.
- Finally, the depression had been tackled by individual governments each applying their own remedies. Apart from the League of Nation's World Economic Conference of 1935, there was virtually no international co-operation to deal with the depression. It would appear that a lesson was learned from this as since 1945 there has been an increasing tendency for governments to co-operate in economic affairs.

QUESTIONS

1. **Objectives 1 and 2**

(a) Assess the relative importance of the following causal factors of
the depression:

- The effects of the First World War.
- The collapse of world primary produce prices.
- International indebtedness.
- The Wall Street Crash.

(b) Which of these causal factors were

(i)   long-term,
(ii) short-term?

(c) How far do the causal factors interlink?

(Total = 20 marks)

2. **Objectives 1, 2 and 4**

Study the sources below and then answer the questions:

Source A

THE CRISIS

HIS MAJESTY'S RETURN

A LONG CABINET

MEETING

NO DECISION

The Times 24 August 1931

Source B

A NATIONAL CABINET

MR. MACDONALD GOES ON

ALL PARTIES TO SERVE

ONE PURPOSE ONLY

MAINTENANCE OF CONFIDENCE

The Times 25 August 1931

Source C

'There is no doubt that, for some time past, we have been living above our means' (Philip Snowden's Budget Speech, 10 September 1931).

(a) Study Source A.

　(i)　What was 'the crisis'?
　(ii)　Why was there a long cabinet meeting?　　　(5 marks)

(b)   Study Source B

   (i)   What was the 'National Cabinet'?
   (ii) Why was the 'maintenance of confidence' needed?

(4 marks)

(c)   Study Source C.

   How did Snowden's Budget attempt to rectify the situation suggested by this quotation?   (5 marks)

(d)   Ramsay MacDonald has been accused of 'betraying the Labour Party' in 1931. Do you agree with this analysis? Give your reasons.   (6 marks)

3.   **Objectives 1 and 2**

(a)   How did the National Government respond to the depression after 1932?   (10 marks)

(b)   How successful were the policies adopted?   (4 marks)

(c)   'The situation was so desperate the Government had no real alternative but to adopt the measures they did'. How far do you agree? Give your reasons.   (6 marks)

4.   **Objective 3**

As a car-assembly worker in Oxford in 1935 describe:

(a)   (i)   your working conditions
      (ii) your standard of living

(b)   Why do you consider yourself to be fortunate to be living in Oxford at this time?

(Total = 20 marks)

5.   **Objective 3**

As an unemployed steel worker in South Wales in 1935 describe your attitude towards the following:

(a)   The Means Test.
(b)   The Special Areas Act.
(c)   Your hopes for the future.

You should base your answer on accurate historical knowledge.

(Total = 20 marks)

THE HOME FRONT DURING
THE SECOND WORLD WAR
1939–45

30.1 INTRODUCTION

The Second World War was a total war which demanded the effort of
the whole nation to ensure survival and, ultimately, victory. It was
also a war where the state necessarily became involved in directing
the economy and organising society: in the words of David Thomson
it produced 'a sense of national purpose', which was used to pursue
'social justice' after 1945. This chapter will concentrate on the Home
Front and the social and economic impact the war had on Britain.

30.2 THE BLITZ AND EVACUATION 1939–41

(a) Unlike the First World War, the civilian population of Britain
was directly threatened by the German Luftwaffe. Cinema audiences
had already witnessed the terrible effects of bombing when the attack
on Guernica (1937) during the Spanish Civil War was reported on the
newsreels; the aeroplanes which did the damage were German. In
1937 the *Air Raid Precaution Act* was passed to make preparations
against such attacks and rearmament was started in earnest. By the
time war actually broke out buildings had been sandbagged, gas-
masks issued and air-raid shelters constructed (the government had
distributed 2.25 million Anderson shelters free of charge). Air Raid
Wardens were appointed to supervise specified areas during an
attack. Identity cards were issued to everyone and information
disseminated on coping with enemy raids. A blackout was imposed at
nights, even car headlights were not permitted. All this was part of
the organisation of Civil Defence which played a vital part during the
Blitz.

(b) After the initial period of the 'phoney war', British cities were under constant attack during the months from September 1940 to May 1941 – The Blitz. London, Plymouth, Coventry, Liverpool, Hull and Southampton were just some of the cities that suffered. An estimated 60 000 people were killed by enemy bombs, and three and a half million houses were badly damaged (or two in seven). People would search out the nearest shelter – in London the nearest underground station provided refuge. Raids were more intermittent after 1941 with retaliatory attacks on a few towns but in 1944 fear was put back into the civilian population when Hitler launched the V1 and V2 flying bombs ('doodle-bugs'). The South-East and London were within range of these weapons and 10 000 people lost their lives.

(c) Evacuation

(i) Since 1938 the government, in the shape of Sir John Anderson, had been laying plans to evacuate young children from the cities, in anticipation of enemy air raids. Parents were required to register with the Local Authority for evacuation to rural counties. Some 1.5 million children, parents and teachers were evacuated between 1 and 3 September 1939, and another 2 million people left the cities to stay with relatives. The evacuees were received at reception centres and then billeted out with local families; arrangements, however, did not always go smoothly. City schools were temporarily closed and one result of this was an increase in juvenile crime.

(ii) Unfortunately many evacuees could not settle in the country-side, and relationships were not always cordial. The country people were shocked at the obvious poverty and deprivation of the urban children, not to mention their bad manners. A Women's Institute publication *Town Children Through Country Eyes* (1940) commented that the condition of Manchester evacuees 'was appalling; clothing was dirty and footgear inadequate, the majority wearing old plimsolls or sandals'. There were also reports of children 'fouling' gardens, hair crawling with lice and bed-wetting.

(iii) When the expected air raids did not materialise in the early weeks of the war, there began a steady return to the cities. By December 1939 almost 1 million evacuees had returned home. Then, in 1940, the Blitz started, which caused another exodus from the cities. In 1944 there was another phase of evacuation following the 'doodle-bug' attacks.

(iv) The historian, Arthur Marwick, is of the opinion that one positive effect of evacuation was that it gave the sheltered rural middle class a deep culture-shock which motivated them to demand better social and environmental conditions for city children. On the other side of the coin, many evacuees came to appreciate the pleasures afforded by the countryside.

30.3 HOW WAS THE LABOUR FORCE MOBILISED?

(a)

(i) The government moved to mobilise the nation, a lesson learned from the First World War, which showed that state regulation was essential in a 'total' war. *The Emergency Powers Acts* (1939 and 1940) provided the government with complete authority to direct the lives of people in the interest of the war effort: in Attlee's words, the government 'demands complete control over persons and property'.

(ii) Initial measures included the introduction of conscription (compulsory military service) for men aged 18 to 40, during the summer of 1939, and a National Register was drawn up under the auspices of the *National Service (Armed Forces) Act*. In September 1939 a number of new government ministries were established, including – Food, Information, Home Security, Supply and Economic Warfare. It was clear by the spring of 1940 that the government was not moving quickly enough. Conscription was going ahead but food and wartime supplies were at dangerously low levels. On 10 May 1940, Neville Chamberlain resigned as Prime Minister, leaving the *Daily Express* to remark that history would give him 'the blame for our lack of war materials and equipment'. Chamberlain was replaced by Churchill's Coalition Government and from this point onwards the state began to organise with an energy hitherto unseen.

(b) On 14 may 1940 Anthony Eden, the newly-appointed Secretary of State for War, called upon all able-bodied men between 17 and 65 and not in the services, to join the Local Defence Volunteers – later to be renamed the Home Guard. Within 24 hours 25 000 men had enrolled, the speed of response being facilitated by the imminent invasion of Britain by Hitler's forces which would, in Churchill's words, 'only be held off by having large mobile forces in readiness'. During the period from May 1940 to December 1944 some 2 million men were given the necessary military training, including the use of fire-arms. At first there were not enough weapons to go round – it was not until 1943 that each man in the Home Guard was equipped with a rifle. This led to the image of a force armed with pitchforks, as presented in the television programme *Dad's Army*. The official duties of the Home Guard were:

● Observing and defending strategic points in the local area, such as roads and factories.
● Sabotaging enemy movements in the event of invasion.
● Attacking small enemy detachments.

As it turned out, the Home Guard was never needed, and when the allied forces had Hitler on the retreat in 1944, the organisation had served its purpose. It was disbanded on 31 December 1944.

(c)   Also in May 1940 Churchill made what proved to be a very astute move when he made Ernest Bevin the new Minister of Labour and National Service. This put Bevin in charge of putting Britain's manpower on a war footing. In many ways Bevin was the ideal choice – he was the leader of the TGWU and a man whom the labour force respected. He was also a man of extraordinary energy and Mark Stephens, in his book *Unskilled Labourer and World Statesmen*, claims that Bevin's achievements as Minister of Labour were 'awe-inspiring'. Judged against the measures listed below, it is difficult to disagree with this assessment:

● The Schedule of Reserved Occupations (first introduced in September 1939) was continued. Those men in vital jobs, for example, miners, agricultural workers, munition workers, boiler-makers and teachers, were not required to join the armed forces. The numbers in reserved occupations were skilfully managed and adjusted as needs required during the course of the war.
● During Bevin's 'reign' the number of workers in key industries was dramatically increased, for example, in the engineering and chemical industries the numbers rose from 3.1 million in June 1939 to 5.2 million in June 1943.
● In March 1941 the *Essential Work Order* was introduced, making it impossible for labour to leave those occupations considered

important for the war effort, for example, dockers. In return, workers received a guaranteed minimum wage.

● In December 1941 the Ministry of Labour introduced measures for the 'extended conscription on Man Power and Woman Power'. Men between the ages of 41 and 51 were now liable for call up. Single women between the ages of 19 and 30 were also called up. They were given the option of joining one of the armed forces (WRNS, WAAF or ATS), the Civil Defence, or factory work. Those choosing the latter were expected to go to any part of the country as required and became known as 'mobile women'. Married women were allowed to volunteer for the forces or employment. In addition, boys of 16 were permitted to volunteer for the Home Guard. These measures were required to secure 'the maximum national effort in the conduct of the war and in production'.

● In July 1943 women between the ages of 46 and 50 were conscripted into employment, the so called 'Grannies Call Up'. Bevin met a storm of criticism over this measure in the House of Commons, being accused of breaking up family life even further. The minister stuck to his guns so that virtually all people between the ages of 14 and 65 (or over) were doing 'their bit' towards the war effort. (In 1943 there was an estimated 23 million in full-time jobs, the Civil Defence and the armed forces.)

● During 1942 coal supplies were dwindling and production was down because of a lack of coal-miners. In October 1942 the *Daily Mail* warned 'it is coal or catastrophe for us, make no mistake'. Bevin announced that conscripts could go down the pits rather than fight. The response was terrible – only 1000 men opted for the mines in the first four months of the scheme! After this a ballot was organised – if a man's number came out of a box he was now told to go underground. Such recruits to the mining industry were nicknamed 'Bevin Boys' and they were the butt of considerable 'mickey-taking' from the regular miners. In the end there were 45 000 'Bevin Boys'.

● With agricultural workers being gradually filtered into the forces, the void was filled by members of the Women's Land Army. This organisation had been started as early as June 1939 but it flourished under Bevin. At its peak the WLA had 200 000 girls working on farms throughout the country.

● Women also did extremely important work in munition factories, working long hours and for lower wages than men. The average weekly wage for men in 1941 was £5 and for women £2.4s. (£2.20).

● The summit of Bevin's achievement was to be seen in the numbers in the armed forces. In 1940 there were 2.25 million in the services, in 1945 there were 4.7 million (which included half a million women).

(d) Why was Bevin so successful in mobilising the labour force?

Historians such as Norman Longmate point out that Bevin's organising and directing of British manpower towards the war effort was second only in achievement to that of Russia. There were a number of reasons for this:

● Bevin had a special relationship with the trade-union movement. He was from a working-class background himself and had risen to be the secretary of Britain's largest union, the TGWU. The direction of labour was generally accepted by the people (with a few exceptions) and there is little doubt that respect for Bevin was a factor in this. An example of this was the 'dilution of labour' where unskilled and semi-skilled men were allowed to do the jobs of skilled workers. This was always a touchy issue with trade unionists yet it was accepted during the Second World War.

● Bevin introduced measures to improve working conditions so that the bitter pill of direction was sweetened. For example, the *Catering Wages Act* of 1943 introduced the Catering Wages Commission to oversee working conditions and wages in hotels and restaurants. Bevin also insisted that factories had personnel officers, welfare officers and canteens, and inspectors were appointed to make sure that he was obeyed.

● Trade unions gained in strength and morale. There was full employment during the war and union membership increased from 6 million (1938) to 8 million (1944). Relationships between the unions and the government were generally excellent. Despite the fact that strikes were made illegal in 1940, there were a few disputes where men withdrew their labour. In theory they should have been prosecuted, but Bevin turned a blind eye in order to maintain harmonious relations. His tact was probably justified by the extenuating circumstances of a total war.

● Bevin also gained gratitude from the workers for getting the *Determination of Needs Act* passed in 1941. This abolished the hated means test; in future those needing National Assistance would undergo a *personal* means test with income from the other members of the family not being deducted from any award that was made.

● As the war progressed the belief developed that post-war reconstruction would be designed to benefit the working classes. Bevin fostered this belief and made his opinion known that social reforms after the war were essential. Again to quote Stephens 'not just a Minister of Labour, but [a] Minister for Labour'.

30.4 WHAT MEASURES WERE TAKEN TO OVERCOME THE SHORTAGE OF FOOD DURING THE WAR AND HOW SUCCESSFUL WERE THEY?

In 1939 about two-thirds of Britain's food was imported, and as an island it was easy for the German navy to block her supplies. The 'U-boats', in particular, sank many cargo vessels, and food was in short supply. The following measures were taken to overcome the problem:

(a) Rationing

(i) This was put into operation on 8 January 1940. It was organised by the Ministry of Food headed by Lord Woolton. Ration books were issued to each citizen. People had to register their name with one retailer from whom they obtained all their rationed food. When a purchase was made the equivalent cost in coupons was extracted from the book; once all the coupons were exhausted the ration quota had been used up.

(ii) In spring 1942 the rations consisted of 6p worth of meat per week (this worked out at about a pound in weight or 450 grams), bacon 4 ounces (100g), sugar 8 ounces (225g), cheese 3 ounces (75g), tea 2 ounces (50g), butter 2 ounces (50g), margarine 4 ounces (100g). The ration of preservatives amounted to one pound (450g) per month. In addition there was a 'points' system. Each person was allocated 16 points for a period of a month which could be spent on items such as tinned fruit, rice and tinned vegetables. Points could be spent at any shop, the snag being that the cost of food in points varied in accordance with supplies (the lower the stocks, the higher the price in points). About 4 ounces (100g) of sweets and chocolates per month could be obtained on the 'personal points' rations scheme. Bread, however, remained unrationed during the war; instead the extraction rate of wheat was raised to 85 per cent so that less grain was used to make flour. The only loaf made was called the 'national wheatmeal'.

(iii)   Rationing was complicated, particularly as the amounts rationed varied according to the supplies in stock. The Ministry of Food kept the public informed via leaflets, posters and the newspapers. However, the system did work. All citizens were able to maintain a balanced diet and no one starved. The poorer people actually benefited as now they could afford foods which had been too expensive before the war. Furthermore, mothers-to-be were entitled to additional milk and eggs, whilst young children were given free milk, orange juice and cod-liver oil. In point of fact the war-time rationing reduced malnutrition and made for a healthier population and rationing also kept the price of food down.

(b)   The Ministry of Food also organised a widespread publicity campaign giving suggestions for 'wartime recipes' and encouraged people to grow their own food to supplement their diet. 'Dig for Victory' and 'Grow Your Own' were just two of the catchphrases used by the Ministry's propaganda. Even the dry moat around the Tower of London was turned over to allotments! The Ministry also published leaflets giving free advice on how to cultivate a garden.

(c)   Another important part of the government's food policy was to encourage home farmers to produce more. From 1939 farmers could obtain a subsidy of £2 per acre to grow wheat; to do this, marginal land was brought into cultivation. The amount of land under arable use increased from 119 million acres (48 million hectares) to 180 million acres (72 million hectares); more machinery was introduced which increased efficiency (tractors increased from 60 000 to 190 000). Livestock farms, with the exception of dairying, declined a little as pasture land was being ploughed up for crops. Furthermore, farmers were given a guaranteed price for their crops. The effects of this were that the population was less dependent on imported food and British farms experienced a period of prosperity.

30.5   HOW WERE OTHER SHORTAGES OVERCOME?

Apart from food the other major commodity shortages were clothes, household goods and petrol. Measures had to be taken to combat this.

(a)   **Clothes** were rationed from May 1941 onwards. Textiles were in short supply as materials were in great demand for military uniforms and blankets, etc. A points system was adopted for the rationing of clothes. The government also introduce utility garments in order to save material and control prices. Clothes, blankets, sheets, etc. were made to 'basic' standards and a limited range of designs. The 'utility' scheme was also applied to furniture to save timber. All utility goods carried a mark 'CC41' so they could be distinguished. Without doubt the idea worked as clothes and furniture were kept to a reasonable price and ensured that there was 'the greatest possible production from limited resources' (Hugh Dalton, President of the Board of Trade). In addition, the population was asked to 'help themselves' by handing clothes down and producing home-made clothes.

(b)   Petrol was rationed immediately the war started, but as time progressed people were asked to lay up their cars to help the war effort (petrol and oil were imported and were needed for aircraft and military vehicles). The major car firms issued detailed instructions on how to put a vehicle into storage.

(c)   Why did the government control prices during the war?

The answer to this is that the government was afraid of runaway inflation which would have reduced the value of money and fired a demand for higher wages. This was achieved by subsidising farmers (so that they did not pass their increased production costs on to the consumer) and maintaining fares and rents at reasonable prices. The Utility Scheme also helped to keep prices down.

30.6   HOW DID THE GOVERNMENT FINANCE THE WAR-EFFORT?

The war was a great strain on Britain's financial resources; overall it has been estimated that each day of the war cost £15 million to finance, and this too at a time when Britain's earning power was reduced by the fact that she could not export so much as in peace-time. The money was obtained in a number of ways.

(a)

(i)   *By borrowing from abroad*

At the start of the war America supplied Britain with goods paid for with dollars. By early 1941 Britain's supply of dollars was almost drained and Churchill visited Washington to seek aid. As a result, in March 1941 President Roosevelt introduced the *Lend-Lease* programme. Under this, America supplied materials, weapons and equipment to Britain and by the end of the war she had loaned goods from America to the value of $27 million. There were, however, some disadvantages to the agreement, notably that Britain was not allowed to export goods made from lend-lease materials. As a result she lost vital markets which proved difficult to recover.

(ii) *Forced loans from the sterling area*

A number of countries who used sterling for their international currency (for example, India, Egypt, Argentina, Brazil) held credit accounts in London. These credit accounts consisted of money which Britain owed to them for various materials. However, Britain withheld payment so that the accounts became 'loans' from these countries, allowing her to fight the war 'with resources greater than her own' (Pollard).

(iii) *Selling of overseas investments*

As the war progressed Britain's exports steadily decreased whilst imports drastically increased. Prior to the war Britain had paid for her purchases via the proceeds of her exports – this was now proving not to be possible. The fact that the war effort was paramount is shown by the fact that the government sold off Britain's foreign investments to the tune of £1200 million. These assets were not retrievable and the loss of them was a serious blow to the economic strength of the nation.

(iv) *Income tax was raised*

This was raised from 42.5 pence in the pound (1940) to 50 pence in the pound (1941). Those in the high income bracket also had to pay surtax at 92.5 pence in the pound. From 1943 onwards income tax was deducted at source (Pay As You Earn), so that the money was available to the government more quickly. Prior to this a wage-earner paid his tax annually. The government also introduced an additional form of income tax called 'Post-war Credits'. A person could reclaim this money after the war by redeeming his credit vouchers. Indirect taxation was also increased. Heavy duties were put on alcohol, tobacco and cinema admission prices and 'Purchase Tax' was imposed on a number of consumer goods from 1940. This was similar to VAT and was payable on items such as clothing, toys and luxury goods. The result of this taxation policy was that Britain was able to cover about 55 per cent of the total cost of the war; proceeds from taxation increased from £920 million in the financial year of 1937–8 to £6179 million in 1944–5.

(v) *Internal borrowing*

Taking the war years as a whole, wages went up by approximately 18 per cent whilst prices were deliberately held steady by the government. People, therefore, had some money to spare – even with taxation at such a high level. The government instigated *National Savings Certificates* and *War Bonds*. People were willing to invest in them as interest was paid on the money they invested. In effect, the amounts invested in these schemes were used to help finance the war.

30.7 IN WHAT WAYS DID THE WAR BENEFIT BRITISH SOCIETY?

Industry was stimulated by the war and this in turn benefited British society:

(a) There was greater emphasis on scientific research which was carried out under the auspices of the Department of Scientific and Industrial Research (DSIR). This brought about advances in a number of industries including engineering, chemicals, agriculture, machine tools, drugs and aircraft production. In agriculture, new fertilisers were developed and the war 'forced' the perfection of Frank Whittle's jet engine which had been invented in 1929. Radio broadcasting made rapid strides and the technical knowledge from this was directed into work on television broadcasting after the war.

(b) New factories were built – often in the 'depressed' areas of the north and Scotland. This investment brought jobs and new expertise to these areas (which was carried on after the war).

(c) Furthermore the war brought a number of improvements to medicine. The Medical Research Council was able to acquire new knowledge about the nutritional value of food and this was very useful to the Ministry of Food in determining its rationing policy. Plastic surgery was developed by Sir Archibald MacIndoe who treated many badly-burned pilots, injured in the Battle of Britain. Progress too was made with administering blood transfusions. In 1928 Alexander Fleming had discovered the drug penicillin which combatted blood-poisoning. His work was developed by Ernest Chain and Howard Florey, but by 1939 no way had been discovered of mass-producing the drug. The war created an urgent need for penicillin, and eventually, in 1943, the American chemical industry developed the means of doing this. Penicillin has, however, benefited society world-wide.

30.8 HOW WAS CIVILIAN MORALE MAINTAINED DURING THE WAR?

(a) The government was only too well aware that high morale among the civilian population was essential to the success of the war. The Ministry of Information issued a host of leaflets and posters to the population, offering advice on a variety of subjects such as 'How to identify enemy aircraft'. Many posters carried catchy slogans designed to show that the country was united against the enemy – 'Let Us go Forward Together', 'Careless Talk Costs Lives' and 'Turn This Raw Material into War Material'.

All of this helped to keep people in good spirits. In fact the nation suffered the hardships of the war with remarkable steadfastness.

(b) Although first-class sport was seriously curtailed during the war, entertainment was available to the public:

- In 1940 the government provided finance for the *Council for the Encouragement of Music and the Arts* (CEMA) – later to become the Arts Council. CEMA supported the nation's orchestras and encouraged dramatic productions.
- Apart from the first fortnight, cinemas kept going during the war years, providing valuable escapism for up to 30 million people per week! The government also provided funds for film-making. Perhaps the most celebrated British film of the period was *Brief Encounter*, which starred Trevor Howard and Celia Johnson.
- BBC radio also played a vital role. Apart from the regular news bulletins, a number of variety programmes were broadcast, including Tommy Handley's ITMA.

● Linked to the radio and cinema there were a number of magazines and comics providing 'escapism'. These included *Radio Fun* and *Flix*.

● Ernest Bevin went out of his way to provide a cheerful atmosphere in factories, instituting 'Music While You Work' among a number of other measures (see Section 30.3(d)).

30.9 WHAT PLANS WERE LAID FOR RECONSTRUCTION?

(a) As early as 1941 a committee was instigated to study 'reconstruction problems' under the direction of the Labour minister, Arthur Greenwood. This committee commissioned Sir William Beveridge (a Liberal) to 'undertake a survey of the existing national schemes of social insurance and allied services . . . and to make recommendations'. Beveridge was a man of considerable ability and foresight and he carried out his task with vigour, presenting 'The Beveridge Report' to Parliament in December 1942. He emphasised the need to eradicate from life five major evils – **want**, **squalor**, **ignorance**, **disease** and **idleness**, suggesting the ways that this might be achieved by a government. Beveridge advocated a wide range of benefits:

● Unemployment pay as long as a man was without a job.
● Widows' and old age pensions.
● Sickness benefit, maternity and funeral grants.
● Family allowances.

All this would be financed by contributions from employees, employers and, in some instances, the state. All citizens would thus be given a minimum standard of living, yet the right of an individual to increase his 'cover' by taking out private insurance would be maintained. Inherent in Beveridge's proposals were the setting up of a National Health Service, policies for housing and town planning, improved education and a commitment to full employment.

(b) The reaction to the 'Report' among the public at large was one of enthusiasm; within twelve months over 500,000 copies had been sold. People came to view the report as the basis for life after the war had finished. Most Labour ministers were fully behind Beveridge, but Churchill adopted a rather indifferent attitude. He declared that the report did have merit but the public should not get carried away as the enemy had yet to be defeated. Historians, such as Marwick, see this indifference as a factor in Churchill's election defeat in 1945.

Other 'opposition' to the report at the time came from the doctors, who were not keen to be any part of a national scheme for a health service, as they felt that their autonomy would be threatened (see chapter 31). The armed forces learned of the report via the Army's education service, ABCA (Army Bureau of Current Affairs). Seminars were held to discuss the implications of the report and in them they saw some reason for the sacrifice they were making.

(c)   Even so, some socialists believed that the report was 'evolutionary' as opposed to 'revolutionary'. A. J. P. Taylor points out that Beveridge was merely reiterating what the Fabians had proposed before 1914. The *Daily Mirror* regarded Beveridge as merely the 'beginning of reconstruction, not the end'. However, a balanced view would be that the report was a 'breakthrough' in the sense that the benefits referred to in Section 30.9(a) were now regarded as a 'right' for all citizens. Attitudes had been redirected. The report also provided a base for the Labour Government (1945–51) to shape post-war society in Britain.

(d)   From 1943 the government began to plan for peace in earnest. Churchill appointed Lord Woolton as Minister of Reconstruction and then declared that he advocated a 'Four-Year Plan' for reconstruction. This was in reality a watered-down version of the Beveridge Report. It has been suggested that Churchill had been reluctant to give his full support to Beveridge for political reasons – Beveridge was a Liberal – and he wanted plans for social change to be seen to be originating from the Conservatives. Woolton soon introduced a plethora of committees in progress, and before the war was over legislation was on the Statute Book.

   (i)   The *Uthwatt Committee* and *Scott Report* put forward ideas on town and country planning, the most important being the reaffirmation of the 'Green Belt' to control the haphazard growth of suburbs.

  (ii)   In 1944 White Papers were brought out on 'Social Insurance' (Parts 1 and 2) 'Employment Policy' and a 'National Health Service'. By 1945 a Ministry of National Insurance had been set up with the aim of administering these proposals.

 (iii)   Legislation passed before the war ended included:

   ●   *Butler's Education Act 1944* (see chapter 18).

- *Town and Country Planning Act 1944* which gave consideration to the development of areas damaged by bombs and also enabled local authorities to clear slums.
- *Housing (Temporary Accommodation Act) 1944* which made £150 million available for the building of temporary houses to make good bomb damage.
- *Location of Industry Act 1945* which gave the government powers to regenerate employment prospects in the depressed areas of the basic industries. This involved encouraging firms to build new factories in these areas.

(e) Why was it considered important to plan 'post-war reconstruction'?

 (i) Perhaps, most importantly, the failures of the government after the First World War were still fresh in the memories of the citizens and politicians alike. Everyone was anxious that the same mistakes should not be repeated and this is illustrated by the fact that planning began at a very early stage.

 (ii) Many British workers had suffered from the depression in the thirties, and on top of this came the stress of fighting a total war. After such sacrifices the natural feeling was one of optimism – the future just had to be better.

(iii) The war had had the effect of dismantling 'class-barriers'. Everyone had to 'muck in', rich and poor alike. This somehow fused society into one and created a level of expectation, that is, that post-war society should have a reasonable standard of living and social justice. A mood of consensus and 'egalitarianism' was dominant. This mood was one reason why the electorate voted the Labour Party into power in the 1945 election (see chapter 31).

30.10 HOW MUCH DAMAGE HAD THE WAR CAUSED?

(a) In 1945 Britain was in a state of exhaustion and it was clear that victory had only been gained at a considerable cost to the nation:

- The war left Britain in debt and with her gold resources reduced. She had also sold off almost one-third of her overseas investments. Furthermore, the British economy had been bled almost to the point of exhaustion.

- Export markets had been lost. Over 400 000 men had been lost in the war.
- Enemy air raids had caused extensive damage to Britain's cities, ports and factories. The housing stock had been chronically depleted.
- A large hole had been made in the size of Britain's merchant fleet. Tonnage was reduced from 18 million tons (17.7 tonnes) to 13 million tons (12.8 million tonnes).
- Very little had been done to improve the railway rolling-stock or factory plants during the war; much of it was now worn out or outmoded. A vast amount of investment was needed to update machinery.

(b) There were, however, some positive effects:

- Society had been united and victory was a morale-booster, giving the nation the stamina to cope with the problem of the post-war world.
- Full employment during the war had created a skilled labour force, 20 per cent larger in size than in 1939.
- Agriculture had made rapid strides and was thoroughly up-to-date.
- Technological progress made in the war could be transferred into peace-time (for example, drugs and aircraft).

30.11 CONCLUSION

Probably the main impact of the war was to involve the government necessarily in the direction of people's lives. In doing so, it had convinced people of the need for a mixed economy which had a considerable degree of planning. The war also convinced the nation of the desirability of full employment and the ideas of Keynes came to be recognised as the way forward into the future. Keynesian ideas dominated government thinking until 1979. The war had, in fact, set the stage for the Labour Party to play a central role in the immediate post-war domestic world. In the words of Pauline Gregg: 'it came into a legacy of controls, direction of labour, rationing and savings campaigns that had made familiar the idea of planning'.

QUESTIONS

1. Objectives 1 and 2

'Bevin's achievements as Minister of Labour and National Service
. . . amount[ed] to the mobilisation and demobilisation of the entire
nation, and a permanent change in relationship of labour to the state'
(Mark Stephens).

(a) Describe the main ways in which the nation was 'mobilised' for
war.   (10 marks)
(b) Explain how the relationship of 'labour to the state' changed
during the war.   (5 marks)
(c) 'Bevin's background helped to make him successful as Minister
of Labour'. How far do you agree? Explain your answer.
(5 marks)

2. Objective 4

Study the sources below and then answer the questions:

Source A   (courtesy BBC Hulton Picture Library)

Source B   (courtesy London Express News and Features Service)

"Now I want you to promise me you're all going to be really *good* little evacuees and not worry his Lordship."

Source C *(courtesy Imperial War Museum)*

Source D

'I was an evacuee for six weeks . . . The main problem between the evacuees and the hosts seems to be the difficulty of adapting the one to the other' (17-year-old evacuee).

(a) Why was Source C published?
(b) In what ways does Source D appear to support Source B?
(c) How far does Source A support Sources B and D?
(d) 'The only reliable source of the four is Source A. This is because it is a photograph'. Evaluate the sources against this statement.
(e) 'There is a rich selection of sources about the Second World War and this, therefore, makes the historian's task very easy when writing about this topic'. Do you agree or disagree? Explain.

(Total = 25 marks)

3. Objectives 1 and 2

'The main concern of the men in the forces is what they are coming home to' (Minister of Labour quoted in *The Sunday Pictorial*, 1 November 1942).

(a) Outline the major themes contained in the 'Beveridge Report' 1942.   (6 marks)
(b) How far, in your opinion, were Beveridge's proposals 'revolutionary'?   (4 marks)
(c) What error of judgement may Winston Churchill have made with regard to the Beveridge Report?   (4 marks)
(d) Why do you think people at the time were so concerned about life after the war had finished?   (6 marks)

4. Objective 3

(a) What might have been the thoughts, feelings and experiences of a ten year old child evacuated from London to Kent in 1939?
(b) The evacuees were often very unpopular with the rural population. How do you account for this at a time when the nation was supposed to be united in its efforts to win the war?

(20 marks)

5. **Objectives 1 and 2**

Explain the importance of **three** of the following in the war:

(a) Civil Defence
(b) The Home Guard
(c) Rationing
(d) Financing the war
(e) Propaganda
(f) Entertainment

(Total = 20 marks)

6. **Objective 2**

Assess the social and economic effects of the war under the following headings:

(a) Short-term consequences
(b) Long-term consequences

(Total = 20 marks)

THE LABOUR GOVERNMENT 1945–51

31.1 INTRODUCTION

On 26 July 1945 the results of the General Election were announced with Labour gaining a landslide victory. Winston Churchill was stunned by his defeat, but the electorate associated him with a party which fostered class division and privilege. It was clear that the British public was of the opinion that the Labour Party was better equipped to implement the social policies which were needed to 'win the peace for the people'. There appeared to be a mood prevalent which said that the mistakes of the post-1918 years and the mass unemployment of the thirties would not be repeated. The Labour Party Manifesto 'Let us Face the Future' captured this mood when it stated that 'the nation wants food, work . . . and labour saving homes, . . . security for all against a rainy day . . . a great programme of modernisation . . . of its factories, . . . its schools, its social services'.

With this sentiment in mind the Labour Government, led by Clement Attlee, the Prime Minister, immediately settled down to its task.

31.2 WHAT IMMEDIATE FINANCIAL PROBLEMS FACED THE LABOUR ADMINISTRATION?

(a) Apart from making good the damage to housing, industry and ports caused by enemy bombing, the new government found itself faced with an immediate financial crisis, which was the direct result of the war. To pay for the war Britain had sold off £1200 million of overseas investments and had borrowed money to such an extent that by 1945 her foreign debts amounted to £3500 million. In addition, her exports had dropped by 66 per cent compared with pre-war levels. Before the war Britain had paid for her high imports by selling goods but she was now unable to do this. Her balance of trade had a deficit of £750 million in 1946 (compared with £43 million in 1938) – bankruptcy beckoned. It was estimated that exports would have to be increased in order to restore the economy to stability – yet industrial plants were run down. Furthermore Britain's earnings from 'invisible exports' were much lower than in 1939.

(b) Superimposed on this precarious position was the fact that Britain had committed herself to a number of financial promises to other nations during the war itself: these promises were based more on Britain's image as a leading world power than her actual ability to fulfil them. In 1944 a conference of 44 allied countries had taken place at *Bretton Woods*, New Hampshire, to discuss world trade and finance after the war. The result of the meeting was an agreement which obligated the signatories to the following conditions:

- Each signatory would contribute an agreed sum into an International Monetary Fund (IMF) – made up of 25 per cent gold and 75 per cent own currency. The idea being that nations could take out short-term loans when they were in trouble.
- Each signatory agreed that by 1949 all currencies should be freely convertible against other currencies. The idea here was to encourage international trade.

This agreement was to have significant effects on the British economy in 1947 (see Section 31.7(b)).

(c)
  (i) In 1945 Britain's problems were compounded by the fact that most of the materials required to rebuild her industries were only obtainable from North America – but she had no dollars to pay for them at that time with her exports at such low levels. On 21 August 1945 the USA informed Britain that 'lend-lease' was to be stopped with immediate effect.

   Britain was put into a desperate financial situation. John Maynard Keynes went to Washington to discuss a loan of dollars from America. After weeks of acrimonious negotiations, Keynes managed to strike a deal, but only by accepting a smaller amount than he asked for and with harsh conditions attached. The Americans agreed to lend Britain $4400 million (which included $650 million to pay off her lend-lease debts) to which Canada added $1250 million. The conditions were that:

- Repayments should be made over 50 years at 2 per cent interest.
- Britain would be asked to make sterling freely convertible within one year of the loan being ratified by the Senate (in effect this worked out to be in 1947).

(ii) Britain did not like the conditions and there was a deal of criticism fired at 'our American allies' from Labour left-wingers who felt that the Americans' actions were based on their contempt for the Labour Party's social policies. Yet, given the situation, Britain was faced with 'Hobson's Choice' – she was desperate for dollars. Furthermore, without this loan there was no way that the Labour Government could start its programme of social legislation which would require large amounts of finance.

31.3 WHY DID THE LABOUR GOVERNMENT NATIONALISE KEY INDUSTRIES?

(a)

(i) The nationalisation of industry was a corner-stone of socialist thinking, and in some ways Attlee's government saw itself as destined to introduce such measures. Nationalisation had been promulgated as early as 1881 by the Social Democratic Federation's (SDF) leader, H. M. Hyndman, but it was not until 1918 that it became a central objective of the Labour Party. The famous Clause 4 of the Labour Party's Constitution of that year stated that the party aimed

> to secure for the workers by hand or by brain the full fruit of their industry and the most equitable distribution thereof that may be possible upon the basis of the common ownership of the means of production, distribution and exchange.

Despite this declaration the Labour Governments of 1924 and 1929–31 did nothing to nationalise industry – even though the Sankey Commission of 1919 actually recommended it for the Coal Industry (see Section 27.3).

In 'Let us Face the Future' the electorate were offered a programme of industrial change which would gradually reorganise the nation's resources 'in the service of the people'.

With a landslide victory behind him, Attlee was the first Labour Prime Minister to have the opportunity of putting nationalisation into effect.

(ii) Apart from the 'socialist theory' argument outlined above, Labour could also put forward a strong case for nationalisation on economic grounds. Many of Britain's major industries had been experiencing a long period of stagnation which resulted in inefficiency and the mass unemployment of the thirties. The coal-mining industry services as an example. Here private ownership had meant hostile labour relations, lack of investment and low productivity. Nationalisation, it was believed, could only serve to rejuvenate the industry and improve relationships between worker and management, bring greater investment in modern machinery (and therefore, better safety) and eliminate wasteful competition.

(b) How was the nationalisation programme implemented between 1945 and 1951?

(i) The Labour Party had no 'blueprint' for nationalisation which could have been implemented immediately the chance arose. As a result the Public Corporation framework, which fell short of the socialist principles outlined in clause 4, was adopted (see Section 31.3(d)).

The Public Corporation Model of Nationalisation

Private Firms taken over by Government

↓

Compensation paid

↓

Government Minister appoints a Board of Directors to run the Industry headed by a Chairman

↓

Annual Accounts have to be published

↓

Profits used for pegging prices to consumers and/or investment in machines

↓

Affairs openly debated in Parliament

This approach was championed by the Lord President of the Council, Herbert Morrison, and was accepted by the Conservative opposition with the minimum of protest. Indeed, Baldwin had used the Public Corporation format when his Conservative Government established the British Broadcasting Corporation (BBC) and the Central Electricity Board (CEB) in 1926. The only nationalisation Bill to be strongly opposed was Iron and Steel (see Section 31.3(c)).

(ii) The first concern to be nationalised in late 1945 was the Bank of England, but it was hardly a revolutionary measure. The Act was the work of the Chancellor of the Exchequer, Hugh Dalton, and provided for a new Court of Directors headed by the Governor, Deputy Governor and 16 directors. In effect, the changes in banking were minimal and the measure met with little opposition.

(iii) Civil Aviation was nationalised in May 1946 with the intention of eradicating private competition. In fact this measure completed the work of Neville Chamberlain who, in 1939, had amalgamated a quantity of small airlines into the British Overseas Airways Corporation (BOAC). Now Labour added British European Airways (BEA) and British South American Airways Corporation (BSAAC). Once again there was very little opposition.

(iv) The nationalisation of the electricity supply went through Parliament in February 1947. This built on to the CEB and established 14 Area Electricity Boards headed by Lord Citrine, the Chairman of the new British Electricity Authority.

(v) In 1946 the *Coal Nationalisation Act* was passed which 'establish[ed] public ownership and control of the coal mining industry'. The Act set up the National Coal Board (NCB) under the Chairmanship of Lord Hyndley, and was to operate as from 1 January 1947. Under the NCB, Britain was divided into 8 regions which were themselves subdivided into 48 Colliery Groups. The measure was seen as a 'triumph' by the miners, especially those who had experienced the bitter disputes with the private colliery owners in the interwar years. The owners, in fact, did well out of the deal, receiving a total of £164.6 million in compensation, but the change in ownership did not sweep away the industry's problems as had been anticipated by the miners (see Secftion 31.3(d)).

(vi) *The Transport Act*, passed in 1947, aimed to provide an 'integrated system of public inland transport and port facilities . . . for passengers and goods'. This involved taking into public ownership the railways (British Railways (BR), Inland Waterways, Road Haulage (British Road Services (BRS)), the London Transport Passenger Service and Harbours and Ports. The whole network would come under the auspices of the British Transport Commission. Alfred Barnes, the Minister of Transport was hopeful that nationalisation would result in the profit-making routes subsidising transport in rural areas.

(vii) In 1948 the *Gas Act* was passed which set up the Gas Council, a public corporation. The country was divided up into Area Gas Boards to organise supply, distribution and the maintenance of plant.

(c) Why was the nationalisation of iron and steel controversial?

(i) In 'Let Us Face the Future' the Labour Party argued that 'private monopoly has maintained high prices and kept inefficient, high-cost plants in existence. Only if public ownership replaces private monopoly can the [iron and steel] industry become efficient'. Nationalisation of iron and steel proved to be the final nationalisation measure to reach the Statute Book in 1949. It was devised by George Strauss, the Minister of Supply, but it was only adopted after a considerable struggle.

(ii) Much of the opposition was based on the fact that, contrary to Labour's statement, the iron and steel industry was not inefficient. It had made a good recovery from the depression and had served the country well during the war. The opposition was determined, therefore, to obstruct the Iron and Steel Bill for as long as possible. Furthermore, the Labour Cabinet was split as to whether nationalising steel was a wise measure; considerable debate took place on the issue throughout 1947–8. The left-wingers argued passionately for it, on 'socialist' grounds, stating that such a major industry belonged to the people.

(iii) In the end, the *Iron and Steel Act* set up the Steel Corporation of Britain in October 1950, under which 92 private firms were taken into public ownership. Compensation of £243 million was paid out to the owners. The Conservatives made it clear that they would denationalise the industry as soon as they returned to power.

(d) How successful was nationalisation?

It was difficult to assess the 'success' of Labour's nationalisation policy as it may be judged from different standpoints.

(i) Judged from the point of view of a socialist, the Labour Government may well be seen to have missed a golden opportunity in 1945. It had a large majority and could have carried through far more radical measures; in the event the nationalisation programme was *ad hoc* in structure and luke-warm in content.

Public corporations did little to alter the traditional management/labour relationship. Workers did not gain a greater say in the running of the industry as Clause 4 wanted. In his book *Arguments for Socialism*, Tony Benn quotes the words of William Straker, a Northumberland miner, who gave evidence to the Sankey Commission in 1919. Straker said that nationalisation of the coal-mining industry must bring the mine workers 'a share in the management of the industry . . . he must feel that the industry is being run by him in order to produce coal for the use of the community, instead of profit for the few people'.

Assessed on this premise nationalisation has been something of an anti-climax for left-wingers in the Labour Party.

(ii) An assessment from an economic standpoint is even more difficult. Supporters of nationalisation claim that the public corporations have provided a high level of management and conditions of work have improved. They would also claim the record of nationalised industries to be satisfactory even though levels of capital investment to update machinery have not been high enough. Furthermore, the definitive argument is 'would these industries have fared better under private ownership?' The opponents of nationalisation point to the problems that the Coal Industry and the Railways have experienced since 1947. The NCB started off badly, having to deal with the coal shortage of 1947, and a lack of manpower (see Section 31.7(b)). Critics also cite the miners' disputes of 1947, 1973 and 1984–5 as evidence that nationalisation has not brought im-proved labour relations. The railways have also been criticised. Labour disputes, poor catering services and an apparent inabil-ity to operate at a profit have plagued the reputation of British Rail (BR). An objective answer to the question of nationalisa-tion is therefore very difficult to arrive at.

31.4   THE WELFARE STATE: NATIONAL INSURANCE

(a)   The Labour Government was committed to putting the Beveridge Report into operation. The realisation of the Beveridge proposals would have the effect of establishing a Welfare State in Britain, completing the work started by the Liberal Governments between 1906 and 1914 (see chapter 25). The Welfare State built by Labour incorporated the idea of 'universality', that is the concept of *all* citizens benefiting from a wide variety of social services organised by national and local government. 'Let Us Face the Future' promised 'to press on rapidly with legislation extending social insurance over the necessary wide field to all'.

(b)   Ironically (in view of his election defeat), Churchill's 'Caretaker' Government of 1945 had already made a start by passing the *Family Allowances Act* in June of that year. This was to pay mothers five shillings (25p) a week for each child in the family from the second born upwards. The Act was to be financed directly by the Treasury. The Labour Chancellor of the Exchequer, Hugh Dalton, rubber-stamped the Act in his first Budget and payments commenced in August 1946. The allowances were payable up to the age of 16 or the child obtaining employment.

(c)   Attlee appointed James Griffiths to be Minister of National Insurance and he guided two far-reaching Acts through Parliament.

(i)   *The National Insurance Act 1946*

This Act had the following features:

- All persons of working age had to pay a weekly contribution which was signified by one one single stamp on an Insurance Card to be kept by the employer. The contribution paid varied according to whether a person was employed or self-employed.
- In return, contributors would be entitled to receive a comprehensive range of benefits in Sickness Benefit, Retirement Pension, Maternity Benefit, Unemployment Benefit, Widow's Benefits, Guardian's (or Orphans) Allowances and death grants.
- The Act introduced, in theory, a national minimum standard of subsistence.

The Act was widely welcomed and the first payments, retirement pensions, were made in 1946, and were set at 42 shillings

(£2.10) per week. Payments were not index linked. One weakness with the Act was that married women and a small section of self-employed workers were not included in the schemes. Whatever its faults, the 1946 National Insurance Act was, in Kenneth Morgan's words, 'a measure which provided a comprehensive universal basis for insurance provision that had hitherto been unknown'.

(ii) *National Insurance (Industrial Injuries) Act 1946*

This measure complimented the National Insurance Act and it followed proposals made by Beveridge. It stated that:

- Contributions would be paid in equal amounts by workers, employers and the state.
- All workers were to be compulsorily covered.
- The funds provided compensation paid by the Ministry of National Insurance (not the employer) to workers injured or disabled due to accidents which occurred at work.
- Tribunals were established to decide on disputed claims.

The Act was passed with little criticism or opposition.

(iii) *National Assistance Act 1948*

This provided a safety-net for those who could not pay contributions (for example, the physically handicapped, the homeless, unmarried mothers) and were, as a result, not covered by the Acts above. It also aimed to help those such as the elderly, who needed 'supplementary' benefits to make a subsistence living.

Those who wanted to take advantage of National Assistance had to apply to the National Assistance Board (NAB), a revamped version of the Assistance Board of 1940. It was this Act which finally buried Chadwick's 1834 Poor Law Act. By 1950 some 1.5 million people were on National Assistance.

(iv) *Why was the introduction of National Insurance a 'great' achievement?*

A number of points can be made here:

- For the first time the whole work force was covered completely by a single-system insurance.
- The idea that the state had a responsibility to protect all its citizens, but particularly the weakest, was firmly cemented in British society.

- The volume of administration and organisation to implement the schemes was collosal and was carried out in a short amount of time. This in itself was an achievement.
- The idea of National Insurance was allied to the policy of full employment, so that only a minority had to draw benefits. This reversed the policy of the 1930s where unemployment was seen as an answer to a depression.
- One criticism, however, may be levelled at the Labour Government. They kept National Assistance and National Insurance as separate units, thereby ignoring Beveridge's proposal of a single 'Ministry of Social Security', which would have facilitated administration (this did not happen until Wilson's Labour Government in 1966).

31.5 THE NATIONAL HEALTH SERVICE

(a) Background

Prior to the Second World War health provision was a mish-mash of components which had developed on an *ad hoc* basis over the years.

(i) There were about 2000 hospitals organised by local authorities and a further 1000 run by voluntary concerns (for example, Cottage Hospitals and Teaching Hospitals). Poor patients could obtain free treatment in local authority hospitals but, in the main, hospitals were not interested in those who could not afford to pay fees. Undoubtedly an element of rivalry and competition existed between the two kinds of hospital.

(ii) There were many private nursing homes which catered purely for the rich.

(iii) Doctors preferred to build up their practices in upper-class areas which meant a shortage of provision in the inner cities. Furthermore, on retirement, doctors 'sold off' their practices to the highest bidder.

(iv) An insured workman (under the 1911 and 1921 National Insurance Acts) could obtain free treatment from his panel doctor. However, this provision did not extend to his wife and family. Workmen outside the insurance scheme also did not qualify for free treatment: they had to pay or go without treatment.

(v) There was some health provision for children under the
auspices of the Ministry of Education. A variety of Acts
provided medical inspection, school meals and milk.

(vi) Mothers and babies came under the Maternity and Child
Welfare Act of 1918. This stated that all births had to be
notified to the Local Authorities Medical Officer of Health
who would then arrange for a Health Visitor to advise the
mother on the health of her offspring.

(b) The Second World War

The Second World War highlighted the shortcomings in the system
when the Blitz resulted in a large number of casualties. This led to all
hospitals being put under the Emergency Hospital Scheme organised
by the government. This move, together with the Beveridge Report,
made people think along the lines of a National Health Service.

(c) The Role of Aneurin Bevan

(i) In 1945 Bevan became the Minister of Health and Housing,
pledging to carry out the promise made in 'Let Us Face the
Future' that 'the best health services should be available for all
. . . Money must no longer be the passport for the best
treatment'. As with National Insurance, the principle of 'universality' was to be applied. Bevan, however, faced a monumental task drawing all the various strands into a unified
system and, furthermore, he had to overcome the stubborn
resistance of the British Medical Association (BMA). Bevan's
National Health Service intended to provide the complete
range of medical services including hospital treatment and
dental services free of charge. Drugs, spectacles and dentures
would also be free. The whole service would be financed
mainly by taxes, with a small section being funded by National
Insurance contributions. Bevan was totally committed to this
scheme and fought hard between 1946 and 1948 to make sure
that his 'beloved Health Service' came into existence. That he
succeeded was a tribute to his stamina, determination and tact.
The National Health Act was passed in 1946 to come into
operation in 1948.

(ii) *Bevan's National Health Service – The Structure:*

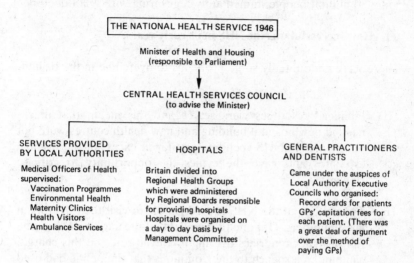

THE NATIONAL HEALTH SERVICE 1946

Minister of Health and Housing
(responsible to Parliament)

CENTRAL HEALTH SERVICES COUNCIL
(to advise the Minister)

SERVICES PROVIDED BY LOCAL AUTHORITIES	HOSPITALS	GENERAL PRACTITIONERS AND DENTISTS

Medical Officers of Health supervised:
  Vaccination Programmes
  Environmental Health
  Maternity Clinics
  Health Visitors
  Ambulance Services
	Britain divided into Regional Health Groups which were administered by Regional Boards responsible for providing hospitals Hospitals were organised on a day to day basis by Management Committees	Came under the auspices of Local Authority Executive Councils who organised:
		  Record cards for patients
		  GPs' capitation fees for
		  each patient. (There was
		  a great deal of argument
		  over the method of
		  paying GPs)

(d) The opposition of the British Medical Association

The BMA, led by its secretary, Dr Charles Hill, was bitterly opposed to the National Health Act for the following reasons:

- They feared that the status of doctors would be akin to that of 'civil servants' and that they would be told by the NHS where they had to work.
- They were highly suspicious that the government intended to pay them a set salary.
- They also objected to the prohibition of the sale of practices (Bevan's intention was to achieve a more equitable distribution of doctors between rich and poor areas).

Negotiations and meetings between the government and the BMA were acrimonious, with the BMA running a propaganda campaign against Bevan. In the end Bevan made a few concessions: Doctors would be paid 'a capitation fee' (a sum for each patient they had registered) but doctors could still take private patients and there would be a number of 'pay-beds' in each hospital. These reassurances lessened the opposition of the BMA, and by June 1948 92 per cent of the GPs in Britain had registered with the NHS. Out of 3000 hospitals in Britain, 91 per cent had come into the NHS fold – only 236 remained outside. The NHS came into operation on the appointed day in July 1948. The public responded enthusiastically with some 30 million people immediately registering with NHS doctors.

(e)   How successful was the NHS in its early years?

There were undoubtedly some problems to overcome in the beginning.

 (i)   Financial resources were scarce and this meant that much-needed new hospital building and new health centres were not built. In 1949 NHS spending was far in excess of the original estimates and gave the cynics the opportunity to criticise Bevan.

 (ii)   The novelty of the NHS caused people to visit their doctors in large numbers. Opponents claimed that the nation had become full of hypochondriacs overnight. Bevan rejected this charge, claiming in a speech to the Commons that the public had used the system intelligently, and that 'abuses had been few and far between'.

(iii)   The issue of cost came to a head in 1950 when Britain became involved in the Korean War, and more money was needed for the Defence Budget. The NHS spending for 1950 amounted to £351 million. In April Hugh Gaitskell, the Chancellor of the Exchequer, announced in his Budget that charges would be made on NHS dental treatment and spectacles. There was a bitter debate within the Labour Cabinet with Bevan believing that his colleagues had abandoned their socialist ideals. He resigned in protest along with Harold Wilson (President of the Board of Trade) and John Freeman (Junior Minister of Supply).

(iv)   Overall, Bevan's achievement was astounding. The NHS is still intact today and, despite financial cutbacks, offers a medical care second to none. It was been argued that few politicians would have had the necessary skill to set up such a mammoth undertaking, and override the opposition of the BMA. It is, without doubt, one of the most far-reaching pieces of legislation ever achieved. E. P. Thompson sums up Bevan's contribution to the NHS by stating that 'he fought every inch of the way for resources . . . and founded the service on authentic socialist principles; a free service and to each according to his needs'.

31.6 HOW SUCCESSFUL WAS THE LABOUR GOVERNMENT IN OTHER AREAS OF SOCIAL REFORM?

(a) Housing

'Let Us Face the Future' made a bold promise that Labour would 'proceed with a housing programme with the maximum practical speed until every family in this land has a good standard of accommodation'. The Labour Government, however, found great difficulty in delivering the required number of houses to satisfy the needs of the nation:

(i) On coming to power the housing shortage was acute. In addition to the backlog of 1939, bomb damage had left the country short of an estimated 1.25 million houses. (See Section 30.10)

(ii) There was a shortage of building materials and labour. As well as houses the nation needed new factories and hospitals. The demand was just too great to overcome in a short space of time.

(iii) Housing was made part of the Ministry of Health and this proved too big to deal with – even for someone with the ability of Bevan.

(iv) Bevan's housing policy was to foster the building of new council houses for the working classes with rents held to 10 shillings (50p) per week. The finance would come partly from the Exchequer (in grants to local authorities) and partly from the rates. Bevan ruled that council houses and private houses should be built in the ratio of four to one. This was a mistake as it restricted the number of houses which could have been built overall.

(v) As a consequence of these problems, house-building was slow to progress. To overcome the shortage temporarily, some 500 000 prefabricated buildings were erected. A number of families, however, were forced to resort to squatting.

(vi) In an attempt to improve matters, Attlee made a personal intervention into housing policy by setting up a Housing

Production Executive (April 1946). The statistics suggest that this was to some extent a successful move:

Year	No. of new dwellings
1947	139 000
1948	227 000
1949	197 000
1950	198 000
1951	194 000

(vii) In 1951 housing was divorced from the Ministry of Health and a new government department, The Ministry of Housing and Local Government, was born under the leadership of Hugh Dalton.

When Labour left office in 1951 there was still a shortage of houses, and in basic terms of 'houses built' their record was 'moderate'.

(b) The environment

The issue of town planning and land utilisation also required urgent attention. Little regard had been paid in the 1930s to controlling urban growth, with the result that large cities had been allowed to expand in a haphazard, chaotic manner. As a long-term policy Labour advocated 'land nationalisation' but felt that this could only be achieved in stages. The starting point was to control land utilisation and to keep a firm grip on town planning – ideas which were contained in the Uthwatt Report of 1945. Three important Acts were passed by the Labour Government:

(i) *The New Towns Act 1946*

New Towns were the brainchild of Sir Patrick Abercrombie. To prevent urban sprawl 'green belts' were to be instituted around large cities, like London, where building would be strictly restricted. The outer edge of the green belt would provide the sites for New Towns which would be planned communities. Industry and people would be encouraged to move out of the cities to the New Towns in an attempt to reduce the problem of over-population. Their ideas were contained in the *New Towns Act* which stated that:

- The government could take over an area of land for the construction of a New Town.
- The planning and building of such towns would be carried out under the auspices of a Development Corporation.

Fourteen New Towns were started between 1946 and 1950 and completed by the Conservative Governments of the 1950s. Stevenage (1946), Harlow, Hemel Hempstead, Crawley (1947), Hatfield, Welwyn (1948), Basildon and Bracknell (1949) were to take overspill from London. Peterlee was started in 1948 to take overspill from Newcastle. East Kilbride and Glenrothes, to relieve Glasgow and Edinburgh, were begun in 1947.

(ii) *Town and Country Planning Act 1947*

This Act required local authorities to produce plans which anticipated how the land under their jurisdiction would be utilised in the foreseeable future. They had to consider private and public housing, industry, agriculture and recreation. They were given increased powers to preserve buildings of historical value and to purchase land compulsorily. From now on planning permission would be needed for any building to be constructed or extended.

(iii) *The National Park and Access to the Countryside Act 1949*

Under this Act areas of natural beauty were to be set aside for the enjoyment of the population. Such areas were to become National Parks and would be subject to austere planning restriction in an attempt to minimise industrial development and pollution.

(c) Education

(i) When Labour came to power, Butler's Education Act (1944) was already on the Statute Book (see Section 18.9). It fell to Ellen Wilkinson, the Minister of Education from 1945–7, and her successor George Tomlinson, to administer the introduction of the Act. Both these Ministers were to be a disappointment to the left-wing element of the Labour Party. As the LEAs put the 1944 Act into practice, it became evident that the

11-plus examination would be a central feature in selecting pupils for secondary education – grammar schools or secondary modern. It also became obvious that this examination tended to favour children from middle-class homes. Furthermore, the number of grammar school places varied from area to area. In Wales it was estimated that 33 per cent of 11-year-olds achieved a grammar school place, whereas in Surrey only 15 per cent were successful. Often children 'failed' the 11-plus and found themselves labelled as 'failures'; other children 'passed' the 11-plus only to find it difficult to cope with the academic pressures of a grammar school.

(ii) Many in the Labour Party were unhappy with the system advocating the abolition of grammar schools and the 11-plus and the introduction of comprehensive schools, catering for all abilities. Miss Wilkinson believed that grammar schools provided clever working-class children with a fine educational diet. She was severely criticised by left-wing groups for her 'short-sightedness'.

It was not until the 1950s that the comprehensive movement gathered momentum. In addition, many socialists were dismayed to see that the public school system was continuing unchallenged.

Robin Pedley, in his book *The Comprehensive School*, accuses Labour's thinking of being 'a generation out of date' and that Wilkinson and Tomlinson were 'sincere but ill-equipped Labour ministers'. This assessment may well be accurate given the fact that the Labour Government 'was pledged to social reform'.

(d) Other legislation

Finally, Labour implemented a number of individual Acts.

(i) *The Trades Disputes Act 1946* – this swept away Baldwin's Trade Dispute Act of 1927 which had been designed to weaken trade unions. From henceforth trade-union members were to 'contract out' from the political levy to the Labour Party (rather than 'contract in') and Civil Service Unions were permitted to be affiliated to the Trade Union Congress (TUC).

(ii) *Legal Aid and Advice Act 1949* – under the people could obtain free legal aid if they could not pay a solicitor. One side effect of this Act was to increase the number of divorces.

(iii) *The Parliament Act 1949* – limited the power of the House of Lords. From now on they could delay Bills for a period of up to one year only.

31.7 FINANCIAL AND ECONOMIC POLICY 1945–51

(a) What 'broad' policies were adopted?

In order to finance the Welfare State measures and restore Britain's economy to stability, the Labour Party adopted a number of approaches which would be daunting in any period – but the conditions which prevailed between 1945 and 1951 made them very difficult to achieve, particularly as they were interdependent.

(i) *Full employment*

After the experience of the thirties the government wanted to avoid mass unemployment at all costs. Labour committed itself firmly to a policy of full employment – 'No more Dole queues'. Between 1945 and 1951 unemployment was kept at below 2 per cent, a praiseworthy achievement. Yet there were dangers inherent within this policy, as full employment can lead to a high turnover of labour and also lull the nation into a mood of complacency and indifference.

(ii) *Suppressed inflation and controls*

With full employment, the purchasing power of the population was stimulated, creating a real danger of inflation (rising prices) as well as demand outpassing supply. This danger was increased by the fact that many people had wartime savings which they were now itching to spend.

The government's answer to this was to keep taxation high and to continue rationing so that goods were not available to purchase ('suppressed inflation'). Other factors also contributed to the need to continue food rationing such as the world shortage of rice and wheat in 1946. The following controls were implemented at one time or another:

- In July 1946 bread was rationed for the first time with adults being restricted to two loaves per week.
- Meat rationing was maintained until 1951.
- Clothes rationing continued until 1949.
- Petrol rationing continued.
- There was rationing on potatoes, jam, eggs, milk.

(iii) *'Cheap Money'*

As if to walk a tight rope, Hugh Dalton (Chancellor of the Exchequer 1945 – November 1947), deliberately adopted a policy of cheap money. This meant that money could be borrowed at low interest rates (on average 2 per cent) to invest in industrial reconstruction. This policy could possibly lead again to inflation as businesses expanded. At the time, however, Dalton argued that cheap finance was necessary to pay for new houses, factories and hospitals.

(iv) *Maintaining a favourable balance of trade*

In order to achieve a favourable balance of trade, exports had to exceed the value of imports. Thus Labour restricted certain imports (which fitted in with suppressed inflation) and encouraged an export drive at the cost of depriving the home market. If exports were high then Britain would be solvent and able to pay for her imports.

(b) Why was 1947 a difficult year for the Labour Government?

Until the end of 1946 Labour's policies were having a degree of success. Exports were up by over 100 per cent compared with the 1938 level. The year 1947, however, was a disaster.

(i) *The severe winter and the fuel crisis 1946–7*

For some time critics had been warning the government about low productivity in the coal-mines. Manpower was in short supply and miners were only working a five-day week. Emmanuel Shinwell, the Minister of Fuel and Supply, claimed that everything was in hand, only to be caught out by one of the worst winters on record, that of 1946–7. Between January and March Britain was under a blanket of snow, and temperatures remained well below freezing. At a time when electricity was in high demand both from industrial and domestic consumers, power stations were actually forced to close down as they had no coal to burn. Factories were forced to shut down or work truncated weeks. The effect was catastrophic, with reduced productivity, a loss of export earnings to the tune of £200 million and rising unemployment.

Farmers also suffered with much lievstock dying in the severe conditions. The government and country had suffered a crippling blow and, for the first time, arguments started in the Cabinet. Shinwell was dismissed in October 1947 and there was a feeling that the government's confidence had been seriously undermined. Worse was to follow!

(ii)   *The convertibility crisis 1947*

In April 1947 Dalton presented his Budget. It was not a Budget to deal with the present situation. With imports up and exports down, Dalton needed to curb home demand for products, but he failed to do this. He also continued the 'cheap money policy'. As a result, Britain's solvency continued to be heavily dependent on the American loan 'begged' by Keynes in 1945. The loan was rapidly running dry and one of the terms came into operation in 1947; sterling became freely convertible against other currencies. Foreign countries observed that Britain was in economic trouble and began to withdraw sterling from London and bought dollars instead.

The summer of 1947 saw a drastic fall in Britain's dollar and gold reserves and she was on the brink of bankruptcy. In August the USA agreed to suspend convertibility to keep Britain solvent; at this point Britain had approximately 400 million dollars of the loan left.

Initially Dalton blamed Britain's financial plight on the convertibility issue, failing to pay enough attention to the underlying trends of falling exports, loss of world markets and high imports. By November 1947 he had begun to see the problems and his autumn Budget contained a change in thinking with heavier taxation, increases in food rationing, and reduction in imports. He leaked details of this budget to a journalist from the *London Evening Star* and as a result was forced to resign as Chancellor. He was succeeded by the Minister of Economic Affairs, Sir Stafford Cripps.

(c) What was the policy of austerity?

Cripps told the nation that it would have to undergo a period of hardship, with people having to make personal sacrifices in their standard of living so that more goods could be sold abroad – this was the 'policy of austerity'. It was nothing new to the long-suffering British. Cripps put a number of measures into operation:

(i) A campaign to increase productivity in Britain's factories.

(ii) An intensification of the export drive. Cripps did not hesitate to aid the growth of the mixed economy where private industry flourished.

(iii) Government spending cuts were implemented. The Budget of April 1949 reduced the amount of Treasury money for local authority housing programmes, maintained a high level of taxation, and fixed food subsidies at £465 million.

(iv) Cripps also managed to get the TUC to agree to a wage-freeze (as from March 1948). The agreement was generally accepted, although some union members showed their disapproval by unofficial strikes, such as the London Dock strike of 1949.

Cripps' policy brought some success. There was an improvement in the balance of payment situation. A deficit of £443 million in 1947 was transformed into a surplus of £30 million in 1948. There can be little doubt, however, that Britain's slight recovery was also explained by the injection of American money under the Marshall Aid Plan which took effect from April 1948. The American Secretary of State (General Marshall) set up the Plan to pump dollars into Europe to allow it to recover from the war. Marshall Aid was used by Cripps to pay for vital imports.

(d) What was the devaluation crisis of 1949?

In 1949 yet another financial crisis was in evidence. Britain's dollar and gold reserves continued to fall rapidly during the summer months; she was still not earning enough dollars on her own, even though industrial productivity and exports were increasing. The choice to be made was between cutting back imports to such a level that there was a drastic fall in the standard of living or to sell more goods. Cripps chose the latter, and on 18 August 1949, to encourage the economy in this direction, he decided to devalue the pound (with the agreement of the IMF). Instead of being worth $4.03 the £ would now be worth $2.80. The anticipated effect of this devaluation was explained by Cripps in a radio broadcast on 19 September. 'An English motor car is exported to the United States; its price is £300 sterling. An American buyer will pay $1,200 if the exchange rate is $4 to the £, . . . but suppose the rate was only $3 to the £ . . . he would only pay $900'.

Thus Britain's exports would be cheaper, and in theory this should have the effect of increasing British sales. However, the effect of a lower rate of exchange on imports would be to make them more expensive. Cripps further explained how this would affect the British consumer:

[We will] have to pay more pounds . . . for the same quantity of dollar goods . . . [which includes] wheat and flour . . . from North America . . . [The Government cannot afford to increase the subsidy on these, so] . . . the four and a half penny loaf [2p] will have to go up to 6d [2.5p].

Cripps had to take a deal of criticism over the decision to devalue, but he was decisive in his action and realised that something had to be done to save Britain from bankruptcy. In the short term the measure seemed to have some success as exports were increased in 1950.

(e) How did the Korean war affect the Labour Government?

In February 1950, a General Election returned Labour to power with their majority drastically reduced. In June 1950 Labour suffered yet another blow. The outbreak of war in Korea resulted in the United Nations (UN) sending an army to repel the Chinese invasion on South Korea. Attlee committed the British Government to supporting the UN with troops and arms. In April 1951 the new Chancellor of the Exchequer, Hugh Gaitskell, proposed to spend £1,500 million on rearmament. This was a staggering amount and the only way to raise so much money was to make economies elsewhere. The NHS and other items of social welfare were the victims (see Section 31.5(d)). It appeared that Labour had come to the 'end of its Socialist road'. A further election of October 1951 returned the Conservatives to power.

31.8   CONCLUSION – WHAT WAS THE ACHIEVEMENT OF THE LABOUR GOVERNMENT?

(a)   First and foremost, the Labour Government constructed a universal Welfare System within which its citizens were cared for from the 'womb to the tomb'. This in itself was a major achievement, but to build such a system in a time of financial difficulty makes it even more awe-inspiring.

(b)   Historians argue, however, as to how well the Welfare State was put together. Kenneth Morgan sees the construction of the Social Services in terms of a 'mosaic' whereas Marwick feels that it was something more akin to 'crazy-paving'. His opinion is probably nearer the mark. There was no real integration of the Welfare Services – for example, between National Insurance and the NHS. (The NHS itself was made up of three different sections – GPs, local authorities and hospitals.)

(c)   It may well be that the Labour Government missed the opportunity to produce a fully-planned economy. There were some measures passed like the *Distribution of Industry Act* in 1945, which attempted to direct industries to the old development areas of the 1930s (South Wales for example) – but by and large the government was extremely naïve in its efforts to plan economic growth and direct the economy. A Central Economic Planning staff under Sir Edwin Plowden was set up in 1947 but it had little effect. The ineffective nature of Labour's planning was highlighted by the fuel shortage of 1947, a situation which could have been avoided. For some reason the Labour Cabinet wanted to avoid any direct planning involving the private sector.

(d)   It is also arguable that Labour missed the chance to implement much greater schemes of industrial democracy in its nationalisation programme. The work force, however, gained no more say in organising British industry than they had before.

Such criticism, however, is probably harsh. Few administrations in British History worked harder. By 1951 the government had well and truly exhausted itself – Attlee, Cripps and Bevin all felt the pace. Cripps died in 1950 after illness, and Bevin in 1951 (shortly after losing the post of Foreign Secretary). The overall impression of this government is summed up by Kenneth Morgan: 'It was without doubt the most effective of any British Government . . . a landmark in the history of Modern Britain'.

QUESTIONS

1. Objectives 1 and 2

(a) Why was the Beveridge Report drawn up in 1942?
(b) Describe the main Acts which led to the setting up of the Welfare State.
(c) How successful was the Welfare State in overcoming the problems described in the Beveridge Report?

(Total = 25 marks)
(Southern Examining Board)

2. Objectives 1 and 2

(a) What financial problems faced the Labour Government between 1945 and 1951? (8 marks)
(b) How did the Labour Government cope with these problems? (12 marks)

3. Objectives 1 and 2

(a) What is meant by nationalisation? (4 marks)
(b) How and why did the Labour Government carry out its policy of nationalisation between 1945 and 1951? (10 marks)
(c) 'Labour's nationalisation programme was not radical enough and to many socialists represented a missed opportunity'. Is there any evidence for this viewpoint? Give reasons for your answer. (6 marks)

4. Objective 3

You have been asked to interview an elderly person about life in Britain between 1945 and 1951. Write an account of the conversation. You may consider:

● Austerity and rationing
● The winter of 1947
● The beginning of the National Health Service and National Insurance
● Entertainment
● Unemployment
● Education
● Family life

(Total = 25 marks)

5. **Objective 1**

What policy did the Labour Government adopt towards:

(a) New Towns
(b) Education
(c) The environment
(d) Trade unions?

(Total = 20 marks)

6. **Objective 4**

Study the sources below and then answer the questions:

Source A   (courtesy of London Express News and Features Service)

"*Now don't forget—anyone hanging around with a wistful look in their eye—let 'em have it—bing, bang!*"

Source B   *(courtesy of London Express News and Features Service)*

"MAKE WAY!"

Source C   *(courtesy of London Express News and Features Service)*

"Dentist says if there are any more of you thinking of fitting one another up with National Health teeth for Christmas presents you've had it."

Source D   (courtesy of London Express News and Features Service)

"I'LL ATTEND TO THE FOUNDATIONS LATER"

Source E

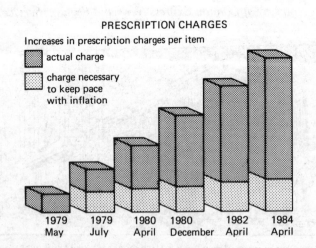

PRESCRIPTION CHARGES

Increases in prescription charges per item

- actual charge
- charge necessary to keep pace with inflation

| 1979 May | 1979 July | 1980 April | 1980 December | 1982 April | 1984 April |

(a) What point is the author of Source A making?   (2 marks)

(b) How does Source A illustrate that some aspects of life in 1945–51 were no better than during the years of the Second World War?   (2 marks)

(c) What point is the author of Source C trying to make?

(2 marks)

(d) In what way does Source D contradict Source B? How can this be explained?   (5 marks)

(e)   (i)   What would Aneurin Bevan have made of Source E?

(ii)   What leads you to think this source might be biased?

(2 marks)

(f) How useful would you find the following sources if you were asked to write an extended essay on the Labour Government 1945–51?

● Secondary source textbooks which gave the basic facts of these years.

● Statistics on employment figures, inflation rate

● Speeches made by politicians at the time

● Opinions and judgements on the work of this government made by political commentators.

(10 marks)

CHAPTER 32

COMMUNICATIONS AND TRANSPORT SINCE 1840

32.1 INTRODUCTION

(a) In 1840 the quickest method of travel was the railway, the postal services were only just on the point of improvement, the press was limited in output, and there were no telephones, radios or television. In the mid-1980s we do not think twice about receiving mail and newspapers daily or telephoning the other side of the world or watching events on the television 'live' from distant locations. We live in an age of mass communication which has come about in the last 150 years.

(b) The fact that such rapid progress has taken place in this period can be explained by a web of interrelated factors as the diagram below shows:

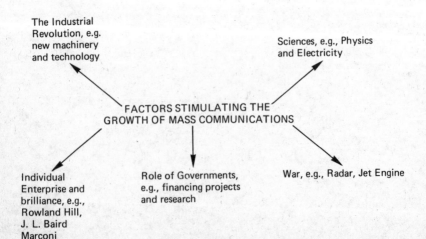

The Industrial Revolution, e.g. new machinery and technology

Sciences, e.g., Physics and Electricity

FACTORS STIMULATING THE GROWTH OF MASS COMMUNICATIONS

Individual Enterprise and brilliance, e.g., Rowland Hill, J. L. Baird Marconi

Role of Governments, e.g., financing projects and research

War, e.g., Radar, Jet Engine

This chapter will provide a brief survey of main developments in communications since 1840, including the growth of the mass-media (radio, television, cinema and the press).

32.2 HOW IMPORTANT WAS ROWLAND HILL (1785–1879) IN THE DEVELOPMENT OF THE POSTAL SERVICE?

(a) Before 1840 the postal service was limited by the following features:

(i) In most cases the receiver of the mail had to pay the cost. This meant that the postman had to knock on each door and collect money, thereby making his delivery round painfully slow. Sometimes people were reluctant to pay, particularly those on low wages.

(ii) The cost of a letter was calculated by the number of sheets and the distance over which it travelled. For a single sheet letter to be conveyed a distance of 298 miles (480 kilometres) the charge was one shilling (5p).

(iii) Some people, such as MPs, had the privilege of being allowed to use the postal service free of charge. This was often abused.

(iv) In some areas mail had to be collected from a Receiving House.

In 1837 Rowland Hill, a schoolmaster's son from Kidderminster, published a booklet called *Post Office Reform: Its Importance and Practicality*. Hill argued:

● Letters should be pre-paid by the sender.
● There should be a low standard rate of charge for a letter based on the weight of half an ounce; Hill suggested a charge of 1d (0.5p) irrespective of distance.

Hill argued that good communications were vital for an industrial nation and a low uniform rate would enable all people to make use of the system. The result would be increase in mail traffic and rising profits.

(b) Hill received strong support from the business fraternity – merchants and bankers – who organised meetings to publicise the proposal of a 'uniform penny postage'. The Whig government was not wildly enthusiastic but, in the end, the Penny Post became law on 10 January 1840. One of the first groups to benefit from it was the Anti-Corn Law League. To indicate that the sender had prepaid, a black gummed stamp was to be affixed to the letter – the famous Penny Black.

(c) The introduction of the Penny Post had the effect of increasing mail traffic but revenue actually decreased at first. In 1839 76 million letters were delivered; by 1865 this had risen to 642 million. In 1840 the Post Office received £1 634 000 in revenue, but in 1845 the figure raised was only £720 000. From 1875 revenue increased each year as Hill had originally forecast.

(d) All sections of society benefited from the Penny Post; relations could keep in touch and businessmen could advertise their products. In 1865 the first pillar box was introduced in London (the idea is usually credited to Anthony Trollope) thus eradicating the idea that people had to go to Post Office to send a letter. The rapid delivery of mail from town to town was aided by the growth of the rail network and steamship companies fought for the Atlantic mail contract (see chapter 13). Gradually offices increased in number and glances at any county directory of the mid nineteenth century such as Kelly's provides an insight into the postal service at the time. At Avington, Hampshire: 'Post Office – Mrs. Harper, sub postmistress. Letters through Alresford arrive at 8.15 am. and 3.10 pm. . . . letter box cleared at 6.30 pm on weekdays and 10.00 am on Sundays'.

(e) The traditional view of Rowland Hill makes him out to be 'the great pioneer' but M. J. Daunton, the Post Office historian, makes a number of interesting points:

● Hill's proposals had, in fact, been put forward in 1832 by Robert Wallace (MP for Greenock), who argued that an inefficient postal service hindered trade. At the time a number of reforms were being discussed by the government.
● Hill was often looked upon as an outsider by Post Office employees. When he published his *Post Office Reform* he was working as the Emigration Secretary to the South Australian Commission. He later obtained a position in the Treasury and then, in time, became Secretary of the Post Office.

Hill was not very popular. His critics regarded him as conceited, an 'empire-builder' and a poor manager of men. Daunton assesses Hill as an 'amateur propagandist', an opinion which appears to be justified.

(f) In the mid-1980s the Post Office deals with over 10 000 million letters each year. There are over 22 000 Post Offices which provide a range of services from paying pensions and allowances to selling TV licence stamps. The sorting of mail is being increasingly mechanised aided by the use of post codes.

32.3 WHY WAS THE INVENTION OF THE ELECTRIC TELEGRAPH IMPORTANT?

(a) In 1837 Charles Wheatstone and William Cooke invented the electric telegraph which enabled messages to be sent along wires. To begin with a complicated method of transmitting words was used, but in 1838 Samuel Morse introduced a code of 'dots and dashes' (Morse Code) which was much easier to operate; the code was widely adopted.

(b) The speed of the electric telegraph was first demonstrated by an employee of the Great Western Railway on 1 January 1845. A suspected murderer boarded the Paddington train at Slough. The telegraph operator sent a telegraph message to Paddington who contacted the police and the man, John Tawell, was arrested when the train arrived in London.

(c) In the 1850s electric telegraph companies began to compete for business and it was not long before most large towns were connected. This meant that urgent messages could be sent via telegraph, written down at the receiving office and then delivered to the door. The telegraph was also used by newspaper reporters who wanted their editors to receive their story rapidly. In 1870 the operating of the telegraph service came under the control of the Post Office by which time submarine cables linked Britain with Europe and America. The age of mass communication had dawned (see below);

1805   NEWS OF THE BATTLE OF TRAFALGAR TOOK *17 DAYS* TO REACH ENGLAND, USING MESSENGERS ON HORSEBACK AND SAILING SHIP

1815 NEWS OF THE BATTLE OF WATERLOO TOOK *3 DAYS* TO REACH ENGLAND FROM BELGIUM, USING MESSENGERS AND SAILING SHIP

1881 PASTEUR DEMONSTRATED ANTHRAX VACCINE AT POUILLY-LE-FORT IN FRANCE. A REPORT WAS SENT TO ENGLAND BY THE CORRESPONDENT OF *THE TIMES* USING ELECTRIC TELEGRAPH. THE REPORT WAS PUT THROUGH FROM PARIS AT 9.30 pm ON 2 JUNE. IT APPEARED IN *THE TIMES* ON 3 JUNE.

32.4 HOW DID THE TELEPHONE COME INTO BEING?

(a) In the mid nineteenth century a German named Reis devised a telephone – that is, an instrument which sends sound along a wire – but for some reason he faded into obscurity.

In 1876 however, a Scotsman – Alexander Graham Bell, produced a similar device in Boston, Massachusetts. He returned to Britain and demonstrated his invention to Queen Victoria, receiving the 'royal seal of approval'. In virtually no time at all his invention was commercially developed with several telephone companies already in business by the 1880s. Telephone exchanges provided women with careers as operators. In 1912 private telephone companies were taken over by the Post Office (except for the one in Hull) and also in this year the first automatic exchange was opened.

(b) The potential and uses of the telephone were soon demonstrated. Businesses found them to be essential and society at large was able to benefit. The early types of telephone are well illustrated in the television series *All Creatures Great and Small* with James Herriot's surgery often receiving an emergency call from a worried farmer. It took some time for many of the rural areas to be connected; a resident of Easton (Hampshire), writing in his diary on 28 August 1912, stated 'Telephone connected from my house to Avington House and Itchen Abbas station – a wonderful invention'.

(c) In the present century the following developments have taken place:

- In 1958 Queen Elizabeth II opened the new Subscriber Trunk Dialling System (STD) enabling the caller to dial long distant calls direct without going through the operator.
- In 1963 the International Subscriber Dialling System was introduced. Initially this provided a direct link between London and Paris, but it has now spread world-wide to over 130 countries.
- In 1962 the *Telstar* satellite enabled Europe to be linked with America. By 1982 Britain had over 25 000 satellite and cable links with countries throughout the world.
- In the mid-1980s there are over 30 million telephones in Britain with over 25 000 million calls being made annually.
- The latest development is the installation of cables made from thin sinews of glass (optical fibres) which are able to carry more calls at the same time.

One interesting point to note from the historian's point of view is that each telephone conversation made is 'lost' evidence as they are not recorded. We shall never know the contents of many telephone conversations between people in high places!

THE MASS-MEDIA (Radio, Television, Cinema and the Press)

32.5 WHAT HAVE BEEN THE MAJOR DEVELOPMENTS IN BROADCASTING?

(a) The radio

(i) The forerunner of radio broadcasting came in 1864 when it was discovered by James Clerk Maxwell (1874–1937) that sound could be sent via electromagnetic waves and wires were, therefore, not essential. It took a number of years before an Italian, Guglielmo Marconi, developed Clerk Maxwell's work. In 1899 Marconi succeeded in sending a wireless message in Morse Code to France, but the real breakthrough came when, in 1901, a message was sent over the airwaves from Poldhu (Cornwall) to Newfoundland. Marconi established his own company to manufacture wireless equipment.

(ii) The first practical use of wireless telegraphy was for shipping. As with the electric telegraph, there is a famous incident involving a criminal. This time it was a Dr Crippen, who in 1910, after having murdered his wife made good his escape for Canada via an ocean liner. A wireless message was sent to the captain and Crippen was arrested as soon as the vessel docked. He was brought back to Britain, found guilty, and executed. In 1912 the *Titanic* went down on her maiden voyage. The SOS message was sent out via the ship's wireless to shipping in the area to pick up survivors.

(iii)   Once the thermionic valve had been invented by John Fleming in 1919 it became possible to broadcast people's voices via the wireless. The first 'crystal set' had headphones so that it was possible for only one person to listen in at any one time. In 1922 the British Broadcasting Company was formed with bases in London, Birmingham and Manchester. Radio programmes were now broadcast – news information and entertainment. In December 1926 the company came into public ownership and was renamed the British Broadcasting Corporation (BBC). It charged licence fees to finance its operations and was under the directorship of John Reith. The radio played a vital part in maintaining the morale of the nation during the Second World War.

(iv)   In the 1960s the BBC was challenged by off-shore 'radio pirate-ships' such as Radio Caroline. These stations broadcast non-stop pop music and, helped by the invention of the transistor radio, gained a large audience. These radio ships were made illegal in 1967 by the *Marine Broadcasting Offences Act*, but they had the effect of shaking up 'the establishment'. In September 1967 the BBC revamped its structure with one channel devoted to pop music (Radio 1) and in 1972 the *Sound Broadcasting Act*, inspired by Christopher Chataway, Minister for Posts and Telecommunications, sanctioned the setting up of local commercial radio stations. These would be financed by advertisements and under the auspices of the Independent Broadcasting Authority.

(v)   In the mid-1980s there are over 40 independent radio stations throughout the country with a further 28 local stations operated by the BBC. A wide range of programmes is now provided but radio audiences have declined in the face of competition from television.

(b) Television

(i) In October 1925 John Logie Baird, using a collection of primitive and make-shift equipment (including old radio parts and a biscuit tin), managed to transmit a black and white image using electromagnetic waves – the television was born. It took some 11 years, however, before the invention was developed enough to transmit programmes to the public. In 1936 the BBC opened a transmitter at Alexandra Palace (North London) using a system designed by V. K. Zworykin, an American. During the Second World War no television programmes were broadcast, and this hindered the quick development of the medium.

(ii) In 1954 the Television Act was passed; this broke the monopoly of the BBC by introducing the following measures:

● The formation of the Independent Television Authority (ITA) – renamed Independent Broadcasting Authority (IBA) in 1972 – for the purpose of transmitting television programmes.
● ITA was to be financed by attracting advertisements.
● The country was divided into 14 regions for the purpose of broadcasting. Each region was under the control of an independent company responsible to the ITA.

(iii) By 1960 the television had become an integral part of daily life with 10,475,000 sets in use. Independent Television (ITV) tended to provide a diet of escapist entertainment programmes with 'soap operas' such as *Coronation Street* and quiz programmes like *Take Your Pick* and *Double Your Money*.

In 1962 the Pilkington Committee, set up to report on British broadcasting, contended that television transmitted too many mundane programmes and should increase the educational programmes – documentaries, current affairs, etc. As a result, the BBC instituted 'BBC2' in 1964 to provide more educational programmes.

(iv) In 1978 the Annan Report recommended further changes in television broadcasting, and as a result Independent Television introduced Channel 4, catering for minority interests (ethnic groups, drama, pressure groups, music).

(v) In the early 1980s there were almost 20 million television sets in Britain and an average viewing period of three hours per night per person. The content of programmes was still under fire with Mrs Mary Whitehouse aiming to 'clean up' television by reducing the amount of violence and sex shown. A new development in 1983 was the introduction of Breakfast Time television on both BBC and ITV. In the future the choice of viewing will probably be increased by the expansion of cable television operated by private companies and 24-hour viewing.

32.6 THE CINEMA

(a) Why and how did cinema-going develop?

(i) In 1896 the first silent moving film was shown in London. 'Movies' were slow to develop at first as they were of poor quality and very brief. They were more of a novelty as shown by this quote from the *Hampshire Chronicle* (16 January 1909):

> On January 7th the employees on the Avington Estate with their wives and families were invited by Sir John and the Honourable Lady Shelley to a bioscope [cinema] entertainment which included scenes depicting the flight of Wilbur Wright's aeroplane.

(ii) By the time the First World War broke out (1914) the potential of the moving picture had been realised. Scenes from the front were shown in British cinemas (many of these films may now be viewed at the Imperial War Museum). By 1920, Charlie Chaplin with his bowler hat and bow-legged walk had become the first real 'film star'. Cinemas were now to be found in most main towns.

(iii) In 1927 Al Jolson starred in the first talking move *The Jazz Singer*. This was a breakthrough as subtitle frames would no longer be needed. The 1930s saw a dramatic growth of the film industry based on Hollywood in America and Elstree and Pinewood in Britain. Major films such as *Gone With the Wind* attracted large audiences and film stars such as Clark Gable were idolised. Audience figures for 1935 were 20 million per week, increasing during the Second World War to 30 million as the cinemas remained open.

(b) Why has the cinema declined?

In 1982 the weekly attendance at Britain's 1400 cinemas totalled about one million people – a drastic decline. The reasons for this are manifold:

  (i) Television provides a variety of home entertainment for the cost of the annual licence fee.

 (ii) In the 1980s video-recorders have become popular. People can hire films on video or tape television programmes – reducing further the demand for the cinema.

(iii) The effects of the declining audience numbers have been catastrophic for the film industry:

> ● Cinemas have been forced out of business – closed or converted into bingo halls.
> ● The loss of box-office revenue has forced the film industry to operate on low-cost budgets, reducing the quality of films. Britain's film industry has been in the doldrums for some time and only a few major successes have been achieved recently, notably Richard Attenborough's *Gandhi* – claiming eight Oscar awards in 1983.

32.7 THE PRESS

(a) Early developments

  (i) In 1702 the *Daily Courant* was published. As the first daily newspaper it was limited in scope, consisting of a single broadsheet and catering for the middle and upper classes. Few of the labouring class were able to read but the government still imposed a stamp duty on newspapers throughout the eighteenth century, making them too expensive for the workers.

 (ii) In 1785 *The Times* was first published by John Walter. By the end of the nineteenth century it had gained a reputation for being outspoken, but its circulation was small (about 60 000 copies in 1850). Probably its most famous editor was John Thadeus Delane (from 1841 to 1877). During this period *The*

Times attacked the Poor Law (by revealing the scandal of the Andover workhouse), the Public Health Board, and the mismanagement of the Crimean War. William Russell sent back despatches from the Crimea revealing the terrible medical facilities and the poor communication between the army and the War Office. This appalled the British public and such was the uproar that Florence Nightingale was sent to Scutari (see Section 19.9(f)). The influence of the press on forming public opinion still remains.

(iii) In 1851 Julius Reuter opened the first News Agency in London. He was the first to realise the potential of the electric telegraph. Until this time a newspaper gathered foreign news by distributing reporters around the world to send despatches back if and when necessary – a costly and slow method. Reuter's idea was cheaper, more efficient and quicker. He opened offices in major capital cities sending news around the world by electric telegraph. He profited by selling the news to newspaper editors.

(b) Broadsides and ballads

(i) In the early nineteenth century newspapers were not written for the working man. There were a few 'radical' publications which he could perhaps afford but he was mostly dependent on 'broadsides' for the news.

(ii) Broadsides consisted of a single sheet, and were sold in alehouses or on street corners. They were cheap and popular, containing 'the news of the day'. A variety of topics would be dealt with – political, religious items, stories, law and order, etc. They were often satirical and critical of the government. By law the printer's name had to appear on the broadside but often the content was so inflammatory that he adopted a pseudonym for fear of being in trouble with the authorities. One such Winchester printer attempted to disguise himself by printing his address as 'Sheep-skin Street' the real location being 'Parchment Street'! 'Litanies' were sometimes performed – an event or story was acted out in a dialogue between two 'patterers' (people who sold broadsides).

(iii) Broadsides are very important sources to historians of the nineteenth century as they are virtually the only documents providing evidence for the attitudes, values and lifestyles of the working classes of the time. Most source-material for the early nineteenth century consists of documents reflecting the official 'viewpoint', for example, the Swing Riots of 1830. There is much evidence from the landowner's side – letters, diaries, circulars from the Home Office – but little reflecting the motives and attitudes of the labourers. Broadsides declined after about 1860 when the British 'popular' press began to grow.

(c) The growth of the popular press

(i) By 'popular' press we mean newspapers and magazines which contain some news but at the same time carry a large amount of entertainment and features, including illustrations. This type of newspaper developed due to a number of factors:

- In 1855 the government abolished the stamp duty on newspapers, making them cheaper.
- In 1870 Forster's Elementary Education Act introduced state education up to the age of 10 (later extended to 14) which had the effect of spreading literacy.
- Technical advances such as the steam-printing-press enabled the newspaper industry to mass produce on a larger scale.
- The railways could distribute the newspapers nationwide.

(ii) A number of individuals exploited these circumstances. Among them were:

Alfred Harnsworth (1865–1922), who introduced the first popular newspaper, the *Daily Mail*, in 1896, charging a half-penny per copy. The followed this by publishing the *Daily Mirror* in 1903. Harmsworth was created Lord Northcliffe and was thus the first 'press baron'. *Arthur Pearson (1866–1921)* was responsible for starting, in 1900, the *Daily Express*, which was later taken over by Max Aitken (Lord Beaverbrook).

By the late 1930s newspaper circulation exceeded ten million copies daily, and it was clear that the editors and owners could exert a powerful influence on public opinion.

(d)   Modern developments

(i)   In 1949 a Royal Commission on the Press reported that newspaper editors should be answerable for what they printed. This led to the establishment of the Press Council in 1953 with the objectives of defending freedom of the press and conducting inquiries into complaints received against individual newspapers.

(ii)   In 1977 the McGregor Commission expressed concern about the way that the press was developing. It criticised the fact that the national press was coming under the control of a few owners and it warned the unions against the dangers of overmanning.

(iii)   The late 1970s and early 1980s have seen a circulation war between the popular tabloid press (papers such as the *Sun*, the *Mirror*, the *Mail*) with various devices such as 'bingo' being used to attract readers, as well as claims of 'exclusive stories'. The emphasis has thus become one of entertainment (rather than information or news), and a number of people feel that the quality of the press has declined as a result. In the autumn of 1986 the balance was redressed slighlty with the introduction of *The Independent*, a new quality newspaper.

(iv)   A confrontation between the print unions and management occurred in January 1986 with the dispute at the News International Company owned by Rupert Murdoch (see chapter 33).

32.8   DEVELOPMENTS IN TRANSPORT 1900–1950

This section will deal with railways, aeroplanes and the hovercraft (for the motor-car industry, see chapter 26).

(a)   The railways

(i)   *The Railway Amalgamation Act 1921*

During the First World War the railways had been run by the state. When they were returned to private ownership the government took the opportunity to rationalise the network.

The Act stated that the existing 120 private companies were to be amalgamated into four large companies:

- The London and North-Eastern Railway (LNER).
- The London, Midland and Scottish Railway (LMS).
- The Southern Railway (SR).
- The Great Western Railway (GWR).

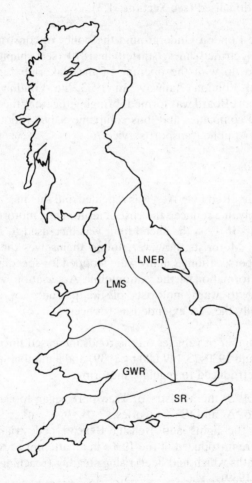

(ii) The railways were beginning to face a serious challenge from road transport and in the 1930s the major companies attempted to update their image by:

- Electrifying track with would mean less pollution (SR led the way with the electrification of the London-Brighton line in 1933).
- Producing large streamlined locomotives on a design pioneered by Sir Nigel Gresely. In 1936 the *Silver Jubilee* achieved a top speed of 112 mph (181 kmph), and the *Mallard* broke the world speed record for a steam locomotive 126 mph (203 kmph). In 1947 the railways were nationalised (see Section 31.3).

(iii) On the London Underground the policy of constructing deep tube electrified lines, started in 1890 (see chapter 12) was stepped up with the opening of the Bakerloo Line and the Central London Railway. In 1933 the London Passenger Transport Board was formed, bringing together the five underground companies and 'bus companies, thus rationalising the capital's public transport service.

(b)   The roads

(i) Once the 'Red Flag Act' was repealed and the mass production assembly line reduced the cost of motor cars, motoring became popular. In 1904 the speed limit was increased to 20 mph (32 kmph). Motorists, however, found themselves the victims of police persecution as many were stopped for speeding. This led to the formation of the Automobile Association who initially set out to warn motorists of the presence of the police: gradually the AA extended its services.

(ii) The number of vehicles on the roads increased throughout the 1920s and 1930s (3 149 000 by 1939) and a number of measures were introduced to regulate motoring:

- In 1920 the Ministry of Transport began to classify roads into 'A' and 'B' categories.
- Traffic lights and Belisha Beacon pedestrian crossings were introduced in the 1930s in an attempt to reduce road deaths which had been rising steadily (reaching over 7000 in 1939).
- The 1930 Road Traffic Act was passed. This introduced compulsory third party insurance and stated that all people applying for a licence had to prove themselves physically fit.

- The Driving Test was introduced in 1934.
- The 1933 Road and Traffic Act stated that goods vehicles had to be licensed.
- In 1935 the speed limit in built-up areas was set at 30 mph (48 kmph).

(iii) The economic and social effects of the motor car began to be felt from the 1920s. They included:

- The growth of 'ribbon development suburbs, and 'dormitory villages' on the edge of towns. The motor car meant that people could commute into work daily.
- The traffic jam, particularly at 'rush hour' and holiday periods.
- The relocation of industry away from raw materials and closer to markets. The motor vehicle permits door-to-door delivery.
- Noise pollution and air pollution.
- Assembly-line mentality.
- The decline of railways and horse-drawn vehicles (see section 33.7).

(c) Air travel

(i) In December 1903 Wilbur and Orville Wright succeeded in flying 'a heavier than air' machine at Kitty Hawk, North Carolina. Rapid progress followed. By 1909 Louis Blériot had flown the English Channel at a height of approximately 100 feet (30 metres). The First World War stimulated research into developing aircraft so that by 1918 speeds of 150 mph (240 kmph) were commonplace.

(ii) In 1919 John Alcock and Arthur Whitten-Brown just managed to cross the Atlantic from Newfoundland to Ireland. Other epic journeys included Charles Lindbergh's flight across the Atlantic in 1927 and Amy Johnson's flight from Britain to Australia in 1930.

(iii) A number of commercial airlines were set up after 1919 but the first company of any size was Imperial Airways founded in 1924 and supported financially by the government. By 1932 it was operating routes to Australasia, India and Europe. In 1935 British Airways was formed and then in 1938 the two companies were joined to make the British Overseas Airways Corporation (BOAC) (see Section 31.3).

(iv)   Another major breakthrough (stimulated by the needs of the Second World War) was the perfection of the jet engine by Frank Whittle which was to revolutionise both military and civil aircraft .

(v)   Air travel has reduced travelling time considerably and has had the effect of 'shrinking the world'. The rise of air travel spelt the decline of the world's ocean-going ship routes.

(d)   Hovercraft

(i)   The hovercraft, invented by Christopher Cockerill in 1953, operates by floating on a bed of air; it can move either on land or water. Cockerill could develop his work because of financial backing from the government-sponsored National Research Development Council. In 1959 the first crossing of the Channel was achieved, and by the late 1960s many hovercraft were operating on ferry routes throughout Britain, for example, Portsmouth to the Isle of Wight and from Scottish islands to the mainland. Regular services were also operating between the Channel ports, taking about 35 minutes to cover the distance between Dover and Calais. Today the enlarged SRN-Super 4, built by British Hovercraft, is capable of taking over 400 passengers and 55 cars.

(ii)   Despite these developments it is probably true that the hovercraft has not yet been used to its full potential. The idea of a huge craft to take goods and freight has not really materialised. With the anticipated construction of the Channel Tunnel it is possible that the hovercraft's cross-Channel routes will be threatened.

32.9   CONCLUSION

There is no doubt that progress in the development of mass communication has been staggering over the last 150 years. The future should open up new horizons . . . Space Travel? The revival of supersonic air travel? Cable television on a national basis? Further refinements of information technology? Domestic telex service? . . . Time will tell!

QUESTIONS

1. Objectives 3 and 4

Study the sources below and then answer the questions:

Source A

THE POOR LAW CATECHISM

Q. What is your name?
A. A Pauper.
Q. Who gave you that name?
A. The Board of Guardians, to whom I applied in the time of distress, when first I became a child of want, a member of the workhouse, and an inheritor of all the insults that poverty is heir to.
Q. What did the Board of Guardians do for you.
A. They did promise two things. First, that I should be treated like a convicted felon, being deprived of liberty, and on prison fare. Lastly, that I should be an object of oppression all the days of my life.

Source B

INVITATION TO SUNDAY SCHOOLS

O come, come away,–
From labour now reposing,
Let anxious care awhile forbear;
O come, come away,
Who does not wish to die a fool
Must early come to Sunday School,
And learn the Saviour's rule,
So come, come away.

O come, come away,–
The Sabbath day's returned,
Which calls on all to come to School,
So come, come away,
Your Teachers then with joy shall know
You wish to taste those joys below.
Which Christians only know,
So come, come away.

O come, come away,
Let's search the sacred treasure,
Which David said would not mislead,
O come, come away,–
Such toil will gain its own reward,
In blessings from our gracious Lord,
For faithful is his word.
So come, come away.

Then come, come away,–
The glorious is dawning,
When Christmas all both great and small,
Shall cry come away,
Come take your palms through Jesus won
And hail the saviour on his throne,
And shout the work is done,
Some come, come away.

(a) Why, do you think, the two broadsides (Sources A and B) were published?

(b) Were broadsides and ballads popular amongst all sections of society in the nineteenth century? Explain your answer.

(c) 'Broadsides and ballads are usually biased in their content and, as such, are of limited use to the historian'. Do you agree or disagree? Explain your answer.

(Total = 20 marks)

2. **Objectives 1 and 2**

(a) Describe the developments in **two** of the following during this period:

- Newspapers
- The cinema
- Radio
- Television

(b) How did these developments affect society?

(Total = 20 marks)

3. **Objectives 1 and 2**

(a) Outline developments in the following during the twentieth century:

- Road transport
- Air
- Railways
- Hovercraft

(12 marks)

(b) Why do people now refer to the 'shrinking world'? (8 marks)

4. **Objectives 1 and 2**

(a) How did the 'penny post' change the postal service in Britain?

(8 marks)

(b) Describe how the inventions of the electric telegraph and telephone came into being. (8 marks)

(c) Why were the above two inventions important to society?

(4 marks)

5. **Objectives 1 and 2**

Read the following sources and then answer the questions:

Source A

> I still have amongst my junk a little home made crystal set, which
> worked lovely with the iron bedstead for aerial and the gas stove
> for earth, and which told me and my wife (each with one earphone
> to the ear) what was really happening.
> (An Old Age Pensioner recalling his experience of the General
> Strike 1926)

Source B

> Within months aerials were appearing on one house after another,
> and the first question when you met anyone was; 'Have you got a
> wireless?' All over the country, as though from nowhere, hordes of
> young mechanics were available to install a set, to build a set and to
> attend to repairs. As sets improved so did transmission. The
> engineers worked to provide better quality. On the programme
> side, the BBC went further than any othe radio organisation in the
> world.
> The difference that the radio has made in the lives of the listeners is
> enormous. It has changed people's habits to fit the break-up of
> family life by providing entertainment for all.
> (Vivien Ogilvie, *Our Times*)

(a) (i)   Who pioneered wireless communication?   (1 mark)
     (ii) What was the wireless used for before public broadcast-
           ing?   (4 marks)
(b) How can you tell that the writer of Extract A trusted the BBC?
     Why were people more likely to trust the BBC than
     newspapers?   (2 marks)
(c) (i)   When was the BBC founded?   (1 mark)
     (ii) Who was its first Director-General?   (1 mark)
     (iii) What were the aims of the first Director-General?
                                                         (2 marks)
(d) How was the BBC financed?   (2 marks)
(e) What evidence is there in Source B that the BBC provided
     employment?   (2 marks)
(f) Explain 'the difference that radio has made in the lives of the
     listeners' in the 1930s.   (10 marks)
                                                (Cambridge Board)

6. **Objective 2**

(a) Why have developments in the means of communication been so rapid in the last 100 years?

(b) Which invention in the field of mass communication do you think has provided the biggest breakthrough for mankind? Give your reasons.

(c) 'We now live in a world where news travels so rapidly that there is little else left for man to achieve'. How far to do you agree with this statement?

(Total = 25 marks)

BRITAIN
1951–86

33.1 INTRODUCTION: THE FESTIVAL OF BRITAIN

(a)   On 3 May 1951, King George VI, speaking from the steps of St Pauls's Cathedral, declared the Festival of Britain officially open. The centre piece of the festival was a huge exhibition on the south bank of the River Thames, which cost the taxpayer £11 million to stage. The displays on show illustrated 'Modern Britain', reflecting the latest developments in industry, transport, housing, education, the arts, the sciences and technology. By the time the exhibition closed on 30 September 1951 it had attracted 8 455 863 visitors. In addition, hundreds of local events (pageants, displays, dances, etc.) were organised throughout the country.

(b)   Ostensibly, the festival was organised to celebrate the centenary of the Great Exhibition of 1851, but the Labour Government also saw it as a boost to the morale of the nation after a period of post-war 'austerity' and also an opportunity to show that Britain was still competing with the world. A number of cynics, including Winston Churchill, said that the festival was nothing more than socialist progaganda and an extravagence the nation could ill afford. Despite such opposition, the general atmosphere evoked a sense of optimism and a feeling that Britain could look forward to the future with confidence. Herbert Morrison, Labour's Foreign Secretary, triumphantly announced that the festival 'is a great national effort to show the world how much we have achieved, are achieving and are going to achieve'.
   A brief survey of events (and that is all it can be in a book of this length) will enable us to judge whether the optimism of 1951 has been fulfilled.

33.3   THE BRITISH ECONOMY SINCE 1951

Over the period as a whole successive governments have been plagued by four main problems:

- Inflation
- Unemployment
- Adverse balance of payments
- Slow economic growth

(a)   What economic policies did the Conservative Governments of 1951–64 adopt?

(i)   *'Butskellism'*

Initially, the Conservatives continued in the same vein as Attlee's Labour administration, spending money on social welfare, and following a 'mixed' economic philosophy with nationalised industries existing side by side with private businesses. The only real departure from this was the denationalisation of iron and steel and road transport in 1953. The continuity of policy inspired *The Economist* to use the term 'Butskellism', a word which owed its origin to the name of the outgoing Labour Chancellor of the Exchequer, Hugh Gait*skell*, and the new Tory incumbent of the position, R. A. *But*ler.

(ii)   *Stop-Go policies*

R. A. Butler completed the removal of wartime controls when he abolished food rationing in 1953–4. There was also an improvement in the balance of payments and a fall in unemployment from 450 000 in 1953 to 280 000 in 1954. Affairs took a turn for the worse in 1955 when inflation began to bite and the government introduced measures to cut state spending and control hire-purchase agreements, that is, they tried to 'slow down' the economy by reducing domestic demand in an effort to boost exports.

In 1957 Harold Macmillan declared that the Conservatives wanted an atmosphere of 'freedom' to encourage individual enterprise. When the export trade showed signs of improving he introduced 'go' policies to encourage the growth of the economy. He reduced interest rates and removed hire-purchase restrictions, claiming that the British people 'had never had it so good'. Income tax was also reduced giving the population more money in their pockets to purchase goods.

Two points of concern, however, were that inflation reached 6 per cent in 1957–8 and that British productivity was lower than her main competitors, particularly Japan and Germany. Imports began to flood into Britain and once again the brakes were applied to the economy. In 1961 the new Chancellor of the Exchequer, Selwyn Lloyd, introduced a nine-month 'pay-pause' to keep down wages which, in turn, would contain inflation – or so it was hoped. At the same time a longer-term measure was introduced with the establishment of the National Economic Development Council (NEDC) or 'Neddy'. This body had TUC support and was to supervise the future development of the economy. In July 1962 the National Incomes Commission was set up to control wage claims. Neither of these measures could prevent unemployment nearing the 600 000 mark in 1963.

In 1963–4 Reginald Maulding, Selwyn Lloyd's successor as Chancellor, deliberately brought back expansionist 'go' policies hoping to create jobs. He cut income tax and reduced interest rates. Unfortunately Maulding's measures resulted in increased imports, rather than exports. By 1964 the balance of payments deficit was over £600 million. In addition, wage increases were running at 5–6 per cent and fuelling inflation.

(b) How did Harold Wilson's Labour Government 1964–70 tackle Britain's economic problems?

Wilson announced that Labour would adopt new policies to steady the economy and that they would abandon the stuttering 'stop-go' approach. Things turned out to be rather more difficult than he anticipated.

(i) Deflationary measures

Wilson tried to wipe out the balance of payments deficit by obtaining a loan of $1000 million from the International Monetary Fund. In November 1964 the new Chancellor of the Exchequer, James Callaghan, introduced the following measures:

● Income tax was increased by 2.5p in the £.
● The bank rate was increased from 5 per cent to 7 per cent.

- Petrol was increased by 2.5p per gallon (4.5 litres).
- A tariff of 15 per cent was imposed on all imports except food and raw materials (which went against GATT and EFTA).

These measures did not work immediately. More foreign loans had to be obtained in May 1965 and a new 'Capital Gains Tax' was introduced in April 1965. By this time the balance of payments deficit had been reduced to £49 million, but further difficulties were just around the corner (see Section (iii) below).

(ii) *The Department of Economic Affairs*

Headed by George Brown, this new department was set up to mastermind Labour's economic planning. Among its measures were:

- The NEDC was retained as the main planning body.
- The National Incomes Commission was replaced by the Prices and Incomes Board under Aubrey Jones.
- The Industrial Reorganisation Corporation was set up with a fund of £150 million to help ailing industries.
- In September 1965 Brown published *Labour's National Plan*.

This set growth targets for British industries over a period of five years in the anticipation of achieving a growth of 3.8 per cent each year. The plan never got off the ground. In many ways it was far too optimistic given the difficulties the economy was facing in the mid-1960s. Brown left the DEA in 1966 and became Foreign Secretary.

(iii) *Devaluation 1967*

One problem with the British economy was that service industries were expanding at a much faster rate than manufacturing industries. To try and arrest this, Callaghan introduced Selective Employment Tax in 1965. This taxed each employee to the tune of £1.25, payable by the employer (manufacturing industries were able to claim it back).

The economy continued to have difficulties. The seamen went on strike in 1966 which had a drastic effect on Britain's trade figures. Foreign countries lost confidence in Britain and began to withdraw their money from London. Wilson imposed a wage freeze for six months starting in July 1966.

By November there was no sign of improvement and surprisingly the 15 per cent import tariff was abolished, encouraging an increase in imports. With heavy debts, and an inability to sell goods abroad, urgent measures were called for. Consequently, on 18 November 1967 the £ was *devalued* from $2.80 to $2.40. The effect was to make British exports cheaper.

(iv) *Reduction of government spending 1968–9*

At the same time as devaluation Roy Jenkins replaced Callaghan as Chancellor of the Exchequer, and over the next two years he attempted to reduce government spending:

● Prescription charges were reimposed.
● Taxes were increased.
● Hire-purchase was restricted.
● Credit was more difficult to achieve.

By 1970 Britain's balance of payments had improved, with exports up by 8 per cent. Unemployment, however, was increasing steadily and inflation still lurked.

(c) How did Edward Heath try to solve Britain's economic problems and how successful was he between 1970 and 1974?

On coming to power in June 1970, Edward Heath, the Conservative Prime Minister, said, after a meeting with top-ranking officials at Croydon, that he would be looking to allow a greater degree of individual freedom and less state interference in the economy. This approach suggested that Heath would expect industry to stand on its own two feet. Heath also stated his wish to terminate incomes policies expecting wages and price levels to be kept stable by 'market-forces' and competition. As with Wilson, things did not quite work out.

(i) *The Rolls-Royce crisis 1971*

Rolls-Royce was under contract to manufacture the RB211 engine for the Lockheed Tristar aeroplane. In 1971, however, the company ran into serious financial difficulties, and could not pay for the raw materials needed to build the engine. The government was obliged to step in and pay off the debts of Rolls-Royce; following this the company was nationalised. Senior ministers were left with red faces at this undoubted 'U-turn'.

(ii) *Upper Clyde shipbuilders*

In 1971 the work force took over four shipyards on the River Clyde after the government announced its intention to withdraw financial support which would have caused the closure of the yards. This action forced the government to think again, and in 1972 it granted a subsidy of £40 million to keep the yards working.

(iii) *Growing inflation*

Anthony Barber, the Chancellor of the Exchequer, followed a policy of cutting government spending so that reductions in taxation could be made. The theory was that people would have more money to spend, demand would be stimulated and the economy would expand. By 1972 it was clear that this approach was not working. The unions had taken advantage of the abolition of an incomes policy and huge wage increases had been granted. Together with an increase in the price of basic world food commodities (because of crop failures) these wage increases brought a serious increase in inflation (9.2 per cent on average during 1973). Unemployment in 1972 reached 899 000. As a result, Heath was forced to revert to controlling wage demands and in April 1973 he set up the Pay Board which was to work in conjunction with the Price Commission (established to oversee price rises). Wage increases were to have a ceiling of 7 per cent except for 'special cases' (the so-called Stage III).

(iv) *The oil crisis*

Nothing appeared to be going right for Heath. Although unemployment fell between 1973 and 1974, in October 1973 came a crushing blow which was beyond the control of any government. Following the Yom Kippur War between the Arab States and Israel, the Arab-dominated Oil Producing and Exporting Countries (OPEC) put up the price of oil and held back supplies to the West as a reprisal for their support of Israel. The result was to aggravate further the inflation situation. Petrol in Britain doubled in price and manufactured goods went up as a result of increased transport costs being passed on to consumers. In 1974 inflation reached 16.1 per cent.

(v) *The miners' strike 1974*

The miners demanded a pay rise which was in excess of the government's 'Stage III' ruling. The National Coal Board and the government felt duty-bound to resist the demand. The miners rejected an offer from the NCB and went on strike. The result was the imposition of a three-day week and Heath felt that the crunch had come. He called a General Election for March 1974 and the result was a narrow victory for the Labour Party.

That Edward Heath had failed was down to a mixture of misjudgement and misfortune.

(d) What policies were adopted by the Labour Governments 1974–9?

Harold Wilson must have felt a sense of *déjà vu* as he took office for a second time. This time there was to be no ambitious National Plan; the problem of 'stagflation' (a stagnating economy with raging inflation) had to be tackled with immediate measures. The miners were given a substantial pay rise and a normal working week was restored. Meanwhile, in the absence of any wage restraint, other unions won large pay awards. By 1975 inflation had reached 25 per cent.

(i) *Incomes policy again and foreign loans*

To combat inflation it was agreed with the TUC that wage increases would be restricted to £6 per week across the board. Unemployment continued to rise and the loans were obtained from the IMF to tide the country over. Meanwhile money was withdrawn from London by foreign investors and the Chancellor of the Exchequer was forced to cut government expenditure – even social welfare was affected, a bitter pill for the Labour left-wingers to swallow.

(ii) *The Industry Act 1975*

This established the *National Enterprise Board* with the brief of looking after the state's business interests and bailing out 'lame duck' companies. It provided financial assistance for British Leyland Motor Cars, Rolls-Royce and Ferranti. Despite this measure and further borrowing there was no upturn in the economy – things were as bleak as ever.

(iii)   *The winter of discontent 1978–9*

In 1976 James Callaghan became Prime Minister after Wilson had resigned to make way for new blood. In 1977 Callaghan announced a wages ceiling of 10 per cent (inflation was running at 15.9 per cent) and then in July 1978 stated that wage increases would be kept to 5 per cent. This time the trade unions did not co-operate. During the winter of 1978–9 a number of strikes took place, the most serious being the lorry drivers. In the election of March 1979 Callaghan was voted out of power by an electorate who saw the trade unions as the 'villains of the piece'.

(e)   How did Margaret Thatcher approach Britain's economic problems 1979–86, and with how much success?

(i)   *Monetarism*

In 1956 Milton Friedman and a group of economists at Chicago University published *The Quantity Theory of Money – a Restatement* in which they argued that the supply of money had to be rigorously controlled to check the rate of inflation. Margaret Thatcher adopted this policy – known as monetarism – and a whole barrage of government expenditure cuts were made. A leading Conservative, Nicholas Ridley, stated that 'bringing down the rate of inflation can only be done by restricting the money supply'. In practice, monetarism brought savage cuts in public spending including health, education and housing. Government borrowing was also restricted and wage increases limited.

(ii)   *How successful?*

The answer to this question is really a matter of opinion. Mrs Thatcher's policies have resulted in:

- Some growth in the economy.
- An improvement in the balance of trade.
- A gradual reduction in inflation to 3 per cent in May 1986, the lowest for 20 years.

However, the price for this progress has been massive unemployment on a scale worse than the depression years of the 1930s. In May 1986 unemployment in Britain stood at 3.2 million with vast amounts of money being paid out in 'dole' payments.

The Annual Register 1985 summed up the Britain of the mid-1980s when it wrote that

> The country was ever more clearly becoming divided into the growingly prosperous – those in employment, especially those working in expanding industries and services or living in the less afflicted areas, and the growingly poor – the unemployed and those dependent on declining industries and living in depressed areas of the North and Midlands. A Two Nation Syndrome was afflicting the economy and the social structure [of Britain].

33.3 TRADE UNIONS 1951–86

Trade-union membership increased from 9 535 000 in 1951 to 12 300 000 in 1981. The numbers of trade unions, however, declined from 735 to 461, mainly as a result of amalgamations. Thus, the movement came to be dominated by a small number of 'giants' which included the TGWU (2 million members in 1977) the GMWU and the AEU.

(a) Why did the trade unions clash with management and the government in the 1960s?

(i) During the early 1950s the unions followed a policy of co-operation and there was a period of relative peace. This pattern was disturbed in 1955 when there were major disputes in the docks and on the railways. As the 1950s progressed signs of conflict began to surface as the unions obtained wage increases above the level of inflation. When Selwyn Lloyd imposed the 'pay-pause' in 1961 the writing was on the wall: the scene was set for a full-scale clash in the 1960s.

(ii) During 1964 the unions suffered a major setback with the *Rookes v. Barnard Case* – this occurred when Douglas Rookes, an employee of BOAC, and member of the Association of Engineering and Shipbuilding Draughtsmen (AESD) told the union he wanted to resign his membership. The union, however, had an agreement with BOAC that they would not strike if they were permitted to have a 'closed shop' arrangement (that is, all employees had to be in the union). The officials of the AESD told BOAC that they would call out their men if Rookes was not dismissed from his job. BOAC promptly fired Rookes who then sued the union for damages and won. The decision shocked the trade-union movement, as they believed that under the Trade Dispute Act of 1906, they could not be sued for damages. This put the legal position of trade-union leaders in some doubt. In 1965 the Labour Government passed a Trades Dispute Act which restored the legal immunity of officials; they could no longer be sued for threatening to strike.

(iii) In the mid-1960s the unions found themselves up against a Labour Government which was determined to have an 'incomes policy' in order to control inflation. Between 1967 and 1969 the number of strikes increased (many of them unofficial) as the unions demonstrated their determination to win high wage increases. In 1968 the Donovan Report on Industrial Relations was published. It recommended a policy of arbitration, negotiation and conciliation between the government and the unions, rather than a policy of coercion. To this end the Report proposed that a Commission for Industrial Relations should be established. The government duly acted upon this and appointed George Woodcock as Chairman.

(iv) In 1969 Mrs Barbara Castle, Secretary for Employment and Productivity, published a White Paper, *In Place of Strife*. She was seeking the co-operation of the unions to enable the government to overcome the growing ills in the economy. She wanted to give the government the power to:

- Impose settlements where management and unions could not agree.
- Order a ballot prior to any strike.
- Impose a 'conciliation' pause of 28 days before a strike could take place (this was to allow further negotiation to take place).

Such was the furore and opposition to these proposals from both the unions and members of the Labour Party that they had to be abandoned. The government was deemed by many to be unable to control the trade unions and this was probably one of the reasons why the Conservatives won the 1970 General Election.

(b) **Why was there no improvement in industrial relations during the early 1970s?**

(i) The new Conservative Government was quick to pass legislation to control the unions. In 1971 the *Industrial Relations Act* was passed. It stated that:

- Unions had to register with 'The Registrar of Trade Unions and Employees' Association' who had the power to vet rule-books.
- Workers were to receive compensation if they were unfairly dismissed.
- Unions were not to be allowed to have 'closed-shops'.
- The National Industrial Relations Courts (NIRC) would be set up to settle disputes. It had the power to call strike ballots and order a 'cooling off' period. Any union failing to comply with the Court would be fined.

(ii) The Act turned out to be counter-productive. Instead of curbing the unions it had the effect of embittering industrial relations. The majority of unions refused to register and publically stated their opposition to the Act. In 1972 NIRC found itself with plenty of work to do:

- In March the TGWU was taken to the Court for 'blacking' containers in Liverpool. The TGWU, however, refused to take any notice of the Court and was fined £50 000 for contempt.
- In April the NUR threatened a strike if a pay demand was not met by British Rail. NIRC imposed a 'cooling off' period and told the union to hold a strike ballot. The result turned out to be a staggering reversal for the Court with the railwaymen voting by six to one to support a strike. The 'cooling off' period was never imposed again.
- In July five London dockers continued to black containers after being told otherwise by the Court. As a result they were imprisoned and became 'martyred' as the 'Pentonville Five'. There followed a national dock strike in protest.

(iii) *Trouble in the coal industry 1972 and 1974*

In January 1972 the NUM called a national strike in an effort to win a substantial wage increase. Power-stations unable to receive regular supplies of coal were unable to meet domestic and industrial demand for electricity. The government imposed a three-day working week and Lord Wilberforce was appointed to investigate the miners' claim. He reported in favour of the miners in February, concluding that mining was a dangerous occupation and should therefore be well paid.

In January 1974 another strike took place in the coal industry, when 81 per cent voted in favour of industrial action (see section 33.2(c)(v)). Once again the issue was a wage increase higher than the rate of inflation. The government again introduced the three day week and rationed the supply of electricity. This time, though, Edward Heath put the issue to the electorate; the result, in March 1974, was a narrow Labour victory. On coming to power the new Labour government granted the miners a large wage increase. This brought a short-lived period of industrial peace.

(c) What efforts were made to obtain industrial peace between 1974 and 1979? Why did they fail?

(i) In 1974 the Labour Government abolished the Industrial Relations Act (1971) and negotiated the *Social Contract* with the unions. This was an agreement to co-operate with each other in the interests of restoring calm to industrial relations. In return for the government removing the Act the unions stated that they would be moderate in wage demands and would keep within the rate of inflation. In July 1975 the TUC agreed to accept a flat-rate ceiling on wage increases of £6 per week hoping that this would help to reduce inflation.

(ii) The *Employment Protection Act 1975* was a further measure to bring sanity to the situation. It said that:

● Workers could take grievances (for example, unfair dismissal, sex discrimination) to industrial tribunals.
● Unions were to be registered on an official list kept by the Certification Officer, thereby giving them bona fide status.
● The Advisory, Conciliation and Arbitration Service (ACAS) was given statutory status with the power to arbitrate between two parties in dispute.

(iii) In 1976 the unions agreed to 4.5 per cent as the guide line for pay increases but in 1978 their patience ran out when a ceiling of 5 per cent was suggested by James Callaghan. There followed the 'winter of discontent', as referred to above.

(d)   What policies did the Conservatives adopt towards trade unions between 1979 and 1986? How successful were they?

(i)   Margaret Thatcher had made an election pledge that a Conservative Government would pass legislation to reduce the influence of the unions. Consequently, in 1980 the *Employment Act* was passed with the following terms:

- In future 'closed shops' would have to be approved by 80 per cent of a union's membership, otherwise they were illegal.
- 'Secondary' picketing was severely restricted (this was the practice of men from other unions picketing in a dispute that did not directly concern them).
- Government funds were to be made available for unions to hold strike ballots.
- Codes of practice were laid down on the issues of the 'closed shop' and picketing.

(ii)   In 1982 a *Second Employment Act* was passed:

- All 'closed shops' (not just new ones) were to be illegal if they did not have the backing of a secret ballot, with a majority of 85 per cent in support.
- Industrial action with the purpose of persuading an employer to accept a 'closed shop' agreement was made illegal.
- Compensation was to be made available to any worker who had been dismissed (between 1974 and 1980) for refusing to join a trade union in a 'closed-shop' situation.
- The meaning of the term 'trade dispute' was narrowed down to mean simply a dispute between worker and management. Strikes called where the employer was not in dispute with his workers were to be illegal.

(iii)   These two Acts had the effect of polarising public opinion with some people strongly in favour whilst others were bitterly opposed to them. Between 1983 and 1986 a number of head-on collisions occurred:

- In January 1983 the Water and Sewerage Workers staged a four-week strike and achieved a startling victory. They succeeded in winning a payrise of 10.4 per cent (the initial offer by the employers was 7.3 per cent) and a 38-hour week.

● In 1983 Mr Eddy Shah, proprietor of the Messenger Printing Group, which published local newspapers, became involved in a long-running battle with the trade unions. Not wishing to have a 'closed shop' situation in his workshops he dismissed six workers who were members of the National Graphical Association. This he was legally entitled to do under the Employment Acts of 1980 and 1982. However, the NGA regarded the 'closed shop' as an integral part of their policy and imposed a picket on Shah's Warrington factory.

Other trade unionists came from all over Britain to put their weight behind the NGA and thus were indulging in 'secondary picketing', also outlawed under the two Acts above. Shah gained a High Court injunction to stop the picketing which had produced some ugly incidents. The NGA refused to obey, intensified the picket and was further fined a total of £150 000 for contempt. Matters then escalated further when the NGA called out its members in Fleet Street which resulted in the High Court confiscating the union's assets (put at £10 million).

Feelings were now at fever pitch. Len Murray, Secretary-General of the TUC, worried about the legal implications of the dispute, stepped in and persuaded the NGA to call off a national strike planned for December 1983. The dispute left deep wounds. Trade unionists believed that they were only defending their traditional rights. Others argued that workers should not be subject to a closed shop and should have the right to choose whether they wished to join a particular trade union. What clearly worried the more moderate members of the TUC (and Labour Party) was that the dispute was, in fact, breaking the law and this could not be condoned.

● On 10 March 1984 the National Union of Mineworkers, led by Arthur Scargill and Mick McGahey, went on strike in protest at the NCBs intended plan to close 20 collieries with 20 000 miners losing their jobs. The closure plan had been drawn up by Ian MacGregor, Chairman of the NCB. The strike turned out to be a bitter and violent struggle.

At first the NUM had solid backing from its membership, but as time wore on Scargill began to be criticised for apparently condoning violence on the picket-line and for not holding a ballot before the strike. Recriminations were rife and mining families were split over the issue. Gradually miners began to seep back to work – as they were unable to pay household bills or adequately feed their families. Mr Norman Willis, the new Secretary-General of the TUC, was shouted down by angry miners at Aberavon when he criticised the amount of violence on the picket lines.

On 5 March 1985 the executive of the NUM called off the strike by a narrow majority. They made it clear that they would fight to obtain an amnesty for those miners who had been dismissed by the NCB during the strike. An estimated 25 million working days had been lost and the scars of the strike would take decades to heal.

The Nottinghamshire miners, unhappy at the NUM's no-ballot policy broke away and formed the Union of Democratic Mineworkers (UDM). Throughout the strike the government had refused to intervene and try to negotiate a settlement. The strike will probably go down as the most bitter industrial struggle in trade-union history.

● In January 1984, Sir Geoffrey Howe, the Foreign Secretary, stated that no person employed by the Government Communication Headquarters (GCHQ) in Cheltenham was to belong to a trade union. The government was fearful of industrial action causing a security risk to the nation (no one would be monitoring world events and foreign radio stations). Employees were offered £1000 to rescind their union membership. The House of Lords ruled that the government was within the law to do this but the TUC were unhappy with the decision, referring the matter to the European Commissioner of Human Rights (May 1985).

(iv) *Fortress Wapping* – For some time there had been an uneasy atmosphere in the Fleet Street newspaper industry with the print unions resisting new technology, whilst demanding high wages. This issue was at the centre of a dispute which arose in January 1986 involving Mr Rupert Murdoch, the owner of 'News International' (which prints *The Sun*, *The News of the World* and *The Times*), and the major print unions – SOGAT 82 and the National Graphical Association. Mr Murdoch announced that he was moving his company from Fleet Street to new premises at Wapping where he had installed the latest printing technology. He intended that any worker transferring with him might be asked to sign a 'no strike agreement'. The unions expressed their opposition to this and Mr Murdoch replied by dismissing 5500 workers. He then opened his Wapping Plant using labour from other unions and non-union labour, stating that the NGA would never be allowed in. The print unions then put a picket line on the Wapping Plant which had barbed wire on its perimeter walls to keep out the 'undesirables' (hence 'Fortess Wapping'). The objective of the picket was to try and dissuade workers going into the plant and also to try and stop delivery lorries making an exit. There was violence on the picket lines but the dispute remained dead-locked.

(v)   The success of these policies is difficult to assess. Historians in the future will be better placed to make judgements. However the government pointed to the fact that the number of trade-union disputes was reduced between 1979 and 1986 and that this was a measure of success. Opponents of the government argued that their policies resulted in confrontation and conflict and only succeeded in dividing the nation.

33.4   EDUCATION SINCE 1951

(a)   How and why did 'comprehensive' schools develop?

(i)   The official definition of a comprehensive school is 'one which is intended to cater for all secondary education of all the children in a given area'. Hence there is no selection at 11-plus, and no attempt to categorise children according to their ability. Before 1965 most Local Education Authorities organised their schools on the Tripartite System (see chapter 18) – only a few comprehensive schools existed:

Provision of secondary schools in 1961

Grammar schools ⎫	
Technical schools ⎬	5400 in number
Secondary schools ⎭	
Comprehensives	138 in number

However, public opinion gradually observed the way that the 11-plus examination could disadvantage children and a growing lobby for comprehensive education materialised.

(ii)   Among the arguments in favour of comprehensive schools were that they:

- Would be larger and therefore able to provide a much wider curriculum.
- Would remove selection at 11-plus and therefore be fairer.
- Provide equality of opportunity for all individuals.
- Would not condemn a child as a 'failure' at 11-plus.
- Would provide a broader social education allowing children from all types of background to mix.

Opponents of comprehensive schools expressed a number of fears stating that they would result in:

- Poor academic achievements (a tendency for the less able to 'bring down' the brighter pupils).
- Too large in size and therefore impersonal.
- Difficult to manage and organise.

(iii)   On 12 July 1965, the Secretary of State for Education, Tony Crossland, issued Circular 10/65 which made comprehensive education the official policy of the government, and requested LEAs 'to prepare and submit plans for reorganising secondary education in their areas on Comprehensive lines'. By 1968 66 per cent of the LEAs in England and Wales had responded by sending their 'Comprehensive Reorganisation Plans' to the Department of Education and Science (DES) for approval.

(iv)   LEAs were free to adopt a comprehensive system best suited to their needs. The following types of Comprehensives appeared:

- Straight-through schools from 11 to 18
- Schools which took children from 11 to 16, with those wishing to have a sixth form education transferring to a Tertiary or Sixth Form College
- Middle schools, taking children from 8 to 12 and then transferring to upper schools from 13 to 18.

(v) In 1970 Margaret Thatcher, the Secretary of State for Education, issued Circular 10/70 which stated that LEAs were under no obligation to reorganise on comprehensive lines. Then in 1974 Labour reversed the policy once again, insisting that LEAs submit proposals for comprehensive reorganisation. By the 1980s 90 per cent of state secondary schools were comprehensives, although some LEAs have said that they would favour a return to a selective system (for example, Solihull, Hereford and Worcester).

(b) An outline of some of the most important educational reports since 1951

There has been a surfeit of inquiries into all aspects of education since 1951.

(i) In 1956 the Central Advisory Council for Education, under the chairmanship of *Sir Geoffrey Crowther*, was asked to investigate 'the education of boys and girls between the ages of 15 and and 18'. Its findings were published in *The Crowther Report: 15–18* in 1959. It suggested that many youngsters between these ages did not receive an adequate education and many left school at 15 without the necessary basic skills to cope with the outside world. In addition, Crowther expressed concern about the sixth form curriculum in English schools claiming that it 'introduces specialisation too early . . . Not only may specialisation begin before a boy knows his own mind but . . . before anybody can give valid advice on what his best course is'. Crowther recommended that the compulsory school-leaving age should be raised to 16 (by 1968 at the latest) and that the nation should aim to have 50 per cent of its children in full-time education to the age of 18 by 1980, (the actual figure achieved was 29 per cent). The school-leaving age was raised to 16 in 1972.

(ii) *The Robbins Report of 1963* concerned Higher Education. The government was concerned that too few students had the opportunity to attend university because of the lack of places. Robbins recommended:

● That the number of places in higher education should reach 560 000 by 1980–81, of which 350 000 would be in universities.

● That a Grants Commission should be established to oversee the awarding of grants.

The Robbins Report was accepted by the government and was implemented. In the mid-1960s a number of new universities were opened including York, Warwick, Essex, Kent and Sussex. In addition, a number of other institutions were given university status, for example, Bradford College of Advanced Technology. The numbers of polytechnical colleges and colleges of education were also increased. A further extension of the Robbins philosophy was the establishment of the Open University in 1969 based at Milton Keynes, the main aim of which was to give those adults who had missed out earlier in life the opportunity to study and gain a degree. Courses were modular in design and taught via course-books, television and radio programmes, and seminars at local centres.

(iii) *The Newsom Report of 1963* entitled *Half our Future* concentrated on the average and below-average secondary pupil between the ages of 13 and 16. Among its recommendations were that:

● The school-leaving age should be raised to 16 'for all pupils entering the secondary schools from September 1965'.
● Extra-curricular activities should be extended.
● Schools should be 'adequately' resourced.
● Every school should present every pupil with a certificate of achievement when they leave 'irrespective of any external examination they may take'.

Although the Newsom Report was thoroughly discussed in education circles it had little immediate impact.

(iv) In 1967 the *Plowden Report* was published. Entitled *Children and their Primary Schools* it considered 'Primary education in all its aspects, and the transition to secondary education'. It recommended that:

● Educational Priority Areas (EPAs) should be established where children were environmentally deprived. These EPAs should receive extra funding.
● Learning in primary school should be a combination of 'individual, group and classwork . . . [we] welcome the trend towards individual learning'.

This report was generally welcomed by the educational world although many people wondered if LEAs would be able to finance the priority areas. As it turned out a large number of inner-city areas were given EPA status and there was a move towards 'child-centred' or individual learning in primary schools.

(v) In 1972 the *James Report* recommended that teachers should receive one full term off school every seven years to undergo refresher training; this was not implemented.

(vi) Finally in 1975 the *Bullock Report – A Language for Life* published its findings on the 'teaching of reading in school and the other uses of English'. Among its many recommendations were that each school should:

- Devise a reading policy for all its pupils.
- Devise a policy for 'language across the curriculum' in schools.
- Have better resources (that is, staffing) to achieve a higher standard of the use of language.

Once again wide-spread debate was stimulated with many schools taking the initiative and appointing a teacher to develop the policies advocated by Bullock.

(c) What changes have taken place in examinations between 1951 and 1986?

(i) In 1951 the School Certificate was superseded by the General Certificate of Education (GCE) which was divided into Ordinary Level and Advanced Level. The GCE was administered by a number of Examining Boards throughout the country (for example, London, Cambridge, Oxford) and schools had a free choice as to which syllabuses they adopted.

(ii) The GCE was academically weighted and was therefore more suited to pupils in grammar schools. Children in secondary modern schools did not take any examinations and left school without any formal qualification. To try to overcome this the Certificate of Secondary Education (CSE) was introduced in 1965. This was organised by Regional Examination Boards (for example, East Midlands Regional Examination Board) and was aimed at average pupils. A Grade 1, however, in CSE was accepted as equivalent to a GCE 'O' level pass grade. The CSE differed from GCE in that classroom teachers were involved in the setting and marking of examination papers.

(iii) By the early 1970s it was clear that the examination system needed streamlining. There was a multitude of syllabuses and uniform standards were difficult to apply. Furthermore, in comprehensive schools it was often very difficult for teaching staff to decide which examination to enter 'borderline' children for and 'double-entry' was often the solution. Thus the idea of one common examination for all 16-year-old pupils was suggested by the Schools Council in 1975. Some boards carried out 'feasibility studies' but not until the 1980s did the idea start to be a reality when Sir Keith Joseph, Secretary of State for Education, announced that the new GCSE would be examined for the first time in 1988. One of the main features of the examination was that 'national criteria' (general and subject-specific) were drawn up to bring a greater degree of conformity between the various examining boards. The establishment of the GCSE was supervised by the Secondary Examinations Council (SEC).

(d) What was the 'great debate'?

 (i) In 1976 Her Majesty's Inspectorate published their views about 'standards' in schools in England and Wales. There was a growing concern that schools were not providing the right kind of curriculum for the modern world and furthermore, they appeared to resent any criticism of the system.

(ii) Shirley Williams, Secretary of State for Education, and Prime Minister James Callaghan, therefore initiated a 'great debate' into education. How would our schools be improved? Callaghan made a speech at Ruskin College, Oxford, in October 1976 in which he said the nation must seek to improve standards in schools to meet the demands of modern life.

(iii) The great debate was concluded in 1977 with the publication of a Government Green paper which urged that the curriculum and methods of assessment should come under close scrutiny. The question of educational standards remained a major issue in 1986.

(e) What recent trends have there been in education?

(i) The 1980 Education Act stated that parents were to have greater representation on school governing bodies and that pupils from working-class backgrounds should be given financial aid to enable them to obtain a place in an independent school (this was called 'The Assisted Places' scheme).

(ii) In 1981 the government made it policy that every school should have at least one computer – the so-called 'Micros in Schools' scheme. By December 1984 this was achieved. In 1980 the 'Microelectronics Education Programme' was started in order to 'promote the study of microelectronics in schools'.

(iii) In 1983 the Manpower Services Commission, anxious to give young people a more appropriate education for the industrial world, launched 'The Technical and Vocational Educational Initiative'. Money was made available to develop courses for 14 to 18-year-olds such as Business Studies, Information Technology, Design Technology and Personal Education. By 1986 the scheme was well established.

(iv) Despite these developments, the government came in for fierce criticism from parents, teachers and LEAs for the cuts in spending in education. An HMI report in May 1986 revealed that many of Britain's schoolbuildings were dilapidated and that schools were short of books and basic equipment. In addition, Higher Education had been squeezed having absorbed a reduction in income of 2 per cent per year; as a result, whole departments in some institutions were axed. The number of foreign students in British universities declined drastically and it became increasingly difficult for British students to gain a place. Critics pointed out that Higher Education was the key to Britain's future industrial prosperity and future generations would pay the price for the short-sighted cutbacks.

(v) There was a long-running dispute between the teachers on the one hand and the LEAs and the government on the other. The central issue was pay, with the teachers claiming that their salaries, compared with other professional groups, had been eroded by 30 per cent since the Houghton Pay Award of 1974. Voluntary duties and out-of-school activities were stopped and selective strikes were held. The dispute was brought to an uneasy truce when ACAS intervened and the outcome was a salary award of 6.9 per cent. Following this, negotiations were begun about teachers' conditions and contracts.

(vi) By May 1986 education had become a major political issue. Such was the concern about the state education system that Mrs Thatcher replaced Sir Keith Joseph with Kenneth Baker as Secretary of State for Education in an effort to improve matters. Critics of the government declared that it had deliberately run down the state system in order to give a boost to the independent sector. Supporters of the government's policy argued that schools should be accountable for their performance and should learn to give value for money.

33.5 INDUSTRIAL DEVELOPMENTS 1951–86

(a) The coal industry

(i) The fortunes of the coal industry fluctuated in this period. During the 1950s a number of collieries were closed as the demand for coal decreased in the face of competition from nuclear power and oil. By the late 1960s the National Coal Board had embarked on a programme of modernisation to make British pits more efficient and cost effective. The industry received a boost in 1973 when OPEC cut back supplies of oil to the West, and this led to the NUM and NCB publishing the *Plan for Coal* in 1974. This was an agreed plan for the development of the industry over a period to 1984; it envisaged large-scale investment in the industry, including the opening of new fields.

(ii) Some progress was consequently made but the NCB found it difficult to make a profit. In 1983 the new Yorkshire coalfield near Selby was opened and plans were laid to exploit large reserves of coal in the Vale of Belvoir. However, in 1982–3 the NCB could do no better than keep its losses down to £11 million over the year. Ian MacGregor thus decided to slim down the industry further and in doing so, precipitated the miners' strike of 1984–5. Following the miners' defeat in this strike, pit closures were announced with 4000 miners being made redundant in south Yorkshire in the summer of 1986.

(iii)   Despite these problems it can be argued that the British coal industry has a promising future:

- Coal will not be exhausted for another 300 years, whereas coal and natural gas will run out in the twenty-first century
- After the Chernobyl Nuclear Explosion (April 1986) the government may review its policy on nuclear energy and build more coal-fired power-stations.

(b)   Shipbuilding

(i)   This industry has undergone a rapid decline since its halcyon period immediately prior to the First World War. In the modern period British yards were unable to maintain a good record of industrial relations and this resulted in the British industry gaining a reputation for unreliability, often failing to deliver the goods on time. A further setback was the fact that the Japanese and South Koreans dominated the construction of the super oil-tankers during the 1960s. Britain could not compete with the low-wage economies of these countries and consequently, lost ground. The output from British yards tended to be limited to cargo vessels, tugs and warships for the Navy. In the 1970s oil-rigs were constructed in British yards in response to the exploitation of the North Sea oil and natural gasfields.

(ii)   In 1985–6 British shipbuilding hit an all-time low. Already in the doldrums, the industry only managed to obtain orders for 23 million tonnes of shipping during the year as opposed to the 200 000 million tonnes they had hoped to attract. The industry was faced with a world recession. The era of the super-tanker had declined and the Japanese yards (supported by massive financial aid from major banks) continued to win the lion's share of the world market. By 1986 Britain was producing just 1 per cent of the world's tonnage. In the light of this background the government announced in the spring of 1986 that 3500 jobs would be abolished in British yards. The following areas were affected:

Yard	Redundancies	Total work-force
Appledore, Devon	95	645
Ferguson-Ailsa (Troon)	325	780
Govan (Clydeside)	495	2 345
N.E. Shipbuilders (Sunderland)	925	3 005
Smith's Dock (Middlesborough)	1 295	1 365
Clark Kincaid (Wallsend)	360	890

The redundancies left a work-force of 5535 in British yards.

(iii) The job-losses were made harder to bear as the areas affected were already ones of high unemployment. Critics of the government stated that British shipbuilding would be dead within a year. The government defended their action on British shipbuilding by arguing:

- Orders were simply not there to be won, and thus British yards had an over-capacity.
- Despite £1400 million being invested in the industry, the decline in fortunes had not been averted.
- Other countries, such as Sweden, were suffering from the same problem.

(c) Textiles

(i) Both the cotton and woollen industries declined in this period for two main reasons:

- Competition from abroad.
- Competition from synthetic (man-made fibres).

Wool is now the most important natural fibre, being concentrated in West Yorkshire and Scotland. The Lancashire cotton industry has been cut back drastically, employing only 45 000 workers (compared with 150 000 in 1962).

(ii) The manufacture of synthetic fibres in Britain was pioneered by Courtaulds and ICI who started manufacturing rayon, nylon and terylene. Momentum was gained during the 1960s and by 1986 a whole range of man-made fibres had been created including 'Orlon' 'Acrilan' polyester, polypropylene and polyethylene.

(d) Iron and steel

(i) Between 1951 and 1970 the iron and steel industry prospered, with steel production rising from 16 million to 28 million tonnes and iron from 12 million to 18 million tonnes. This was despite the denationalisation of the steel industry by Churchill's government in 1953. During the 1950s Scunthorpe, Corby and Margam were developed as steel centres. In 1967 the industry was nationalised for a second time with the British Steel Corporation (BSC) taking over the vast majority of the furnaces (a few private companies producing specialised products, for example, stainless steel, were allowed to continue independently). BSC invested a large amount of money in installing the basic oxygen and electric-arc processes which speeded up production.

(ii) Since the 1970s, however, the steel industry has been in the doldrums because of a decline in the shipbuilding and motor-car industries. The industry has been forced to cut back, with works closing down – Consett, Shotton, Corby, Sheffield, Rotherham, Ebbw Vale all suffering. The major plants are now centred at South Teesside, Ravenscraig, Llanwern, Port Talbot, Sheffield and Scunthorpe (and even these have lost some furnaces). In 1978 production slumped to 20 million tonnes, and in 1986 Britain was producing less steel per annum than she had done in the 1950s.

(iii) Non-ferrous metals have steadily increased in importance with aluminium, titanium (used in the electronic and aircraft industries) and a number of alloys being developed. These metals are light but strong and are essential to modern technology.

(e) The motor-car industry

(i) Although the number of motor vehicles on the road has increased rapidly since 1950, the British motor-car industry has never been completely free of problems. In the 1950s it was realised that the industry had too many firms producing too many models and this prompted a number of amalgamations. In 1952 the British Motor Corporation was formed by the merger of Austin and Morris, followed by the amalgamation of Jaguar and Daimler. One important model introduced by BMC was the Mini, a cheap economical car. In the later 1960s the government-sponsored Industrial Reorganisation Corporation inspired Leyland Motors and BMC to join together to form British Leyland. This caused a deal of controversy, as during the 1970s this huge company found it difficult to operate at a profit and suffered from poor industrial relations.

(ii) Since the 1970s the British motor industry has found it increasingly difficult to hold on to its share of the market. Fierce competition from abroad has caused a number of assembly plants to close, including Speke, Solihull and Abingdon (all Leyland) and Linwood (Talbot). A number of other centres such as Oxford (Leyland), Luton, Ellesmere Port (Vauxhall) and Dagenham (Ford) have been forced to reduce their labour force. In 1983 more than half the cars sold in Britain were imported. The Japanese have captured a large slice of the British market – Datsun, Nissan and Toyota in particular, making decisive inroads. In 1986 Nissan opened a new plant in Washington (Tyne and Wear) capable of producing 100 000 cars in a year. They have been allowed into Britain because of the number of jobs they will provide in the North-East.

(f) The aerospace industry

Britain has a better record of achievement in this industry, producing helicopters, aircraft (military and civil), hovercraft and guided weapons. In 1978 the British Aircraft Corporation, Hawker-Siddeley and Scottish Aviation were merged to form British Aerospace. This was originally a nationalised organisation but in 1981 the government sold half of its shares to private individuals. Among the successes of the industry have been:

- The Harrier Jump Jet.
- The Tornado combat aircraft (produced in collaboration with Italy and West Germany).
- The supersonic airliner 'Concorde' (produced in conjunction with the French). This airliner went into service in 1976 and

although a superb technological achievement, it has not been a commercial success. There are no plans, at present, to develop another supersonic airliner.

● The high quality of Rolls-Royce engines.
● Its contribution to the European Space Agency which deals with the manufacture of satellites and space research.

(g) The chemical industry

This industry has made good progress since 1951 and by 1982 was the second most important producer in Europe with a total work force of 360 000 and exports valued at over £6 million. Among the products made are dyes, plastics, detergents, adhesives, fertilisers and cosmetics. In 1981 ICI accounted for one-third of Britain's chemical output. One major development was the expansion of oil refineries in Britain which began about 1950. The large oil companies such as Esso, Shell and British Petroleum spent huge sums on building refineries in the knowledge that it was cheaper and safer to import crude oil rather than petrol. Among Britain's largest refineries are Milford Haven, Stanlow, Fawley, Killingholme, Teesport, Grangemouth and Llandarcy.

(h) Electrical and electronic engineering

(i) Since the Second World War electrical engineering has made staggering progress. The industry began to manufacture televisions and transistor radios on a mass-scale in the 1950s and has not looked back since, with the technology becoming more sophisticated day by day.

(ii) There is now a wide range of domestic appliances ranging from deep freezers and food-blenders to video recorders and Hi-Fi systems.

(iii) The electronics industry also manufactures instruments – radar equipment, telecommunications equipment (telephones, telex, satellites, etc.). One important breakthrough in 1964 was the invention of optical fibres used in electrical cables for the transmission of electricity.

(iv) The computer industry has made incredible progress. The industry was stimulated by the Second World War and development work was undertaken at Manchester University in the

1950s. In 1969 came the silicon chip and the start of the microprocessor industry. By the 1980s computers were used in a huge range of businesses, including factories, offices, schools, building societies, telecommunications, etc. and one company which dominates the mainframe computer industry is the American-owned International Business Machines (IBM). The computer has brought the age of information technology, with such systems as 'Prestel' and 'Times Network' being developed for the rapid call-up of data.

(v) Britain was prominent in the 'home-computer boom which took off in 1980. The leading individual in this venture was Clive Sinclair who produced a range of cheap microcomputers including the ZX80. This 'boom' suddenly dried up in 1985 and Sinclair found himself in financial difficulties. The education market has been dominated by the 'BBC-B ' model.

(vi) Allied to the use of microcomputers has been the development of sophisticated office machinery including electric typewriters, photocopiers, microfilm readers and word processors.

(vii) In 1981 the electronics and electrical engineering industry, despite facing major competition from abroad (especially Japan), employed 700 000 people and had total sales of almost £12 million.

(i)   Service industries

These industries, which include advertising, wholesaling, retailing, catering, tourism, consultancies and the media, have increased in importance. In 1982 they were responsible for employing over 60 per cent of the total work force.

(j)   The privatisation of industry

In 1979 the Conservative Party, in keeping with its political philosophy, announced that a programme of privatisation would be put into operation. This involved the selling of public assets to private shareholders. This has proved to be very controversial but the government claim that private industry is more competitive and that the selling of shares has raised large amounts of capital for the Exchequer. Some of the concerns which have been affected are British Telecom (51 per cent of the shares sold to private shareholders, raising £1357 million in 1985), Amersham International, British Aerospace, British Petroleum, Cable and Wireless, Britoil, Forestry Commission and New Town Development Corporations (sale of land). Margaret Thatcher informed the House of Commons in February 1986 that:

> Since the Conservative Government came to power in 1979 a total of twelve major companies, comprising some 20% of the state commercial sector had been privatised, and that by the end of the current Parliament [that is, not later than mid-1988] a further 20% should have been transferred to the private sector. (Keesing's Contemporary Archive, April 1986, p. 34319)

(k) What developments have taken place in agriculture since 1951?

(i) The Labour Government (1945–51) made a firm commitment to the future of British agriculture when it passed the *1947 Agriculture Act* which stated that:

- The government would give farmers subsidies to help them invest in modern methods.
- There would be a guaranteed minimum price for farm products which would be reviewed annually.
- A new body, the National Agricultural Advisory Service (NAAS) would advise farmers as to how to manage their farms.

The Act was a 'shot in the arm' for British agriculture which was given the confidence to make rapid strides in the 1950s and 1960s.

(ii) Farms became fully-mechanised, with more tractors (500 000 in 1981), combine harvesters (57 000 in 1981), seed-drills and mechanical milking parlours. This in turn has meant a decline in the numbers of workers employed in agriculture (from 800 000 in 1952 to about 500 000 in 1982). Chemical fertilisers and pesticides came to be used on a much wider scale with output and yields increasing accordingly. In the fenland areas of Lincolnshire and Cambridgeshire, farmers took up hedge-rows in order to make use of every available metre of land. Factory farming methods (for example, battery hens) were widely adopted. These measures brought a great deal of

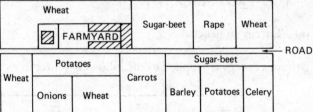

Features
Large rectangular fields
Fertile Peat Soil
No hedgerows
Fields separated by drainage ditches
Size: about 250 acres (100 hectares)

A typical Cambridgeshire fen farm in the 1960s

protest from conservationists and animal-right campaigners who argued that the British farmer was cruel, over-commercial and obsessed with profit-making. The farmers were able to argue that his increased efficiencies benefited the country as they were providing over half the nation's food requirements. In the 1970s and 1980s British farming has been at pains to adopt a responsible attitude towards balancing the conservation issue with the economic side of the argument.

(iii) *The European Economic Community (EEC)*

Britain's membership of the EEC has meant that her agriculture has become subject to the Common Agricultural Policy (CAP). This sets out the following points:

● Subsidies to be paid to EEC farmers in order that they receive a guaranteed price for their products.
● An import tariff on food brought into the EEC from non-member countries.
● Grants to be made available to help farmers develop their activities (for example, the British hill farmer).
● Surplus stocks of food to be bought up by the EEC.

The CAP has produced a deal of controversy with member states often arguing as to how the financial cake should be cut (in 1982 CAP used over 60 per cent of the EEC's total budget). In addition, the policy has encouraged farmers to grow large amounts of food as they know that even if the market price collapses they will be able to sell to the EEC. The effect of this has been the much publicised 'butter mountains' and 'wine lakes'. Doubtless the controversy will continue.

33.6 ENERGY SINCE 1951

(a) Energy in general

Britain's energy is supplied by the following sources:

Primary sources		Secondary sources
Coal		Electricity
Oil	used	
Natural gas	to	Coke
Nuclear power	produce	
Water-power		Town gas

The main trend since 1951 has been the continued decline of the use of steam-power and an increase in the use of oil, natural gas and nuclear power. As a primary source of energy, coal remains important (see below and Section 33.5).

Primary energy consumption (percentages)

	1972	1982
Oil	48.0	35.6
Coal	36.2	35.5
Natural gas	12.1	23.0
Nuclear power	3.1	5.1
Hydro-electric power (HEP)	0.5	0.1

(b) Oil

(i) Before the mid-1970s the vast majority of Britain's oil requirements were imported from the Middle East. The political dangers of the dependence on this source of energy has already been referred to in Section 33.2(c)). From the late 1960s, however, off-shore exploration in the North Sea revealed substantial deposits of oil (and natural gas) which were commercially viable. By 1984 almost 30 North Sea oilfields had been referred to in Section 33.2(c)). From the late 1960s,

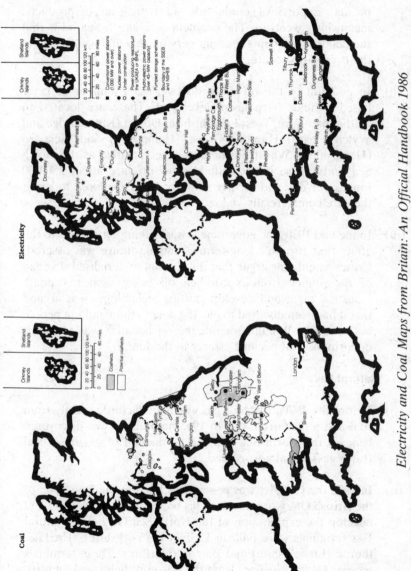

Electricity and Coal Maps from Britain: An Official Handbook 1986
(reproduced with the permission of the Controller of Her Majesty's Stationery Office)

per day. These discoveries provided the country with something of a bonanza. Britain was able to cut back on some of the foreign imports, with the major oil companies making large profits. Exports of crude oil and petroleum by-products, meanwhile, went up. The problem with North Sea oil is that the deposits are being used up very quickly and will dry up in the twenty-first century.

(ii) In addition to the off-shore discoveries, a number of land-based oilfields have been developed. These are located in Nottinghamshire, West Lincolnshire, Dorset (Kimmeridge and Wytch Farm), Humbly Grove (Hampshire) and Herriard (Hampshire). Whilst nowhere near as lucrative as the North Sea finds, these inland oilfields now produce about 250 000 tonnes per day and further sites are being explored to see if they are commercially viable.

(iii) In the mid 1970s the government was making statements to the effect that Britain's long-term economic future was assured. Critics would now argue that this has not materialised. Instead of the money from North Sea oil being used to update industrial plant and develop existing technology, it is argued that it has been diverted to pay the dole to three million people out of work. Whether or not the oil bonanza was a wasted opportunity will become clearer in the future.

(c) Natural gas

(i) Before the 1970s Britain's gas was manufactured mainly from coal and a little from oil. In 1965 natural gas was discovered beneath the North Sea and the production of gas from coal (town gas) has almost ceased.

(ii) In 1972 the Gas Act was passed which led to the formation of the British Gas Corporation. This body was to co-ordinate and develop the exploitation of the North Sea Gasfields. Natural Gas terminals were built at Easington (Yorkshire), Theddlethorpe (Lincolnshire) and Bacton (Norfolk). These terminals receive gas via pipelines from the off-shore fields and, in turn, they distribute it inland through a pipeline network.

(iii) In recognition of the fact that Natural Gas is not a finite resource the BGC are investing large amounts of capital into researching methods of making gas from low-grade coal and oil.

(d) Nuclear power

(i) Britain's first nuclear power-station was opened in 1956 at Calder Hall, Cumbria. Nuclear fuel (uranium) is used to create heat to produce steam. The steam drives a turbine which, in turn, generates electricity for the national grid.

(ii) The development of Britain's nuclear power-stations has been achieved in two phases:

- 1962–71 saw the construction of power stations based on the Magnox reactor. These were located at Bradwell, Hunterston, Sizewell, Dungeness, Berkeley, Hinkley Point, Trawsfynydd, Chapelcross, Windscale and Wylfa.
- After 1971 Britain changed her opinion about the Magnox reactor after corrosion had been found. Instead power-stations based on the 'Advanced Gas-cooled Reactor' were constructed. These included Hinkley Point B, Hunterston B, Dungeness B, Hartlepool and Heysham. All these power-stations proved difficult to build and in most cases their completion dates were delayed. In addition they proved to be very expensive.
- The latest development is the adoption of the American pressurised water reactor, with plans to build a new nuclear power-station at Sizewell in Suffolk.

(iii) The first power-stations in Britain were built away from large centres of population because of the risk of explosion and resulting nuclear fall-out. In the 1970s, however, the feeling grew that the dangers of nuclear power were known and containable; consequently locations near to towns at Heysham and Hartlepool were built.

(iv) Attitudes towards nuclear energy have changed radically during the 1980s. The general public have been made aware of a number of accidents and 'near-misses' in British nuclear power-stations. Further questions were asked about the disposal of nuclear waste and the effects of radiation leaks on the people who lived near to nuclear power stations. Radiation leaks at Windscale (1957) and Three Mile Island (America) in

1977 were considered alarming. Then in April 1986 a horrific explosion at a Russian nuclear power-station at Chernobyl (near Kiev in the Ukraine) brought a world-wide outcry against nuclear power. Nineteen people were killed directly in the explosion and over 200 were detained in hospital suffering from serious burns. The fire took almost three weeks to extinguish and the population around the area (some 90 000 people) was evacuated. Mikhail Gorbachev, the Soviet leader, was severely criticised in the Western press for not publishing the full facts quickly enough. The fall-out resulting from the explosion reached a distance of 1000 miles, with the Scandinavian countries and northern Scotland being affected. The unknown factor is the number of people who will die in the next 20 years as a result of radiation-related diseases such as cancer. The result of Chernobyl will be a re-examination of nuclear energy policies throughout the world. British Nuclear Fuels Ltd has reaffirmed that nuclear power-stations are not a risk. However, in the light of Chernobyl, many people were seeking the closure of all nuclear power-stations and calling for greater efforts to be made to develop 'new' forms of energy such as solar and tidal power.

33.7 TRANSPORT DEVELOPMENTS

(a) Roads

Over the period as a whole Britain's roads have increasingly become more crowded with some 20 million vehicles in use. Among the major developments have been:

(i) New motorways and bridges

The first stretch of motorway in Britain, the Preston bypass, was opened in 1958, followed by the M1 in 1959, which linked London and Birmingham. Motorway transport is quicker and more direct. In the mid-1980s the M25 which encircles London was opened to bring the total amount of motorway in Britain to approximately 1860 miles (3000 km). This is not so extensive as once envisaged – costs have spiralled since 1970 and conservationists have delayed a number of projects.

In addition, motorways have proved to be expensive to maintain and there have been problems with surfaces cracking.

'Contra-flows' and 'lane closures' are now common occurrences for motorway users. Unfortunately, motorways have not resulted in a better standing of driving. Multiple accidents have happened, particularly in fog, where motorists have driven at high speeds. 'Motorway madness' is thus a new phrase in the English language.

Three major road suspension bridges have been opened in this period – The Forth Bridge (1966), the Severn Bridge (1966), and the Humber Bridge (1981). The Humber Bridge caused a deal of controversy. As it does not actually link any major industrial areas it has been referred to 'as the bridge to nowhere'.

(ii) Bypasses

The first bypass in Britain was opened in 1935 skirting the eastern side of Winchester, but they did not become a common feature of the landscape until the 1960s. To deal with the increasing pressure of the motor vehicle in town centres a number of measures have been introduced including ring roads, pedestrian precincts, parking meters, one-way systems and computer-controlled traffic light systems. With the number of large 'juggernauts' on the roads (maximum weight is now 38 tonnes) the bypass has become essential if historic buildings in congested towns are to be protected. Kent, in particular, has suffered in this respect with large lorries heading for the Channel ports of Dover and Folkestone.

(iii) Road safety

Speed limits in Britain are set at 30 mph (48 kph) in built-up areas and 70 mph (113 kph) on motorways.

The wearing of seatbelts was made compulsory on 31 January 1983. Although some people believed this was an infringement of an individual's freedom, there is evidence to suggest that many lives have been saved as a result of this measure.

In 1967 the 'breathalyser' was introduced by the Labour Government. This too has had a beneficial effect, discouraging many from 'drinking and driving'. There are those, however, who would like to see a law introduced stating that drivers should not drink at all.

Another controversial matter was the pollution caused by the lead content of petrol and the effects this has on the health of people living in urban areas. There are now plans to make lead-free petrol compulsory by the 1990s.

(b) Railways

(i) By the early 1960s it was clear that the railway network needed to be pruned. There were too many passenger lines operating at a loss and the amount of freight carried was declining in the face of fierce competition from the roads. In 1963 the chairman of the British Railways Board, Dr Richard Beeching, publishing *The Beeching Plan*. This said that if British Rail was to compete and become more efficient the following measures were needed:

● The scrapping of steam-locomotives, to be replaced by diesel and electric trains.
● The closure of over 2,000 stations and 4,960 miles (8000 km) of loss-making track.

There followed a gradual closure of lines, often in the face of fierce opposition. Many station-masters' houses were sold as private dwellings, track dismantled and cuttings filled in to reclaim the land for agricultural purposes.

(ii) During the period from 1970 onwards, British Rail tried hard to revamp its image and capture a greater share of the freight traffic. Among the measures taken were:

● Computer-operated signals and marshalling yards.
● More lines electrified including the London to Liverpool route (1966).
● The introduction of the freightliner services for goods traffic. A number of 'freightliner' depots were constructed where lorries would deliver containers. These containers were loaded on to the freightliner trains and could be loaded onto lorries at the other end.
● The introduction of 'Merry-Go'Round' trains. These would travel continuously between the coalfields and the power-stations delivering fuel.
● The installation of 'Inter-City Services', a fast service between Britain's major cities. An important part of this service was the introduction of the High Speed Train in 1976 which operated on some routes. These locomotives travel at a speed of 125 mph (201 kph). A further develop-

ment, however, the 'Advanced Passenger Train', has had to be abandoned. It was to be capable of maintaining speeds of 150 mph but minor disputes, technical problems and increasing costs caused BR to drop the scheme.

(iii) Urban railways operate in London, Glasgow and Liverpool. The most recent development has been the construction of an electric railway network which links 40 urban stations in Tyneside and serves the commuter market.

(iv) The 1980s, however, has proved to be difficult years for British Rail. The amount of freight and passenger traffice has declined gradually and there has been increasing pressure to cut back and give greater value for money. The amount of financial support from the government has dropped by a third. The result has been a decline in the amount of rolling stock.

BR rolling stock

	1977	1982
Locomotives	3 610	3 016
Coach vehicles	21 580	16 889
Freight vehicles	166 935	45 000

The effects of this have been reductions in the workshops of the *British Rail Engineering Ltd (BREL)*. In May 1986 British Rail announced a total of 7650 redundancies at workshops in Glasgow, Doncaster, Wolverton and Eastleigh. The General Secretary of the National Union of Railwaymen (NUR), Mr Jimmy Knapp, stated that the redundancies were being made in preparation for the privatisation of British Rail. The government refuted this charge and pointed out that the redundancies would save BR £30 million a year.

(v) The Channel Tunnel, a long-discussed project, eventually became a realistic possibility when on 25 January 1986 Margaret Thatcher and President Mitterrand of France signed an agreement. They announced their joint support for the construction of a railway tunnel under the Channel by the Channel Tunnel Group and France Manche Group. The cost of the project was to be met by private finance.

(c) Air travel

(i) Air travel has expanded dramatically in this period, with over 44 million passengers passing through Britain's airports in 1982. The British aviation industry is controlled by the Civil Aviation Authority which looks at safety and the regulation of services. The largest airport in Britain is Heathrow, London, followed by Gatwick and Manchester Ringway. Such has been the pressure on Heathrow and Gatwick that in the 1970s a search was started for a site to build a third large London airport. Four sites were considered by the Roskill Commission in 1971 – Cublington (Buckinghamshire), Thurleigh (Bedfordshire), Nuthampstead (Hertforshire) and Foulness (Essex). Opposition to all four sites from conservationists was fierce; airports mean noise pollution and air pollution. The Commission made a split decision with a majority favouring Cublington and a minority favouring Foulness. In the end the government rejected both and postponed the decision. In June 1985 a Government White Paper, however, stated that Stansted was favoured as the site for London's third airport. Ultimately it was hoped that Stansted would be extended to accommodate up to 15 million passengers per year compared with the present 2 million. In early 1986 Heathrow's Terminal Four was opened, designed to deal with massive numbers of passengers. The government have ruled out a fifth terminal as was once proposed.

(ii) In 1972 British Airways was formed by amalgamating BOAC and BEA. There are plans, however, for British Airways to be sold off to private operators.

(iii) Among the most successful airliners during the period 1951–86 have been:

● The De Havilland-built 'Comet' (1950s).
● The Boeing 747, an American-built aeroplane capable of carrying 400 passengers and aptly nicknamed the 'Jumbo Jet'.
● Concorde (see Section 33.5(f)).

(iv) Several attempts have been made to provide cheap air travel to capture the tourist market. The most celebrated was by Freddie Laker. In the late 1970s he began to operate cheap trans-Atlantic flights with his Sky-Train service. By 1982, however, he had been forced out of business by opposition from the large airlines and became bankrupt. In 1986 British Airways and British Caledonian were being forced to make economies by reducing their work forces.

33.8 WHAT SOCIAL PROBLEMS FACE MODERN BRITAIN?

(a) Race relations

(i) From the 1950s and 1960s the number of immigrants entering Britain began to increase, attracted by the possibility of employment. The vast majority of these immigrants came from New Commonwealth countries such as the West Indies, India, Pakistan and Bangladesh. Most of these people went to live in areas such as London, Birmingham and Bradford where the best job opportunities were to be found at the time.

(ii) Unfortunately, Britain has not achieved a harmonious record of race relations. Politicians spoke out against immigration, in particular Enoch Powell, declaring that the black immigrants would take employment from white people and in 1966 the fascist National Front Party was formed. In 1968 there were 1.1 million Commonwealth immigrants in Britain and the government acted to try and control the rate at which people entered Britain. *The Immigration Act of 1971* stated that immigrants could enter only if:

● They obtained a work permit (for a period of one year at first).
● They had dependents or relatives in Britain.

In 1983 the *British Nationality Act* was put into operation with the overall intention of keeping immigration under control.

(iii) Social investigations and Census returns have shown that Commonwealth immigrants, by and large, were channelled into manual employment and that a great deal of racial discrimination was evident, not only in employment but also in housing, education and public life. In an attempt to combat this the Race Relations Act was passed in 1976. This stated that:

● It was against the law to 'incite racial hatred'.

- It was against the law to 'discriminate on grounds of colour, race or ethnic or national origin in the provision of goods, facilities and services in employment, in education, in housing, etc.'.

The Act also set up the Commission for Racial Equality with the task of trying to harmonise race relations and bringing discrimination to an end. It has the power to investigate any charge brought to its notice which claims racial discrimination.

(iv) A happier side to the question of race relations is the number of black sportsmen and women who have represented England, particularly in soccer and athletics. John Barnes and Viv Anderson led the way, playing international football for England, and Tessa Sanderson, Daley Thompson and Sonia Lannaman have performed superbly for the British athletic squad.

(b) Unemployment

(i) This has been the greatest single problem facing Britain in the 1980s. Unemployment is unevenly distributed, with the North/South divide again in evidence. The worst-affected areas are the North-West, Northern Ireland, Tyneside, West Midlands and Central Scotland. The South, South-East and East Anglia have escaped lightly. In 1986 a *Daily Telegraph* report revealed the difference in life styles between Winchester (4 per cent unemployment) and Consett (23 per cent unemployment). In Winchester the vast majority of 16-year-olds are able to gain employment or a college place; whereas in Consett some young people have been unable to find work in five years. A similar situation exists on Merseyside. At least the Liverpudlians maintain their sense of humour. Stan Boardman, a Liverpool comic, asked a 20-year-old what his last job was – 'A school prefect' came the reply!

(ii) The cost of unemployment has given rise to great concern:

- In 1983 dole payments cost an estimated £17 000 million.
- Studies have shown that depression, alcoholism and drug-taking have increased.
- It is also claimed that unemployment has helped to increase the rate of crime.

(iii) Measures taken to try and combat the problem of the 'depress- ed' regions of Britain and unemployment have included:

Regional Aid – those areas of Britain worst affected by indus- trial stagnation of the old basic industries have been given regional aid by the Central Government. Grants and subsidies were given to firms establishing industry in these areas. The areas were categorised according to the rate of unemploy- ment – 'Special Development Area' (with the greatest need), 'Development Area' and 'Intermediate Area'. Overall, however, this has only been a partial success as the amount of money available in grants has been cut back and the size of assisted areas reduced.

The Youth Training Scheme – this originally started as the Youth Opportunity Programme (YOP) in the mid-1970s but the Conservative Government of 1979 revamped the idea. The Youth Training Scheme (YTS) is sponsored by the Manpower Services Commission and firms are encouraged to take on 16-year-olds and give them a basic training and work exper- ience for two years. The youngsters receive a weekly wage of £25. This scheme attracted much debate. At its best it does provide a scheme and a job at the end of the two years, at its worst it is a provider of cheap labour.

(c) Inner city problems

(i) On 2 April 1980 rioting took place in the St Pauls's area of Bristol. The trouble followed a police raid on a club which was suspected of being the centre of drug traffic. Most of the club members were West Indian, but the ensuing riot involved white people as well as black. The Home Secretary, William Whitelaw, commented that 'all the evidence suggests that it was not in any sense a race riot'. Forty-two arrests were made with 12 people taken to court, all of whom were acquitted.

(ii) On 10 April 1981 serious rioting took place in Brixton, South London, leading to over 200 arrests and widespread criminal damage to property – arson and looting. A public inquiry was established under Lord Scarman, but before he could report further trouble took place in July 1981 in Southall, London, and Toxteth, Liverpool, where police used (CS) gas in an effort to disperse the crowd. Mr Whitelaw stated in the House of

Commons that 'the police were faced with concerted violence by white and black youths hurling missiles including petrol bombs'. Following Toxteth there were further disturbances in Leeds, Bradford, Birmingham and Wolverhampton. Michael Heseltine was given the job of investigating the social conditions of Merseyside.

(iii) In his report Lord Scarman stated that the riots had occurred in 'inner city areas which . . . [have] a high ethnic minority population, high unemployment, a declining economic base, a decaying physical environment, bad housing, lack of amenities, social problems . . . and a high rate of crime and heavy policing'. He went on to say that he did not believe the disturbances constituted a race riot, although black people in these areas felt harrassed and discriminated against. Lord Scarman called for restoration of relations between the community and police.

(iv) In the autumn of 1985 more disturbances took place – in the Handsworth district of Birmingham, in Brixton, and on the Broadwater Farm Estate, Tottenham, London. The estate, designed in the 1960s, has been described as 'a concrete jungle' and rioting started when police searched the home of Mrs Cynthia Jarrett, who collapsed and later died. The scenes which followed were extremely ugly with P.C. Keith Blakelock being stabbed to death, an action which was universally condemned. The Home Secretary, this time Douglas Hurd, again denied that the riots were 'racial'. He expressed the government's intention to strengthen public order and to improve conditions in Britain's inner cities.

(v) The riots motivated the Church of England to publish *Faith in the City, a Call for action by Church and Nation* (December 1985). The report expressed similar views to Lord Scarman, commenting on 'social disintegration' and 'physical decay' in the inner cities. The Report urged the government to improve employment opportunities and increase the rate-support grant to such areas. Meanwhile public attention also focused on whether or not the police should be armed with plastic bullets.

33.9 CONCLUSION: THE FUTURE

The Britain of the mid-1980s faces a number of problems. In September 1986 there were signs of Mrs Thatcher's popularity waning and an upturn in the fortunes of the Labour Party. The country appeared to be disillusioned with monetarism and Mrs Thatchers's uncompromising attitude. Furthermore, the Social Democratic party (formed in 1981)/Liberal Alliance was attracting considerable support as it showed signs of developing definite policies. Problems which the next government will have to face include unemployment, nuclear energy, the north/south divide, racial unrest, housing, educational provision, economic growth and inflation. Returning to the initial observation at the start of this chapter, the optimism of 1951 has only been partially justified. We now live in a push-button, materialistic, technological age with high living standards. But one must ask how Herbert Morrison would have reacted to the problems above which now appear to plague contemporary Britain.

QUESTIONS

1. **Objectives 1 and 2**

(a) Why was the Festival of Britain held in 1951?   (4 marks)
(b) What parallels is it possible to draw between the Festival of Britain (1951) and the Great Exhibition of 1851?   (8 marks)
(c) How far, in your opinion, has the optimism of 1951 been fulfilled?   (8 marks)

2. **Objective 4**

You have been asked to collect ten sources of evidence about 'Life in Britain in the 1980s'.

(a) List the ten sources you would include.
(b) Explain why you have selected them.
(c) Do you think your sources would provide any problems for a future historian who was using them to write a history of the 1980s?

(Total = 25 marks)

3. **Objectives 1 and 2**

(a) Why has there been a move towards comprehensive education in the last 30 years? (6 marks)

(b) Explain the importance of the following educational issues:

● The Plowden Report
● The Great Debate
● The introduction of the GCSE (10 marks)

(c) What educational developments do you think will take place in the future? (4 marks)

4. **Objective 1**

What developments have taken place since 1951 in:

(a) Agriculture
(b) Transport
(c) Industry?

Give specific examples wherever possible in your answer.

(Total = 25 marks)

5. Objectives 1, 2 and 4

World use of various sources of energy 1950–82

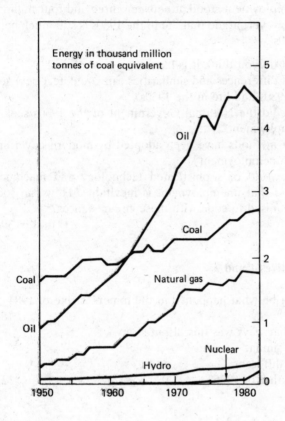

Energy in thousand million tonnes of coal equivalent

Study the graph and using your own knowledge answer these questions:

(a) What reasons can you suggest for the great increase in the use of all the sources of energy shown in the graph?

(b) How can you explain the fact that the use of oil has increased much faster than the use of the other sources shown?

(c) Choose **one** of the sources of energy shown in the graph and explain what problems or dangers have arisen due to its increasing use.

(d) Which source of energy do you think has the best future in front of it?

(Total = 30 marks)
(Southern Examining Group)

6. **Objectives 1, 2 and 3**

'In 1932 Unemployment peaked at the three million mark . . . In 1986 Unemployment stood at between three and four million. Many people, however, argue that life in the 1980s is still much better than in the 1930s'.

(a) What do you think it is like to be unemployed?
(b) What differences and similarities can you detect between life in the 1980s and life in the 1930s?
(c) How did the National Government of the 1930s seek to curb unemployment?
(d) What methods have been adopted by modern governments to curb unemployment?
(e) In a world of sophisticated technology and machinery it is argued that unemployment is inevitable. How can society be reorganised to cope with these circumstances?

(Total = 30 marks)

7. **Objectives 1 and 2**

(a) Describe what happened in the miners' strike of 1984–5.

(8 marks)

(b) In what ways was this dispute
   (i) similar
   (ii) different
   from that of 1926? (12 marks)

8. **Objectives 1 and 2**

(a) Why does Britain appear to have had a poor race relations record in recent years? (12 marks)
(b) What measures have been taken to improve race relations and what more needs to be done? (8 marks)

9. **Objective 1**

Explain the following policies which have been adopted by governments to deal with Britain's economic problems since 1951:

(a) 'Stop-Go' policies of the 1950s
(b) Economic planning of the Labour Governments 1964–70

(c) Income policies of Labour 1974–9
(d) Monetarism of the Conservative Government 1979–86

How successful have these policies been?

(Total = 20 marks)

10. **Objectives 1 and 2**

On 31 December 1979 *The Daily Telegraph* said that 'trade union power . . . has been the biggest domestic political issue of the decade' (that is, the 1970s).

(a) Is there any evidence to support this view?
(b) Does the statement hold true for the 1980s?

Explain your answer.

(Total = 20 marks)

BIBLIOGRAPHY

GENERAL REFERENCE

Clapp, B. W., *Documents in English Economic History: England Since 1760* (Bell, 1976)

Cook, C. and Stevenson, J., *The Longman Handbook of Modern British History 1714–1980* (Longmans, 1983)

Douglas, D. C. (ed.), *English Historical Documents: Vol. XI (1783–1832), Vol. XII (1833–1874), Vol. XII (1874–1914)* (Eyre and Spottiswoode)

Mitchell, B. R. and Deane, P., *Abstract of British Historical Statistics* (Cambridge University Press, 1971)

CHAPTER 1: POPULATION

Deane, P., *The First Industrial Revolution* (Cambridge University Press, 1965)

Deane, P. and Cole, W. A., *British Economic Growth 1688–1959* (Cambridge University Press, 1967)

Flinn, M. W., *British Population Growth, 1700–1850* (Macmillan, 1970)

Malthus, T. R., *Essay on the Principle of Population as it affects the Future Improvement of Society* (Dent, 1982)

Morris, J. A., *The Growth of Industrial Britain (1700 to the Present Day)* (Harrap, 1971)

Thomas, C. J., *Population* (Open University, Second Level Social Sciences Course: Statistical Sources, Unit 3, 1975)

Tranter, N. L., *Population since the Industrial Revolution: The Case of England and Wales* (Croom Helm, 1973)

CHAPTER 2: THE AGRARIAN REVOLUTION 1750–1850

Addy, J., *The Agrarian Revolution* (Longman, 1967)

Chambers, J. D. and Mingay, G. E., *The Agrarian Revolution* (Batsford, 1966)

Hammond, J. L. and B., *The Village Labourer* (Longman, 1979)

Jones, E. L., *Agriculture and Economic Growth in England 1650–1815* (Methuen, 1967)

Kerridge, E., *The Agricultural Revolution* (Allen and Unwin, 1967)

Mingay, G. E., *English Landed Society in the Eighteenth Century* (Routledge and Kegan Paul, 1963)

Parker, R. A. C., *Enclosures in the Eighteenth Century* Aids to Teacher No. 7 (Historical Association, 1967)

Speed, P. F., *The Growth of the British Economy 1700–1850* (Wheaton, 1980)

Thompson, F. M. L., *English Landed Society in the Nineteenth Century* (Routledge and Kegan Paul, 1963)

Turner, M., *English Parliamentary Enclosure* (Archon Press, 1979)

Wright, P. A., *Old Farm Implements* (David and Charles, 1961)

CHAPTER 3: THE INDUSTRIAL REVOLUTION

Ashton, T. S., *The Industrial Revolution 1760–1830* (Oxford University Press, 1948)

Checkland, S. G., *The Rise of Industrial Society in England 1815–85* (Longmans, 1964)

Cowie, L. W., *Industrial Evolution 1750 to the Present Day* (Nelson, 1970)

Deane, P., *The First Industrial Revolution* (Cambridge University Press, 1965)

Hartwell, R. M., *The Causes of the Industrial Revolution in England* (Methuen, 1967)

Rostow, W. W., *The Stages of Economic Growth* (Cambridge University Press, 1960)

CHAPTER 4: THE TEXTILE INDUSTRY 1700–1850

Addy, J. J. and Power, E. G., *The Industrial Revolution* (Longman's 'Then and There' Source Book, 1976)

Bruton, F. A., *History of Manchester and Salford* (S R Publishers, 1970)

Gregg, P., *A Social and Economic History of Britain 1760–1972* (Harrap, 1973)

Habakkuk, H. J. and Postan, M. (eds), *The Cambridge Economic History of Europe: Volume VI* (Cambridge University Press, 1965)

Harvie, C., *The Industrial Revolution* (Open University, Second Level Arts Course: 'The Age of Revolution', 1972)

Inglis, B., *Poverty in the Industrial Revolution* (Hodder and Stoughton, 1971)

Jenkins, D. J. and Ponting, K. J., *The British Wool Textile Industry* (Heinemann, 1982)

Lythe, S. E. G. and Butt, J., *An Economic History of Scotland 1100–1939* (Blackie, 1979)

Murphy, B., *A History of the British Economy 1740–1970* (Longmans, 1973)

Parker, St J. and Reid, D. J., *The British Revolution 1750–1970* (Blandford, 1972)

Power, E. G., *A Textile Community in the Industrial Revolution* (Longmans, 1969)

CHAPTER 5: THE LUDDITES

Dickinson, M., *Britain, Europe and Beyond 1700–1900* (Macmillan, 1979)

Longmate, N., *Milestones in Working Class History* (BBC, 1975)

Thomis, M., *The Luddites: Machine Breaking in Regency England* (David and Charles, 1970)

Thompson, E. P., *The Making of the English Working Class* (Penguin, 1968)

Urban Sylvanus, *The Gentleman's Magazine, 1813*

White, R. J., *Waterloo to Peterloo* (Penguin, 1968)

CHAPTER 6: THE COAL INDUSTRY

Buxton, N. K., *The Economic Development of the British Coal Industry* (Batsford Academic, 1978)

Davies, H., *George Stephenson: A Biographical Study of the Father of Railways* (Quartet, 1977)

Hale, D. and Vickers, M., *Coal Mining* (Arnold, 1979)

Musson, A. E. and Dickinson, M., *The Growth of British Industry* (Batsford, 1978)

Raistrick, A., *Industrial Archaeology* (Paladin, 1973)
Victoria County History, Durham, Vol. II (Oxford University Press, 1967)
Victoria County History, Staffordshire, Vol. II (Dawsons of Pall Mall, 1968)

CHAPTER 7: THE IRON INDUSTRY 1700–1850

Ashton, T. S., *Iron and Steel in the Industrial Revolution* (Manchester University Press, 1963)
Court, W. H. B., *A Concise Economic History of Britain* (Cambridge University Press, 1965)
Gale, W. K. V., *Iron and Steel* (Moorland, 1977)
Hale, D. and Vickers, M., *Iron and Steel* (Arnold, 1979)
Raistrick, A., *Dynasty of Ironfounders: The Darbys of Coalbrookdale* (Longmans, 1953)
Rowley, T., *The Shropshire Landscape* (Hodder and Stoughton, 1970)
Scrivenor, H., *History of the Iron Trade* (Cass, 1967)
Trinder, B., *The Iron Bridge* (Ironbridge Gorge Museum Trust, 1979)

CHAPTER 8: THE POTTERY INDUSTRY 1700–1900

Archer, S. M., *Josiah Wedgwood and the Potteries* (Longmans, 1973)
Buchanan, R. A., *Industrial Archaeology in Britain* (Allen Lane, 1974)
Kelly, A., *The Story of Wedgwood* (Faber and Faber, 1975)
Lane, P., *Documents in British Social and Economic History 1750–1850* (Macmillan, 1968)
Sekers, D., *The Potteries* (Shire, 1981)
Sekers, D., *The Guide to the Gladstone Pottery Museum, Stoke-on-Trent* (Gladstone Museum, 1982)
Victoria County History, Staffordshire, Vol. II (Dawsons of Pall Mall)

CHAPTER 9: THE DEVELOPMENT OF POWER 1700–1850

Briggs, A., *The Age of Improvement* (Longmans, 1959)
Buchanan, R. A., *Industrial Archaeology in Britain* (Allen Lane, 1974)

Langdon-Davies, J., *James Watt and Steam Power* (Jackdaw No. 13, 1967)

Law, R. J., *The Steam Engine* (HMSO, 1965)

Musson, A. E. and Dickinson, M., *The Growth of British Industry* (Batsford, 1978)

Rundle, R. N., *Britain's Economic and Social Development from 1700 to the Present Day* (University of London, 1973)

The Newcomen Society, *Thomas Newcomen: Engineer 1663–1729*

CHAPTER 10: ROAD TRANSPORT

Brenchley, D. R. and Shrimpton, C., *Archive Teaching Units: Travel in the Turnpike Age* (Newcastle University, 1968)

Cameron, A. D., *Thomas Telford and the Transport Revolution* (Longmans, 1979)

Pearce, M., *Keele Teaching Units No. 1: Thomas Telford* (University of Keele, 1971)

Pearce, M., *Thomas Telford: Lifelines No. 10* (Shire, 1973)

Rolt, L. T. C., *Thomas Telford* (Longman, 1958)

Tames, R., *The Transport Revolution in the Nineteenth Century; Roads and Canals* (Oxford University Press, 1970)

CHAPTER 11: CANALS

Aickman, R., *The Story of our Inland Waterways* (Geoffrey Dibb, 1967)

Bagwell, P., *The Transport Revolution from 1770* (Batsford, 1970)

Bode, H., *James Brindley: Lifelines No. 14* (Shire, 1973)

Denyer, R., *Introducing the Kennet and Avon Canal* (Kennet and Avon Canal Trust, 1971)

Farnsworth, W., *On Location: Canals* (Mills and Boon, 1973)

Matts, M., *The Canal at Foxton* (Foxton Boat Services, 1970)

Metcalfe, L., and Vince, J., *Discovering Canals* (Shire, 1968)

Pick, C., *Canals and Waterways* (Macdonald Educational, 1977)

Tames, R., *The Transport Revolution in the 19th Century: Roads and Canals* (Oxford University Press, 1970)

CHAPTER 12: RAILWAYS

Bagwell, P., *The Transport Revolution from 1770* (Batsford, 1970)
Barnes, E. G., *The Rise of the Midland Railway 1844–1874* (Allen and Unwin, 1966)
Coleman, T., *The Railway Navvies* (Pelican, 1968)
Jeans, J. S., *History of the Stockton to Darlington Railway* (Frank Graham, 1974)
May, T., *The Economy 1815–1914* (Collins, 1972)
Perkin, H., *The Age of Railway* (Panther, 1970)
Ray, J., *A History of Railways* (Heinemann, 1969)
Sherrington, C. E. R., *A Hundred Years of Inland Transport* (Cass, 1969)
Simmons, J., *Railways of Britain* (Macmillan, 1968)
Tames, R., *The Transport Revolution in the Nineteenth Century: Railways* (Oxford University Press, 1970)
Tames, R., *Isambard Kingdom Brunel: Lifelines No. 1* (Shire, 1972)

CHAPTER 13: THE DEVELOPMENT OF SHIPPING 1800–1939

Bagwell, P., *The Transport Revolution from 1770* (Batsford, 1970)
Court, W. H. B., *A Concise Economic History of Britain* (Cambridge University Press, 1965)
Deeson, A. F. L., *An Illustrated History of the Steamship* (Spurbooks, 1976)
Lewenhak, S., *Steamships and Shipbuilders in the Industrial Revolution* (Longmans, 1976)
Palmer, M. D., *Ships and Shipping* (Batsford, 1971)
Richards, D. and Quick A., *Britain 1815–1945* (Longman, 1967)
Ridley, A., *An Illustrated History of Transport* (Heinemann, 1969)

CHAPTER 14: FACTORY REFORM

Battiscombe, G., *Shaftesbury: A Biography of the Seventh Earl 1801–85* (Constable, 1974)
Best, G. F. A., *Shaftesbury* (Batsford, 1964)
Gibson, J., *Chadwick and Shaftesbury* (Methuen, 1971)
Henriques, U. R. Q., *The Early Factory Acts and their Enforcement* (Historical Association, 1971)
Pike, R. E., *Human Documents of the Industrial Revolution in Britain* (Allen and Unwin, 1966)
Ward, J. T., *The Factory Movement* (Macmillan, 1962)

CHAPTER 15: SOCIAL AND ECONOMIC CONDITIONS IN BRITAIN 1793–1822

Darvall, F. O., *Popular Disturbances and Public Order in Regency England* (Oxford University Press, 1934)

Langdon-Davies, J., *Peterloo and Radical Reform* (Jackdaw No. 17, 1967)

Marlow, J., *The Peterloo Massacre* (Rapp and Whiting, 1969)

Patrick, J., *Waterloo to the Great Exhibition: British Society 1815–51* (John Murray, 1981)

Peacock, A. J., *Bread or Blood* (Gollancz, 1964)

Thompson, E. P., *The Making of the English Working Class* (Penguin, 1968)

Walmsley, R., *Peterloo: The Case Re-opened* (Manchester University Press, 1969)

White, R. J., *Radicalism and its Results 1760–1837* (Historical Association, 1968)

White, R. J., *Waterloo to Peterloo* (Penguin, 1968)

CHAPTER 16: THE POOR LAW 1750–1948

Anstruther, I., *The Scandal of the Andover Workhouse* (Geoffrey Bles, 1973)

Brundage, A., *The Making of the New Poor Law: The Politics of Inquiry, Enactment and Implementation 1832–39* (Hutchinson, 1978)

Dawson, K. and Wall, P., *Society in Industry in the Nineteenth Century – A Documentary Approach: The Problem of Poverty* (Oxford University Press, 1969)

Digby, A., *The Poor Law in Nineteenth Century England and Wales* (Historical Association, 1982)

Finer, S. E., *The Life and Times of Sir Edwin Chadwick* (Methuen, 1952)

Lewis, R. A., *Poor Relief in Staffordshire 1662–1840* (Staffordshire County Council, 1975)

Poynter, J. R., *Society and Pauperism: English Ideas on Poor Relief 1795–1834* (Routledge and Kegan Paul, 1969)

Styles, S. J., *The Poor Law Society* (Macmillan, 1985)

Watson, R., *Edwin Chadwick: Poor Law and Public Health* (Longman, 1974)

CHAPTER 17: LAW AND ORDER 1700–1900

Ashley, B., *Law and Order* (Batsford, 1967)
Cockburn, J. S., *Crime in England 1550–1800* (Methuen, 1977)
Gibson, J., *John Howard and Elizabeth Fry* (Methuen, 1971)
Johnson, D., *London Peelers and the British Police* (Jackdaw No. 88, 1970)
Mayhew, H., *London Life and the London Poor* (Dover Publications Inc., 1968)
Reith, C., *A New Study of Police History* (Oliver and Boyd, 1956)
Speed, P. F., *Police and Prisons* (Longmans, 1968)
Wilkes, J., *The London Police in the Nineteenth Century* (Cambridge University Press, 1977)

CHAPTER 18: EDUCATION 1750–1944

Barnard, H. C., *A Short History of English Education 1760–1944* (University of London, 1961)
Dent, H. C., *A Century of Growth in English Education 1870–1970* (Longman, 1970)
Maclure, S., *Educational Documents 1816–1968* (Chapman and Hall, 1966)
Pedley, R., *The Comprehensive School* (Pelican, 1969)
Ray, J., *The Growth of Schools: 1750 to the Present Day* (Nelson, 1972)
Robottom, J., *Education for the People* (Longman, 1974)
Speed, P. F., *Learning and Teaching in Victorian Times* (Longman 1974)

CHAPTER 19: PUBLIC HEALTH IN BRITAIN 1750–1900

Allday, R. K., *The Story of Medicine* (Ginn, 1971)
Calder, J. M., *The Story of Nursing* (Methuen, 1971)
Finer, S. E., *The Life and Times of Sir Edwin Chadwick* (Methuen, 1952)
Flinn, M. W. (ed.), *Report on the Sanitary Conditions of the Labouring Classes of Great Britain 1842* (Edinburgh University Press, 1965)
Hartley, L. P., *History of Medicine* (Blackwell, 1984)

Hodgkinson, R., *Science and Public Health* (Open University, Second Level Science Course: Science and the Rise of Technology Since 1800, 1973)

Longmate, N., *Alive and Well* (Penguin, 1970)

Schools' Council History Project, *The Medical Revolution* (Holmes McDougall, 1976)

Tonge, N. and Quincey, M., *Cholera and Public Health* (Macmillan, 1985)

Watson, R., *Edwin Chadwick: Poor Law and Public Health* (Longmans, 1974)

CHAPTER 20: TRADE AND TRADING POLICY SINCE 1750

Bagwell, P. and Mingay, G. E., *Britain and America 1830–1939* (Routledge, 1970)

Beales, D., *From Castlereagh to Gladstone 1815–1885* (Nelson, 1969)

Ensor, Sir Philip, *England 1870–1914* (Oxford University Press, 1936)

Gash, N., *Sir Robert Peel: The Life of Sir Robert Peel after 1830* (Longmans, 1972)

Hair, P. E. H., *The Atlantic Slave Trade and Black Africa* (Historical Association, 1978)

Hill, C. W., *An Illustrated Life ofJoseph Chamberlain: Lifelines No. 11* (Shire, 1973)

Huggett, F. E., *What They've Said About Nineteenth Century Reformers* (Oxford University Press, 1971)

McCord, N., *Free Trade: Theory and Practice from Adam Smith to Keynes* (David and Charles, 1970)

McCord, N., *The Anti-Corn Law League 1838–46* (Allen and Unwin, 1975)

Thomson, D., *Britain in the Nineteenth Century (1815–1914)* (Penguin, 1963)

Titley, D. P., *Machines, Money and Men* (Hart-Davis, 1969)

Woodward, Sir Llewellyn, *The Age of Reform 1815–1870* (Oxford University Press, 1962)

CHAPTER 21: WORKING-CLASS MOVEMENTS

Adelman, P., *The Rise of the Labour Party 1880–1945* (Longman, 1972)

Briggs, A., *Chartist Studies* (Macmillan, 1959)

Browne, H., *The Rise of British Trade Unions 1825–1914* (Longman, 1979)

Dawson, K. and Wall, P., *Society and Industry in the Nineteenth Century – A Documentary Approach: Trade Unions* (Oxford University Press, 1968)

Gammage, R. C., *History of the Chartist Movement 1837–54* (Merlin Press, 1969)

Gard, E., *British Trade Unions* (Methuen, 1970)

Hobley, L. F., *Working Class and Democratic Movements* (Blackie, 1970)

Lichtheim, G., *A Short History of Socialism* (Fontana/Collins,1970)

Lovell, J., *British Trade Unions 1875–1933* (Macmillan, 1977)

Mather, F. C., *Chartism* (Historical Association, 1965)

Moore, R., *The Emergence of the Labour Party 1880–1924* (Hodder and Stoughton, 1978)

Pelling, H., *A Short History of the Labour Party* (Macmillan, 1961)

Pelling, H., *A History of British Trade Unionism* (Pelican, 1984)

Royle, E., *Chartism* (Longmans, 1980)

Shapiro, H., *Keir Hardie and the Labour Party* (Longman, 1971)

Thompson, D., *The Chartists* (Temple Smith, 1984)

Trade Union Congress, *The Story of the Dorchester Labourers* (1957)

Ward, J. T., *Chartism* (Batsford, 1973)

CHAPTER 22: INDUSTRIAL DEVELOPMENTS 1850–1914

Best, G., *Mid-Victorian Britain 1851–75* (Weidenfeld and Nicolson, 1971)

Court, W. H. B., *British Economic History: Commentary and Documents 1870–1914* (Cambridge University Press, 1965)

Jones, R. B., *An Economic and Social History of England 1770–1970* (Longmans, 1971)

Robbins, K., *The Eclipse of a Great Power* (Longman, 1983)

Saul, S. B., *The Myth of the Great Depression 1873–1896* (Macmillan, 1969)

Thomson, D., *England in the Nineteenth Century 1815–1914* (Penguin, 1963)

Yglesias, J. R. L., *London Life and the Great Exhibition* (Longman, 1964)

CHAPTER 23: AGRICULTURE IN BRITAIN 1815–1914

Adams, L. P., *Agricultural Depression and Farm Relief in Britain 1813–52* (Cass, 1969)
Caird, J. R., *The Landed Interest and the Supply of Food* ([1878] Cass, 1967)
Cobbett, W., *Rural Rides* (Penguin, 1967)
Fream, W., *Elements of Agriculture* (John Murray, 1897)
Hobsbawm, E. and Rudé, G., *Captain Swing* (Lawrence and Wishart, 1969)
Hopkins, H., *The Long Affray: The Poaching Wars 1760–1914* (Secker and Warburg, 1985)
May, T., *Agriculture and Rural Society in Britain 1846–1914* (Arnold, 1975)
McConnell, P., *The Agricultural Notebook* (Crosby Lockwood, 1897)
Orwin, C. and Whetham, E., *The History of British Agriculture 1846–1914* (David and Charles, 1964)
Peacock, A. J., *Bread or Blood* (Gollancz, 1964)

CHAPTER 24: THE EMANCIPATION OF WOMEN

Brendon, P., 'Mrs Pankhurst – The Vote and the Violence' (an article in the *Sunday Telegraph*, 5 August 1979)
Kazantzis, J., *Women in Revolt* (Jackdaw No. 49, 1968)
Liddington, J. and Norris, J., *One Hand Tied Behind Us* (Virago, 1978)
Marwick, A., *The Deluge* (Penguin, 1965)
Read, D., *Edwardian England* (Historical Association, 1972)
Rover, C., *Women's Suffrage and Party Politics in Britain 1866–1914* (RGP, 1967)
Snellgrove, L. E., *Suffragettes and Votes for Women* (Longman, 1964)

CHAPTER 25: THE SOCIAL REFORMS OF THE LIBERAL GOVERNMENT 1906–14

Cook, C., *A Short History of the Liberal Party 1900–76* (Macmillan, 1976)
Cross, C., *The Liberals in Power* (Barrie and Rockliff, 1963)
Read, D., *England 1868–1914: The Age of Democracy* (Longman, 1979)

Rowland, P., *The Last Liberal Governments: The Promised Land 1905–10* (Barrie and Jenkins, 1968)
Rowland, P., *The Last Liberal Governments: Unfinished Business 1911–1914* (Barrie and Jenkins, 1971)
Rowland, P., *Lloyd George* (Barrie and Jenkins, 1975)
Wilson, J., *Campbell-Bannerman: A Life of Sir Henry Campbell-Bannerman* (Constable, 1973)

CHAPTER 26: THE FIRST WORLD WAR (1914–18) AND ITS EFFECTS

Marwick, A., *The Deluge* (Penguin, 1965)
Marwick, A., *Britain in a Century of Total War 1900–67* (Penguin, 1968)
Medlicott, W. W., *Contemporary Britain 1914–64* (Longman, 1967)
Pollard, S. F., *The Development of the British Economy 1914–1980* (Arnold, 1983)
Taylor, A. J. P., *English History 1914–45* (Penguin, 1970)

CHAPTER 27: THE TRADE UNIONS 1914–39

Arnot, R. P., *The General Strike of May 1926: Its Origins and History* (EP, 1975)
Gard, E., *British Trade Unions* (Methuen, 1970)
Marwick, A., *The Deluge* (Penguin, 1965)
Marwick, A., *Britain in a Century of Total War 1900–67* (Penguin, 1968)
Morris, M., *The British General Strike 1926* (Historical Association, 1973)
Skelley, J., (ed.) *The General Strike 1926* (Lawrence and Wishart, 1976)
Stephens, M., *Ernest Bevin: Unskilled Labourer and World Statesman* (Transport and General Workers' Union, 1981)
Tames, R., *The General Strike* (Jackdaw No. 105, 1972)
Taylor, A. J. P., *English History 1914–45* (Penguin, 1970)

CHAPTER 28: INDUSTRY BETWEEN THE WARS 1919–39

Constantine, S., *Unemployment between the Wars* (Longman, 1980)
Marwick, A., *The Deluge* (Penguin, 1965)

Marwick, A., *Britain in a Century of Total War 1900–67* (Penguin, 1968)

Mason, S., *Agrarian Britain 1700–1980* (Blackwell, 1984)

Pollard, S. F., *The Development of the British Economy 1914–1980* (Arnold, 1983)

Robbins, K., *The Eclipse of A Great Power* (Longman, 1983)

Stevenson, J. and Cook, C., *The Slump: Society and Politics During the Great Depression* (Cape, 1977)

CHAPTER 29: THE WALL STREET CRASH AND THE DEPRESSION OF THE THIRTIES

Harrison, A., *The Framework of Economic Activity* (Macmillan, 1970)

Hyde, H. M., *Baldwin: The Unexpected Prime Minister* (Hart-Davis, 1973)

Keesing's Contemporary Archives:
  Volume 1 (1931–4) (Keesings, 1934)
  Volume 2 (1934–7) (Keesings, 1938)
  Volume 3 (1937–40) (Keesings, 1941)

Marquand, D., *Ramsay MacDonald* (Cape, 1976)

Marwick, A., *The Deluge* (Penguin, 1965)

Marwick, A., *Britain in a Century of Total War 1900–67* (Penguin, 1968)

Medlicott, W. W., *Contemporary Britain 1914–64* (Longmans, 1967)

Mowat, C., *Britain between the Wars* (Methuen, 1975)

Skildesky, R., *Politicians and the Slump: The Labour Government of 1929–31* (Macmillan, 1967)

Taylor, A. J. P., *English History 1914–45* (Penguin, 1970)

Thompson, D., *England in the Twentieth Century* (Penguin, 1969)

CHAPTER 30: THE HOME FRONT DURING THE SECOND WORLD WAR 1939–45

Calder, A., *The People's War: Britain 1939–45* (Cape, 1969)

Calder, A., *Britain at War* (Jackdaw No. 66, 1973)

Gregg, P., *The Welfare State* (Harrap, 1967)

Keesing's Contemporary Archives:
  Volume 5 (1943–5) (Keesings, 1945)

Kelsall, F., *How We Used to Live 1936–53* (Macdonald, 1981)

Longmate, N., *How We Lived Then: A History of Everyday Life During the Second World War* (Hutchinson, 1971)

Pike, A. and Pike A., *The Home Front in Britain 1939–45* (Tressell, 1985)

Thomson, D., *England in the Twentieth Century* (Penguin, 1969)

CHAPTER 31: THE LABOUR GOVERNMENT 1945–51

Benn, A. W., *Arguments for Socialism* (Cape, 1979)

Burridge, T., *Attlee: A Political Biography* (Cape, 1986)

Childs, D., *Britain Since 1945: A Political History* (Methuen, 1986)

Craig, F. W. S. (ed.), *British General Election Manifestos 1918–66* (Political Reference Publications, 1970)

Gregg, P., *The Welfare State* (Harrap, 1967)

Keesing's Contemporary Archives:
>   *Volume 6 (1946–8)* (Keesings, 1948)
>   *Volume 7 (1948–50)* (Keesings, 1950)

Marwick, A., *British Society Since 1945* (Pelican, 1984)

Monk, L. A., *Britain 1945–70* (Bell, 1970)

Morgan, K. O., *Labour in Power 1945–51* (Oxford University Press, 1984)

Pedley, R., *The Comprehensive School* (Penguin, 1969)

Pollard, S. F., *The Development of the British Economy 1914–1980* (Arnold, 1983)

Seaman, L. C. B., *Post-Victorian Britain 1902–51* (Methuen, 1975)

CHAPTER 32: COMMUNICATIONS AND TRANSPORT SINCE 1840

Daunton, M. J., *Royal Mail: The Post Office Since 1840* (Athlone, 1985)

Hennessey, R. A. S., *Transport* (Batsford, 1973)

HMSO, *Britain: An Official Handbook* (1984)

James, A., *The Post Office* (Batsford, 1970)

James, A., *Sir Rowland Hill and the Post Office* (Longman, 1972)

James, A., *Newspapers and The Times in the Nineteenth Century* (Longmans, 1976)

Ray, J., *A History of British Transport 1700–Present* (Heinemann, 1969)

Schools Council History Project, *Britain 1815–51* (Holmes McDougall, 1976)

Thomas, D. St J., *The Motor Revolution* (Longman, 1961)

Titley, D. P., *Machines, Money and Men* (Hart-Davis, 1979)

Wilkerson, M., *News and Newspapers* (Batsford, 1970)

Worlock, D. R., *Post-Haste: The Post Office from 1500 to the Present Day* (Nelson, 1972)

CHAPTER 33: BRITAIN 1951–86

Fothergill, and Vincent, *The State of the Nation* (Pluto Press – Pan Reference, 1985)

HMSO: *Britain: An Official Handbook* (1982, 1983, 1984, 1985, 1986)

Hodson, H. V. (ed.), *The Annual Register 1985* (Longman, 1985)

Keesing's Contemporary Archives: 1982, 1983, 1984, 1985, 1986 (Keesings)

Lane, P., *Post-War Britain* (Macdonald Educational, 1971)

Rae, W. P. and Coutts, N. C., *Contemporary Files: The United Kingdom* (Heinemann, 1980)

Sedgwick, P. J., Steeds, D. and Williams, L. J., *Britain Since 1945* (Hutchinson, 1982)

Simpson, W. O., *Changing Horizons: Britain 1914–80* (Stanley Thornes, 1986)

INDEX

A

Abercrombie, Sir Patrick   612
Acts of Parliament
  Abnormal Importations Act
    1931   563
  Agricultural Credit Act   551
  Agricultural Marketing Act 1931   565
  Agricultural Rate Act 1928   551
  Agriculture Act 1920   550
  Air Raid Precaution Act 1937   577
  Artisan's Dwelling Act 1875   10, 317,
    492
  Balfour's Act (Education)
    1902   291–5
  British Nationality Act 1983   687
  British Shipping Assistance Act
    1935   566
  Broad Wheel Act 1753   126
  Butler's Act (Education) 1944   295,
    590, 613
  Catering Wages Act 1943   582
  Children's Act 1908   494
  Climbing Boys Act 1864   209
  Coal Mines (Eight Hours Act)
    1908   497, 533
  Coal Mines (Minimum Wages) Act
    1912   387, 497
  Coal Mines Act 1919   524
  Coal Nationalisation Act 1946   602
  Combination Acts 1799, 1800
    (repealed 1824; amended
    1825)   222, 232, 370, 371
  Conciliation Act 1896   381
  Conspiracy and Protection of
    Property Act 1875   377, 492
  Corn Production Act 1917   549
  Corrupt Practices Act 1888   471
  Cotton Spinning Industry Act
    1936   566
  County (Rural) Police Force Acts
    1839 1856   225
  Criminal Law Amendment Act
    1871   376
  Cultivation Production Act 1917   549
  Custody of Infants Act 1839   466
  Defence of the Realm Act 1915   513
  Determination of Needs Act
    1941   582
  Distribution of Industry Act
    1945   620
  Education (Administrative Provision)
    Act 1907   294, 493
  Education (Provision of Meals Act)
    1906   294, 493
  Electrical (Supply) Act 1926   546
  Emancipation of Slaves Act
    1833   339
  Emergency Powers Acts
    1939–40   523, 530, 579
  Employers and Workmen Act
    1875   377
  Employment Acts 1980, 1982   659
  Employment Protection Act
    1975   658
  General Enclosure Acts
    1801–45   26–7
  Parliamentary Enclosure Acts
    1760–80   25–6
  Endowed Schools Act (1869)   25–6
  Equal Pay Act 1971   464
  Factory Acts   11; Factory Act Health
    and Morals of Apprentices
    1802   200; Factory Act
    1819   200; Factory Act 1833
    (Althorp)   204, 282–3, 387;
    Factory Act 1844
    (Graham)   205; Factory Act
    1847 (Fielden)   205; Factory Act
    Factory Act 1850 (Grey)   206;
    Factory Act (Lace Works)
    1861   206; Factory Act 1878
    (Disraeli)   206
  Family Allowances Act 1945   605
  Fisher's Act (Education) 1918   294,
    517
  Forster's (Education) Act 1870   11,
    286–90, 469, 637
  Friendly Societies Act 1855   375, 406
  Friendly Society (Consolidating) Act
    1875   406
  Gaol Act 1823   264
  Gas (Nationalisation) Act 1948   603

712

Acts *contd.*
Gilbert's Act 1782　240
Grammar Schools Act 1840　286
Horticultural Products Act 1931　564
Housing and Town Planning Act 1919　517
Housing of the Working Classes Act 1890　317
Housing (Temporary accommodation) Act 1944　591
Immigration Act 1971　687
Import Duties Act 1932　335, 564
Industrial Relations Act 1971　657–8
Industry Act 1975　653
Iron and Steel (Nationalisation) Act 1950　603
Labour Exchanges Act 1909　499–501
Legal Aid and Advice Act 1949　615
Limited Liability Acts 1855, 1862　442
Local Government Board Act 1871　315
Local Government Act 1888　131, 459, 469
Location of Industry Act 1945　591
Marine Broadcasting Offences Act 1967　632
Married Woman's Act 1882　467
Married Woman's Property Acts 1870, 1882　467, 470
Maternity and Child Welfare Act 1918　608
Matrimonial Causes Act 1857, 1878　467
Merchant Shipping Acts, 1850, 1876, 1893　187
Metropolitan Police Act 1829　257
Middlesex Justices Act 1792　255
Mines Act 1842　206–8
Mundella's Act (Education) 1880　290
Municipal Corporations Acts 1835, 1869　259, 286, 308, 469
Munitions Act 1915　513
National Assistance Act 1948　606
National Health Act 1946　608–9
National Insurance Acts 1911, 1945　492, 497–9, 501, 605
National Park and Access to Countryside Act 1949　613
National Service (Armed Forces) Act 1939　579
New Towns Act 1946　612
North Atlantic Shipping Act 1934　566
Navigation Acts 1651, 1660　336, 345
Nuisance Removal Act 1848　312
Old Age Pensions Act 1908　494

Parliament Acts 1911, 1949　495, 615
Payment of Members Act 1911　383
Penal Servitude Act 1853　267
Poor Law Amendment Act 1834　243, 387, 606
Prison Acts 1835, 1877　264, 268
Prisoners' (Temporary Discharge) Act 1913　478
Public Health Acts 1848 1872 1875　10, 312, 316, 492
Race Relations Act 1976　687
Railway Amalgamation Act 1921　638
Railways Act 1844　167
Railway Gauge Act 1846　167
Reciprocity of Duties Act 1823　344
Red Flag Act 1865　429, 640
Reform Act 1832　232, 387, 469
Registration of Births Act 1836　205
Regulation of Railways Act 1889　167
Representation of People's Act (1918)　480
Road Traffic Acts 1930, 1933　640–1
Roses Act 1793　406
Safeguarding of Industries Act 1921　335
Sandon's Act (Education) 1876　290
Sanitary Act 1866　315
Second Reform Act 1867　287, 315, 399
Secret Ballot Act 1872　399, 475
Seditious Meetings Act 1817　229
Settlement Act 1662　239
Sex Discrimination Act 1975　464
Shops Act 1911　496
Six Acts 1819　228
Smallholders and Allotment Act 1908　459
Smallholdings Act 1893　459
Sound Broadcasting Act 1972　632
Special Areas Act 1934　567–9
Standstill Act 1934　567
Sugar Subsidy Act 1925　550
Television Act 1954　633
Third Reform Act 1884　399
Tithe Commutation Act 1836　442
Torrens Act 1868　317
Town and Country Planning Acts 1944, 1947　591, 613
Trade Boards Act 1909　496
Trade Disputes Act 1906　383, 404, 656
Trade Disputes Act 1927　533
Trade Dispute Act 1965　656
Trade Union Acts 1871, 1913　376, 383, 533

Transport Act 1947   603
Unemployment Act 1934   567
Unemployment Insurance Act
    1920   514, 518
Union Chargeability Act 1865   248
Wheat Quota Act 1932   565
Workmen's Compensation Act
    1906   497
Addison, Dr Christopher   517
Advisory, Conciliation and Arbitration
    Service (ACAS)   658–9
aerospace industry   673
agent provocateurs   228–9, 397
agriculture
    1750–1850   21–37
    nineteenth century   437–60
    1914–30   549–551
    1931–9   565
    1939–45   584
    since 1951   676
    Agrarian Revolution   23–37
    Depression (1837–1914)   453–60
    distress (1815–50)   439–48
    during French wars (1793–1815)   221,
        438–9
    Parliamentary enclosure   25–30
    Golden Age of   448–53
    propagandists   36–7
    Royal College of   450
    Royal Society of   450–1
aircraft industry since 1951   548
Air Raid Wardens   577
air travel   641–2
Albert, Prince Consort   316, 416–19
Alcock, John   641
Alexandra Palace   633
Allen, Ralph   155
Allan, William   374
Amalgamated Society of Carpenters and
    Joiners   376
Amalgamated Society of
    Engineers   374
American Civil War (1861–5)   185,
    422, 425, 431, 449
American economy in the 1930s   554–7
American War of Independence
    (1776–83)   337
Anderson, Sir John   526, 577–8
Andover Workhouse Scandal   246, 636
Annan Report 1978   633
Annual Register 1985   655
Anti-Corn Law League   334, 347–50,
    392, 628
Anti-Poor Law Committees   387
Anti-Suffrage League   475
Anti-Sweating League   496
Applegarth, Robert   374

Arch, Joseph   378
Arkwright, Richard (1732–92)   58–9,
    195, 198
Arnott, Dr Neil   310
Arnold, Thomas   285
arterial system   310–11
Ashworths of Bolton   198
Asquith, H. H.   476, 492–4
Astor, Lady Nancy   481
Attlee, Clement   248, 515, 534, 579,
    598, 600–1, 611, 619–20, 648
Attwood, Thomas   386, 389, 392, 390
autarchy   541
Automobile Association   640
Avington, Hampshire   447–8, 628, 634

B

Baird, John Logie   626, 633
Bakewell, Robert   33
Baker, Arthur Octavius   443
Baker, Kenneth   669
Baker, Robert   307
Baldwin, Stanley   528–33, 559–60, 602,
    614
Balfour, Arthur J.   354, 476
Bamford, Samuel (1788–1872)   225
Bank of England   559, 561, 602
Barnes, Alfred   603
Barnes, James   144
Basic industries   423–8, 541–5, 562
Battersea Teachers' Training
    College   282
Beale, Dorothea   286, 466
Beaverbrook, Lord (Max Aitken)   637
Becker, Lydia (1827–90)   471–2
Bedford, Duke of   36, 460
Bell, Alexander Graham   630
Bell, Andrew   279–80
Bell, Henry   182
Bell, Patrick   35
Bell, Richard   404
Bell, Thomas   61
Bentley, Thomas   108
Bentham, Jeremy   226, 242–3
Benz, Carl   429
Besant, Annie   33, 379, 400, 467
Bessemer, Henry (1813–98)   427–8
Bevan, Aneurin   608–11
Beveridge, Sir William   501, 513, 589,
    605–7
Bevin, Ernest   528–9, 535, 580–1, 589
bicycles   430
Billington-Grieg, Theresa   473
Birkenhead, Lord   528
Birkinshaw, John   156
Bismarck, Otto von   431
Black Friday (1921)   524–5

Black, Professor Joseph 117
Blanc, Nicholas le 429, 431
Blanketeers, March of 227
Bleriot, Louis 641
Blitz, The 577, 608
Board Schools 287–8
Boer War (1889–1902) 354, 491
Bondfield, Margaret 481
Booth, Charles 491
Boulton, Matthew 47, 108, 117, 198
Bow Street Runners 228, 255, 259
Bradlaugh, Charles 11, 379, 467
Bramah, Joseph (1748–1814) 423
Brandeth, Jeremiah 227
Bretton Woods 599
Bridgewater, Duke of
  (1736–1803) 109, 141–2
Bright, John (1811–89) 348, 350, 353,
  396
Brindley, James (1716–72) 142–3,
  145–6
British Airways (BA) 641
British and Foreign Schools
  Society 280, 289
British Broadcasting Corporatiion
  (BBC) 531, 588, 602, 632–3
British Electricity Authority 602
British European Airways (BEA) 602
British Gazette, The 530–1
British Iron and Steel Federation
  (1934) 566
British Medical Association
  (BMA) 502, 608–9
British Motor Corporation 673
British Overseas Airways Corporation
  (BOAC) 602, 642, 655
British Railways (BR) 603–4
British Road Services (BRS) 603
British South American Airways
  (BSAAC) 602
British Steel Corporation 672
British Sugar Corporation (BSC) 550
British Transport Commission 603
British Worker, The 531
Broadhurst, Henry 378, 400
broadsheets 222
broadsides and ballads 636
Brougham, Henry 280
Brown, George 650
Bryce Report 291, 433
Brunel, Isambard Kingdom 162,
  182–3, 426
Buckingham and Chandos, Duke
  of 448
Buddle's exhaust fan 85
Bull, George 202
Bullock Report (1975) 666

Burdett, Sir Francis (1770–1864) 225–6
Burke, Edmund 221
Burns, John 400, 403
Burt, Thomas 399
Buss, Frances 286, 466
Butler, R. A. 648
Butler, Samuel 285

C
cable television 634
Caird, James (1816–92) 450–3
Caledonian Canal 146
Callagham, James 654, 659, 667
Campbell-Bannerman 475, 492
canals 140–9
Capital Gains Tax 650
Caroline, Radio 632
Castle, Barbara 481, 656
Castlereagh, Lord 231
Carron Ironworks 98, 229
Cartwright, Edmund (1743–1823) 61
Cartwright, Major John
  (1740–1824) 225
Cartwright, William 72
Catch-Me-Who-Can 156
Cato Street Conspiracy (1820) 228
Census Returns 12–13
Central Committee for Woman's
  Suffrage 471
Central Economic Planning 620
Central Electricity Board (CEB) 546,
  602
Chadwick, Edwin · 242, 258, 303,
  306–16
Chain, Ernest 322, 588
Chamberlain, Joseph (1836–1914) 317,
  353, 560, 564–5, 579, 602
Champion, H. H. 400, 403
Channel tunnel 642, 685
Charity Schools 279
Chartism 204, 232, 261–2, 368,
  386–98
chemicals 429
  1919–39 548–9
  since 1951 674
  chemical fertilizers 450–1
Chernobyl 670
child labour 110, 195–210
chloroform 323
cholera epidemics 306, 314
Churchill, Randolph 433
Churchill, Winston 492–3, 496, 499,
  525, 528, 530, 533, 586, 598, 605,
  647
cinema 627, 631, 634
Citrine, Lord W. 528, 535, 602
Civil Aviation 602

Civil Defence 577, 581
Clarendon Commission (1861) 286
Clarkson, Thomas 339
climbing boys 208–9
clippers 184–5
Clynes, J. 528
coal mining industry 80–90, 93, 423–4, 542–3, 657
coastal shipping 140
Cobbett, William (1763–1832) 202, 225, 246, 441, 443, 445
Cobden, Richard (1804–65) 347–9, 392
Cobden–Chevalier Treaty (1860) 334, 352
Cockerill, Christopher 642
Cockerton Judgement (1901) 291
Coke, Thomas of Holkham 36
Cole, Henry 416
Colling Brothers 34
Collison, William 381
colonial system 336
Committee of Privy Council (on Education) 282–4
Common Agricultural Policy (CAP) 677
communications since 1840 626–42
Communist Party of Great Britain (CPGB) 526, 532, 534
comprehensive schools 614, 662–4
conscription 579
Conservative Party 354–5, 377, 476, 495, 507, 525, 559–60, 590, 619, 648–9, 651–5, 657–60
Cook, A. J. 527–9
Cooke, William 629
Co-operative movement 368
  consumer co-operatives 408
  producer co-operatives 407
Corn Laws 205, 223, 224, 334, 346–51, 442, 444, 448, 454–5
Cort, Henry (1740–1800) 81, 96
Cotchett, Thomas 56
cotton 50, 333, 419, 543–4
Councils of Action 530, 522
Courant, Daily 635
Cowper-Temple Clause 288
Cranage, Thomas and George 96
Crawshay family 99
Crimean War (1854–6) 283, 324, 449
Criminal Investigation Department (CID) 259
Crippen, Dr 632
Cripps, Sir Stafford 617–8, 620
croppers 72
Cross, Richard 317
Cross, The 142–3

Crowther Report (1959) 664
Cruikshank, George 131
Crystal Palace 417
crystal set 632
Culley, George 34
Cunard, Samuel 181, 183–4, 189

D
Daily Express, The 579
Daily Herald, The 570
Daily Mail, The 474, 502, 529, 581
Daily Mirror, The 590
Daily News, The 479, 496
Daimler, Gottlieb 429
Dale, David 59
Dalton, Hugh 602, 612, 616–17
Dame schools 278
Darby Family of Coalbrookdale 46, 81, 94, 95
Davies, Emily 466
Davison, Emily Wilding 478
Davy, Sir Humphrey 85, 322
Defoe, Daniel 124
Delane, John Thadeus 635
denationalisation 648
Department of Economic Affairs 650
Department of Scientific and Industrial Research (DSIR) 548–9, 587
Depression of the 1930s 14, 355, 517, 591, 305, 535, 548, 554–73
Derby, Lord 416
Derbyshire Rising (1817) 227
Despard, Charlotte 473
Development Corporations 613
Dickens, Charles 209, 247, 281, 467
diseases 110, 301, 304–8, 312–325
Disraeli, Benjamin 349
Doherty, John 202, 372
Domagk, Gerhard 322
domestic system 53–55
doodle bugs 578–9
driving test 641
Drummond, Flora 477
Duncan, William 312
Dunlop, Marion Wallace 477

E
East India Company 336
Economy Committee (May) 588
Eden, Anthony 515, 579
Eden, Frederick Morton 241, 405
Edison, Thomas 428
education 277–96
  elementary education 278–295
  secondary education 278, 281, 285–6, 290–6
  since 1951 662–9

Edwards, George 228
Ehrlich, Paul (1854–1915) 322
Elder, John 186
Eldon, Lord 230
electoral system 223–4
electric telegraph 628, 631
electrical/electronic engineering since
    1951 674
electricity 428, 546–7
Elizabeth II, Queen 631
Ellman, John 34
emancipation of women 464–481
Emergency Budget (1931) 560–1
Emergency Hospital Scheme 608
emigration 2, 15, 445
Empire, The British 340, 354, 422, 564
Employers' Parliamentary Council 381
Engels, F. 44, 420
engineering 422–3, 428, 432
Essential Work Order 580
European Economic Community
    (EEC) 16, 332, 335, 356–8, 677
European Free Trade Association 356
evacuation during Second World
    War 577–8
examinations 666–7
Exchange Equalisation Fund 565
Eye, John 141

F
Fabian Society 400, 491, 501, 590
Factory Acts 11, 200, 204–6
factory conditions and reform
    of 194–210
factory system 55, 59, 194, 368
Fair Trade League 335, 353
Faraday, Michael 304
Fascist party 572
Fawcett, Millicent 471
Ferranti 653
Festival of Britain 647
Fielden, John 198, 202, 204–5, 209,
    246, 390
Fielding, Henry (1707–54) 255
Fielding, John 255
finance 422, 438, 442, 512, 516–17,
    519, 544–73, 585–6, 598–600, 615–19
Fitzwilliam, Lord 75
Fleming, Alexander 322, 588
Fleming, John 632
Flemish immigrants 52
Florey, Howard 322, 588
Foley, Cissy 474
Forster W. E. 287
franchise, the 469–481
Franco-Prussian War (1870–1) 422,
    449

Frankland, Lewis Thomas 244, 310
Friedman, Milton 654
Freeman, John 610
free trade 332, 341–358, 422, 431, 541,
    549, 563
French Revolution (1789) 219, 221
French Wars (1793–1815) 37, 47,
    219–23, 240, 256, 340, 438
friendly societies 368, 371, 405–7
Frost, John 393
Fry, Elizabeth (1780–1845) 253, 263–4
Fulton, Robert 182

G
Gaitskell, Hugh 610, 619, 648
gaols 261–8
Garrett-(Henderson), Elizabeth 468
Gas Council 603
Geddes, Sir Eric 519
General Agreement on Tariffs and
    Trade (GATT) 335, 356
General Strike (1926) 392, 521, 523,
    526–34, 542
George, Henry 400
George III, King 37
George V, King 559
George VI, King 646
Gilbert, John 142
Gilbert Unions 247
Gilchrist, Percy 427, 431
Gilchrist-Thomas, Sidney 427
Gladstone, William E. (1809–98) 167,
    287, 351, 416, 438, 512, 516, 525,
    527, 557, 561–2, 599, 617–18
Gott, Benjamin 63, 198
Gordon Riots 1780 256
Goulden, Emmeline (Pankhurst) 472
Gore-Booth, Eva 474
governesses 465–6
Graham, Sir James Robert George
    311
grammar schools 281–2, 293, 295
Grand Junction Canal 143
Grand National Consolidated Trades
    Union (GNCTU) 372–3
Grand Trunk Canal 142
graveyards 305, 311–12
Great Exhibition (1851) 351, 416–19,
    647
Great Western Railway (GWR) 639
green belts 612
Greenwood, Arthur 589
Gresely, Sir Nigel 640
Grey, Edward 473
Grey, Lord 232
Griffiths, James 605
Guest, John 99

H

habeas corpus, suspension of
(1817)   229
Hackworth, Timothy   156
Hadow Report (1926)   294
Hall, Sir Benjamin   314
Hall, Y. T.   87
Hamilton, Lord   499
Hampden Club   226
Hanway, Jonas   209
Hardie, James Keir
(1856–1915)   402–4, 476, 502
Hargreaves, James (1720–78)   58
Harney, George Julian (1817–97)   391,
396
Harmsworth, Alfred (1865–1922)   637
Hart, Judith   481
Harvey, William   318
Hasker, Thomas   130
Hearth Tax   4
Heath, Edward   651–3, 658
Hedley, William   156
Hetherington, Henry (1792–1847)   386
Hill, Dr Charles   609
Hill, Octavia (1838–1912)   317
Hill, Rowland (1785–1879)   626–7
Hoare, Samuel   560
Home Front during Second World
War   577
Home Guard during Second World
War   580–1
Homfray, Samuel   99, 156
Hornby v. *Close*   375
Horner, Leonard   205
Horrocks, William   61
Horsfall, Williams   73
Horsburgh, Florence   481
housing   110, 301–4, 308–9, 316–17,
517–18, 611
hovercraft   642
Howard, John (1726–90)   253, 262
Hudson, George   166
Hume, Joseph   371, 396
Hunt, Henry (1773–1835)   225, 227
Huskisson, William (1770–1830)   11,
231, 334, 344–5
Huntsman, Benjamin (1704–76)   100
Hussey, Obed   451
Hyndley, Lord   602
Hyndman, H. M.   400, 472, 600

I

Imperial Airways   641
Imperial Chemical Industries (ICI)   548
income tax   219, 223, 586, 649
Independent, The   638

Independent Broadcasting Authority
(IBA)   632
Independent Labour Party (ILP)   403
Independent Television (ITV)   633
Independent Television Authority
(ITA)   633
indoor relief   239
industry
since 1951   669
between the wars (1919–39)   541–51
depression in 1875–1914   430–5
developments between
(1850–1914)   415–35
during French Wars (1793–1815)   221
electrical   546–7
engineering   422
film   634–5
Industrial Revolution   43–49
iron and steel   91–101, 419, 426–8,
545
motor car   547–8
nationalisation of   600–4, 620
new industries in the nineteenth
century   545–9, 563
optimist *v.* pessimist debate   47
shipbuilding   117–19, 544–5, 566
staple/basic   423–8, 541–5
sweated   495–6
textiles   50–79, 424–6, 544
inflation   220, 654, 658
inner-city problems since 1951   689–90
International Monetary Fund
(IMF)   599, 649, 653
International Subscriber Dialling   631
inventions
Arkwright's water frame (1769)   58–9
Bessemer's Converter (1856)   180
bicycles   430
Cartwright's power loom (1785)   60
Crompton's mule (1779)   59
Gilchrist-Thomas basic process
(1879)   180, 427
Hargreave's spinning jenny
(1764)   58
Horrock's power loom (1803)   61
Kay's flying shuttle (1733)   57
locomotives   155–60
Nasmyth's steam hammer (1839)   426
Neilson's hot blast (1828)   426
Robert's self-acting mule (1825)   60
Siemens–Martin's open hearth process
(1867)   180, 427
Whitney's cotton gin (1793)   61
Whittle's jet engine 1929   587, 642
invisible exports   341, 352, 420
Irish Potato Famine (1845–6)   11, 205

iron and steel industry 91–101, 419, 426–8, 545, 566, 672
Ironbridge 95
iron ships 180–1

J
James Report 1972 (teachers) 666
Jarrow March (1936) 570
Jenkins, Roy 651
Jenner, Edward (1744–1823) 319–20
Jex-Blake, Sophia 468
Johnson, Amy 641
Jolly George incident (1920) 522
Jones, Ernest (1819–78) 391, 394, 396
Joseph, Sir Keith 667, 669
Joyson-Hicks, W 528, 533
Junta, The 374–5, 399
Justices of the Peace 253

K
Kay, John (1704–64) 57
Kay, Shuttleworth, Dr James 282, 310
Kelly, William 60
Kempthorne, Sampson 245
Kennedy, Annie 473
Keynes, John Maynard (1883–1946) 573, 592, 599, 617
Kingsley, Charles 209
Knight, Anne 470
Koch, Robert (1843–1910) 319

L
Labour Exchanges 499–501
Labour Government, The (1945–51) 598–620, 647, 649–51, 653–4, 656–8
Labour Party, growth of 398–405
Labour Representative Committee 404
laissez-faire 9, 47, 74, 126, 143, 166, 187, 201, 202, 203, 204, 209, 210, 242, 247, 254, 278, 280, 289, 309, 312, 315, 369, 401–2, 405, 415, 422, 452, 491–2, 494, 499–500, 513, 515, 517
Lancaster, F. W. 429
Lancaster, Joseph 279–80
Lancet, The 314
Lansbury, George 476
Lavassor, Emile 429
law and order 253–68
Lawes, John Bennet 451
Lefevre, John, George Shaw 244
Lend–Lease programme 586, 599
Leon, Daniel de 385
Le Veil, Colonel 255
Liberal Government (1906–14) 248, 475–6, 491–503

Liebig, Justus von 451
Lindbergh, Charles 641
linen industry 50, 52
Lister, Joseph (1827–1912) 323
Liston, Robert 323
Liverpool, Lord 228–9
Liverpool–Manchester Railway (1830) 158
Lloyd George, David 476, 478–9, 492–495, 498, 500–3, 513, 515, 517, 523–4
Lloyd, Selwyn 649, 655
Local Education Authority (LEA) 292–9
Local Defence Volunteers 579
Lombe, John 56, 195
London and North East Railway 639
London Democratic Association 390–1
London Dock Strikes (1889) 380, 460
London gas workers' strike (1889) 380
London Midland and Scottish Railway (LMS) 639
London Passenger Transport Board 640
London Society for Women Suffrage 470
London Underground Railway 640
London Working Men's Association 386
Lovett, William (1800–77) 386, 388–9, 394
Lowe, Rev. Robert 242, 284, 287
Luddites (1811–12, 1816) 71–79, 221
Lyons v. *Wilkins* (1896) 381–2

M
Macadam, John Loudon (1756–1836) 129
MacDonald, Ramsay 404, 476, 528, 531, 559–62
McDougall, Colin 246
MacGregor, Ian 660–9
MacIndoe, Sir Archibald 588
McKenna Duties (1915) 335
Macmillan, Harold 515, 648
Malthus, Thomas 6, 201, 242–3, 405
Mann, Tom 385, 400
Manus, Siegfired 429
Marconi, G. 429, 626, 631
Marshall Aid 618
Marshall, William 37
Martin, Pierre 180, 427
Marx, Karl, Marxism 48, 400
mass media 626–38
match girls' strike 379, 460
Maudling, Reginald 649
Maudslay, Henry (1771–1841) 119, 423

Maxwell, James Clerk (1874–1937)   631
May, Sir George   558
Mayhew, Henry   420
Mayne, Richard (1796–1868)   258
means test, the   567, 569
Medical Research Council   587
Meikle, Andrew   35
Melbourne, Lord   373
mercantilist system   332–3
Metcalfe, John (1717–1810)   128
Metropolitan Police Force   257–61
Milk Marketing Board   565
Mill, J. S.   226, 351, 470
Miners' Federation of Great Britain
   (MFGB)   380, 385, 523–4, 527,
   532
Mines Report (1842)   207
miners' strike (1974 and 1984–5)   654,
   660–1, 669
Ministry of Agriculture   459
Ministry of Food   513, 583–4, 588
Ministry of Housing   612
Ministry of Information   588
Ministry of Labour   514
Ministry of Munitions   513
Ministry of National Service   514
Ministry of Transport   640
Mond-Turner Talks (1927–30)   534
monetarism   654
monitorial system   279–80
Morant, Robert   291–2, 493
Morris, William   400
Morrison, Herbert   602, 647
Morse code   629, 631
Morton, William   323
Mosley, Oswald   572
motor-car industry   429, 547–8, 640–1,
   672–3
Murdoch, Rupert   638, 661
Murdoch, William   81, 117
Murray, Len   660
Mushet, Robert (1811–91)   427

N
Napier, General   389, 392
Napier, Robert   184, 181
Nasmyth, James (1808–90)   119, 426
National Agricultural Labourers Union
   (NALU)   378
National Association for the Protection
   of Labour (NAPL)   372
National Anti-Suffrage League   474
National Assistance   582
National Assistance Board (NAB)   606
National Charter Association   393, 396
National Coal Board (NCB)   602, 604,
   660–1, 669

National Debt   220
National Economic Development
   Council (NEDC)   649–50
National Enterprise Board   653
National Free Labour Association   381
National Government   559–62
National Health Service   589, 590,
   607–10, 619
National Insurance   605–7
National Land Company   394
National Research Development
   Council   642
National Savings Certificates   587
National Savings Schemes   516
National Shipbuilding Security Ltd   566
National Society for Promoting
   Education to the Poor   280
National Union of Women's Suffrage
   (NUWSS)   471–2, 474, 477, 479
nationalisation of industry   600–4, 620
natural gas   680
Navigation Laws (1651, 1660)   336
navigators (navvies)   144, 163–5, 171
Need, Samuel   59
Neilson, J. B. (1792–1865)   426
New Model Unions   374–8
Newcastle Commission   283
Newcomen, Thomas (1663–1729)   83,
   115
Newgate Prsion   261, 263
New Lanark Mills   59
New Poor Law   239–45, 372
Newport Rising (1839)   391–3
Newsom Report (1963)   665
newspapers   627, 635–8
Newton, William   374
New Towns   612–3
New Unions   378–81
Nicholls, George   242, 244
Nightingale, Florence (1820–1910)   324,
   467, 636
Normanby, Lord   312
Northern Star, The   393, 391
Northcliffe, Lord   513, 637
Norton, Caroline   466
Norwood Report   295
nuclear power 1951–86   681–2

O
Oastler, Richard   201, 205, 209, 246,
   378
O'Brien, James Bronterre
   (1805–64)   390
O'Connor, Feargus (1794–1855)
   389–92, 394, 396
Oil Producing and Exporting Countries
   (OPEC)   652, 669
oil since 1951   678

Oldknow, Samuel 198
open-field system 21
Open University, The 665
Organisation for the Maintenance of
  Supplies (OMS) 526, 529
Osborne Case 383, 405
Ottawa Agreements 1932 564
outdoor relief 239, 243–48
Owen, Robert 198–9, 202, 209, 280,
  340, 372, 407

P
Paine, Tom 221–2, 466
Palmer, John 130
Palmerston, Lord 267
Pankhurst family 472–4, 476–9
parish apprentices 195
parish constables 254
Parliamentary Reform 223–5
Parks, Josiah 451
Parsons, Sir Charles 186, 428
Pasteur, Louis (1822–95) 319–21, 630
Patterson, William 182
Paxton, Joseph 417
Pay Board 652
payment by results 283–4
Payne, William 254
Peabody, G. (1795–1869) 316
Pearson, Arthur (1866–1921) 637
Pease, Edward 157, 400
Pechey, Emma 468
Peel, Robert 231, 257-61, 334,
  345–51, 416
Peel, Robert Senior 198, 200
Pelham, Henry, 5th Duke of
  Newcastle 283
Penal Code 256–7
Penny Black 628
Pethick-Lawrence, Mr and Mrs 473,
  478
People's Charter 386–7
Peterloo Massacre 1819 227
Philosophic Radicals 226
Pilkington Committee (1962) 633
Pitt, William the Younger 219, 334,
  343
Pitt–Vergennes Treaty 343–4
Place, Francis 231, 371, 386
Plimsoll, Samuel (1824–98) 187
Plowden, Sir Edwin 620
Plowden Report on Primary Education
  (1967) 665
Plug Riots (1842) 389, 393
pocket boroughs 224
police force
  Bow Street Runners 255, 259
  law and order 253–68
  Metropolitan, formation of 232

Political and Economic Planning Group
  (PEP) 571
Poor Law 238–49, 440, 443
  Andover workhouse scandal 247,
    636
  Anti-Poor Law Committee 246
  Board of Guardians 243–5
  Commission 243–8, 310
  Commissioners 241–5
  New Poor Law 239–45
  Old Poor Law 239
  Poor Law Report (1834) 242
population 1–20, 430
  birth rate 1, 5, 15
  death rate 2, 6, 15
  demography 2
  emigration 2, 11, 15
  immigration 15
  infant mortality rate 2
  life expectancy 2, 307–8
  migration 2
  rural depopulation 30
  statistics 2
  trends 4, 10, 13
Post Office 627–8
Post War Credits 586
Potter, George 376
pottery industry 105–13
Pounds, John 283
poverty 238
power 114–20
  animal 115
  for industry 545–6
  nuclear 681–2
  oil, 1951–86 678
  steam 114
  water 114
  wind 114
prescription charges 651
Press, The 631, 635–8
Price Commission 652
Prices and Incomes Board 650
primary education 295, 665–6
Primrose League, The 471
Public Corporation Model 601
public health 301–25, 636
public schools 281, 285–6
purchase tax 219, 223, 444,
  587

Q
Queen Mary, The 566

R
race relations 687–8
Radicals 225–231
Radical Suffragists 474

radio 626, 631–2
Ragged Schools Movement 283
Raikes, Robert 279
railways 155–73, 419, 638–40
Rainhill Trials (1829) 160
rationing 513, 583–4, 616
Red Friday (1921) 525
Reith, John 632
Rennie, John 144, 159
replacement boom 512
Revised Code 284
Reynolds, Richard (1735–1816) 95
Ricardo, David 201
Richmond, Duke of 349
Ridley, Nicholas 654
riots
  Anti-Poor Law 246
  Cold-Bath Fields 258
  Ely and Littleport (1816) 226, 446
  Gordon (1780) 256
  Luddites (1811–12, 1816) 71–9, 254
  Newport rising (1839) 392–3
  Peterloo massacre (1819) 227
  Plug (1842) 389, 393
  Rebecca riots (1842–3) 128
  Spa Fields (1816) 226
  Swing (1830) 242, 254, 262, 446, 637
roads 124–31, 640
  condition of 124–8
  development (1840–1986) 640–1
  regulations 640
  stagecoach travel 124, 130–1
Robbins Report on Higher Education
  (1963) 664
Roberts, Richard (1789–1864) 60, 61
Robinson, Frederick 344
Roebuck, John 98
Rolls, C. S. 429
Romilly, Samuel (1757–1818) 257
Rookes v. *Barnard* 655
Roosevelt, F. D. R. 586
Roper, Esther 474
rotten boroughs 224, 232
Rowan, Colonel Charles 258
Rowntree, Seebohm 491
Royal College of Agriculture 450
Royal Mail 130, 170, 184, 627–9
Royal Society of Agriculture 450–1
Royce, F. M. 429
Russell, Lord John 350
Russell, William 636

S
Sadler, Michael Thomas 202, 209
Salvation Army 491
Samuel, Sir Herbert 525, 532, 559–60, 563
Sanitary Reform Movement 310

Sankey, Sir John 524, 560
satellite communication 631
Savery, Thomas (1650–1715) 83, 84, 115
Scagg, Thomas 451
Scargill, Arthur 660
Selective Employment Tax 650
Semmelweis, Ignaz 323
Senior, Nassau 203, 242, 283
Seven Years War (1756–63) 336
Shaftesbury, Lord 202, 204–9, 267, 283, 312
Shah, Eddy 660
Shaw, G. B. 400
Sheffield Outrages (1866–7) 375
Sherman, Edward 131
Shinwell, Emmanuel 616
shipping 179–90, 420, 592
  coastal 140
  shipbuilding 177–90, 516, 544–5, 566, 570, 670
Short-Time Committees 202, 204, 206, 39
Sidmouth, Lord 230, 231
Siemens, William 180, 427
silk industry 50
Simon, Sir John 315–6, 531
Simpson, James Young (1811–70) 323
slavery 337–9
Slesser, Sir Henry 532
Smiles, Samuel 405
Smith, Adam (1723–90) 47, 201, 240, 333, 342–5
smuggling 342
Snow, Dr John 314
Snowden, Philip 476, 523, 558–61, 563
Social Contract 658
Society for the Promotion of Christian
  Knowledge (SPCK) 279
Southern Railway (SR) 639–40
Southwood, Smith, Dr 207, 312
Social Democratic Federation 400, 600
Socialism 400–4
Socialist League 400
Sorel, Georges 385
Speenhamland System 6, 221, 223, 240, 242, 444
Spence, Thomas (1750–1814) 226
Spencean Society 226
Spens Report 294
standard of living 420, 591, 618–19
statute labour 125
steam power 114–20
  in agriculture 452
  effect on economy 119
  engines 83, 84, 156–90
  pump 115–6
Stephens, Joseph Rayner 246, 386

Stephenson, George 86, 156–9, 163
Stephenson, Robert 159–60, 163
Stockton–Darlington Railway
  (1825) 157–8
Strauss, George 603
strikes 379–80, 521–35, 618, 662, 655
Strutt, Jedediah 59, 198
Stubbs, George 108
Sturges, Joseph 391
Subscriber Trunk Dialling System
  (STD) 631
Suez Canal 186
Suffrage Movement 469–80
Sun, The 638
Sunday Schools 279
Swan, Joseph 428
Swales, A. B. 528
sweated industries 495
Swing Riots (1830) 242, 262, 372, 637
Symington, William 181
Syndicalism 385, 405

T
Taff Vale case 382, 404
tariffs (customs duties) 332–3, 344,
  353–4, 541, 544, 564, 650
Tariff Reform League (1903–6) 353–4
Taunton, Lord 286
telephone 626, 630, 633
Telstar 631
television 626, 631
Telford, Thomas (1757–1834) 128–9
Ten Hours' Movement 201–5
Tennant, Charles 61
textiles 50–79, 416–17
  1951–86 671
  bleaching 61
  cotton 50, 55–61
  domestic system 53
  dyeing 61
  factory system 55
  linen 50, 52
  machinery, inventions 56–61
  printing 61
  silk 50
  wool 50, 55, 61
  worsted 51
Thatcher, Margaret 481, 654, 664
Thistlewood, Arthur 228
Thomas, J. H. 528, 560
Thring, Edward 285
Thorne, Will 380
Thornton, Henry 339
Tillett, Ben 380
time, standardisation of 170
Times, The 205, 227, 228, 246, 261,
  316, 324, 349, 395, 468, 493, 495,
  558, 635–6

Titanic, The 632
Tolpuddle Martyrs 262, 373
Tomlinson, George 613
Townshend, Viscount 33
Toynbee, Arnold 44
trade
  balance since 1951 654
  clubs 369–70
  free 332, 341–58, 422, 541, 549, 563
  invisible 340–1
  patterns 1919–39 512
  protectionism 332, 352–5, 563–64
  slave (triangular trade) 337–8
  with EEC 332–5, 356–8
  with EFTA 356
  with Empire 340
trade unions 368–92, 460, 521–5,
  655–62
Trades Union Congress (TUC) 376–8,
  401, 521, 525, 529–35, 559–60, 614,
  618, 649, 653, 658, 660
transport in the nineteenth century
  canals 140–9
  railways 155—73
  roads 124–31
  shipping 179–90
transport in the twentieth century 626,
  638–42
transportation 262
Treaty of Rome (1957) 356
Trevithick, Richard
  (1771–1833) 1566–7
tripartite system 295–6, 662
Triple Alliance 385–6, 524
Trollope, Anthony 628
Tull, Jethro 34
turnpike trusts 124, 126–31
Turner, Ben 535

U
underground railways 169, 640
unemployment 222, 499–501, 518, 557,
  561, 567–71, 607, 615, 654, 671,
  685, 688–9
Union of Democratic
  Mineworkers 661
United Nations 619
Utilitarianism 226, 242
Utility Scheme 585

V
vaccinations 6, 320–1
Victoria, Queen 417, 630
Vincent, Henry (1813–78) 391–2

W
Wade, General 128
Wade, John 225

wages and incomes 110, 421, 444, 455–7, 650, 653
Walker, Samuel 99
Wall Street Crash 520, 554–7
Walter, John I (founder of *The Times*) 635
Walter, John II (Andover scandal) 247
wars
  American Civil War (1861–5) 185, 449
  American War of Independence (1776–83) 337
  Boer War (1899–1902) 354
  Crimean War (1854–6) 283, 324, 449, 467, 636
  First World War (1914–18) 14, 189, 479–80, 512–12, 521, 591, 634, 641
  Franco-Prussian War (1870–1) 442, 44
  French Wars (1793–1815) 37, 47, 219–223, 240, 256
  Korean War (1950–3) 610, 619
  Second World War (1939–45) 535, 577–92, 608, 642–3
  Spanish Civil War (1936–9) 577
Waterloo, Battle of 219, 439
Watt, James (1736–1819) 47, 61, 81, 84, 108, 116, 181
Webb, Sidney and Beatrice 248, 368, 400, 501
Wedgwood, Josiah (1730–95) 105–10, 142
Welfare State, The 248, 503, 605–10, 615
Wellington, Duke of 439, 448
Wells, Horace 322
Wells, H. G. 400

Western, Charles 439
Westminster Committee 226
Wheatstone, Charles 629
Whitbread, Samuel 280
Whitehouse, Mary 634
Whitney, Eli 61
Whittle, Frank 642
Whitten-Brown, Arthur 641
Whitworth, Joseph (1803–87) 423
Wilberforce, Lord William 280, 658
Wilkinson, Ellen 613
Wilkinson, John (1728–1808) 98, 117
Williams, Shirley 481, 667
Wilson, Harold 607, 610, 649, 653–4
Wilson, Havelock 403
wireless, the 631
Wollstonecraft, Mary 466
women, emancipation of 464–82
  Women's Freedom League 473
  Women's Land Army 549, 582
  Women's Social and Political Union (WSPU) 472–8
Wood, John 201
Woodcock, George 656
woollen industry 50–65, 544
Woolton, Lord 583
Workhouses 239–47
Worlidge, John 34
Worsley Canal 141–2, 146
Wright, Wilbur and Orville 634, 641

Y
Young, Arthur 36, 124
Youth Training Scheme 689
Ypres, Battle of 513

Z
Zworykin, V. K. 633